D0217882

WITHDRAWN
UTSA LIBRARIES

CULTIVATED POWER

PENN STUDIES IN LANDSCAPE ARCHITECTURE

John Dixon Hunt, Series Editor

This series is dedicated to the study and promotion of a wide variety of approaches to landscape architecture, with special emphasis on connections between theory and practice. It includes monographs on key topics in history and theory, descriptions of projects by both established and rising designers, translations of major foreign-language texts, anthologies of theoretical and historical writings on classic issues, and critical writing by members of the profession of landscape architecture.

Cultivated Power

Flowers, Culture, and Politics in the
Reign of Louis XIV

ELIZABETH HYDE

PENN

UNIVERSITY OF PENNSYLVANIA PRESS

Philadelphia

Publication of this volume was assisted by a grant from the Getty Grant Program.

Copyright © 2005 University of Pennsylvania Press
All rights reserved
Printed in the United States of America on acid-free paper

10   9   8   7   6   5   4   3   2   1

Published by
University of Pennsylvania Press
Philadelphia, Pennsylvania 19104-4011

Library of Congress Cataloging-in-Publication Data

Hyde, Elizabeth.
   Cultivated power : flowers, culture, and politics in the reign of Louis XIV /
Elizabeth Hyde.
        p.   cm. (Penn studies in landscape architecture)
     Includes bibliographical references (p.) and index.
     ISBN 0-8122-3826-5 (cloth : alk. paper)
     1. Louis XIV, King of France, 1638–1715.   2. Gardens, French—History—
17th century.   3. Gardens, French—History—18th century.   4. Gardens—France—
History—17th century.   5. Gardens—France—History—18th century.   6. Symbolism
of flowers.   7. France—History—Louis XIV, 1643-1715.   I. Title.   II. Series.

SB457.65.H94   2005
712'.0944'09032—dc22   2004043089

Library
University of Texas
at San Antonio

For my parents, curious florists themselves

For my husband, who is not, but who has been devoted and supportive anyway

And for my daughters in hopes they will be

CONTENTS

INTRODUCTION

In 1688 Jean Donneau de Visé presented to King Louis XIV an exquisite manuscript entitled *History of Louis le Grand, contained in the rapport that [is] found between his actions, & the qualities, & virtues of flowers, & of plants*[1] (see plate 1). The manuscript was a magnificent object. Its nearly one hundred pages were elaborately bound in a cover of tortoiseshell with brass inlay crafted by Louis Boulle, the French master of marquetry. The pages within were covered with delicately rendered, gold-framed watercolor portraits of flowers, herbs, and trees. Each plant addressed the king in accompanying texts, celebrating his accomplishments by comparing his deeds to its own botanical features and medicinal properties. The book was a masterpiece of late seventeenth-century flower painting, calligraphy, and marquetry and therefore was a gift suitable for presentation to a king. It was also a tour de force in courtly flattery. For Donneau de Visé, publisher of the seventeenth-century Parisian periodical *Le Mercure Galant*, was seeking to be named an official historian to Louis XIV, and the manuscript was his plea for patronage. Yet why would Donneau de Visé have sought an appointment by comparing the king to flowers, symbols most often identified with ephemerality and femininity, not everlasting royal power?

Fending off the ephemerality of political goodwill born of short-lived memory was, of course, Donneau de Visé's goal in writing the history of Louis XIV's reign. Several floral species included in the text outlined the benefits of such an endeavor on Donneau de Visé's behalf. In boasting of its own exquisite fragrance, the tuberose said that it perfumed the air long after the plant began to flower. The publication of the king's works in an official historical account would have the same effect on his posterity as the lingering perfume of the tuberose. Said the flower to the king:

> As soon as one begins to publish [reports of] the great projects that you often make for the tranquility of the Earth, and for the advantage and the glory of France, one is surprised . . . at the first noise that spreads from these projects, which [is no longer heard as time passes]. But when one comes to examine them in succession, and as they begin to produce results for which they were conceived, it is then that they appear more extraordinary, and that one discovers with pleasure the grandeur and the beauty, and that as the good that arises from them is of long duration, one can with justice compare them to my flowers, which are born in one season and last into another.[2]

The iris, too, made the case for a comprehensive history of the king's reign. After explaining that it existed in an infinite number of colors and varieties and had many medicinal uses, the iris said to the king: "The enumeration of the qualities, and virtues, through which I contribute to the health of men, would be too long to make in their favor, and those who have undertaken to make your panegyric are often forced to remain limited to only titles of your principal actions, and their works were not permitted to be of the size that they resolved to make them, in elaborating on each one [of your actions]."[3] Donneau de Visé, of course, offered to resolve this state of affairs by giving the principal actions of the king their full due in a series of comprehensive histories to be written by himself.

Donneau de Visé's case for both his talents as a historian and the necessary role to be played by documented history in ensuring the lasting legacy of Louis XIV was well received—he was given the appointment. The flowers, it seemed, had been effective in conveying his plea for patronage. Donneau de Visé, though, was not the first to realize the iconographic utility of flowers. Indeed, Louis XIV's own panegyrists had begun to use floral symbolism well before the Sun King came to rule over the horticultural and architectural magnificence of Versailles. As early as 1661, the young king danced in Isaac de Benserades's *Ballet des Saisons* as "Le Printemps" to the following verses:

> The young vigor of Spring
>> Dissipated bad times,
>> All the mutinous and strange winds
>> Who amid thick fog
>> Caused great tempests
>> Have been banished forever,
> And in the air is a profound peace.
>> This season who strongly pleases
>> Sends to the cold northern climates
>> Winter who surrenders to war,
>> And produces for our posterity
>> In the most noble place on the Earth
>> The great and immortal Flower
> Who spreads his odor over all of Europe.[4]

In the passage, Benserade mixed metaphors, comparing the young king to spring, the season of rebirth, fertility, and potentiality most frequently identified with flowers, and to the *immortelle*, or everlasting flower, the one species whose beauty was capable of defying death and decay. The ballet proved prophetic in that Louis XIV would go on over the course of his long reign to "spread his odor over all of Europe," both in the form of the often-imitated aesthetic legacy of Versailles and, with greater immediacy for his European neighbors, with the pungent aroma of gun smoke and cannon powder expended in the repeated attempts to extend the boundaries of France. In the ballet, then, the floral symbolism functioned as a means of communicating the military power of Louis XIV.

While Benserade celebrated the bellicosity of the springtime warrior king, the Jesuit writer René Rapin argued the opposite case, expressing hope that Louis XIV would usher in a period of springlike prosperity and peace. In his *Hortorum libri IV*, a georgic verse celebration of flowers, forests, water, and orchards first published in Latin in 1665, Rapin connected the horticultural successes of Louis XIV to a cultural rebirth of European, and specifically French, civilization that would be the king's lasting legacy. Rapin argued that Louis would lead Europe and France out of the constant warring that had plagued the continent for much of the late sixteenth and seventeenth centuries, and thereby usher in not only a new era of peace, but also a new golden age, the prosperity and civility of which would be reflected in gardens the likes of which had not been seen since antiquity. Rapin wrote (quoted here in John Evelyn's seventeenth-century English translation):

> When *France* her former riches shall regain,
> If our affairs should prosper once again;
> Then by the bounty of a lasting Peace,
> Our labours may be crown'd with more success.
> The World of late in Warrs has bin ingag'd,
> And stern *Enyo* through all *Europe* rag'd;
> Famine, and Pestilence, and Feavers raign'd,
> The blushing fields with civil Gore were stain'd.
> The gods were all averse, who can remount
> Those crimes, which do the reach of thought surmount?
> The violated Laws, the broken faith,
> And Nations guilty of their Sov'rains death?
> And heavier ills then these had yet remain'd,
> If *Lewis* from the gift of Heav'n obtained;
> Had not with pow'rful arms, and greater mind,
> Repair'd our fortune, ere it quite declin'de,
> Then having stretch'd his bounds from shore to shore,
> That he might arts and manners too restore,
> And through the World the golden age renew;
> The rains of Justice great *Lamon* to you
> He gave, and you ore his Tribunals plac't:
> When led by you *Astraea* shall, at last,
> Return to us agen, as we have cause
> To hope from the beginnings of your Laws;
> Then shall the Earth in her first glory be;
> And those new arts and methods which by thee
> T'improve their Plants the Husbandmen receive,
> Shall ever in they native Soil survive.

> Thus much of Gardens, I at *Clermont* sung,
> In thee sweet *Paris*; treading all along
> Those sacred steps; which *Virgil* led before,
> When blest in her affairs, in her King more,
> Ore willing Nations *France* began to sway:
> And made the universe her Pow'r obay.[5]

For Rapin, the flourishing of the garden arts in the France of Louis XIV attested to the return of peace, order, and justice made possible by the leadership of the king. Rapin's vegetal symbolism thus, too, spoke of Louis XIV's power—his power to herald the arrival of nothing less than a Virgilian second golden age.

The use of floral imagery to such varied ends by Donneau de Visé, Benserade, and Rapin speaks of the malleability of floral symbolism and tempts one to dismiss the proliferation of floral imagery as mere ornament. But in using flowers to communicate historical memory, military might, and the rebirth of civilization, the three men also were complimenting the king in the highest terms possible for significant accomplishments. Flowers were useful for such purposes precisely because of the cultural meanings that flowers had acquired in early modern Europe. Indeed, one may safely speak of a new "culture of flowers"[6] in the early modern period that encompasses changes in the cultivation, uses, and symbolism of flowering plants. For in the sixteenth and, increasingly, into the seventeenth and early eighteenth centuries, as this book demonstrates, flowering plants captivated Europeans of all sorts and ranks from gardeners to kings—including Louis XIV. The flowers, many imported into European gardens for the first time, were celebrated not only for their beauty, form, color, and fragrance, but also for their rarity, exoticism, tastefulness, expensiveness, and difficulty of cultivation. To acquire and cultivate such blossoms successfully demonstrated the horticultural proficiency—and taste—of their owner. At the same time, the new cultural significance of flowers imbued traditional floral symbolism and imagery with powerful meanings like those illustrated by Donneau de Visé, Benserade, and Rapin.

This intersection of flowers as material objects collected and cultivated in the garden and the cultural meanings projected onto those flowers in the construction of identity is the subject of this book. It is a history of flowers in a particular time and place. The chapters that follow trace the evolution of this culture of flowers over the course of the early modern period in France from the traditional associations of flowers with beauty, ephemerality, and femininity, to their rise in popularity, and ultimately to their utility in the royal gardens of Louis XIV as markers of his might in military, political, and aesthetic arenas. In other words, this work demonstrates that flowers became invested with such cultural and, therefore, political power that courtiers such as Donneau de Visé could successfully compare the king to anemones and pansies, while Louis XIV himself adroitly appropriated flowers and their symbolism to further his own absolutist ends.

Accounting for the new meanings attached to flowers in the early modern period raises broad interdisciplinary questions about larger changes in European notions of nature. Such changes were exemplified by interest in agricultural improvements, by fascination with horticultural developments fed largely by the availability of new species, by the celebration of the pastoral in literature and the landscape in painting, and through the philosophical contemplation of the relationship between humans and the natural world.

The sixteenth and seventeenth centuries, in particular, witnessed a renewed attachment to the soil demonstrated by the publication of manuals to guide European elites in the proper management of the country estate. Olivier de Serres published one of the most important of these works in 1600 under the title *Le Théâtre d'agriculture et mesnage des champs.* In it he outlined the parameters for establishing and furnishing the four types of gardens to accompany a properly situated *château*: the vegetable, medicinal, fruit, and flower gardens. The vegetable, medicinal, and fruit gardens would ensure the self-sufficiency of the well-run estate and thereby contribute to the reconstruction of the French economy. But Olivier de Serres (in drawing inspiration from long-lost gardens of Roman antiquity), did not overlook aesthetic pleasures to be gained from the gardens. The flower garden, or "bouquetier" as he called it, was to contain "all sorts of plants, herbs, flowers, shrubs in compartments or parterres, and . . . *cabinets*, according to the inventions and fantasies of the lords, [and was intended] more for pleasure than for profit."[7] De Serres's work on estate management appeared at a historical moment in France when an audience particularly receptive to his ideas was emerging. The decades of religious wars that had devastated France in the sixteenth century had come to an uneasy end, allowing for attempts to rebuild the ravaged French landscape and economy to go forth. De Serres's practical information on the planning and operation of productive manors was therefore timely and important. He offered one of the first systematic treatments of agriculture as a science. His advice, for example, on the plantation of mulberry trees to sustain silkworms in hopes of generating a silk industry in France even captured the attention of Henri IV, who, with his chief minister, the Duc de Sully, hoped to grow the French economy by promoting the manufacture of goods.

In addition, De Serres's work was published at the same time that the elites of early modern France entered a period of nostalgia for an idyllic pastoral existence. The celebration of the pastoral was epitomized by the immense popularity of *L'Astrée*. Published in four installments between 1607 and 1627, the multivolume romance by Honoré d'Urfée told of unrequited romance between numerous shepherds and shepherdesses played out in an idealized natural setting far removed from the increasingly urban centers of French culture. The idealization of the rural was rooted, too, in the landed wealth of the old French nobility who, over the course of the seventeenth century, would see their political power and actual wealth eclipsed by the upstart *noblesse du robe* ("nobles of the robe") who owed their recent acquisition of noble titles to their ability to purchase them from a perpetually cash poor monarchy or to their ability to serve the king and his government in some professional capacity. The old nobility, the *noblesse d'épée* ("nobility of the sword"), a name stemming from its ancient origins as regional military rulers) and the nobles of the robe were both conscious of the meaning of landed wealth in early modern France. The nobles of the sword clung to it as the marker that separated them from the more recently ennobled nobles of the robe whose wealth was more likely than not rooted in banking or trade. At the same time, the nobles of the robe, recognizing the cultural significance of landownership, sought to emulate the nobles of the sword by buying and improving estates.

Renaissance thinkers may have rediscovered the glory of humanity and nature, but it was left to thinkers in the sixteenth, seventeenth, and eighteenth centuries to impose order on the concepts of humanity and nature and to explore the relationship between the two. Early modern thinkers contemplated, even celebrated, their uniquely human ability to apply arts and culture to nature. Familiar oppositions between nature and culture, or nature and art, were held up as intellectually intriguing concepts and disciplines about which one should ideally profess knowledge and understanding. The frontispiece of Etienne Binet's 1621 *Essay des merveilles de Nature et des plus nobles artifices: Pièce très-nécessaires à tous ceux qui font profession d'eloquence*, a manual, of sorts, on cultivating eloquence, represents visually the early modern opposition between art and nature and the relationship of both to notions of culture and flowers. In the engraving, the iconographical representation of "Art" stands above scientific and mathematical instruments emblematic of the learned skills and arts of man. In opposition to her stands "Nature," a woman with a cornucopia in one hand, the sun in the other, and a group of flowers beneath her. Placed above both figures, however, is "Eloquence," who is framed by elaborate bouquets of flowers arranged in exquisite urns. As the title of Binet's work suggests, the work was intended to help the reader become conversant in human arts and works of nature in order to master the art of rhetoric.[8] Flowers, as indicated on the frontispiece, belonged to the realm of nature. But gathered into bouquets in fanciful urns, or elegantly described and celebrated in Binet's prose, they signified eloquence. In other words, the "cultivated" flowers communicated Binet's learning, his civility, and his own cultivation. Humans could improve nature, but the manipulation of nature—even if only on paper—could contribute equally to the improvement of humanity.

The three works by Olivier de Serres, Honoré d'Urfée, and Etienne Binet, iconic in their respective genres, are each paradigmatic of the celebration of the natural world and the place of humans in it that enraptured early modern Europeans. Taken together, the works bring into focus the complex intersection of nature, art, and culture manifested in so many aspects of early modern European culture. In the seventeenth and eighteenth centuries, Europeans constructed increasingly elaborate formal gardens, published and purchased large numbers of instructional manuals and lavishly illustrated folio volumes about the plants that filled those gardens, commissioned increasing numbers of landscape and still-life paintings, studied formally and informally botany, zoology, anatomy, and other natural sciences, and assembled public and private collections of plants and animals from all over the world.

With equal passion and curiosity, many Europeans also collected and cultivated flowers. Oddly, while Olivier de Serres's work reflected many of the developments in early modern agriculture and horticulture, his thoughts on furnishing the flower garden were already outmoded. The "bouquetier à fleurs" of antiquity, he informed his readers, had served as the repository of all the finest ornaments, beauties, and rarities. But, he lamented, it was not possible at the beginning of the seventeenth century to know how to cultivate all of the different rare and beautiful flowers that had filled the gardens of ancient Greece and Rome. Instead, he maintained, while "waiting for more ample knowledge" of the specimens, he recommended that gardeners plant well-known flowers and "fleurs sauvages," or wildflowers, which could be found in uncultivated meadows. Domesticated in the garden, these flowers, he assured his reader, could achieve beauty and honor while inflicting neither trouble nor cost on the *seigneur*.[9] De Serres suggested violets, daisies, marjoram, thyme, hyssop, sage, chamomile, and mint as suitable plants for the flower garden.

De Serres may have frowned upon the money needed to acquire more extravagant flowering plants for the flower garden. Or perhaps he gave precedence to species requiring little care and attention. Whatever his reasons, however, few would have followed De Serres's advice on selecting flowers. For by the early seventeenth century, the acquisition of new, rare, exotic, and expensive flowers had become quite the fashion. Over the next two centuries, new (and some old) species such as tulips, hyacinths, anemones, ranunculi, carnations, narcissi, and irises were hoarded by collectors, bred to improve blossoms and create new varieties, bartered and sold in a burgeoning flower trade, and cultivated in pots and elaborate gardens in order that their glorious colors, strong perfumes, and great variety be displayed.

Such "florists' flowers," as they came to be called, were regarded by those who cultivated and collected them as the finest ornaments of nature, "les étoiles de la terre," or the stars of the earth.[10] Those who made the cultivation of these treasured blossoms their passion labeled themselves "curious florists" and consciously constructed an identity for themselves around their floral fervor. The conjunction between the literal cultivation of flowers and new symbolisms attached to flowers in the early modern period suggests that the cultivation of flowers contributed to the "cultivation" of the self in early modern France. For the application of the human arts to nature expressed in the cultivation of flowers was equally an exercise in the art of the construction of the self. As symbols of the superlative ("the stars of the earth"), flowers effectively conveyed the refinement and curiosity of those who cultivated them. So effective were flowers in communicating these values that, by the end of the seventeenth century,

Louis XIV himself could be counted among the "curious florists," including them in his gardens and constructing nursery systems for their cultivation. Flowers became an important component of the gardens at Versailles and were drafted into Louis XIV's iconography of power.

These florists' flowers, then, are situated at the nexus of a number of vital aspects of early modern culture including nature, the arts, science, politics, and even economics. Thus positioned, flowers, a seemingly benign part of the material world, offer the scholar of early modern Europe a unique perspective from which to gain a greater understanding of the role of material culture, consumption, and cultivation in the construction of cultural—and increasingly, political—identities shaping the early modern world. Specifically, exploring the cultural meanings of flowers exposes the ambiguous—and ever-changing—gendering of nature and material goods, the process by which such goods acquire meaning in the seventeenth century, and the transferal of such meaning from the cultural to the political realm.

This book's investigation of the intersection of these themes and ideas as they collide in the consumption of flowers in the early modern period has benefited from many important works that have touched upon this nexus in one way or another. Much, of course, has been written about the efforts of early modern Europeans to control, tame, exploit, and simply understand the natural world around them, including Keith Thomas's *Man and the Natural World*. More recently, Simon Schama's *Landscape and Memory* has shed light on the endurance of history and myths of nature in the human condition.[11] Initial early modern efforts to comprehend the rapidly expanding natural world often took the form of collections of natural history specimens, including flowers. This work has therefore been influenced by Antoine Schnapper's *Le Géant, la licorne, et la tulipe: Histoire et histoire naturelle*, volume 1 in the series "Collections et collectionneurs dans la France du XVIIe siècle," and Krzysztof Pomian's *Collectors and Curiosities: Paris and Venice, 1500–1800*, works that reconstruct the world of the "curious" and their *cabinets*. This study, however, goes beyond establishing the "curiosity" for flowers and the identification of "curious florists" to explore the sociability that grew among male flower enthusiasts in early modern Europe and the implication of that sociability for the new meanings attached to flowers.[12]

As this book demonstrates, European curiosity about the natural world was distinctly gendered, though not always in expected ways. It argues that the world of flowers was initially feminine but, over the course of the early modern period, was co-opted by the male world of curious sociability. Several important works on the role of women in the natural sciences place this transition in context, the earliest and most influential of which is Carolyn Merchant's *Death of Nature: Women, Ecology, and the Scientific Revolution*. Merchant examines the transition from a society defined by the female natural world to one ruled by science, mechanics, and learning, a notably male domain. In the years since its initial publication, numerous studies have emerged, championing the means by which women were able to exploit their deeply rooted relationship to nature and the plant world in order to carve a niche for themselves in the burgeoning world of science and learning.[13] The investigation of the early modern European culture of flowers recovers an important and exceptional chapter in the gendering of the natural world.

In exploring the politicization of the natural world, specifically through the study of the means by which gardens, flowers, and floral symbolism were drawn into the celebration of Louis XIV, this work has, of course, been influenced by the now classic studies of Ludovican iconography. Jean-Marie Apostolidès' *Le Roi-machine: Spectacle et politique au temps de Louis XIV*, Jean-Pierre Néraudau's *L'Olympe du Roi-Soleil: Mythologie et idéologie royal au Grand Siècle*, and Peter Burke's *The Fabrication of Louis XIV* offer important insight into the deliberate construction of the king's image. Chandra Mukerji's *Territorial Ambitions and the Gardens of Versailles* examines more directly the reflection of the king's military and economic exploits and policies in the construction of the king's image in the gardens of Versailles. The study of the political uses of floral symbolism at the court of Louis XIV, however, raises important questions about how the image of the king, in his gardens and on royal medals, was fabricated. For I demonstrate that in resorting to flowers to communicate the power of the king, the king's panegyrists were drawing upon the new culture of flowers that had emerged around the curious florists. Instructive here has been the work of Abby E. Zanger. In her *Scenes from the Marriage of Louis XIV: Nuptial Fictions and the Making of Absolutist Power*, she demonstrates the means by which royal iconographers and panegyrists necessarily drew upon supplementary images and themes to bolster the representation of the not yet absolutist king,[14] making the case for any critical analysis of Louis's language and machinery of power to consider their broader cultural and historical context.

The history of the flowers, themselves, has been explored largely as a part of the history of botany or of art. Historians of science and art have noted that the development of the science of botany was highly dependent on the ability to produce naturalistic representations of the flowers and plants studied.[15] Though floral still life painting was popular among viewing audiences and has been the subject of numerous exhibitions, art historians have only recently begun to look beyond long-held prejudices that regarded flower painting as a less artistically challenging and intellectually inferior endeavor. Works by Simon Schama, Norman Bryson, and Paul Taylor offer interpretations of flower painting in the context of the cultural meaning of flowers in the Netherlands.[16]

The role of flowers in the early modern garden has received increasing attention. Georgina Masson's "Italian Flower Collectors' Gardens in Seventeenth-Century Italy" first demonstrated that early modern flower cultivation and collecting was an intriguing cultural phenomenon. Elisabeth Blair MacDougall continued Masson's investigation of Italian flower gardens in her 1994 *Fountains, Statues, and Flowers: Studies in Italian Gardens of the Sixteenth and Seventeenth*

Centuries in which she studies inventories, horticultural treatises, planting lists, and an album of painted flowers related to a little-known flower garden at Rome's Palazzo Barberini. Mark Laird has focused on the reconstruction of early modern flower gardens in France and England. Laird, working with the few planting plans that have been found for early modern gardens, has produced watercolor elevations drawn to scale in order to help understand what the early modern flower garden looked like. His work, *The Flowering of the Landscape Garden: English Pleasure Grounds, 1720–1800*, goes a long way toward restoring flowers to our understanding of garden history. Brent Elliott's *Flora: An Illustrated History of the Garden Flower* brings together the botanical history of flowers and their introduction into Western gardens.[17]

But the history of flowers is more than their inclusion in the garden or their depiction on canvas. The challenge to understand flowers within the broader cultural context through which they have been consumed, cultivated, and celebrated in history remains. In recent years a few scholars have begun to make the broader cultural role of flowers and floriculture the focus of their investigations,[18] the most important of which is Jack Goody's 1993 work, *The Culture of Flowers*. His exhaustive anthropological study explores the meanings attached to flowers in cultures ranging from antiquity in the Near East, to modern Western Europe and America, and modern Africa and China. Goody devotes considerable attention to the fall and rise of flowers in medieval Christian thought, to the importance of floral symbolism in the Renaissance, and to the general recovery of floriculture in early modern Europe. Goody's work, which "map[s] out 'culture areas' marked by an emphasis on broadly different uses of flowers, rising above the local characteristics of individual 'cultures,'"[19] must be the starting point for any investigation of flowers in context of cultures, both historical and contemporary.

In considering the place of flowers in early modern Europe, Goody primarily investigates "crowns in the Italian Renaissance," the Dutch tulip mania and still life painting, and flowers in the English tradition. He devotes considerable attention to flowers in England where, deemed simultaneously dangerously pagan and popish by the Puritans, they were caught in the midst of the complicated politics of Reformation religion.[20] However, the breadth of Goody's work, by necessity, leaves much work yet to be done. One therefore, for example, eagerly awaits the appearance of Anne Goldgar's *Tulip Mania*, a work that promises a more subtle investigation of the Dutch tulip mania and those Dutch flower enthusiasts who fueled it than has yet appeared.[21]

This study, *Cultivated Power: Flowers, Culture, and Politics in the Reign of Louis XIV* explores the social and cultural context of flowers within early modern French culture. Early modern France was the undisputed European leader of courtly life and fashion, serving as the model to be aspired to by monarchs all over Europe. And, although while the aesthetic preeminence of the French formal garden is widely known, less familiar is the role of flowers within those gardens. For from the end of the sixteenth century through the seventeenth, reaching an apex in the reign of Louis XIV, flowers were incorporated into French formal gardens on a scale unequaled anywhere in Europe. *Cultivated Power* recovers this history of flowers in the French garden, but also joins the equally important conversation about nature, gender, art, and politics in early modern culture. To achieve this interdisciplinary goal, the work therefore incorporates a wide range of documents and printed sources, many of which have seldom been consulted by historians. Archival records of royal gardeners, and specifically of flower gardeners, have yielded a wealth of information on flower purchases and planting schemes for early modern French gardens, revealing not only the floral species included in flower parterres, but also significant amounts of money expended on furnishing them. Together with early modern instructional gardening manuals, they allow for the reconstruction of the place of flowers in the early modern formal pleasure garden. Early modern European flower collectors and gardeners wrote numerous guides to the cultivation of flowers that reflect trends in flower collecting and cultivation that shaped the fashionability of different species. These manuals, and especially their rich dedications and prefaces, proved to be an invaluable source for understanding the motivations of the curious florists who felt it necessary to defend their floral preoccupations. In so doing, these early modern floriculturists lay open the means by which their interest in flowers displayed their refinement and civility. Similarly, the incorporation of flowers into decorative and fine arts, into portraits, emblems, and devices, demonstrates the aesthetically pleasing uses of flowers in conveying that civility. Court panegyric literature, including the *livrets* of court ballets and operas, the published descriptions of royal fêtes and gardens, royal devices, and unique works such as Donneau de Visé's *Histoire de Louis le Grand*, reveal how flowers became political vehicles, trading on their cultural distinction to enhance the glory of the king.

Ultimately, it is this interdisciplinary approach, the combining of archival, printed, and visual sources, that exposes the broad yet powerful symbolic value of flowers in early modern France. In reconstructing this complex culture of flowers—who collected and cultivated them, why, and what that cultivation conveyed—this study demonstrates that understanding the history of flowers in the early modern period has implications for our comprehension of the rich texture of early modern society that extend far beyond floriculture. First, in exploring the ambivalent gendering of flowers and floriculture in Chapters one and two, in which seventeenth-century men sought to appropriate flower culture and symbolism for themselves, this study suggests that the female proclivity for botany in the late eighteenth and nineteenth centuries, the subject of much recent scholarship, is less exceptional than it might seem. In other words, it is men's encroachment on the world of flowers in the seventeenth century that is unique. The distinction conferred by floral cultivation was too great in the seventeenth and eighteenth centuries to be ignored by curious and fashionable men. But by the end of the eighteenth century, as floriculture ceased to be fashionable and it no longer benefited men to demonstrate an interest in flowers, flower culture was once again relinquished to women.

The history of early modern French floriculture also reveals the complexity of the roles played by nature and material culture in early modern Europe. The criteria developed by curious florists on the breeding, cultivation, and consumption of flowers suggests that consumption itself was increasingly regarded as an art through which floriculturists not only cultivated the flowers in the garden, but also authored their own cultural identities around that floral consumption. For in early modern Europe, flowers acquired a degree, in Pierre Bourdieu's words, of "cultural capital" through which flowers became capable of conferring on one a degree of cultural power, or "distinction."[22] But, as the culturally rich gardening manuals make clear, in order to lay claim to the distinction offered by flowers, it was necessary to master their cultivation. The study of those who did seek such floral distinction also reveals a common sociability that demonstrates the limits of traditional social order. For curious florists, drawn from a broad spectrum of French society, defy description by traditional markers of rank in a society generally assumed to be governed rigidly by one's status at birth. The cultivation and collection of flowers therefore reveals the implications of the creation of such cultural identities for the political realm.

Finally, the investigation into the appropriation of floral culture by Louis XIV and his court helps to refine the understanding of the means by which the king used taste and culture to persuade his subjects of his greatness. Just as the king funded academies of the arts to produce works flattering to the monarchy, and employed the likes of André Le Nôtre, Charles Le Brun, and Louis Le Vau to provide the architectural staging for the courtly drama of baroque politics, he also orchestrated the display of flowers at his court. His panegyrists sang the praises of those flowers in ballets, operas, and emblems, cleverly converting the king's perpetual display of ephemeral flowers into a demonstration of the king's power. Further, the traditionally feminine traits of flowers—especially their fertility and implied prosperity—were incorporated into expressions of the prosperity of his own reign. Yet in demonstrating that the king's use of flowers and floral symbolism was shaped, too, by the new culture of flowers, this study questions traditional notions that the king was the arbiter of taste in the seventeenth century. For in joining the already formed ranks of the "curious florists," Louis XIV was hardly breaking new ground. Rather, he very wisely incorporated into his language of power a phenomenon already validated by those elite members of French society that he most needed to persuade of his glory. What emerges, then, is a far more complex picture of the king's use of taste, culture, and consumption to glorify his reign than has been conventionally assumed.

The first chapter, "Disorderly Flowers," explores traditional aspects of floriculture and floral symbolism that gave some seventeenth-century flower collectors pause. Flowers had long symbolized beauty and fertility, but those traits were accompanied by darker, more dangerous qualities. For beauty was notoriously short-lived and served as a reminder that death would come to all. And the fertility implied by the flowers that promised the fruits of prosperity was inherently sexual. The beauty and fertility of flowers also led to their identification with women and the realm of nature. Using sixteenth- and seventeenth-century representations of flowers and women, the chapter establishes the contribution of gendered floral metaphors to powerful though ambivalent images of women, flowers, and nature. In signifying beauty and decay, fertility and sexuality, femininity and female power, flowers and women together were potent reminders of the unruliness and dangers of the natural realm—and women.

Chapter 2, "Refashioning the Culture of Flowers in Early Modern France," explores the reconfiguration not only of the gendering of flowers in early modern culture, but also the reconfiguration of floral symbolism. As new, expensive, and fashionable flowers emerged in Western Europe, they captured the attention of men who had the money, connections, and curiosity to obtain them. And those men quickly co-opted the power inherent in floral symbolism but remained anxious about its feminine connotations. Through the sentiments expressed by the early modern male flower enthusiasts, the chapter demonstrates the "curious florists'" successful refashioning of the culture of flowers. By associating it with the male realm of curiosity and collection, floriculture came to signify the taste and reason of those who engaged in it. The chapter reveals, too, that a degree of sociability formed around those who fashioned themselves as "curious florists." Importantly, it demonstrates that those "curious florists" were drawn from a broad spectrum of early modern social ranks, including men from royal, noble, and bourgeois lineage, thereby demonstrating the existence of meaningful cultural identities that transcended the traditional social order in seventeenth-century France.

The third chapter, "Cultivating the Flower," investigates more fully flowers as material objects in a society increasingly driven by the act and art of consumption. For to partake of the cultural distinction conferred by the cultivation of flowers, "curious florists" had necessarily to furnish their gardens with those species deemed worthy by their fellow collectors. Through the discussions among flower collectors expressed in flower gardening manuals, the chapter explores the criteria by which "florists' flowers" came to be judged—not only to distinguish superior specimens from the mediocre, but also to distinguish among themselves those florists conscious of fashion and the art of consumption, and those who were not. The chapter further examines how fashion shaped floriculture. By demonstrating the means by which "curious florists" attempted to produce new varieties and colors of their favorite species, together with their efforts to describe their creations accurately through the act of naming, the chapter reveals the work of the "curious florists" to be driven by fashion not only for certain colors and exoticism, but also for the application of art to nature.

Chapter 4, "Cultivating the Man," illuminates the social practices and displays through which curious florists sought to lay claim to the taste and reason conveyed through the familiarity with floriculture. The chapter first recovers the aesthetic importance of flowers in the French formal gardening tradition by exploring the connection between the display of flowers in the garden and the ways in which flowers were valued and celebrated in early modern France. The chapter then explores the incorporation of flowers into portraits and emblems as the most elaborate and direct means of expressing one's identity through flowers. Finally, the chapter concludes with a discussion of the relationship between flowers and print. For the authorship of manuals on the cultivation of flowers, as well as more philosophical ruminations on floriculture, like the authorship of new floral species in one's garden, made possible the display of one's own cultivation. The chapter as a whole, then, reveals the many means by which flowers could express effectively and beautifully one's identity as a person of learning and taste.

The fifth and final chapter, "Cultivating the King," betrays the impact of the new culture of flowers on Louis XIV and the iconography drafted into his glorification. Through the study of royal financial and gardening records, the chapter establishes the indisputable importance of flowers in the royal gardens and reveals a little-known royal system of nurseries and forced cultivation constructed for the proper furnishing of the royal flower beds. The chapter ultimately exposes the fertile collision of material culture and symbolism in the realm of the political by demonstrating the means by which the flowers growing in the royal parterres were incorporated into the literary, painted, and printed celebration of the reign of Louis XIV. By literally fulfilling the floral praises of the likes of Benserade and Rapin quoted earlier, the gardeners of Louis XIV therefore made real and more powerful the notion that Louis XIV truly was leading France into a new golden age.

The book ends with an epilogue on flowers in the gardens of Louis XV, and specifically on the creation of a garden devoted to the cultivation of fine hyacinths, the most fashionable species in the eighteenth century, at Choisy. In demonstrating that Louis XV and his gardeners resorted to the acquisition of hyacinths through a Dutch mail-order service, the epilogue makes clear the contrast in the means by which the Sun King and his successor made use of floriculture. Louis XV would have the most sought-after blossoms in the Choisy parterres, each one an expensive, named variety. But their role in the machinery of royal celebration ended there. For, as the book demonstrates, Louis XIV and his gardeners, eager to lay claim to the distinction offered by the cultivation of flowers and be identified among the curious florists, created extensive nurseries in Paris, at Versailles, and in the south of France for the propagation of flowers intended for the royal parterres. But those parterres were no simple displays of floricultural wealth. They signified the king's taste, learning, and curiosity while at the same time offering his panegyrists a seemingly endless and aesthetically pleasing source of symbol-laden ornament. In demonstrating the use of flowers in the celebration of the king in context of the broader early modern French culture of flowers, this book exposes the means by which Louis XIV cultivated power.

CHAPTER 1

Disorderly Flowers

In 1668 the newly formed French Académie royale des sciences commissioned the noted engraver Abraham Bosse, along with flower painter Nicolas Robert and Louis Claude de Chastillon, to produce engravings of botanical specimens in the Jardin du roi to accompany the academy's *Descriptions de quelques plantes nouvelles* and *Mémoires pour servir à l'histoire des plantes*.[1] Among those images completed by Bosse was his version of the mandragore, or mandrake (figure 1). The engraving's richly textured leaves and delicate flowers were an accurate rendering of the plant's appearance aboveground. But the academicians found fault with the representation of the plant's root, which bore a strong resemblance to the torso and thighs of a female body. The work did not represent the male plant as the caption indicated. It was, they declared, "a ridiculous affectation. It must be corrected."[2] The engraving of the mandragore was subsequently reworked to eliminate the anthropomorphic references, but the Académie's condemnation of Bosse's original work marks a transitional moment in the study of natural history. The planned publication of the engravings as part of the royally sponsored botanical histories was one of the more ambitious projects that exemplified the increasing interest in the systematic investigation of the natural world and the application of the knowledge gained. That Bosse, whose works serve modern historians as exquisite records of the social and material world of seventeenth-century France, chose to render the mandragore in such way as to hint at the plant's uses and reputation demonstrates that flowers—both the physical specimens and the symbolisms they evoked—were laden with powers not yet confined to the realm of memory.

Bosse's version of the mandragore was not unique; others before him, including Basilius Besler and Johann Theodor de Bry, both important figures in the history of botanical illustration, had chosen to represent the plant in the same manner.[3] Their works, like Bosse's, referred to the plant's rich popular and medical lore that maintained that the mandragore existed in "male" and "female" forms, the differences of which were manifested in the shape of each plant's root. While the root of the "male" mandragore consisted of a single body, the root of the "female" version separated into two sections resembling legs; the female was considered to be the more dangerous version of the plant. Simply gathering the plant for use could expose one to its lethal powers, for it was believed to emit a deadly shriek when pulled from the ground.[4] Once harvested, the mandragore was employed in the treatment of a number of conditions including infertility. It was also thought to be useful as an aphrodisiac and was, therefore, clearly associated with sexuality. Even more troubling, the plant was implicated in the

FIG. 1   Abraham Bosse, *Mandragore*, 1676. Paris, Bibliothèque Nationale de France, cliché C 20687.

practice of witchcraft, for it was believed that witches utilized the plant to induce deep sleep in their husbands thereby allowing women to sneak away undetected at night to attend Sabbat meetings at which, it was thought, witches engaged in sexual unions with the devil.[5] Bosse's representation of the flower, like others before it, emphasized the imagined likeness between the "female" mandragore and the dangerous sexuality of the human female by adding human trunk-like and even pubic features to the hairy two-legged root. Within a single plant were brought together the most potent fears preoccupying sixteenth- and seventeenth-century Europeans. Bosse and his contemporaries lived in a European society still subject to outbreaks of the plague and other virulent diseases. They were still fighting, theologically and militarily, over the religious questions raised by the Reformation and the legitimacy of the new Protestant sects. They could still remember the "monstrous regiment of women," described by John Knox—the accidental dynastic rise to political power of a number of women in the sixteenth and early seventeenth centuries. And they had seen the climax of the witch craze, during which thousands of Europeans, mostly women, had been convicted of commerce with the devil and executed.

The medical and diabolical attributes of the mandragore are only the most extreme powers, ranging from the pharmacological to the sensory to the symbolic, that were inherently connected to flowers in the early modern European imagination. The early modern understanding of flowers owed much to the inheritance of traditional medical practices, medieval Christian floral symbolism, and the newly recovered, though fragmentary, knowledge of floriculture in classical antiquity.[6] When, in the sixteenth and seventeenth centuries, flowers, some recently introduced to Western Europe, became highly desired objects of collectors and fashionable additions of the formal garden, they entered early modern culture with an ambiguous mix of traditional, Christian, and classical symbolic baggage that both denigrated flowers as symbols of the ephemeral and celebrated them as the beautiful creations of the Christian God or gods and goddesses of antiquity. Flowers, too, were part of the yearly rituals of crop fertility central to traditional or popular Western culture.[7] Efforts to strike a balance between the earthy pagan past of flowers, Reformation-era Christian sensibilities, and changing concepts of nature are revealed through intriguing subtexts of a broad social conversation on flowers and floriculture contained in sources ranging from flower gardening manuals, moral treatises, and even dictionaries to emblem books, popular prints, and formal paintings. Through this rich discourse on floriculture, seventeenth-century flower enthusiasts and French society in general defined a new culture of flowers that brought order to the floral realm, even making them suitable for celebrating important people. But in defining that new culture, flower enthusiasts or collectors, like the members of the Académie royale des sciences uncomfortable with Bosse's mandragore, had to confront the historical meanings of flowers and the symbolic and real powers they embodied.

FLORAL SEDUCTION: DEATH, SEX, AND FLOWERS

The discourse around the uses of the mandragore was centered in the debate over who controlled nature. Women were believed to be closer to nature, whereas men—the thinkers, theologians, artists, builders, and rulers of society—were thought to be more closely aligned with culture and the forces of civilization.[8] But the fear inherent in the belief that women used the mandragore to drug their husbands in order to participate in the practice of witchcraft suggests that male leaders of society were concerned that women, in harnessing the power of the mandragore, were harnessing the power of nature herself. Increasingly, however, from the Renaissance forward, educated men took a strong interest in unlocking the secrets of nature and in so doing, mounted a challenge to the notion that nature was the domain of women. But the conventions they challenged were deeply rooted in tradition.

The medical uses of plants and flowers were, of course, ancient. Knowledge about such uses of plants in the arts of healing were passed down as tradition from mother to daughter, as knowledge of herbal healing was essential in any good mistress of the household; from father to son (or apprentice) if the father was an apothecary by profession; and from brother to brother within the monastery, for, as with many types of learning that had disappeared from European culture after the fall of Rome, it was within the cloister walls that much knowledge about the medicinal properties of plants resurfaced, especially during the Carolingian Renaissance of the eighth and ninth centuries. Monastic gardens therefore included herbs, along with vegetables, fruit trees, and grapevines, despite the fact that some Christian theologians questioned intervening through herbs in the healing process—for the power to cure belonged to the realm of God.[9] Nonetheless, monasteries remained the seat of medical studies until the establishment of universities devoted to the study of medicine in Padua, Pisa, Bologna, and Montpellier.

To facilitate the study of the medicinal herbs, including new plants brought back to Europe from the Americas and the Near East, the professors and doctors affiliated with the universities established botanic gardens in hopes of exploring what beneficial properties the plants might hold.[10] The first botanic gardens were attempts to raise new specimens along with known species in what functioned as living encyclopedias. Richer de Belleval, who held a newly created chair in anatomy and herbal medicines at the university at Montpellier, founded the first French botanic garden.[11] As early as 1597, a botanic garden was planned in Paris, but the Jardin royal des plantes médicinales was not constructed until 1626.[12] The garden became the center for the study of plants by the Académie royale des sciences where members undertook chemical "distillations" of the plants in their collection. By the late seventeenth century, members of the academy debated the extent to which the society should devote itself to the detection of medical and other practical applications of plants, as opposed to the study of plant structure and classification,[13] but plants themselves remained at the center of their focus.

Yet the tendency to view the botanic garden as a purely scientific endeavor signaling the emergence of the scientific revolution is premature, for other motivations existed as well. John Prest explains: "It might appear . . . that in the

Botanic Garden, one stands in the presence of the beginnings of modern science, the collection of data, and that patient, detailed observation of causes and their effects. These are, indeed, the directions in which the Garden ultimately led, but reference to modern science does not describe the motivation with which it began. Contemporaries interpreted the foundation of these encyclopaedic Gardens in a context of the re-creation of the earthly paradise, or Garden of Eden, with which this story begins."[14] Central to Renaissance Christian humanist and hermetic thought was the notion that God's expulsion of Adam and Eve from the paradise that was the Garden of Eden had resulted in humankind's seemingly irreparable loss of the totality of God's creations and, as a result, the loss of the key to understanding God's Truth.[15] By reuniting the plants dispersed after the Fall, Renaissance and early modern thinkers hoped to recover an important key to understanding the universe while at the same time unlocking the earthly powers of plants, be they medicinal or nutritive.

Flowers were almost universally celebrated as one of God's supreme creations. But theologians, Catholic and Protestant alike, felt that the manner in which one appreciated flowers, as well as the ways in which one used flowers, was crucial in determining their compatibility with Christian goodness. Flowers had been used in ancient Roman civic and religious rituals and were, therefore, easily incorporated into early Christian practices. By the eve of the Protestant Reformation, flowers had become thoroughly entrenched in Christian rituals: floral chaplets were worn during weddings, flowers were used during funerals, and bouquets of flowers, taken as offerings to the altar, decorated church buildings. But Protestant reformers became suspicious of flowers within the church. Initially, strict Protestant sects sought to ban flowers along with the paintings and statues that Protestants expelled from their churches as idolatrous. The Puritan iconoclasts of England were particularly bothered by the presence of flowers, and attempts were made to ban them from civic and religious rituals. They were ultimately unsuccessful, but the targeting of flowers by Protestant and Catholic reformers alike points to an uneasy ambivalence about flowers in early modern culture.[16]

For while the plant kingdom was credited with a lofty position in Christian cosmology, it was also acknowledged that flowers held the power to turn the attention of the faithful toward more worldly matters. The aesthetic pleasures afforded by flowers—chiefly their visual beauty and fragrance—were believed to hold considerable power over the senses and hence over one's ability to exert self-control. Cesare Ripa described the symbol signifying "Beauty" in his well-known emblem book: "A Lady hiding her Head in the Clouds, and the rest of her Body is scarce visible, by reason of the Splendour that environs her. She stretches one Hand out of the Light, with a Lilly, and holds out a Ball and Compasses with the other. Her Head in the Clouds shews that nothing is more *impossible* to be *declar'd*, nor nothing *less known*, being a Ray of Divinity. The Lilly denotes *Beauty*, the Ball and Compasses denote that Beauty consists in *Measure* and *Proportion*.

The Flower *moves* the Senses, and *recreates* the Spirits; so does Love *move* the Soul to Enjoyment."[17] In Ripa's representation of beauty, the visually pleasing flower not only symbolized one's beauty, but also the sensory response stimulated by beauty. In other words, floral beauty, like a woman's beauty, had the power to influence the actions of those captured by its spell.

But the beauty of flowers was, like that of women, unavoidably—even notoriously—short-lived. Ripa used flowers in the emblems for "Fugacitá: Soon Fading" and "Vita breve: Short Life." In the depiction of "Fugacitá," a woman carried "a Nosegay of Roses; part of which fall to the Ground, fading and discolour'd." Ripa offered further explanation: "The Rose, in the Morning, buds, is fragrant, and flourishing; and, in the Evening, languishes and fades; a true Emblem of the Frailty of sublunary Things."[18] Similarly, in order to illustrate "Short Life," Ripa included a garland in the emblem which "shews the *Frailty* of Man, that

FIG. 2.   Jacques Lagniet, *Il faut mourir* [*One must die*], seventeenth century. Paris, Bibliothèque Nationale de France, Cabinet des Estampes, cliché C 4994.

loses his Strength as Flowers fade in a moment."[19] The use of flowers to express the brevity of beauty and hence of life was a common sentiment in the *memento mori* culture that was preoccupied with earthly sin, death, and salvation. A seventeenth-century popular print by Lagniet uses flowers in a gruesome but playful reminder that death will come to all. In the engraving, two fashionable gentlemen are depicted, one sniffing a bouquet of roses (figure 2). The caption reminds one that "From the bud comes the Rose, and from the Rose, the rose hip."[20] When the print is turned upside down, the viewer sees that the gentlemen have become fleshless skulls.

The use of flowers to express the shortness of life reached its apogee in early modern still life *vanitas* paintings.[21] Dutch and Flemish flower painters dominated the genre, producing hundreds of the commercially popular works for a broadening public eager to purchase them.[22] The Netherlandish works might consist of elaborate bouquets in which, upon close examination, one could find rotting petals and insect-riddled leaves as evidence of encroaching decay. Others were less subtle in communicating the *memento mori* message, including with a bouquet or even a single blossom a skull or an hourglass. French still life painters, too, produced *vanitas* paintings. One work, attributed to Philippe de Champaigne, included a single red and white tulip, a skull, and an hourglass. The choice of the tulip as the floral symbol would also have served as a critique of the waste of money (as serious as the foolhardy waste of time) in the speculation in the Netherlands in the 1630s. Lubin Baugin's *Still Life with Game Board,* now in the Louvre, included an indictment of the five senses within its *vanitas* message. In the painting, the five senses were metaphorically represented by their usual attributes, including flowers for the sense of smell, yet each symbolic object in the painting was simultaneously a symbol of the brevity of life.

The most celebrated seventeenth-century French painter, Nicolas Poussin, explored the dark theme in a composition of the goddess Flora.[23] Poussin completed a rendition of Flora in 1631 that was heavily dependent upon Ovid's telling of the metamorphoses of his tragic characters into flowers. In the work, the goddess prevailed in a garden illuminated by Apollo whose life-giving warmth crossed the horizon. Yet it was Flora who offered an immortality of sorts by turning the figures, depicted at the moment of their deaths, into flowers. From left to right, a priapic herm looked on as Ajax fell on his sword, bleeding into the earth what would become a flower; Clytie watched Apollo cross the sky at the moment when she was transformed into the sunflower; and Echo and Narcissus, gazing at his reflection in a bowl of water, occupied the center foreground of the painting. Beyond Flora, Hyacinthus contemplated the flower bearing his name while holding his injured head; Adonis inspected the hound-inflicted bite from which would sprout the anemone; and the love of Smilax and Crocus, shown staring into each other's faces, would remain unconsummated as both were turned into flowers.

Although Anthony Blunt found in the painting a "light-hearted delicacy" unequaled in any of Poussin's other works,[24] others have suggested a darker reading. The art historian Troy Thomas, through a study of the floral metamorphoses included in Poussin's *Realm of Flora* in conjunction with the editions and interpretations of Ovid's work available to Poussin, argued convincingly that as the victims shown were all defeated by their own vanity or passion, the painting should be read as a cautionary tale. Thomas explained: "In placing side by side images of death and the enduring forces of life and regeneration, Poussin calls upon the observer to contemplate the meaning of mortality in a larger context. The picture is a poetic and evocative depiction of the unhappiness of love, of the closeness of love to death, and, in depicting humans turned to flowers, of the limited scope of human immortality in the ceaseless cycle of nature." Thomas continued, "Poussin's themes of love, death, and rebirth are richly linked in the subtle fusion of two genres, one moral and one reflective: *vanitas* and elegy."[25]

Thomas's argument is convincing and offers a valid explanation of Poussin's interpretation of Ovid's characters. While Poussin's moralizing treatment of Flora was atypical of most French painted representations of the goddess, it did reflect the moralistic and intentionally Christian tone expressed in some seventeenth-century gardening texts.[26] For the writers of early modern flower gardening manuals did not overlook the floral metaphor for death, drawing connections in their celebration of floriculture between flowers, women, and death. Charles de la Chesnée Monstereul, author of an early work on the cultivation of tulips, explained the importance of contemplating the similarities between women's and floral beauty: "The most beautiful and virtuous woman of the world, (as well as tulips) will be abandoned for an ugliness [or wickedness]." He continued: "Some people in our age ask what is the use of this short-lived beauty; what utility [is there] in the connections between the beauty of women and of flowers; does one not see that their lustre passes in an instant and that possession of it is very short."[27] For La Chesnée Monstereul, a flower was properly appreciated if its short life (and therefore its reminder to look after the soul) was recognized, just as women (and adoring men) were wise to keep in mind that outward beauty would not be rewarded in the afterlife. The short-lived display of tulips in the garden could serve, argued La Chesnée Monstereul, as a moralizing presence.

If the physical beauty of flowers was capable of distracting one from the care of the soul, the fragrance of flowers was regarded as even more sensual and therefore more dangerous. Franciscus de Grenaille explained in his *Plaisirs des Dames*, "if you smell their odor, your soul will remain so delighted that you will no longer have the strength to look at their colors."[28] The fragrance of a flower could affect the heart—and the brain. The early modern conception of sensory experience owed much to classical and medieval Christian inheritance. Ancient Greeks and Romans believed that smells, because of the proximity of the nose to the brain, were very powerful. The association of particular smells with the humors, sweet and spicy with hot and dry, putrid odors with cold and wet, explained the effects of odors on the brain.[29] The ancients therefore valued fragrances and made use of them in religious observances.[30] Early Christians thus regarded perfumes as idolatrous and luxurious, but the use of incense was so ingrained in late antique culture that, by the sixth century, fragrances were fully incorporated into Christian worship.[31] Indeed, despite Christian suspicion of sensory fulfillment, smell came to signify the holiest of worshipers among medieval Christians.

The "odor of sanctity," a sweet fragrance emitted by the saintly, or more commonly the pleasing aromas given off by the bodies of those saints miraculously undecayed even years after death, distinguished the specially blessed. The "odor of sanctity" survived into the early modern period. One seventeenth-century French saint was reported to have perfumed with the fragrance of her own body everything she touched, and her scent increased when she was in a state of ecstasy.[32] The notion that aromas projected one's essence was so ingrained in French culture that words about smell were figuratively used to comment on one's character. In his *Dictionnaire universel*, Antoine Furetière wrote that the word *odeur* could be used in reference to "moral things, and signify good or bad reputation."[33] Pierre Richelet, in his *Dictionnaire François*, also included *estime* and *reputation* as synonyms for *odeur*.[34] The connotations for the word *parfum* were even stronger and more complimentary. Furetière wrote that "Perfume, is said figuratively [to refer] to things which agreeably flatter the spirit. The perfume of praises. Prayer rises to heaven as an agreeable perfume."[35]

Yet early modern clerics continued to regard olfactory fulfillment with disapproval. The renowned Jacques Bénigne Bossuet, bishop of Meaux, cited in his *Traité de la concupiscence* a woman in Proverbs who invited a lover to her bed sprinkled with sweet-smelling flowers and herbs. The story, explained Bossuet, demonstrated the dangers of "pleasant odors [that] prepared to weaken the soul and attract it to sensual pleasures." Although the fragrant aromas of flowers, he continued, "do not appear to represent a direct offense against modesty, . . . nonetheless they can cause [the soul] to let go and distract its attention from what should be its natural occupation."[36] The fragrance of flowers, then, could be used as an agent of seduction. Not surprisingly, floral fragrances, emanating from flowers themselves or from expensive perfumes distilled from them, were becoming increasingly popular among the privileged.[37]

The seductive qualities of sweet-scented flowers were also explored in popular prints devoted to the sense of smell. The images flirted with the powerful temptations facilitated by flowers and their perfumes. Abraham Bosse represented the sense of smell with, predictably, flowers, a garden, and sniffing dogs—typical attributes of smell—but also a man and woman strolling together with a bouquet of flowers. Their interlude is related to the sense of smell through the role played by the bouquet of scented flowers accepted and sniffed by the man (figure 3). Other images playfully attested to the effectiveness of flowers and perfumes in seduction. As the verse accompanying an anonymous late seventeenth-century depiction of smell explained:

FIG. 3. Abraham Bosse, *Odoratus, L'Odorat* [*Smell*], seventeenth century. New York, Metropolitan Museum of Art, Harris Brisbane Dick Fund, 1926 (26.49.24).

> I love to smell flowers,
> They are a delight for coquettes.
> But they give them the vapors,
> Thus I like best [to offer] *fleurettes*.[38]

"Fleurettes" were defined by Furetière's *Dictionnaire universel* as "small ornaments of language, and sweet terms which one ordinarily uses to cajole women, or to make love to them."[39] As the caption to another Bosse representation of *L'Odorat* read, the sense of smell "was the subtle enchantress of the other senses,"[40] and flowers were the primary tool used in the aromatic seduction (figure 4). The Sieur de Grenaille, whose *Plaisirs des Dames* was dedicated to Henrietta Maria, queen of England, in hopes that it would help the queen protect her honor while in France "while the men are occupied with making war,"[41] cautioned the queen and other women of honor against receiving flowers. Grenaille argued that while the short-lived beauty of the flower ought to encourage contemplation of the state of one's soul, every suitor truly hoped that "the odor of flowers purifies the mind of his mistress, producing there the image of her lover."[42] The odor of the flower was supposed to persuade, or even to seduce, the woman.

If the fragrance and beauty of a single flower could sway a lover, the bou-

L'ODORAT.

La Deesse des fleurs ne sçait pas l'art de plaire,
Comme cette beauté que tu vois peinte icy,
Et c'est auec raison qu'vn bouquet elle flaire,
Estant de l'Odorat le portrait raccoursy.

Mais bien que se flattant au milieu des delices,
Elle semble n'aimer que les bonnes senteurs;
Ses regards toutes fois ont beaucoup de malices,
Et sont des autres sens les subtils Enchanteurs.

A.Bosse.in et sc.   le Blond excud auec Priuilege du Roy

FIG. 4.   Abraham Bosse, *L'Odorat* [*Smell*], seventeenth century. New York,
Metropolitan Museum of Art, Harris Brisbane Dick Fund, 1930 (30.54.27).

quet of beautiful flowers gathered together into one bunch could be even more dangerous. Floral bouquets were given to women as tokens of love, yet, warned the moralist Grenaille, the gift of a bouquet, or, more importantly, the acceptance of one, was an ambivalent gesture that, while complimenting a woman's beauty, compromised her reputation. Bouquets worn by women to ornament their décolletage, according to Grenaille, served also as a temptation to men. In Grenaille's opinion, "The bouquet and the breast that carries it are two subjects of corruption."[43] Grenaille further explained: "That as it is not the crowns that embellish heads, but rather the heads that embellish the crowns, one should think equally that it is the breast of a lady that embellishes the bouquet, and not the bouquet that embellishes the Lady. If there is a bosom, it should be covered, as there are others who would allow the beauty to be discovered, and that it is very difficult to render invisible the two mountains of love."[44] Grenaille thus argued that the flirtatious disguising of the breasts with flowers was an invitation by the woman and a temptation to the man to uncover them.

The application of sexual connotations to the word *bouquet* was not limited to Grenaille. According to Furetière, one could use "bouquet" in the phrase "that she has a bouquet on the eye" in reference to a house in order to communicate that the house was for sale. Similarly, it could be used as an allusion to one's daughter to imply that "she is [available] to marry," the bouquet referring to the daughter's marriageability. In another reference to the transaction that the exchange of a bouquet implied, one could use the phrase "return the bouquet," meaning to "to settle one's debt." Offering a bouquet was thus clearly connected to the exchange of property or services or of the fulfilling of an obligation. Finally, Furetière remarked, "One says also, that a woman carries the bouquet to her husband, when she is unfaithful to him."[45] The bouquet therefore exemplified transactions of all sorts, including marital and sexual ones of an amoral nature.

Despite the moralizing warnings over the seductive powers of flowers, over the course of the seventeenth and into the eighteenth century flowers were increasingly enlisted by women in the enhancement of their beauty. Incorporated by women in their efforts to produce favorable responses to their beauty, floral-based perfumes, powders, and oils as well as flowers themselves were essential elements in the fashionable woman's *toilette*. Pierre-Joseph Buc'Hoz remarked in his eighteenth-century *Toilette de Flore, ou essai sur les plantes & les fleurs qui peuvent servir d'ornement aux dames*, "flowers are today one of their principal ornaments."[46] His publication included a list of flowers useful in various elements of the *toilette*, as well as recipes for oils, powders, and perfumes to be made from them. Buc'Hoz's list contained, in addition to those flowers useful in the preparation of cosmetic concoctions, various blossoms "to ornament the toilettes of women."[47] A woman's beauty was thus complimented not only by the floral applications to her visage, but also by the flowers she carried with her or displayed at her *toilette*, where she might receive visitors.

As potent as flowers could be in the art of seduction, they were just as importantly associated with its fruits. That is, as the botanical precursors to a plant's fruit, flowers were also symbols of fertility. Thus the flower, known to be the necessary precursor to plant reproduction, was a natural symbol with which to associate female humans. Ripa depicted "Hope" as a woman "crown'd with a Garland of Flowers," explaining that "the Flowers denote *Hope*, they never appearing without some Hope of Fruit."[48] Women's bodies were commonly explained and described in medical literature by resorting to the language of gardens and cultivation. For example, Thomas Bartholin wrote in his anatomy, "The Womb is like a Garden or Field, which receives, preserves, and nourishes the Seed; and therefore Aristotle calls it the Field of Nature."[49] The metaphor was reinforced linguistically through words used to refer to women's bodies and bodily functions[50] and visually in illustrations of women's anatomy.[51] According to Furetière's *Dictionnaire universel*, "fleur" could be used to refer to menstrual flow. Furetière wrote, "One also calls *flowers* the ordinary purgations of women, their monthlies, their menses."[52] The word "fleur" was also used to refer to a woman's virginity. "One says also, that virginity is a flower that one can cut only once," explained Furetière.[53] In a seventeenth-century print by Le Pautre, a gallant lover standing in a formal parterre offers to a woman a bouquet of flowers that he places in her decolletage. The woman, who holds up a gathering of flowers in her skirt, responds to his overtures saying, "That if you place a kiss on my mouth// you could cause me the loss of my flowers."[54] Nicolas Venette used the word in a similar way in his *Tableau de l'Amour*, a sex manual for married couples. Venette explained in his "Eloge de la Virginité" that "it is a pretty flower poorly guarded in a walled garden."[55] Even the sexuality of the Virgin Mary was represented by vegetal symbols; the white lily was generally included in portrayals of the Annunciation to signify her purity, just as the scene frequently included a room opening into a closed garden to remind the viewer of her chastity.[56]

The anatomical relationship between women's bodies and flowers was visually interpreted in Matthieu Merian's engraved depiction of the anatomy of a pregnant woman (figure 5). The image displayed the fetus within the womb by pulling back layers of skin, abdomen, and finally the uterus to reveal the fetus in such a manner that the layers resembled petals of a flower, with the fetus forming the center of the blossom. A stem extended downward from her trunk, rooting her firmly to the earth. The various features of the woman's body were labeled to convey the proper anatomical information, but the image contained more than simple anatomy. The pregnant woman was about to bring forth the fruit of a sexual union. She was literally flowering, and by doing so she was fulfilling her destiny, her highest calling as a laywoman, by becoming a mother.[57] Yet the woman in the engraving held a piece of fruit in one hand, reminiscent of her predecessor in sin, Eve. In the background, a wrecked ship lay beached upon a shore—she had tasted the fruit and was a fallen woman. For her "flowering," then, the woman had sinned. The flowering woman in Merian's engraving revealed much about, indeed embodied the paradox of, early modern womanhood. Unable to achieve

FIG. 5. Matthieu Merian, *De Foetu Formato* [*Formation of the fetus*]. From Adriaan
van den Spiegel, *Opera quae extant, omnia*, Amsterdam: Johan Blaeu, 1645. Boston,
Francis C. Countway Library of Medicine, Harvard Medical Library.

motherhood in the chaste manner of the Virgin Mary, earthly women sacrificed their chastity in order to bear children. The flowering of the woman's body implied not only the chaste fertility of Mary, but also the female sexuality of Eve.

The ambivalent floral attributes associated with women and flowers—beauty, sensuality, fertility, and sin—were also embodied in the guise of Flora, the ancient goddess of flowers who enjoyed a resurgence in popularity in the early modern period. Flora's own sexual reputation heightened the connections between the sexual connotations of women and flowers. Early modern scholars of classical literature disputed Flora's uncertain ancestry; the moral standing of the goddess depended on which version of her heritage one believed. The Floralia, or floral games, were held annually in honor of Flora in ancient Rome from April 28 to May 3,[58] and, according to Ovid's *Fasti*, were characterized by "greater wantonness and broader jests" because "the gifts that she brings lend themselves to delights." Ovid continued: "A rakish stage fits Flora well; she is not, believe me she is not, to be counted among your buskined goddesses. . . . She is none of your glum, none of your high-flown ones: she wishes her rites to be open to the common herd; and she warns us to use the life's flower, while it still blooms; for the thorn, she reminds us, is flouted when the roses have fallen away."[59] By Ovid's account, the high-spirited, popular Flora was originally a young nymph named Chloris who attracted the attentions of Zephyr, one of the winds. Ovid included Flora's narration of her own history in his *Fasti*: "I who now am called Flora was formerly Chloris: a Greek letter of my name is corrupted in the Latin speech. Chloris I was, a nymph of the happy fields where, as you have heard, dwelt fortunate men of old. Modesty shrinks from describing my figure; but it procured the hand of a god for my mother's daughter. 'Twas spring, and I was roaming; Zephyr caught sight of me; I retired; he pursued and I fled; but he was the stronger, and Boreas had given his brother full right of rape."[60] For enduring the dishonor done to her by the wind, Zephyr rewarded her with marriage and immortality. Flora continued: "However, he made amends for his violence by giving me the name of bride, and in my marriage-bed I have naught to complain of. I enjoy perpetual spring; most buxom is the year ever; ever the tree is clothed with leaves, the ground with pasture. In the fields that are my dower, I have a fruitful garden, fanned by the breeze and watered by a spring of running water. This garden my husband filled with noble flowers and said, 'Goddess, be queen of flowers.'"[61] Thereby empowered by her wind husband, Flora governed in the realm of flowers, crops, and even honey, while occasionally exercising her powers by turning unfortunate lovers and passionate mortals into various floral species.[62]

Ovid's account of the origins of the Floralia and the goddess of flowers, however, was not the only version of her story. According to Julius S. Held, Lactantius, Minucius Felix, and Arnobius all wrote of a less honorable Flora who had gained notoriety as a wealthy prostitute. Boccaccio repeated their allegations in both his *De Claris Mulieribus* and *Genealogy of the Gods*, explaining that the courtesan had founded the floral games and that the Roman Senate had fabricated the history of Chloris in order to hide the dishonorable origins of the festival.[63] Boccaccio wrote, "For some say that she spent all the flower of her youth and the beauty of her body in brothels among panderers and wretched young men in public prostitution, and with lust and cajolery, as such women do, she stripped this or that simpleton of his riches, and by gnawing and picking in every direction she came into such great wealth." Others, according to Boccaccio, say that the keeper of the Roman temple of Hercules lost a bet to Hercules for which he paid with dinner and "the noble prostitute Flora." Flora was told by Hercules that "she would receive payment for her services from the man she would first see on leaving the temple in the morning. As she left the temple, she met . . . a very wealthy young man, who fell in love with her and took her to his house. She stayed with him a long time, and when he died she was his heir. . . . This quibbling," continued Boccaccio, "does not matter to me, as long as it is clear that Flora was a rich prostitute."[64] The prostitute, he claimed, left her fortune to the people of Rome on the condition that they celebrated her birthday. "At these games in the presence of the people," wrote Boccaccio, "among other foul things there were naked prostitutes who practiced their art in pantomime with various lewd gestures to show how Flora had acquired her wealth."[65] He continued, "After some time, the Senate, knowing the origin of these games and being ashamed that the city which was already mistress of the world should be branded by this foul blot and that the whole city rushed to praise a prostitute, and knowing that it could not easily wipe this out, in order to hide their ignominy and disgrace added to it a detestable but droll fiction,"[66] the story of Chloris the nymph transformed into the goddess Flora.

Both interpretations of Flora's heritage were known in early modern Europe. Boccaccio's works, as we have seen, disseminated the view that Flora was originally a Roman courtesan. Meanwhile, Ovid's *Metamorphoses* and *Fasti* had been available in Latin (and later in French translation) through the Middle Ages, during which they were interpreted as moralizing tales. In the sixteenth century, some humanist scholars moved away from Ovid as moral censure, instead exploiting the tales for their erotic content. This interpretation continued into the seventeenth century, during which they allowed for expressions of libertinage;[67] they were repeatedly translated and published over the course of the century.[68] The *Métamorphoses* in particular were very popular, despite the "querelle d'Ovide," a debate over whether or not such risqué pagan works constituted appropriate reading material in Christian society.[69]

Representations of the goddess in paint and print reflected both interpretations of her past. Sandro Botticelli's famous *Primavera*, painted in the 1470s or 1480s, included on the right side of the painting Zephyr in pursuit of Chloris, who was then transformed into a flower-clad Flora spewing blossoms from her mouth. The painting has been interpreted variously as a "model of behavior" for the new bride of Lorenzo di Pierfrancesco de Medici,[70] an exercise in

Neoplatonic thought, and a simple celebration of the marriage.[71] From within the painting that depicts, from right to left, Zephyr, Chloris, Flora, Venus, the Three Graces, Mercury, and a cupid, many have sought to tease a narrative that explains the presence of each figure. Mirella Levi D'Ancona argues that Zephyr and Chloris, who becomes Flora, together represent earthly, physical love being transformed through marriage. From the center of the painting to the left, Venus stands under a cupid who aims an arrow at Chastity, one of the Three Graces, next to whom can be found Mercury, perhaps the intended groom, who looks upward toward divine love. Levi D'Ancona's analysis of the meticulously rendered flowering plants reinforces this interpretation of the figures in the work: the floral species refer symbolically, in Greek, Roman, and Italian Renaissance texts, to the transfer of earthly love and fertility to divine love as the eye passes from right to left.[72] Within Levi D'Ancona's reading of the painting, as with most interpretations of it, however, Chloris and Flora in the Botticelli masterpiece represent Ovid's account of Flora to signify honor and chastity in marriage as exemplified by the nymph turned goddess.[73]

The alternative heritage of Flora and the Floralia was also incorporated into Renaissance painting. Julius S. Held argues convincingly that Titian's notable portrait, now in the Uffizzi, of a partially disrobed woman grasping a handful of blossoms depicts Flora as a prostitute or perhaps even one of Venice's notoriously cultivated and sought-after courtesans.[74] He also points to a tradition of portraiture stemming from the morally compromised Flora.

Other images are more difficult to interpret. Mid-sixteenth-century paintings such as the *Triumph of Flora* by an anonymous artist now known as the "Maître de Flore," and the also anonymous *Allegory of Love*, now in the Louvre, depict the goddess surrounded by her floral subjects.[75] Yet in both images, the goddess is portrayed in a more erotically charged manner than in Botticelli's rendition. Both appear nude and are surrounded by cupids. In the *Triumph of Flora*, she reclines beneath a tree, her lap filled with blossoms. In the *Allegory of Love*, Flora is partially hidden behind flowering plants. Zephyr whispers into her ear while she points to a cupid struck by an arrow.

However these images of Flora were intended to be interpreted, it is clear that floral symbolism of the Renaissance and early modern period drew from both traditions. Whether Flora was originally a Greek goddess or a Roman courtesan, her power stemmed from her sexuality. Either she was given her power over the kingdom of flowers in compensation for Zephyr's rape and as a reward for serving chastely as his wife, or she earned her power and influence as a wealthy prostitute.

Flora's rule, extending as it did over fertility and the cultivation of gardens and crops, naturally was celebrated along with spring, the planting season. The Floralia, or floral games celebrated in ancient Rome in honor of Flora, were held annually in the last days of April into early May. Not only were Flora and flowers associated with spring, but personifications of Spring and Flora were often indistinguishable. Spring, too, carried flowers as her principal attribute, and both Flora and Spring celebrated the potential fertility and rebirth offered by the beginning of the agricultural cycle. Cesare Ripa included a garland of flowers in his representation of the season.[76] Similarly, Abraham Bosse illustrated the four seasons as the four ages of man, with Spring depicted as a young woman standing before a garden, picking flowers from a bouquet offered by a cherub or cupid. A verse accompanied the image:

> During the springtime of your age,
> Follow the love who follows you.
> Treat carefully the flowers that he gives you as pledge
> Or else you will lose those that bear fruit.[77]

The flowers and the young woman symbolized youth, fertility, beauty, and love.

Spring was also believed to be the season for love. Traditional May Day rituals, including the crowning of the May Queen with flowers, celebrated fertility.[78] Pseudo-medical marriage texts such as Nicolas Venette's *Tableau de l'amour* maintained that men and women were more amorous in the spring. Venette explained, "It is this nice season in which all of nature through its greenery and its flowers exudes production. Then the blood boils in the veins of one and the other sex. . . . We can therefore say that Spring is the season in which men and women are most amorous."[79] Because of the importance of fertility in the season, women were particularly associated with springtime. Indeed, the season marked a period of relative power for women, during which they could, according to local custom, assert power over their husbands.[80]

Representations of Spring therefore stressed both love, flowers, and the power of seduction. A mid-seventeenth-century engraving by Jean Le Blond, for example, depicted a woman with flowers in her hair and a bouquet in her hand and was accompanied by the words,

> At the return of Spring the trees recover
> Their greenness, that winter had rendered hoary;
> The rays of the sun banish the coldness,
> And the beautiful Adonis makes love to Venus.[81]

A late seventeenth-century example of *Le Printemps* by H. Bonnart directly incorporated a flower-adorned Flora attended by youthful Zephyrs offering a basket of blossoms. The verse added, "Flora, accompanied by two zephyrs who joke with her: the Poets feign that it is these agreeable winds who bring back the spring, and that their loves with Flora give birth to the flowers that embellish the season."[82] Similarly, the break of dawn could bring flowers—or at least the dew that quenched their thirst. In an allegory of Dawn executed by Jean-Baptiste de Champaigne for the Tuilleries palace, exquisite flowers rain from the hands of Aurora (plate 2). The coming of dawn, like the arrival of spring, signified by the blossoming of flowers offered a cleansing rebirth and the promise of plenty.

All of these images explore and exploit the relationships between flowers and women, their fertility, and sexuality—in short, between women and the essence of nature. The fertility of women and flowers was a reference to the larger cycle of life played out in nature—that of birth, fertility and sexuality, and death. Flowers were thus a reference to the natural, the uncivilized. The sixteenth-century Huguenot painter Jacques Le Moyne de Morgues, who survived an expedition to Florida in 1564 where he observed native peoples, fauna, and flora, illustrated the connection between women and flowers in the early modern imagination in his depiction of an ancient Pict female (plate 3). In the painting, Le Moyne represented the young Pict, one of the earliest ancestors of the Europeans, as a primitive creature, unclothed except for her belt, scabbard, and the floral tattoos that covered her body. The flowers—anemones, roses, tulips—that adorned her were exotic and rare in the sixteenth century, uncultivated and even unknown in ancient Britain. The work was a product of his historical imagination. Yet to depict the young woman living in a state very close to nature, in a society untouched by modern civilization, he dressed her in flowers, thereby demonstrating the very natural affinity between women's bodies and flowers. Although at first glance the floral tattoos veil the anatomical attributes of her sexuality, the artfully placed blossoms accentuated her fertility.

TRADING ON THE POWER OF FLOWERS

The very basic associations drawn between women, their bodies, and flowers in the early modern mind extended beyond the representation and symbolism of women, flowers, and fertility. Indeed, the connection between women and the procreative elements of nature symbolized by flowers were reflected, too, in women's work in the flower trade to the extent that some male flower enthusiasts were troubled by it. The cultivation of flowers, like the cultivation of foodstuffs, was traditionally identified with the female on a number of levels, the most prevalent of which was the very practical role of women in the production of food and household goods. Traditional culture in Western Europe had long before assigned women responsibility for the household or "kitchen" garden. In early modern Europe, mistresses of the estate cultivated herbs and flowers needed for oils, powders, perfumes, and medicines, as well as flavorings used in the production, preparation, and preservation of vegetables, fruits, and seasonings. The Ménagier de Paris, for example, in the household management book he composed for use by his young wife, directed her to mind the garden, advising her on when and how to plant individiual vegetables and flowering herbs. He even included instructions on how to "keep roses in winter."[83]

Nearly two centuries later, Charles Estienne and Jean Liébault similarly proclaimed in the *Maison Rustique*, a classic estate management manual of the sixteenth century,[84] that the mistress of the estate was "tied to matters within the house and base court . . . as the husband is tied to do what concerneth him."[85] Responsibilities connected to the "house and base court" included the care of farm animals (with the exception of the horses), insects (bees and silkworms), and plants, and the eventual processing and preservation of the food and fibers produced by them. Explained Estienne and Liebault, the woman was in charge "of ordring of the kitchin garden: and keeping of the fruites, herbes, rootes, and seedes."[86] These flowers and herbs flavored food, were added to flour in years of bad harvests, and were used in the "naturall remedies which she shall acquaint herselfe withall for the succour of her folke in their sicknesses." The flower garden itself was deemed "the most delectable thing for recreation belonging unto our French farmes . . . in respect that it serveth for the chiefe Lord whose the inheritance is to solace himselfe therin, as also in respect of their service for to set Bee-hives in."[87] Although it is not clear whether the cultivation of the distinct flower garden of Estienne and Liebault's ideal estate belonged to the duties of husband or wife, women were likely responsible for its maintenance. Working-class women were employed outside the home as weeders.[88] Women's responsibility for the flower and herb gardens, then, was a serious one, as their success was vital to the health and productivity of the manor.

In urban areas, fresh flowers and herbs could be purchased in the marketplace, along with the expected butter, eggs, and produce from surrounding farms. Flowers and herbs (called *jonchées*, from the verb *joncher*, meaning "to strew") were scattered on the floors of homes and public buildings to absorb dirt and freshen the air. They were also gathered into bouquets as offerings to the church, or formed into garlands and chaplets (or crowns constructed of flowers and vines) to adorn people and tables in times of celebration or feasting. Fresh flowers were in such demand for these uses as to warrant the founding of guilds and corporations to control their sale. And just as women controlled the sale of their own farm produce, so did they dominate the market for flowers and herbs. *Jonchées*, or sweet-smelling plants scattered on floors, could be purchased from *bouquetières*, or women flower sellers. The women flower sellers conducted their business from established city markets or in the street. A *bouquetière* might also be given a contract to maintain the *jonchées* for a specific public building. The flower seller Colette la Moinesse, for example, was employed in 1430 "to strew fresh herbs, from the month of May until the end of September, for several rooms in the old Hôtel de Ville."[89]

Throughout the Middle Ages, flowers had been used to make chaplets or crowns worn by men and women in civic and religious ceremonies and public processions.[90] The demand for chaplets led to the founding in the twelfth century of a corporation or guild known as the "chapeliers de fleurs." Most guild members were women, many of whom were married to gardeners. It is not clear whether the women or men cultivated the roses, marigolds, pinks, lilies, wallflowers, columbine, and violets (all fairly common flowers) that were regularly incorporated into the crowns,[91] although Boileau reports that "the women would search for flowers in the gardens on the outskirts [of town], weaving them into crowns and selling them in the city."[92] By the fifteenth century, however, floral chaplets were no longer fashionable and the guild ceased to function.

When flowers became popular again in the seventeenth century, the sale of fresh flowers, as in the Middle Ages, fell to the female *bouquetières*. Although in 1642 a Parisian man, Jean Pertuissard, was named "bouquetier ordinaire de l'Hôtel de Ville," and thereby awarded the right (in addition to duties with cannon and other artillery) to distribute bouquets at the Hôtel de Ville during the fireworks celebrating the feast of Saint Jean,[93] most flower sellers were women. Indeed, although no incorporated guild of *bouquetières* existed in the early seventeenth century, a strong network of female flower sellers flourished. Jean Pertuissard contracted with Claude Baujard, a woman identified as a "maîtresse bouquetière à Paris," or mistress flower seller, to furnish the bouquets each year for the celebrations held at the Hôtel de Ville, including that of Saint Jean.[94] According to their agreement, the two shared both the expenses and profits, suggesting that while Pertuissard had received the commission from the city, he required the services of someone in the flower trade to supply the needed bouquets. He therefore turned to a *bouquetière*. For the most part, however, women dominated even the most prestigious parts of the fresh flower market. Marguerite François was identified as "ouvrière de la Reine en fleurs," or worker in flowers for the queen, in 1619,[95] and in 1650 a contract was drawn up between Marie Flocourt, "*bouquetière* to the queen," and Perrette Duquesne "for the service of the king, the queen, and the duc d'Anjou."[96]

Notarial records thus reveal the network of women flower sellers, but they offer little evidence to the kinds of goods sold by the *bouquetières*. For insight into the nature of their trade, one can turn to the few images of flower sellers produced in the seventeenth century. In the first half of the century, Jacques Linard painted images of women, perhaps as allegories of the element "earth," constructing bouquets from fresh flowers.[97] In the late seventeenth century, the engraver Nicolas de Larmessin visually interpreted the *bouquetières* as purveyors of both fresh and artificial flowers in the series of "Costumes grotesques et les métiers." Typical of the engravings by Larmessin in that the tradesperson was playfully constructed of the objects in which he or she traded, the two women flower sellers executed by Larmessin were covered with garlands, nosegays, and flower arrangements. One was composed of naturalistically rendered blossoms closely resembling those depicted in still life paintings (figure 6). The other, however, wore plumes and chaplets similar to artificial flowers made of fabric and feathers, while carrying a large basket (figure 7). The fanciful portrait depicted the woman constructing bouquets of artificial flowers in the basket and binding them with string or wire.[98] Though fantastical renderings, the images reveal that *bouquetières* could be engaged in the trade of fresh flowers or in the construction and sale of artificial blossoms increasingly popular for the decoration

N. de l'Armessin javen. et Sculp.

Habit de Bouquetiere

Se vend à Paris Chez N. de l'Armessin Rüe S.ᵗ Iaques devant la Rüe de la Place a la Coupe d'Or. Auec Privilège du Roy. 1695

FIG. 6.   Nicolas de Larmessin, *Habit de Bouquetière*, c. 1695. Paris, Bibliothèque Nationale de France, Cabinet des Estampes, cliché C 75957.

Habit de Bouquetiere

Se vend à paris Chez la Vefue N.de l'armessin Rüe St Jacques à la Pomme d'Or   Auec priuil du Roy.

FIG. 7.   Nicolas de Larmessin, *Habit de Bouquetière*, c. 1695. Paris, Bibliothèque Nationale de France, Cabinet des Estampes, cliché C 75958.

of homes and clothing. Flowers made of silk were displayed at Versailles in the seventeenth century. The demand for artificial flowers, and specifically those faithfully representing individual species of flowers, increased dramatically in the eighteenth century. Women might be taught artificial flower-making as a pastime. But women, both *bouquetières* and others, made and sold such artificial flowers for a living. Illustrations in Diderot's *Encyclopédie* include not only patterns for the construction of such flowers, but also an image of a flower-manufacturing workshop in which women and children worked at the trade[99] (figure 8). The division of labor was made even more clear by Larmessin's male gardener (*jardinier*). The gardener was constructed of and covered with potted plants, fruits, vegetables, and gardening tools. Live specimens meant to be planted in the garden were purchased from and planted by men.

The gendered division of labor in the flower trade and the control of flower selling by women meant that women flower sellers contracted their own young, female apprentices. In 1609, for example, fifteen-year-old Etienne Gallier was apprenticed for four years to *bouquetière* Marie Dabenet.[100] Similarly, Claude Baujard, who would later work with Jean Pertuissard at the Hôtel de Ville,

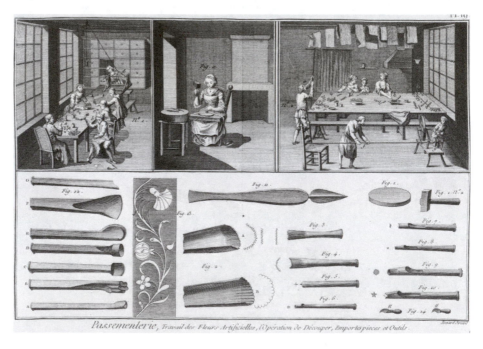

FIG. 8.   Benard, "Passementerie, Travail des Fleurs Artificielles, l'Opération de Découper, Emportes pieces et Outils, [Passementerie, making artificial flowers, the process of cutting them out, punches and tools]" From Denis Diderot, *Encyclopédie, ou dictionnaire raisonné des sciences, des arts et des métiers. Recueil des planches, sur les sciences, les arts liberaux, et les arts méchaniques, avec leur explication*, vol. 3, 1765. Image courtesy of author. Photograph by John Blazejewski, Index of Christian Art, Princeton University.

was apprenticed in 1620 to Guillemette Rabache.[101] In 1631 Renée Chevallier contracted to serve an apprenticeship to Claude Trevian, "bouquetière chapelier en
fleurs."[102] Marie Desmaretz took a series of apprentices in the early seventeenth
century, including Madeleine Seye, age eleven, for eight years in 1611,[103] and in
1616, eight-year-old Marguerite Girault for ten years and fourteen-year-old
Nicole Hadé for four years.[104]

Women flower sellers, like other women merchants, were frequently the
wives or daughters of men in similar or complementary trades.[105] *Bouquetières*
who made and sold artificial flowers might be married to men who worked with
fabric and ribbon, for some *bouquetières*, hearkening back to the traditional
bouquetières-chapelières guild, sold both fresh flowers and artificial flowers used
in floral hats and crowns.[106] Both husband and wife would thus have been
employed in the decoration of dresses and hats with ribbons, feathers, or flowers. Bonne Petit, according to a 1607 apprenticeship contract, and Barbe
Moucheny, a flower seller active in the 1630s, were both married to "tissutier-
rubanniers."[107] Many, however, were associated with gardeners.[108] *Bouquetières*
Jeanne Dufour and Michelle Compagnon were married to Nicolas Alix and Jean
Langot respectively, both "gardeners in the faubourg St. Jacques,"[109] while Etiennette Callier was married to a "marchand granier," or seed merchant.[110] In 1629
the same Etiennette Callier took as an apprentice Antoinette Driau, who was
placed there by Quentin Monsion, gardener at the Hôtel d'Epernon.[111] In 1607
Bonne Petit accepted as an apprentice Marie Alix, the daughter of Nicolas Alix,
gardener in the faubourg St. Jacques, and, according to the apprenticeship
agreement, his wife Jeanne Dufour, "also a mistress flower seller."[112]

By the mid-seventeenth century, women flower sellers were so numerous
in Paris that they were incorporated as a separate guild in 1677.[113] The corporation was one of three exclusively female guilds in old regime Paris.[114] According to the statutes registered in 1678 and reconfirmed until the guild lost its
monopoly in 1776,[115] "No girl or woman can become a mistress [flower seller]
if she has not served her time as an apprentice at the establishment of one of
the mistress flower sellers for four years." The apprenticeship was to be followed
by the creation of the customary masterpiece. Daughters of *bouquetières*, however, could be admitted without the production of the "chef-d'oeuvre."[116]

The statutes of the guild also regulated who could sell flowers, what kind
of flowers could be sold and by whom, and where the flowers could be offered
for sale. *Bouquetières* primarily hawked their wares at the main Parisian market
in Les Halles,[117] as well as in smaller marketplaces around the city. The right
to sell and display "bouquets, chaplets, crowns, [and] garlands of flowers" was
reserved for *maîtresses bouquetières*, although when violets, roses, and pinks were
in season, "all sorts of persons" could sell them as long as the specified blossoms
were not mixed with other flowers. Members of the guild of gardeners, the "Com-
munauté des Jardiniers," were also forbidden from displaying and selling cut or
potted flowers near the boutiques of *bouquetières*, although they could take cut

flowers to Les Halles and potted flowers to the markets on the Quay de la Megisserie on Wednesdays and Saturdays.[118]

Bouquetières and gardeners were threatened with the confiscation of their
merchandise if they hawked flowers in streets and outside churches.[119] Jacques
Savary des Bruslons reported in his early eighteenth-century *Dictionnaire universel de commerce*, however, that the *bouquetières* did sell their bouquets of "fleurs
naturelles," or fresh flowers, in "the halls [covered markets] and markets of the
city, or at the doors of the principal churches . . . for the finery of women."[120]

Savary des Bruslons also reported that, despite the regulations against it, a
number of perambulatory flower sellers sold flowers in the streets "in order to excite
the charity [of passersby], and obtain alms from them."[121] Although *bouquetières*
were forbidden by statute from selling their wares to such "personnes sans qualité," or people of such low status,[122] by the end of the eighteenth century, the
poverty-stricken flower girl had become a fixture on the streets of Paris and an
object of sympathy for wealthy philanthropists.[123] The guild status of the *bouquetières*, together with the privileges and protection offered by it, was revoked
in 1776, and the flower market was thrown into turmoil.[124] With the trade no longer
under control of guild and government regulations, flowers were sold freely on
the streets, especially by young, poor girls. By the nineteenth century, the flower
girl had even become the subject of literary works such as Paul de Kock's 1839
La Bouquetière des Champs-Elysées and Nicholas Mullen's 1880 *Janet, the Flower
Girl*. In each work, the lower-class, but virtuous, flower girls were rescued from
their public trade and poverty by wealthy, newly discovered relatives.[125]

Unlike nineteenth-century flower girls, seventeenth-century women flower
sellers had guild status and therefore a degree of economic power and inde-
pendence. The sale of their wares in the public markets of Paris afforded them
high visibility. That visibility, however, tinged their reputations with an air of
impropriety. There is no evidence that early modern French flowers sellers were
equated with prostitutes as they were in ancient Rome, where flower sellers were
reputed to have sold sex as freely as flowers.[126] Nor were the early modern *bouquetières* as physically, sexually, and economically vulnerable as the nineteenth-
century flower girls of the street who lacked the protection of both family and
guild. Yet an air of licentiousness lingered around the flower sellers and the bouquets that they sold. The Sieur de Grenaille asserted that blame for the corruption
of both parties in a seduction lay partly with the *bouquetière* who constructed
and sold the bouquet: "Thus if flowers enter a bouquet, it is not of their own
inclination, but because of the caprice of the flower seller who supports the fol-
lies of men because they are essential to her livelihood."[127] Women who made
and sold bouquets, the flowers that went into their construction, and the women
who accepted bouquets colluded, in the view of the moralist Grenaille, to create a web of seduction.

In the mentality of early modern Europe, then, flowers (linked with women)
could simultaneously imply not only fecundity, abundance, and beauty, but also

sin, sexuality, and death. The ambivalence of the symbolism of flowers was echoed in the use of women to illustrate vices and virtues in early modern culture. Sarah Matthews Grieco has demonstrated that specific traits came to be symbolized by women in what amounted to a visual library of moral qualities. In particular, she has noted that women could symbolize both maternalistic "Nature" and nature run amok. Grieco acknowledges the ambivalence of the images of women and nature and demonstrates the complexity they impose on the understanding of women in Renaissance and early modern culture.[128] Yet even positive images of woman as "Nature" were always inferior to man and "Culture."[129] According to Carolyn Merchant, "In early modern Europe, the assumption of a nature-culture dichotomy was used as a justification for keeping women in their place in the established hierarchical order of nature, where they were placed below the men of their status group. The reaction against the disorder in nature symbolized by women was directed not only at lower-class witches, but at the queens and noblewomen who during the Protestant Reformation seemed to be overturning the order of nature."[130] Merchant's words contain several important points. First, the identification of women with the "Nature" side of the nature-culture divide ranked them beneath men and culture. Second, argues Merchant, the disorder seen in both women and nature served as evidence condemning both. Just as women's association with nature was evidence of the inferiority of their sex, women who upset the order of nature by exerting political or other types of power offered proof of the dangerous susceptibility of nature to outside forces.

Despite the connotations of disorderliness—or perhaps because of them— women took full advantage of the power with which nature had endowed them, in part by representing themselves as Flora, Spring, or other deities related to women's connection with nature. The notions of fertility and birth and rebirth were not unimportant; indeed, they were powerful concepts in a Europe seeking to recover political, social, and religious stability after the devastating wars of religion that had dominated much of the sixteenth century. Prosperity and fertility were essential to domestic tranquility, for Western European countries were still teetering precariously between famine and the ability to feed, if inadequately at best, the bulk of their populations. Queen Elizabeth I of England, for example, was portrayed as Flora or with floral attributes in an effort to suggest that England and her queen were in the midst of a glorious eternal springtime.[131] To celebrate Elizabeth, Sir John Davies of Hereford composed a series of poems collectively titled *Hymnes to Astraea* that presented the queen in the guise of Astraea, the goddess representing the zodiac sign for the constellation Virgo, identified by Ovid as a symbol of the golden age of the past, and by Virgil as the symbol of the golden age of the future.[132] Astraea was therefore identified with Spring, May, and Flora. In addressing Flora, Davies asked her to lead Beauty, Virtue, and Majesty to the flowers in the royal gardens of Greenwich so that they might gather them to honor Astraea.[133] Davies writes Hymne IX to Flora:

E mpresse of flowers, tell where a way
L ies your sweet Court this merry *May*,
I n *Greenwich* garden Allies:
S ince there the heavenly powers do play,
A nd haunt no other Vallies.
B *ewty, Vertue, Majestie,*
E loquent Muses, three times three,
T he new fresh houres and Graces,
H ave pleasure in this place to be,
A bove all other Places.

R oses and Lillies did them draw,
E r they divine *Astraea* saw;
G ay flowers they sought for pleasure:
I n steede of gathering crownes of flowers,
N ow gather they *Astraeas* Dowers,
A nd beare to heaven that treasure.[134]

For Davies the flower-filled gardens of the queen were a suitable means of honoring her reign. The floral and garden motif was also incorporated into portraiture. In one portrait of the Virgin Queen attributed to Marcus Gheeraerts I, she is depicted in front of a doorway opening onto a closed garden, symbolism often associated with Mary's virginity. Holding an olive branch and standing upon a sword, the queen is shown wearing a gown covered in naturalistically rendered flowers.[135]

While Elizabeth I of England used floral symbolism to demonstrate both her virginal purity and the fertile potential and prosperity of her reign, queens who did not rule outright used floral symbolism to refer to the power they held through their fertility. For example, representations of Marie de Medici, on the occasion of her marriage to Henri IV, king of France, drew upon floral imagery. In a formal portrait of the Italian princess by Ambroise Dubois, she wears a blue cape covered in golden fleur-de-lys while holding a red lily, as a symbol of the Medicis, and the white lily of the French kings. The flowers implied the peace and prosperity promised by a union of the French royalty with Florentine money. In a 1601 print celebrating the royal marriage, Marie and Henri IV are shown at the ceremony in the presence of the priest and two attendants. At the top of the print, a vine links the stylized fleur-de-lys to a naturalistic lily while cupids fill the air with flowers that fall through the air and blanket the floor. Beneath the image, the caption reads, "Now that you are Queen in the Kingdom// of the greatest King of Kings this happy Alliance// promises to render very happy fruits to France// from flowers that she has joined to the scent of your beauty."[136] In the print, flowers symbolic of the royal family of France were combined with celebratory wedding flowers whose presence anticipated the hoped for production of royal fruit—an heir to the throne to secure the new Bourbon line of succession. Years after the production of that royal fruit, an anonymous engraving (see figure 29) celebrated Marie de Medici's successful role in the proliferation of the Bourbon lineage by depicting her at the base of a "family tree" blooming with lilies. Her offspring sprouted from each of the liles while a plaque proclaimed, "I cover by my shadow all of the earth."[137]

Twenty-three years after the marriage of Henri IV and Marie de Medici, the marriage of their daughter Henrietta Maria to Charles I of England was similarly portrayed. In the engraving, the couple was flanked by the flowers symbolic of their families: the red rose for the English prince and the white lily for the French princess. The caption explained, "Crimson rose dedicated to Venus// From now on conjoined to the silver flower// Of this beautiful lily, portrait of chastity.// What you want, that from this marriage// We hope that from a race well born// that of a son perfect in valor and goodness."[138] Again, the floral heraldry joined floral symbols of fertility. Later in her reign, Henrietta Maria portrayed Flora in the masque "Chloridia." The 1631 collaboration of Ben Jonson and Inigo Jones was inspired by Ovid's *Fasti*, and concluded with a chorus singing

> Chloris the queen of flowers,
> The sweetness of all showers,
> The ornament of bowers,
> The top of paramours![139]

The naming of Chloris or Henrietta Maria as the "paramour" of the king has been interpreted as a reference to Neoplatonic ideas of natural love and beauty leading to the understanding of divine love.[140] Yet it is difficult to accept that Jonson's Flora would not have reminded courtiers of Ovid's beautiful, sexual though chaste, and fertile Flora. Her performance as the pagan goddess raised the ire of Puritans who would eventually overthrow the English monarchy.[141]

The use of Flora and floral imagery by these queens played, of course, on the hopes that they would be fertile, for the continuation of the dynasties into which they married depended upon their ability to provide an heir to the throne. And the fertility anticipated in the various representations of the queens enhanced the image of their respective kings whose own legitimacy was bolstered by the belief that his legacy would soon be secured with the production of an heir. Indeed, Abby Zanger has argued, by looking at the examples of the marriages of Louis XIII and Louis XIV to Anne of Austria and Marie-Thérèse, respectively, that images and texts celebrating the marriages necessarily strengthened the position of the king during the precarious period of his rule before he had generated a more stable future.[142]

Henrietta Maria's daughter Henrietta-Anne (d'Angleterre, as she was known) was also depicted as Flora. Married to Philippe, duc d'Orléans, the brother of Louis XIV, she was potrayed as Flora in Jean Nocret's group portrait of the French royal family in which each family member was shown in mythological guise.[143] Rumors at the court of Louis XIV held that the king was attracted to his brother's wife, and it was only the transfer of his affections to her lady-in-waiting, Louise de la Vallière, that quieted talk of their flirtation. But the legacy of Flora and the French royal family did not end with the early death of Henrietta-Anne, for the guise of the floral goddess was soon associated with Louise de la Vallière, who became the king's official mistress. The position of *maîtresse en titre* combined moral impropriety with real power in the hands of the woman who held it. In a court society in which the king's mistress was openly flaunted, if not accepted, the acknowledged access of the mistress to the king meant that she could exert influence on behalf of those who courted her favor. Louise de la Vallière may have danced as Flora in the *Ballet des Saisons* and was depicted as such in a small watercolor in the Musée Carnavalet. Her successor, (Françoise) Athénais de Rochechouart, marquise de Montespan, who was Louis XIV's mistress from the late 1660s through the late 1670s, was depicted as Flora in a portrait miniature by Jacques Bordier.[144] Then in 1689, Françoise Marie de Bourbon, the Mademoiselle de Blois, the legitimized daughter of Louis XIV and Madame de Montespan, performed as Flora in the ballet *Le Palais de Flore dansé à Trianon devant Sa Majesté le 5 janvier 1689* by Michel Richard Delalande. Pierre Mignard painted the young performer in costume (see plate 4). In the portrait (now in the Louvre), the Mademoiselle de Blois wears a crown of flowers and gathers jasmines, tuberoses, and orange blossoms, favorites of Louis XIV, in her skirt. The Mademoiselle de Blois became the duchesse d'Orléans in 1692 when she married Philippe II, the duc d'Orléans and eventual regent of France upon the death of Louis XIV. The marriage took place despite the strong objections of the duke's mother, Elisabeth Charlotte, duchesse d'Orléans, who communicated her dislike in her letters explaining that the Mademoiselle de Blois and her brother were "the children of a double adultery . . . and the children of the most wicked and desperate woman on earth."[145] Elisabeth Charlotte's opinion of her daughter-in-law did not improve. In describing her daughter-in-law she wrote, "As for my son's wife, she is the most disagreeable person in the world; her figure is all askew, her face is ugly, and she is unpleasant in everything she does, and yet she fancies that she is beautiful, primps herself all the time, and is full of *mouches*. When I see all of this and think that she is nothing but mouse-droppings, I must admit that I find it a bit upsetting."[146]

At the court of Louis XIV, then, Flora as courtesan reigned. The king's Floras were, of course, suspected of using their beauty and sexual relationships with the king to bring undue influence upon him. But even those who drew upon the powers of nature governed by the chaste goddess Flora were not immune from criticism. Elizabeth I—as Astraea, Flora, Spring, or the rose of England—could not ensure that eternal springtime would continue to reign in her land because she herself did not marry and never bore an heir. Those suspicious of Henrietta

Maria's continental tastes and Catholic religion complained of her portrayal of the pagan Chloris. In combining the traditional symbolism of flowers as short-lived but powerful beauties capable of swaying the senses of the reasonable, the biological role of flowers in fertility and prosperity along with early modern stereotypes of women as oversexed fading beauties who might use flowers to supplement their own charms in the art of seduction, flowers and women together evoked nature unchecked and uncivilized. To some, these women did indeed represent, if not nature turned upside down, then a part of nature, like the mandragore, that not only could not be controlled by men, but also could even be dangerous to them.

CHAPTER 2

Refashioning the Culture of Flowers in Early Modern France

Women's reign over the realm of nature did not go uncontested in the sixteenth and seventeenth centuries; indeed, by the end of that period, the rule of Flora could be proclaimed at an end. In the sixteenth and seventeenth centuries, men across Europe took a greater interest in the natural realm. Spurred in part by the influx of new plant and animal species from the Americas and the Near and Far East, pharmacists and doctors gathered new plants for their potential pharmacological traits. The science of botany began to emerge among those who studied plants with scholarly rigor, and collectors coveted newly desirable natural history specimens. The cultivation of flowers in early modern Europe was not immune from these developments, and flowers became one of the primary objects of study and collection. Yet women were not, by and large, among those who collected and cultivated the newly fashionable flowers. Indeed, references to women collectors of fine flowers, especially in continental Europe, are quite rare: in his 1644 tulip-cultivating manual,[1] the Sieur de La Chesnée Monstereul cited a "Demoiselle" who named her tulips after ancient Romans, and Henrietta Maria, queen of England, imported French flowers to fill her gardens in England[2] where, even into the eighteenth century, women were involved in the cultivation of flowers. But the traditionally female orientation of flower culture remained troublesome to some. In 1675 a cleric, writing under the pseudonym "F.B. Sieur de L'Ecluse" in deference to the sixteenth-century botanist and tulip grower Clusius,[3] published a flower gardening manual entitled *La Flore sainte et l'apologie de Flore et des floristes contre les critiques: Avec un traité de la culture des principales fleurs*. In this eccentric work, distinguished by its lengthy defense of floriculture,[4] F.B. identified the reign of the rose, the flower named by the goddess Flora to serve as queen of all the flowers, as one cause of the moral and floral dilemma in which he found himself. The selection of the rose to rule in the floral realm had been recounted in numerous texts recalling the pagan era of Flora.[5] But the rule of the rose was problematic on at least two fronts. First, the Sieur de l'Ecluse maintained, her rule as queen allowed for "a Monarchy resembling that of the Amazons, who did not want a king,"[6] and, second, a pagan goddess had conferred her powers upon her. In short, the rule of the rose was tainted by her gender and her pagan origins. F.B. proposed a solution to both problems in which a Christian king could be named. "Now that the reign of innocents is over," he wrote, the carnation (*oeillet*), symbolically associated with Christ and known as the flower of God,[7] would rule as king and "take hold of the reigns of this monarchy."[8] In addition, the carnation would preside over an extended "cour illustre" including the rose as his queen, the ranunculus as the dauphin, the anemone as infanta, the lily and iris as princes of the blood, with other fashionable flowers comprising the remainder of the royal household.

The disorder within the floral realm identified by F.B. is not surprising given the French recognition of the Salic Law, their interpretation of which prohibited women from ruling as queen.[9] The recent regencies of Bourbon France, including those of Marie de Medici and Anne of Austria, had been marked by political and military turmoil. But F.B. went further, suggesting that the realm of flowers was Amazonian, a domain of women, and this posed a problem for him. Though F.B. acknowledged that "the passion that a great many of honest people have for [flowers] . . . is without doubt the most pure & the most innocent of all the passions,"[10] he worried that his own reputation as a cleric would be sullied by the association of flowers with either Flora, the pagan goddess, or Flora, the Roman courtesan.[11] F.B. therefore devoted nearly forty pages of his flower gardening manual to a discussion and interpretation of the history of flowers in Western civilization and the quandry in which he and his fellow florists found themselves. He reviewed the uses of flowers in antiquity as revealed by classical texts:

> Add to the utility that we receive from flowers the ancient custom of making and carrying the crowns, garlands, & bouquets, principally for girls, for whom they serve as ornament. Strabo says that this custom comes primarily from Vibonne, in Calabria, where Proserpine retreats for the abundance which is there: And Ovid gives to Europe this occupation of making festoons and garlands, in the prairies of Phénicie, when she was ravished by Jupiter. Pliny, in the first book of his history, says that the first who were entertained by the crowns of flowers were the Sicyoniens, by the imitation of the famous flower seller Glycéra, who was liked by an excellent painter from Sicyone, named Plausias, who attempted to imitate in his paintings the bouquets which she made, with so much art, & who represented her in a painting so well ornamented with chaplets of flowers, that one could never see any more admirable.[12]

He also acknowledged the role flowers in Christian practice and its origins: "The church of Jesus Christ followed the usage of antiquity, since by unanimous consent, & by a custom that the heavens authorized themselves, one uses flowers in order to decorate temples, altars, and sacred ornaments; one strews with them the churches and the streets in solemn processions; one embellishes the torches and flames, & one crowns with them the images of the saints as if there were nothing in all of nature more pure, more simple, more innocent, making them an agreeable offering to God."[13] Despite the appropriation of flower culture by early Christians, to the frustration of F.B., gardeners continued to invoke the pagan Flora. He asked of his fellow flower enthusiasts: "What blindness is yours, [if you do not see] the state of the flower that heaven made, since God has deliberately changed bread into flowers, by an amazing miracle, in favor of an innocent girl, and inspired a group of religious to change the name of one of their sisters, into that of flora, in order to substitute for a pagan divinity, and to give by this means a patron saint to florists through which they can honor without crime, and cultivate the flower so saintly?"[14] F.B. further proposed that florists instead honor a certain Saint Flora, a thirteenth-century nun,[15] whose sanctity had been revealed by God through the miraculous transformation of bread she was secretly and disobediently supplying to starving villagers into "very beautiful & rich *fleur de lys* & Roses."[16] While the starving peasants may have wished their bread back, the goodness of the Christian Saint Flora was revealed, making her preferable, argued F.B., to the pagan goddess.

Amateur florists had no formal organization in France through which they might recognize a patron saint, although the *bouquetières* and gardeners both worked under the protection of Saint Fiacre, a legendary Irish monastic hermit who labored to produce a miraculous garden.[17] Although F.B. hoped that other florists would transfer their veneration of the goddess to the saint, he did not believe it was likely to come to fruition. He therefore devoted a number of pages of his text to an exploration of the true identity of Flora. He attempted to answer the question of her origins and weighed the evidence for the cases of both the goddess and the courtesan, finally concluding that even if the Floralia had been held in honor of the prostitute, then the prostitute herself had been named after Flora, the chaste wife of Zephyr. Ultimately, what mattered most to F.B. was the chastity of Flora, saint or goddess.

The strong gendering of the floral tradition and the wrangling for control over it, as exemplified by F.B.'s text, reveals that flowers and floral symbolism were culturally valuable in early modern France. As new flowers made their way to Western Europe from exotic lands, the cultural meaning of flowers was refashioned to accommodate the changing aspects of floriculture. Ownership and cultivation of spectacular new blossoms required geopolitical influence, scientific knowledge, economic opportunity, and cultural refinement. Early modern society afforded little opportunity for women to engage in such undertakings, and the flower was a powerful symbol and useful metaphor too valuable to be left to women. By problematizing the relationship between women and flowers, men opened the door for new interpretations of their treasured blossoms to come forth. Throughout the seventeenth century, men who had become intrigued by flowers played with ambiguous floral symbolism, and altered it, as F.B. proposed in his treatise, to meet their own cultural and even political needs. Flowers and men of elite society collaborated in the construction of social and cultural identities, offering up new meanings safely removed from their disorderly heritage and entirely suitable for men to stage their learning, wealth, taste, and power.

The potency of the real and metaphorical association of women and flowers posed to early modern male flower growers both a challenge and an example. First, if the cultivation of flowers was to reflect well on their own social identities, they had to address the female tradition of flowers and construct their own cultural meaning of flower cultivation. Second, these male flower enthusiasts had to find ways to appropriate for themselves the tremendously adaptable and powerful symbolism offered by flowers. Their efforts to do so were neither systematic nor collaborative in any organized manner. No watershed moment in the early modern history of flower cultivation marked a shift in the reordering of the floral realm, thereby hampering attempts to narrate a change chronologically. Certainly, the dispute over Abraham Bosse's mandragore (noted in Chapter 1) heralds the attempt to remove the plant from the disorderly, female world of nature and transplant it into the male world of science. But the symbolic potential offered by flowers and flower cultivation survived, if the meanings attached to it changed. The male flower growers of early modern France did not entirely dismantle the female world of flowers. Men dominated trade in expensive and fashionable flowers, bulbs, and seeds, but women continued to sell fresh flowers in the streets; and Flora, goddess and courtesan, survived to serve Louis XIV at Versailles. Nonetheless, it is possible to discern the emergence of a male culture of flowers in the seventeenth century, defined not so much in opposition to the female world of flowers, but superior to it. As early as the late sixteenth century the gardening and estate management manual by Charles Estienne and Jean Liebault drew a distinction between the kitchen garden, the woman's domain, and the "garden of pleasure or flower garden" which "serveth for the chiefe Lord [of the manor] . . . to solace himselfe therein."[18] And in an engraving in Nicolas de Bonnefons's *Jardinier françois*, a man and a woman, husband and wife, are depicted overseeing the work being done in their formal garden. The woman extended her hand toward the *potager*, or vegetable garden, while the man opened his in the direction of the formal parterre, or ornamental garden terrace.[19] The flower parterre had become a male domain. By cultivating flowers, male flower connoisseurs would demonstrate throughout the early modern period their ability to resist the seductive forces of nature and even learn how to control her.

CURIOSITY AND FLOWERS

In 1688 a flower collector named N. Valnay published a manual on the cultivation of flowers entitled *Connoissance et culture parfaite des tulippes rares, des anemones extraordinaires, des oeillets fins, et des belles oreilles d'ours panachées*. In the introduction to the guide, the author expounded on the "taste" for flowers as it compared more favorably to "other more fashionable curiosities" such as paintings, medals, and porcelains. "Look at [paintings] as long as you please," he explained, "you always come to the same thing. The variety and this annual game of flowers are much more satisfying. All the beauties of the art of painting are in the design, execution, and coloring. I defy the entire academy of painting to imagine a flower . . . and to execute in the last perfection that which we have shown it, and [they will] never approach the colors of flowers." "A painting is one," he continued, "a bulb multiplies. . . . A well-worn medal, of which its flaw makes in part its merit, which is something old, is modern in comparison to flowers; they are the creation of the world." It is the same, maintained Valnay, with porcelains, too. For, he claimed, "when one mixes reason with taste, the beautiful flowers hold the first rank among the pleasures of sight."[20] The flowers that had once connoted raw nature and female sexuality were, by 1688, being touted by Valnay as the object of choice among those who claimed a degree of reason and taste! *Raison* and *goût*—two of the most important markers of civility and culture in seventeenth-century France! But how and why did such a transformation in the cultural meaning of flowers take place?

The emergence of a culture of flowers celebrating reason and taste, of which Valnay was a part, was rooted in the renewed interest in natural history and curiosities that spread, like so many other cultural movements, from Italy[21] across Europe during the sixteenth century.[22] During the Renaissance, Italian humanists and then humanists throughout Europe expanded their search for and quest to own antiquities beyond manuscripts and sculptures to include antiquities of all sorts, books produced with the newly invented printing press, scientific instruments, natural history specimens, and exotica brought by traders and explorers from around the world.[23] Those who collected natural history specimens might organize, store, or display their treasures in their cabinets, which might be either the elaborately decorated pieces of furniture by that name or, increasingly, the often exquisitely decorated rooms, also called the cabinet, that these men reserved for their studies and the housing of their collections. But once installed in the cabinet, the items were not forgotten. Rather, the items, like all of the specimens they collected, were meant to be studied, contemplated, and shared with others who were similarly curious about natural history.[24] It was through this collection and observation of specimens that these men sought to understand the natural world, and through that understanding could come, perhaps, revelations about God's world or greater control over the earthly world.

The interaction between these curious men followed conventions originally associated with courtly society. Etiquette manuals that proscribed manners of polite interaction governed exchanges of conversation, correspondence, and gifts between the learned just as they did for polite society. By the seventeenth century in Italy, writes historian Paula Findlen, "masters of etiquette took as a given the connections between social and learned conventions."[25] The learned constructed networks through which they shared both specimens and information through lively but polite correspondences, the culture of which peaked with the eighteenth-century "Republic of Letters," and the display of social status came to require a degree of learning. In France, the worlds of the erudite and the social elites came together in the salon culture that took shape in the seventeenth century, the most famous example of which was the salon hosted by Catherine de Vivonne-Savelli, the Marquise de Rambouillet.[26]

Historian Peter Miller has cautioned against extending Findlen's model too far into the seventeenth century in France, arguing that beginning in the 1620s the learned and the increasingly fashionable salon culture began to diverge. Miller maintains that while salon culture adopted the interactive modes of learned society, the substance—genuine erudition and the values of scholarship—were abandoned.[27] It can be argued that Miller overdraws the distinctions between the salons and the erudite *doctes*. Erica Harth, in *Cartesian Women*, has demonstrated that serious intellectual matters were taken up in the salons where women played a significant role.[28] But Miller does highlight an important point in making his comparison: the intellectual world of universities and academic societies, unlike the salons, were characterized by the absence of women.[29] The study and collection of natural history, as we will see, bridged salon, academic, and aristocratic culture, but women were largely excluded, not only in France, but across Europe.[30] The collection of flowers was no different from the study of other aspects of natural history; although women sold fresh flowers and were associated symbolically with them, they did not participate in the collection of flowers that became fashionable among men in the late sixteenth and seventeenth centuries.

Learnedness was not the only quality associated with collecting and curiosity. As Valnay wrote, reason *and* taste led one to the veneration of flowers; and taste in seventeenth-century France was shaped largely by salon culture. The salons were frequented by the *honnête homme*, or honorable gentleman, who was upheld in seventeenth-century France as a social and cultural ideal whose behavior served as a model of taste and learning appropriate for the intimate world of the salon or the public display at court (although *honnêteté* was also held up in opposition to the "uncivilized" royal court of the early seventeenth century). The gentleman was distinguished by his taste which was exhibited through his behavior, material consumption, and appearance. Writes Jean-Louis Flandrin, "Possession of political, economic, or military power did not necessarily imply a leading position in society, where birth, wealth, brilliance, and other qualities all contributed to distinction." He continues: "The seventeenth century invented good taste. . . . Good taste became the primary social virtue, a matter of inner being as well as outward appearance. Politeness and polished speech concerned only behavior towards others. But taste affected what a man was, what he felt about the world."[31] And the collection of flowers offered many opportunities for the display of one's taste.

How flower enthusiasts viewed themselves can be discerned partially from the monniker they chose for themselves. In the preface to his tulip manual, La Chesnée Monstereul addressed his readers as "curieux floristes."[32] The term *fleuriste*, or "floriste," as La Chesnée Monstereul spelled it, was a new term in the seventeenth century used to describe a person who collected or cultivated flowers.[33] Pierre Morin, the celebrated seventeenth-century flower collector and seller,[34] was identified as a *fleuriste* in the title of his 1651 *Catalogues de quelques plantes a fleurs qui sont de present au jardin de Pierre Morin le jeune, dit Troisième; Fleuriste*.[35] By the eighteenth century, a professional flower gardener might be referred to as a *jardinier fleuriste*[36] to indicate that he was a master gardener specialized in floriculture. But in the seventeenth century, the terms *fleuristes* and *curieux fleuristes* were more often than not applied to collectors and cultivators of rare, exotic, and expensive flowers such as fashionable tulips, anemones, ranunculi, carnations, hyacinths, and auriculas that, not surprisingly, came to be labeled "florists' flowers."[37]

The term *fleuriste* was frequently used in conjunction with the adjective *curieux*. Valnay, for example, directed his readers to the "premier curieux riches en Tulippes" and the "grand Curieux en Anemones,"[38] and he referred to his fellow florists as "nos curieux,"[39] or "our curious." A 1683 flower gardening manual by J.L. was produced, according to its title, for those "curious in all sorts of things."[40] Ballon and Garnier's 1692 flower gardening treatise addressed the great "number of persons who are curious" about flowers,[41] and as late as 1775, Robert-Xavier Mallet prefaced his *Beauté de la Nature, ou fleurimanie raisonnée, concernant l'art de cultiver les oeillets* with the claim that he published his work "for the advantage of *Curieux Fleuristes*."[42]

Whether labeled as "curieux fleuristes," or merely "fleuristes," what distinguished the flower connoisseurs was their *curiosity* in flowers. The connection between flowers and curiosity was even noted in seventeenth-century French dictionaries. According to Antoine Furetière's 1690 *Dictionnaire universel*, a *fleuriste* was someone "who is curious about rare flowers, or those who traffic in them."[43] Similarly, the *Dictionnaire des arts et des sciences* published in 1694 by the Académie française identified a *fleuriste* as "the one who is curious about flowers, who is acquainted with their properties, and who knows the manner in which he must cultivate them."[44] Curiosity itself was also identified with flower collecting or cultivating. Furetière's *Dictionnaire universel* and the dictionary of the Académie française both cited enthusiasm for flowers in their discussions of curiosity.[45] Furetière's entry for *curieux* listed the various items in which one might be curious:

> CURIOUS, is said also of he who has amassed very rarest, most beautiful and most extraordinary works of art and nature. He is an enthusiast [*curieux*] in Books, in medals, in prints, painting, flowers, shells, antiquities, in natural objects.[46]

The Académie similarly named flowers as objects of curiosity, even singling out tulips for special mention:

> CURIOUS. He who is most eager and is at great pains to learn, see, possess new, rare, and excellent things. Very *curious*. Extremely *curious*. *Eager (curieux)* to know. *Eager (curieux)* to see. He is a flower, tulip *enthusiast (curieux)*, *interested (curieux)* in the latest news. A paintings, picture, medal *enthusiast (curieux)*. *Interested (curieux)* in books, busts. She is *interested (curieuse)* in clothes, in linen.[47]

According to the dictionary entries, then, an interest in flowers implied curiosity, and one's curiosity could be demonstrated through an interest in flowers.

In the definitions of curiosity, flowers were considered alongside the equally popular collection of natural history specimens, *objets d'art*, medals, and books. The Renaissance humanist quest to recover the texts and artifacts of antiquity and the sixteenth-century tradition of the *Kunst- und Wunderkammern* had only grown in the early modern period. Krzysztof Pomian has even labeled the period an "age of curiosity."[48] In the seventeenth and eighteenth centuries, curiosity was still characterized by the study and collection of objects. The curious not only collected antiquities, medals, and paintings, but were also increasingly occupied with objects related to natural history. Fossils, shells, animals, and, of course, flowers were deemed natural wonders, rarities to be hoarded and displayed by those who had the money, knowledge, and taste to acquire them. Collecting and cultivating rare flowers was thus an activity identified with the impulse to learn, or to gather information about the world in written or material form.[49] The demonstration of such erudition implied by the collection of flowers could therefore place one among the learned and elite men in early modern society.

The concept of curiosity was not, however, uniformly celebrated in early modern French culture, and neither was curiosity about flowers. In the Netherlands, the collection of flowers was ridiculed in numerous pamphlets and popular prints as a supremely foolish activity guaranteed to separate one from one's hard-earned money. Such censure is hardly surprising, given the disastrous financial consequences of the collapse of the Dutch bulb market in 1637.[50] But in France, flower collectors were criticized not for their financial irresponsibility (though the great expense of flowers is often noted),[51] but for the nature of their interest in flowers. Pomian argues that the intellectual impulses driving curiosity were regarded as less than admirable, less than rigorous by certain segments of French society. He demonstrates that while the term *curiosité* implied an interest in learning, it had pejorative connotations, too, that were inherent in the Académie's definition.[52] Curiosity was suspect because it was driven not by intellectual or scientific rigor, but by fashion, desire, and passion. Curiosity and collecting therefore belonged in the milieu of the *mondain*, among the men of the world, the amateurs, rather than among the *doctes*, or the erudite, the scholarly elite. Not surprisingly, René Descartes viewed curiosity and the curious as impediments to the properly methodical search for scientific truth outlined in his *Discourse on the Method*. Descartes wrote in the portion of the *Discourse* devoted to the "Things Required for the Investigation of Nature": "For, as to volunteers, who, out of curiosity or desire to learn, might perhaps offer themselves to help him, aside therefrom that they usually have more promises than achievements and that they only make fine suggestions none of which ever results in any success, these volunteers would inevitably like to be paid off by the explanation of various difficulties, or at least by compliments and useless conversations, which could only cost him so much of his time that he would thereby lose."[53] But in the seventeenth century, Descartes and his followers anticipated a scientific community yet to take shape, a systematic manner of thinking yet to be imposed on the world of arts, letters, and science still inspired by curiosity and collecting. With Cartesianism in its infancy, curiosity remained the primary approach to learning about the world. Pomian writes: "Moreover, it should be stressed that learned culture in the sixteenth and seventeenth centuries consisted chiefly of the practice of curiosity in all these many forms, and the moralisers and philosophers simply confirm this with their incessant attacks on it."[54] Although the academic or intellectual elites may have increasingly looked down on curiosity, it was still regarded as evidence of learning among the "mondain," or the worldly and fashion-conscious elite in seventeenth-century France, who themselves would have scoffed at the pedantic tendencies of the *doctes.*

But the scholars were not the only critics of the fashion of curiosity. Moralists, too, found fault with the curious because they seemed to be governed by the whims of fashion; and it was on these grounds that most French critics of flower collecting found fault. As early as 1641, Franciscus de Grenaille criticized the florist in his *Plaisirs des Dames*:

> The bouquet is a product of men as well as of heaven and the earth. The pleasure of our women comes from the concerns of several great gardeners. There are those spirits for whom curiosity is a love who sometimes care less for their house than a parterre, and who forget about the upkeep of their life in order to maintain their flowers. It is said that a rose was born from the wound of the feet of the goddess of Love, but it is the hand of those of whom I speak who give birth to all other terrestrial beauties. If the air seems to threaten us with some tempest, they fear more for their garden than for their person, and they do not desire fine days in order to live a long time, but in order to see their carnations live. In the morning they greet them with the dawn[;] they would disdain seeing the sun in comparison with their carnations if the sun did not give them a new brilliance, & the night which is the mother of repose is the subject of their worry, because they fear that its coldness stifles these rare beauties that the heat vivifies. For the rest, when the sky does not send them its dew, they form a rain over the earth that they distill with a watering can. They try to surpass nature by artifice, & nevertheless their artifice always acts by the forces of nature. They are not content themselves to raise their creations in the gardens, they even carry them into their *cabinets* & make them live without violence in taking them outside of their element. They make commonly [easily] that which Semiramis would call a miracle, that is to say parterres suspended in the air.[55]

For Grenaille, florists' neglect of their own safety and comfort for the sake of their flowers, together with their fruitless attempts to outdo nature, was incomprehensible. In 1648, flower collecting was ridiculed in a collection of anonymous verses titled *Les Franc grippés* that lampooned various trends and fashions, including the mania for flowers.[56] Florists were also satirized by Jean de la Bruyère in his famous *Caractères*. In an attack on fashion, he parodied flower collecting by describing the daily activity of a curious florist:

The florist has a garden in the faubourg, where he goes shortly after the sun rises until he goes to bed; you would think that he planted himself there and had taken root among his tulips and in front of the *Solitaire* [a tulip]; he stares, he rubs his hands, he bends down, he looks at it more closely; he has never seen anything so beautiful; his heart is filled with joy; he leaves [the *Solitaire*] for the *Orientale*, then he goes to the *Veuve*, he moves on to the *Drap d'or*, from there to the *Agathe*, from where he finally returns to the *Solitaire*, where he rests, sits down, loses himself, and forgets his dinner; . . . it has a beautiful shape or a beautiful calyx; he contemplates it, he admires it; God and nature are in all that which he does not admire, he does not go beyond the bulb of his tulip which he will not abandon for a thousand *écus*, although he will give it to you for nothing when tulips are neglected, and carnations have prevailed. This reasonable man, who has a soul, a cult, and a religion, returns to his home tired, starving, but very pleased with his day's work; he has seen his tulips.[57]

Thus the utter devotion exhibited by the florist for his tulips would fade as quickly as the flower passed out of fashion. For La Bruyère, the florist's curiosity was driven not by intellectual inquisitiveness, but by the florist's desire to follow popular trends.

Although La Bruyère criticized his florist for his fickle tastes, he also pointed out the florist's failure to recognize the goodness and power of God and nature as embodied by the tulip. Yet it was precisely on such moral precepts that those who were interested in flowers defended vehemently their floral passions, by both explaining the merits of flower collecting and by distinguishing themselves from those whose motives for flower collecting were less than noble or were lacking in curiosity. Valnay, for example, qualified his list of the "grands curieux en Anemones" by adding "I know that Monsieur the Prince and Monsieur the Marquis de Seignelay have many anemones, but I do not know if they are curious about them."[58] As with other curiosities, simple ownership was not enough to merit the cultural distinction conferred by flower collecting. Rather, it was necessary to display some understanding of the nature of the object, its origins, or its history.

La Chesnée Monstereul, in a chapter of his *Floriste François* entitled "Of the differences between true florists and the ignorant curious," distinguished "true florists from a certain lot of people who carry [only] a little curiosity and like flowers."[59] A true florist, he maintained, was one who respected the toil required in the successful cultivation of flowers and recognized in his flowers the work of God. An imposter, on the other hand, could be compared to "vain lovers who believe that they merit the affections of women without having the trouble of acquiring them, and possess the treasure of their beauty without costing them anything."[60] The distasteful behavior of such false florists, La Chesnée Monstereul continued, could take several forms: "There are florists who, less discreet than bees who visit flowers without damaging them, go as swine digging and pecking our parterres in order to remove [from them] the riches by their authority or irksome demands;

and after they have ravished the beauties against the wishes of those who conserved them, they want to pass among the true florists. . . . There are people who sacrifice to unknown gods and who in the temple of Flora worship divinities who are foreign to them. There are ignorant curious who possess treasures without knowing their value."[61] For La Chesnée Monstereul, the most serious fault with such behavior was the veneration by the "curieux ignorans" of the beauty of the tulip while failing to recognize neither the "cause nor the dignity of the subject to which they give their admiration." Having served metaphorically as a "Chemist, who separates the pure from the impure, in order to know the dignity of the one, by the contempt of the other," La Chesnée Monstereul explained, "I want to rebuff these people, and not admit them to the catalogue of true florists."[62]

Such distaste for "curieux ignorans" was echoed in other countries. Samuel Gilbert explained in his 1682 *Florists Vade-mecum* that the flower gardening manual was intended not for "those that think the Divertisement [of flower cultivation] too easie or effeminate," but for those true florists who "have some understanding in or love to Flowers."[63] Gilbert's defense suggests that English florists were subjected to accusations of effeminacy, but his concern seems to have been unique to him, despite the fact that the *hônnete homme* in France was subjected to similar charges. It is possible that Gilbert's statement reflected the participation of greater numbers of English women in the collection of flowers, the most famous of whom were Mary Capel, duchess of Beaufort, and Mary Delany. Charles Evelyn even published *The Lady's Recreation: or, the Third and Last Part of Gardening Improv'd* in 1717.[64] Henry Van Oosten suggested yet another distinction in his *Dutch Gardener*:

> We ought to distinguish between the true Sons and Lovers of Flora, and those who trade and deal in Flowers: The latter are alike all other Tradesmen; they'll promote the Growth of Flowers as long as they can put off the Commodity to good Advantage: and these stand in need of no Instruction from me. The Design of this Book is, to serve the young Lovers of Flowers, or those who are just commencing that pleasant Study; and considering that they are prompted to it by an instinct of Nature, their Number would doubtless be much greater, if they were not afraid of being impos'd upon, or of being ridicul'd, by those who know no better.[65]

For Henry Van Oosten, profit motive proved to be the discriminating characteristic. Those who sold flowers for a living could not be counted among the true florists.

Others defended the status of the *curieux fleuristes* by defending the status of the flowers themselves. The prefaces to many flower gardening manuals consisted of polemical defenses of flower collecting as an innocent pleasure that delighted the senses while allowing for the contemplation of the miracles of God through his works of Nature that they were accused of overlooking. Valnay favorably compared flowers to other fashionable "curiosities." He maintained that rare flowers were more rare, and therefore more desirable, than "autres curiositez."

The author of *La Culture des fleurs* went further, arguing that flowers were both superior to the arts and compatible with Christian values: "Of all the occupations which relax the spirit, the most innocent is that of the florists which without a doubt today [commands] the eagerness of a great number of the most honorable [*honnêtes*] people in all sorts of state.... The brilliance, the odor, & the variety meet in the parterres as a reward for the troubles and the diligence of those who are involved in cultivating them."[66] He then added that the cultivation of flowers was superior to the arts of painting, embroidery, and perfume-making because they were all attempts to imitate Nature, whereas flowers were Nature's original creations. He suggested to his readers: "Regard the Heavens as the Father of flowers, the earth as their Mother, and air and water as their nourishment. Whatever it is that we cannot see in our silks, our wools, our cloth, neither our fabrics, nor the liveliest shades, & the brightest that Europe can borrow from other parts of the world, have finally deceived the sense of sight until it has confounded the inventions of art with the productions of which Nature adorns the compartments of our parterres."[67] Finally, he concluded that one could find religious perfection in the garden: "You know well (my dear reader) that your parterre is a figure of your soul, and that one day it will serve in your condemnation in the judgment of God, if you neglected to cultivate the Plant of your Garden.... The world is a garden, or the nursery of the great God, it is there that he opens every day that flowers to be placed on the altars of his glory, and in making the ornaments of his Paradise."[68] To the author, the time spent in careful cultivation of the flower parterre was an opportunity to reflect on the state of one's soul and contemplate salvation.

The Sweet Society of the Curious Florists

Members of the French clergy were among those who cultivated and collected flowers. F.B., the Sieur de l'Ecluse, believed the interest in flowers to be compatible with Christian devotion, if only Flora, goddess or courtesan, could be replaced with Saint Flora. And the Jesuit René Rapin wrote a gardening manual modeled on Virgil's georgics entitled *Hortorum libri IV cum Disputatione de Cultura Hortensi*, the largest "book" of which was devoted to flowers.[69] Although Rapin drew criticism from some for his interest in flowers and antiquity,[70] he was a member of the Society of Jesus, and the Jesuits, from their foundation in the early sixteenth century, had valued rigorous intellectual pursuit, though they specifically championed neo-scholasticism. But even their celebration of Thomas Aquinas led them to an Aristotelian approach to the understanding of and interest in nature. Rapin unapologetically defended himself in his *Hortorum libri IV* (here quoted from the seventeenth-century translation from Latin into English by John Evelyn): "The mention of the Heathen Deitys, by a

Christian Authour, perhaps will seem absurd to those, who are ignorant of the *Genius* of Poetry, which by the services of the gods, and a feigned terrour of their decrees, ought sometimes to elevate the mind, that it may create admiration; and for this the liberty that is usually allowed the Muses is warrant enough, if we had not that of Religion too, which neither thinks it self, or morality injured, by that licence which a Poet takes to set off the truth, by the beauty and gracefulness of fiction."[71] For Rapin, then, poetry—even that inspired by the Ancients—could lead to God. He added that "the Soul must be excited, that so the mind . . . being raised to a Poetique height, may breath forth divine raptures."

Rapin also specifically addressed those who questioned his passionate curiosity for horticulture:

> Yet if I appear too curious, I can defend my self by the authority of all those Greeks, who have written of Flowers, or their Culture. What can be more elegant then the description which *Nicander* makes in the second of his *Georgicks* of those Gardens in the territories of *Pisa*, which were water'd by the river *Alpheus*? In which he so often makes use of those ornaments, which Poetry derives from its fabulous times. It is almost incredible how copious and eloquent the rest are in that argument, of whom *Athenaeus* makes mention in his 15th book. Those who in verse treated of flow'ry Garlands, as *Cratinus, Hegesias, Anacreon, Sappho, Pancrates, Chaeremon, Eubulus*, and innumerable others.[72]

For the Jesuit Rapin, not only were the ancients a model for writing about flowers, but also the very justification for doing so.

F.B.'s anonymity makes it difficult to determine his religious order and therefore his theological underpinnings,[73] but the examples of F.B. and Rapin together demonstrate the breadth of seventeenth-century religious attitudes toward antiquity in general and enthusiasm for flowers in seventeenth-century France in particular. Both F.B. and Rapin felt it necessary to defend their interest in flowers and both were able to make a case for the religiosity and piety inherent in their celebration of flowers. Jean Franeau illustrated the presence of God in the flowers of his *Jardin d'hyver* by including an illustration of the passionflower in which a crown of thorns literally sprouted from the plant. Even Huguenots, whose Calvinist faith might have precluded them from engaging in flower collecting, produced *curieux fleuristes*, among them Pierre Borel and the duc de Sully.[74]

In defending their floral connoisseurship, then, the *curieux fleuristes* put forth an admirable list of personal qualities that could be demonstrated through their interest in flowers. If their curiosity did not necessarily endear them to the erudite scholars of the Académie française or philosophers like Descartes who advocated the practice of pure science, it nonetheless placed them among the "learned" elite of the *mondain*. Their veneration of flowers and, thereby, nature as an example of the powers and wonder of God demonstrated their piety. But the collection of the expensive floral specimens also allowed for the display of personal wealth, and by engaging in the mania for fashionable flowers, the *fleuristes* demonstrated their adherence to the dictates of fashion. Taken together, the qualities revealed by the inquisitive (and conspicuous) consumption of the *curieux fleuristes* provided proof of their taste, an essential trait for the *honnête homme* in seventeenth-century France. Despite the few erudite critics and moralists who questioned the expensive, impious, and trendy aspects of curiosity and flower collecting, flower collectors themselves held up flowers as an innocent means of knowing God, understanding nature, and displaying their civility. To return to the words of Valnay, the collection of flowers displayed one's reason and taste.

The desire to lay claim to such qualities through the collection of flowers in the fashioning of one's self in the seventeenth century implies that the collection and cultivation of flowers could confer cultural status or distinction. Sociologist Pierre Bourdieu has argued that the expression of one's taste could bestow social or cultural status, or "distinction," on an individual or a group. Bourdieu explains: "Taste . . . [is] one of the most vital stakes in the struggles fought in the field of the dominant class and the field of cultural production. This is . . . [in part] because the judgement of taste is the supreme manifestation of the discernment which, by reconciling reason and sensibility, the pedant who understands without feeling and the *mondain* ('man about town') who enjoys without understanding, defines the accomplished individual."[75] The curious florists did indeed establish criteria to allow for the judgment not only of the worthy and unworthy flower, but also the worthy and unworthy collector according to the flower collector's expression of both reason and taste. The ability of flower collecting and cultivating to confer such cultural distinction no doubt contributed to the participation in the world of the *curieux fleuristes* of men from all ranks of French society. Any list of known seventeenth-century flower collectors demonstrates that among their ranks were men of a broad range of wealth and status, including gardeners, pharmacists, doctors, and nobles of both robe and sword. Indeed, Antoine Schnapper, in the course of his study of collecting in seventeenth-century France, found that flowers were collected by a broader social group than any other object.[76] This could be due in part to the relative affordability of flowers, when compared to the paintings, medals, and antiquities sought by some collectors; but it also points to the near universal appeal of flowers in seventeenth-century French society.

Some floriculturists were connected to the collection and cultivation of flowers by profession. For others, flowers were a diversion. Yet all sought to be distinguished by their curiosity and thereby included among the *curieux fleuristes*. Jean-Baptiste Dru addressed the varied group of flower collectors in his catalogue: "But as two means serve the acquisition of flowers, purchase and exchange, . . . I will accommodate each of the two means, [for] those who wish (as well as what I desire myself) to be contented with this praiseworthy curiosity. . . . I would not know how to express the number of persons of wit, who, charmed by the agreeable diversions furnished by plants, give themselves to their culture, in order to distract them from their greatest affairs & from their most serious studies: & one even finds someone who has made them their principle occupation, their dearest study & their diversion all together."[77] Dru did not distinguish between those who made flowers their trade and others who merely collected them, suggesting that curiosity could be demonstrated by men of any status. It could even be found in a gardener in one's employ; in fact, it was a desirable quality. Louis Liger counseled his readers on hiring a good gardener, explaining, "A Flower Gardener who should be naturally curious, should satisfy honorably the curiosity of those who demand to see the flowers in his garden."[78]

Jean Robin, gardener to Henri IV and Louis XIII, was sufficiently "curious" to assemble a famous collection of rare flowers and plants that was eventually appended to the royal collection of plants in the Jardin royal des plantes médicinales.[79] The Morin brothers, and most notably Pierre, were also gardeners and plant traders whose curiosity was celebrated. Pierre Morin, the greatest flower trader in Paris, published catalogues of his collection of rare and fashionable flowers, and called himself a "*fleuriste.*" Morin was neither a master gardener nor a *bouquetière*, of course. Rather, he uniquely carved out a living for himself by cultivating, selling, and trading flowers. With his earnings, he indulged all of his curiosities, for Morin's collecting impulse was not limited to flowers. John Evelyn, who visited Morin's garden in Paris in 1644, described Morin's possessions: "The tulips, anemones, ranunculus's, crocus's, &c. are held to be of the rarest, and draw all the admirers of such things to his house during the seasons. He lived in a kind of Hermitage at one side of his garden, where his collection of purselane and coral, whereof one is carved into a large Crucifix, is much esteemed. He also has bookes of prints by Albert [Durer], Van Leyden, Cal[l]ot, &c. His collection of all sorts of insects, especially of Butterflys, is most curious; these he spreads and so medicates that no corruption invading them, he keepes them in drawers, so plac'd as to represent a beautifull piece of tapestre."[80] Morin was neither noble by birth nor a scholar, but he was clearly a part of the social milieu of the curious.

For some, interest in plants and flowers stemmed from their professional status as doctors and pharmacists, for whom knowledge of plants, but not necessarily fashionable flowering plants, was essential. Seventeenth-century floriculturists frequently touted the medicinal properties of flowers in their collections, but, by and large, the most fashionable species (especially tulips) had little to offer the sick. Such impracticalities did not dampen the enthusiasm for these flowers among seventeenth-century botanists, pharmacists, and doctors. Jean-Baptiste Dru, who identified himself as the "Herboriste du Roy," published in Lyon a catalogue of his collection that included lengthy lists of tulips, anemones, and irises.[81] Paul Contant, who first published *Le Jardin & Cabinet Poëtique* in 1609, identified himself and his father as "maistre apoticaires."[82] Among those *curieux* with whom Contant corresponded was Pascal le Coq, a member of the faculty of medicine and founder of a botanical garden in Poitiers, who collected anemones and obtained tulips from Clusius himself.[83] And Huguenot Pierre Borel, given the title "médecin du roi" in 1655, included a large collection of dried floral specimens in his notable *cabinet de curiosité*.[84]

Even the doctors in the employ of the king at the Parisian Jardin royal des plantes médicinales demonstrated a less than professional interest in flower collecting. Although it was widely known and lamented by *curieux fleuristes* that tulips had no practical uses, a plan of the royal botanical garden printed in Guy de la Brosse's 1636 *Description du Jardin Royal des Plantes Medecinales* included a special "Jardin a tulipes," a small enclosure on the left side of the garden. The medicinal garden thus housed a collection of essentially useless tulips that were nonetheless deemed valuable enough to protect with walls. The description of the garden suggested that other flowers were incorporated into the botanical garden. According to Guy de la Brosse: "The first two parterres and those nearest the building are planted with all sorts of evergreens and perennials, as well as flowers more pleasing than others, and the two others [are planted] in many sorts of shrubs that lose their leaves in winter."[85] Fashion and aesthetic beauty merited a place even in the scientific garden.

Most *curieux fleuristes*, however, had no professional relationship to flower collecting and cultivation. Yet even among them, the breadth of the French social spectrum was represented. For example, François de Ranchin, a chancellor at the university in Montpellier who corresponded with the noted collector and erudite Nicolas Fabri de Peiresc, collected all sorts of curiosities and cultivated a garden of rare flowers.[86] The abundant surviving correspondence between Peiresc and other fellow *curieux* identified a number of flower enthusiasts including Claude Menestrier and Cassiano dal Pozzo.[87]

The clergy, as we have seen, were also avid flower collectors. The learned and eloquent René Rapin and F.B. Sieur de l'Ecluse, the anonymous author of *La Flore sainte, et l'apologie de Flore*, were both members of the clergy and passionate flower gardeners. Peiresc was also in contact with flower-collecting men of the church. He corresponded with Nicolas Tudert, a clergyman attached to Nôtre Dame and member of the Parlement of Paris, who collected anemones and tulips,[88] and a Jacobin friar named André traded flowers with Peiresc.[89]

The new bureaucratic servants of the king, many of whom were nobles of the robe, were particularly well represented among the ranks of the curious florists. Louis Boulanger dedicated his work *Jardinage des Oeillets* to Geoffrey Lullier, "Chevalier Seigneur of Orgeval & of Mal-maison, Councillor of the King in his Councils of State & Privy, & Master of Ordinary Requests of his House," to whom he wrote, "As a very faithful and former magistrate of our kings, all of your industrious occupations have had no other goal than the immortalization of the fleur de lys of France, & your innocent entertainments have kept you busy in the cultivation of carnations in the terrestrial paradise of your agreeable abode in Paris."[90] The Monsieur de Valnay was himself the "Controller of the King's Household" during the reign of Louis XIV, and his flower gardening manual identified among the Parisian curious Monsieur Desgranges, "Controller general of the Treasury of His Majesty's Household," Monsieur Caboud, "Advocate to the Council," Messieurs Descoteaux and Breart, "Officers of the King," Monsieur le Verrier, "Recorder for the Consuls," and Monsieur Charpentier, "Lieutenant General of Compeigne."[91] And the duc d'Aumont, first gentleman of the chamber, collected flowers in addition to paintings and medals.[92]

Even the most important ministers of the kings of France could be counted as *curieux fleuristes*. The duc de Sully, first minister of Henri IV, collected anemones.[93] The Cardinal de Richelieu (who even had tulips named after him)[94] maintained a flower garden within his large garden at Rueil;[95] and Nicolas Fouquet featured an extensive flower parterre in his garden at Vaux-le-Vicomte.[96]

Flower collectors could also be found among those whose veins pulsed with royal blood. The Grand Condé was a noted collector of anemones, and it was reported that he cultivated flowers while imprisoned at Vincennes during the Fronde.[97] Henri de Bourbon, duc de Verneuil, the legitimized son of Henri IV and Henriette de Balzac d'Entraigues, collected flowers.[98] And Gaston, duc d'Orleans, established a botanical garden at his palace in Blois and gathered an impressive flower collection in the gardens of the palais du Luxembourg.[99] When Nicolas Robert painted the portrait of the duc d'Orléans, he included a florilegium alongside the armor, arms, armillary, and books that signified his military valor and learnedness, while floral pendants flanked the image of the duke (figure 9). Finally, the most eminent citizen of France in the seventeenth century, Louis XIV himself, amassed extensive flower gardens.[100] No one could dispute, in the seventeenth century, that flower collecting was an activity pursued by "personnes de qualité."[101]

This group of "personnes de qualité" who counted themselves among the *curieux fleuristes*, as we have seen, proffered the innocence of flower collecting, the veneration of God that could occur through the cultivation and contemplation of flowers, and the fact that the ancients had glorified blossoms in verse as defenses against those who questioned their undue devotion to flowers. By the late seventeenth century, however, they added additional defenses—French achievements in the realm of floriculture and the inclusion among their ranks of their king. Writing in 1688, Valnay explained that "le bon goût des Fleurs," the "good taste for flowers," had become so widespread in France that French florists rivaled and surpassed those of other countries. In addition, he wrote: "Before the reign of Louis XIV was the beauty of gardens known [in France]? It seems that the Arts and their retinue were waiting for all times in order to flower in this [era], & because our monarch merits as many crowns as all the Heros, he has brought forth flowers more beautiful than have ever been seen, in order to serve as models to the clever architects of his trophies."[102] The anonymous author of *La Culture des fleurs* also cited the king's interest in flowers: "the care of flowers is [the most] exquisite in the commerce of the world; since the greatest of kings and heros, who can, as sovereigns have the use of fashion, as well as all that is

FIG. 9. Nicolas Robert, *Gaston, duc d'Orléans*, seventeenth century. Paris, Bibliothèque du Museum d'Histoire Naturelle. France/Bridgeman Art Library.

of good taste, and has made [the care of flowers] the object of his attention during the leisure time that the interested public grants him for his refreshment."[103] As Valnay and the author of *La Culture des fleurs* implied, if the Sun King himself demonstrated such good taste in collecting flowers, then he and the other flower collectors could only be above criticism.

But what does the consumption of flowers across such a broad spectrum of French society, ranging from the gardener florist to the king, suggest about the place of flower collectors in the context of the broader social order in seventeenth-century France?[104] The three orders or estates, the first estate (clergy of noble and non-noble birth), the second estate (the nobility), and the third estate (everyone who did not fit into either of the first two categories) into which the French peoples were divided, served as the hierarchical foundation of early modern French society. One's political, legal, and financial rights and privileges were determined by one's estate. But the social hierarchy of seventeenth-century French society was more complex than its division into only three orders might suggest. For divisions within, between, and irrespective of the three estates broke down over the course of the century. As structured as French society was, the political necessities of Bourbon rule—the kings' need for a talented bureaucracy, loyal nobility, and increasing amounts of money—meant that one could attain noble rank through the purchase of noble titles or offices. Louis XIV issued more *lettres de noblesse* than any of his predecessors or successors.[105] Seventeenth-century French society, therefore, experienced a period of relative fluidity in social status, increasing people's need to distinguish themselves from those whom they (rightly) feared were encroaching upon their traditional position of privilege. Within the nobility itself, identity as a member of an ancient family of the nobility of the sword distinguished one from the recently ennobled nobility of the robe, whose bourgeois origins as a councilor or secretary to the king, a member of the judiciary, or a financial officer were too recent to be forgotten.

But even the robe-sword distinction does not fully explain the increasingly complex social identities that emerged during the first half of the seventeenth century. Noble members of the French royal court were increasingly set apart from those frequenting the Parisian salons who valued grace, wit, comportment, civility, and fashionability above title. Learning was also valued in the salons. But professional scholars increasingly sought to distance themselves from those members of the nobility and the third estate who valued learning, but who pursued it out of curiosity, as amateurs. Thus the dichotomy between noble and non-noble was complicated in the seventeenth century by the emergence of competing categories of distinction: nobility of the sword versus nobility of the robe, court versus salon, *doctes* (scholars) versus *mondains* (educated and worldly "men about town"),[106] all of which contributed to a complex set of intersecting cultural hierarchies within the ruling classes of ancien régime France.

Flower collecting, as we have seen, existed in France at the convergence of these competing social groups. That the curious florists came from such varied social groups demonstrates that flower collecting was not defined by social order or class. Rather, it reveals the unification of a seemingly diverse set of men around a common set of ideals. Their ideals—curiosity, erudition, honor, and taste—constituted an identity around which these men could converge that superseded rank. Indeed, the literal and figurative meeting of their minds around the subject of flowers was perhaps the most valued aspect of their shared passion. For flower collectors, the opportunity to converse and correspond about and to contemplate the object of their enthusiasm was critically important. In 1647, for example, Louis Boulanger wrote in his *Jardinage des Oeillets*:

> The pleasure that there is to be had from raising something beautiful and rare, beyond the benefit it provides to its master, is to see it be visited by many gardeners, in the hopes of drawing something sweet, & to court a quantity of persons of condition & of merit, who come to examine all the parts, remark on the foliage, distinguish the colors, and find, or hide its faults, according to their spirit, generous or envious, which animates them. And all this with the small silver needle which develops the marvels of it, without altering its beauty by touching it with a hot hand.
>
> I wish this good fortune to all those who cultivate carnations on the condition that they would have the charge that it will be drawn according to nature [drawn accurately] by some adept brushstrokes, & that they conserve for us the genus, if not in a matter of fact, at least in paint.[107]

Charles de La Chesnée Monstereul argued the same point in his 1644 tulip-cultivating manual, *Le Floriste François. Traittant de l'origine des Tulipes*. He paused in the text to contemplate what the future held for curious florists if tulips became readily available to the general populace: "If tulips were rendered common, it would only take away the most praiseworthy commerce between men, and deprive them of the sweetest society that existed among men of honor. . . . How much does their rarity contribute to the wish to understand [them] by curious minds? How many agreeable visits? How many sweet conversations? And how many sound interviews? Certainly, it is the sweetest life in the world to meditate among the flowers, to consider the marvelous effects of Nature, and the power of its author."[108]

The "sweet society" of French flower enthusiasts celebrated by La Chesnée Monstereul was not a formal organization. As he proceeded to explain, Flemish florists formed confraternities in each town under the protection of Saint Dorothy. Held in "grande veneration," the confraternities provided society and conversation for those sharing an interest in flowers. In the Protestant Netherlands, flower sellers and collectors gathered under different circumstances: "The Dutch, in consequence of their religion, practice another order[;] they assemble every year on a certain day on which they know when the tulips are in their perfection; & after having visited the gardens of the florists, at the end of a feast among them, they elect one of a company who is the judge of the different [tulips] which were raised in the year.[109] Florists' societies were also formed in England and Ireland where they flourished into the nineteenth century.[110] In France, however, apart from the professional guilds formed by persons selling flowers for a living (such as *jardinier-fleuristes* or *bouquetières*),[111] there were no such organizations for French flower enthusiasts. Yet La Chesnée Monstereul suggests that flowers did serve as the instigation for erudite conversation among his friends and peers.[112] The society about which La Chesnée Monstereul writes was far removed from the marketplace of the *bouquetière* or the flowers in the utilitarian kitchen garden for which the mistress of the manor was responsible. On the contrary, he was specifically addressing his fellow curious florists who collected rare and fashionable flowers that conferred on their collectors a degree of cultural cachet. Through his interest and expertise in these flowers (specifically, in the case of La Chesnée Monstereul, tulips), La Chesnée Monstereul and his fellow flower connoisseurs laid claim to a place in early modern French society where learning and taste were highly valued.[113]

Historians have sought in the sociability described by La Chesnée Monstereul the roots of the burgeoning citizenship that would characterize the reorganization of French society in the eighteenth century. Recent scholars have looked to salon culture in the early eighteenth century as the predecessor to the civic culture of the Enlightenment that found its home in taverns, coffeehouses, and salons alike. Dena Goodman has studied the influence of women as the patrons and hostesses of these salons in shaping the new sociability;[114] and Anne Goldgar has explored the fellowship created among those who took part in the "Republic of Letters."[115] In the quest to extend the search even earlier for evidence of a changing social order, Peter Miller maintains that the origins can be traced to the world of the intellectuals he describes in *Peiresc's Europe*. Miller explains that the values of "constancy, conversation, friendship, and benificence"[116] championed by the erudite collectors and thinkers like Peiresc and his friends expanded beyond learned society to the polite society cultivated in seventeenth-century salons, and eventually to eighteenth-century civil society.[117] Daniel Gordon, in *Citizens without Sovereignty*, has looked to the seventeenth century for the origins of eighteenth-century sociability, but argues that seventeenth-century sociability is distinct from its eighteenth-century counterpart in that it lacks any political sensibility. In studying the lexicography of the word *societé* and its variants *sociabilité* and *social* in seventeenth- and eighteenth-century France, Gordon has determined that *societé* was the most frequently used variation in the seventeenth century. Gordon also argues that it is possible to distinguish between five ideal types of sociability, ranging from the most basic, "sociability as the love of exchange," or "the pursuit of convivial interaction for the immediate pleasure it affords[,] . . . a pure love of fellowship that has no political significance and that precludes political activism," to the politicized sociability "as the propagation of absolutism," to the consciously apolitical idea of sociability "as the recovery of *logos*." In the seventeenth century, he concludes, sociability primarily took the form of convivial interaction "that precludes political activism."[118]

Yet it is difficult to divorce sociability from politics in a court society in which proximity and access equaled power. The flower gardens and collections of early modern France were sites of sociability, both literally in the garden itself, as seen in a drawing for the frontispiece of a flower gardening manual in which

FIG. 10.   Hubert François Gravelot, *Gentlemen Discussing Tulips*. Preparatory drawing for frontispiece to Fréard du Castel, *L'Ecole du Jardinier Fleuriste*, 1764. Washington, D.C., Dumbarton Oaks Research Library and Collection.

two gentlemen converse over a bed of tulips, and metaphorically in the conversation about flowers that filled personal letters and published books (figure 10). One's behavior during a promenade in the garden was sufficiently important to be included in conduct manuals. The author of the *Nouveau traité de la civilité qui se pratique en France parmi les honnêtes-gens* wrote of how to walk in the garden with men of different ranks in groups of two or more and warned readers against picking flowers: "It is a great incivility, when one is in the garden . . . to cut there fruits or flowers," although he added that if a flower or piece of fruit was presented, it could be accepted.[119]

Men from the full spectrum of early modern social groups—from the academies to the salons to the royal administration—collected and cultivated flowers. But, as we have seen, flower collecting also extended beyond each of those groups. What role might the "sweet society" of curious florists have played in the transformation of French society in the seventeenth and eighteenth centuries?

It would be preposterous to propose that the collection of flowers resulted in the dismantling of the ancien régime social order. But it is possible to discern in the mania for flowers the formation of an identity based upon a shared culture. The collection of flowers provided a focal point around which those with similar cultural values, manifested or displayed through their cultivation of flowers, could gather, converse, and lay claim to an identity not based upon social rank, office, or birth status.

The conviviality around flowers was described by René Rapin in his *Hortorum libri IV* in his celebration of both Gaston d'Orléans and the anemone:[120]

> Victorious *Gaste* so this flower did grace,
> That in his *Luxemburgh* he gave it place;
> Call'd for the Pots; nor could at meals refrain,
> With it himself and Court to entertain.[121]

Not only, then, did the duc d'Orléans decorate his table with anemones, but the fashionable blossoms were the subject of conversation among his dinner guests.[122] Was the sociability of the curious florists political? Certainly it was not political in any modern sense. Civic engagement was not expected of the curious, but, increasingly, effectiveness at court and in the government demanded the very qualities celebrated by the curious florists. The participation of the king and members of his bureaucracy in the collection and cultivation of flowers suggests a connection between the cultural and the political. The sociability constructed around the cultivation of flowers reveals the possibilities existent in seventeenth-century France for the creation of a cultural identity that transcended traditional French social order well before the emergence of eighteenth-century civil society.

CHAPTER 3

Cultivating the Flower

When Jean-Baptiste Dru published the contents of his flower garden under the title *Catalogue des Plants, tant des tulips, que des autres fleurs, qui sont à present au Iardin du sieur Iean Baptiste Dru, Herboriste du Roy* in 1649 and again in 1653, he explained, "I would not know how to express the number of persons of wit, who, charmed by the agreeable diversions furnished by plants, give themselves to their culture, in order to distract them from their greatest affairs & their most serious studies: & . . . one even finds someone who has made them their principal occupation, their dearest study, and their diversion all together." In turning to floriculture for diversion, distraction, study, these *fleuristes,* as Dru labeled them, were "the persons who join the knowledge [*connoissance*] of flowers to the intelligence [*intelligence*] of their culture."[1] As Dru makes clear, a curious florist was one who combined two kinds of intellectual faculties. "Connoissance," according to the *Dictionnaire de l'Académie française* of 1694, was the "idea, imagination that one had of some thing or some one." One might have, according to the dictionary, "knowledge of precious stones, paintings, the knowledge of business."[2] For the curious florist, "connoissance des Fleurs" implied an appreciation of flowers, an understanding of their beauty, rarity, and history. The "intelligence de leur culture" implied something different. "Intelligence," according to the *Dictionnaire*, was an "intellectual faculty, the capacity to perceive, to understand."[3] And the "culture" of flowers meant the growing (or cultivation) of flowers in the garden. The "intelligence of their culture" was an understanding of how to grow flowers—how to raise them from seed to blossom and care for them in such a way as to ensure the same in the following year. For Dru, a curious florist necessarily combined the two kinds of knowledge about flowers.

In requiring of its curious the ability to germinate seeds, force bulbs, water, fertilize, transplant, multiply, and variegate flowering plants, floriculture was peculiar among the curiosities popular in early modern Europe. The collection of paintings, medals, coins, antiquities, precious stones, fossils, shells, books, prints, and manuscripts required the acquisition of the item and then its proper storage or display. One might study or contemplate the piece, write about it, compare it to other specimens of its kind. But such collections generally demanded no additional labor—certainly no manual labor—on the part of the owner. The florists, however, like those whose horticultural interests tended toward fruit trees, or those who maintained a menagerie of live animals, were responsible for maintaining the very life of the objects of their curiosity. The curious florist might also study, contemplate, write about, and display his flowers, but the failure to cultivate the plant properly could mean the loss of one's treasure, whatever money it cost to aquire, and what status it brought to the collector. As Antoine-Joseph Dezallier d'Argenville described in *La Théorie et la pratique du jardinage*[4] (in an account not too far removed from La Bruyère's satirical description), the activities required of the successful florist were, if not arduous, certainly intensive:

> It is these tulips, these anemones, & c. which demand such care and such pain, in order to have the pleasure of seeing them last twelve or fifteen days at the most. Let us imagine a mysterious man, always anxious, always concerned, who gets up at night in the frost in order to cover his flowers, who works, waters, and weeds his *plates-bandes* [border flower garden] continually, who passes the earth through a fine sieve, & prepares [the soil] differently for each species, who makes a written record of the order of his *plates-bandes*, with the name and portrait of each flower, which, as soon as the flowers have passed, takes up the bulbs, & dries them in boxes and drawers each one in its case, & envelopes them in paper, & who . . . guards his flowers as a treasure, & he does not allow those with jealous eyes to approach, one has a true idea of a great florist.[5]

D'Argenville's description of the floriculturist and the extravagant care lavished on his flowers was not inaccurate. Curious florists did need to understand how to care for their specimens and how to bring them to flower. Even if a flower collector or enthusiast employed a gardener to carry out manual labor, the gardener was very likely unversed in the care and cultivation of the rare specimens in the collector's garden. Louis Liger's suggestion that one look for a gardener who was himself "curious" speaks to the prevelance of gardeners who were not.[6] The responsibility for the proper care of the flowers, or, at the very least, the proper instruction of the hired gardener, therefore fell to the collector.

In performing manual labor, however, the curious florist had to maneuver difficult cultural terrain. If flower collecting and cultivating were connected to expressions of taste and reason, one might be tempted to conclude that the performance of manual labor necessary for successful cultivation would detract from such social and cultural distinction. After all, soil preparation, working with fertilizers, and weeding were tasks performed by professional gardeners—guildsmen. Most likely, those gardeners would assign such menial jobs to their journeymen and apprentices. Or they might hire poorly paid day-laborers to carry them out. In early modern French society, manual labor was regarded as lowly. For the nobleman, the stakes were high: derogation, or the loss of one's noble rank or title, could occur if one engaged in manual labor for profit. But tilling the soil was an exception, as it did not necessarily bring dishonor to one's rank. According to Charles Loyseau, whose 1610 *Treatise on Orders* described the legal and social structure of the three orders, or estates, into which French society was organized, explained: "Activities leading to the forfeiture of nobility are those of the pleading attorney, clerk of the court, notary, sergeant, clerk, merchant, and artisan of all trades except glass-making. . . . What is at issue here is the fact that these activities are performed for profit. . . . Tilling the fields does not derogate from nobility, not because of its utility (as is commonly thought) but because nothing a gentleman does for himself, and without taking money from another, implies derogation."[7]

Historian Pierre Goubert explains further, however, that "farming evades derogation within certain limits, provided it is practised in the enclosed '*parc*' or over an area of one or two 'plough-lands' (*charrues*)—not more than twenty hectares—or within a 'capon's flight' radius of the manor, although taking land in farm always means derogation. . . ."[8] Tilling the soil in the pleasure garden surrounding one's chateau, then, did not bring with it the risk of losing one's rank. Indeed, in the seventeenth century, French nobles devoted considerable money and effort toward "improving" their estates through the construction of new chateaus and the elaborate gardens that surrounded them.[9]

The risks facing the *honnête homme* were trickier to avoid. For the *honnête homme*, the "man of means," the "galant man, who . . . has an air of worldliness, who knows how to live,"[10] was governed to a greater extend than the nobility by "the rules of decorum, of good manners."[11] The successful *honnête homme* perfected "a manner of acting just, sincere, courteous, obliging, civil"[12] exhibited with grace and ease. Such qualities were not compatible with the dirty fingernails of garden work and the study necessary for growing rare and sometimes difficult flowers. It is not clear how the *honnête homme* surmounted the social dilemma of work. He may not have soiled his hands in the garden, preferring to offer instruction to his hired gardener. Or he may have taken care not to be seen working in his garden. The ambiguities of working in the garden are illustrated by premier flower collector Gaston d'Orléans who, as brother of the king, was at the top of the hierarchy of nobility in France *and* was also a part of Parisian salon culture where the rules of *honnêteté* were perfected. The duc d'Orléans could be spotted working in his walled flower garden at the palais du Luxembourg in Paris. And yet when John Evelyn described the gardens there, "In sum, nothing is wanting to render this palace and gardens perfectly beautifull & magnificent; nor is it one of the leaste diversions to see the number of persons of quality, citizens and strangers, who frequent it, and to whom all accesse is freely permitted, so that you shall see some walkes & retirements full of gallants and ladys; in others melancholy fryers; in otheres studious scholars, in others jolly citizens. . . . What is most admirable is, you see no gardners or men at worke, and yet all is kept is such exquisite order as they did nothing else but work; it is so early in the morning, that all is dispatch'd and don without the least confusion."[13] Evelyn celebrated the gardens for the splendor displayed without any evidence of the labor required. Nonetheless, the descriptions by Dru and the satirization by La Bruyère demonstrate that florists were willing to risk ridicule to work in their parterres to bring their flowers to blossom.

The Florists' Flowers

For Evelyn and the curious florists, the fruits of the labor—the fine flowers within the garden—were more important that what it took to achieve them. Nonetheless, one's energies in the garden could be directed in ways that would allow the florist to lay claim to the taste and reason implied by the collection and cultivation of flowers. One's reason could be communicated through the successful cultivation and broader understanding (*connoissance*) of the flower. One's taste could be displayed through the flowers chosen to grow in one's garden. The curious florist had to demonstrate the embodiment of taste by discriminating among flower species in building a collection of only the finest and most fashionable species and varieties. Discrimination was central to the ability of taste to convey distinction, and, as Pierre Bourdieu has observed, "It is no accident that, when they [tastes] have to be justified, they are asserted purely negatively, by the refusal of other tastes. In matters of taste, more than anything else, all determination is negation."[14] Within the realm of the curious florist, discrimination and distinction converged around the cultivation of the most fashionable species, labeled "florists' flowers," and the emergence of criteria by which varieties and individual specimens of the "florists' flowers" might be judged against each other.

The flowers designated as "florists' flowers" generally included tulips, anemones, ranunculi, carnations, auriculas, and, by the eighteenth century, hyacinths. D'Argenville wrote: "The curiosity for flowers turns principally on Tulips, Anemones, Ranunculi, Bears' Ears, & Carnations. The Curious hardly make a case for our other flowers, which, although less varied in their species, cede nothing to them in the vivacity of colors, the pretty forme, odor, duration, & agreement with which they furnish the gardens."[15] But even within the small group of flowering plants that interested the curious florists, fashions, crazes, and vogues for particular species, varieties, forms, and colors fluctuated over time, demonstrating that despite the condemnation of critics like La Bruyère, seventeenth-century patterns of consumption and shifting aesthetics reveal a growing concern for following fashion.[16] Indeed, taste and fashion became increasingly important in the seventeenth and eighteenth centuries as old identities fell away or lost relevance. Jean-Louis Flandrin suggests that "no doubt this had something to do with the fact that the great lords lost the major part of their old political and military powers in the seventeenth century; thus their primary role became that of great consumers. And the various classes that composed the social elite in the seventeenth and eighteenth centuries found it easiest to communicate with one another by means of consumption and luxury."[17]

Taste and fashion in seventeenth-century France were shaped largely by the baroque aesthetic that highly valued the new or novel. Writes José Antonio Maravall, "the baroque proclaimed, cultivated and exalted novelty."[18] The quest for novelty fueled interest in the exotic, a category of distinction brimming with possibility as European explorers and traders brought back previously unknown plants, animals, and material goods from the Americas, Africa, and the Far East. The quest for the new or novel also shaped the interest in variety in both the familiar and the exotic. Further, Maravall argues that the more difficult the attainment of novelty or fashion was, the more highly it was valued: "The taste for the difficult occupied a preferential position in baroque mentality; in judging any work whatsoever, it gave a prominent role to the qualities of novelty, rarity, outlandishness, the breaking of norms. All these traits . . . were connected in that they each derived from a longing for novelty, just as this longing in turn originated from the tendency to seek out difficulty."[19]

The collection, cultivation, and consumption of flowers meshed neatly with such modes of consumption. For the florists' flowers were not only novel and exotic, but they also offered many difficult challenges in their successful cultivation and in the efforts to produce new varieties, new colors, and new shapes to feed the never-ending quest for the novel. The quest for the new, different, and difficult is woven into the manuals and treatises composed by the curious florists. For in addressing the form, color, fragrance, uses, history, and even symbolism of their favorite flowers, early modern florists reveal the aspects of floriculture they believed capable of demonstrating their taste, fashionability, and reason. Through their discussions of the flowers in their gardens, the exotic, the difficult, and the aesthetics of floral connoisseurship and fashion take shape.

The mania for flower collecting began, according to the story most frequently repeated by *fleuristes* (and modern historians),[20] in a suitably exotic manner. In 1554 Ogier Ghiselin de Busbeq, ambassador from Emperor Ferdinand I of the Holy Roman Empire to the Turkish court of Sulieman the Magnificent, observed a flower he called the *tulipam*. While traveling from Adrianople to Constantinople, Busbeq reported "an abundance of flowers everywhere—narcissus, hyacinths, and those which the Turks call *tulipam*—much to our astonishment, because it was almost mid-winter, a season unfriendly to flowers. . . . The Turks pay great attention to the cultivation of flowers, and do not hesitate, although they are far from extravagant, to pay several aspers for one that is beautiful. I received several presents of these flowers, which cost me not a little."[21] He returned with bulbs or seeds to Vienna. By 1559, herbalist Conrad Gesner reported seeing them growing in Augsburg;[22] then in 1573, Busbeq gave several tulips to the famous botanist, Charles de l'Ecluse, or Clusius, as he has become known, who installed them in his collection in Vienna and later in his botanic garden in Leiden.[23] Another account of the introduction of tulips to Western Europe stated that a shipment of bulbs was sent in 1562 to Antwerp where most of them were mistakenly eaten until the remaining few were rescued by a merchant, George van Rye.[24] La Chesnée Monstereul provided yet another account in his 1654 *Floriste François*. The seventeenth-century tulip enthusiast claimed that the tulip grew (with a "very agreeable odor") in the Indies from where it was brought to Portugal.[25] But Busbeq and Clusius are still given primary credit for the introduction of the flower.

Whatever route the tulip took to Western Europe, by the late sixteenth century the tulip had become indisputably the most prized flower in the Netherlands, Flanders, and England. By the early seventeenth century, it had conquered France. It is not known precisely when tulips were introduced into French gardens, but several tulips were pictured in Pierre Vallet's 1608 *Le Jardin du Roy Tres Chrestien Henry IV Roy de France et de Navare dédié à la Royne*.[26] Within decades the flower became wildly popular, and speculation on the rapidly changing, highly unstable new varieties resulted in the tulip mania that swept the Netherlands in the 1630s and the 1637 crash of the tulip market.[27]

But the Dutch tulip mania was only one (if the most dramatic) chapter in the history of flowers in early modern Europe. Although the tulip continued to be one of the most desirable flowers throughout the early modern era, other flowers, too, experienced periods of tremendous fashionability. As the floriculturist N. Valnay explained, "I am particularly attached to the rare tulip, to the extraordinary anemone, to the fine carnation, & to the variegated bears' ears, & I cherish the knowledge and culture of them so strongly that I have enterprised to speak about them," and, in fact, these four flowers formed the chapters of his 1688 book on cultivating fine flowers.[28] Pierre Morin, whose famous garden and collection of flowers became a destination for curious tourists, included in his *Catalogues de quelques plantes a fleurs* tulips, ranunculi, irises, and anemones as well as a few cyclamens and auriculas.[29] Ballon and Garnier provided their readers with chapters on anemones, pinks, tulips, auriculas, tuberoses, and ranunculi in their 1692 treatise on growing flowers.[30]

Tulips, carnations, anemones, ranunculi, hyacinths, and auriculas, in addition to irises, narcissi, and lilies were the most important florists' flowers in the early modern period, although the flowers grown by a particular collector or gardener could vary according to individual taste. And individual taste could lead one to particular species, or brilliantly colored flowers, or strongly fragrant flowers. Pierre Morin noted diplomatically: "Color and fragrance are the two principal qualities for which flowers are loved: but to know which of the two is preferable, is a question [for debate]. There are people who do not love flowers if they do not smell good, and they are those who prefer carnations to the tulip. Others, on the contrary, . . . are rejuvenated only by rich colors. . . . They are those who most esteem the tulip, over the rose or carnation."[31] Personal preferences aside, however, botany and fashion dictated a fairly limited number of worthy flowers. Other species could be and were included in flower gardens, but the "florist's flowers" were those deemed most valuable. According to the anonymous F.B. Sieur de l'Ecluse, these "principalles fleurs" alone "could be sufficient to ornament a garden, content the passion of a [flower] enthusiast, & form a pretty monarchy over the Empire of Flora." Other flowers, he explained, were like the stars compared to the sun, "the simple subjects compared to princes, & soldiers compared to the generals of armies."[32]

The tulip, despite the scandal of the 1637 market crash, remained the most popular, most collected flower, in large part because of its great variety (figure 11). Pierre Morin explained in 1651: "Among the most beautiful flowers, there is not one which has the diversity of color and manner of the tulips: those who name [tulips] Queens of Flowers are within their rights."[33] Not just any example of the queen of flowers was deemed worthy of fine gardens, however. The striped or variegated varieties demanded the highest prices and occupied the places of honor. In P. Cos's 1637 Haarlem tulip book (which includes fifty-four watercolor tulips together with their weight and price), the most fantastically yet clearly colored were the most expensive. Cos recorded the price of 1,520 guilders for a white tulip with red stripes, and a white tulip delicately fringed in red sold for 2,000 guilders.[34] Whereas a mottled red, pink, and white tulip brought only 300 guilders, a clear purple or brownish and white tulip called "Viceroy" (*Viseroij*) sold for between 3,000 and 4,200 guilders depending on the weight of the bulb.[35] Even the cheapest bulbs included in Cos's book were expensive—a pale pink and white tulip was available for 65 to 90 guilders,[36] a price well beyond average Dutch earnings.[37]

Although the prices in P. Cos's book were recorded at the height of the tulip mania and tulip prices fell quickly afterward to a fraction of what they had been, choice tulips continued to be favorites in the gardens of collectors. They remained expensive enough to preserve their elite reputation. By 1654 the

FIG. 11.   Nicolas Cochin, Tulips. From *Livre nouveau de fleurs tres util pour l'art d'orfevriere et autres*, Paris: Baltazar Moncornet, 1645. By permission of the Houghton Library, Harvard University.

Sieur de La Chesnée Monstereul could look back at the tulip speculation with amazement, but still assert that the tulip remained the "empress" of flowers: "Tulips have always been very highly regarded, & particuliarly by the Flemish and Dutch . . . who in the year 1637 expected to enter into commerce with them as [if they were] diamonds and pearls, but the state, by a political maxim, had a different opinion; they saw to it that the public sale and resale [of tulip bulbs] was forbidden."[38] Yet he celebrated the flower only pages later: "It is without a doubt that the tulip has been raised legitimately above the other flowers and takes its rank among them as the sun does among the stars; since with the Curious it passes for the empress of flowers."[39]

"Empress" or not, tulips were still subject to discriminating tastes of fashion; the French, like the Dutch before them, distinguished fine tulips from ordinary ones. Valnay enumerated the categories into which the best tulips were divided: "There are six sorts of tulips that can be marked with three colors of background. It is about them that this memoir is written. The tulips bound with a white ground are the springlike colors, those bound by a dark ground are the bright variegated, those bound with a pink ground are the perfect random ones, those bound with white and black ground are the random ones for the second bed, those with a white and pink ground are the tricolors, & those with a dark ground are the tulips for seed."[40] Standards by which tulips were judged had not changed much by the eighteenth century. Spelling out the categories of fine tulips in his 1764 *The Dutch Florist*, Nicholas Van Kampen explained:

> The variegated late-blowers are . . . beyond dispute the most diversified, beautiful, and perfect of all. There is an almost infinite number of sorts of them, which are reduced by florists to five classes, viz.
>
> 1. Tulips with a white bottom, striped with brown, called Baguette primo.
> 2. Such as have a white bottom, striped with brown, called Baguette rigaut.
> 3. Those with a white bottom, striped with violet, and blackish brown, called Bybloemen.
> 4. Those with a white bottom, striped with rose-colour, vermilion and ruby.
> 5. Such as have a yellow bottom, striped with different colours, called Bizarres. . . .
>
> The colours ought to be lively and bright: Those that are most valued and in greatest request are the black, golden yellow, purple violet, rose, and vermilion colours. Tulips whose flowers are finely striped and variegated with three colours, distinct and unmixed, with very strong and regular streaks, without any tinge of the colour of the breeder, are the finest bizarres, and may be called perfect Tulips.[41]

Robert-Xavier Mallet, writing in the eighteenth century, argued that a fine tulip ought to be judged by more than just its color. Although he noted that "taste is very inconstant in the flower: as for me, I do not like to keep the bizarres in all colors," he explained: "The beauty of the tulip consists essentially in the form of a goblet & in the beauty of its plant. Its leaves must be neither too long, nor too short, nor too big, & that is so it will lie down [only] a little on the ground. Its stem should be moderately tall in the bizarres, less so in the *baguettes rigaux*. The colors & the variegations of tulips should be broken cleanly, into large patches, & be as brilliant on the outside as within. The six petals that form the corolla should be spaced, regularly arranged, resembling well the goblet."[42] With such stringent qualifications required of the flowers, Van Kampen felt the need to ask: "But where is the flower to be [found] that possesses all these properties? Such a one indeed has never yet been seen; and even those which are esteemed the finest, almost always are deficient in some of these perfections."[43]

For all the praise heaped on even the most beautiful tulip, florists argued that the flower was not without fault. Most significantly, the tulip lacked a pleasing fragrance. Many curious florists openly lamented this problem in their otherwise celebratory discussions of the flower. The Sieur de La Chesnée Monstereul, who believed that tulips had originated in the Indies where they had "a very agreeable odor," blamed the colder climate of Western Europe for the shortcoming: "If the tulips had conserved in this cold country the sweet odor it had on its island, [together with] its utility & beauty, one could say with truth that this flower possesses itself all the perfections of the others."[44] Etienne Binet argued that the lack of fragrance was no unfortunate accident of nature; rather, he suggested, "Nature has wisely given [the tulip] no odor, because if, with such beauty, she had infused it with the sweetness of fragrant flowers, men who are only mad about them would be entirely and hopelessly in love with them."[45] The *curieux fleuristes* thus found ways to make the shortcoming a positive trait.

Though tulips were the only flower to have instigated such widespread financial speculation and monetary disaster, they were not the only species to attract enthusiastic and loyal followers. Carnations (*oeillets*) (see figure 39) were the subject of the earliest treatise written in French about a single species: Louis Boulanger's *Jardinage des oeillets* was published in 1647. Boulanger opened the treatise by hailing the carnation as the ruler of the floral kingdom:

> Until now the flowers have always disputed
>> Who carried the scepter in their small kingdom,
> The battle is over, the carnation has won.[46]

To those who favored the tulip or rose over the carnation, Boulanger offered the following argument: "[The carnation] . . . is held in highest esteem, all the more so since it is at no point disrobed before our eyes for the space of nine or ten months, as the tulip (nonetheless so highly esteemed) to show besides after eight or ten days its radiating scarlet and its enamel of diverse colors, since at all times it displays a pretty green, blooms even stronger in the winter, & at no point bloodies our hands when cutting them as does the rose with its thorns."[47]

Unlike tulips, carnations and pinks were not new to Western Europe. Part of the *Dianthus* class that includes pinks, carnations, and clove gillyflowers (a medium-sized flower with a strong clove scent), they are believed to have originated in Europe. According to Brent Elliott, evidence of cultivated carnations, derived from *Dianthus caryophyllus,* surfaces as early as 1460 in Spain.[48] All three related species—carnations, pinks, and gillyflowers—were present in late medieval gardens, but all became extremely popular in the early modern period. Indeed, it is difficult to determine in many cases if florists are describing pinks, carnations, or gillyflowers in their manuals.[49] Selective breeding in the sixteenth and seventeenth centuries led to the development of larger, double, striped, and varicolored blossoms and transformed a fairly common flower into a florists' variety. "Interest & curiosity have invented many means of variegating . . . the diverse colors of Flowers in our Gardens," Boulanger informed his readers.[50] Pinks, from *Dianthus plumarius,* became more popular in the eighteenth century.

Unlike the easily cultivated tulips, the successful cultivation of the most elaborate pinks and carnations offered the early modern floriculturists a real challenge. Gardening manuals, accordingly, offered lengthy instructions on how to grow them. Robert-Xavier Mallet stated in his *Beauté de la nature, ou fleurimanie raisonnée, concernant l'art de cultiver le oeillets,* "As the Carnation is the flower of greatest merit and the most difficult to cultivate, it will be the principal object and most detailed of my first treatise."[51] Boulanger offered chapters on how much sunlight the flower required, what sort of earth it preferred, how frequently it should be watered, how to conserve the flower during the winter, how to multiply one's carnations by seed, and how they were to be properly layered ("marcoter," or reproduced by cuttings). He even enumerated eight diseases that frequently afflicted the carnation and discussed how to treat them.[52]

Valnay sought to ease the worries of potential growers by offering simpler instruction: "Monsieur Morin and Monsieur Charpentier, Lieutenant General of Compeigne, have written on the carnation. I have written after them not because they have not written enough; on the contrary, I speak only to show that the cultivation of this flower is no longer a thing so painful as these authors have made it." The "size of their treatises, and their long dissertations on the slightest rules which are often useless," he continued, led him to decide to produce simpler guidelines. After all, he concluded, "experience puts us above all of their work, & one governs at present with more facility two or three hundred pots of carnations, when they have governed, according to them, about thirty."[53]

Unlike most other florists' flowers that were planted in gardens, carnations and pinks were regularly planted in pots which were then placed at symmetrical locations in the formal garden or displayed indoors. Gardening manuals therefore also concerned themselves with the suggested pots to be used, correct soil with which to fill the pots, and proper drainage. The author of the *Nouvelle instruction pour la culture des fleurs* explained: "The Pot contributes a great deal to the beauty of the carnation and its conservation. *First*, to its beauty, because many make use of pots that are too large or too small and can be visibly perceived to be at fault. If the pot is too large the carnation takes too much nourishment, and [produces] shoots with strong roots, but small buds that will not make a large flower. If the pot is too small, the carnation lacks nourishment and restrains its roots so much that its growth will be impaired. The most suitable pot should be one of medium size, neither too low nor too high, containing about as much dirt as that contained in the form of a hat."[54] For florists living near Flanders or Artois, Mallet recommended pots manufactured by the Sieur Vaterlot in Lille; for others he offered appropriate dimensions for pots to be obtained from one's local potter.[55] Illustrations of the potted carnation also frequently showed the flowers surrounded by a wire cage for support.[56]

Cultivators of pinks and carnations were as discriminating as tulip fanciers in judging their flowers. The carnation's first blossom of the season was usually its finest, prompting Valnay to write, "The first flower is always the largest, it is unique in the hopes of the Curious, who neglects the others."[57] But persuading the tightly formed petals packed in the bud of the blossom to spread open presented another problem unique to the species. As a solution the *Nouvelle instruction pour la culture des fleurs* suggested the use of a special tool produced for that purpose.[58] Thomas Hale (alias of John Hill), however, proposed an alternative:

> When the Buds appear for flowering, the inner Cup must be opened in three or four Places, to favour the regular spreading of the Petals; and it must be defended from Wet, and too much Sun, by a Glass Cap; covered occasionally with a Piece of Bays.
>
> After this a Paper or Card Collar may be placed under the Petals; and the Gardener must from Day to Day, as they disclose themselves, favour their spreading, that they may be supported everywhere by the Collar, while they hide it compleatly; and he is afterwards to lay the several Petals handsomely one upon another; they will remain as they are placed, and make a very regular Appearance.[59]

Once the difficulties of carnation cultivation were surmounted, however, the florist was rewarded with a delightful flower. Argued Sieur Robert-Xavier Mallet in his 1775 *Beauté de la Nature, ou Fleurimanie Raisonnée, Concernant l'art de cultiver le Oeillets*:

> No one can disagree that it is without contradiction the most beautiful and the most brilliant of all the flowers, without wanting, however, to show disregard to the other flowers. Apart from the fact that the carnation is quite varied in its colors, it is the plant most agreeable to the sense of sight, as much as by its form as by its greenness and the majesty of its stem. . . . Its sweet, aromatic, and gracious odor surpasses all of the perfumes in the world. One must admire its colors, their nuances, the regularity of its markings, and its admirable form. It is,

finally, the flower of flowers, which can preferably be offered to the greatest princesses of the land.[60]

The difficulties encountered in producing such fine pinks and carnations only enhanced their desirability, and carnations remained fashionable and expensive throughout the early modern period. Mallet advertised his own pinks for sale at the end of his book, informing readers that lesser varieties could be purchased for prices ranging from 6 francs, to 3 livres, and 30 sols, while he reserved for himself those of such "a rare beauty of which he does not mark with a price."[61] Although Mallet's eighteenth-century prices could not compare to those commanded by the tulip in the seventeenth, he nevertheless either deemed it wise not to print the value of his rarest, finest blossoms, did not intend to sell them, or judged them to be priceless.

The brightly colored anemone (*Anemone coronaria* and *A. Pavonia*) rivaled tulips and carnations in the gardens of seventeenth- and eighteenth-century curious florists (figure 12).[62] Yet admirers of anemones, too, felt it necessary to defend the anemone against the virtues of tulips. The seventeenth-century British florist John Rea remarked: "The Wind-flower, or *Anemone*, by which name it is generally received and known, for the delicacy of form, richness of colour,

FIG. 12.   Nicolas Robert, Anemone. From *La Guirlande de Julie*, Paris, 1641. Paris, Bibliothèque Nationale de France, Manuscrits, fonds français NAF 19735.

and excellency of variety, next to the *Tulips*, deserveth to be esteemed."[63] Valnay added in his *Connoissance et culture parfaite des tulippes rares, des anemones extraordinaires, des oeillets fins, et des belles oreilles d'ours panachées* of 1688, "The ease that there is in knowing the beauties of the anemone, & even in raising it, has given us many more Curious in this Flower than in the Tulip. . . . I like and know thoroughly the two flowers," he explained, "but one [the anemone] has a great deal more taste and delicacy than the other."[64]

Though native to southern and eastern Europe eastward to Asia, anemones, like the tulip, came to Western Europe through Turkey.[65] Yet French curious florists repeatedly credited flower collector Bachelier with having brought the finest florists' varieties of anemones to France from the Indies. Valnay explained: "Anemones come to us from the Indies; the great curious [enthusiast] in flowers Monsieur Bachelier brought them [from there] around forty years ago. . . . Our illustrious curious diligently visit the garden of Monsieur Bachelier, because they know its many rarities."[66] Jean Donneau de Visé, too, reported that Bachelier had brought the flower from the Indies, writing in 1688: "It has been nearly fifty years since the first anemone was imported from the Indies into France, by Monsieur Bachelier, the great flower enthusiast. We admire its flowering, its vivacity, & the enamel of its flowers. The beauty of the anemone, which has seeds in abundance, increased during eight or ten years, and during all this time Monsieur Bachelier wished neither to sell them nor give them [away], one found ways of surpassing him, & the most beautiful cultivated Anemones were brought to the point of perfection, where they are, & will be even more admired and sought after."[67] Anemones were, however, cultivated in Paris long before Donneau de Visé and Valnay assert. The catalogues of Jean Robin's collection of plants, including the 1601 *Catalogus stirpium tam indigenarum quam exoticarum quae Lutetiae coluntur a J. Robino botanico regio* and the 1623 or 1624 *Enchiridion Isagogicum ad facilem notitiam stirpium, tam indigenarum, quam exoticarum* . . . included twenty-six anemones in 1601 and fifty-five varieties in the later edition.[68] Reference to anemones could also be found in Olivier de Serres's *Le Théâtre d'agriculture et mesnage des champs* of 1600.[69]

Despite the confusion over the origin of anemones in the French garden, there was little doubt that the anemone brought a brilliant variety of color to the parterre. Valnay wrote that those who visited the garden of Monsieur Bachelier "were marveled to see the flowering of the Anemones. The merit of the novelty & the vivacity of the enamel [coloring] of the flowers was ravishing."[70] Correspondence between humanist Nicolas-Claude Fabri de Peiresc, his brother, and the Genoese architect Bartolomeo del Bianco included a celebration of the anemone. Peiresc wrote, "of all the plants, it seems to me that the variety of anemones passes all the others; it is true that to have all [of them] in a garden makes a beautiful effect."[71]

Though anemones, like tulips, were valued for their variety, they, too, were subjected to standards according to which the best were judged. A fine anemone, explained the author[72] of the *Nouvelle instruction pour la culture des fleurs*, "should be large, and dappled; & the plush should form a dome as in the poppy."[73] The author added: "There are anemones that vary, which are variegated one year by large patches that show off the large leaves, the *béquillons* outlined, another year everything will be weepy, & another year the great leaves will be ticked, and the *béquillons* pure. These anemones are preferable to the others, because from the same bulbs you have differences, as if they were from other plants."[74] The qualities of the best anemones were similarly described in Ballon and Garnier's *Nouvelle instruction facile pour la culture des figuiers:* "To begin . . . , their beauty depends in the first place on the disposition of their petals: [its beauty is] greater if it is curly, greater if it is pretty; its *tousse* low and well garnished to make it all pleasing to see. An anemone, in order to be beautiful, should be large and mottled, and tall in proportion to its girth. It should carry its flower without bending. The brilliance of its colors is a quality that is liked no less than in other flowers; not only in that it does not fail to have the color of fire, rosy pink, white & other brilliant colors; there are in them marvelous browns."[75]

Pierre Morin described the anemone in greater detail in his *Catalogues de quelques plantes a fleurs*:

> One can see a great variety of anemones: some carry large leaves in their greenery, which are named ivy anemones, the other smaller ones which we call the leaves of parsley, some have single flowers, others double, and of so much color that it is marvelous. The double parsley-leaved ones are again divided into two species: because there are many (& they are the most common) which carry ordinarily on their flowers five or six big and wide petals, which surround an infinity of other narrow petals which are called *pluche* or plush: & others which carry also many tiny short filaments, which are held attached to the base in the flower between the said petals and plush, surround all the parts; these can be called *Fraise*, or ribbon. The other double anemones of the parsley leaves do not carry large petals on their flowers, nor plush, nor *Fraise* either: but their flower is composed of a multitude of medium-sized petals, in the manner of the edged anemones; & we have named them *Hermafroites* [*sic*: possibly hermaphrodite], because they have in them the nature of the said plush anemones in their leaves, & with the edging in their flowers.[76]

Morin then listed twenty-seven different varieties that could be found in his collection.

Thus fine anemones, florists agreed, were valued for the brilliance of their color, the profusion of pleasantly balanced petals, and the contrasting filaments in the center. The best examples of them were grown in France or the Netherlands. James Justice advised the readers of his *The British Gardener's Director, Chiefly Adapted to the Climate of the Northern Counties* of 1764: "This Flower is one of the Beauties of the Spring, which I would advise you to get from France or Holland, they having by far greater Varieties of this Flower than what are raised in Britain, whose Colours, as far as I have seen, are confined to Reds and Whites;

whereas abroad I have seen great Varieties of Blues, Purples, and brownish Colours, most admirable intermixt, and most other colours, excepting yellow, which is as rare to see, as a blue Ranunculus."[77] By the late eighteenth century, however, interest in anemones began to wane. The Reverend William Hanbury lamented in his *A Complete Body of Planting and Gardening*:

> Inferior in beauty to none, though perhaps the least cultivated of any of the seven capital shed flowers, is the Wind-Flower; for which no other reason can be assigned, than the inattention it has mostly met with, perhaps, in the great regard and over-care of the other sorts; and which if taken off, and the nature of the flower duly weighed, reason would direct us to shew it more respect than it has hitherto met with; for its charms in its variety of colours are transcendent, and its composition is of such a nature as to form (if the phrase may be allowed) a conscious beauty. There is a certain freedom or ease in this flower that is not common; they blow with those truly admired flower the Ranunculi at all their times; but the proportions required to establish a compleat flower of that kind, give it rather a stiff formal look. Nothing of this is to be found in the Anemone; and without defaming the preceding flowers, for that turn in those is perfection, the Anemone shews itself without that stiff look in its varieties of all colours, (yellow excepted) large and double, in all its natural luxuriance and ease, waving with every wind its petals of so delicate a nature, so soft and susceptible as to be affected by every breath of air, opening and shutting, and gently obeying the direction and impulse of such externals.[78]

The anemone, however, did not return to the levels of popularity it had enjoyed in the seventeenth and early eighteenth centuries.[79]

While the anemone declined in popularity in the eighteenth century, other species, most importantly the hyacinth and the auricula, reached new levels of fashionability. Nicholas Van Kampen wrote: "Among all the ornaments of a flower-garden, the Hyacinth merits the first place. It commands the admiration of every beholder, who cannot without pleasure observe the sweetness and vivacity of its various colours, the arrangement and duplicity of the petals, and the elegant disposition of the florets."[80] Although Mallet championed the *oeillet* as the most worthy flower in *Beauté de la Nature*, he conceded that hyacinths were also fine flowers: "As the double hyacinth is the flower which disputes by its beauty the preference for carnations, although unjustly, it is not very just to place it in the second rank of flowers of the first order: this is why I am presenting here its culture that is very simple, after that of the Carnations."[81] Given the new popularity of hyacinths in the eighteenth century, many devotees wrote manuals devoted exclusively to the hyacinth. In 1752 George Voorhelm, "fleuriste d'Harlem," published *Traité sur la jacinte. Contenant la maniere de la cultiver suivant l'expérience qui en a été faite*, and in 1765 a *Traité sur la connoissance et la culture des jacintes* was published by "l'Auteur du *Traité des Renoncules*," in Avignon. The Marquis de Saint Simon published in 1768 *Des Jacintes, de leur anatomie, reproduction et culture*, the title page of which depicted a seated florist gazing intently at his blooming hyacinths while coins, pearls, his dog, and other treasures lay dismissed at his side.[82]

The hyacinth, also native to Turkey and western Syria, became known in Western Europe in the sixteenth century and was counted among the finest florists' flowers by the seventeenth. They did not reach the height of fashion until the eighteenth century when they became highly desirable in England, France, and the Netherlands, selling for as much as £100 per bulb in England.[83] "The double hyacinth has [spread beyond] Haarlem in Holland; they are sold at present equally in Paris and in many towns of Flanders and Brabant," observed Mallet.[84] Prominent florists such as Dirk and Pieter Voorhelm of Haarlem sold a huge variety of hyacinths by advertising them on broadsheet-style catalogues[85] and, with other Dutch growers, led in the production of new and fancier hyacinths. Mallet explained from a French perspective: "We have obligations to the Dutch for this plant; it is in forcing the seeds that they managed to furnish us with the beautiful varieties that we admire."[86] He added, however: "It seems that each country is favorable to certain plants: we have the advantage over them in carnations."[87] The Reverend William Hanbury agreed: "The Dutch pride themselves upon the Hyacinth, as the chief or mistress of all flowers, and boast that they alone are possessed of its true nature and management. Certain it is, they bring a blow to very great perfection; they raise infinite numbers from seeds, and obtain numerous fresh sorts of prodigious value, by which their stock, both in number and value, is greatly encreased. . . . It has been too justly lamented, that our skill in the management and ordering of these flowers falls vastly short of that of the Dutch florists."[88]

Of all the hyacinths cultivated in the early modern period, among them shades of blue, pink, and white, it was the doubled varieties of all these colors that attracted the most attention and sold for the highest prices in the eighteenth century. Hanbury elaborated on their newfound popularity:

> Fashion, by which most things at different times are affected, influences also the Hyacinths, and some particular sort will always have the run, and be most esteemed, as being the fashionable sort, whilst others, perhaps of better properties, are less regarded. But in all flowers, never was the height of fashion carried to so great a degree of absurdity, as in these flowers. Strange to tell! The large Double Hyacinths have not been many years in fashion! The Single ones were only deemed valuable; and those noble full flowers were thrown away as fast as they shewed their multiplicity of petals, and loaded with the opprobium of large cabbages.[89]

Saint Simon's *Des Jacintes* even included a diagram illustrating nine *fleurettes* (or individual flowers on the stem) doubled to various degrees, as well as three cross sections of the same[90] (figure 13).

A fine hyacinth, however, was more than just doubled. "Symmetry and proportion constitute the chief beauty in most things; and thus it is with the

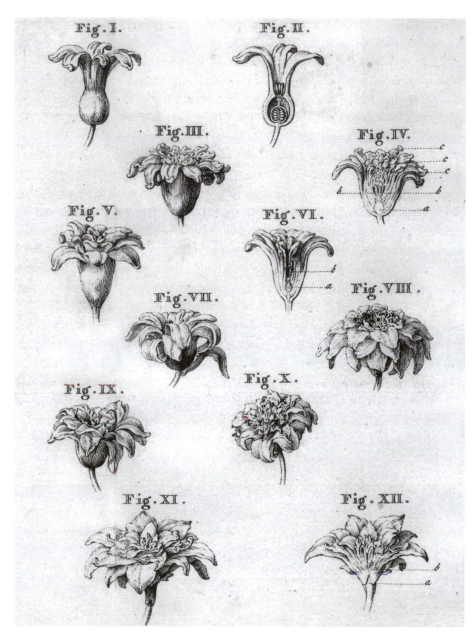

FIG. 13.   Maxmilien Henri, Marquis de Saint Simon, Hyacinth fleurettes. From *Des Jacintes, de leur anatomie, reproduction et culture*, Amsterdam, 1768. Washington, D.C., Dumbarton Oaks Research Library and Collections.

Hyacinth," explained Hanbury. "A few bells, however beautiful," he continued, "irregularly placed on an ill-proportioned and almost naked stalk, will compose a flower of a very awkward appearance amongst others of different properties."[91] In addition, he continued, "These beautiful spikes are most enchanting when the figure they represent is truly such, broadest at the base, and diminished gradually to a point; and it could be wished all Hyacinths in particular had this property." However, he cautioned that "indeed, though these are in general the standing properties of a good Hyacinth, yet the rules are not too strictly to be adhered to, as there are many valuable flowers that will not answer to all of them; and the florist who raises from the best of seeds must not expect to have one flower in a thousand that can, in every respect, bear the test of such criticism. The laws, therefore, are left to be softened, and dispensed with at pleasure."[92]

Only one other flower, the auricula (of the *primula* family), was subjected to such high degrees of critical standards in the eighteenth century. The auricula, or bears' ears, as the flower was also known, had been popular in the seventeenth century. John Parkinson remarked in his 1629 *Paradisi in Sole*: "The Beares eares or French Cowslips must not want their deserved commendations, seeing that their flowers, being many set together upon a stalke, does seeme every one of them to bee a Nosegay alone of it selfe; and besides the many differing colours that are to be seene in them . . . which increase much delight in all sorts of the Gentry of the Land, they are not unfurnished with a pretty sweete sent, which doth adde an encrease of pleasure in those that make them an ornament for their wearing."[93] But by the eighteenth century, the incredible popularity of the auricula had sparked competitions among growers of the flower, and even led to the construction of special stages upon which the blossoming plants were displayed.

The auricula was native to Europe and was known to grow in the Alps,[94] yet its "perfection" was claimed by florists in several countries. Hanbury argued in 1770 that the English were the most proficient growers of auriculas. He boasted: "The pride of our English florists is the [auricula], as there is no nation that ever boasted such variety, to form a large Collection, all raised by their own industry and skill. So that while the Dutch are boasting of their grand tulips, hyacinths, &c. we may lay claim to a greater honour, in our improvement of these delightful plants; for the Auricula, if we regard its sweetness of odour as well as beauty, must claim the precedence, and stands in our gardens the glory of all flowers, the carnation not excepted."[95] James Justice also wrote of the British role in raising auriculas, but suggested that the Dutch had taken over as the primary growers of the flower. He explained in his 1764 *The British Gardener's Director*: "This Flower was formerly the pride of the English Gardiners and Florists; that is, they had the greatest good Fortune in raising the best seminal Varieties, and that to such a Degree of Perfection, that I have known a single Plant of a good new raised Seedling, sold for seventy Guineas. The Dutch Florists envious of the good Fortune of the English, in raising so many fine Varieties of this Flower, sent to England and purchased their best Flowers, from which they have raised many admirable Varieties, which they value very high."[96]

The author of *A Treatise on the Culture and Management of the Bear's Ear, or, Auricula Ursi*, also related the story of the Dutch acquisition of English auriculas, but asserted that the English florists were working to recover the position of superiority in the cultivation of auriculas. He explained:

The Auricula was once the pride of the English gardeners and florists; and such excellent flowers were by them raised from seed, that a single plant has been sold for more than fifty pounds. But as fashion prevails in every thing, and we are apt to grow tired of the greatest beauties, the Auricula was neglected, and the English gardens were for some times deprived of one of the most lovely productions of nature.

The Dutch gardeners, prudently attentive to their interest, and wisely considering that this beautiful flower could not long remain in exile, but must certainly soon find its way again into the gardens of the curious, bought up all our best plants, and from them raised so many seminal varieties, and such excellent flowers, that we have been forced to apply to them again to adorn our sheds, and purchase the produce of our own flowers at most extravagant prices.

The Auricula thus restored to us, is now again become the chief ornament of our flower-gardens; and no garden is esteemed compleat without a stage of these delicate beauties.[97]

Some Englishmen, however, continued to look to the Dutch for new varieties. The author added: "So insatiable are the expectations of a florist, that many send annually to Holland for plants, in hopes of obtaining finer flowers than they have already, or of meeting with something new to add to their collections."[98]

The French, meanwhile, prided themselves on the reportedly French origin of the flowers. Valnay wrote in his 1688 flower gardening manual that "the Bears' Ear is French,"[99] but argued that it did not necessarily follow that the French excelled in their breeding: "We are not the first to have known their beauties. One must render justice to whom it is due, the Flemish are more attached to them than we [are]; there are those who raised on the island in Flanders the first variegated ones; but after we purchased them, we have sown many, & are at present very rich in this flower."[100] Robert-Xavier Mallet made a similar observation in 1775, explaining that "the Liegois are our masters in this genre of flowers, as much as for the taste for the species; although this flower was naturally French, the Flemish have made more of a case for them than we, who prefer carnations and double hyacinths."[101] Regardless of who produced the best auriculas, however, the nationalistic wrangling over the flower demonstrates the seriousness with which the florists took their passion for flowers.

The passion for auriculas was not unlike that for other florists' flowers, in that auriculas were lauded for the varieties of color in which they existed. So great was their variation that the author of the *Treatise on the Culture and Management of the Bear's Ear* argued that "a compleat collection of Auriculas is never to be obtained by one person's cultivation alone; he may sow and increase his plants by offsets his whole life-time, and at last be in possession of but few sorts."[102] Collectors paid particular attention to the color combinations found between the center or eye of the flower and the outer part of the petals. Over the course of the seventeenth century, red, purple, crimson, and buff-colored auriculas overtook yellow ones as the most sought after. And although striped ones were highly popular in the late seventeenth century, they were surpassed in the eighteenth century by blossoms edged in green.[103]

As the Reverend Hanbury pointed out in his *Complete Body of Planting and Gardening*, exactly what constituted a fine auricula was subject to the whims of fashion: "Fashion . . . alters the more trivial properties [of the auricula] at pleasure; and what is a perfection at one time or place, at another shall be called a defect. Nay, the very leaves are often by fashion made the chief characteristics of a good flower; and tho' the real flower has every such perfection, if the leaves do not answer such a particular description, it is rejected."[104] Nonetheless, Mallet attempted to summarize the qualities desired in the bears' ear. The leaves were to be fanned out evenly around the plant, the stem was to be large and sturdy in order to support its bouquet of blossoms, and the flowers had to be large in number and of a "beautiful color & agreeable to the sense of sight."[105]

Displaying one's auriculas to their best advantage was just as important as having fine specimens. Thus auricula connoisseurs invented the auricula "stage," which allowed them to showcase a large number of flowering auriculas grown in pots, while sheltering the flowers from wind, rain, and strong sun. Thomas Mawe explained the importance of protecting the delicate blossoms in his *Every Man His Own Gardener*: "The meally dust which covers these flowers, composes a principal part of their beauty; this must therefore be preserved upon them; the least shower of rain would easily wash it off; it is also liable to be blown off by the winds; and the sun, if permitted to shine freely on the flowers, would occasion them soon to fade."[106] According to Mawe's recommendations, just as an auricula began to bloom, it was to be placed on the stage to be displayed. He offered his readers instructions for the construction of such a stage:

> The stand, or stage, should have from three to five or six ranges of shelves, about six inches broad, rising theatrically one above another, from the front, the back being generally placed against a wall, pale or other building; it must be constantly covered at the top, but the front and two ends must only be covered occasionally. There should be some canvas or mats fastened to the top of the front and ends, by way of curtain. . . .
> By thus placing your auricula pots on a covered stage, it not only preserves the flowers much longer in beauty, but you also more readily view them, and they shew themselves to much greater advantage than when placed on the ground.[107]

An example of an auricula stage was provided on the frontispiece of Guénin's 1738 *Traité de la culture parfaite des oreilles d'ours ou auricules*[108] (figure 14). So important was the auricula stage to the florist's garden, explained "A Florist," author of *A Treatise on the Culture and Management of the Bear's Ear*, that "as these stages are generally placed in some conspicuous part of the garden, many people have been at a great expence to render them ornamental."[109] Some, he noted, painted the stages green, but it was necessary to find the correct shade of green. The "Florist" recommended "an olive-colour or faded green, for if your green be too

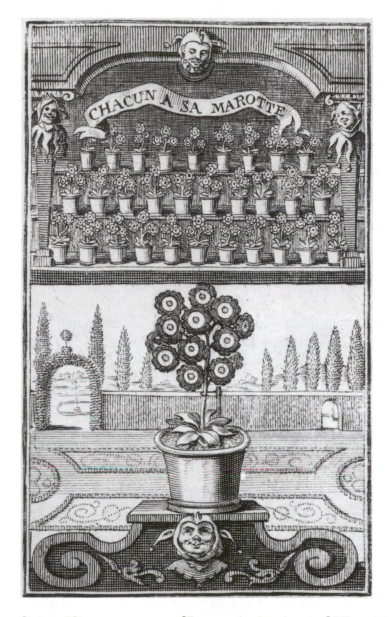

FIG. 14.   Guénin, "Chacun a sa marotte [Everyone has his obsession]." From *Nouveau Traité de la Culture parfaite des Oreilles d'ours ou Auricules*, Paris, 1738, title page. Paris, Bibliothèque Nationale de France.

lively, it will not sufficiently contrast the green leaves of your flowers."[110] For others, however, a simple green stage was not ornate enough. "Some persons," the Florist continued, "ornament the insides of their stages with paintings of landscapes &c." Yet the author did not recommend the practice, explaining, "This I can by no means approve of, as their colours will interfere too much with those of the flowers. Let the inside of your stage therefore be painted with some dark colour that will serve as a back ground to your flowers, and by such well-chosen contrast render the appearance more beautiful and lively."[111]

The "Florist's" critique of overly ornamental auricula stages, together with the exacting standards articulated for the blossoms of each species of the florists' flowers by their respective enthusiasts and collectors, demonstrates the means by which curious florists distinguished not only between worthy and unworthy flowers, but also between the truly tasteful florists and the less worthy collectors. By defining the standards of color and form for fine flowers, the florists defended their ranks against mere pretenders to the cause and attempted to preserve the status of their own collections; and they demonstrated their possession of knowledge and understanding of the flowers they cultivated. But just as learning and skill were revealed through the cultivation of flowers, so did the curious florists reveal themselves to be motivated by fashion. Brent Elliott has demonstrated that although some of the flowers to capture the attention of the curious came from Turkey or other eastern lands associated with the exotic in the early modern European mind, other flowers such as the anemone and the auricula were found in Europe. But only when anemone cultivars arrived in Western Europe from Turkish sources did Western Europeans become enamored with them.

UNLOCKING THE DOOR TO THE TEMPLE OF FLORA

The increasingly specific criteria by which seventeenth- and eighteenth-century florists defined fine floral specimens suggests that the number of flowers circulating in early modern Europe was increasing, too. But it took many years, even decades, for the most desirable species to become widely available. Collectors were anxious about sharing their rarities. La Chesnée Monstereul had worried that if tulips became common, the sociability, or "sweet society," as he called it, that existed among flower collectors would be lost. Some were motivated by financial losses resulting from the multiplication of rare specimens. Dezallier D'Argenville described curious florists who "value a bulb of tulips as high as a hundred *pistoles* & more, & the same in order to render their beautiful bulbs unique, often have the malice to crush their offshoots"[112] in order to preserve the rarity and therefore the status and monetary value of the original bulb. Others, however, did not want to share their specimens at all, or at least until they had multiplied their stock. Such was the case with Monsieur Bachelier, the curious florist credited in French flower gardening manuals with having introduced anemones into France. According to Valnay, Bachelier wanted to perfect his anemones for several years before sharing any of his seeds. "But," writes Valnay, "the ardor of the other Curious was too vehement for such a long period," so one flower collector hatched a plan to obtain seeds from Bachelier's collection.

> The invention of one of our Curious Counselors in Parlement that helped him to have the seed of the Anemones, despite the hard refusal of Monsieur Bachelier, is

too witty to be forgotten. The seed [of the anemone] very much resembles down, as it carries the same name, & when it is all mature, it attaches easily to wool fabric; this Counselor went to see the flowers of Monsieur Bachelier when the seeds were ripe, he went enrobed in a cloth of the Palais, and commanded his lackey to let it trail. When the gentlemen were near the Anemones, [when] the conversation [was fixed] on a plant that attached sight elsewhere & by a turn of the robe, he brushed some of the heads of Anemones that left their seeds on the wool. He entrusted the lackey to immediately pick up the train of the robe, the seeds were caught in the binding, & Monsieur Bachelier did not suspect anything as nothing appeared to have been done.[113]

The subterfuge perpetrated by the unnamed member of the Parlement would not have been regarded as honorable behavior, as it demonstrated character traits ill befitting those who wished to be counted among the ranks of La Chesnée Monstereul's "sweet society." But the incident reveals the lengths to which curious florists were prepared to go to grow their collections.

Fortunately, deception was only one means of obtaining flowers. The flower mania depended on the seemingly endless varieties of "florists' flowers" to perpetuate interest in the flowers, but also on the development of a flower trade capable of meeting the ever-increasing demand. Throughout the early modern period, trade in flowers responded, becoming more and more sophisticated not only in the sale of cut or fresh flowers, but also in the marketing of florists' flowers. The tulip mania of the early seventeenth century led to the establishment in the Netherlands of "colleges," groups organized specifically to trade tulips, as well as public tulip auctions, both of which played into the rampant speculation on the rare bulbs.[114] Even after the collapse of the Dutch tulip trade, the Netherlandish commercial development of the flower trade was regarded with envy. James Justice even recommended studying the Dutch and Flemish commercial flower businesses in his 1764 *The British Gardener's Director*. In offering "some general Directions to Florists, or to those Persons who make the propagating and cultivating these Flowers their Trade and chief Business,"[115] Justice recommended that the prospective florist be prepared to spend a good deal of money to launch the business and "spare no Cost to purchase the best Flowers; and if he should take a Trip to Holland and to Flanders, to see and observe their Methods of cultivating their Flowers, it would be well worth his Travel and Expences."[116]

French commercial floriculture could not compare to the highly organized Dutch example. The 1617 purchase of several tulip bulbs in Paris, for example, was deemed important enough to warrant the registration of an official notarized contract and bill of sale between engraver Simon de Poelenbourg and "arboriste" René Morin.[117] After all, rare bulbs were expensive. But most transactions were handled more casually, with curious florists seeking out a variety of sources, including *bouquetières*, *jardiniers-fleuristes*, and, most importantly, each other in order to add to their prized collections.

The *Statuts et ordonnances* of the flower sellers suggest that although some *bouquetières* sold potted flowers, they primarily sold cut flowers. For potted plants, seeds, and bulbs, one was best served by a *jardinier*, or preferably, a *jardinier-fleuriste*, or gardener who specialized in the cultivation of flowers. Records of the incorporation of the "Communaute des jardiniers" date back to 1473; their rules were reconfirmed by each ruler from Henri III through Louis XIV.[118] To counter the decline in the fashionability of flowers in chaplets and *jonchées* in the late Middle Ages, gardeners added skills to make their services more marketable to Renaissance gardeners such as building trellises and garden pavilions.[119] Thus, by the eighteenth century, gardeners fell into four categories: "flower gardeners" ("jardiniers fleuristes"), "merchant gardeners of trees" ("jardiniers marchandes d'arbres"), "garden planters" ("jardinier planteurs"), and "market gardeners" ("maraîchers").[120] Apprenticeships lasted four years after which the former apprentices served for two years as journeymen. Much like most other guilds, only males could become master gardeners. Their statutes did, however, allow the widows of gardeners to continue in the trade, although widows were not permitted to accept new apprentices.[121] Women were also commonly employed by gardeners performing manual day labor such as weeding.[122]

According to Jacques Savary des Bruslons, Parisian gardeners sold their plants, trees, fruit trees, and shrubs, most of which were cultivated in the *faubourgs* and fields outside of the city, everyday at Les Halles, but also on Wednesdays and Saturdays on the quay de la Vieille Vallée.[123] In *Le Livre commode contenant les adresses de la ville de Paris et le trésor des almanachs pour l'année bissextile 1692*, however, Abraham du Pradel directed his readers to the faubourg Saint Antoine for gardeners "who sell flowers, trees, & shrubs for the ornament of gardens."[124] There, he said, could be found several gardeners including "Les Sieurs Julier & Guyot et petit Claude, rue de Pincourt; Chevalier, rue des Amanders; Tremel & Grebey, rue de la Raquette; les Breton, rue de Charonne; du Puis, Juby & Hely, rue de Baffoy; Gaumont Jacques & du Buisson grande rue de Fauxbourg," among others. He also recommended consulting the Sieur Billette, "Gardener to the King" (whose wife was "Flower Seller to His Majesty"), for "very beautiful flowers . . . & very beautiful shrubs." Flowers and fruit trees from the south of France, such as oranges, lemons, jasmines, tuberoses, narcissi, and hyacinths, were available at "chez les Provençaux" at the "cul de sac Saint Germain l'Auxerrois rue de l'Arbre sec."[125]

Seeds for choice flowers, according to Pradel's directory, were available on Wednesdays and Saturdays on the quay de la Megisserie.[126] Louis Liger, in his gardening manual *Le Jardinier Fleuriste et Historiographe*, advertised the services of a Madame le Fevre, "seed merchant," who, in addition to selling vegetable and herb seeds, offered "all sorts of seeds for the most beautiful flowers, Anemones of all varieties, & the most rare, of the most esteemed Tulips, & the finest Ranunculi."[127]

For other supplies and services, Pradel listed gardeners who excelled in the construction of "cabinets & ornements" out of trellises. Terra-cotta pots were available from Sieur du Vivier in the faubourg Saint Antoine, while faience pots

could be purchased from the potters at Saint Cloud, although if one wanted violet and white faience, he recommended the "Fayancerie de Rouen."[128]

The flower trade was also international, and a number of gardening manuals advised their readers on successful international transport of plants or
bulbs ordered from abroad. Transporting living specimens could be difficult. In
the first half of the seventeenth century, the Italian flower collector and Jesuit
priest Giovanni Battista Ferrari included in his *De Florum Cultura*, a Latin flower
gardening manual, an engraving of a special crate for shipping flowers. Labeled
a "capsula ambulatorio assere flores transferens," the box was designed to protect flowers and floral bouquets in transit.[129] The twelfth chapter of George London and Henry Wise's *The Retir'd Gard'ner*, a compilation and translation of Louis
Liger's *Le Jardinier François* and *Le Jardinier Solitaire*, was devoted to "How to
observe all Sorts of Flowers in Transporting them from Foreign Countries." "A
Florists Curiosity," read the text, "is not to be confin'd to his own Country, nor
to such Flowers as he can find there; he should seek abroad, and deal with Neigh-
boring Nations for what he has not of his own."[130] Gardeners were advised to
pack roots or cuttings of plants in dry moss, and place them, carefully labeled,
in strong boxes for shipping.

So important was the acquisition of specimens from foreign countries
that an entire text was devoted to the subject. In 1770 John Ellis, who prided himself on his correspondence with Carl Linnaeus, published in London *Directions
for Bringing Over Seeds and Plants, from the East-Indies and Other Distant Countries, in a State of Vegetation*. Ellis proposed a method of packing and shipment
"communicated to me some years ago by the celebrated Professor Linnaeus" which
would prevent seeds from rotting or sprouting en route. He also cautioned his
readers that Chinese traders had been known to take advantage of European plant
hunters by selling them already decayed seeds.[131]

Despite such diversification and specialization in the flower trade, the flower
markets were neither steady sources of large numbers of flowers, nor able to supply the rare and extremely expensive exotic flowers sought by the most curious
florists.[132] Flower collectors instead traded with each other to increase their own
collections. As a result, a network of personal relationships developed that were,
among most florists, regarded as pleasant, rewarding exchanges—the "sweet society" described by La Chesnée Monstereul. Antoine Schnapper has demonstrated,
for example, how the personal letters of Peiresc reveal an extensive and friendly
network of floral exchanges.

Within published flower gardening manuals, the florists advertised each
other's collections as well as their own, as sources for the highly sought-after plants.
Emanuel Sweerts's 1612 *Florilegium*, published in Frankfurt, was not only a
visual record of his collection, but also a sale catalogue (although no prices were
recorded).[133] Sweerts addressed his potential buyers simultaneously in Latin,
Dutch, German, and French: "Gentlemen who desire to buy books, plants, or
flowers, narrated in these said Books, can be found at the fair of Frankfurt in

front of le Roemer: or [at his] house in the town, inside the boutique of the author Emanuel Sweerts, but after the fair in Amsterdam . . . Emanuel Sweerts lives on the Bloemgracht."[134] In Paris, René Morin's *Catalogus plantarum horti Renati Morini inscriptarum ordinae alphabetico,* one of the earliest such catalogues, appeared in 1621.[135] Jean-Baptiste Dru, "Herboriste du Roy," listed his extensive collection in his *Catalogues des Plantes, Tant des tulipes, que des autres fleurs,* in the text of which he commented on the two primary means of enhancing one's own collection—money and exchange.[136] Pierre Morin, brother of René,[137] published several catalogues describing his collections, including his 1658 *Remarques nec-essaires pour la culture des fleurs . . . Avec un Catalogue des Plantes rares qui se trou-vent à present dans son Jardin,* and the *Catalogues de quelques plantes a fleurs qui sont de present au jardin de Pierre Morin* of 1651. N. Valnay directed the readers of his *Connoissance et culture parfaite des tulippes rares* to specific gardeners, him-self among them, for the best of each flower included in his manual. For the "pur-chase [and] the exchange" of tulips, Valnay recommended his own collection, in addition to "M. Desgranges, Controlleur général de la Tresorie de la Maison de sa Majesté & de Monsieur Caboud Avocat au Conseil." For anemones, he suggested again himself, Desgranges, and Caboud, as well as "Monsieur Descoteaux & Monsieur Breart Officiers du Roy, Monsieur Demauges, Mon-sieur le Verrie Gressier de Consuls, Monsieur Lobinois Officier de Monsieur, & Monsieur Roland." The best carnations in Paris, he continued, were available from Descoteaux, himself, Breard, and Caboud, while he and Descoteaux main-tained the best collections of bears' ears.[138]

Flower collecting and gardening were therefore based largely on personal relationships with other flower enthusiasts. Claude Mollet wrote in the 1670 edi-tion of his *Théâtre des Jardinages,* "I have seen that some curious Gardeners visit one another amiably, & do research on that which they can have in their Gar-dens, to see if they have some species of flowers or of fruits that one or the other does not have, in order to come to terms among them."[139] The anonymous author of *A Treatise on the Culture and Management of the Bear's Ear* explained, "A compleat collection of Auriculas is never to be obtained by one person's culti-vation alone." "A variety of fine flowers," he continued, "are only to be obtained by purchase or exchange. At the time of bloom therefore visit the gardens of the curious, you will find florists enough who will exchange flowers with you, as by this means each florist will enrich and increase his collection."[140]

Ultimately the eighteenth-century marketplace responded to the increased demand for expensive and fashionable flowers. In the eighteenth century, the flower gardening manual that included a catalogue evolved into a placard-style catalogue, a cheaper and more easily disseminated format. In 1739 Nicolas Van Kampen of Haarlem produced an extensive catalogue and price list that included large selections of hyacinths, tulips, ranunculi, anemones, narcissi, crocuses, lilies, frit-illaries, irises, crown imperials, cyclamen, aconite, and gladioli.[141] In the 1740s, Dirk and Pieter Voorhelm, florists also based in Haarlem, began to circulate flower and price lists in Dutch and French. A 1746 catalogue by the Voorhelms, for example, included more than three hundred sixty different auriculas,[142] and their hyacinth catalogue of the same year listed more than two hundred of them. The Voorhelms counted among the recipients of their flower lists Louis XV of France. From the 1746 hyacinth list, the king's gardeners ordered 403 bulbs of twenty-five varieties.[143] Indeed, the royal gardeners began a correspondence with the Voorhelms and used their firm to supply the hyacinths for Louis XV's extensive hyacinth garden at Choisy. The catalogue facilitated the growth of an international network of flower sellers, thereby fulfilling demands that an international network of friends and acquaintances could not. By the late eighteenth century, one could even have fresh flowers delivered to one's home. The *fleuriste* Sieur Regnault, for example, advertised in a 1781 *Annonces, affiches et avis divers, ou Journal Général de France* that for 6 livres per decoration and two days' notice, he would "garnish with flowers the tables in apartments and renew them."[144]

Despite such innovations, the collection of florists' flowers remained a personal, sociable activity. The frontispiece for a 1764 tulip-cultivating manual depicted two gentlemen deep in discussion over a bed of tulips that were clearly the object of their attentions (see figure 10).[145] The flowers remained a source of personal pride and had even become a focus of mild national identity. The careful and ardent discussions of what constituted a quality bloom were matched only by claims put forward by florists of England, France, and the Netherlands that theirs were the finest tulips, or auriculas, or anemones. If the acquisition of flowers became easier in the eighteenth century, their ability to foster conversation and convey taste remained intact.

The work of the florist had only begun, however, once a specimen had been acquired, for the flower had to be cared for, multiplied, and, according to some collectors, "improved." Early modern flower collections usually took one of two forms. Either the curious florist attempted to amass as many different species of plants as possible, or he sought to gather in his garden different varieties or colors of the same species.[146] Pierre Morin, the most important flower collector in seventeenth-century Paris, described his collection in both ways, perhaps hoping to advertise his holdings to different clientele. His collection, as described in his *Catalogues de quelques plantes a fleurs,* included one hundred different tulips, twenty-four ranunculi, seventy-one irises, and twenty-seven anemones.[147] Yet his *Remarques necessaires pour la culture des fleurs* included extensive lists of plants categorized as "fragrant flowers," "flowers of the best odor," "fragrant herbs," "bulbous plants," "more curious tuberose plants," and, finally, a list of "some flowering plants."[148] The two catalogues of Morin's collections would have appealed to two different kinds of collectors and collections. Those less preoccupied with fashionable flowers, and hence more interested in obtaining the broadest range of botanical specimens, would have favored the *Remarques necessaires.* But most curious florists would have been more interested in his first catalogue. For them, it was the continual selective breeding for new colors, striped or variegated blossoms, double flowers, and stronger scents that fueled the fires of floral passion.

Fashion, as we have seen, valued what was novel or rare, and the bizarrely colored, fantastically striped, or wildly doubled caused the greatest sensation. Single-colored tulips were regarded simply as bulbs that could be used for breeding variegated varieties.[149] Fashion also determined the popularity of different colors of flowers. Louis Boulanger wrote in his manual on carnations: "Interest & curiosity have invented many means of variegating . . . in diverse colors the flowers of our gardens, as in making roses green, yellow, and blue, & similarly in a very short time two or three colors have been given to one carnation, besides its natural tint."[150] As Boulanger's statement reveals, florists were always in search of blue, green, and even black flowers, the same rare colors advertised in bulb catalogues today. Black or brownish tulips were also always in demand. In the seventeenth century, anemones in vermilion and scarlet accented with pink were popular; in the eighteenth century, blue and purple varieties were highly sought after. In auriculas, collectors sought red, purple, crimson, and brownish or buff-colored blossoms.[151]

Attaining this broad range of fashionable colors, however, was difficult, especially given the lack of concrete scientific information about genetics. Botanists and floriculturists would not understand the complexity of selective breeding until the nineteenth century.[152] Adding to the mystery of breeding flowers was the unexplainable rapidity with which tulips were prone to "breaking," or producing multicolored flowers. It was not understood that "breaking" was caused by a virus transmitted by aphids, making it impossible to predict how a tulip bulb would "break" or how long the bulb would continue to produce variegated flowers. Therefore the cultivation of wildly colored tulips was fraught with mystery and uncertainty.

The absence of scientific information about selective breeding, however, did not stop the authors of flower gardening manuals from sharing with readers their methods of, or opinions on, such matters. Nor did the fact that most curious florists regard flowers as God's creations interfere with their belief that nature was best if improved by the arts of man. Theologically, early modern Europeans believed that God had given humans power over plant and animal life. Indeed, the idea that nature should be improved was central to the early modern way of thinking about the natural world.[153] Aesthetically, writes José Maravall, "The baroque individual . . . always preferred nature transformed by art to simple nature."[154] Among the subjects frequently discussed in flower gardening manuals, then, were instructions on how to perfect nature—how to achieve those new colors and doubles.

The methods prescribed by gardeners and collectors varied widely. Sir Hugh Plat offered his readers advice on making "single flowers doubled" by the phases of the moon. According to Plat, gillyflowers, pinks, roses, daisies, and tulips could double if one followed his instructions: "Remove a plant of stock gilliflowers when it is a little wooded, and not too green, and water it presently; do this three dayes after the full [moon], and remove it twice more before the change. Do this in barren ground, and likewise three dayes after the new full Moon, remove again; and then remove once more before the change: Then at the third full Moon . . . remove again, and set it in very rich ground, and this will make it to bring forth a double flower."[155] Giovanni Battista Ferrari's early seventeenth-century Italian manual on floriculture included entire chapters on improving odor and color.[156] Louis Boulanger, too, listed several different methods employed by florists. "For example," wrote Boulanger, "they have pulverized coarse soil, cut it in the sun, & watered it little after the space of fifteen or twenty days with red water, or yellow, or another tint, then . . . they sow the seed of this flower of a color contrary to the artificial water."[157] Others, he reported, mixed seeds of the carnation with the roots of wild chicory in hopes of producing a blue carnation, "as beautiful as it is rare," or combined carnation seeds with seeds of variegated flowers in hopes of striping their carnations.[158]

Stephen Blake, in *The Compleat Gardeners Practice,* described altering the colors of red and white tulips by planting each with a mixture of wild herbs, sheep manure, and pigeon manure. He reported, however, that contrary to the advice of others, an experimental mixture of a white tulip, lettuce, solendine leaves, chamomile, white thistle, and sweet peas planted with a red tulip did not alter the tulip's color. Blake concluded that colors contrary to the nature of the flower would not affect the color of that flower.[159] He was also unsuccessful in altering floral colors by inserting pigments into the plant through an incision.[160]

Blake similarly purported to be knowledgeable in the alteration of the scent of flowers. He recommended that florists interested in attempting to do so direct their experiments toward flowers that naturally had little or no scent such as "flowerdeluces, scarlet-beans, emrose or Tulips, because they are flowers that Ladies love to have so nigh to their noses, which have little or no sent [*sic*], and it would be a rare art to cause them to have a sent."[161] Others, he warned his readers, advised florists to mix cloves, mace, cinnamon, musk, "amber-grease," and Damask rose-water, and apply the solution to tulip bulbs for "it would make this Flower exceed all Flowers, for there is nothing wanting in this Flower that nature did bestow in any other, except sent." Unfortunately, Blake reported, "I can assure you that you will lose your labour and cost: My reason is, as I said before, plants do not contract any substance, as it is either sweet or sowr, black or white, but into its own sent, colour and forme that God and Nature gave it."[162]

Not all, then, approved of attempts to alter the scent or color of flowers. "I have known several Persons that have spent a great deal of time in enquiring into this Knowledge," wrote Henry Van Oosten, "but because those Florists have been but of indifferent Parts, and their defective Insight has been but a little above the Knowledge of the Ignorant, the Goddess Flora has esteemed them not worthy of her Mysteries, and locked up the Door of her Temple from them."[163] Some gardening manuals therefore advised florists against tampering with expensive bulbs and plants. Boulanger, after recounting the practice of a "subtil fleuriste" who attached to one carnation plant shoots of diversely colored blossoms, in order to "ravish the eyes of the ignorant who do not know the cause of the diverse paints," concluded that such violations of the bulbs "sometimes causes the death of that which [the florist] was trying to give life, punishing in this way the curiosity of a hand too bold."[164]

In addition to cautioning against harming the flower, Boulanger also reminded the florist that the flower was the work of God and best appreciated as such. Boulanger admonished, "my dear Reader, I invite you to worship innocently with myself, . . . as God has so composed all the creatures so that one cannot examine the least of them, without encountering immediately some supernatural feature of his love and power."[165] More responsible gardening manuals therefore suggested that florists approach the quest for new varieties conservatively, through careful selective breeding. They advised that if one was seeking to raise double hyacinths, for example, that all singles be thrown away, and suggested that to increase one's stock of double or uniquely colored flowers, seeds, cuttings, or bulb offshoots be gathered only from such plants.

If a flower collector was successful in multiplying his collection, then he had to devise a method for managing its growing numbers. Flower gardening manuals therefore offered specific plans for growers to follow in order to keep track of one's large variety of holdings. John Rea, in his 1676 *Flora: seu De Florum Cultura,* suggested that the florist construct an octagonal "Somer-house, roofed in every way, and finely painted with Landskips, and other conceits, furnished with Seats about, and a Table in the middle." The structure was useful, he explained, for several reasons: "[The building] . . . serveth not onely for delight and entertainment, to sit in, and behold the beauties of the Flowers, but for many other necessary purposes; as, to put the Roots of *Tulips* and other Flowers in, as they are taken up, upon Papers, with the names upon them, until they be dried, that they may be wrapped up and put in Boxes, in order as you dispose them; for shelter, in case of a sudden shower of rain; and divers other purposes you will find this House to be fit for."[166]

James Justice offered more detailed descriptions in his *British Gardener's Director* for such a structure: "In the Great Flower-garden, a good Florist must build a proper Root-room." "And off from that in the same Range," he continued, "a good handsome chamber or two for his own Convenience, that, when his Flowers are in Bloom, or when his Roots are in the Root-room, he may ly in those Chambers to take Care at Nights of his Goods there." The structure, built in proportions to the "Pleasure of the Proprietor," was to include a strong door large enough for crates to pass through, with windows facing north, south, and west. The dimensions of the building were left to individual taste, but Justice felt that in a proper "Root-room," there should be Shelves on two Sides by the Windows from Top to Bottom, on which there should be placed Drawers, divided . . . to hold the different Sorts of Tulips, Hyacinths, Ranunculus, Anemonies, and Polyanthos Narcissus's: And upon these Drawers, and upon their several Division, should be pasted, written or printed Paper Labels, telling the Names of the Flower-roots contained in every Division or Apartment of these Drawers. . . . The Place where the Anemonies and Ranunculus's ly [sic], should be near a Fire, in case of violent Frosts in those Months only before they are planted, and to exclude all Frosts from them, which would prejudge and rot their Roots before they are planted in the Ground. . . . The Drawers in this Root-room should be only five Inches deep, that the Roots may ly single therein, and not in Heaps, or one above another; and they should be very close at Bottom, but as airy above as may be, that the Air and Wind may have free Access to them.[167]

Nearly as important as the condition of the bulbs was their security. The bulbs of rare flowers, after all, commanded great prices, and some flower growers stooped to dishonorable means to enhance their collections. Justice added to his description of the "Root-room" that "upon these Shelves and Drawers, there should be folding Leaves of Timber and Cases trelaced with Wire for Air, and well locked, to exclude too busy Hands. The Windows of this Root-room should have fixed Iron fine Trelaces, and strong Timber-covers over them, to shut or lock at Night."[168]

The care taken to label and keep separate different colors and varieties of flowers points to another problem at the center of flower breeding: how to define or label accurately each variety in the absence of any systematic plan for naming. Even the doctors of medicine from the royal Jardin des plantes acknowledged the shortcomings of seventeenth-century nomenclature and vocabulary. In the *Memoires pour servir l'histoire des plantes* published by members of the Académie royale des sciences, Dionys Dodart wrote, "The necessity of finding proper terms, especially in the Descriptions, made us think of taking the liberty of introducing some new manners of speaking, or of reestablishing some old words when the proper words were lacking."[169] The issue of naming and describing were also matters of great consternation to curious florists throughout the early modern period. The problem was discussed frequently in gardening manuals, and each florist was eager to propose a better system.

Louis Boulanger included a lengthy discussion of the "diverse names that the Curious gave to flowers" in his *Jardinage des Oeillets,* exploring the variety of sources florists consulted for names. In addressing his own carnations, Boulanger wrote, "I had the happy memory of Themistocles who greeted each of his citizens by their proper names. Like Cyrus and Scipio I call all the soldiers of the large army by their surnames in war. And as with Cyneas Ambassadors of Pyrrhus, I speak to the entire Senate."[170] Indeed, several of the names in his collection were classical in origin. Ceasar, Pompey, and Alexander were potential carnation names. For those favoring contemporary European politics, Boulanger offered "Royal, Prince, Duc, and Archi-Duc." The variety of names

was such that Boulanger remarked: "They alone command entire armies of cap-
tains and soldiers. Without beating the drums he raises Swiss regiments. They
are governors of many towns, of Rouen, of Tours, of Bordeaux. He creates
Republics and Kingdoms, of Parisians, of Picards, and the Portuguese. Without changing religion, he is today a Capuchin, and tomorrow a Huguenot, or
anti-Huguenot."[171] As the names cited by Boulanger illustrate, the curious did
not shy away from referring to politics or even highly contentious religious debates
in naming of their specimens.

The Sieur de La Chesnée Monstereul reported a similar diversity in the
naming of tulips, although he detected differences in Dutch and Parisian naming practices. In Holland, he maintained, the republican tulip enthusiasts named
their flowers after army officers, whereas in Paris the curious florists were more
likely to choose names from kingdoms, provinces, and towns.[172] But these
observations were hardly the rule, as he also cited "un autre Curieux & grand
Floriste" who selected names of foreign lands such as "Orientale, . . . la Chinoise,
la Venitienne, [et] l'Angloise." A "Demoiselle"[173] gave her tulips the names of
Romans, and another florist used the names of famous painters. Noble family
names such as "Pamphilie" were possibilities, as were various "femmes fortes"
names including mythological characters such as Prosperine, Old Testament figures such as Dorotée, and the regal L'Imperatrice.[174] Boulanger even reported
that "Monseigneur the Cardinal Richelieu, who after his great duties goes to
refresh his spirits among the flowers, and the beautiful enamel of the gardens,
does not disdain to give the name Jean Scime, of Gaignepain, and the Chancellor."[175] And in the catalogue of his own tulips printed at the end of the book,
La Chesnée Monstereul listed the "Monstereulle, striped with lively crimson,
on a great deal of white" (no doubt one of his own productions), "Virginie, striped
with rosy-pink tones on white, with detached patches which resemble drops of
blood," and one named after the Cardinal himself, "Richelieu," which was
richly striped with "violet washed over white."[176]

The great diversity in naming tulips and other florists' flowers, however,
revealed a problem at the heart of flower collecting (and, more broadly, early modern botany): it was impossible to be sure that a new and different variety was truly
new and different. In other words, the lack of a system for naming allowed each
collector to name his own specimens, so that two bulbs, differently named, could
easily be of the same variety and produce identical blooms. La Chesnée Monstereul discussed the problem at length, illustrating the situation for his readers and proposing proper guidelines for naming flowers:

> Of all the species and types of tulips, there are those which [serve as] paragons, &
> those which become more beautiful in perfecting them: then the curious, who have
> brought them [to this point], can give them a name; & conserve always that of their
> species, adjusting that of the Paragon. For example, one can say such and such
> *paragonnée*, or the paragon of such and such, so that the name that they give them

is adjusted to that of the species (those who always demur to a general rule) & that the name should agree with the form, color, & perfection of the tulip. . . . thus Monsieur Robin gave the name Agate Robin to an Agate Tulip that he perfected, & to which (it was further embellished) has since been given the name of Agate Royalle. The Agate Morin was named by Monsieur Morin the Elder, after he perfected it. And thus each should name the tulip by judgment, & not by fantasy.[177]

The problem with this method, according to La Chesnée Monstereul, however, was that tulips were given many different names, despite the fact that they were identical. Thus the "difference would be only in name, & not in color."[178]

Valnay proposed a more systematic means of keeping track of one's specimens over multiple growing seasons.

[Although] one must give names to your most beautiful tulips, you can wait if you want so that your *hazards* have variegated cleanly for two successive years, in order to not name them uselessly; but you must describe your principal *hazards* perfectly in order to see in the following year their constancy, their progress, or their diminution. In which case in place of wool, you must tie at the bottom a small piece of card, on each of which you have a sign relative to your memory, on which you will put their portaits.

Thus, for example, you would write number 1. bizarre color, nuanced with tan, brown & bright, variegated with very beautiful golden yellow in large patches, medium vase or large vase, beautiful form, high or medium stem, green-circled bottom or otherwise, stamens of blue . . . , bright yellow pistils, . . . broke in 1688, & the same for other numbers.[179]

Valnay's systematic record of the blooms produced by each bulb over a series of years would ensure that the tulip in question was stable in color and could be given an appropriate and original name.

The difficulty of distinguishing between new varieties and duplications continued into the eighteenth century. English flower gardener John Cowell began the discussion of flowers in his 1730 *Curious and Profitable Gardener* with a letter from P. Belandine, a "Curious Gentleman," expressing his dismay with the naming crisis because the names failed to describe the blossoms accurately. In the letter, P. Belandine reported:

Abroad our very Curious Flowerists have Lists of all the great Personages, Castles, and Cities by them; and when a good Flower happens to come in their Garden, they give it a name from them that shall in the two first Letters signify what Colours it is mark'd with: and so when they read their Catalogues over, every Name is, as it were, a Painting of the Flower. The Method is, to make a Table as follows, viz.

For White, put the Letter W
For Yellow put [the letter] Y
. . . A Flower with White abounding, and mark'd with Crimson, may be called William the Conqueror; the W in William expressing the White abounding, and

the C the Crimson: or, in a different manner, the same Flower might be named the Wonder of Constantinople. . . .

A Flower striped with Crimson and Purple, may be called the Charming Phyllis, or the Curious Ptolomy.[180]

The complex system described by Belandine, however, did not gain followers.

In 1764 Nicolas Van Kampen, writing in *The Dutch Florist*, saw no need for a revised system. He, too, reported, "The florists of different countries have very different methods of distinguishing their flowers," but he found the Dutch system to be superior. The British, he explained, named their flowers after British noble titles, resulting in the frequent duplication of names, though he added that the British sometimes appended the name of the cultivator to the flower, "a tolerable good method to prevent . . . confusion arising from the scarcity of their names." Van Kampen then described a French system that he found to be totally unacceptable: "The French distinguish their flowers by numbers only, or at most by the name of the principal colour; but this method occasions too much confusion, because a great number of different flowers may have the same denomination, as every florist markes his own with the same numbers. We would not therefore advise, but rather absolutely reject, the use of figures, as very defective." Yet the Dutch system, which he favored for the "prodigious multitude of names" it incorporated, was no more descriptive. Van Kampen continued: "The method practised by the Hollanders is preferable. They not only denominate their flowers from the principal colours, but also add the names of the greatest kings, and bravest generals, the gods, goddesses, nymphs, illustrious persons, and others, celebrated in the most famous poets, and ancient historians."[181]

In the end, Van Kampen wrote that the Dutch gave their flowers "such names . . . as denote their value."[182] Underlying Van Kampen's statement was the reality that florists gave their flowers such names to increase their value. His observation could easily be applied to the rest of European flower collectors. Florists sought to identify their creations with historical, mythological, or religious figures or with fashionable and exotic places in order to elevate the status of particular bulbs. It did not hurt, either, for florists to demonstrate their knowledge by throwing around the names of Roman senators, biblical heroes, and contemporary political figures. In occasionally naming specimens after themselves, the florists attempted to elevate their own status by claiming credit for the flower's creation. For in applying the practical knowledge about flowers, the "intelligence of their culture," as Dru had described it, the curious florists had demonstrated the application of the art of the floriculturist to the flowers of nature. Through the "improving" or refinement of flowers—the breeding of new varieties, attempts to alter the color and fragrance of the old, and the choice of names—the curious florists had taken raw nature and cultivated her.

Plate 1. Jean Donneau de Visé, *Histoire de Louis le Grand contenüe dans les rapports qui se trouvent entre ses actions, & les qualités, & vertus des fleurs, & des plantes*, 1688, title page. Paris, Bibliothèque Nationale de France, Manuscrits, fonds français 6995.

Plate 2.   Jean-Baptiste de Champaigne, *Aurora*, seventeenth century. Paris, Louvre.
Copyright Réunion des Musées Nationaux/Art Resource, New York.

Plate 3.   Jacques Le Moynes de Morgues, *Young Daughter of the Picts*, c. 1585. New Haven, Yale Center for British Art, Paul Mellon Collection. USA/Bridgeman Art Library.

Plate 4. Pierre Mignard,
Mademoiselle de Blois,
seventeenth century. Paris,
Louvre. Copyright Réunion
des Musées Nationaux/
Art Resource, New York.

Plate 5. Laurent
de La Hyre,
*Allegorical Figure
of Grammar*, 1650.
London, The
National Gallery.

Plate 6.   Carpet with floral design, French, Savonnerie, second quarter of the seventeenth
century. New York, Metropolitan Museum of Art, Gift of Mr. and Mrs. Charles
Wrightsman, 1976. (1976.155.111). Photograph © The Metropolitan Museum of Art.

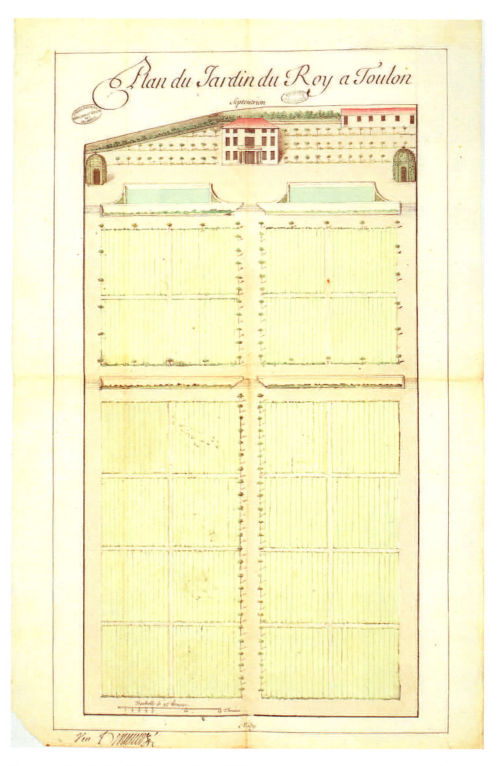

Plate 7.   *Plan du Jardin du Roy a Toulon* [*Plan of the Garden of the King in Toulon*], c. 1683.
Document conserved in Paris, Centre Historique des Archives Nationales, O¹2124¹.
Cliché atelier photographique du Centre Historique des Archives Nationales.

Plate 8.   Charles de la Fosse, *Clytie Turning into a Sunflower*, 1688. Versailles, Châteaux de Versailles et de Trianon. Copyright Réunion des Musées Nationaux/Art Resource, New York.

Plate 9.   Anonymous, *Design for a fan, Lady [possibly Madame de Montespan] in a richly decorated interior*, c. 1670. London, Victoria and Albert Museum.

Plate 10.　Jean Donneau de Visé, *Histoire de Louis le Grand*, 1688, dedication page. Paris, Bibliothèque Nationale de France, Manuscrits, fonds français 6995.

CHAPTER 4

Cultivating the Man

In 1650 the French artist Laurent de La Hyre painted an allegorical representation of grammar as part of a series on the liberal arts for Gédéon Tallement's Parisian *hôtel* (see plate 5).[1] To illustrate grammar, La Hyre depicted a woman who with one hand held a ribbon bearing the inscription "A meaningful and literate word spoken in a correct manner" and with the other watered two terracotta pots in which anemones and primulas grew.[2] La Hyre's choice of the cultivation of flowers as a symbol of the cultivation of words and language was based in a tradition dating to antiquity in which the development of virtue and intellect was envisioned as the nourishment of a seed—one's potential—into a "tree" of knowledge and wisdom. The allegory was given new life by Renaissance humanists for whom it offered not only a framework in which they could, self-consciously, imagine their own era as the maturation of the seeds planted in antiquity, but also a metaphor for the humanist approach to the education of the mind and soul.[3] For La Hyre, the cultivation of flowers illustrated the cultivation of language and, through it, the cultivation of the mind.

Seventeenth-century floriculture existed in a metaphorical space between the cultivation of the mind and the cultivation of the flower. While cultivating flowers allowed for curious florists to demonstrate their knowledge about and ability to grow flowers, it also allowed them to participate in the world of collecting and curiosity and display their taste and awareness of style and fashion. In other words, it allowed them to lay claim to the symbolic cultivation that flowers and La Hyre's painting implied.

The appearance of cultivation was increasingly important as the social structure of elite society changed over the course of the seventeenth century. Challenging the traditional nobility (the nobles of the sword), for whom distinction came through one's birth into a noble family, were the new noble families (the nobles of the robe), whose rank came from the performance of professional or financial service to the king and government. For the nobles of the sword and the *honnêtes hommes* of the salon, civility, grace, and taste were qualities with which one was born. Everyone else, and especially nobles of the robe and those aspiring to political and cultural power, needed to believe that civility and taste could be acquired or learned.[4] In exploring early modern guidebooks on civility, Roger Chartier has noted that in the seventeenth century there was disagreement over whether civility could be acquired or was an inherent quality. "Interpreted according to social order," writes Chartier, "the notion of *civilité* thus came to have an ambiguous status during the seventeenth century."[5] He continues: "The concept of *civilité* stands at the very heart of the tension between appearance and existence that epitomizes baroque sensibility and etiquette. The *civilité* of the seventeenth century, poles apart from a conception that perceived outward behavior as an exact and necessary translation of the disposition of one's inner being, is best understood as above all a social seeming. Every man must strive to be as he seems, and thus adjust his moral nature to the appearances demanded by his position in the world."[6] One had to appear to have taste and civility, but one also had to live up to those appearances.

In order to live up to the appearance of civility, one had to cultivate one's spirit, intellect, and manners. Cultivation, stemming from the verb *cultiver*, implied action—the act of cultivating something. According to Furetière, "One must cultivate the spirit of young people," or one might cultivate "friendship" or "knowledge."[7] Similarly, according to the *Dictionnaire de l'Académie française*, "One says figuratively, *To cultivate the spirit, to cultivate memory. To cultivate judgment*" and "*Cultivate knowledge, friendship, good manners.*" One might also "*Cultivate the Arts & the Sciences*, so to speak, To make them flower."[8] One could therefore cultivate the arts, knowledge, and the self—and in the process, make one's self flower, or flourish.

Increasingly over the course of the early modern period, the appearance of grace, taste, and cultivation was expressed through material culture. That is, the consumption of material goods allowed for the demonstration of taste.[9] Cultivating the appearance of civility on the part of those who were not assumed to have been born with it was not without risk: Molière, for example, notoriously ridiculed clumsy attempts to acquire and exhibit refinement;[10] and florists, as we have seen, distinguished between true and ignorant curious.[11] But the collection and cultivation of flowers were well suited for such expressions. Flowers required cultivation in the literal sense *and* allowed for the demonstration of one's own cultivation in the metaphorical or symbolic sense. Materially, flowers had much to offer, too: the variety of colors, fragrances, and forms of flowers made them aesthetically interesting in the age of the baroque; and their rarity, exoticism (or perceived exoticism), and cost heightened their fashionability and desirability. But just as importantly, in requiring the care and the attainment of knowledge about them from all of their enthusiasts, flowers were, if not a social leveler, at least an interest that could be cultivated among all who could afford them, regardless of titular status or birth. One's cultivation could be communicated in the gardens first and foremost where the flowers were grown, in the homes decorated with increasing personal interest in décor and material display, in the painted expressions of personal identity, and, finally, could be shared through the medium of print.

The Theater of the Goddess of Flowers

The anonymous author of the *Nouveau Traité pour la culture des fleurs*, which combined "the manner of their cultivation, multiplication, and conservation" with "their marvelous properties, & their medicinal virtues" explained to his reader that the flower garden required constant attention and careful planning to ensure that the flowers were displayed to their best advantage. "For this agreeable Theater of the Goddess of Flowers," he wrote, "has much grace when the beauty of the flowers is accompanied by an exact *politesse*."[12] But how *politesse* was to be achieved in the flower garden was not entirely clear. For gardening manuals are surprisingly vague in describing how flowers were to be exhibited or even planted in the garden. Customarily, numerous pages were devoted to the care and cultivation of flowers and to the plotting of the increasingly elaborate *broderie*, the scrollwork patterns created with boxwood, herbs, colored earth, pebbles, and sand covering the parterres of the formal garden. But few, if any, manuals discussed in any detail how to showcase the hard-won blossoms. Nonetheless, a few guidelines and suggestions can be found, through which it is possible to discern how and where flowers were planted in early modern French gardens and what aesthetic principles guided their display.

The simplest display of flowers was in the window, where they had been cultivated for centuries. Window boxes were so common in the Middle Ages that edicts were issued in 1388 and 1539 in Paris forbidding residents to use them out of consideration for the people walking on the street below. According to the edict: "Because the many proprietors and tenants throw waters over their fences, on their gardens, pots of carnations, rosemary, marjoram, and other things, which can become inconvenient, and also that one cannnot simply see where the said waters are flowing: we forbid all persons of whatever estate, quality, or condition they are, from putting in the windows any pots for gardening, on pain of 100 Parisian sols fine."[13] Nevertheless, window boxes remained popular in the early modern period. As late as 1783, Louis Mercier wrote that in spite of laws forbidding them, Parisians remained attached to their window boxes, a "hommage" offered to Pomona and Flora by those exiled from the countryside.[14] Mercier wrote: "The love of the countryside and of agriculture, common to all men, is manifested in the immense lot of laborers who live in the city. He raises in the air a small garden three feet long; he places in the windows a pot of flowers; this is a small tribute sent from afar to nature. He cultivates in a case the carnation & the rose. Six shoots of green console him for the loss of enameled tapestries [of the parterre] & replace the sight of thick & flowering woods."[15] When police inspectors passed, explained Mercier, the pots were taken inside, then "replaced when [the police] have passed." Window boxes were of particular consolation, continued Mercier, to women who chose not to venture into the streets and public gardens of the city: "The woman who does not leave her chamber, looks for this fortunate hour & smiles with joy when the bud of an isolated flower comes to open up at the start of the day. She calls her neighbor in order to share with her this phenomenon."[16]

Gardening manuals suggested appropriate plants to be included in window boxes. Hugh Plat instructed his readers to plant sweet marjoram, basil, carnations, or rosemary in pots to be placed on shelves outside windows.[17] Thomas Fairchild devoted an entire chapter to "Ornaments and Decorations for Balconies and the Outsides of Windows in Large Streets" in which he proposed using polyanthus, auriculas, wallflowers, stocks, pinks, carnations, and honeysuckle to brighten windows.

Flowers were also cultivated indoors. Hugh Plat, for example, suggested that carnations and roses could be grown inside if they were placed in "a roome that may some way be kept warme, either with a dry fire, or with the steam of hot water conveyed by a pipe fastened to the cover of a pot . . . now and then exposing them in a warme day . . . in the sun."[18] He reported that he himself, "by nipping off the branches of Carnations, when they began first to spire, and so preventing the first bearing, have had flowers in Lent by keeping the pots all night in a close roome, and exposing them to sun in the day." Thomas Fairchild, in *The City Gardener*, advised London dwellers on plants that could be persuaded to grow in the polluted city air and suggested using the chimney space for flower cultivation when no fire was burning. "The Chimneys which are generally dress'd in Summer with fading Bough Pots," he proposed, "might be as well adorn'd at once with living Plants, as I have observ'd at her Grace's the late excellent Dutchess of Beaufort."[19] He proposed the construction of a "Pyramid of Shelves" for the display of potted orange and other fruit trees, myrtle, and aloes. He recommended that boxwood be trained into pleasant shapes within which could be placed "white Lillies taken up in Bunches, just as they are coming into Flower, and potted they will make a good Show, and will last beautiful a long Time, and perfume the House almost as well as a Tuberose." Similarly, one could use pots of campanulas "which last in flower a long Time, and make a fine Appearance with their long Spikes of blue Flowers and yield a grateful Scent."[20]

Early modern flower connoisseurs also forced bulbs to enjoy indoors in the winter. Nicholas Van Kampen wrote: "In winter, nature sunk again into her former languishing condition, and stript of all her charms, wears the most melancholy aspect." "Yet this season is not without its advantages," he continued, explaining, "it may be considered as a time of tranquillity, in which we may force upon nature, and, in spite of the rigours of winter, produce in that season all the beauties of spring."[21] The beauties to which he referred were hyacinths, tulips, narcissi, irises, and crocuses that he successfully cultivated in glasses or, preferably, china pots: "The pots are china of three inches diameter, and four or five deep; which depth is sufficient to make the bulbs flower. Seven or eight inches is height enough for the glasses or bottles, and the mouths must be proportioned to the size of the bulbs, which are to be put into them about the middle of October, taking care that the bottom of the bulb touch the surface of the water, that the fibres may shoot into it."[22] Van Kampen reported great success in forcing bulbs. He wrote in his manual:

At the present time (the 1st of February) our room is set out like an amphitheater, being furnished with an hundred pots and glasses of flowers, lively and beautiful as they can be in the natural season. The Narcissus are very pretty, and with their beautiful colours seem to rival, and (if it were possible) eclipse, the lustre of the Hyacinths, which arise with noble splendour, attended with an agreeable fragrancy, and whose bright colours, vermillion, azure, white, and sanguine red mixed together, dazzle the eye; whilst the sweet Jonquilles embalm the whole room with aromatic perfumes. Thus by industry we are able to exhibit a pleasant garden in a chamber, and that at a season when nature bound in winter's icy fetters lies torpid and incapable of acting.[23]

James Justice also advised his readers on the forcing of bulbs in winter. "I shall now proceed to show a Method invented within these few Years," he promised, "whereby Persons, who are fond of Flowers, may have Hyacinths and Oriental Narcissus blow in their Chambers in Winter, when, by the Rigour of the Season, there are no Flowers in the open Ground, to gratify our Passion for Flora's Productions."[24] Justice suggested that specific varieties of hyacinths and narcissi could be forced to bloom in glasses "which are now made in Plenty for that Purpose, and which are sold in most of the Seed-Merchant Shops here."[25] Within two weeks, he reported, one should see roots sprouting from the bulb.

Robert Furber, in his 1734 *Flower Garden Display'd*, however, proposed a much more elaborate planting pattern. He reported that, in earthenware basins painted to resemble Delft pottery, he planted in the middle of them "a strong Root of Crown Imperial. . . . Round the Crown Imperial I placed some Tulips, and round them a Ring of double white and blew Hyacinths, between them I put in some Anemonys, then a Ring of white and of yellow Polyanthus Narcissus, then a Ring of large double Daffs, a Ring of different colour'd Crocus; and lastly, a Ring of double Snow-drops: On two Sides, against each other were two Roots of Hipatica's, and on the two opposite Sides against each other, were some Roots of Fretillaria's."[26] For his work, Furber claimed to be rewarded with flowers blooming from the twelve days of Christmas until the middle of March. He also reported successfully forcing hyacinths and narcissi in glasses which "will supply the curious Ladies with most agreeable Perfumes for their Chambers, Parlours, &c. and with Nosegays to adorn their Bosom at Christmas."[27]

Just as important as forcing bulbs indoors, however, was the manner in which these flowers were displayed. Delft potters in the Netherlands and faience producers in France both responded to the demand for flower receptacles. In the eighteenth century, their works became increasingly elaborate and decorative. Nicholas Van Kampen referred to his display of forced bulbs as an "amphitheater."[28] He recommended to his readers that in order to "make a shew, the flowers should be disposed in a pyramidal form, upon semicircular shelves, rising one above another, and gradually diminishing. This arrangement forms a grand mountain of flowers, which will strike the eye most agreeably."[29] The idea of the "theater" or "amphitheater" was designed to highlight the blooming flowers and to create veritable living bouquets.[30]

Robert-Xavier Mallet also described the creation of a "theater" of flowers, although his was composed of potted summer-flowering plants. After guiding the reader through the cultivation of auriculas (which required a stage), he demonstrated that ranunculi and carnations could also be arranged gradationally, explaining that the auricula "is the first flower to be entered into the theater among those of the premier order: following is the ranunculus in the pyramid, & then the carnation completes it." Mallet explained that the flowers could be combined into a single display that would bloom for months: "By this means a florist who has a tendency toward these three genres of flowers, with knowledge & precision, can, nearly without interruption, have the agreeable power of garnishing his theater from the month of April until the end of August."[31]

Valnay described a similar, though more ornate "Theatres de Fleurs" of his own creation whereby using cut tulips he "found the means of making to be seen together & easily a mass of striped [tulips] mixed together according to their different colors & arranged one next to the other, in a manner that . . . a single glance diverts the eye with everything that one very large garden can produce in rarities."[32] The theater of flowers, explained Valnay, could be composed of tulips, anemones, carnations, or bears' ears. He offered his readers a precise description of a display he had seen: "In the middle of a room on a very large table, he made a theater of five or six long tiers of 4 to 6 pouces & raised one over the other at the same height, he covered them with a green carpet, & cut the striped [tulips] perfectly so that he put each one in a small flask with water after [the blossoms] have entirely opened. Then he arranged all of the flasks on the tiers. He cut the tulips for this purpose when they were in flower for some time, since if he cut them too early, they would not open in the water, they tighten immediately. . . . These theaters . . . make an extraordinarily agreeable effect."[33]

As early as 1713 (though quoted here from the 1739 edition), Dezallier d'Argenville cited both sorts of theaters.

> One other means that the curious, & . . . the florists by profession, place their work, to see them more easily, & to cultivate more freely certain favorite flowers, is that which is named the theater of flowers. It consists of an assemblage of planks or of steps that they want always raised one behind the other, to see to it that the eye & the hand could carry everywhere without any obstacle. One reserves them particularly for the bears' ears & for the carnations; & as these flowers have greater need than the others of being covered [when] it rains, & from strong Sun, the theater is always accompanied by a small roof of planks or of oiled cloth. . . .
>
> There are also some curious who have another kind of theater which they call the pyramid of flowers: after the most beautiful [flowers] adorned for some time the parterre, they cut them & display them in vials on the steps of a pyramid that they constructed on purpose in the middle of their room, & there with the help of water & the shade they prolonged for a good bit their duration.[34]

For those lacking the flowers to fill an entire series of shelves, potters produced a variety of vases designed to achieve the theatrical effect on a smaller scale. An eighteenth-century faience vase from Marseille was designed to hold cut flowers, both in a large central cavity, as well as on the sides where individual stem holes would maintain the shape of a floral arrangement (figure 15). And a mid-eighteenth-century faience bulb pot from Sceaux arranged the bulbs in two rows, one raised above the other as the advocates of the "theatres des fleurs" suggested (figure 16).

Incorporating flowers into the formal garden was of even greater concern for the florists. In the sixteenth century, the Italian style of formal garden was

FIG. 15.   Flower vase, Marseille, eighteenth century. Paris, Musée des Arts Décoratifs.

FIG. 16.   Bulb pot, Sceaux, mid-eighteenth century. Paris, Musée des Arts Décoratifs.

admired and adapted in France just as Italian humanist learning, philosophy, and the arts had gained favor. The Italian architectural garden, which stressed symmetry, sculpture, and fountains rather than (but not to the neglect of) horticulture, influenced the construction of large formal gardens such as those built at Blois, Amboise, Ancy-le-Franc, Anet, Chenonceau, Chantilly, Saint-Germain-en-Laye, and Fontainebleau.[35] Despite the devastating Wars of Religion that preoccupied the French people and ruling society from 1560 to 1589, the French garden continued to grow in importance. Catherine de Medici expanded royal gardens, utilizing them for elaborate court entertainments or garden festivals.[36]

Little is known about the plant material used in French Renaissance gardens, or how flowers were incorporated into them, but gardening manuals such as Olivier de Serres's *Le Théâtre d'agriculture* and Charles Estienne and Jean Liébault's *L'Agriculture et maison rustique*, printed repeatedly in the second half of the sixteenth century, described not only the management of a country estate, but also the construction of a formal garden. The gardens that they described allowed for the inclusion of flowers. According to Estienne and Liébault (in an English translation from 1600):

> The most pleasant and delectable thing for recreation belonging unto our French farmes is our flower garden, as well in respect that it serveth for the chiefe Lord whose the inheritance is to solace himselfe therin, as also in respect of their service for to set Bee-hives in. It is a commendable and seemely thing to behold out at a window many acres of ground well tilled and husbanded, ... but yet it is much more to behold fair and comely proportions, handsome and pleasant arbours and as it were closets, delightfull borders of lavander, rosemarie, boxe, and other such like: to heare the ravishing musicke of an infinite number of prettie small birdes ... and to smell so sweet a nosegaie so neere at hand: seeing that this so fragrant a smell cannot but refresh the Lord of the farme exceedingly.[37]

By distinguishing the formal garden from the cultivated fields and the flower garden from the kitchen garden, Estienne and Liébault testify not only to the existence of the pleasure garden in the country estate, but also to the importance of flowers within the garden.

Estienne and Liébault indicated that the flower garden was to be divided into two sections, one for herbs and flowers "used to make nosegaies and garlands" and one for "sweet smelling herbes, whether they be such as beare flowers, or if they bear any, yet they are not put into nosegaies alone but the whole herbe with them."[38] Gardens of the first type included violets, gillyflowers, daisies, marigolds, lilies, daffodils, Canturbury bells, anemones, corn flag, mugwort, and purple velvet flowers—flowers valued for their beauty and scent, and suitable for bouquets and garlands. The herb or scent garden included wormwood, rosemary, marjoram, balm, mints, pennyroyal, hyssop, lavendar, basil, sage, savory, rue, tansey, thyme, camomile, anise, and horehound.[39] But the placement of flowers in a garden specifically designated for them demonstrates that floriculture had entered a new era—flowers could be regarded as the raison d'être for some gardens. Each garden, they recommended, should be organized into labyrinths or mazes for which several complex designs were included, although they cautioned that not all of the flowers and herbs named were suitable for the fashionable and elaborate scrollwork patterns of which most parterres consisted, as some were too tall and unruly.[40]

Because the curious florist appreciated flowers for their seemingly endless variety, their pleasant odors, their brilliant colors, and their rarity, it was therefore only natural that the display of flowers in gardens highlighted the qualities for which flowers were valued. The most basic tenets on the place of flowers within the French parterre, an ornamental section or terrace of a garden, suggested planting patterns that featured color, fragrance, and variety. Charles Estienne and Jean Liébault recommended distinguishing between the kitchen garden and the pleasure garden by separating them with an alley.[41] Noting that flowers belonged in the pleasure garden, Estienne and Liébault added that placed near the château, the flower garden could be enjoyed by the lord from the window of his apartment. As perspective and scale became more important through the seventeenth century, the placement of the flower garden as close to the palace as possible remained an important tenet in the French gardening tradition.

Claude Mollet, who created formal parterres for Henry IV at Fontainebleau, Saint-Germain-en-Laye, and the Tuileries and thereby set the style for elaborate and intricate *parterres en broderie* in the first half of the seventeenth century, suggested in his *Théâtre des jardinages* that taller flowers be separated from the others in compartments not filled with elaborate *broderie*. Mollet, who compared a good *parterre en broderie* to a Turkish tapestry, explained: "Short flowers, such as violets, all sorts of marguerites, or daisies, sweet williams, double camomile, anemones, hyacinths, primaveras, pansies, and all sorts of small low flowers are more appropriately planted in all sorts of compartments of broderie than others, in order that the gardener can observe symmetry."[42] However, while naming the plants and flowers that could be used in the realization of broderie and those that were best excluded, Mollet offered no specific suggestions as to where flowers could be used within the delicate *parterre en broderie* so characteristic of his work and fashionable in the late sixteenth and the first half of the seventeenth century.

André Mollet, gardener to the queen of Sweden and the son of Claude Mollet, was more precise. The younger Mollet advised that in the construction of the "jardin a fleurs": "It is expedient that one separates [the garden] into two parts; one part for flowering trees, such as roses, . . . French marigolds, peonies, and other large flowers that will obscure the shorter flowers in the middle of the ensemble; and the other part for short flowers, and rare flowers, such as carnations, double pinks, crown imperials, martagons, tulips, anemones, ranunculi, auriculas, iris, and others, which can be further divided in order that each species can best be separated."[43] To these general instructions, Mollet added individual parterre designs accompanied by written descriptions of their plantation. The eighth design, for example, "is also a *parterre en broderie* 40 toises [historical measure equaling 6.5 feet] square; with a fountain 7 toises in diameter; the *plates-bandes* of 6 feet with the corners in the circle in the middle, in the center on which are marked 8 pedestals where statuary can be placed. And, in the middle of such *plate-bandes*, one may plant in intervals, small well-clipped evergreens, between which one may plant all sorts of short flowers such as tulips, anemones, ranunculi, and others.[44] Thus, in order to maintain the integrity of the delicate *broderie*, flowers were relegated to the borders, called *plates-bandes*, of the design where they were planted between small evergreens or, according to other designs, between small flowering trees. It has been assumed that flowers, confined to the borders, planted between topiaries, were not important elements of the early seventeenth-century French garden; however, by subordinating flowers to the overall design of the parterre and placing then in borders, the flowers could be admired at a close proximity while not detracting from the *broderie*. The coexistence of *broderie* and specially designated flower beds is illustrated in the garden depicted on the frontispiece of Daniel Rabel's *Theatrum florae* (figure 17). In Rabel's formal garden, rectangular flower parterres, symmetrically placed, alternate with *broderie*.[45] Within the beds, one can discern tulips, fritillaries, and other fashionable flowers.

Flowers were also displayed in *pièces coupées*, or cut work, as illustrated in Johann Walther's 1663 *Florilège de Nassau-Idstein*, in which the flowers were planted in fruit-shaped beds outlined in box,[46] and in the garden on in Jean Franeau's *Jardin d'hyver*.[47] The flower gardens of both Liancourt and Vaux-le-Vicomte were executed in this style (figures 18 and 19). Although the gardens at Vaux and Liancourt consisted primarily of the delicate tracery of *broderie*, flowers were featured in geometrically shaped beds. In the geometric beds at Liancourt, flowers of many varieties were allowed to bloom together in a lush display dedicated to flowering plants. Similarly, Israel Silvestre's engraved illustration of the flower parterre at Vaux demonstrated that although the flower garden was only a part of André Le Nôtre's larger creation, the flowers were given their own parterre. In contrast to the fine arabesques of the central parterre of the garden, the flowers of the flower parterre were not confined to borders; rather, they filled each shape freely.

Louis Liger addressed the placement of flowers within cut-work compartments or borders in his 1706 *Le Jardinier fleuriste*: "There are those who have been so curious, that, after having mark'd out Borders and Compartments proper to put Flowers in, they have computed the number of them to know how many each Border or Compartment would hold, when planted at Four inches Distance one from the other; and also not contented with the Particular, have planted in strait Lines, and at equal Distance alternatively, as well spring Flowers, as Summer, Autumn, and Winter; and tis, to the end that their Gardens might not at any time be deprived of Flowers."[48] Liger suggested to his reader, then,

FIG. 17.   Daniel Rabel, "Deliciae domini nec quid sperare habebat [The delights of the lord, nor yet what he hoped to have]." From *Theatrum florae*, Paris: Apud Petrum Firens, 1627. Image courtesy of author. Photograph by John Blazejewski, Index of Christian Art, Princeton University.

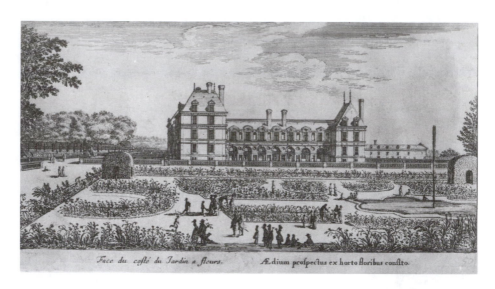

FIG. 18.   Israel Silvestre, "Face du costé du Jardin a fleurs [Face of the château on the side of the Flower Garden]" at Liancourt. From *Differentes veues du chasteau et des jardins, fontaines, cascades, canaux et parterres de Liencourt* [*sic*], 1656. New York, Metropolitan Museum of Art, Purchase, Anne and Carl Stern Gift, 1959 (59.642.118).

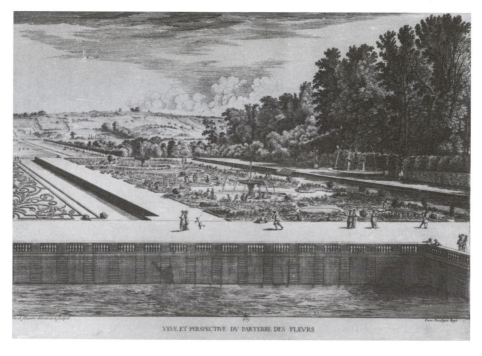

FIG. 19.   Israel Silvestre, "Veue et perspective du parterre des fleurs [View and perspective of the flower parterre]" at Vaux-le-Vicomte, seventeenth century. Paris, Bibliothèque Nationale de France, Cabinet des Estampes.

that flowers be planted at regular intervals, with different species combined so that flowers would be blooming at all times. Liger added, however: "Tho' I recommend this way of Planting Flowers, 'tis not that I pretend to establish it as a general Rule, that must always be observed; every one is at liberty to follow what Fancy he likes best, provided his Design be good; that is to say, that the Flowers which cast deep Roots be not mingled with those that have but middling ones, especially among the bulbous Sort; and that he always observes to put Ranunculus's and Tulips a-part from one another. This Separation will have a wonderful Effect, whereas if they are planted all together, they will not afford half the Pleasure to the Eye they would otherwise do."[49]

Liger's assertion that different flowers be separated in the same border was not a strict rule. In fact, there was considerable debate among writers of flower gardening manuals as to what flowers ought to be combined. S.A., author of *Jardinier portatif, ou la culture des quatre classes de jardins*, explained the variety of positions on the matter:

> There are those curious who, after having traced the pieces of their parterres or *plates-bandes* destined for flowers, in making a calculation in order to know that the compartments can contain them, have planted them at eight *doigts* [inches] from one to the other, & who, not content with that, plant equally & at equal distances the flowers which are early, by another which comes in summer or later, so that they succeed one to the other, their gardens seem always garnished with flowers. Others, in order to plant regularly, first draw on a chart the design and plan of the gardens, & plant according to measure the bulbs and roots in plots or *plates-bandes* of their parterres, they mark them in the same manner in which they figure on the map, so that they better know the quality of the flowers in each plot or *plates-bandes*.[50]

According to S.A., then, motive, or when one wanted flower beds to be in bloom, governed planting patterns in some gardens. The author of the *Nouveau traité pour la culture des fleurs* argued, as Liger had done, that certain species be displayed separately for aesthetic reasons. Although he suggested that "the Tulips & the Anemones can be placed around the beds near the borders, & the other Flowers in the middle, mingled with other species: And in this manner in each plot the diversity of Flowers will be gay & very pleasing to the eye,"[51] he warned that not all flowers should be planted with the others.[52]

John Rea also recommended separating species of flowers, but mostly for the purpose of tracking one's prized specimens: "Now for planting the Beds in the Fret, you must . . . place the Roots so, as those of a kind set in several Beds may answer one another; as in the corners of each Bed, the best Crown-Imperials, Lillies, martagons, and such tall Pionies, and round about them, several sorts of Cyclamen; the rest with Daffodils, Hyacinths, and such like: the streight Beds are fit for the best Tulips, where account may be kept of them: Ranunculus and Anemonies also require particular Beds; the rest may be set all over with the more ordinary sorts of Tulips, Frittillaries, bulbed Iris, and all other kinds of good Roots."[53] Rea therefore mixed his more common flowers, but planted his finer ones in separate beds.

Other florists also favored diversity in the flower bed. Ballon and Garnier wrote, "arrange and sort the Bulbs by the mélange of different colors, [for] the effect of them will be very agreeable when the flowers come."[54] J.L., author of a flower gardening manual published in Paris in 1683, also preferred the diversity of color and flowers in a flower garden. For the proper furnishing of a flower border he suggested: "In each of the said borders, & at a distance of less than four good *doigts* & more if you plant there bunches of bears' ears, distance them one after another at a half-foot or more, between them plant Iris of Persia, double & single jonquils, crocus, snow-drops, *Bizantines*, blue, white, and musk hyacinths to provide perfume, & marguerites in divers colors, & each in equal portions: in the rest . . . one must plant tulips, . . . in another all bears' ears, in another all double hepaticas, in another all cyclamens, . . . fritillaries, . . . in others all amaranths, in another all anemones, in another all ranunculi."[55] He added, however, that the ultimate rule governing the plantation of flowers in the garden was to observe the principle of symmetry. He concluded, "The best order for making beautiful flower gardens is to avoid confusion in them, . . . to guard its overall symmetry, that is to say to accommodate and arrange well the flowers, so that they always have an opposite & are equal in quantity, & the number of beds respond one to the other."[56] As long as flower gardeners adhered to the basic principles of formal gardening, the plantation of flowers within them was a matter of taste.

Flowers were also included in formal gardens in pots and vases that were then displayed at prominent points in the parterre. Gardening manuals frequently offered instruction on planting flowers, most frequently carnations, tuberoses, and auriculas in pots.[57] For example, André Mollet's description of his seventh plan in *Le Jardin de plaisir* calls for "*plates-bandes* of 6 feet with blocks of stone properly spaced on which you can place pots or vases of flowers."[58]

For insight on how curious florists and the gardeners in their employ interpreted the suggestions put forth in the flower gardening manuals in their own parterres, it is possible to turn to the handful of surviving planting plans dating from the period. Though cryptic and incomplete, fragmentary plans of the garden of flower collector and dealer Pierre Morin, of the royal garden at the Grand Trianon, and of Marly offer the best evidence for how real gardens were planted.

The garden of the *curieux fleuriste* Pierre Morin was described by two English visitors—first by John Evelyn, who recorded his 1644 visit in his travel journal, and then by Richard Symonds, who sketched a rough outline of the garden in 1649.[59] Morin's activity in the rare flower trade in the seventeenth century is recorded in the catalogues of his collection. Published in 1651, his *Catalogues de quelques plantes à fleurs qui sont de present au jardin de Pierre Morin* included a list of one hundred different tulips, twenty-four ranunculi, seventy-one irises, and twenty-seven anemones.[60] In 1658 Morin published through Charles de Sercy, a Paris bookseller specializing in gardening manuals, *Remarques necessaires pour la culture des fleurs*, in which he included a calendar for the gardener, a discussion of plants according to their climatic tolerances, and the catalogue of his holdings.[61] Morin listed plants ordinarily found in the "jardin de plaisir" as well as those cultivated in the "jardin des curieux." The garden of the curious florist, he explained, should include crocuses, crown imperials, fritillaries, gladiolias, hyacinths, irises, lilies, narcissi, martagons, tulips, and anemones."[62]

Morin's own garden, as described by John Evelyn who visited Morin's home in 1644, consisted of "an exact oval figure, planted with cypresse cutt flat & set as even as a wall: the tulips, anemonies, ranunculus's, crocus's, &c. are held to be of the rarest, and draw all the admirers of such things to his house during the seasons. He lived in a kind of Hermitage at one side of his garden, where his collection of purselane and coral . . . is much esteemed."[63] Evelyn's description is echoed in the sketch by Richard Symonds, which illustrates the oval plan with beds radiating out from the center fountain. Symonds's key explained that the small ovals, labeled "C," were "beds compassd with box wherin the middle grow all sorts of rare Tulips[,] . . . flowers, herbes, rare all."[64] Morin's flower collection, then, was displayed in small beds outlined with boxwood. Although it is not possible to speculate how, within each bed, the flowers were planted and intended to be seen, it is clear that Morin's tulips, anemones, ranunculi, and crocuses competed with no *broderie* or tracery; rather, they were featured in simple beds similar to *pièces coupées*, their own beauty and rarity the focus of attention.

Planting plans have also survived from the royal gardens of Louis XIV. The most famous and frequently cited example is that of the 1693 planting plan for the Trianon de marbre (figure 20).[65] The rare planting plan reflects a *plate-bande* or border of a larger parterre in which parallel rows of spring-flowering bulbs alternate with rows of summer-flowering perennials. The flowering bulbs, tulips, hyacinths, and narcissi labeled "A," "B," "C," alternate in a single row, while the two alternate outer rows were to be planted with smaller perennials including sweet rockets, speedwell, sweet williams, hyacinths, cornflowers, pasque flowers, and spring violets. The center row was planted in feverfew, bellflowers, wallflowers or carnations, white lilies, and valerian. In all, 96,000 flowers were called for in the proper furnishing of the lavish border. In the spring, then, the Trianon garden would consist of rows of tulips, hyacinths, and narcissi, but in the summer it would be a colorful mix of perennials with a row of taller flowers in the center, and shorter plants on the edges.

Another planting plan concerns the planting of a border at the royal garden at Marly (figures 21 and 22). The "Memoire des plantes vivaces, plantes annuelles, et oignons de fleurs propres a garnir les petit costiere le long des allées du Jardin Roialles de Marly" details the use of flowering bulbs, perennials, and annuals in the gardens at Marly.[66] Similar to the now famous planting plan from

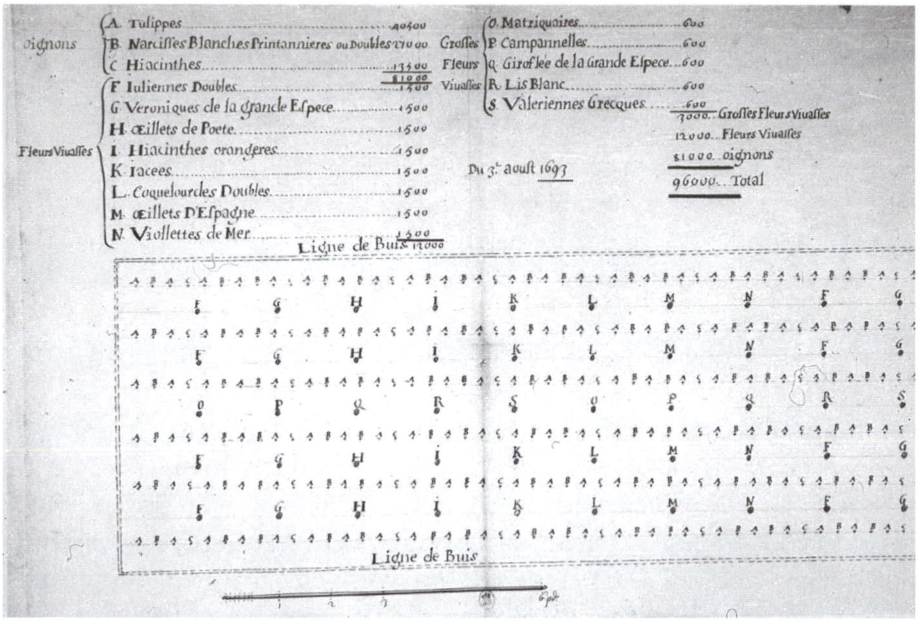

FIG. 20. Planting plan for the Trianon garden, 1693. Paris, Bibliothèque Nationale de France, Cabinet des Estampes, cliché B 11189.

the Trianon, the Marly plan called for rows of flowering bulbs alternating with plantations of perennials and annuals, while incorporating a greater variety of flowers described in fuller detail than at Trianon. The flowering bulbs were planted in a twelve-bulb sequence of a yellow narcissus, red and yellow tulip, white narcissus, blue or white hyacinth, double white narcissus, tulip, narcissus, red or white *bosuelle*,[67] white narcissus, blue or white hyacinth, double white narcissus, with tulips, hyacinths, *bosuelle* in the center, another hyacinth, and finally another tulip, across the width of the flower bed. Planted between the rows of bulbs were series of statice, pinks, pansies, and violets, bears' ears, basil, and statice; pansies, pinks, and statice; or pansies, immortelles, and statice. The accompanying instructions, bearing the name Olivier,[68] explained that the flowering bulbs would bloom in March, April, and May, and the annuals and perennials would be in flower from April through September, and even into October and November. The flower bed was to be colorful "in all seasons."[69]

The floral planting plans from the Trianon and Marly gardens demonstrate that flowers did indeed find a place in the baroque and classical gardens of seventeenth-century France. That place was determined as much by the aesthetic value placed on flowers in early modern France as on the architectural principles of the formal garden. Within the pleasure garden, they were preferably displayed outside the elaborate *broderie* of the parterres, either in borders or *plates-bandes*, in cut-work or shaped beds, or even in pots. These flower beds might intermingle with the *broderie*, but they were best placed closer rather than far-

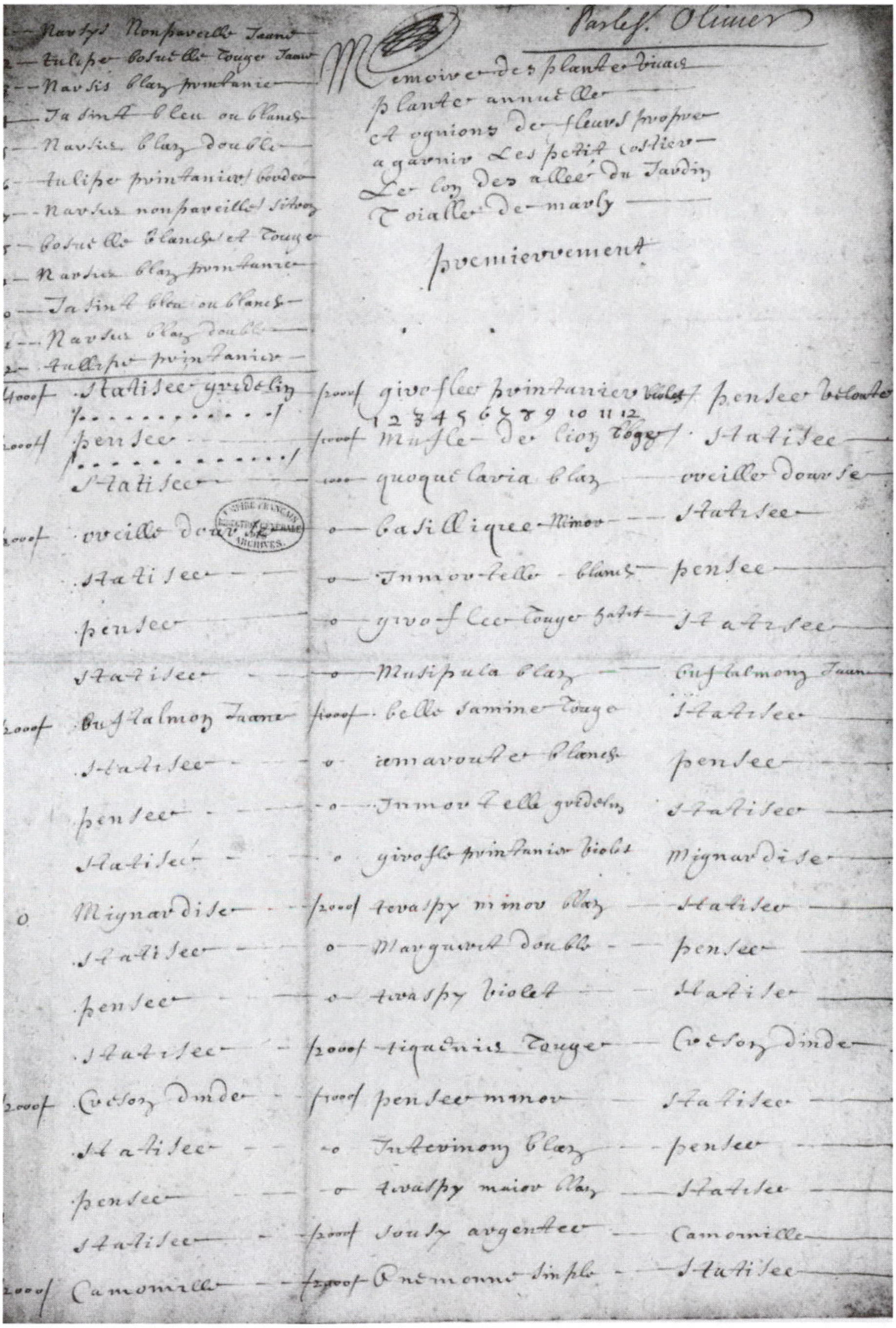

FIG. 21. "Memoires des plantes vivaces, plantes annuelles, et oignons des fleurs propres a garnir les petit costiere le long des allées du Jardin Roialles de Marly [Memorandum on perennials, annuals, and flowering bulbs appropriate for furnishing the small bed along the avenues of the Royal Garden of Marly]," c. 1700. Document conserved in Paris, Centres Historiques des Archives Nationales, O^{1}2102^1 cotte 4, page 1. Cliché atelier photographique du Centre Historique des Archives Nationales.

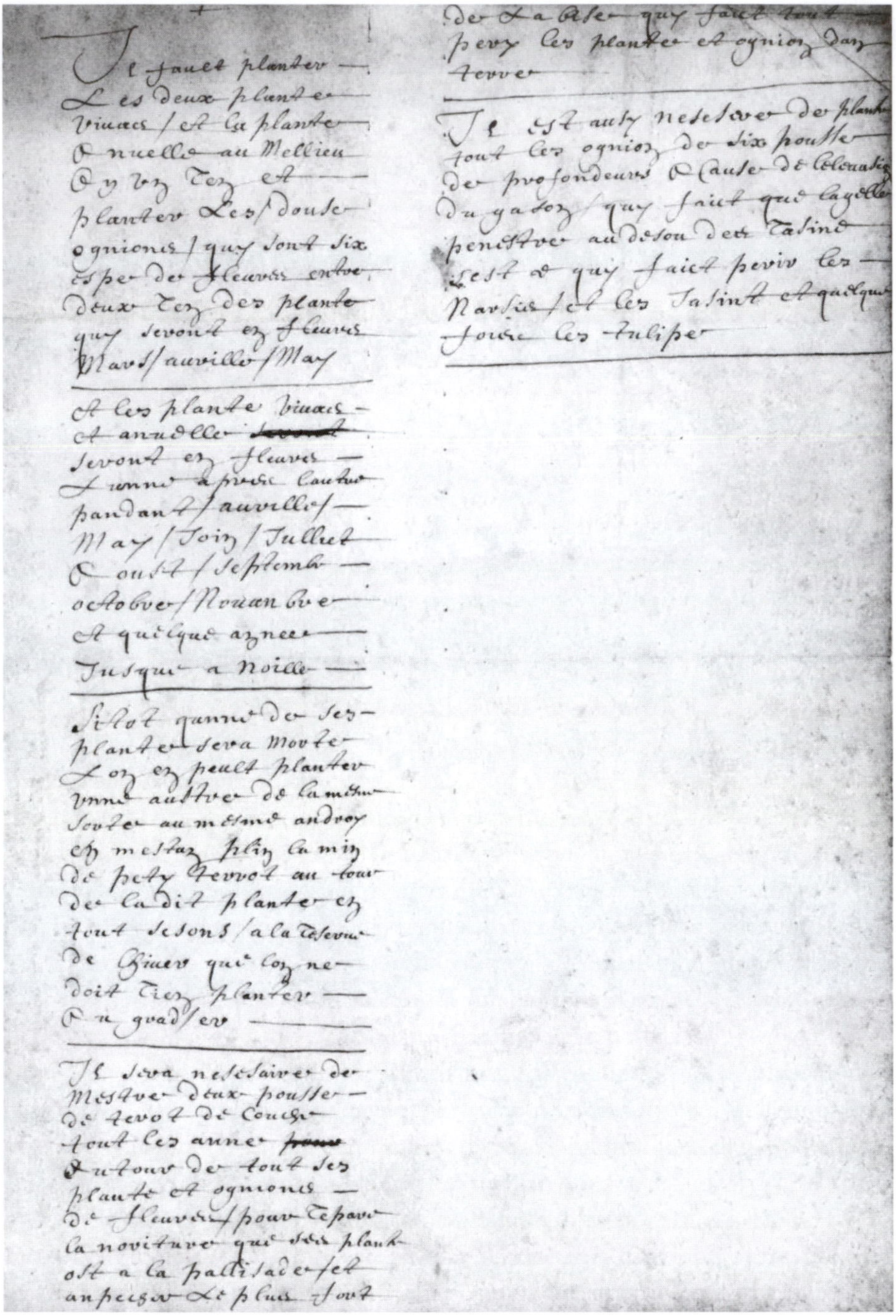

FIG. 22.　"Memoires des plantes vivaces, plantes annuelles, et oignons des fleurs propres a garnir les petit costiere le long des allées du Jardin Roialles de Marly [Memorandum on perennials, annuals, and flowering bulbs appropriate for furnishing the small bed along the avenues of the Royal Garden of Marly]," c. 1700. Document conserved in Paris, Centres Historiques des Archives Nationales, O¹2102¹cotte 4, page 2. Cliché atelier photographique du Centre Historique des Archives Nationales.

ther from the châteaux. Most intriguingly, within the individual flower parterre, specimens were selected and displays were planned for the same aesthetic principles for which flowers were appreciated. Just as curious florists admired the variety of colors in which flowers existed, so the flower beds were designed to celebrate that variety. Finally, floral plantations were coordinated to allow for a continual display of blooming flowers from springtime into autumn. The manual labor of the gardeners and weeders might have been hidden from public view, but the manipulation of flowers to produce the many colors and endless display communicated unquestionably the efforts of the curious florist to transform Nature into Art. If the flower garden was indeed the "Théâtre de la Déesse de fleurs," it was also the stage upon which collectors and florists performed their craft.[70]

Nature into Art

The formal gardens in which flowers were displayed were the crowning achievements of those who sought to bring perfection to the realm of nature. But the arts, too, offered the means to express one's taste in flowers. For seventeenth-century aesthetics both were increasingly shaped by and contributed to the new impulses to observe, study, and collect the material parts of the natural world. The most direct expression of the relationship between the curiosity for flowers and the arts were the attempts by numerous curious florists to achieve a visual record of the contents of their collection. Those who could afford to do so commissioned professionally painted images of their beloved blossoms. One of the earliest of these painted *florilegia* was produced in 1608 for, and perhaps even by, Jean Le Roy de la Boissière, a nobleman from Poitiers.[71] Le Roy or the artist he employed covered forty-eight leaves of vellum with brilliantly colored flowers. Some pages were devoted to the depiction of a single species; other pages illustrated several species or different varieties. The naturalistically rendered flowers demonstrate an attention to botanical detail even though some pages have ornamental borders filled with plants and animals reminiscent of medieval illuminated manuscripts. The species represented include tulips, carnations, and other flowers, such as fritillaries, lilies, and iris, popular with curious florists. One page of tulips included three different blossoms, each, however, representative of the popular variegated varieties. On the title page of the work, flowering plants, insects, and a rabbit frame his family's coat of arms. Tellingly, the decorative border also includes the attributes of both kinds of labor necessary for the production of such a volume: juxtaposed to the hoe, rake, and shears of the gardener who cultivated the flowers in the garden were the easel, palette, and paintbrushes of the artists who rendered the blossoms in paint. In the *florilegium* of Jean Le Roy, nature and art came together not only in the perfection of the flowers in the garden, but also in the creation of the fine volume of paintings.

Jean Le Roy de la Bossière's volume was not unique. Indeed, it is possible that he was also responsible for an album of eighty-six paintings recording the botanical collection of Thomas Garnier, an apothecary in Poitiers.[72] Daniel Rabel, who enjoyed royal patronage through much of his career, also produced flower paintings. He was sent by Marie de Médici to Madrid to paint a portrait of Anne of Austria prior to her marriage to Louis XIII;[73] and he was employed to design sets for the performances of court ballets. Gaston d'Orléans hired him to render painted images of flowers in his collection, suggesting, as Lucia Tongiorgi Tomasi and Antoine Schnapper argue, that Rabel's works laid the foundation for the *vélins*, Gaston's collection of flower paintings on vellum most frequently identified with later contributions of Nicolas Robert.[74] In Germany, Basil Besler created his *Hortus Eystettensis* in 1613 for Johann Konrad von Gemmingen, prince bishop of Eichstatt, to record the flowers in his garden.[75] Similarly, Count Johann of Nassau at Idstein hired Johann Walther to paint his flowers and garden. In Walther's rendition of the count's flower parterres, the flowers are planted in fruit-shaped flower beds. Walther produced two nearly identical copies of the work in the 1650s and 1660s, one including 133 flower portraits, another sixty-five.[76]

The most successful painter of flower studies, however, was undoubtedly Nicolas Robert. Little is known of Robert's training or career. Though born in France, in 1640 he illustrated *Fiori Diversi*, a book of flower etchings published in Rome.[77] Yet by 1641 he became known throughout the fashionable circles in Paris for his flower paintings in the *Guirlande de Julie*, a small gift that was celebrated in the seventeenth century as "one of the most illustrious gallantries that has ever been made."[78] The work was, indeed, one of the most exquisite productions of the flower mania. In 1641 Charles de Montausier left on the table of Julie d'Angennes, the object of his affections and daughter of Catherine de Vivonne-Savelli, marquise de Rambouillet, the fashionable *salonnière* or *precieuse*, the small book called *La Guirlande de Julie*. The gift was a collection of madrigals and flower paintings bound in deep red leather and enclosed in a perfumed case.[79] Montausier had solicited from his friends in Rambouillet's circle poems simultaneously celebrating specific flowers and his beloved Julie.[80] Among those contributing verses were no lesser talents than Tallement des Reaux, Malleville, Godeau, Colletet, Chapelain, and Charles de Scudéry.[81] To copy the contributions of the different poets into fine script, Montausier sought the services of Nicolas Jarry, a noted calligrapher.[82] To complete the treasure, Nicolas Robert painted thirty delicate and charming flower portraits, among them the crown imperial, rose, narcissus, amaranth, carnation, thyme, jasmine, lily, jonquil, hyacinth, sunflower, pansy, crocus, lily of the valley, iris, snow-drop, poppy, everlasting, two tulips, and the anemone (see figures 12 and 23).[83]

The *Guirlande de Julie* became instantly famous,[84] and Robert found a new patron in Gaston, duc d'Orléans.[85] He succeeded Rabel in rendering portraits of the flowers in Gaston's collection. It would take Julie d'Angennes many more years to accept Montausier's proprosal of marriage, but the privately commissioned *Guirlande de Julie* had become part of the French cultural tradition

FIG. 23.   Nicolas Robert, *La Guirlande de Julie*, 1641, title page. Paris, Bibliothèque Nationale de France, Manuscrits, fonds français NAF 19735.

from its inception, for the small volume was created out of the convergence of multiple cultural impulses, including the cultural meaning of flowers in early modern France. The Neoplatonic love poems in the form of madrigals employed the contemplation of the beauty of flowers to honor the physical, or outer, beauty of Julie d'Angennes that was symbolic of her inner beauty. This literary celebration of nature and the flower was symptomatic of the interest in the pastoral that had become popular in seventeenth-century France, particularly since the enthusiastic reception of Honoré d'Urfé's *L'Astrée*, published in three parts in 1607, 1610, and 1619.[86] At the same time, Robert's flower paintings were executed with attention to botanical realism and demonstrated familiarity with early modern floricultural preferences. Yet Robert's flowers were rendered so delicately that they equaled the finest paintings in aesthetic beauty. Indeed, the work bridged the narrow gap between the taste for botanical flower studies and more decorative flower paintings such as floral still lifes that had rapidly gained popularity in the early seventeenth century in decorating châteaux and *hôtels*. Finally, the volume, perfumed and bound in delicate red leather, was itself a luxuriously restrained objet d'art emblematic of the civilizing processes at work in learned Parisian circles. In short, the work was the perfect gift for an arbiter of taste, as Julie d'Angennes surely was, in early seventeenth-century France. The *Guirlande de Julie* thus resonated deeply with the literary salon tradition, the world of flower collecting, and the fashionable, wealthy, and well-bred who demonstrated taste and civility in the conspicuous and self-conscious selection of art, objects, gardens, and furnishings to surround them.

Flowers and floral motifs were not confined to the page in the seventeenth century. Indeed, fresh-cut flowers, painted flowers, and even woven flowers adorned the increasingly sumptuous trappings of early modern elite lifestyles. Fresh flowers adorned the *chambre bleue*, the room where Madame de Rambouillet, mother of Julie d'Angennes, held her salon,[87] and other *précieuses* incorporated floral decor in their fictional settings.[88] Madeleine de Scudéry, for example, described the setting of one of her literary works in the following manner: "Everything is magnificent in her [home]; . . . her cabinets are full of a thousand rarities, which make visible the judgment of those who chose them; the air is always perfumed in the palace: diverse magnificent baskets full of flowers make a continual springtime in her chamber."[89] And Anne-Marie-Louise-Henriette d'Orléans, duchesse de Montpensier (La Grande Mademoiselle), included in her *Relation de l'isle imaginaire et l'histoire de la princesse de Paphlagonie* a "lair surrounded with large vases of crystal full of the most beautiful flowers of springtime, which last always in the gardens which are next to the temple."[90]

The real and imagined floral paradises of the salon and literary pastoral wildernesses were echoed in paint on the walls and ceilings of fashionable palaces and *hôtels*.[91] Floral decoration could be as simple as the painted *plafonds à la française* popular in early seventeenth-century France in which the exposed surfaces of ceiling beams were covered with decorative (and frequently floral) motifs. A fine example survives in the *grande salle* of the *rez-de-chaussez* of the Parisian Hôtel de Sully, built between 1625 and 1630. On its roughly hewn beams, floral bouquets, decorative cartouches, and landscapes were rendered with charming simplicity reminiscent of the floral still lifes by Jacques Linard.[92] This decoration of the ceiling and window frames, believed to date to 1634 when the *hôtel* was acquired by Maximilien de Béthune, duc de Sully (1559–1641), finance minister of Henri IV, was complemented by a series of tapestries devoted to the seven liberal arts.[93] Similar floral decoration was executed for the Hôtel d'Aumont in Paris.[94] Not coincidentally, both the duc de Sully and the duc d'Aumont collected flowers.

Many other interiors included flowers painted on the walls. One of the earliest examples of painted floral decoration dates to the late sixteenth or early seventeenth century in the Burgundian château Ancy-le-Franc, built in 1544 by Sebastiano Serglio. In a *cabinet* decorated in the late sixteenth or early seventeenth century, somewhat stylized (but still recognizable) flowers were painted on a gold background over the entire lower register of the room.[95]

Painted flowers might also cover the paneling between history paintings or portraits.[96] The use of flowers in the early seventeenth-century château of Cormatin in Burgundy is typical. As in the Hôtel de Sully, flowers adorned the *plafonds à la française* of the cabinets and chambers of Cormatin. Even more flowers were rendered on panels in the *cabinet* dedicated to Saint Cecilia, the sumptuous retreat for Jacques du Blé, the marquis d'Huxelles. The scheme of the room was organized around Saint Cecilia as the allegory of Harmony, who reigned triumphantly over Force, Temperance, Fame, and other human vices. Some of the larger panels in the *cabinet* were given over entirely to bouquets in elegant vases and urns, and displayed on trompe l'oeil tabletops. Smaller panels placed around the allegorical portraits were covered with floral garlands and festoons.[97]

Floral ornament was similarly incorporated into the Burgundian residence of the notoriously failed courtier Roger de Rabutin, comte de Bussy. Banished from court for, among other indiscretions, uttering unflattering comments about Louis XIV's mistress and penning the slanderous *Histoire amoureuse des Gaules*, Bussy-Rabutin created in his château a fanciful and satirical metaphorical representation of his life in exile. In addition to a portrait gallery of worthy men and a room devoted to views of grand palaces of France and devices, Bussy-Rabutin adorned his private *cabinet*, the circular "tour dorée," with three rows of paintings. The lower included scenes from Ovid's *Metamorphoses*, the upper contained copies of portraits of the most important members of court, including Anne of Austria, the queen mother, Maria Theresa, the queen, the Grande Condé, and Louis XIII.[98] In the middle, however, were portraits of ten women from court with whom the count was acquainted.[99] The portraits were framed with painted borders covered with cupids bearing bows and arrows, flower-filled urns, and flower bouquets tied with blue ribbons.

Flowers were also used in the grand style of decoration popular in the later decades of the seventeenth century and characterized by the work of Charles le Brun at Vaux-le-Vicomte. Throughout the château built by Louis le Vau for Louis XIV's finance minister Nicolas Fouquet, Le Brun echoed the flowers in André Le Nôtre's flower parterres in the garden. In the chamber of Madame Fouquet, garlands of flowers were draped around the ceiling decoration, while bouquets filled cornucopias on paneling on the wall. In the Hercules room, which featured a ceiling painting of Hercules welcomed to Olympus by Jupiter, Diana, and Juno, putti held sumptuous trompe l'oeil bouquets. The muses depicted by Le Brun on the ceiling of the "Salon des Muses" were draped with floral garlands in a manner anticipating Le Brun's use of painted flowers at Versailles.[100] And finally, a *cabinet* on the ground floor not only included gilded wall panels covered with garlands and bouquets of flowers, but also featured on the ceiling an allegory of "Sommeil," with her floral attribute, the poppies that aided her sleep.

Flowers might also cover the floors of fine homes. Scholars have sought to link the evolution of parterre designs to the fashionable and expensive carpets covered in arabesques imported from Turkey in the seventeenth century. But if the floor coverings from the Orient influenced garden design, the taste for flowers and floral motifs also exerted influence on French carpets. In the mid-seventeenth century, the Savonnerie workshops produced carpets covered with bouquets similar to those rendered in still life paintings (see plate 6). The design of a Savonnerie carpet dating to the second quarter of the seventeenth century consists of baskets and blue and white porcelain vases holding rich bouquets. Filled with accurately portrayed arrangements of tulips, anemones, narcissi, carnations, and other fine flowers, the bouquets are reminiscent of the flower paintings of Jacques Linard. In the later seventeenth century, when the workshop was drafted into the production of carpets for Versailles and other royal palaces, the floral motifs incorporated into the carpets came to resemble the rich, sumptuous style typified by Charles Le Brun.

But flowers were more than just sumptuous framing devices or decorative motifs. Though they were commonly used to adorn and enhance the decorative schemes in seventeenth-century châteaux, they were also featured in increasingly frequent allegorical representations of Flora, Spring, and even Aurora (see plate 2). Flora made an early appearance in the French palace. Francesco Primaticcio, lured to France from Italy by François I, created in the 1540s a fresco of Flora on the ceiling in the Galerie d'Ulysses at Fontainebleau.[101] The goddess of flowers was also depicted in a fresco by Niccolò dell'Abbate and Primaticcio in the *salle de bal* of Fontainebleau, in a tapestry series of "The God's Arabesques," and in a rendition of *The Triumph of Flora* by an artist now known only as the "Master of Flora." Henri IV continued the precedent of depicting Flora at Fontainebleau by commissioning a Flora from Ambroise Dubois for the Cabinet du Roi[102] (figure 24). In Dubois's painting, the classically attired goddess, attended by flower-bearing cupids, embraces a vase of flowers. A window opens onto a formal garden with a *parterre à broderie*. And Poussin produced two portrayals of Flora (see Chapter 1). Yet Poussin's moralizing treatment of Flora is neither typical of, nor consistent with, the ways in which Flora was popularly (and decidedly more lightheartedly) incorporated into the many new *hôtels* constructed in Paris in the seventeenth century.[103] The goddess of flowers was depicted in numerous homes, sometimes as part of larger allegorical schemes such as the four seasons or five senses, in other instances as an independent decorative motif. Mazarin commissioned a Flora from the Italian Francesco Albani

FIG. 24. Attributed to Ambroise Dubois or his workshop, *Flora*, c. 1600. Cambridge, Mass., Fogg Art Museum, Harvard University, Cambridge, Mass. Courtesy of the Fogg Art Museum, Harvard University Art Museums, Gift of Sydney J. Freedberg in recognition of his long and treasured association with the Fogg Museum. Copyright President and Fellows of Harvard College, Harvard University.

for the ceiling of a "petite galerie" of his Parisian palace.[104] Among the renditions of the goddess in the Marais, the most fashionable section of Paris in the seventeenth century, was Eustache Le Sueur's Zephyr and a chariot-drawn Flora on the ceiling of the Place Royale (now the Place des Vosges) residence of the marquis de Dangeau.[105] Anne de Villars hired Nicolas Loir to decorate the ceiling of her room in the Hôtel de Vigny on the rue du Parc Royal with a trompe l'oeil dome opening to the sky, around which he painted allegories of the four seasons.[106] As expected, flowers featured prominently in the depiction of spring and even summer. The four seasons were also allegorized above the doors in a room in the Hôtel de Chaulnes in Place Royale.[107] Flora, seated on a cloud from where she sprinkled flowers offered by a putto, was painted on the ceiling of the "Cabinet en auvalle" of the *hôtel* of Etienne Landais at 5 rue du Mail.[108] A similar composition was also executed on the ceiling of the home at 36 rue Vieille-du-Temple.[109] Finally, the ceiling of the "Cabinet des Miroirs" of the Hôtel de Lauzun included an oval central panel depicting Flora strewing flowers down from a trompe l'oeil sky that was surrounded by arabesques, cupids, and rich flower garlands.[110]

The Floras floating on clouds above the *cabinets* and salons of elite Paris sprinkled flowers upon the playfully learned who delighted in ornamenting their chambers to reflect their wealth, learning, and taste. The depiction of Flora, like that of other gods, goddesses, and allegories, not only illustrated a knowledge of mythology[111] and symbolism of fertility and rebirth, but also an interest in love and beauty characteristic of both the pastoral and Neoplatonic ideals of the seventeenth century. And, on purely aesthetic terms, the goddess and her requisite flowers offered a display of brilliant color and luxuriousness characteristic of baroque taste. Flora's popularity, however, also implied awareness of the flower mania of the early modern period. The sheer profusion of flowers in the décor of elite seventeenth-century homes makes it tempting to dismiss the omnipresent floral garlands, festoons, and Floras as mere ornament. Certainly, the fashion for floral décor had spread beyond the scope of those who were genuinely curious about flowers. But no one in the seventeenth century would have failed to recognize that the blossoms, incorporated into the sumptuously (and botanically) rendered festoons and garlands that draped around historical figures or crowned the myriad numbers of muses, graces, Venuses, Auroras, and Floras, were among the finest, rarest, most expensive, and most fashionable flowers available. No one could dispute that such flowers had become part of the visual vocabulary of taste and refinement.[112]

Painted flowers were not always, however, elements of larger decorative schemes. Liberated from paneling, the self-contained floral still life compositions so popular in early modern Europe were widely collected. Although the floral still life is commonly associated with Flemish and Dutch painters, French artists were also highly successful in the genre.[113] Early seventeenth-century painters such as Jacques Linard, painter and "valet de chambre du Roy," and Jean-Michel Picart painted vases or baskets of flowers. Not only did Linard include flowers (symbolizing the sense of smell) in an allegory of the five senses which could also be interpreted as a *vanitas* painting, but he also painted baskets overflowing with fashionable flowers such as tulips, anemones, ranunculi, cyclamen, roses, primroses, and carnations. Picart produced bouquets of flowers in

elegant though simple vases.[114] Floral still life paintings increased in popularity and prestige in the late seventeenth century through the work of Jean-
Baptiste de Monnoyer and his pupil Jean-Baptiste Belin de Fontenay, whose grand
compositions depicted flowers in grand settings—on marble pedestals, for
example, or in gilded urns and porphyry vases. Louis XIV favored their style;
many works by Monnoyer and Belin de Fontenay were incorporated into the
decoration of Versailles and the Grand Trianon.

Still life painting was not viewed, however, as a sophisticated form of art.
Indeed, in the context of the hierarchy of genres of painting, it was regarded
as an inferior pursuit. André Félibien explained in the *Conferénces de l'Académie
Royale de Peinture et Sculpture* in 1668 that

> the representation of a body which is made by simply tracing its lines or mixing
> colours is considered mechanical work. This is why it is that, just as there are dif-
> ferent Workers in this Art who apply themselves to different subjects, so, as they
> occupy themselves with things which are more difficult and more noble, they escape
> from that which is most base and common, and ennoble themselves by a more illus-
> trious labor. Thus someone who paints landscapes perfectly is superior to another
> who only makes fruits, flowers or shells. Someone who paints living animals is more
> to be esteemed than those who only represent things which are dead and motion-
> less; and as the figure of man is the most perfect of God's works on earth, so it is
> also certain that whoever makes himself the imitator of God by painting human
> figures, is much more excellent than all the others.[115]

Given such critical reception in the official circles, it is easy to dismiss the
importance of still life painting. But the genre, if not deemed challenging by
critics of art, gave expression to early modern French tastes for flowers and decorative painting.

The question of how thoroughly still life paintings should be gleaned for
symbolic meaning is frequently debated. The flower was often used in such paintings as a symbol of vanity or brevity of life,[116] and indeed some flower paintings were obviously meant to be thus interpreted. Yet many have rightly
cautioned against reading too stridently symbolic content. Simon Schama
argues that the Dutch taste for still life painting had to be considered in context of their "strong cultural predisposition towards seeing the description and
representation of natural phenomena as an enrichment of Christian belief."[117]
Such "predisposition" therefore allowed the Dutch, Schama explains, to see in
their still life paintings both Aristotelian cataloguing of worldly goods and a Neoplatonic celebration of the works of God. "The still-life painter," he continued,
"could thus use all of his or her skills in the creation of an illusion that would
be, at one and the same time, an account of the infinite ingenuity of the Creator and a version of the axiom that the terrestrial world remained but a shadow
of the celestial."[118]

Whereas Schama argued that the floral still life painting was thereby imbued with a subtle symbolic expression of Dutch culture, Paul Taylor, who made an intriguing attempt to compare the cost of floral still life paintings to that of flowers in the seventeenth century in the Netherlands, concluded that the success of flower paintings (and their respective painters) had little to do with their cultural meaning.

> We have seen that the floral still life could be responded to in a variety of ways in seventeenth-century Holland. For some, the rarity and beauty of the flowers would have been the most appealing feature. For others, the religious symbolism would have outweighed such worldly frivolity. Both these aspects of the flower piece must have contributed something to its popularity: but they were not the ones on which the main appeal of the genre was based. The most successful flower painters did not reach their positions of eminence by painting only the rarest blooms. . . . Nor did true Christian sentiment guarantee success. . . . It was the artist's facility as an illusionist which sold paintings. This was what the public wanted.[119]

Although it is likely that consumers did indeed favor the most beautifully rendered flower paintings, Taylor does not adequately address why the demand for such paintings existed in the first place or consider the broader cultural significance of flowers in Dutch culture.

Norman Bryson, in a series of essays on still life, attempted to explain both the cultural meaning of the contents of still life paintings and the importance of the physical paintings themselves. Dutch flower painting, according to Bryson's interpretation, existed simultaneously in three economic spaces: that of the botanical garden producing the flowers, speculation in the flower trade, and the commercial value of the painting itself.[120] Bryson's example is useful in understanding not only floral still life, but all painted flowers in early modern France. But one must add to Bryson's paradigm the "cultural capital," to borrow Pierre Bourdieu's term, of flowers. Into French flower paintings one must read an awareness of floriculture, participation in the flower mania (if not speculation as occurred in the Netherlands), and the wealth demonstrated in acquiring the floral painting or decoration. The identification of floriculture and flower collecting with curiosity, the degree to which "persons of quality" engaged in activities around flowers, and the fashionable ornamentation of homes with floral decoration suggest that one must add to the broadly defined "economic space" the cultural capital inferred by all things floral. If flower painting was deemed, as Félibien explained, inferior to history painting, it was hardly inferior in its ability to comment upon the cultural distinction of the owner.

The cultural cachet of decorative floral painting, like that of flower collecting and flower books, provided subtle testimony to one's learning and taste, wealth and fashionability.[121] It is not surprising, then, to find that flowers were deliberately included in the least subtle expressions of identity, the portrait and the device. The incorporation of flowers in portraiture took a variety of forms. In the early seventeenth century, many northern European (mostly Flemish) portraits were surrounded with garlands or wreaths of flowers, such as Rubens's portrait of the Madonna and Child, now in the Louvre, or Jan Brueghel's *Garland of Flowers with the Virgin, Infant Jesus, and Angels* in the Prado.[122] For paintings of this type, flower painters were frequently employed to ornament the already rendered figures. But French portraitists, too, depicted their subjects surrounded by flowers. Jean-Baptiste Colbert, Louis XIV's "surintendant des bâtimens," was depicted in a watercolor portrait with a garland of all of the most fashionable flowers around him.[123] Catherine d'Angennes, the countess d'Olonnes, was depicted as Diana in a miniature portrait, but the image was framed by enamel flowers, while flowers covered the back of the miniature as well. More commonly, however, flowers were included as personal attributes in portraits. Nicolas Robert, for example, depicted festoons dangling from the cartouche framing his portrait of his patron, Gaston, duc d'Orléans.[124] In the painting (see figure 9), which accompanied the *vélins*, Gaston was shown with scientific instruments and military paraphernalia to signify his learning and military successes, while the flowers attested to his interest in floriculture and botany.

Flowers were also incorporated into the body of portraits. Madame de Rambouillet and her daughter Julie d'Angennes, the recipient of the *Guirlande de Julie*, were shown exchanging a crown of flowers. Seated before a classically inspired backdrop, the mother and daughter were attended by a cupid fluttering above them. Flowers were similarly incorporated into another portrait of d'Angennes by Claude Deruet, who depicted the young woman as a shepherdess, crook in hand and accompanied by a small flock of sheep. She holds a chaplet of flowers in her hand. The roses, sheep, and temple of Vesta in the background, according to Anthony Blunt, were all symbols of innocence,[125] and all contributed to Julie's representation as Astrée, a popular character among the *précieux*.[126]

It was not uncommon for portraits of seventeenth-century persons to depict them in allegorical garb, with the sitter assuming the persona of a season or goddess of classical or literary fame. Flowers were featured in such portraits, too. It is hardly surprising, given the degree to which flowers and Flora were incorporated into creating pleasing and fashionable atmospheres in châteaux and *hôtels*, that women should have chosen the goddess who so beautifully called to mind love, beauty, springtime (and thus youth or rejuvenation), and fertility.[127] All were desirable qualities and therefore would have been appropriately complimentary to the sitter.

Indeed, throughout the seventeenth century, flowers were increasingly incorporated into portraits of women. When Julie d'Angennes was depicted as Astrée, for example, flowers helped set the stage for the role of the shepherdess. Others were shown not necessarily as Astrée or as a shepherdess, but merely holding a bouquet. Marie-Anne de Bourbon, the princesse de Conti, was, for example, depicted by Pierre Gobert taking flowers from a formal bouquet to add to a floral crown that she held. Pierre Mignard, who waited out the royally favored Charles le Brun by painting, among other commissions, a large number of portraits, decorated many of them with flowers. Marguerite de Sévigné, the future Madame de Grignan, was painted by Mignard with a bouquet of orange blossoms in her hand, perhaps in honor of her marriage to the comte de Grignan in 1669. And Marie Mancini was depicted with an elaborate bouquet in the foreground and a large nosegay attached to her dress. Elisabeth Charlotte, the second wife of Philippe d'Orléans, was painted with two of her children by Mignard. She was shown plucking a blossom from a floral arrangement while her daughter holds a rose in the lap of her mother.[128] Indeed, any survey of Mignard's work reveals enough flowers sprinkled, offered, and contemplated by women to fill a garden. As fashionable interchangeable symbols of beauty, love, and fertility,[129] flowers were well suited for the portrayal of women. After all, the success of a portrait depended on its ability to communicate something of the sitter in a language understandable to the viewer.[130]

Portraits in which the sitter was represented as the goddess Flora, a popular guise among prominent women in the seventeenth century, also, of course, included flowers. Henrietta-Anne (d'Angleterre), whose mother Henrietta Maria famously portrayed Chloris (of Flora) in Ben Jonson and Inigo Jones's masque *Chloridia*[131] and who was herself the first wife of Philippe, duc d'Orléans, was depicted as Flora in Nocret's mythological group portrait of the court.[132] Louise de la Vallière was painted as Flora by Jean Petitol. And Mademoiselle de Blois, the legitimized daughter of Louis XIV and Madame de Montespan, played Flora in the Ballet de Flore and was painted in her costume which was decorated with orange blossoms and jasmines (see plate 4).

Devices and emblems, both popular in seventeenth-century France, also incorporated flowers into expressions of identity.[133] The emblem was a personal symbol that indicated particular qualities about a person or that person's identity. They were suitable adornments, according to the Jesuit scholar Pierre Le Moyne's 1666 *De l'art des devises*, "in the Court *Fêtes*, in the entries of Kings & Queens, & in other occasions, or with painting & embroidery, with marble & gilding."[134] And flowers were deemed particularly suitable for devices. Pierre Le Moyne included in his work a collection of devices, together with his interpretation of them which he called his "Cabinet de Devises." He later produced a "Jardin de Devises." Le Moyne wrote, "It is the title that I give to this second collection of devices made of diverse flowers."[135] "In each device," Le Moyne explained, "the flower speaks; all of its words have a double meaning; & they [could not] pertain more to the person for whom they speak."[136] Le Moyne spelled out, for example, the distinguishing characteristics of the anemone and the person who could appropriately incorporate them into a personal emblem: "One will never see tissue more delicate than [the petals] of the Anemone: the heat & the cold offend it equally. . . . It is the proper figure for a tranquil and moderate soul: [a soul] as incapable of excess as of absence: [someone] who behaves neither warmly nor with coldness: [someone] who keeps a distance from extremes: & who never gives in to any passion."[137] Then the anemone, spoke:

> I have a delicate body, as I have a tender heart;
> To my temperament my spirit is equal;
> The smallest excess results in a great harm;
> And my instinct inclines me to defend myself.
> Although I savor the sun,
> I avoid with equal care,
> Either the extreme heat, or the extreme cold;
> And material of temperate air,
> From which Nature composes me,
> Suffers nothing that is not moderate.[138]

Le Moyne included similar devices for the violet, narcissus, crown imperial, rose, lily, iris, carnation, poppy, tuberose, campanelle, jasmine, and sunflower.

Floral devices were included, like floral garlands and the goddess Flora, in the decoration of châteaux. A notable example can be found at the château of Cheverny, where floral devices by Jean Mosnier[139] decorated the lower register of one chamber. And a floral motif was incorporated into Bussy-Rabutin's *salle des devises*. Positioned near a painting of the sun, one flower stands erect and in full bloom, its caption reading, "In your presence I thrive." Opposite the fresh flower is a dying one with the caption, "In your absence I die." Some have interpreted the device as an expression of longing felt by Bussy for his favorite daughter,[140] but the device could just as easily be read as a metaphor for his exile. At court in the presence of the Sun King, he thrived, whereas in exile he withered away.[141]

Norman Bryson argued that the lesser status of the flower painting was based in part upon its inability to tell a story. "While history painting is constructed around narrative," Bryson wrote, "still life is the world minus its narratives or, better, the world minus its capacity for generating narrative interest."[142] Flower paintings could not tell a story in the literal sense. But flowers incorporated into the decoration of the garden, *hôtel*, and *cabinet*, in the adornment of portraits, and in the composition of devises did constitute a language capable of communicating one's learnedness, wealth, and taste. That language, expressed visually and built upon traditional floral symbolism, floral mythology and allegory, contemporary floriculture, and the cultural capital of flowers in early modern Europe, allowed for the construction and articulation of identities of seventeenth-century French elites.

"Jardin d'Hyver," or Flowers in Print

The notion of the garden as a theater (explored earlier in this chapter) was only one of many garden metaphors employed in the early modern period. Some, like

Abraham Bosse's *Le Iardin de la Noblesse Françoise dans lequel ce peut ceuillir leur manierre de Vettements* of 1629, played with the notion of the garden as a fashionable collection or repository of specimens of many sorts. On his title page, Bosse employed the garden, fashionable in itself, as the setting for his collection of fashionable noble styles of dress from which to pick[143] (figure 25). Less frivolously, in 1517, the French humanist Guillaume Budé exploited the floral motif in the presentation of his manuscript *Le Livre de l'institution du prince* to Francis I. In the work he addressed his patron, writing, "as if I am in a great meadow in the month of May and am cutting the flowers most distinguished by odor or color or eminence over the others in order to make a chaplet and present it to your majesty in place of a great present that a rich man could give."[144] Budé's flowers were metaphorical references to the lessons of history and statecraft that he imparted to the king in the manuscript. Budé's use of the chaplet as a metaphor for the flowers of wisdom he intended to impart foreshadowed the *Guirlande de Julie* with its construction of a garland of floral poems. But many other uses of garden metaphors reflected serious philosophical and religious epistemologies of the Renaissance and early modern periods. Within the broad range of vegetative and horticultural metaphors in the humanist approach to learning, flowers held specific meanings. Flowers, as the horticultural "ornaments of the earth," were the linguistic equivalent of the rhetorical flourish. According to Antoine Furetière's *Dictionnaire universel*, the word *fleur* could be used to describe language. Furetière wrote, "One names *flowers* of rhetoric, the figures, the ornaments of discourse. He used all the flowers of his rhetoric to persuade me of his opinion. The *flowers* of speaking well." Furetière added, "This word serves also as a title to many books. The *Flowers* of Saints. The poetic *flowers*, &c."[145] The "flowers" of saints to which Furetière referred belong to a genre of writing that consisted of collections of sayings and commonplaces gleaned from classical texts, or, in the case of Furetière's saintly flowers, from the writings of church fathers and saints. These textual florilegia became increasingly popular in the Renaissance during which humanist educators encouraged their students to compile their own flowers of philosophy and theology.[146]

French writers expanded the notion of rhetorical flowers to include contemporary poetry. Men in Toulouse had competed in the Floralia, or floral games, since the fourteenth century. Named after the more populist, even raucus, Roman floral games that marked the completion of the planting season and looked forward to a fertile growing season, the Toulouse version consisted of a poetry contest held in early May in which the winners were presented with a golden violet, a silver eglantine, or a silver marigold.[147] In 1694 Louis XIV awarded the ancient literary society with royal patronage and the official name of the Académie des Jeux Floraux.

Numerous collections of poetic florilegia, such as *La Parterre de la rhetorique François, emaillé de toutes les plus belles fleurs d'eloquence qui se montrent dans les oeuvres des orateurs tant anciens que modernes, ensemble le verger de poësie, ouvrage tres-*

Text within the image:

Le Iardin de la Noblesse Françoise
dans lequel ce peut Ceuillir
leur manierre de Vettements

A° 1629 Auec Preuilege du Roy

A PARIS chez Melchior Tauernier Graueur et Imprimeur
du Roy pour les Tailles douces demeurant en Lisle du
Palais sur le Quay qui reguarde la Megisserie a l'Espic d'Or.
Bosse in. et fecit.

FIG. 25.   Abraham Bosse, *Le Iardin de la Noblesse Françoise dans lequel ce peut Cueillir leur manierre de Vettements* [*The Garden of the French Nobility from which one can pick the manner of their clothing*], Paris: Melchior Tavernier, 1629, title page. Image courtesy of author. Photograph by John Blazejewski, Index of Christian Art, Princeton University.

utile à ceux qui veulent exceller en l'un et l'autre art,[148] played upon the flower as a metaphor for eloquence. Many frontispieces of such works used flowers as a visual expression of eloquence. The title page of Pierre Le Moyne's *Les Pein-tres Morales* included a parterre of *broderie* in which were planted flowers.[149] Jean Puget de La Serre's *Bouquet des plus belles fleurs de l'eloquence* title page, engraved by Crispin de Pas, too, made visual reference to the flower as eloquence. The title page took the form of a bouquet of fashionable flowers (figure 26). The title was printed on a petal of the centrally placed tulip, while the names of authors included in the anthology, the authors La Serre held up as examples on which to model one's own prose, were named individually on the flowers that comprised the bouquet. The fritillary, crocus, anemone, lilies, iris, narcissus, and carnation that made up the bouquet represented the works of Guillaume du Vair, J. Davy du Perron, and François de Malherbe, among others, whose writings were included in the volume.[150] Each poet had become a flower of eloquence within the metaphorical bouquet that was the book.

But the connection between the "flowers of rhetoric" and the flower in the bouquet was more than metaphorical. Increasingly in the seventeenth-century, flowers and rhetoric merged through the pens of rhetoricians and curious florists alike. The rhetorician Etienne Binet addressed the intersection of flowers in the garden and flowers on the page directly. In his *Essay des merveilles de Nature et des plus nobles artifices, pièce très-nécessaires à tous ceux qui font profession d'eloquence*, he argued that eloquent writing required knowledge of the natural world[151] and lamented that his culture lacked a richness in vocabulary necessary for writing about the marvels of nature. He explained that just as Nature enameled the fields with flowers, so the "Fathers" (of antiquity) filled their writing with rhetorical flowers so beautifully that it was difficult to judge which was more beautiful than the other. His contemporaries, Binet reported sadly, knew neither Greek nor Latin botanical terms, and even in French, "they know neither their names, nor the parts of Flowers, nor speak of things so delicate, and so ordinary. When the most high-class have named the Rose, and the Lily, and the Carnation, and the Bud and the leaf," they could say no more because "that is all that they know."[152] For Binet, the task was to unite the metaphorical flowers of rhetoric with the living flowers that so fascinated his contemporaries. His solution was to provide those contemporaries with the vocabulary necessary to speak and write eloquently about flowers—to allow them, as he made clear, to move beyond the obligatory rose and lily. In the pages that followed, Binet presented to his readers a lengthy collection of nouns and adjectives and phrases that could be used not only to describe accurately the botanical features of flowers, but also to better exploit floral motifs in their writing.

Armed with the words necessary to describe accurately and eloquently the flowers in the garden, flower enthusiasts eagerly entered the increasingly prestigious realm of authorship and print. The print medium had much to offer florists, for the cultivators and collectors of flowers in early modern France faced

FIG. 26.   Jean Puget de la Serre, *Le Bouquet des plus belles fleurs de l'Eloquence* [*The Bouquet of the Most Beautiful Flowers of Eloquence*], Paris, P. Billaine, 1624, title page. Paris, Bibliothèque Nationale de France.

obstacles to the enjoyment of their floral passions that collectors of medals, antiquities, and shells did not: once a flower bulb or seed had been acquired, it had
to be coaxed into flowering in order that the collector might reap its aesthetic
and botanical rewards. Even then, the flowering plant could be enjoyed only for
the short time that it blossomed. Thus curious florists needed, in addition to the
floricultural knowledge necessary to grow their treasured plants, a means to share,
display, and enjoy their flowers throughout the year. The medium of print fulfilled all these requirements. Flower gardening manuals and florilegia communicated in printed form not only information useful to the florist in cultivating
flowers, but also the distinction conferred by flower gardening in every season
of the year. Such publications suggest the extent to which an interest in flowers spread beyond the cultivation of flowering plants, while illustrating the
degree of cultural sophistication held, or perhaps sought, by curious florists. Early
modern flower books were guides to both floricultural and civilizing processes
that also allowed for the display of cultural distinction. And the improvements
to the French language that Etienne Binet sought to encourage mirrored the
improvements made in the men who cultivated and wrote about the flowers.

The production of gardening manuals was nearly as old as printing itself,
although the nature and contents of the manual changed over time. The earliest gardening manuals offered some instruction, but essentially were humanist
treatises celebrating the idyllic rural life. Translations of Italian works such as
Francesco Colonna's *Hypnerotomachie ou Discours du Songe de Poliphile* and
Pietro Crescenzi's *Le Bon Mesnagier* were reprinted numerous times throughout the sixteenth century. The popularity of French works such as Charles
Estienne and Jean Liébault's *L'Agriculture et la maison rustique* (originally published in 1570) and Olivier des Serres's *Le Théâtre d'agriculture et mesnage des champs*
(1600) reflected the growing taste in France for life on the country estate and
its requisite gardens.[153]

In the seventeenth century, the publication of gardening manuals increased
while the genre fragmented into subgenres as authors addressed more specialized topics and audiences in a decidedly more instructional tone. Works such
as Jacques Boyceau's 1638 *Traité du jardinage selon les raison de la nature et de l'art*,
Claude Mollet's *Théâter des jardinages, contenant une methode facile pour faire des
pepinieres, planter, elever, enter, gresser, & cultiver toutes sortes d'arbres fruitiers
avec les fleurs qu'il faut mettre dans les parterres*, first published posthumously in
1652, and his son André Mollet's *Le Jardin de Plaisir* of 1651 confined themselves
to the creation and cultivation of a garden (as opposed to the management of
an entire country estate).[154] The works offered patterns for the creation of
parterres and knots, listed plants appropriate for each part or type of garden, and
offered some horticultural information.

The works by Boyceau and the Mollets were published in large format and
assumed that their readers were constructing immense gardens adjoining their
country châteaux. Thus these early books offered advice on the layout or "situ-

ating" of the garden, not information about more practical horticultural questions on fertilizing soil or germinating seedlings. Such publications concerned themselves with achieving the aesthetic qualities desired in seventeenth-century gardens. Boyceau's work, dedicated to Louis XIII, described a formal garden divided into one section devoted to pleasure and beauty and another called the "Jardin utile," or "useful garden." In the pleasure garden, Boyceau imagined a luxurious garden "that was enriched with fountains, embellished with canals and streams, grottoes and subterranean places, aviaries, galleries decorated with painting and sculpture, the orangery, the alleys and walkways well arranged, covered or uncovered, lawns and yards for games of ball, and exercises for people . . . well disposed around the parterres."[155]

As it became increasingly fashionable to be knowledgeable about gardening, manuals provided more detailed horticultural instruction, especially in the cultivation of fruit trees and flowers. Such manuals assumed that a professional gardener would be hired to direct the creation and upkeep of one's garden, while asserting that it was necessary for the reader to know how to hire a good gardener and properly oversee his work. In offering suggestions on how to pick a "naturally curious" gardener, Liger assumed that the reader of his volume would be the owner.[156] The format of gardening manuals, too, responded to the demand for the functional as smaller, more practical volumes were produced in greater numbers. For example, Nicolas de Bonnefons's *Le Jardinier françois* was purposely printed in a small format so that it might be carried into the garden where it was needed. Bonnefons wrote, "That is why (Madames) I hope that you are grateful to me for having addressed this instruction to you, [for] I have printed [the work] in a small volume so that you . . . can carry it without inconvenience, in order to confront the work of your gardener with this small book, and judge his capacity or negligence."[157] Although English floriculturists responded to the growing number of English women gardening and cultivating flowers by publishing a number of texts specifically for them, Bonnefons's work is unique in seventeenth-century French gardening literature in its dedication to women readers, for which there was apparently less demand.[158] But its attention to the utility of the volume is characteristic.

Publishers also began to address increasingly specific audiences. Numerous works were written especially for and by the curious florists. In 1658 Pierre Morin authored *Remarques necessaires pour la culture des fleurs*. The 1682 *Nouveau traité pour la culture des fleurs* and the 1692 *La culture des fleurs* were published anonymously, while in 1688 N. Valnay produced his *Connoissance et culture parfaite des tulippes rares*.[159] These works, and others like them, were intended to guide the reader through the cultivation of the rare and fashionable florists' flowers, offering criteria for distinguishing the best blossoms from lesser specimens and the latest information on cultivating the plants. The print industry responded to further specialization in the milieu of flower enthusiasts by publishing a number of treatises devoted entirely to individual species. Louis Boulanger's *Le Jardinage des oeillets* appeared in Paris in 1647 educating the reader on the finer points of growing carnations, and the Sieur de La Chesnée Monstereul's *Le Florist françois. Traittant de l'origine des tulipes* was published in Caen in 1654 for those who favored the tulip and wanted to learn more about its cultivation and history. In 1738 Guénin produced a *Traité de la culture parfaite des oreilles d'ours ou auricules.* For those seeking advice on the cultivation of hyacinths, a florist might consult George Voorhelm's *Traité sur la jacinte* or the Marquis de Saint Simon's *Des Jacintes, de leur anatomie, reproduction et culture.*[160] In these publications, florists not only instructed fellow flower collectors on the cultivation of the species in question, but also defended their favored flower against those who touted another.

In addition to providing for the dissemination of information on the cultivation of flowers, print also allowed for the easy and accurate reproduction of images of plants and flowers. The use of illustrations in printed works was older than that of the earliest gardening manuals. Indeed, herbals, or compendiums of the uses of herbs dating back to the late fifteenth century, included images of individual herbs for the purpose of their identification.[161] Herbals included instructions for the cultivation of, but more importantly, the medicinal uses of herbs that were then illustrated in woodcuts. The introduction of the woodcut increased the scientific value and utility of such works, offering for the first time a visual guide to identification of a particular plant. Woodcuts were, however, limited in the degree of detail that they could represent, and what detail they could include was dulled with each impression.[162]

The use of line engraving and etching, invented in the fifteenth and sixteenth centuries respectively,[163] changed the nature of the illustrated gardening manual. The ability to reproduce highly detailed and precise images brought the artistic and aesthetic tendency for naturalism to the printed botanical work, resulting in representations realistic enough to identify individual species of plants and flowers and even distinguish between varieties. It did not take long for florists to take advantage of the possibilities offered by printed engravings; by the early seventeenth century, books of elaborately engraved florists' flowers began to appear. These florilegia (literally, flower books)[164] subordinated the text to the image (in many cases, eliminating text altogether) and were printed in large format with a high degree of botanical accuracy.[165]

The most notable early printed florilegium was Pierre Vallet's *Le Jardin du Roy tres Chrestien Henry IV Roy de France et de Navare dedie à La Royne*, published in Paris in 1608. Containing more than seventy-five elegant engravings, the work depicted rare and desirable flowers from the royal garden on the Ile de la Cité tended by Jean Robin. The plates illustrated tulips, lilies, iris, and carnations on which the flowers were labeled in Latin. The work, whose printed flowers did not "fear the cold breath of winter, nor the shock of winds, nor the harshness of the drying and withering rays of the sun,"[166] not only preserved and disseminated a record of the king's collection of flowers, but also served as patterns for "those who want to paint or illuminate, or embroider & make tapestries"[167] from the floral designs. Crispin de Passe's 1614 *Hortus Floridus*, too, contained charming portraits of flowers and insects. It was so popular that it was translated from Latin into French, Dutch, and English by 1615,[168] and its engravings were so highly regarded that they were copied and inserted into numerous other florilegia.[169] Another flower album, Langlois's *Livres de fleurs ou sont representées toutes sortes de tulippes; narcisses, iris, et plusieurs autres fleurs*, was published in Paris in 1620. The flowers depicted in the work, including twenty-three plates of tulips, twenty-two irises, three fritillaries, five crocuses, twenty-one narcissi, a rose, poppy, sweet pea, and crown imperial, were intended for those interested in the most fashionable species.[170]

The 1622 *Theatrum florae* by Daniel Rabel stylistically resembled Vallet's earlier florilegium more than those of de Passe and Langlois. Rabel's engraved collection of flowers in the *Theatrum florae*, likely based on paintings now in the Bibliothèque Nationale de France, were well received: subsequent editions were printed in 1627 and 1633.[171] His volume was not limited to the depiction of fashionable florists' flowers. The frontispiece (see figure 17), framed by vine-covered trellises, allows the viewer to peer into a formal garden parterre that included arcades, grottoes, parterres *en broderie*, and flower beds. In the foreground, Flora and Vertumnus hold implements of their work while between them a rich bouquet of florists' flowers demonstrates their success.

Jean Franeau's florilegium, the *Jardin d'hyver ou cabinet des fleurs* included engravings of a wider variety of flowers, including hepaticas, bears' ears, hyacinths, anemones, fritillaries, narcissi, lilies, tulips, irises, cyclamen, carnations, pinks, and passionflowers. Published in Douai in 1616, Franeau's work differed from the others in that each engraving was accompanied by an elegy composed in honor of the flower. Franeau explained in the dedication of the work his purpose in writing it: "As the Gardens & domestic parterres, amid the rigor of a rude and cold winter, among the ice, hail and snow, are rendered more sterile, & when Nature has taken back her flowers from us, . . . I have represented [with] the ink of my pen the most remarkable flowers, to participate in this sad season." "That is why," Franeau added, "that on the door or frontispiece of these faithful lines & portraits, I have put the inscription of Garden of winter or cabinet of flowers."[172]

Franeau's choice of the elegy—a form of poetry characterized by its mournfulness or lament for the dead—is appropriate given that the volume was framed as the celebration of the short-lived flowers driven underground by winter's harshness. Yet Franeau's comparison of his book to a *cabinet* is instructive: the engravings of the flowers served as visual records of the flowers in Franeau's garden. By gathering the images into a volume, Franeau was imposing permanency on the flowers, allowing them to be enjoyed in one's collection (of flowers or books) year round. The *cabinet*, generally a repository of one's prized possessions or a private retreat, could be a piece of furniture with compartments for the safekeeping and display of objects, a room for the solitary enjoyment of the collector where one's treasures were housed, or even a garden where botanical, sculptural, and engineering wonders were exhibited. It was not uncommon for gardens to serve as *cabinets*, yet flowering plants could only be displayed when in bloom.[173] Franeau's work and other florilegia like it not only preserved in perpetuity the contents of one's garden, but also resulted in books themselves worthy of collecting.[174]

The florilegia was more than a fine book, more than a catalogue of the florist's collection. They also served as pattern books for amateurs and professional artisans.[175] Pierre Vallet's *Le Jardin du Roy tres Chrestien Henry IV* demonstrates the many layers of usage combined in a single publication. Like Franeau, Vallet comments on the ability of his work to provide floral gratification in every season: "The name of perpetual Springtime is all the more suitable, because the flowers by which it is embellished do not fear the cold breath of winter, nor the shock of winds, or even the . . . drying and withering of the rays of the sun." The flowers, he continued, "have imitated those that are bred within the superb and delicious gardens that his Majesty has cultivated by Jean Robin, his herbalist."[176] Vallet's engravings therefore record the contents of the garden of the king and Robin, allowing them to be admired even in winter. Yet the work was dedicated to Marie de Medici. Vallet, the embroiderer to the king, must have known that the queen herself took pleasure in embroidery and particularly in working floral designs. His book was therefore not only a pictorial record of the flowers in the king's garden, but also a pattern book. In the beginning of the book, Vallet included an "Advertisement to those who wish to paint or illuminate, or embroider and make tapestries from this book," in which he explained that in order to serve better those who wanted to reproduce the flowers according to nature, he included the appropriate colors for each flower in the book. The first eighteen pages of the text were thus given over to identifying those colors for the painter or embroiderer.[177] There is evidence that Vallet's book was indeed put to such use: in one extant copy of the publication, plate 16, an engraving of a *Lilium purpureum subalbidis oris*, was painted in rough accordance with the prescribed color list.[178] The nineteenth and eighty-fifth plates in the same volumes were painted, too, but not completed. In addition, several of the flowers bear imprints or pinpricks outlining them, suggesting that the images were traced or possibly transferred with chalk dust onto fabric in order to be embroidered.

Vallet's work was not the only collection of floral engravings produced for multiple purposes. Crispin de Passe's *Hortus Floridus* included guidelines for painting the flowers,[179] and Guillaume Toulouze, himself the "Maistre Brodeur de Mont-pelier," published the *Livres de fleurs, feuilles, et oyzeaux* in 1656 for his fellow professional embroiderers.[180] Nicolas Cochin's *Livre nouveau de fleurs tres util pour l'art d'orfevrier et autres* was intended to serve as a pattern book for artisans decorating gold objects and jewelry.[181] The *Livre de fleurs & de feullies pour servir a l'art d'orfevre* by François Le Febvre also included delicately rendered floral designs perfectly suited for engraving gold objets d'arts, and Jean Vauquier's

Livre des fleurs propre pour orfevres et graveurs included floral designs for specific shapes and functions including circles and bands to go around vases, urns, and clock faces.[182] In addition, the notable and pioneering entomologist Maria Sybilla Merian supported herself by publishing floral pattern books such as her *Neues Blumen Buch*, printed in Nuremberg in 1680, in which naturalistic flowers were depicted in wreaths, garlands, and bouquets of flowers in vases or gathered by a ribbon.[183]

The proliferation of floral pattern books for artisans attests to the fashionability of floral motifs in the decorative arts. But other books were intended to instruct amateurs in the creation of flower paintings as a form of recreation. Catherine Perrot, a member of the royal academy of painting, composed two instructional manuals including *Les Leçons Royales ou la maniere de peindre en mignature les fleurs & les oyseaux* published in 1687, and the 1693 *Traité de la migna-ture*.[184] The works were written, explained Perrot, to accompany the floral engravings of her teacher, Nicolas Robert.[185] She wrote: "Although Monsieur Robert, of whom I was a student, is not the only florist who has excelled, nevertheless I have always preferred his works to those of other florists, because he best represents the nature of flowers and birds."[186] Armed with Robert's engravings to color, Perrot also advised her readers to obtain their paints from the *veuve* Foubert, and included prices the amateur painter might expect to pay for them. The two volumes, dedicated respectively to Madame la Dauphine (Victoire, princess of Bavaria, 1660–1690) and Madame la Princesse de Guimené, each demonstrated that they were written for amateur flower painters: they suggest that flower painting had become a fashionable pastime for the elite. In the "Epistre" of *Les Leçons Royales*, Perrot named the dauphine as one of "all the persons of quality who have an inclination for painting in miniature," although she added that "common persons will be no less obliged to have these agreeable lessons."[187]

Charles Boutet's *Ecole de la mignature, dans laquelle on peut aisément à peindre sans maitre*, published in Lyon in 1679, was also written to guide the reader through the intricacies of flower painting. Boutet suggested that his readers purchase the engravings of Nicolas-Guillaume la Fleur, but he also included general instructions for reducing any design into miniature form.[188] He explained that flowers were particularly agreeable to paint "not only by the brilliance of their different colors, but also by the little time and trouble that one employs in making them."[189] To instruct his amateur painters, he included chapters on achieving likenesses of the most fashionable flowers such as roses, tulips, anemones, carnations, lilies, hyacinths, peonies, narcissi, jonquils, tuberoses, jasmines, and more common flowers such as violets and pansies. Painting flowers in miniature was easy and therefore enjoyable, Boutet claimed, but also very fashionable. He added, "the greatest number of persons of quality who [seek diversion] in painting, stick to flowers."

Painting flowers was not the only fashionable pastime related to floriculture. Some attempted to capture floral fragrances in perfumes and oils. Perfumes were important in the early modern period not only as a means of disguising unpleasant oders, but also as an element of fashion. And in the late seventeenth century, floral fragrances replaced heavier musk and civet-based scents as the most preferred.[190] Simon Barbe's *Le Parfumeur françois, qui enseigne toutes les maniere de tirer les odeurs de fleurs*, published in Lyon in 1693, provided information necessary to make perfumes "for the diversion of nobles," as well as for clergy, wigmakers, and bathers. His work was not, therefore, intended for professional perfume makers, but for those "persons of condition and those who have an honest leisure to fill their time and [alleviate] their boredom in the countryside, when they can employ the abundance of flowers to make perfumes at a just price."[191]

Others sought not to preserve the scent of flowers, but the flowers themselves. An author writing under the initials F.L.D.T.R. published in Paris in 1690 *Secrets pour teindre la fleur d'immortelle en diverses couleurs, avec la maniere de la cultiver*. F.L.D.T.R. included instructions for raising to maturity the *immortelle*, or everlasting, which could then, according to his directions, be dried, dyed, and displayed in bouquets. Recipes for dyes, techniques for producing striped or marbled blossoms, and two methods for constructing bouquets formed the subjects of chapters in the book.[192]

The enthusiasm for flowers thus extended far beyond the cultivation of flowers, and the opportunity to market the phenomenon more broadly was not lost on publishers. Charles de Sercy, for example, printed a large series of gardening texts under the title *Théâtre du jardinage*. Moderately priced between 10 and 15 sols each, the twenty books in the series ranged in subject from general gardening texts, to fruit tree instruction, to manuals on individual flowers, to F.L.D.T.R.'s treatise on drying and dyeing everlastings.[193] Sercy also sought to sell new editions of classic gardening texts in a series including new editions of Bonnefons's *Jardinier françois*, Claude Mollet's *Théâtre des jardinages*, Pierre Morin's *Remarques necessaires pour la culture des fleurs*, and Charles de la Chesnée Monstereul's tulip manual. The publication of floral pattern books and commercially marketed volumes on flower painting, perfume making, and dried flower arranging suggests that the fashionability of flowers had indeed moved beyond the ranks of the curious florists. Such publications reveal that interest in flowers was widespread, though concentrated among "personnes de qualité," and extremely fashionable, be it for flowers grown in the garden, reproduced in embroidery or paint, or depicted in lavishly illustrated florilegia. But just as flowers and floral fashion were not confined to the curious florists, those curious florists could not refrain from sharing with their readers their learning on a broad spectrum of themes. The flower books suggest also that curious florists were an intellectually elite, well-educated group who took advantage of opportunities offered by print to express their learnedness. For flower gardening manuals and related books were just as likely to include discussions of religious doctrine and displays of classical learning as they were to contain practical instruction on the planting and care of flowers. The books both displayed the learned status of their writers and readers and illuminated the cultural significance of flowers as well.

The tulip manual of Charles de la Chesnée Monstereul, the carnation book by Louis Boulanger, and the anonymous *Culture des fleurs* each combined the espousal of Christian morals with the celebration of their favorite flowers and instructions on caring for them. Boulanger concluded his *Jardinage des oeillets* with a chapter entitled "Reflexions Chrestiennes" which consisted of eight reflections on the moral lessons realized through cultivating carnations. The reflections, ranging from the work and close attention needed to bring a carnation to flower, to the short-lived beauty of the blossom, compared the flower and its cultivation to the cultivation of one's soul. Boulanger's final principal is typical of all eight: "Finally, in order to end these pious thoughts, the most beautiful flowers, and the most pompous carnation that nature has ever produced, is not immortal, but after fifteen days, or a month of splendor, after the astonishment of all the curious, after all the vanity of those who raised them, after . . . so much care and caresses. Its flowers wither, & this carnation fades; so that it is no longer more than a bit of straw & manure."[194] Boulanger continued, explaining that the finest flower and the most illustrious Christians must face the brevity of life, brevity that even the must sumptuous monuments to lives and deeds could not change. Such Christian tenets were so central to Boulanger's text that they were cited in the permission given to publish the work. The "Approbation," signed by Cornuty and Thevart, both "Docteur[s] Regent en la Faculté de Medicine de Paris," read, "This book entitled, *Le Jardinage des oeillets*, made and composed by L.B. for his curiosity, and for the precise observation of nature, and of the cultivation of the carnation, mixed with some moral considerations, merits being printed."[195]

While the religious nature of La Chesnée Monstereul's *Le Floriste françois. Traittant de l'origine des tulipes* was not singled out by the censors, they "found [in it] nothing contrary to the faith of the Catholic, Apostolic, and Roman Church, nor good morals."[196] In his treatise, La Chesnée Monstereul pondered the short duration of the life of the flower (and thus symbolically of man), and the glory of God's work that could be seen through flowers. The thirty-second chapter of his celebration of the tulip argued that to scorn flowers was to offend God. "This divine author of all things on the third day created plants," La Chesnée Monstereul explained, "among which the tulip without doubt appears as the premier in dignity, and the most beautiful ornament of the terrestrial paradise, making (according to the text of Moses) a sort of reflection on his divine works, considering their beauty, and the perfection in which he created them, judge them well."[197]

Like Boulanger and La Chesnée Monstereul, the author of *La Culture des fleurs* used the conclusion of his text to deliver a moralizing sermon on the lessons to be learned from the contemplation and cultivation of flowers. The anonymous writer, however, drew a more direct correlation between the flower garden and the soul. He first asked his readers to ponder the significance of sin. "I pray that those who read this treatise," he wrote, "reflect on the marvels of nature in the single production of flowers, and consider that without the sin, [Eve] would have cost us nothing: all the earth would be a garden of delights, one would not even know at all brambles, nor thorns, nor thistles."[198] Following comparisons of the soul to the parterre and the world to the garden, the author implored his fellow florists to "search the whole ensemble, my dear reader, cultivate it, with that of our hearts, and in making a bouquet, which is the only union, that we should support, with the grace of Jesus Christ, to which we [should] devote all our desires, all our thoughts, all our affections."[199]

For all of the Christian doctrine found in flower gardening manuals, however, one was just as likely to encounter a lesson in the culture and mythology of antiquity intertwined with horticultural teachings. The goddess Flora might be invoked or the mythological origins of various floral species discussed, while florists such as La Chesnée Monstereul commented on the uses of flowers in ancient Rome.[200] The presence of Greek mythology side by side with advice for growing flowers in Rapin's *Hortorum libri IV cum Disputatione de Cultura Hortensi* is not surprising, given that Rapin's book was, by his own admission, inspired by and patterned after Virgil's georgics. Indeed, the poetic form of the georgic was characterized not by its celebration of the pastoral way of life, but rather of agriculture and its inherent works. It was only fitting, then, that Rapin's instruction on the preparation of soil for a flower garden (in John Evelyn's 1672 translation into English),

> Break with the Rake, if stiffer clods abound,
> And with ir'n rollers level well the ground.
> Nor yet make haste your borders to describe;
> But let the earth the Autumn show'rs imbibe;
> That after it hath felt the Winter cold,
> You may next Spring turn up, & rake the mold[201]

be followed by, for example, the myth of the creation of the hyacinth:

> If sharper cold give leave, about this time
> The Hyacinth shoots up from *Phoebus* crime.
> At Quoits he playing, by *Eurota's* side,
> Chanc'd the boy's tender temples to divide.
> *The God and youth at once appalled stood;*
> *He through his guilt, and he through want of bloud;*
> From which, in pity of his angry fate,
> A flow'r arose, which oft [does] change its state,

And colour; and to one peculiar kind,
No more then to one season is confin'd.[202]

As a learned poet and Jesuit scholar, Rapin's juxtaposition of practical soil preparation with the ancient histories of flowers is understandable and demonstrates his fascination with the georgic form of poetry—and the layered functions of gardening manuals.

Also intriguing is Louis Liger's 1704 *Le Jardinier fleuriste et historiographe, ou la culture universelle des fleurs, arbres, arbustes, & arbrisseaux, servans à l'embellissment des jardins: Ensemble la maniere de dresser toutes sortes de parterres, berceaux de verdures, des bosquets, boulingring, portiques, patte d'oye, colonnes, & autres piéces, qui pour l'ordinaire accompagnent les jardins des maissons de campagne, les plus magnifiques; le tout enrichi d'un grand nombre de figures demonstratives.* The lengthy title of the work suggests much of its content: it was a practical gardening manual listing tools and techniques necessary for the successful cultivation of flowers. In addition, however, Liger composed each flower's "history," which amounted to its mythological creation, to which was appended an "application," or moral. After informing his readers about bringing anemones to blossom, for example, Liger related the history of the anemone:

> *Anemone* was a Nymph of great Beauty; *Flora* being jealous of her, envy'd to see her become the Admiration of all Men; therefore commanded her to retire into *Greece*, where her Beauty was not less taken notice of than in her Native Country. Her Charms surpass'd those of all others; she had a Thousand ravishing Qualities, but which were nevertheless fatal to her.
>
> This Nymph, being an Enemy to Melancholy and Confinement, went out one Day to take the fresh Air, in a Field shaded with a neighbouring Copse: 'Twas there that being alone, and enjoying the Privilege of her Retirement, she left her bosom half open to receive the gentle Breezes which offer'd themselves to be admitted.
>
> *Zephyrus* did not fail to be among them, which made *Flora* so exceedingly jealous of her Husband, that she could not look on *Anemone* but with Indignation: And therefore, once and for all, to put an end to this Familiarity, she immediately chang'd her into a Flower that bears her name, which even at this Day will not open its Leaves kindly unless *Zephyrus* blows upon it, who likewise on his part, 'tis said, never cares to abandon her, whatsoever condition she be reduc'd to.[203]

While Liger's moral, oddly, was not about immodesty, but rather that "True Love will not only appear during Life, but also will shew it self after the Object belov'd is dead," he nonetheless demonstrated knowledge of and interest in classical mythology through his discussion of flowers.

One might regard Liger's inclusion of these "histories" of flowers conjoined with practical gardening information as an example of what Michel Foucault described as "pre-classificatory," or pre-Linnaean thought. According to this interpretation, the flowers, their physical description, their mythology, and their care and cultivation were all jumbled into one text presumably because early modern thinkers (and gardeners) had no conceptual framework for distinguishing between the different kinds of information about flowers.[204] Yet this is a limited, negative reading. Considered as testimony to the cultural meaning or understanding of flowers in the early modern period, a much different reading of Liger, or even Rapin, emerges. The mythology of flowers was included with its cultivation instruction because flowers and goddesses belonged to the same social milieu. The readers gleaning the works for practical gardening advice were equally adept in the language of myth and allegory. Writing or reading about flowers allowed for the display of both kinds of learning.

It should be noted that some publications about flowers were written in both French and Latin. Jean Robin, gardener to Henri III, Henri IV, and Louis XIII, published in 1601 his *Catalogus stirpium tam indigenarum quam exoticarum quae Latetiae coluntur a J. Robino botanico regio*. In 1611 Paul Reneaulme published the learned and elegantly illustrated *Specimen Historiae Plantarum* in Paris.[205] And Pierre Morin's brother René produced in 1621 the *Catalogus plantarum horti Renati Morini inscriptarum ordine alphabetico*. In 1659 Denis Jonquet produced a catalogue of a botanical garden near St. Germain-des-Pres in Paris under the title *Hortus, sive index onomasticus plantarum quas excolebat Parisiis*, the frontispiece of which depicted Louis XIV as Apollo riding his chariot over the botanical garden as "Hortus Regius" (figure 27). And of course René Rapin's *Hortorum libri IV* was published in Latin and, though very popular, was not translated into French until the late eighteenth century. The majority of the texts, however, were published in French, suggesting that the flower-cultivating public most certainly extended beyond (but included) the more limited population of learned flower collectors literate in Latin.

The publication of texts on cultivating flowers, together with the collection of both the flowers and their books, existed in both the highly learned community of Latin scholars and the more worldly, though increasingly educated and fashion-conscious, social elites. The bridging of the realms of *doctes* and *mondains* in the social milieu of the curious florist is thus reflected in the writings published out of the interest in flowers. Pierre Bourdieu has argued that by the second half of the seventeenth century, "the growing authority of the *mondains* and of the court, combined with the tendency of high society to become more cultivated, reduced the distance between *doctes* and *mondains*." "This led," he continues, "to the rise of a new species of man of letters, typified by the Jesuits Rapin and Bouhours, masters of rhetoric who were themselves both *doctes* and *mondains*, who frequented artists and aristocrats and helped to produce a synthesis of the demands of the court and the academy."[206] The publications generated around the mania for flowers, intended for curious florists drawn from all quarters of elite society, bear out Bourdieu's assertion. The status attached to furnishing one's garden with expensive flowers, adorning one's portrait with them, or reading the

HOC NVMINE FLORET

Hortus Regius.

FIG. 27. "Hortus Regius." From *Hortus, sive index onomasticus plantarum quas excolebat Parisiis*, 1659, frontispiece. Paris, Bibliothèque Nationale de France, cliché E 29297.

"histories" of those flowers engaged one with a world of learning and taste. Books on flowers, like the flowers growing in the garden, or those incorporated into one's personal device, served as a vehicle for the expression of one's distinction. The medium of print, simultaneously disseminated information on how to cultivate those flowers and offered instruction, available for purchase, on the cultivation of one's self.

CHAPTER 5

Cultivating the King

In 1688, N. Valnay reported in his *Connoissance et culture parfaite des tulippes rares* that in 1685 Monsieur le Chevalier de Saint Mory, an "illustrious and grand" curious florist, presented to Louis XIV specimens of his new multicolored auriculas. The striped varieties, according to Valnay, were so new that "His Majesty, who admired them, was surprised that such beautiful flowers existed in his country without him knowing about them."[1] One might read the episode as anecdotal evidence of the absolutist king's attempt to know and control every aspect of his realm, right down to the coloration of the auriculas cultivated in France. But viewed from the perspective of the curiosity for flowers, the encounter between Saint Mory and the king reveals the king's interest in floriculture and illustrates the extension of the sociability among florists to the realm of the political. Valnay flattered the king in his flower gardening manual: "Before the reign of Louis XIV was the beauty of gardens known there? It seems that the Arts and their retinue were waiting . . . in order to flower in this [era], & because our monarch merits as many crowns as all the Heroes, he has brought forth flowers more beautiful than have ever been seen."[2] By 1688, fine and fashionable flowers did indeed fill the royal gardens. But the presentation to Louis XIV of auriculas so newly developed that they were unknown to the king reveals that the curious florists were the driving force in the breeding of new varieties of flowers. They were shaping the taste for fine flowers, and the king was following their lead. But why would the cultivation of a newly fashionable auricula have merited the attention of the king?

Much has been written about Louis XIV's use of the arts and sciences to construct and simultaneously record his own history.[3] The Sun King's absolutist machinery of royal celebration drew upon the talents and services of architects, painters, gardeners, engineers, scientists, poets, musicians, historians, weavers, and tailors in the expression of a broadly defined, but singularly glorious, statement of the king's greatness. The king's patronage, too, led the thinkers, artists, and artisans in the construction of lasting monuments to French culture under Louis XIV.[4] But in identifying the most appropriate means to communicate his power, the king necessarily had to draw upon symbolic languages of power that would be understood by those whom he ruled. The peasants of early modern France would have understood expressions of military might, the presence of the tax farmer, and demonstrations of long-held traditions of royal benificence such as the "king's touch," the belief that the king could cure sufferers of scrofula by laying his hands on the victims of the disease. For the increasingly well-educated and wealthy elites of French society, the ranks of which included ancient noble families, newly ennobled government officers, and the increasingly influential financial elites, a different language was necessary. Like his predecessors and fellow monarchs across Europe, Louis XIV drew upon the language of allegory and history. In the early years of his personal reign, Louis XIV favored comparisons drawn between himself and Alexander the Great. From 1661 to 1668, Charles Le Brun labored to produce a grandiose series of paintings on the history of Alexander the Great for Louis XIV.[5] Le Brun's paintings of Alexander were copied and disseminated in engraved prints and tapestries,[6] and the king danced the role of Alexander in a 1665 court ballet by Isaac de Benserade. In the realm of allegory, Louis XIV favored comparisons between himself and Apollo, choosing to represent himself again and again as the Sun King.

In the 1670s, however, allegorical and historical representations of the king became less frequent.[7] Indeed, as the king aged and his successes grew, he sought less problematic means through which to glorify his reign. Comparing the middle-aged king to the young and daring Alexander would have proved awkward. Instead, Louis and his panegyrists moved away from mythological and historical heroes and boldly offered up Louis XIV himself as the unequaled monarch "Louis le Grand." Le Brun could therefore cover the ceiling of the Hall of Mirrors in Versailles with panels demonstrating Louis XIV's own military victories. In the shift away from historical and mythological characters, Louis XIV in one sense laid claim to a loftier historical legacy for himself. But he also demonstrated an understanding of alternative languages of cultivation, identity, and power that resonated with the elites of French society. And expressions of his power increasingly bridged the two symbolic languages by combining traditional allegories and contemporary expressions of taste and reason. In building the unparalleled gardens of Versailles, for example, Louis simultaneously demonstrated his miraculous, symbolic power over Nature as Apollo riding his chariot out of the fountains of the park, and his knowledge of architecture, horticulture, and hydrological engineering. Flowers were perfectly suited to express both kinds of glory. By the time that Louis XIV had succeeded to the throne of France, as we have seen, flowers had become markers of cultural and social distinction through their ability to communicate taste, learning, beauty, and wealth. In a society such as early modern France, in which one's social and cultural standing could easily be equated with or lead to political influence and power, the extension of the cultural status of the coveted blossoms into the realm of the political was not surprising. As patrons of the arts and sciences, as builders of palaces and gardens, the Bourbon kings, and especially Louis XIV, were greatly aware of the political importance of culture in its material and symbolic forms. Louis XIV not only engaged in the mania for flowers, but in doing so, he put the cultural meanings of flowers to good political use. Indeed, in the years to come, Louis as Alexander the Great, Apollo the Sun King, and finally and most importantly as Louis le Grand, successfully enlisted ephemeral flowers into the drafting of his own historical legacy.

Royal Precedents

The use of floral symbolism to express political loyalties or identify dynasties was neither new in the seventeenth century nor limited to France. In Renaissance Italy, the Guelph party adopted the red lily as its symbol, while the Ghibelline supporters were distinguished by the white lily.[8] In England, the Wars of the Roses ended with the marriage of Henry VII and Elizabeth of York and the combination of their two respective symbols, the white rose and the red rose, into the Tudor red and white blossom.[9] In France, the most important symbol was, of course, the fleur-de-lys, which, by the early modern period, had already been identified with the French monarchy for centuries. As early as 1250 the symbol had taken on its stylized shape and was used by royal family members and institutions alike in government documents and heraldry. At the same time, the history of the fleur-de-lys was being written backwards to augment its legitimacy. By the late thirteenth century, it was suggested that Charlemagne had used the symbol, and by the early fourteenth century it had been attributed to Clovis and his legendary conversion to Christianity.[10] The complex history of the symbol of the French monarchy continued to be debated into the early modern period. Antoine Furetière cited in his 1690 *Dictionnaire universel* a number of early modern texts on the symbol's history: "The Critics who have written [on the fleur-de-lys] are Chiflet, Father Tristau de Saint Amand, Father Ferrand, de la Roque, de Ste. Marthe, Du Tillet in his collection on the Oriflame, Du Cange on the history of Joinville, Father Menestrier, & the Jesuit Father Rousselet, who has amassed all the other said Authors on the fleur-de-lys."[11] Despite the uncertainty of the symbol's history, the identification of the fleur-de-lys with the French monarchy, and therefore the French state, was so strong that, as Furetière continued, "*Lily*, is said figuratively, & poetically for the kingdom of France, which one calls the empire of the lily because of its army, as one says also the *Eagle*, for the [Holy Roman] Empire, the *Rose*, for England, &c."[12]

The Chiflet cited by Furetière was almost certainly Jean Jacob Chiflet, who published in 1658 the *Lilium Francicum, Veritate Historica, Botanica, et Heraldica Illustratum*, a text that traced the history of the fleur-de-lys as it appeared on medals and coins and in devices. Chiflet, a collector of medals, examined medals from the newly discovered tomb of Childeric and argued that the stylized fleur-de-lys was actually a corruption of a symbol incorporating a swarm of bees. In his work, he explored the botanical heritage of the fleur-de-lys in an attempt to solve the debate over whether or not the stylized symbol was really a lily, or an iris, or, the bees.[13] However, in juxtaposing the symbolic with the botanical, Chiflet's investigation of the fleur-de-lys betrayed the complexity that had developed in the use of flowers and floral symbolism by early modern French kings, a complexity mirrored in his own illustrations (figure 28). He investigated the symbolic *and* botanical heritage of the fleur-de-lys in much the same way that curious florists had done with other floral species. Similarly, the Bourbon kings of France conflated the symbolic and naturalistic aspects of flowers into a single strong, political emblem that drew from the ancient use of emblems and modern floriculture. The stylized fleur-de-lys remained central to the Bourbon scheme of glorification and symbolism, but its effectiveness was bolstered by the naturalistic lily and the many other flowers that were drafted into the service of the kings of France.

In the sixteenth century, interest in real flowers (versus the stylized fleur-de-lys) emerged among members of the French royal family and powerful nobility. Influenced by Italian styles,[14] grand châteaux such as Blois, Amboise,

FIG. 28.   Johanne Jacobo Chiflet, The Lily and the Fleur-de-lys. From *Lilium Francicum, Veritate Historica, Botanica, et Heraldica Illustratum*, Antwerp: Balthasaris Moreti, 1658, 117. Washington, D.C., Dumbarton Oaks Research Library and Collections.

Ancy-le-Franc, Anet (the palace of Diane de Poitiers), Chenonceaux, Fontainebleau, and the Tuileries were all constructed in this period, and all were surrounded by increasingly elaborate gardens. In the late sixteenth century, Henri III patronized the work of Jean Robin, whose collection of rare flowers was cultivated in the king's garden on the Ile de la Cité.[15] The floral symbolism of the French monarchy, including the fleur-de-lys and the flowers in the royal gardens, were complemented allegorically by the goddess Flora who lent her support, with increasing frequency, to the kings of France by gracing their walls, canvases, and tapestries. At Fontainebleau, for example, the gardens were complemented by Francesco Primaticcio's *Flora, Goddess of Gardens*, a fresco in the Galerie d'Ulysse (executed 1541–1547 and destroyed by 1739), while another Primaticcio Flora (1551–1556) decorated the Salle de Bal. Flora was also incorporated into several tapestries for the château.[16]

Henri IV, the first Bourbon king, continued to support Jean Robin, who had been placed in charge of the gardens at the Louvre, in addition to his duties overseeing the collection on the Ile de la Cité.[17] Pierre Vallet's 1608 *Le Jardin du Roy Tres Chrestien Henry IV Roy de France et de Navare dédié à la Royne*, the earliest French printed florilegium, depicted flowers from the king's garden.[18] The volume was dedicated to Henri IV's new queen, Marie de Medici, to whom he wrote, "You are the flower of all the queens . . . , you are the divine flower of Florence, who unites with the lilies of France by order of Heaven, to produce the flowers of life, the flowers of health, . . . the flowers of peace."[19] Vallet not only compared the queen to a flower, but also singled her out as the flower of all queens, crediting her, the flower of Florence, with bringing the flower of peace to the lily of France. In addition, through the natural association of flowers with fertility, he celebrated the role of the queen as the bearer of heirs to the Bourbon throne. Vallet's floral comparison was the highest of compliments. But more than that, Marie's role as harbinger of peace, key to the alliance between Medici money and Bourbon rule, and the bearer of a future heir, was expressed through floral symbolism in the joining of the two lilies.

Ambroise Dubois repeated the floral metaphor in a portrait of Marie de Medici as Minerva.[20] The portrait, perhaps executed for display at Fontainebleau, depicted a majestic Marie carrying the red lilies of Florence, while a putto or cherub presented her with the white lilies of France. Significantly, she was draped in a robe covered in the French fleur-de-lys. The botanically rendered floral symbols of the two realms, together with the stylized fleur-de-lys, symbolized peace and the alliance of France and Florence through marriage. Floral images were used to portray the queen's political significance through the malleable symbolism of flowers again in a print in which her offspring literally sprouted from lily blossoms that bloomed on her lily "family tree" (figure 29). The caption, reading "I cover by my shadow all of the earth," referred not only to her fertility, but also to the fact that her children sat on the thrones of France and England.[21]

The political use of naturalistically rendered flowers (versus the stylized

FIG. 29.   Anonymous, *Je couvre de mon ombre toute la terre* [*I cover with my shadow all the earth*], seventeenth century. Paris, Bibliothèque Nationale de France, Cabinet des Estampes, cliché G 153900.

fleur-de-lys) in the representation of France was not limited to queens. An engraving of Henri IV by Jacques de Fornazeris depicted the king on horseback, the glorious victor in the religious wars.[22] In the left corner of the engraving, the fleur-de-lys identified the Gallic hero as king of France. The symbol was mirrored in the opposite corner by a naturalistic lily. The botanical lily thus offered to the king its own botanical worthiness or horticultural splendor, reinforcing in the viewer's mind the king's gardens furnished with fine flowers. Meanwhile, the fleur-de-lys signified Henri as the true king of France. In the engraving, as in Dubois's portrait of Marie de Medici, botanically rendered flowers and their symbolic counterparts worked together to glorify the monarch and the state. In addition to flowers and the fleur-de-lys, monarchs continued to favor depictions of the goddess Flora. Ambroise Dubois added to her almost traditional presence at Fontainebleau with a painting of the goddess in a pose strikingly similar to his portrait of Marie de Medici. Pierre Dan wrote in 1642 that the *chambre du roy* at Fontainbleau contained "on the chimney a very beautiful painting representing the goddess Flora,"[23] presumably the painting by Dubois depicted in figure 24.[24] The floral theme begun by Primaticcio in the sixteenth century was thus continued into the seventeenth.

Henri IV knew that flowers, in addition to their symbolic utility, were economically and scientifically valuable as well. The vast numbers of new and exotic species of flowers and plants brought back to Western Europe by explorers were a source of curiosity and, some thought, power. And Henry IV knew the benfits of more effective management of French agricultural and horticultural resources. The first Bourbon king actively supported the work and ideas of Olivier de Serres, whose agricultural handbook *Le Théâtre d'agriculture et mesnage des champs* became a standard text on French estate management, by promoting De Serres's scheme for cultivating mulberry trees as food for silkworms to encourage a French silk industry. Furthermore, in 1597 Jean Robin was given the opportunity to plan a medicinal or botanical garden in Paris. Although his plans were not executed,[25] Robin did continue to collect and cultivate rare species, many of American origin, in his garden and in the royal garden, as well.[26]

Louis XIII, too, adhered to the notion that royal wealth and power could be obtained through botanical knowledge. Pierre Vallet issued an expanded volume of flowers in the king's garden under the title *Le Jardin du Roy Louis XIII*.[27] And in 1626, with the enthusiastic support of Louis XIII, the Jardin royal des plantes was founded as a repository of botanical specimens and a place to study them in hopes of discovering their pharmacological secrets. The garden, to which were transferred many of Robin's plants, flourished and the collection quickly grew in size.[28] In 1636 Guy de La Brosse, the *médecin ordinaire du Roy* and *intendant* of the garden, published a catalogue of its holdings that not only advertised the garden's rarities for other flower enthusiasts, but also celebrated in print the king's accomplishments of a botanical nature. The *Description du Jardin Royal des Plantes Médecinales* described the layout and buildings of the garden and included a list of the different species grown there. La Brosse's description of the parterre facing the main building of the garden suggested that the plants were organized for botanical and pharmacological study. According to La Brosse, "The plants are arranged in such a manner in their quarters and parterres in such symmetry that they are put in order of their species according to their genres, so that anyone knowing a species can certainly say what genre it falls within."[29]

The use of naturalistically rendered lilies as symbols of the king and the kingdom of France too continued into the reign of Louis XIII. In an image of Marie de Medici, the young Louis XIII, and possibly his queen, Anne of Austria, during a "reception held for the queen at the Louvre where their majesties took the open air on the balconies," the lily of France sprouted out of the crowned head of the king, visually linking "the excellence of the celestial and royal fleur de lys."[30] If the king of France was the lily of France, it was the role of his chief minister, Cardinal Richelieu, to protect that lily. The successes of Cardinal Richelieu in leading France through the tumultuous Thirty Years' War were extolled in an early seventeenth-century engraving by Ganière that depicted

FIG. 30.   Jean Ganière, *Embleme sur l'extirpation de l'heresie, et de la rebellion par les soins du Cardinal de Richelieu* [*Emblem on the elimination of heresy, and of rebellion through the care of the Cardinal Richelieu*], seventeenth century. Paris, Bibliothèque Nationale de France, Cabinet des Estampes, cliché C 155952.

Richelieu carefully tweezing caterpillars and other pests from the lily of France while the eagle of the Holy Roman Empire and the lion of Spain were held in check by heavy chains (figure 30). The image specifically referred to Richelieu's victories against the Huguenot forces, most importantly at the seige of La Rochelle that effectively ended the military and political power of the French Protestants, and in the popular rebellions erupted around France mostly over the increasing burden of taxation, both of which disrupted the delicate internal order of France. The accompanying verse explained,

> O how useful his work is to our Repose!
> Through them on all sides have been buried
> These stinking insects, and these villainous reptiles
> Who tarnished the beauty of our LILY.
>   TO conserve the Royal and Divine Flowers,
> (Treasure dear to the French and preciously earned)
> He wearies not at all from tearing away the thorns
> that the hands of faction sow in our fields.[31]

By trampling underfoot the thistles of faction and revolt that threatened to crowd out order while plucking the "stinking insects" and "villainous reptiles" that threatened to literally eat away at the most Christian kingdom, Richelieu ensured a well-managed national parterre in which the lily of France flourished.[32]

Louis XIII's brother Gaston, duc d'Orléans, who established a well-known botanical garden at his château in Blois, furthered royal interest in flowers and botany. His collection of flower paintings, the *vélins* by Daniel Rabel and Nicholas Robert, was bequeathed to Louis XIV, who continued to add to it.[33] The number of paintings of the rare, exotic, and popular plants in the royal gardens reached into the hundreds. Between 1668 and 1674, for example, when the *vélin* collection was being augmented by Monseigneur, Louis de France, dauphin and son of Louis XIV, the Sieurs Villement and Bailly, working under the instruction of Nicholas Robert, produced 590 paintings of which 184 were birds and 406 flowers and plants. Among the flowers preserved on paper were hellebores, gladiolus, asters, iris, lilies, narcissi, heliotropes, anemones, tulips, auriculas, amaranths, violas, cyclamen, peonies, and ranunculi,[34] all highly prized and popular flowers. By the reign of Louis XIV, then, the royal family had already established a tradition around plants and flowers through which botanical flower collections were supported with royal patronage and stylistically and naturalistically rendered flowers were used to symbolize the French monarchy.

FLOWERS IN THE GARDENS OF LOUIS XIV

Louis XIV inherited the *vélins*, the Tuileries and Fontainebleau gardens, the Jardin royal des plantes médicinales, and Versailles from his predecessors, yet it was during his rule that these flowers and gardens blossomed into magnificent and politically potent expressions of his power. On the walls of his palaces could be found naturalistic, though fantastically rich, painted blossoms. The pantheon of gods and goddesses enlisted in the service of the king prominently included Flora, the goddess of flowers. And traditional floral symbolism was combined with floricultural commonplaces in the creation of beautiful, fashionable, and clever devices and metaphors glorifying the king. Garlands of flowers—cultivated, painted, and poetic—were woven into the very structure of the baroque state.

First and foremost, Louis XIV filled his garden parterres with tens of thousands of colorful and fragrant flowers, thereby providing a living, growing foundation upon which the elaborate floral symbolism of royal power could function effectively. The presence of flowers in the French classical garden has been, with the exception of the repetition of several well-known contemporary reports on the profusion of flowers in the gardens of the Trianon palace, largely unexplored. This lack of emphasis on flowers is not difficult to understand. The unifying architectural harmony of the seventeenth-century French formal garden perfected by André le Nôtre was a truly innovative expression of seventeenth-century French aesthetics, and has therefore dominated discussions of the French garden. Further, although the architectural plan of the garden has been easy to reconstruct, representations and descriptions of the flower plantations were few. Seventeenth-century observers of the main park of Versailles failed to describe the flowers in the garden nearly as often as contemporary historians have ignored them. Madeleine de Scudéry's 1669 description of the gardens in *La Promenade de Versailles* mentions flowers only when writing, "This magnificent garden, as well as the others, has vases of flowers on the terraces."[35] Le Nôtre himself, according to the duc de Saint-Simon, remarked that parterres of flowers were superficial ornaments fit only for the enjoyment of nursemaids who looked at gardens only through a château window.[36] Even Louis XIV's directions for touring the gardens of Versailles, written in the king's own hand six times between 1689 and 1705, paid little attention to vegetation and flowers. The king's *Manière de montrer les Jardins de Versailles*, as his instructions have become known, was designed to usher the spectator from vista to vista, grand perspective to grand perspective.[37] The king's instructions took the visitor from the Grand Canal, to the center of the garden to best view the Trianon palace, and then into the Trianon in order to admire the garden from various perspectives. But at no time did Louis XIV ask his visitors to stop to admire his collection of expensive flowers or recommend the savoring of the strong floral aroma, or point out the elaborate parterres.

From such accounts, one might be tempted to doubt the presence of flowers in the gardens of Versailles at all. But the financial records of the king's household demonstrate the extensive use of flowers in the royal parterres. Documents generated by the king's gardeners in charge of furnishing the royal gardens, together with financial records of the king's expenses, reveal unquestionably that immense sums were expended in order to fill the king's gardens with thousands and thousands of flowers.[38] And the examination of the means by which those flowers were used suggests that the flowers growing in the gardens played a vital part in celebrating Louis XIV's accomplishments.

The role played by flowers at Versailles is best understood by considering how floral motifs were incorporated into the decoration of the palaces and where flowers were planted in the grand parc. The growing use of flowers in the gardens and palace of Versailles corresponded to the physical and political expansion of the château in the 1660s and 1670s. Between 1661 and 1664, the interior of Versailles was renovated and the basic outlines of the garden were established. As early as 1664, Louis XIV chose Versailles as the setting of the first of several court entertainments, or fêtes, indicating the important role the palace and its gardens would play in the staging of his reign. Louis's interest in Versailles only increased, and he decided, against the wishes of Colbert who favored the Louvre, to enlarge the palace. Eventually implementing Louis le Vau's "Enveloppe" plan to increase the size of the château while preserving Louis XIII's original structure, the construction created larger state apartments and lodging for the court by enclosing three sides of the hunting lodge, leaving exposed the brick and stone of only the back *cour de marbre* facing away from the gardens. Le Vau's *enveloppe* was completed by 1674; by 1678 Louis XIV established the seat of the French government at Versailles. This required the addition of Mansart's wings to the *enveloppe* and his "Galerie de Glace," or Hall of Mirrors, to the garden façade.[39]

The décor of the newly enlarged interior of the palace included an ostentatious display of flowers, inspired, it has been suggested, by an attempt to recreate the garden fêtes inside.[40] Le Brun's work on the ceiling of the Galerie des Glaces was typical of the ornamental use of painted flowers in Versailles in that many of the putti draped heavy garlands of lush flowers around the historical figures, which were often framed by carved and gilded flowers.[41] Piganiol de la Force recorded the presence of a statue of Flora along with Ceres and Pomona in the chapel of Versailles, and another in the *appartement des bains*.[42] And in the apartment of Monseigneur, or Louis, the grand dauphin, Piganiol de la Force reported, "On the chimney there is the Triumph of Flora, by Poussin."[43] Nicolas Poussin's painting, now in the Louvre, depicts the goddess Flora, drawn in a chariot, leading a triumphal procession of nymphs and lesser gods and goddesses gathering and offering flowers to her. The dauphin was a noted collector of porcelain *objets*, bronze sculptures, and medals[44] and patron of the *vélins* project and may therefore have valued floral images.[45] As a celebration of antiquity and flowers, the work obviously complemented the iconographical and horticultural scheme of Versailles and its gardens.

Freshly cut flowers were also used in the decoration of Versailles. In 1674 Louis Germain, the gardener placed in charge of the *pépinière du Roule* (the royal nursery in Paris) and of feeding the royal swans on the Seine, was paid 1,793 livres for supplying flowers for the Versailles apartments of the king and the queen from 23 July to 23 December of that year.[46] And according to Abraham du Pradel (the pseudonym of Nicolas de Blegny), the wife of le Sieur Billette, a "jardinier du roy," was "bouquetière de Sa Majesté." Pradel added that the couple could ordinarily be found at court,[47] suggesting that their services were regularly required at Versailles.[48] And in September 1690, 24 livres were paid to Mathieu Lambert, "fayancier," for nine "cuvettes" made of porcelain "which he delivered to the chimneys of the apartment of the queen in order to put flowers in them."[49] It is not clear how or where these fresh flowers were displayed in the royal apartments of Versailles, but the art historian Guy Walton has suggested that baskets and vases of cut flowers and forced bulbs were placed on candle stands that were not in use during the day.[50]

A 1673 inventory of royal belongings indicates that artificial flowers, too, complemented the interior décor of Versailles. The *inventaire générale* included an entry for "one hundred seventy-one other bouquets of diverse kinds of flowers from China, made of a single rolled cord of silk."[51] There is no indication of how or where the silk flowers were displayed in the grand palace of Versailles. It is possible, however, that they were arranged in bouquets placed on pedestals, on mantels, or even on the tops of bed canopies where one might expect to find plumes of ostrich feathers.[52]

The flowers decorating the interior of Versailles were echoed in the gardens. Flowers, in accordance with seventeenth-century theory and practice of gardening, were planted in parterres nearest to the château where they could be enjoyed at close proximity and observed from the advantage offered through the windows on upper floors of the royal châteaux. For the main park of Versailles, this meant that flowers were incorporated into the parterres adjacent to the main part of the palace. In a 1714 plan of the garden, the parterre to the left of the center of Le Vau's *enveloppe* labeled "Parterre de fleurs à l'Angloise" suggested that the *broderie* (or elaborate boxwood or herbal scrollwork) of the parterre, the only *broderie* in the main park, featured floral plantations.[53] Flowers were also incorporated into the "parterre du nord," the parterre occupying the position symmetrically opposed to the "parterre de fleurs," as well as in the parterre in front of the fountain of Latona, and in the parterres occupying the ground in the center of the much celebrated Orangerie. Although no detailed description of the method or pattern of flower plantations in these particular parterres has been discovered, the flowers were most likely planted in borders as illustrated in Etienne Allegrain's painting of the "parterre du nord."[54] Commissioned in 1688,[55] the painting suggests that the geometric shapes comprising the parterre were largely composed of grass plots, whereas borders were furnished alternately with topiaries and flowering plants. Within the borders, flowers could be closely admired while their irregular sizes and shapes would not destroy the geometry and symmetry of the overall design.

Records of royal expenditure reveal large numbers of flowering plants destined for the Orangerie and the *bosquets* in the larger park. In addition to the numerous cases of orange trees sent to the Orangerie, in 1686, 153 "lauriers roses" and 112 "grenadiers à fleurs doubles" were planted there.[56] And in 1683, 2,000 tuberoses, 2,000 narcissi, and 1,500 hyacinths were shipped from Toulon to the Orangerie.[57] Flowers were also sometimes incorporated into the *bosquets*, the "rooms" of the garden created by hedges and trees of which the vast majority of the gardens at Versailles consisted. In 1690, for example, 600 hepaticas and 750 primroses were planted in the *salle du conseil* (a "room" in the garden later renamed the Obelisk Grove).[58] In 1691, to the same *bosquet* were added 100 bears' ears or auriculas,[59] and in late 1692 various flowering bulbs.[60] The *salle du bal* was also specially outfitted in 1691 with 100 double *geroflées*, 300 carnations or double pinks (*oeillets*), and 2,150 double white *juliennes*, or sweet rockets.[61]

The proliferation of flowers inside the palace of Versailles and in the gardens of the main park was overshadowed, however, by the literally tens of thousands of flowers that filled the gardens and décor of the smaller palaces built by the king on the periphery of the park of Versailles. As soon as Louis XIV gave Versailles a larger role in the life of the French court and government, the king sought the place and means through which to retreat from its public spaces. The result was a series of smaller auxiliary palaces including the Trianon de Porcelaine, its successor, the Trianon de Marbre, and the château of Marly. It was at these smaller, more exclusive retreats that flowers played their most important role in the staging of the king's glory.

Jean-Marie Apostolidès has suggested that the atmosphere of wonderment and sumptuousness created by the display of rare and luxurious goods in the staging of the royal fêtes, for which the gardens were utilized in the 1660s and 1670s, influenced the decoration of the palaces and gardens of Versailles.[62] Certainly this was true of the palaces of the Trianon and Marly, for there the flowers that had festooned and garlanded the feasts and theaters of the fêtes took center stage, giving the small châteaux and their gardens a distinctive floral character. Indeed, greater numbers of flowers were used in the Trianon and Marly gardens than anywhere else in the royal gardens. In a 1683 shipment of flower bulbs to royal gardens, the 5,500 bulbs for the main park of Versailles and the Orangerie represent only a small fraction of the 65,000 bulbs sent from Toulon to royal gardens. The destination of the remaining 60,000 is telling. Of the 65,000 tuberoses, narcissi, hyacinths, and jonquils imported from southern France in 1683, 18,000 were sent to the Trianon, 15,500 to Clagny,[63] 7,000 to the Tuileries, 3,000 to St. Germain, 6,000 to the *pépinière du Roule*, and 5,500 to the Orangerie (Marly was not yet under construction).[64] Only 5,500 of the 65,000, then, were intended for the main park of Versailles, and those were designated for the Orangerie. Trianon and Clagny, very small, relatively private, and exclusive châteaux appended to Versailles, received the greatest numbers of flowers.

The royal flower expenses recorded in the *Comptes des bâtiments* only support this conclusion. Between 1668 and 1710, payments were made for at least 530 orders for individually named floral species or "diverse flowers."[65] Of these payments, almost 30 percent were for plantations at Trianon, 24 percent for Marly, a little more than 5 percent for the *pépinière du Roule* (the king's nursery in Paris),

1.5 percent for Clagny (for which expenditure declined after 1677 following the fall from favor of Madame de Montespan), and only 4.2 percent was designated for the gardens of Versailles (see Table 1). As many as 30 percent of the flowers were destined simply for "les jardins des Maisons Royales." Their ultimate destination cannot be known. Yet even if payments in this category were biased toward Versailles and away from the many other royal gardens at the Tuileries, Fontainebleau, Saint-Germain, Choisy, Saint-Cyr, as well as Trianon, Marly, the *pépinière du Roule*, and Clagny, it is unlikely that the gardens of the main park of Versailles were the sole recipient of the entire category of flowers for gardens of the "maisons royales." It is probable that the plants were sent to the *pépinières* (nurseries) in Paris and at Trianon, and then distributed among the many royal gardens, of which Versailles was only one.

TABLE 1. Destination of Flowering Plants Purchased, 1668–1710

Gardens of the Royal Households	29.8%
Trianon	29.4%
Marly	23.8%
Pépinière du Roule	5.3%
Versailles	4.2%
Clagny	1.5%
Miscellanous	6.0%
Total	100.0%

Analysis of money expended on flowers as recorded in the *Comptes des bâtiments* reveals only a slightly different picture (see Table 2). Of the 163,529 *livres* spent on flowers from 1668 to 1710,[66] more than 52 percent was spent on flowers for the "jardins des maison royales," 23 percent on Trianon, nearly 14 percent on Marly, and not even 3 percent on Versailles. Although these numbers suggest that it is possible that greater sums of money could have been expended on the main gardens of Versailles, again, once the floral resources were divided among the royal gardens, it is likely that such sums could not compare to the great expenditures directed toward the Trianon and Marly.

TABLE 2. Royal Expenditure on Flowering Plants, 1668–1710

Gardens of the Royal Households	86,454 livres	52.9%
Trianon	37,945 livres	23.2%
Marly	22,540 livres	13.8%
Pépinière du Roule	6,336 livres	3.9%
Versailles	4,284 livres	2.6%
St.-Cyr	747 livres	0.5%
Clagny	356 livres	0.2%
Miscellaneous	4,867 livres	2.9%
Total	163,529 livres	100.0%

The smaller châteaux appended to Versailles—Trianon, Clagny (in the early years at Versailles), and Marly (in the later years)—and their proportionally smaller gardens were more suitable for the display of flowers. After all, unless flowers were displayed within the confines of the *bosquets* in the main park of Versailles, or in the parterres nearest the palace (as they were), the exquisite and expensive blossoms would have been lost in the grand scale of the expansive gardens. In the smaller gardens, they could be featured; and so large numbers of a wide variety of flowering plants found their way to Trianon and Marly where they not only felled the parterres with color, but also colored the reputation of the pleasure palaces.

If Versailles was public, political architecture, then the Trianon de Porcelaine seemed its converse. Begun in 1670, the small palace was constructed at the end of the perpendicular extension to the Grand Canal. The Trianon was actually five separate pavilions, each covered in blue and white tiles intended to resemble expensive and fashionable Chinese pottery (figure 31). The pavilions were situated in a formal garden. A surviving plan of the retreat suggests that the Trianon pavilions were used for small court entertainments and dinners. Probably drafted to aid in the planning of a dinner party, each room was labeled according to the food or the people served there, including a room for soup, one for entrées and hors d'oeuvres, one for fruit, another for the dessert table, and, finally, one for the table of the princes and the seigneurs. The two smaller pavilions were

Veüe et perspectiue de Trianon de Versailles

FIG. 31. Nicolas de Poilly, "Veue et perspective du Trianon de Versailles [View and perspective of the Trianon at Versailles]." From Adam Perelle, *Chasteaux and Gardens in France*, plate 79. Washington, D.C., National Gallery of Art, 1981.69.10, Gift of Robert H. Thayer.

given over to sweets and preserves.[67] Another plan of the Trianon de Porcelaine identified a room in the central and largest pavilion as the "chambre des Amours."[68] Historians have connected the title to Louis XIV's apparent inspiration for constructing the palace—his new *maîtresse en titre*, (Françoise) Athénais de Rochechouart, marquise de Montespan, who had replaced Louise de la Vallière in the affections of the king. Even after Montespan lost favor with the king and was replaced by Françoise d'Aubigné, the marquise de Maintenon, and the Trianon de Porcelaine was replaced with the larger Trianon de Marbre, the Trianon continued to be identified with the king's mistresses and love of women. Attendance at Trianon entertainments was by invitation only, and those invitations were issued most frequently to the king's favorite women at court. To the great frustration of the duc de Saint-Simon, the invitations were not extended to husbands.[69]

The Trianon was popularly known to seventeenth-century courtiers as the "Pavillon de Flore"[70] and the "palais du Flore." The epithets were appropriate in that, as described in Chapter 1, the king's mistresses, who reigned at the Trianon, were often represented as Flora, the courtesan. But "Pavillon de Flore" also made reference to the fact that Flora, the goddess, aided by the gardeners of Louis XIV, had transformed the Trianon gardens into an idyllic paradise reminiscent of the atmosphere staged temporarily in the royal fêtes where previously unimaginable displays of flowers appeared as if by magic.[71] For the Trianon served, more than anywhere else at Versailles, as a showcase for the royal floral collections and displays of floral wealth. The palace and the gardens were constructed and filled with flowers so quickly that even the jaded courtiers were astonished. André Félibien wrote, "This palace was regarded first, by all the world, as an enchantment; because even though it had not been started at the end of winter it was found done at springtime, as if it came out of the earth with the flowers in the gardens that accompany it."[72]

The gardens of the Trianon were not unusual in their plan, but were unique in the degree to which they featured flowers. In accordance with the conventions of seventeenth-century flower gardening, flowers filled parterres of *pièces coupées*, or shaped beds enclosed by boxwood, that were situated near the pavilions (figure 32).[73] A lower parterre similarly incorporated borders of orange trees and flowers. On the left of the central axis nearest the canal, terraced beds flanked the steps leading to the water, greeting the visitors with an overwhelming display of fragrant flowers. Indeed, so strongly perfumed were the Trianon gardens that Saint-Simon remarked, "All of the compartments in each of the parterres were changed every day, and I have seen the king and the entire court driven out of the garden, although it is vast and built in terraces overlooking the Canal, because the scent of tuberose hung so heavy in the air."[74] Fragrant flowers were particularly important at the Trianon de Porcelaine. In 1671 a pavilion known as the "Cabinet des Parfums" was constructed in the gardens of the Trianon. Situated behind and to the right of the Trianon, the colonnaded Cabinet des

FIG. 32. Plan of the Trianon de Porcelaine, c. 1680. Paris, Bibliothèque Nationale de France, Cabinet des Estampes, cliché H 186630.

Parfums is visible in figure 31. The fragrant flowers in the parterres were supplemented with flower-filled pots and vases: the *Comptes des bâtimens* reports that in August 1673, the widow Siffait, "chaudronnier," was paid 2620 livres for "les vases et godets pour le cabinet des parfums." In the Cabinet des Parfums, courtiers could find respite from the sun and, more importantly, experience the fragrances emitted by the king's flowers, perhaps to be convinced of the king's power by the overwhelming scents.[75] After all, as the "subtle enchantress"[76] of the other senses, the sense of smell could leave one vulnerable to temptation, seduction, or persuasion. Michel de Montaigne, in his essay "On Smells," and Jacques Ferrand, author of a seventeenth-century treatise on lovesickness, both reported that Alexander the Great emitted an irresistible fragrance in his sweat.[77] The nectar of the Trianon flowers allowed Louis XIV to encourage by proxy the powers of persuasion in his garden of living perfumes.

To achieve a garden so rich in flowers and perfumes was a spectacular feat, requiring wealth to purchase the exotic plants and the knowledge and technology required to bring them to flower. And the gardens of the Trianon were indeed spectacular. Placed under the direction of Michel Le Bouteux, who designed the parterres and oversaw their furnishing with flowers and orange trees, the state of the flowers was of constant concern to Jean Baptiste Colbert and the king. The minister made a special note in his *Ordres et règlements pour les bâtiments de Versailles* on 24 October 1674 in which he wrote: "Visit Trianon often, see that Le Bouteaux has flowers for the king during all of winter, that he has a number of boys who are obliged to him whom he can press to achieve all the works for the winter. He must render to me an account each week of the flowers he has. Visit Trianon often and keep watch that all of the repairs are done well."[78] That Colbert himself oversaw the plantation of flowers in the gardens of the Trianon points to their importance to his patron, the king.

The flower expenses revealed by the royal account books make it difficult to believe that there was ever a shortage of flowers or that the gardens were poorly stocked. Although yearly floral expenditures were generally not reported separately for the Trianon before 1686,[79] the flower purchases for the "jardins des maisons royales" include thousands of jasmines, tuberoses, and flowering bulbs that were used extensively at the Trianon de Porcelaine. In March 1672, for example, 10,000 tuberoses were purchased, with another 3,200 bought in 1674 and 7,000 narcissi in 1675.[80] Early flower purchases designated specifically for the Trianon included hellebores, jasmines, tuberoses, anemones, tulips, and other flowering bulbs.[81] The Trianon was also the recipient of great numbers of orange trees, and Le Bouteux devised a means of planting the trees in the ground and covering them on the spot to shield them from frost in winter, rather than transporting them across the park to the Orangerie.[82] Flowers were also carefully protected in the Trianon gardens. Plants were wintered under layers of manure and straw and covered with *cloche de verre* to encourage their growth and protect them from frost.[83] In addition to his ingenious protection for the orange trees,

Le Bouteux also employed a "bedding out" method of planting in the gardens. That is, flowers were raised to maturity in pots and then planted en masse in the parterres so that the display was always full but could be changed quickly and easily. Most important, however, it meant that flowers could be planted out of season.

By the 1680s, however, Louis XIV sought a grander, more substantial stage on which to parade his floral wealth. He therefore tore down the porcelain retreat and replaced it with a larger, permanent structure with accommodations for the king and guests to spend the night. The result was the pink marble palace called the Trianon de Marbre. The majority of the construction of the château took place in 1687 by which time Françoise d'Aubigny, Madame de Maintenon, had replaced Madame de Montespan as the king's favorite. As the small palace of the Trianon de Porcelaine gave way to the Trianon de Marbre, so the intimate gardens were accordingly enlarged, in part under the direction of André Le Nôtre.[84] Le Nôtre added to the park the Bosquet des Sources, an odd wooded garden of irregularly placed springs and streams anticipating the highly structured "spontaneity" of the eighteenth-century English landscape garden. The gardens were also expanded to the north with the addition of two parterres and the *jardin du roi*, a private parterre constructed next to the king's apartments (figure 33).[85]

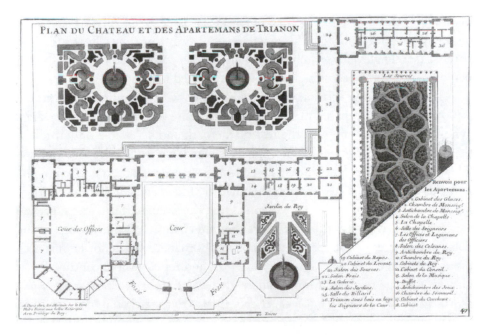

FIG. 33.   "Plan du château et des apartemens de Trianon [Plan of the château and apartments of Trianon]." From Gilles de Mortain, *Les Plans, profils, et elevations, des ville, et château de Versailles, avec les bosquets, et fontaines*, Paris: Chez Demortain, 1716, plate 47. Image courtesy of author. Photograph by John Blazejewski, Index of Christian Art, Princeton University.

Yet the gardens maintained their primary identity as flower gardens and their notoriety for extravagant displays of expensive, aromatic flowers. Piganiol de la Force wrote of the gardens of Trianon in 1701: "the outdoors of this enchanted palace, . . . after the gardens of Versailles & of Marly, nothing in the world approaches the arrangement and the beauty of those of Trianon. In the flowering season everything is perfumed, and one breathes in there only violets, oranges, and jasmines."[86] With the expansion of the gardens at Trianon came a dramatic increase in the purchase of flowers and plants. Between 1686 and 1690, an astonishing 36,639 livres were spent on furnishing the garden with thousands of flowers.[87] Included in the elaborate plantations were wallflowers, pinks, primroses, hyacinths, jasmines, jonquils, juliennes, narcissi, ranunculi, cyclamen, tulips, tuberoses, campanelles, hepaticas, anemones, crown imperials, iris, lilacs, roses, lilies, immortelles, marguerites, and peonies. Purchases in 1686 included 18,850 ranunculi, 10,000 *tulipes bosuelles*,[88] 915 double peonies, 1,200 jonquils, 850 double narcissi, 8,200 hyacinths, 2,000 orange lilies, 1,765 pots of tuberoses, 4,000 cyclamen, and 20,050 double jonquils, in addition to 99,850 assorted flowering bulbs imported from Toulon.[89] In the following years, 1,685 pasque flowers, 1,000 auriculas, 3,976 primroses, 14,000 narcissi, 1,900 white *tulipes bosuelles*, 1,216 "rare" hyacinths, 1,400 iris, 1,200 tulips, 21,300 ranunculi, and 13,700 single late-flowering narcissi were among the larger flower acquisitions intended for the Trianon gardens.[90] The large numbers of flowers were incorporated into densely planted borders. The planting plan of 1693 (discussed in Chapter 4) called for 96,000 plants and bulbs to be arranged in parallel rows of tulips, hyacinths, and narcissi (spring-flowering bulbs), alternating with rows of summer-flowering perennials arranged according to height,[91] depicted in figure 20.

If visitors to the Trianon were overwhelmed with the number and aroma of flowers in the gardens, particular wonder and praise were reserved for the king's own garden, walled off from the rest of the park and accessible only through the rooms of the king and his new mistress, Madame de Maintenon, and visible in figure 33. Le Nôtre himself described the garden in an explication of the new palace and gardens requested by his architect friend and admirer from Stockholm, Nicolas Tessin. Le Nôtre explained that the small parterre was a "private garden, which is always full of flowers that are changed all the seasons in the pots, and one sees neither dead leaves nor shrubs that are not in flower; it is necessary to change as many as one million pots and replace them continually."[92] G. L. Le Rouge reported to the readers of his *Curiositez de Paris, de Versailles, de Marly, de Vincennes, de S. Cloud, et des environs* that one could "observe from this apartment the small royal parterre with a basin in the middle: this beautiful place, which is filled with the rarest and most beautiful flowers in all the seasons, persuades winter not to approach."[93]

Only the most rare flowers were purchased for the king's private garden. Among the flower acquisitions intended for the "jardin du Roy à Trianon" were anemones, double wallflowers, cyclamens, and 26,290 hyacinths purchased in 1688 and 1689.⁹⁴ The hyacinths, specified as "bleue turquin," "bremales hatives," and "tres rares," illustrate that the king was interested in acquiring different species of hyacinths, anticipating (or perhaps encouraging) their immense popularity to come in the eighteenth century.⁹⁵ Louis XIV's most sumptuous display of flowers, then, was reserved for his own "private" garden. In the confines of the king's parterre, Louis XIV as flower collector, as *curieux fleuriste*, reigned supreme, his power over nature unquestioned.

The paradiselike flower-filled gardens of the Trianon gave it a far different character from that of the larger park of Versailles. Although architecturally similar to those of Versailles, the gardens were unique in that they were bursting with colorful, fragrant, expensive, and modish flowers. They celebrated Louis XIV's accomplishments in the floral domain and served as a showcase of rare blossoms and floral wealth, a sanctuary of living perfumes and a colorfully enameled earth. The gardens at the Trianon established the French king as the author of the finest collection of flowers, the owner of the most sumptuous flower gardens, inhabitant of the most fragrant and colorful lover's retreat.

The Trianon captured the imagination of fashionable French circles. The *Mercure Galant* reported in 1673: "Nearly all the great seigneurs who have country homes are having [Trianons] built in their park[,] and private individuals [are building Trianons] in their gardens; the bourgeois have dressed their hovels as the Trianon, or at least some *cabinet* or some turret."⁹⁶ But it ultimately failed to hold the attention of the ever-restless Louis XIV. By 1679 work was begun on the château of Marly northwest of Versailles. Set in a narrow U-shaped valley, this retreat from Versailles was built on a larger scale than Trianon and was intended to accommodate larger, though still intimate and exclusive, parties. Invited guests were lodged in twelve small pavilions constructed on either side of the central axis extending from the château. The traveler Martin Lister described Marly in his late seventeenth-century account of Paris and Versailles: "The two side fronts of the house [Marly] have in prospect large alleys cut through the woods. On each side of the valley, close under the woods, are ranged in a line, six square pavilions, or smaller houses, of the very same form and beauty as the palace itself. They stand at equal distances from each other, not exceeding five hundred paces; those on the right being for gentlemen, and those on the other side for ladies of quality, whom the king appoints weekly to wait upon him, and enjoy the pleasure of this retirement, as it may well be called, from court."⁹⁷

Like Trianon, Marly was a setting for royal entertainments of a more informal nature. Also like Trianon, the lavish gardens of Marly were furnished with expensive flowers. The park at Marly consisted primarily of a central pool and fountain with two long terraces running the length of the pavilions along the central axis. The upper terrace was eventually planted with parallel rows of elms, but the lower terrace consisted of flower beds edged in boxwood for which no expense was spared.⁹⁸ Contemporary descriptions of the flower beds of Marly suggest that they were indeed lushly planted. In a letter to her aunt Sophie, electress of Hanover,

Liselotte von der Pfalz (Elisabeth Charlotte, duchesse d'Orléans) remarked: "I am writing to Your Grace here by my window, looking out on lovely beds of narcissus, tulips, and imperial crowns; the beds are enclosed by two avenues and a horseshoe of white, red, and brown marble. In the middle is a wide stone staircase and on the two sides are also steps decorated with statues and white marble flower pots."[99] Martin Lister added to his account of Marly that, "In the front of these pavilions, and between them, are the finest alleys and walks imaginable, with fountains, and all the decorations of treillage and flowers. Such a display of no vulgar tulips, in beds a thousand paces long, every where disposed over this vast garden, and in their full beauty, was a most surprising scene."[100] The brief, though highly complimentary, descriptions of Marly's flowers offered by the duchesse d'Orléans and Martin Lister are supplemented by the extant planting plan for the Marly beds (see figures 21 and 22). The Marly plan, like that of the Trianon border, consisted of alternating rows of flowering bulbs and perennials and annuals and was designed to be colorful "en tout sesons."[101] That such lavish plans for the Marly flower beds were actually carried out is suggested by royal expense accounts that indicate that from 1690 to 1710 flowers for Marly amounted to nearly 15 percent of royal flower purchases from 1668 to 1710.[102] Among the more significant flower acquisitions in one year (1690) are 5,500 narcissi *non pareilles*, 1,400 narcissi *d'Angleterre*, 107,650 double narcissi *non pareille et d'Angleterre*, 34,300 double white narcissi, 1,100 carnations (*oeillets d'Espagne*), 2,754 double *juliennes*, 2,200 single *juliennes*, 1,300 orange hyacinths, and 1,075 irises.[103]

Flower expenses for Marly remained high through the 1690s, and by the turn of the century the king decided that the gardens at Marly should include a collection of exotic and rare flowers as well. To that end, in 1700 1,500 livres were spent on the purchase of "rare flower bulbs,"[104] and Jean Loitron, a *jardinier fleuriste* long in the employ of the king, was charged with "the maintenance, planting, and cultivation of rare and other flowers in the new garden of Marly."[105] This was followed in 1703 through 1706 with a yearly expenditure of 2,000 livres for additional rare flowers.[106] Flowers were specially imported from the Americas to create what one historian has called a veritable "musée des fleurs."[107] Though supported by the king's enthusiasm and purse, however, the garden languished in poor growing conditions at the chosen site.[108] Louis XIV thereafter turned his attention to assembling a collection of carp that were kept in special pools constructed in the gardens.

But at Marly, as at Trianon, flowers were key to the projection of the king's image as curious florist,[109] and despite the king's interest in fish, Marly remained a primary showplace for Louis XIV's interest in flowers both real and representational. Built in the gardens of Marly was the Bois de la Princesse, a forest of pathways and alleys that opened into several *cabinets*, or small rooms in the garden. One of the best known was the Cabinet des fleurs, intriguingly named to play on the connections between collection (in this case of flowers) and the *cabinet* (either the room or the piece of furniture) where one's collection might be lodged or displayed.[110] The Cabinet des fleurs consisted of a small temple with Ionic columns decorated with flowers painted by Jean-Baptiste Belin de Fontenay.[111] Other fountains and pools in the garden were also ornamented with Fontenay's work.[112] With painted and planted flowers alike incorporated into the creation of the whole desired effect, the gardens of Marly were thus very colorful and very floral. The colors and themes in the gardens were reflected in the interiors of Marly, which were similarly colorful. While Charles Le Brun intended to decorate them with an allegorical scheme similar to Versailles, Louis XIV preferred the gods and goddesses of nature such as Flora, Aurora, Pomona, and the Earth. By 1690 even those schemes were abandoned and the classical personifications of the garden were replaced with cupids, fruits, and flowers,[113] allowing the flowers, fruits (and fish) to testify themselves to the greatness of the king.

FLORAL MERCANTILISM

The British traveler Martin Lister concluded his description of Marly at the end of the seventeenth century writing, "I could not refrain from saying to the Duke of Villeroi, who was pleased to accompany me much in this walk, that surely all the gardens of France had contributed to furnish this profusion of flowers."[114] His compliment could hardly have been more true. The provision of flowers for Versailles, and, indeed, all of the royal gardens, required not only great amounts of money to acquire specimens from all over the country and world, but also the organization of flower cultivation on a grand scale. The flowers favored by the king and his gardeners for use in the royal gardens were expensive and not easily found in the numbers needed to furnish the lushly planted parterres. It was thus necessary for Louis XIV and Colbert not only to seek flowers from wherever they were available, but also to set about creating a supply structure to assure that the king's gardens would be kept in blossom at all times.

Flowers for the royal gardens were acquired from numerous *fleuristes*, gardeners, and traders in Paris and all over France. In 1670 a member of the Trumel family of gardeners was reimbursed for flowers purchased in Toulon, Lyon, and Marseille,[115] and Isaac Blandin bought for the royal gardens 7,560 jonquils from Caen.[116] In the same year orange trees, jasmines, and tuberoses were brought from Lyon to the *pépinière du Roule*.[117] During the following years, orange trees for the Trianon were acquired in Orléans, and additional oranges for the royal gardens were found in Berny.[118] Octavian Henry bought 10,000 tuberoses from Avignon.[119] In 1686, 4,000 cyclamen and lilies were gathered by Pierre Trutry for the Trianon in Dauphine, Auvergne, and Savoye,[120] and M. Chauvelin, the intendant of Picardy and Artois, forwarded 1,034 hepaticas, 352 *jassées*, 15 pansies, and 150 *campanelles* to the king in 1687.[121] As many as 16,300 ranunculi and 50 double anemones were imported from Normandy in 1688.[122]

To gather rare flowers for his collection, the king dispatched his *fleuristes* and *curieux*, armed with the king's purse, farther afield to search for specimens. In 1673 a Sieur Subleau, *trésorier général des galères*, was reimbursed for money spent "to purchase books, flowers, and other curiosities from the Levant for the service of His Majesty."[123] Subleau was again paid in 1675 for the purchase of flowers and animals.[124] American specimens were sought for the collections in the Jardin du roi, the botanical garden in Paris. A "bill for a box of plants and seeds for the garden of the king" sent on board the ship *La Marie* from Guadeloupe to the marquis de Villacerf (the *surintendant*) in 1698 listed twenty-five different plants including white and red lilies, *choux de Madere*, *calbasses de Guinée*, *medecinier de l'amerique*, musque, and acacia.[125] Native French specimens were also sought for the king's gardens. Pierre Truitté was paid in 1689 for "flowering plants that he was going to search for on the mountains of Dauphiné and Piedmont for the garden of Trianon."[126]

But this haphazard means of acquisition was not enough to keep the gardens full. In typical Colbertian fashion, the first minister and the king set in place a system of nurseries that became the largest suppliers of flowers, flowering shrubs, and trees to the royal gardens. Louis XIV's first step came in 1669 with the enlargement and unification of a series of small nurseries or *pépinières* in Paris known as the *pépinière du Roule*. Located in the faubourg Saint-Honoré where Claude Mollet, gardener to Henri IV and Louis XIII, and his son André had established their own nurseries and gardens,[127] the royal nursery became an impressive garden in its own right. Martin Lister reported:

> At my return to Paris, I was shewn the pipinerie [sic], or royal nursery of plants in the Fauxbourgh St. Honoire, by M. Morley, who is master of it, and one of the ushers of the king's bed-chamber. . . . This ground, inclosed with high walls is extremely large, as it ought to be for the supply of the king's gardens; several acres were planted with pines, cypresses, &c. and there were vast beds of bulbous roots and the like. I found but little difficulty in crediting his assertion, that in the space of four years he had sent to Marli, eighteen millions of tulips and other bulbous flowers. He also told me that in furnishing the Trianon (a peculiar house of pleasure) with its parterres, at the extremity of the gardens of Versailles, with flowerpots every fourteen days during the season, required not less than thirty-two [thousand] pots from this nursery.[128]

Lister's account of the *pépinière* illustrates the immensity of this horticultural operation. Yearly accounts of plants requested and provided for royal gardens, together with orders and inquiries from other noble garden owners, support Lister's description. The gardeners of the *pépinière* gathered seeds, bulbs, and young trees that they raised to maturity. Once bulbs could support flowers, or the fruit trees bear fruit, they were dispatched to the numerous royal gardens including Versailles, the Trianon, Marly, Clagny, the Tuileries, and Fontainebleau.

The *pépinière* also served as a centralized gathering and distribution center for flowers, trees, and shrubs for the royal gardens by "contracting out" for the needed supply of plants. For example, in 1684 a Sieur Cottereau presented to Ballon, the royal gardener in charge of the nursery, a statement of the flowers he could provide for the royal gardens (see Appendix A). In the document, an exceptionally rich source because of the detail with which he described different species, Cottereau filled seven pages with numbers of plants required or requested by the royal gardeners together with his prices. For the Trianon, he promised he could produce 100 double white anemones, 100 double white ranunculi, 100 double white ranunculi flecked with pink and violet, 100 blue and yellow aromatic ranunculi, 1,000 ranunculi "*du bagadet* on which the flower is larger than on the others," and 1,000 "giant Roman variegated" ranunculi.[129] Cottereau claimed to be able to obtain 400 "couteront" and 400 "pastout bleüe" from Flanders and Holland, and 5,000 white hyacinths, 5,000 Roman hyacinths, 100 double white hyacinths, 20,000 tuberoses, 4,000 single jonquils, and 10,000 double narcisses all from Provence.[130] Among the variety of other plants listed are 200 narcissi "du Japon couleur de chair," 200 narcissi "du Japon couleur de feu," 1,500 narcissi "[c]alices rouges jaunes odorant," 1,000 iris, 1,000 purple fritillaries, 1,000 white fritillaries, 1,000 black striped fritillaries, daylilies in yellow, red, and violet, martagons, 12 crown imperials, 50 yellow cyclamen, 12 blue fragrant cyclamen "de bonne odeur," 100 white dog-tooth violets, 500 red hellebores, hepaticas, immortelles, pinks, as well as orange and lemon trees, and palms.[131]

By the eighteenth century, the *pépinière* had become so successful that it even entertained requests for shrubs, flowering trees, and flowers from nobility residing in and around Paris, although most requests were refused as the royal gardens took priority over all others, as did providing flowers and shrubs for smaller gardens administered by the *Maison du roi* such as Bellevüe and L'Hôtel des Ambassadeurs.[132] Yet in supplying plant material for the primary royal gardens, the nursery system was so effective that additional (though smaller) royal nurseries were constructed behind the Trianon de Marbre and at Marly. The extent of the nurseries is revealed in a surviving plan that includes, in addition to several plots, a "jardin des fleurs" (figure 34). By 1705 a four-story structure called the Chateau neuf de Trianon was erected in the expanded nursery plots at the Trianon. The size of the building, together with the distribution of its space, illustrates the sophistication and size of the Trianon nursery operation. Two adjoining rooms on each of the four floors were given over to the "Inspecteur des Bastiments," and two rooms on the top two floors were occupied by the "Controlleur des Bastiments," but the majority of the building served the gardens and gardeners.[133] Just as gardeners and *fontaniers*, or workers in charge of maintaining the many fountains of Versailles, were given lodging in the building, so were many plants, bulbs, and seeds. The basement level was dominated by a large orangery. On the *rez-de-chaussée* could be found a spacious *serre*, or greenhouse,[134] for orange trees and flowers. The first floor, too, contained a heated room, this one especially for seeds and rare bulbs. And the majority of the top floor consisted of a *serre* complete with skylights for bulbs and seeds. The *serre* kept seeds and bulbs

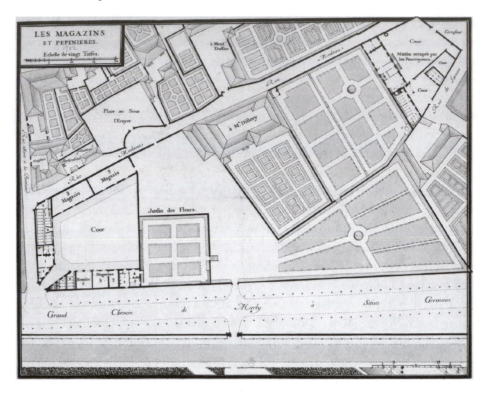

FIG. 34.   *Les Magazins et pépinières* [*Warehouses and nurseries*], 1702. Paris, Bibliothèque Nationale de France, Cabinet des Estampes, cliché H 186270.

warm and dry, and allowed for the forcing of flowers out of season, as well as the wintering over of exotic or delicate flowers and orange trees.

The most enterprising creation of Colbert and Louis XIV, however, was the purchase in 1681 and 1682 of a piece of land in Toulon on the French Mediterranean coast for 11,540 livres[135] for "raising flowering bulbs that must be furnished every year for the gardens of the royal household."[136] During the reign of Louis XIV, Toulon served as an important royal naval base. The royal presence meant that communication networks and personal connections between the king's administration and Toulon were already in place which, together with the city's proximity to southern (therefore climatically milder) flower growing markets, made it an ideal location for a royal acquisition center. In addition, royal gardeners in the south of France could more effectively gather the tuberoses, jasmines, narcissi, and hyacinths that were usually acquired from southern sources. The garden in Toulon would thus serve the king by purchasing small bulbs and seeds and raising them to maturity, after which they would be shipped to royal gardens in Paris and Versailles. Another 8,192 livres was spent on the construction of the garden, walls to enclose it, sheds to hold supplies, and a house for the gardener.[137] An extant plan of the garden indicates that the house was built at the head of the garden, with an axis extending from the center of the house to the end of the garden (see plate 7). On either side of the axis were three large square plots, each quartered and filled with parallel rows for planting. Gardening sheds were placed by the corners of the gardens at the top near the house.[138]

By September 1683, De Vauvré, *Intendant de la Marine*, had established projections for the number of bulbs he anticipated being able to send to the royal gardens (figure 35). De Vauvré estimated that 65,000 bulbs could be provided for Trianon, Clagny, the orangery at Versailles, Tuilleries, St. Germain, and the *pépinière du Roule*.[139] Among the bulbs were to be 30,000 tuberoses, 20,000 *narcisses de Constantinople*, 13,000 hyacinths, and 2,000 jonquils. De Vauvré expected that 800 livres would be needed for the day laborers to prepare the ground, plant the bulbs, and cultivate them; 400 livres for the inspector appointed to oversee the plantations and the packing of the bulbs for shipment; 300 livres for the wages of a gardener who would be sent from Paris; and 700 livres to pay for the packing and transport of the bulbs from Toulon to Lyon.[140]

It was also necessary for the gardeners at Toulon to acquire immature bulbs and seeds that would "increase" over a period of years before shipment to the royal gardens. For this they turned to local merchants and importers. An expense report from 1688 shows that in that year 69 livres 10 sols were paid to Sieur Jean Michel, a French merchant living in Tunis, for 6,000 narcisses; 266 livres 6 sols were paid to diverse private individuals for bulbs which they supplied. Aubert, "Consul de la Nation françoise," was reimbursed for 1,000 tuberose bulbs and 6,000 Roman hyacinths.[141] The king took advantage of the geographical location of Toulon and bought flowers directly from southern sources.

Though it is not clear when the garden began to fulfill its function of sending bulbs to the royal gardens, by no later than 1688 bulbs were being packed and shipped from Toulon to Lyon. André Hermitte, an apparently reliable mule driver, was employed repeatedly during the 1680s and 1690s to transport cases of bulbs to Lyon where they were handed over to Monsieur Du Bois, "commissaire des guerres," who sent them on to Paris.[142]

By 1691 the Toulon garden was shipping thousands of mature bulbs north to the royal gardens. Of a shipment received on 16 August 1691, 6,000 *Narcis de Constantinoples*, 3,000 *jacinthes Romaines*, 2,000 *jacinthes breumales*, 3,000 *jonquilles simples*, and 3,000 *totus albus* were sent to Trianon, while 2,000 *Narcis de Constantinoples*, 1,000 *Jacinthes Romaines*, 2,000 *jacinthes blanches*, and 2,000 *Jonquilles simples* were dispatched to the *pépinière du Roule* in Paris.[143] In February 1692, a shipment of tuberoses was dispatched to Paris, providing 4,000 for the *pépinière du Roule*, 5,000 to Trianon, 2,000 to the Tuilleries, 2,000 to the *orangerie* at Versailles, 2,000 to Fontainebleau, and 3,000 for the *orangerie du Roy au Roule*.[144] In August of the same year, another 20,000 flowering bulbs were divided between Trianon and the royal nursery: the Trianon received 4,500 narcissi, 2,000 *totus albus*, 3,000 Roman hyacinths, 2,500 *hiacinthes brumales*, and 3,000 single jonquils, while the *pépinière du Roule* was sent 1,500 narcissi, 1,000

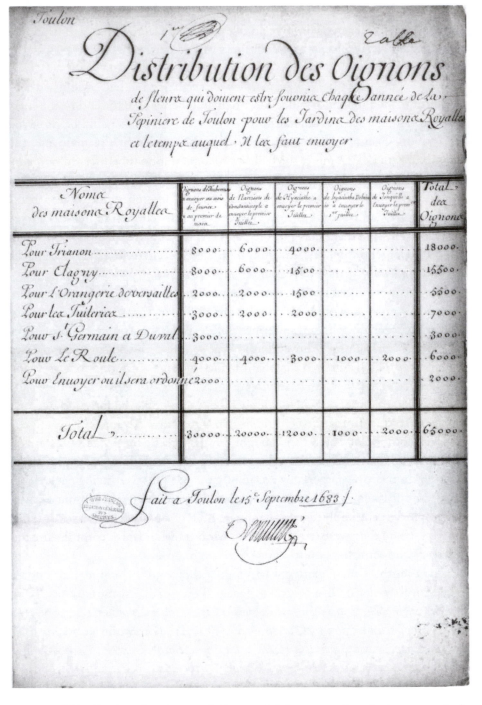

FIG. 35. "Distributions des oignons de fleurs qui doivent estre fournir chaque année de la Pepiniere de Toulon pour les Jardins des maisons Royalles [Distribution of the flowering bulbs which should be furnished each year from the Nursery of Toulon for the Gardens of the Royal Households], 1683. Document conserved in Paris, Centre Historique des Archives Nationales, O[1]2102[1]. Cliché atelier photographique du Centre Historique des Archives Nationales.

totus albus, 1,000 Roman hyacinths, 500 *hiacinthes brumales*, and 1,000 single jonquils.[145] In 1692, then, 38,000 bulbs had made their way from Toulon to the royal gardens; De Vauvré projected that in 1693, only a slightly smaller number could be supplied.[146] Shipments made in July of that year met his estimates; the 21,000 bulbs including 8,000 narcissi, 2,000 *totus albus*, 7,000 hyacinths, and 4,000 jonquils were again divided between Trianon and the *pépinière du Roule*.[147]

Royal gardeners in Paris and at Versailles kept a close watch over the operations of the Toulon garden and expressed great concern for the quality of the bulbs that were being sent. In August 1693, an accounting of the bulbs received at Trianon was made in which the gardener noted that of the 5,500 *narcisses de Constantinople* received, 3,100 were too small to carry flowers that year. Of 1,200 *totus albus*, 600 were too small, maintained the royal gardener, as were 1,250 of 3,750 hyacinths and 700 of 3,000 jonquils.[148] A similar list was drawn up for the bulbs sent to the *pépinière du Roule* in which 800 of 2,000 narcissi, 600 of 2,000 hyacinths, 150 of 500 *totus albus*, and 500 of 700 jonquils were judged too immature to bear flowers.[149] The royal gardener Jacques Robert dispatched a letter on 12 August 1693 to Toulon, informing De Vauvré that the gardener in charge of raising the bulbs was no longer to send those which could not carry flowers. Robert wrote that in the future cases of immature bulbs would not be counted or paid for. As a final note, he added that he did not know whether or not they had received word that Monsieur [Gilles] Ballon, *directeur des plants des parcs et avenues*, had passed away and that his post had been given to a Monsieur Morlay [Morlet], but that in the future business would be conducted through him.[150]

A more formal letter followed on 7 September 1693 from the *surintendant* (by this time Edouard Colbert, marquis de Villacerf)[151] to De Vauvré in Toulon. The superintendent wrote, "I am obliged to inform you, Monsieur, that of the narcissus of Constantinople, Roman hyacinth, and jonquil bulbs, amounting in all to 21 thousand, which were sent from Toulon last July 10, most did not bear [flowers] because they are only *cayeux* which cannot flower."[152] Colbert continued, imploring De Vauvré to be sure that the Toulon gardener complied with his request, as the cost of transporting the immature bulbs to Paris was greater than their value. As a final warning, he reminded De Vauvré, "By the establishment of this garden according to the memorandum that you sent to Monsieur de Louvois [on] 15 September 1683[,] you would furnish every year 65,000 bulbs [whereas] you furnished this year only 24,000 including 3,000 tuberoses, and the expense of the garden is the same."[153]

Despite the complaints about the immature bulbs, the relationship endured and the garden continued to supply flowering bulbs for the royal gardens to the apparent satisfaction of the king's gardeners. No correspondence similar to the complaints of 1693 followed. Shipments continued, and in one 1694 shipment, the Trianon and the *pépinière du Roule* received 3,000 jonquils, 3,000 hyacinths, 3,000 narcissi, and 1,000 *totus albus*.[154] In 1697 De Vauvré sent 1,000 *totus albus*, 3,000 narcissi, 1,500 hyacinths, 1,000 *brumalles*, 2,000 jonquils, and 3,000 tuberoses. The contract with Toulon was renewed in 1697 and again in 1701,[155] although the history of the garden after that date is vague.

The *pépinière* in Toulon had served the needs of Louis XIV well, providing him with a steady and large supply of some of the most important plants in the royal gardens. The Toulon garden's bulbs were of a more ephemeral nature than the woven works of Gobelin or the medals struck in honor of the king, but they were as necessary to the king's program of glory and splendor as the tapestries. The reputation of the Trianon as the "palais du Flore," the image of the king as flower connoisseur and collector, depended on the success of the garden at Toulon and the *pépinière du Roule*. That Colbert turned his mercantilistic principles of managing the national economy to the king's flower beds only emphasized how important flowers were to the glorification of his patron. In the same way that the minister fostered the development of luxury manufactures and industrial enterprises to raise the quality and value of French products and reduce French dependence on imports, Colbert brought order to French floriculture. Colbert and his successor simply created their own supply system to fulfill the king's floral needs and fully exploit their own resources. It is even possible that the king's gardeners made use of the orange blossoms from the Orangerie. Abraham du Pradel's 1692 *Le Livre commode contenant les adresses de la ville de Paris et le trésor des almanachs pour l'année bissextile* directed Parisian shoppers looking for floral perfumes to, among other vendors, the Orangerie on the rue de l'Arbre sec at the sign bearing the royal device where they could purchase the finest "eau de Fleurs d'Oranges."[156] It is not clear whether or not the Orangerie selling perfumes and orange flower water was a royal store, but the *Comptes des bâtimens* reports that in 1686 the widow Jaquin was paid 137 livres 10 sols for ladders used in cutting orange blossoms from the royal orange trees, suggesting that the royal gardeners used the flowers. They could have been displayed in bouquets or distilled into waters and perfumes[157] in a mercantilistic effort to exploit every product of the king's garden.

The establishment of the royal nurseries demonstrates the significance attached by the king to the material demonstration of his floral power, taste, and wealth. Attempts have been made to analyze the role of royal and court consumption in encouraging the development of French manufacturing and consumer habits. Chandra Mukerji has argued that the formal gardens at Versailles embodied "nature . . . as an expression of a culture of mercantile capitalism," whose influence on French, and indeed European, culture stemmed from the public's access to them.[158] Certainly, the nurseries should be interpreted as the floricultural manifestation of the king's mercantilistic economy. The suggestion that the king's mercantilistic flowers shaped French tastes is more problematic given that it was the culture of flowers defined by the curious florists that led to their inclusion in the gardens of the king. Nonetheless, the sophisticated royal nursery system that acquired bulbs, plants, and seeds from sources all over France, together with the royal garden at Toulon that purchased cheap, immature bulbs from Mediterranean sources, points to a highly developed royal floricultural trade fully integrated with the trade networks of French florists. Thus while the French commercial flower trade was unable to fill the demands of the king, French gardeners and florists were incorporated into the royal system on a variety of levels, that could not but have encouraged its development. Though not all of the mercantile flower schemes survived Louis XIV, the king and his ministers put in place royal nurseries, gardeners, botanists, growers, and merchants in order to make the famed gardens as remarkable for their flowers and plant material as for their ingenious architecture.

FLOWERS AND THE "HISTOIRE DU ROI"

While the royal gardeners worked to glorify the king as a curious florist, it was left to royal iconographers and panegyrists to exploit the living specimens for their symbolic potential. In 1671, one future panegyrist, Jean Donneau de Visé, published his dramatic work *Les Amours du soleil*. Performed at the Théâtre du Marais in Paris, the "tragedie en machine" took as its subject the doomed love affair involving Apollo, Clytie, and Leucothoe that was described by Ovid in his *Metamorphoses* and later depicted in paint by Charles de la Fosse for display in the Trianon de Marbre (see plate 8).[159] In the myth, Clytie was transformed into the sunflower who would forever follow Apollo's movements across the sky. In the prologue to Donneau de Visé's play, Apollo addressed the nine muses in their mountain retreat, informing them that he was leaving the mountain to see his beloved Leucothoe. The muses expressed anger and disappointment, but Apollo quieted them by arguing that love and glory required their services. Apollo's words were described in the text: "This God made them know that they could not be abandoned, that their glory grows everyday, and that the Gods should give to France a great king who should make things astonishing for them, who will make the Sciences and the Fine Arts flower again, & who will compensate all those who merit it. He invites them to give all their care to working for his glory, to place him in advance in the Temple of Memory, and place him above all of the demi-Gods."[160] The muses responded by promising their continued service, agreeing to "paint him so well in their works, that the portrait of him will never be lost."[161] Donneau de Visé thus articulated the role of the arts and sciences in glorifying the king of France, who not coincidentally was portrayed as Apollo, the Sun King. In the course of *Les Amours du soleil*, the complicity of the muses, Art, and Nature were demonstrated, for the fifth act took place in the gardens of the king of Persia where "for the embellishment of which Art and Nature seem to have exhausted their marvels." The garden, according to the descriptions provided by Donneau de Visé, included "vases full of flowers in confusion," and an arcade, the herms of which carried on their heads "baskets of gold full of an infinite number of different flowers whose vivacity rejoices the view."[162]

Donneau de Visé's work described the strategy, already being enacted by Louis XIV, of using the arts and sciences to glorify the king and his reign. Louis

XIV's flowers and flower gardens, like those of the king of Persia in Donneau de Visé's tragedy, were the result of the collaboration of art, science, and nature. They displayed the king's ability to create the greatest example of floral collection, cultivation, and display in early modern Europe. Featured in Louis XIV's lavish court celebrations, more lavish building projects, and even in his mercantile programs, flowers constituted an important part of the Sun King's complex iconography. In the Versailles fêtes staged in the early years of his personal reign, flowers contributed to the creation of a luxurious, fanciful, even magical, setting. In later years, flowers ornamented the architectural simplicity of Le Nôtre's gardens at Versailles throughout the year in illustrating the king's mastery of the forces of nature. By building a horticultural network to furnish the enchanting gardens with thousands upon thousands of flowers, the king demonstrated the importance of flowers not only for the achievement of the gardens, but also for the image of the king projected in those gardens. In short, flowers had acquired political meaning. But flowers, the very symbols of the ephemeral, required the assistance of Louis XIV's own seventeenth-century French muses to ensure the flower king's place in the "Temple de Mémoire."

The spectacular display of floral wealth in the royal gardens, made possible by the mercantile organization of the flower trade, was in itself memorable. Because many of the early modern elites whom the king no doubt hoped to convince of his place in history could also be counted among the ranks of the flower connoisseurs and cultivators, they knew the immensity of the king's accomplishments. Indeed, curious florists cited the king's flowers in defense of their own. F.B., Sieur de L'Ecluse asserted that the "invincible Louis returns honor to flowers in his gardens of Versailles, & of his other palaces,"[163] and both N. Valnay and the author of *La Culture des fleurs* included the king's flowers as evidence for the stature of French floriculture in their flower gardening manuals.[164]

The floricultural excesses of the king were dutifully noted in published descriptions of the royal gardens and celebrations produced for those who could not visit in person. Society journals such as the *Mercure Galant*, founded in 1672 by none other than Jean Donneau de Visé, also reported the floral riches of the king's gardens in the context of describing events at court. The periodical devoted considerable space in 1686, for example, to an account of the ambassador of Siam's famous visit to Versailles. In the course of his stay, the ambassador and his entourage were escorted to the gardens at Trianon where, according to the *Mercure Galant*, he saw a flower-filled "galante Maison" that was "destined for conserving there all sorts of flowers as much in Winter as in Summer, the Air there assists Nature so well that it is full in all Seasons." The ambassador was taken to the Cabinet des Parfums: "The Cabinet des Parfums pleased them extremely, because they love strong odors, & they admire the manner of perfuming with flowers."[165] That the ambassador, who hailed from the exotic and legendarily floral and fragrant lands of the East, was impressed by the French king's flowers was a high compliment, indeed.

But Louis XIV was not content to leave the writing of the history of his reign, even its floricultural history, to chance reporting. Rather, he and Colbert, his chief minister and "surintendant des bâtiments," harnessed the creative talents and energy of French writers, poets, composers, painters, designers, and scholars in drafting a carefully constructed image of his rule. Colbert not only took advantage of the Académie française (encouraged by Richelieu during the reign of Louis XIII and given formal royal protection in 1672) and the Académie royale de peintre et de sculpture (founded in 1648), but he also established in 1661 the Académie de danse, the Académie des sciences in 1666, and the Académie royale de musique in 1669. In 1663 Colbert formed the Académie des inscriptions et belles-lettres, or the "petite académie," as it became known, an executive committee of sorts that met twice weekly at Colbert's home in order to direct projects intended specifically to glorify the king. Initially the group consisted of Jean Chapelain, François Charpentier, the abbé de Cassagnes, and the abbé de Bourzeis; Charles Perrault soon joined them. Among the academy's accomplishments can be counted the supervision of André Félibien's descriptions of the royal fêtes and the palace of Versailles, the direction of the *Médailles sur les principaux événements du règne de Louis le Grand*, or the history of the king as recorded by medals,[166] the oversight of decorative schemes for tapestries to be woven at the Manufactures Royale des Gobelins (under the direction of Charles Le Brun), and the coordination of the iconographical schemes for royal fêtes, ballets, and operas. Indeed, when Philippe Quinault was charged with the production of *livrets* for Lully's "tragédie en musique," he was instructed to work directly with the "petite académie."[167]

The material successes of the king's flower gardeners made possible the deployment of numerous symbolic expressions of the king's power. And in the thorough and careful coordination of the royal iconography constructing the "histoire du roi,"[168] as the academicians described their task, they did not fail to take advantage of the floral splendor displayed in the royal gardens. In the gardens of both Marly and the Trianon, Louis XIV maintained the most spectacular displays of flowers that early modern Europe had yet seen, and he did so during the years when flowers were at the zenith of their popularity and fashionability in elite circles. The anemones, tulips, ranunculi, hyacinths, jasmines, tuberoses, and orange blossoms coveted since the early years of the seventeenth century were cultivated at Versailles in tremendous numbers, brought to bloom and perfume for the king all months of the year. There the king was the premier curious florist, the ultimate collector and cultivator of flowers whose taste, reason, and curiosity were demonstrated in the garden.

The king did not neglect the more serious aspects of floriculture: under his direction, the Académie royale des sciences undertook the publication of a history of plants in the 1670s to commemorate his interest in floriculture, horticulture, and botany. Nicolas Robert was employed to produce the illustrations for the work which were transformed into fine engravings by Abraham Bosse and Louis de Châtillon. Dionys Dodart, a doctor of medicine at the Université de Paris and member of the academy of sciences, produced in 1676 the *Mémoires pour servir à l'histoire des plantes* to accompany the images which were not printed until 1701.[169] The king also continued to add to the royal collection of the *vélins* left to him by his uncle, Gaston, duc d'Orléans.

But the display of literally thousands of live flowers, continually in bloom, immediately replaced when their petals faded, provided a grand demonstration of the king's ability to transform nature into art, to perform in the "theater of the goddess of flowers." The staging of the king's floricultural magic, as we have seen, took place chiefly in the smaller gardens of Trianon and Marly (and occasionally in the *bosquets* of Versailles). The effect of the delicate blossoms would have been lost in the grand scale of Versailles. But more importantly, flowers may have been especially included at Trianon and Marly to complement the purpose and iconographical programs of each of the exclusive palaces. That exclusivity is vital for understanding the incorporation of flowers into their gardens. Trianon and Marly have been interpreted as the "private" counterparts to the "public" of Versailles,[170] palaces where the king was free from much of the ritual and etiquette of court life. However, to the courtier hoping for a sign of favor in the form of an invitation to Trianon, the small palace offered not freedom from court, but distinction from other courtiers not so honored with an invitation. The Trianon and Marly were not so much "private" as exclusive. As such, their gardens were, as one might expect, furnished with the most exclusive, rare, and special flowers. The flowers thus contributed to the luxury and exquisiteness of the Trianon and Marly settings while helping to create the idea of a magical prosperity. That they were inaccessible to most (while tantalizingly described in contemporary accounts) only enhanced the reputation of the flowers, the palaces, and the king.

Marly and Trianon, both seemingly private, certainly exclusive, were like the *cabinets* of French *hôtels* and palaces. The *cabinet*, as the gentleman's retreat, his innermost room in the succession of salons that constituted his *appartement*, was also the repository for his most treasured possessions, the most coveted collections.[171] As both the room or piece of furniture housing a collection and the man's intellectual sanctuary, the *cabinet* was related in both senses to the garden. *Cabinets* were also, in fact, constructed in the gardens, where collecting artifacts of natural history and the cultivation of collectible plants merged.[172] An anonymous watercolor portrait of Madame de Montespan, the king's mistress who reigned at the Trianon de Porcelaine, interprets the small palace as a *cabinet* for the king (see plate 9).[173] In the painting believed to have been executed to adorn a fan, Montespan reclines on a quintessentially baroque canopied daybed where she is tended by her ladies-in-waiting and a bevy of cupids in a room identified as a part of the Trianon de Porcelaine by the blue and white décor on the windows and shutters.[174] The cupids hold up a gilded mirror for the mistress to see herself in, they dip silver ewers into a massive gilded tub, they fan her with ostrich feathers, entertain her with music played on a collection of musical instruments and verses sung from open song books, sprinkle her with flowers, drape sumptuously woven textiles (rugs and tapestries) across the room, and pull her jewels and silk dresses from a gilded trunk. It is likely that this image was a playful representation of the five senses—the music for hearing, the flowers, dog, and incense burners for smell, the mirrors for sight, the fabrics for touch, and fruits for taste. But it was also a catalogue of curious, fashionable, and expensive goods valued in the seventeenth century. The flowers, birds, mirrors, gilded objets d'arts, musical instruments, and the king's mistress identify the Trianon as a *cabinet*, though more sensual than scholarly, where the king's collection of flowers, blue and white pottery, luxury goods, and women were lodged. Just as seventeenth-century French *fleuristes* praised flowers as the "jewels of the earth," so the king's flowers were the jewels of his gardens. As such, the king's floral treasures belonged in the exquisite and exclusive gardens of the king's inner sanctum where his taste and reason could be displayed in a manner not unlike, though grander in scale, that of other curious.

The flowers in the gardens of Trianon and Marly also offered the king and his panegyrists the opportunity to capitalize on the massive exhibition of flowers by drawing simultaneously upon the botanical aspects of floriculture and the more traditional symbolism of flowers. Flowers allowed the king to evoke and demonstrate literally ideas and images of abundance and fertility. Flowers were, after all, the very symbols of fertility.[175] Requiring peace and prosperity to flourish, the flowers in the royal parterres allowed the king to celebrate his military successes and subsequent (though increasingly infrequent) peace treaties. The blossoms also provided pleasing evidence that Louis XIV's reign marked the beginning of a return to a perpetual springtime in which the earth was forever fertile and productive, or even the return of Virgil's prophesied second golden age. The idea that a monarch's successes could usher in a period of seemingly endless springtime or prosperity that characterized the golden age was not new in Renaissance or early modern representations of monarchy. The most fully developed use could be found in the sixteenth century across the English Channel where Elizabeth I of England was portrayed as Astraea, the just virgin queen whose rule brought the perpetual springtime of the golden age.[176] In France, the reign of the quintessential Renaissance king François I, too, inspired comparisons of his rule to the golden age.[177] And the peace and order imposed by Henri IV after the devastating religious wars of the second half of the sixteenth century in France were celebrated as the return to the golden age of Astraea.[178] Yet no monarch but Louis XIV had the power and resources to produce the physical attributes of the perpetual springtime—to maintain sumptuous gardens like those at the Trianon able to resist the inevitable succession of the seasons and inevitable decay—and therefore be compared to a golden age.

Flowers were a key attribute of eternal spring and the golden era. Ovid described the idyllic golden age as "a season of everlasting spring, when peaceful zephyrs, with their warm breath, caressed the flowers that sprang up without having been planted."[179] And Virgil's prophetic *Fourth Eclogue* described a flower-filled second golden age.[180] Seventeenth-century French engraved allegories of the four ages of civilization prominently featured flowers in their representations of the golden age. Michel de Marolles depicted it as a young woman tending a beehive wearing a garland and crown of flowers. The caption for the print explained, "During the Golden Age, the age dear to heaven,// Flora is eternally crowned with roses."[181] Nicolas Bonnart, too, included flowers in his *L'Aage d'or*, which was explicated in the caption accompanying the image: "We represent [the Golden Age] under the emblem of a pretty and young girl simply dressed, caressing a lamb on which she has placed a garland of flowers, and she plays with a child to mark the innocence of the customs of this age, the beehive represents the sweetness, and the union; the olive branch is the symbol of peace which then reigned."[182] Louis XIV's reign had been hailed at his "miraculous" birth as the long-awaited return to the golden age.[183] In the gardens of Marly and Trianon, where plantations of spring-flowering bulbs and summer-flowering perennials and annuals were coordinated to ensure their flowering "en tout sesons," Louis could demonstrate that the prophesy had been fulfilled.[184]

The flowers in the garden offered living proof of the prosperity of France under Louis's rule, and the king's panegyrists, in fêtes, ballets, operas, paintings, and devices, eagerly exploited the symbolic meanings of those flowers in the iconographical celebration of the king. The fêtes of 1664, 1668, and 1674 took advantage of the gardens of Versailles, for which the *bosquets* were adorned with lush garlands and bouquets of flowers. The rich floral display contributed to the creation of an idyllic and sumptuous atmosphere. But flowers were also incorporated into the program of the fêtes themselves. The 1664 *Plaisirs de l'île enchantée*, held officially in honor of the new queen, Marie-Thérèse, and the queen mother, Anne of Austria, was generally acknowledged to have been a celebration of the love the young king enjoyed for his mistress, Louise de la Vallière. Accordingly, the fête consisted of lighthearted and gallant entertainments, including a *course de bagues* or equestrian tournament, exquisite dinners, the performance of Molière's *La Princesse d'Elide* (a pastoral with music and ballet), a performance of the *Ballet du Palais d'Alcine*, fireworks, mock naval battles, and "autres fêtes galantes et magnifiques."[185]

To create the setting appropriate for such celebrations, the gardens were especially decorated with an "infinite number of flowers" and orange trees.[186] Flowers were also incorporated into costumes worn during the pageantry. The opening day of the fête began with a procession during which Apollo was escorted by the "Four Ages." The Golden Age wore gilded armor which "was also covered in diverse flowers which made one of the principal ornaments of this happy age."[187] Following the *course de bagues*, the four seasons and the twelve signs of the zodiac danced. *Le Printemps*, represented by Mademoiselle Du Parc, wore a green costume that was embroidered with silver and "fleurs au naturel."[188] The allegory of Spring was also accompanied by twelve attendants who "covered with flowers, carried, as the gardeners, baskets painted in green and silver, garnished in a great number of porcelains, so full of preserves and other delicious things of the season."[189] In honoring the queen and her king, Spring invoked flowers:

> Among all the flowers newly enclosed
>> With which my gardens are embellished
> Scorning the jasmines, the carnations, and the roses,
> To pay my tribute I have chosen the lily,
> That in your first years you have so cherished.
> Louis makes them shine in their beds at dawn;
> All the charmed universe respects them and fears them,
> But their reign is more sweet and more powerful still,
>> When they shine on your complexion.[190]

Spring thus paid homage to the lily of France, the fleur de lys and the queen. Over the course of the fête, a celebration of love, flowers were invoked in the evocation of springtime, the eternal springtime of the golden age described by Ovid in the *Metamorphoses*, the return of which was famously prophesied by Virgil in his *Eclogues*.[191]

The fête was so successful that another was held in 1668 to honor the victorious return of the king from the Franche-Comté and the signing of the peace treaty at Aix-la-Chapelle, that ended the War of Devolution fought to contest the Spanish inheritance of Brabant and Flanders by the terms of the Treaty of the Pyrenees. The fête of 1668, too, was held in the gardens and utilized the *bosquets* for ballrooms, theaters, and dining rooms. As in the *divertissement* of 1664, the gardens were specially decorated with flowers.[192] According to royal accounts, 900 livres were paid to Michel Le Bouteux, royal flower gardener, for "the festoons, bouquets, and floral ornaments that he furnished for the decoration of the rooms of the feast, ball, and *collation*."[193] The account of the fête by André Félibien, printed in order to publicize and commemorate the lavish event, described with greater detail the use of flowers. Staged on 18 July in the gardens of Versailles, the celebration included a *collation*, or light meal, in the *bosquet de l'Etoile*, the performance of Molière's *Georges Dandin*, a *souper* in the *bassin de Flore*, a ballet, and a show of fireworks. For the *collation*, the *bosquet* was outfitted with architecturally arranged greenery accented with vases "remplie de fleurs."[194] Baskets and vases filled with flowers decorated the theater constructed for the performance of *Georges Dandin*.[195] And the *souper* was also complemented by a great number of flowers. According to Félibien's account, "On the large cornice . . . were arranged seventy-four porcelain vases, full of diverse flowers," while "on this cornice and tower that forms the opening of the dome hang many festoons all of flowers."[196] The table held eight pyramids of flowers.[197] The *salle de bal* was decorated for the ballet with "grands festons de fleurs" and two sculptures representing Flora and Pomona,[198] all at a cost of 900 livres.[199]

Flowers were incorporated in even greater numbers into the decoration of the gardens for the fête of 1674 given by the king to the court in honor of his second victory in the Franche-Comté as a part of Louis XIV's war against the Netherlands. During the first day of the fête, which included a *collation*, the performance of Philippe Quinault's "tragédie en musique" *Alceste* (the music for which was composed by Jean Baptiste Lully), and a *souper*, guests were treated to the sight of porcelain pots filled with "an infinity of diverse flowers . . . as well as flowers arranged in such a manner which makes many appear among the trees to which they were attached," and "festoons of flowers."[200] The theater, constructed in the *cour de marbre*, was similarly covered with flowers, and "the marble fountain that is in the middle of this court was surrounded by candelabras and vases full of flowers and in the same basin six large porcelain vases filled with flowers."[201] Félibien remarked, "In this way the architecture of the building is lit by so many lights and the ingenious disposition of so many chandeliers and candelabras mixed among the trees and flowers making a rich ornament to this theater."[202]

On the second day of the fête, courtiers were treated to a concert at the Trianon palace where, according to Félibien, "one always finds springtime," and "one always sees there special beauties and the air one breathes there is perfumed with the most fragrant flowers" (figure 36). To the already sumptuous setting were added porcelain vases dripping with blossoms and porticoes hung with large floral festoons, all accented with pots of flowers.[203] Following the concert, the party continued in the *salle du Conseil* where "the island was bordered by seventy-three pedestal tables of flowers carrying crystal candelabras," and columns were garnished with flowers. In addition, one hundred small vases filled with oranges and tuberoses were arranged on the cornices.[204] The *collation* held on the fourth day included garlands of flowers, flowers on pedestals, a cornucopia filled with fruits and flowers, and even a large orange tree loaded with flowers.[205] The evening ended with a *souper* on the *cour de marbre* on which was constructed a large table around the fountain which was decorated with festoons of orange blossoms, tuberoses, and carnations.[206] On the fifth day, garlands of flowers connected seventeen pyramids of flowers and fruits at the *collation*. Meanwhile, the orangery was decorated with porcelain vases filled with diverse flowers for the performance of Jean Racine's *Tragédie d'Iphigénie*. From there the court adjourned to the Grand Canal for a fireworks display incorporating ornamental symbols designed by Charles Le Brun and featuring especially the fleur-de-lys of the French monarchy.[207]

In each of the major fêtes staged by Louis XIV and his architects of splendor, whether held in the name of a king in love or in tribute to his military successes, attempts were made to transform the gardens of Versailles into a sumptuous, fertile, magical, and even exotic, pastoral wonderland. The fête allowed not only for the expression of an ideal space calculated to appeal to the taste of the courtiers for the pastoral,[208] but also for the very conspicuous display of the creation of that ideal world by the king himself. Historians have long sought to interpret the political and cultural role of these celebrations,[209] sug-

FIG. 36. François Chauveau, *Seconde Journée, Concerts de musique, sous une feüillée faite en forme de salon, ornée de fleurs, dans le Jardin de Trianon* [*Second Day, Concert, under a canopy of leaves made in the form of a salon, adorned with flowers, in the garden of the Trianon*]. From André Félibien, *Les divertissemens de Versailles*, Paris, Imprimerie royale, 1676. Image courtesy of author. Photograph by John Blazejewski, Index of Christian Art, Princeton University.

gesting that the series of ballets, operas, collations, suppers, and fireworks displays allowed the monarch to display in one concentrated series of entertainments the breadth of his power. Through a virtually encyclopedic program of events, the courtiers could experience firsthand the glory of the king.[210] Dining under a display of fireworks, the courtiers witnessed the sufficiently great wealth of the king expended on ephemeral pyrotechnics and feasts. Treated to elaborately staged ballets and operas composed for the occasion by the leading French poets, dramatists, and composers, those in attendance observed, and indeed took part in, the flowering of the fine arts in France under the patronage of their king. And the sheer grandiosity of the consumption of foods, costumes, and the temporary but extensive stage sets demonstrated the abundance and prosperity of the king and his reign.[211] The fêtes, then, were a conscientious display of the king's ability to muster the forces and goods necessary to manufacture such luxury.[212] The impact of such conspicuous consumption was heightened by the nature of the material goods consumed. After all, the fantastical setting created in the gardens was constructed of luxury goods and fashioned according to current tastes biased toward the rare and the exotic.[213] Flowers, simultaneously fashionable, expensive, rare, and exotic, were thus eminently suited for use in the fête.

As the symbols of emphemerality,[214] flowers used in such great numbers to orna-ment the entertainments were the ultimate example of royal consumption.

The incorporation of flowers into the scheme of the fêtes offered a display of conspicuous consumption (Félibien's published descriptions of the flowers rendered them even more conspicuous) as well as the obvious aesthetic pleas-ure afforded to the eyes and nose.[215] But just as important was the ability of flow-ers to contribute to another unifying concept of the gardens of Versailles and the *divertissements*: the king's ability to control nature. The official published description of the 1664 fête asserted as much. The king's writers explained that Versailles was "a château that one can call an enchanted palace, so many adjust-ments of art assisted well the cares that nature took to render it perfect."[216] Nature was improved, continued the text, through the imposition of "symmetry, the riches of its furniture, the beauty of its promenades and the infinite number of its flow-ers, as well as its oranges, [that] render this place worthy of its singular rarity."[217] Clearly, the manipulation of nature by the king was an important message to be communicated through the fêtes. Modern scholars of ancien régime France have noted the centrality of nature in these court entertainments. Of the 1668 Versailles celebration, Roger Chartier explained that it "was to be a multiple cel-ebration of Nature, obliterating the customary frontiers between nature and arti-fice." "The entire fête," he continued, "was to be a rustic amusement in which natural beauty would be subjected to the rules of art and decorative artifice would appear to be the work of Nature itself."[218] Within this context, flowers became only more important to the king's programmatic celebrations. In addition to pro-viding proof of the king's expenditure, and pleasure through their bright col-ors and sweet scents, flowers demonstrated through their presence and cultivation the king's mastery of nature in creating the golden age.

The idea of a flower-filled golden age or eternal springtime was similarly evoked in other royal entertainments, including ballets in the 1660s and operas of the 1670s and 1680s. Spring and also the goddess Flora were frequent char-acters in the productions. In Isaac de Benserade's *Ballet des Saisons*, performed in 1661 at Fontainebleau, the four seasons danced, one after the other, until the king, portraying eternal springtime, returned bringing glory, prosperity, and pleas-ure.[219] On 13 April 1669 at the Tuileries palace, Louis XIV performed publicly for the last time in the *Balet Royal de Flore*, also by Benserade, in which he played the role of the Sun to the duchesse de Sully's Flora (who, the court knew, had replaced Madame, Henrietta of England in the role).[220] In the course of the bal-let, Jupiter and Destiny sang to the king and Madame, who represented Flora, on the uses of flowers:

> Young Lily, who seems not to blossom,
>> You have two brilliant jobs;
> You crown love on the beautiful complexion of Flora:
>> And on the brow of the most powerful of Kings,

> Who is followed by Victory,
> You crown Glory.[221]

Flowers and Flora crowned the victories and glory of the king, who, as the Sun, had the power to bring flowers to life.

The "tragédie ballet" *Psyché* prominently featured Flora, too. First performed in 1671, the work was the result of the collaboration of the composer and director of the Académie royale de musique Jean-Baptiste Lully, Molière, Corneille, and Philippe Quinault. In the prologue, l'Amour, Vertumus, Palemon, nymphs, and divinities of the earth and water accompanied Flora as she invited Venus to grace the earth with her presence:

> It is no longer the time of War;
> The most powerful of Kings
> > Interrupts his exploits
> To give Peace to the Earth.
> Descend, Mother of Love,
> Come give to us beautiful days.[222]

Flora was thus a harbinger of political and military spring, signifying peace imposed by the young king.

The prologue to *Atys*, another "tragédie en musique" by Quinault and Lully, also featured Flora. Performed for the first time at Saint-Germain-en-Laye on 10 January 1676 (and again in Paris in April 1676), the opera recounted a tragic tale of honor and love. *Atys* opened with a prologue set in the palace of Time who lamented that it was in vain that he attempted to preserve in his memory the glory of past heroes. Their deeds, he maintained, paled in comparison to the present exploits of Louis XIV. Flora, accompanied by a troupe of zephyrs and flower-bearing nymphs, entered only to be confronted by Time, who questioned, perhaps in reference to Louis XIV's flower nurseries that provided the court with flowering plants year round, why she brought flowers to bloom before winter had departed. Flora responded that it was necessary to grace the king, whom she hoped to please, with flowers in the winter because springtime (not the idyllic eternal springtime) brought the return of Bellona and thus the return of the king to the battlefield. Flora and Time sang together:

> The pleasures introduced beauty to his eyes,
> As soon as [the king] sees Bellona, he leaves all for her;
> > Nothing can stop him
> > When Glory calls.[223]

In *Atys*, even the beautiful productions of the goddess of flowers could not prevent the king from his valiant pursuit of military glory.

Flowers also crowned the victors of war. In 1689 the Trianon palace itself served as the setting for the performance of the ballet *Le Palais de Flore* staged in honor of the glorious return of the dauphin from battle. In the ballet, the *livret* for which was written by Abbé Genest, Fame, Minerva, and Bellona, who had accompanied the dauphin to battle, returned to the Trianon where Flora was making garlands of flowers with which to crown the victors. Glory, "Plaisirs de la Chasse," Diana, and Joy celebrated as well. The setting was described in the introduction to the performance:

> The Palace of Flora & eternal Springtime, which until now have been only in the imagination of Poets, are [now] veritably found here. The Theater of the Trianon knows no more superb decoration than the Trianon itself. The splendor of the marbles and the beauties of the architecture first attach the sight on this grand façade called the peristyle; & the pleasure is intensified by the openings of the arcades, between several rows of columns, one discovers these Fountains, these Gardens, & these Parterres always filled with all sorts of flowers. One cannot remember that it is the middle of Winter, or one believes that he has been transported all of a sudden to another Climate, when one sees the delicious objects which denote so agreeably the abode of Flora.[224]

The ballet began with naiads and sylvan nymphs celebrating the dauphin's triumph. They were followed by Renommée (Renown or Fame), who "had published" the victories of the dauphin, and Minerva and Bellona who accompanied him to the war. All had come to the Trianon palace "to repose in this beautiful place."[225] Glory, Joy, and Pleasure also arrived to honor the dauphin, while Diana invited all to partake in the pleasures of the hunt. In the second entry, Flora, played by Françoise Marie de Bourbon, Mademoiselle de Blois (the legitimized daughter of Louis XIV and his mistress Madame de Montespan and student of Delalande whose portrait was painted in her Flora costume, as seen in plate 4),[226] called for the flowers in her gardens to join her in honoring the returning warrior. A nymph and a zephyr issued her command:

> At the sight of Flora
> You hasten to blossom.
> Come in your pretty hands,
> Fragrant harvest,
> Smiling riches,
> Roses, Jasmines,
> Anemones, Amaranths,
> Kind flowers come to adorn
> The victorious head that she wants to crown.[227]

The flowers in the Trianon garden were thus woven into a balletic crown for the dauphin. The floral celebration was then reinforced by a nymph who added:

Everything flourishes on our banks
 Our gardens are always green.
 Never have we felt
 The outrage of gloomy winter.
 Our Springtime lasts always.
 We have only beautiful days.[228]

The flowers both crowned the dauphin and symbolized the eternal springtime enjoyed by Bourbon France that was demonstrated in the gardens of the Trianon.

While the Trianon had served literally and figuratively as the setting for *Le Palais de Flore*, other staged performances decorated their sets to duplicate or resemble the Trianon. For the 22 March 1688 performance of the opera *Zéphire et Flore*, the *livret* for which was written by Du Boullay and the music by Jean-Louis or Louis de Lully (Jean-Baptiste Lully's son and successor), the prologue took place in a theater that "represents the new Trianon palace, with its gardens."[229] In the course of the prologue, a zephyr labeled the gardens the "most beautiful place in his charming empire."[230] When the opera began, the theater was transformed into an exotic country in Assyria on the banks of the Euphrates where "the brilliance and abundance of flowers that are sown there can be taken easily for the most agreeable place in the empire of Flora."[231] The opera recounted the relationship between Zephyr and Flora, as well as the floral metamorphoses of Ovid's verses, including Clytie's transformation into the sunflower. In the final act of the work, Borée (the north wind) was finally convinced to relinquish Flora to her true love Zephyr, the gentle west wind, thus allowing for their reunion. The Sun addressed the characters, foretelling the beauty awaiting the earth:

 Leave in peace the tender Lovers,
Jupiter by my cares wants to end their torment.
  See rising on the ruins
  Of your terrifying stay
  A brilliant and pompous Palace
  That Heaven intends for his honor.[232]

At that moment the theater was transformed into a "magnificent Palace all adorned with flowers," which was decorated with gold vases filled with "the illustrious flowers in which many heros of [Ovid's] Fable have been metamorphosed, as Adonis [the anemone], Narcissus, & above all Clytie who comes from changing into a marigold [or sunflower]."[233] The allegorical flowers of antiquity were thus represented on stage by the live flowers of the king's gardens.

If the Ovidian theatrical themes drew inspiration from the Trianon gardens, the interior decoration of the Grand Trianon did so even more. The décor was completed in the late seventeenth century with a large number of paint-

ings commissioned especially for the Trianon, including seventy-eight mythological paintings, fifty-one landscapes, a mere five religious works, and twenty-
eight flower paintings.[234] Inside the Trianon, blossoms moved out of the
garlands and floral frames they had formed on the ceilings of Versailles and into
the center of the canvas. Despite the academy's derision of still life painting as
being less sophisticated than history paintings, the palace was decorated with
trompe l'oeil flower paintings by Jean-Baptiste Belin de Fontenay and Antoine
Monnoyer, the most important flower painters in France. Of the twenty-eight
flower paintings in the Trianon, six hung in the *appartement du Roi*, six in the
rooms of Madame de Maintenon and the Salon des Sources, and another six
in the Cabinet du Conseil. Stylistically, all of the paintings were executed in
the grand style of late seventeenth-century flower paintings: exquisite, rare, and
colorful blossoms dramatically arranged in gold, lapis, or marble vases and on
pedestals.[235]

Of the mythological subjects, most of which were executed by François
Verdier, Louis de Bollogne, René-Antoine Houasse, Charles de la Fosse, Jean Jou-
venet, Noël Coypel, and Antoine Coypel, several depicted scenes from Ovid's *Meta-
morphoses* and *Fastes* including Houasse's *Morphée et Iris* (1688), La Fosse's *Clytie
changée en tournesol* (1688; see plate 8), Jouvenet's *Zéphyr et Flore* (1688), Houasse's
Narcisse, Michel Corneille II's *Flore et Zéphyr* (1688), Antoine Coypel's *Apollon et
Daphné* (1688) and *Zéphyr et Flore* (1702), Boullogne's *Junon et Flore* (1706),
Corneille's *Iris et Jupiter* (1706), and Nicolas Bertin's *Vertumne et Pomone* (1706).

Through these paintings, the mythological flowers not only told the story
of their own creation but also glorified the king. The well-known story of
Clytie, for example, illustrated fidelity and homage to the king. Clytie, according to Ovid, was jealous of the sun's affections for and seduction of Leucothoe.
Clytie spread the rumor of Leucothoe's fall, and when the young girl's father
heard of her indiscretion, he buried her alive in rage. The sun, however, was heart-
broken. As a result, continued Ovid:

> The lord of light did not go near [Clytie] any more—his affection for her was
> at an end. From that day she wasted away, for she had been quite mad with love.
> She had no use for the company of the nymphs, but sat upon the bare ground, night
> and day, under the open sky, her head uncovered, and her hair all disarrayed. For
> nine days she tasted neither food nor drink, but fed her hunger only on dew and
> tears. She never stirred from the ground: all she did was to gaze on the face of the
> sun god, as he journeyed on, and turn her own face to follow him. Her limbs, they
> say, became rooted to the earth, and a wan pallor spread over part of her complexion,
> as she changed into a bloodless plant: but in part her rosy flush remained, and a
> flower like a violet grew over her face. Though held fast by its roots, this flower still
> turns to the sun, and although Clytie's form is altered, her love remains.[236]

Clytie was thus turned into a flower whose blossom followed the sun. By the
seventeenth century, the sunflower, whose bloom indeed tracked the position of

the sun, had taken its place in the Clytie myth and was incorporated into expressions of fidelity and loyalty.[237] The Clytie painting for the Trianon by Charles de la Fosse depicted the sobbing nymph watching as Apollo drove his familiar chariot away from her across the sky (see plate 8). In the Trianon de Marbre, the Clytie myth referred generally (though unambiguously) to the loyalty owed to the king by all of his adoring courtiers.

In the "palais de Flore," the goddess Flora was, too, understandably featured in its decoration. Among the depictions of Flora painted for the Trianon was Jean Jouvenet's *Zéphyr et Flore* (1688), intended for the salon,[238] in which a reclining Flora was crowned with flowers by a cupid and presented with a bouquet by a youthful Zephyr. Michel Corneille the Younger's 1688 *Flore et Zéphyr*, placed in either the *salle de musique* or the *chambre des fleurs*,[239] included an enthroned Flora wearing flowers in her hair, holding a nosegay in one hand while picking another blossom from a cornucopia of flowers offered by a cupid with the other. Cupids and shadowy winds brought a basket of flowers to her, while an adolescent winged Zephyr presented her with more blossoms. Antoine Coypel's oval *Zéphyr et Flore* of 1706 differed in that a winged Zephyr came to Flora aloft, floating in the breezes he personified, while sprinkling flowers into the lap of the elegant and graceful goddess. Flora appeared again in Bon Boullogne's *Junon et Flore*[240] in which a seated Flora, flowers in her hair and accompanied by blossom-bearing cupids, handed to Juno what appears to be an anemone, the flower made of Adonis's blood.

Though the paintings of Flora were commissioned for an aging king who was presumably faithful to his last mistress turned morganatic wife, Madame de Maintenon, the very sensual renderings of Flora recall the origins of the Trianon as a lover's retreat for Louis XIV and his mistresses. According to Ovid, Flora became the goddess of flowers only after she was seduced by the wind Zephyr who had powers enough himself to transform her into the deity. In the works by Corneille, Jouvenet, and Coypel, however, the goddess was attended by adolescent Zephyrs. Zephyr no longer attempted a seduction; here Flora was a beautiful, powerful, grown temptress herself. The representations of Flora at the Trianon were not portraits of court beauties, yet few could have forgotten the king's earlier mistresses in Flora's guise. The Flora reigning at the royal court of France was *both* goddess of flowers and courtesan—and both served their Sun King.

Flora and the flowers used in the staging or incorporated into the story of the ballets and operas, painted on the walls, and planted in the parterres thus contributed to the general evocation of Louis XIV's reign as a golden age or eternal springtime where flowers signified prosperity, plenty, and peace as well as love and beauty. But flowers and floral symbolism were also incorporated into specific references to the king's impeccable character and unequaled talent for kingship. For example, floral themes were featured in a series of devices designed for the king by members of his *petite académie*. In 1668 Jacques Bailly completed a richly painted manuscript of *Devises pour les tapisseries du roi*, a sequence of devices that were to be incorporated into a series of tapestries woven for the king at Gobelins. The manuscript consisted of delicate paintings of devices celebrating the king while illustrating the four elements and the four seasons. The paintings were accompanied by verses scripted by Nicolas Jarry and composed by leading royal poets of the Académié des inscriptions et belles-lettres including Charles Perrault, Jean Chapelain, and François Charpentier.[241] Each element, for example, was depicted by devices dedicated to each of four virtues—piety, magnanimity, bounty, and valor—and an overall tapestry design incorporating the devices of the four virtues into a single composition.

Not surprisingly, floral and vegetal images were incorporated into the representation of the element "earth." Piety was illustrated by a sunflower or *girasol* facing the sun. The accompanying text explained that "A Sunflower" was appropriate "to say that his majesty behaves according to the movement of the Sun which he always watches."[242] Drawing on the Apollo/Sun King image as well as the notion of Christian piety and obedience, the sunflower was used to suggest that the king ruled according to the wishes of the heavens (both Christian and Olympian). The explanation was bolstered by the accompanying verses of Perrault:

> In spite of the Elements that imprison me,
> And the law of destiny that attaches me to the Earth,
> In the highest of heavens are my tender loves,
> I have always followed the path,
> Of the divine author of my life,
> And I will follow it always.[243]

The most prominent botanical characteristic of the sunflower—its tendency to follow the movement of the sun—not only suggested that the flower and the king followed the heavens, but also reminded the viewer that the courtier should similarly follow the sun or Sun King. Another botanical image was used to illustrate the king's magnanimity. The fir tree or *sapin* drew upon its natural habitat in high elevations. The caption added, "His Majesty who pleases in the great things and rises straight to glory, as the fir tree which pleases on the highest mountains, grows straight in height without ever warping."[244] The evergreen, growing on the mountaintop, signified the heights of glory which the king of France aspired to and would attain.

Botanical images were incorporated more extensively into the tapestries of the four seasons. Not only were flowers and plants used in the celebration of the king, but the gods and goddesses of the seasons were depicted hovering in Olympian clouds in front of Louis's favorite palaces and gardens, including Versailles as seen from the Orangerie, Fontainebleau, Saint-Germain, and Paris from the banks of the Seine. Four devices, two referring directly to the character of the king, and two illustrating diversions and entertainments corresponding to each season, accompanied the seasons.

The devices for spring, the season most frequently associated with the reign of Louis XIV—indeed, all rulers hoping to evoke images of eternal growth, prosperity, potential, and anticipation of springtime—included a swallow and a parterre of flowers. The swallow signified spring because "this bird . . . brings back spring with himself."[245] The bird was used to reflect on the king because Louis XIV brought peace and prosperity to his kingdom as the king was the harbinger of spring. The swallow was an appropriate symbol for Louis XIV, the manuscript text explained, because, "one can say the same [of the king in] that the king brought back good times and peace after a long and annoying war."[246]

The device of the border of spring flowers was included "to signify that . . . the earth likes flowers as its premiere production & that they are its most beautiful ornament" (figure 37).[247] The king was compared directly to the flowers as "His Majesty is no less the Love and ornament of all the earth."[248] The most common criticisms of flowers, that they were simple ornaments and ephemeral tokens of love, were here turned upside down and used to compliment the king. Just as flowers ornamented the garden, the king was the finest ornament of all, gracing the earth with his presence.

Flowers also figured in the device for the diversion of springtime, the *carrousel*, or court equestrian spectacle that included jousting and other displays of equestrian skill. To represent the *carrousel*, Bailly depicted a lance sticking up out of the ground in a public square (a likely setting for such an event). To complement the idea of the *carrousel*, another device was designed featuring a pink rose. The rose, explained the manuscript, aptly represented the *carrousel* because the rose was both beautiful and dangerous, fragrant and thorny: "One finds in the Rose beauty & pride all at once, & it is like an image of peace and of war joined together, one can say the same thing about the *Course de bagues* [an equestrian tournament] & *carrousels* which are games, but military games in which one must have much strength and skill in arms, [together] with many good looks and good grace, which are the things that meet regally in his Majesty."[249] In Louis XIV, then, could be found not only military might and leadership, but also grace and good looks. The beauty and fragrance of the rose, but also the necessary dangers of the thorns, were embodied in the king. Perrault expressed it more delicately:

> To my attractive, sweet, charming, agreeable air,
> Of the pleasure one feels to the touch,
> My traits at the same time are rendered formidable,
> Without love and without fear one cannot approach me;
> Also among the horror of arms
> One never lives only by charm.[250]

Arms joined grace in the form of the rose and in the body of the king.

Another flower, the lily, was incorporated into the representation of summer. The white lily, though nowhere compared directly to the fleur-de-lys, was

POVR LE PRINTEMPS,

DANS LA PIECE DE LA SAISON DV PRINTEMPS·

Des Fleurs printanieres dans vn Parterre, qui ont pour Ame ce
Mot, TERRÆ AMOR ET DECVS; pour signifier que si
la Terre aime les Fleurs, comme ses premieres productions, &
celles qui font son plus bel ornement, Sa Majesté n'est pas moins
l'amour & l'ornement de toute la Terre.

Si lors que la Terre se pare
De ce present des Cieux si charmant & si rare,
Elle l'aime si tendrement;
N'est-il pas juste qu'on la voye
En faire ses plaisirs, son amour, & sa joye,
Comme elle en fait son ornement?

PERRAVLT·

FIG. 37.   Jacques Bailly, "Pour le printemps, dans la piece de la saison du printemps. Des Fleurs printainieres dans un Parterre [For spring, in the piece of the season of spring. Spring flowers in a parterre]." From *Tapisseries du roy, ou sont representez les quatres elemens et les quatres saisons avec les devises qui les accompagnent et leur explication*, Paris: Sebastien Mabre-Cramoisy, 1679. Princeton, N.J., Marquand Library of Art and Archaeology, Department of Rare Books and Special Collections, Princeton University Library.

identified as the "symbol of candor and sincerity chosen to represent the noble, sincere and generous behavior of His Majesty in all his Actions."[251] Charpentier proceeded to explain that both the shine of the lily (which nothing could dull), and the parallel brilliance of the king, looked to Heaven for direction with unblemished faces that concealed nothing.[252] Candor or sincerity in the king was thus reflected in the glittering whiteness of the lily.

For winter, Bailly devised an emblem around the *perceneige*, or snowdrop, that praised the king's ability to surmount any barrier to his goals as the snowdrop "blossoms in the middle of the snow in spite of the rigors of winter." The manuscript continued, "Those who can speak of the glory of His Majesty [know] that all the obstacles cannot prevent him from shining, & that he flourishes in the middle of difficulty."[253] Chapelain added, "It is in the time most contrary// that I flourish the most."[254] It was in the face of adversity, the snowdrop claimed, that the king flourished and impressed his admirers just as the snowdrop forced its way through snow to blossom.

Bailly, then, drew upon widely known or obvious qualities of particular species of flowers in order to comment on the powers and glory of Louis XIV. Incorporated into the carefully planned compositions, the floral devices not only added fashionable ornament and decoration to the sumptuous tapestries, but also employed commonly understood floral language to celebrate the king. Nature was embellished or interpreted by art, while both, enlisted by the king, brought glory to his reign. The distinction between Art and Nature in Louis XIV's France was the subject of the final device in Bailly's manuscript, a device illustrating diversion in winter. Stage machinery, the manuscript explained, charmed the spectators and "surpassed natural forces."[255] Casscagnes wrote in accompanying verses:

> What marvelous object, what august miracle,
> By its rapid course surmounts every obstacle,
>   Ravishes the eyes and the spirits?
> By a victorious art its force is animated,
> And by its movements it charms Nature
> Which admires it & yields to its price.[256]

The device, depicting a gardenlike set with a palace floating above the stage, suggested that the theater, or, more specifically, the machinery of the theater, enhanced nature. Together art and nature ultimately enhanced the image of the king. The flowers in Bailly's devices and in the king's gardens functioned in much the same way: the king used the art of the gardeners, the painters, and poets to "improve" flowers that dwelled in royal gardens. The flowers in turn cast their beauty, fragrance, and implied prosperity and fertility, in the direction of the king.

Bailly's *Devises pour les tapisseries du roi* used floral symbolism to represent qualities of Louis XIV as the ballets and operas had used flowers, Flora, and floral symbolism to project the idea that the France of Louis XIV was enjoying a perpetual springtime, that the flowers in the gardens of Louis XIV crowned his many achievements. Louis XIV's panegyrists, crafting the king's history in music, paint, and poetry, consciously appropriated the flowers in the king's garden and a newly invigorated floral symbolism to glorify their patron.[257] In retrospect, then, Jean Donneau de Visé's decision to present to the king his *Histoire de Louis le Grand contenüe dans les rapports qui se trouvent entres ses actions, & les qualités, & vertus des Fleurs, & des Plants*[258] in hopes that Louis XIV would be pleased enough with the work that he would name him a royal historian seems a wise one. Donneau de Visé, the author of *Les Amours du soleil* and known in court and urban circles as the publisher of the Parisian news, gossip, and arts paper called the *Mercure Galant*, presented the sumptuous manuscript to Louis XIV in 1688. The manuscript contained portraits of thirty-five different flowers, shrubs, and herbs that spoke directly to the king in accompanying texts copied by calligrapher F. de La Pointe through which they compared their own practical uses to specific accomplishments of the Sun King (see plate 1).

Donneau de Visé's homage to the king began with a dedication in which he referred to Louis XIV's recent recovery from illness,[259] remarking that while other countries around the world celebrate the birthdays of their sovereigns, every day in France was a celebration of Louis XIV.[260] After the dedication, all of the flowers addressed the king as a group, the text of which was framed with an elegant portrayal of Apollo in his chariot riding toward the viewer from which fell a rich garland of flowers (see plate 10).

The celebration of Louis by Donneau de Visé's flowers began much like those in Bailly's *Devises pour les tapisseries du roi* in that the king was lauded for his ability to conquer whatever obstacles might confront him. The flowers indicated to the king that they, too, had overcome the obstacle of the seasons in order to honor him: "Although the seasons separate us, we have today forced the order of Nature to appear before a Prince who always surmounted the obstacles that [Nature] formed, when to postpone the execution of his grand designs, she opposed him with the cold of the harshest winter, . . . & refused to give everything that is necessary for the embellishment of the superb, & delicious palace that makes him today the admiration of all the Earth."[261] The fawning compliments of the flowers referred not only to the florilegium's ability to capture flowers of all seasons into a single composition,[262] but also to the king's wondrous nurseries, greenhouses, and orangeries that kept Louis XIV's gardens colorful and fragrant throughout the year.

The flowers continued, explaining to the king that while it was written in scripture that Jonathan told of trees gathering to elect a king, they had gathered to tell the history of Louis XIV, assuring him that they all owed allegiance to France: "We assemble today, not to elect a king, but to work on the history of a Monarch, who should be praised by all that the Earth produces, since all the Earth is indebted to him. Although we are from different countries, we are all French by inclination, or rather we are all devoted to you, [we] are all in accord in praising you."[263] Donneau de Visé and the flowers reminded the reader and the king that he had successfully furnished his gardens with flowers from all over the world. But they also communicated to the monarch that the presenter of this piece of royal glorification himself in fact hoped to write the history of the reign of Louis le Grand.

Donneau de Visé questioned whether the king would be flattered by the comparison of his great accomplishments to flowers, and he offered up the famil- iar defenses. Many illustrious thinkers and rulers, argued the flowers, had drawn comparisons between men and plants. The flowers maintained that God had cre- ated plants as he had man: "God gives them his benediction, the Heavens and the Earth as the Father & the Mother of Plants; the Earth gives them the body, the Heavens their soul."[264] Cyrus, king of Persia, insisted the flowers, said that man and plants resembled each other, and "Philon le Juif" had written that "God has made man as a plant with reason & wisdom."[265]

The credibility, honorableness, and purpose of the flowers established, De Visé organized the rest of the manuscript so that each species was rendered nat- uralistically in paint much like the royal *vélins*, embellished only by a decora- tive cartouche enclosing the accompanying short text that described the primary botanical features of the specimen. On the opposite page was a lengthier text in which the flower itself addressed the king, praising the king for the qualities he demonstrated as king of France that were reflected in the botanical features of the flower. De Visé included a great variety of flowers, trees, plants, and herbs, some with historical or botanical significance, others favorites of the king (see Appendix B). The first species addressing the king were of Christian importance. The tree that produced myrrh was followed by that which made incense and then the golden branch.[266] These trees were suitable plants for honoring the "most Christian" king.

Next on the list was the fashionable anemone. The plant's description of the king serves as a good example of how Donneau de Visé's work functioned (figure 38). Underneath the painting of the anemone was a short botanical description and history of the plant.

It has been nearly fifty years since the first anemone was imported from the Indies to France, by Monsieur Bachelier, [a] great flower enthusiast. One admires its flowering, its vivacity, and the enamel of its flowers. The beauty of the anemone, that has seeds in abundance, was augmented in eight or ten years, & during all that time Monsieur Bachelier had no desire to sell them, nor give them, a means was found to surprise him, & the beautiful anemones were cultivated to the point of perfection, where they were, & are still most admired, & desired. They endure the cold, & they are most valued when they are a bit hardened. One counts more than twenty sorts of anemones, which have the names of kingdoms, provinces, towns, and of private individuals. . . . They have medicinal qualities and virtues.[267]

FIG. 38.   Jean Donneau de Visé, Anemone. From *Histoire de Louis le Grand*, 1688.
Paris, Bibliothèque Nationale de France, Manuscrits, fonds français 6995.

The history and cultivation of the anemone, reported in the short description, were then incorporated into the homage to the king, beginning with the first importation of anemones into France. The plant boasted, "Heaven gave you to France in the time when I was imported [to France] from the Indies."[268]

The anemone then described the youth of the king in comparison to the maturity of the anemone itself, reached as the result of selective breeding in France. Of the king the anemone wrote, "You had hardly left the cradle when your infant virtues predicted your grandeur." The young king, explained the anemone, demonstrated sweet and charming vivacity, as well as the desire to moderate his play by abandoning pleasures for business.[269] At the same time, the anemone continued, "My beauty was perfected in France during eight or ten years; you continue to form yourself and to work to become [the king] that we see today." The flower thus compared the talents or virtues that were apparent in Louis XIV, even in his childhood, to the rapidity with which the anemone was successfully bred to perfection in France, though wisely adding that while the anemone had been perfected, the king continued to the present day to improve beyond perfection.

The anemone also referred to specific events in the life of the king, in this case to the importance of Mazarin, the king's first minister. The flower explained that while Mazarin was alive, few knew of Louis XIV's talent and skill, since the minister himself seemed to be governing the kingdom. Yet, argued the anemone, when Mazarin died, Louis's qualities quickly became apparent: "[On] the death of this minister . . . you appeared all at once the wisest and most grand of kings." The flower compared the time during which it was perfected by Bachelier and other early floriculturists to the early years of Louis XIV's reign during which Mazarin determined state policy.[270] It was after the death of Mazarin, reminded the anemone, when Louis took the reins of government into his own hands, that it became apparent how a great a king Louis XIV had and would become, just as it was not until curious florists had wrested the anemone from the control of Monsieur Bachelier that the potential of the flower was revealed.

A more botanically inclined comparison followed, in which the anemone spoke of the example Louis set for kings and men around the world. "I am abundant in seeds," said the anemone, like "the infinite number of your actions of piety in inspiring the practice of them, to nearly all those who regard you with attention. These examples excite others to imitate them, in this way you cause the number of the virtuous to multiply."[271] As the anemone multiplied or was increased by the production of seeds, so the king's goodness was enhanced by the many imitators who sought to duplicate his good deeds, his piety, his virtues. Donneau de Visé tied together the reproduction of the flower and its spread across Europe to the knowledge of Louis XIV's greatness across the continent, a knowledge that Donneau de Visé hoped to increase by writing the history of his reign.

The anemone also recalled the reputation of France and the king across Europe. The flower stated, "I am given the names of kingdoms and provinces, where I reign with splendor," adding, "One gives to you [names] of those who conquer peacefully, of the pious, [and] with an infinity of other [names], according to the actions by you that merit them."[272] As anemone varieties (much like other fashionable flowers that were bred in great numbers and colors) were given names of countries and kingdoms, the king of France was given names and titles to mark his accomplishments.

Donneau de Visé similarly used other flowers and plants to write the history of Louis XIV's reign. The orange followed the anemone, exclaiming, "All the sovereigns built in their palaces a place to lodge me; and how you surpass them all in magnificence; one can say that you have raised me to an unequaled degree."[273] Claiming its own place of honor in the king's floral coterie, the orange honored the palace of Versailles and its magnificent Orangerie and therefore the king who built them. The orange continued, "My foliage is always green and you are always your self; that is to say, your great soul is always firm, in that justice and prudence [guide you] in [anything] you undertake."[274] The evergreen foliage of the orange was used to refer to the constancy of Louis XIV, while the orange tree's production of fruit also was drawn into the text: "All of my parts have qualities useful to the body of man; all your virtues, which are the quality of your soul, are at every moment good to all men."[275] The orange also made references to Louis le Grand as the Sun King. "I love the sun," the orange exclaimed, "because I hold from its heat everything that makes me esteemed, that is to say I could not live without you since you represent the great Star, and [because] you have so much rapport with it, that one cannot name it without thinking of you."[276] The orange, incorporating the image of Louis XIV as the Sun King, professed its love for the heat of the sun or the power of the king who provided the heated orangery for protecting the orange trees.

The orange and the anemone, in honoring the king of France through the collusion of botany and allegory, thus drew upon their own role at court on several levels. First, the flowers used their own botanical qualities—the evergreen foliage, perfumed blossoms, and sweet fruit of the orange, and the numerous colors and plentiful seeds of the anemone—to point out the good deeds and virtues of the king. Second, the national and provincial names of anemone varieties were equated with Louis's military successes across Europe. Third, the orange reminded the reader of its tropical tendencies—namely, its love of the sun—thus honoring the king on a symbolic level as Louis the Sun King, Louis as Apollo. Finally, both plants referred to French patriotism. The supremacy of Louis's France was communicated through the anemone's boast that the anemone had been bred to perfection in France in only a few years, as well as by the king's construction of the finest orangerie in Europe. The flowers paid homage to the king's virtues, the king's symbolic program, and to the king's own gardens and flowers.

Similar comparisons followed, each tailored to the specific plant or flower included in Donneau de Visé's *Histoire*. The gentian, "genevrier," sunflower, oak, tuberose, rosemary, "lisimachie," cedar, poppy, olive tree, iris, almond, "arbre qui produit le baume," lily, palm, rose, plantain, cinnamon, honeysuckle, acanthus, pinks, violet, ambrosia, heliotrope, laurel, pomegranate, jasmine, pansy, and narcissus all addressed Louis le Grand, praising his goodness and greatness in much the same manner as the orange and the anemone were drawn into the service of Donneau de Visé and Louis XIV. The palm, cedar, olive, the trees that produced incense and myrhh, and the rose all had religious significance. The oak, acanthus, olive, laurel, iris, ambrosia, narcissus, and pomegranate had rich mythological histories. The lily, iris, anemone, narcissus, and jasmine were important and fashionable in seventeenth-century floriculture, and the lily, orange, sunflower, jasmine, and tuberose had particular significance for Louis XIV.

Accordingly, religious, courtly, historical, and mythological themes were incorporated into the pages of praise for the Sun King, his character, his deeds, and his importance to France. Following the anemone and the orange, the sunflower referred directly to the king's recent recovery from illness.

> That which stays with me suits me perfectly since I turn every morning toward the star that you represent. I [follow] it during the day, and in the evening I turn toward the east, to await its return. As soon as it is eclipsed, I lose all my brilliance, my leaves and flowers become pale, and even my root shows the effects of this eclipse. Your people are the same in regard to you. They lose all their joy, and become languid, when they see that you are menaced by the least malady which is an eclipse for them, since you are hidden sometimes from their sight. All their movements, all their fears, and all their gazes, without ceasing fasten on you, as mine is on this star, marking an inviolable attachment, a great fidelity, and a strong love for you.[277]

The sunflower compared its own behavior in the presence of the sun to that of the people of France whose attentions were focused solely on the Sun King. Both the sunflower and the French people were despondent, said the flower, when the sun passed through an eclipse, or the king, figuratively eclipsed from public view, was ill.

Donneau de Visé also called upon the lily to speak to the king. Though not directly drawing on the legacy of the fleur-de-lys, the lily claimed that no other flower so closely resembled the king. As its stem grew straight and without knots or bends, said the lily, "the straightforwardness of your soul, attracts every day a thousand praises."[278] As the lily's leaves were always green and long, the king's actions were grand and brilliant. But more specifically, added the lily, "I multiply a great deal; no sovereign has ever enlarged his state as much as you: your conquests gave more towns to France than all of your predecessors together have taken during their reigns."[279]

As the lily honored the king for extending the boundaries of France, the rose honored the king's personal and military might through which he purged the country of vice. The rose said to the king, "We are a great ornament to the gardens; you are a great man in the Universe."[280] The flower then compared its thorns and medicinal powers to the king's might: "My syrup purges without violence, you purge your state of all sorts of vices without shedding blood. . . . Nature gives to me thorns to defend myself, you have not only numerous troops to defend your state but also to make all sorts of conquests, when it pleases you to be crowned with new laurels."[281]

But crowning the king was not the only purpose of the manuscript. Donneau de Visé enlisted the flowers in selling the king on the importance of Donneau de Visé's historiographical proposal. The tuberose, for example, boasted of its exquisite fragrance. It perfumed the air, said the tuberose, long after the plant began to flower. The lingering perfume had the same effect, argued the tuberose, as the publication of the king's works and history would have on his posterity. Donneau de Visé suggested through the tuberose: "As soon as one begins to publish the great projects that you often make for the tranquility of the Earth, and for the advantage, and the glory of France, one is surprised . . . at the first noise that spreads from these projects, which [is no longer heard]. But when one comes to examine them in succession, and as they begin to produce results, for which they were conceived, it is then that they appear more extraordinary, and that one discovers with pleasure the grandeur, and the beauty, and that as the good that arises from them is of long duration, one can with justice compare them to my flowers, which are born in one season and last into another."[282] The publication of such works as André Félibien's *Les Divertissements de Versailles*, or the work of Louis XIV's *petit académie* on the *Médailles sur les principaux événements du règne de Louis le Grand*, and most certainly Donneau de Visé's proposed histories of the king's rule—even the *Histoire de Louis le Grand contenuë dans les rapports qui se trouvent entres ses actions, & les qualités, & vertus des Fleurs, & des Plants* through which the tuberose was speaking—would make certain that Louis XIV's legacy would be lasting and widespread.

The machinery of royal glorification was mentioned again by the iris. After speaking of the many colors and varieties of the flower that could be found in countries all over the world and its many medicinal uses, the iris said to the king: "The enumeration of the qualities, and virtues, through which I contribute to the health of men, would be too long to make in their favor, and those who have undertaken to make your panegyric, have often stopped at [mentioning] only the titles of your principal actions, and their works were not permitted to be of the size that they would have resolved to make them, in elaborating on each one [of your qualities]."[283] Donneau de Visé, of course, offered to resolve this state of affairs by giving the "actions principales" of the king their full due in a series of histories to be written by himself.

The *oeillet* or carnation, in addition to praising the king's engineering feat of bringing water to Versailles, echoed the sentiments of the iris, exclaiming that just as the painter of flowers was unable to capture the many colors of the *oeillet*, the historian found it impossible to gather all of the king's deeds into a competent history of his reign (figure 39). Explained the flower: "The painters cannot represent all of my colors, because of their great number, and their variety. Neither these same painters nor all the great historians that your reign has

FIG. 39. Jean Donneau de Visé, Carnation. From *Histoire de Louis le Grand*, 1688. Paris, Bibliothèque Nationale de France, Manuscrits, fonds français 6995.

to offer know how to collect all of your actions." The carnation continued: "As I have many different names, those who want to speak highly of you lack the terms for praising you, and do not know how to find the epithets for all the extraordinary things that should fill all the panegyrics that are made for you."[284] Donneau de Visé, who promised to find the necessary words, was hardly shy in speaking about what he could offer the king if appointed his historiographer.

To conclude Donneau de Visé's grand floral exaltation, Flora herself addressed Louis XIV (figure 40). She began by reassuring the Sun King that her status as the goddess of flowers in no way compromised the homage that the individual flowers had just paid to the king. "One should no longer regard me

FIG. 40. Jean Donneau de Visé, "Flore au roi [Flora to the king]." From *Histoire de Louis le Grand*, 1688. Paris, Bibliothèque Nationale de France, Manuscrits, fonds français 6995.

as their Queen," said Flora, "since they recognize no one but you as their Sovereign."[285] Louis XIV, she implied, had successfully removed flowers from the "Amazonian" rule of Flora. The goddess also assured the king that while the many flowers of provenance from all over the world celebrated his reach outside of France, their foreign origins in no way compromised their loyalty to France and to the Bourbon king. The flowers had said to the king at the opening of the manuscript, "Although we are from different countries, we are all French by inclination, or rather we are all devoted to you, [we] are all in accord in praising you."[286] Flora elaborated, explaining that "those that foreign countries furnished to us, shine today in France with more brilliance than they ever did in their place of origin from where they are drawn."[287] Intriguingly, there were no tulips in Donneau de Visé's work, though they were present in the royal gardens, suggesting that the recent military actions against the Netherlands made tulips less useful in honoring the Sun King and were therefore best left unmentioned.[288] Flowers were thus politicized and nationalized in illustrating Louis XIV's brilliance across Europe and throughout history.

The flowers that Donneau de Visé used to honor the king succeeded in gaining for him the appointment and pension he sought as a royal historian; he eventually wrote histories of several important military engagements during the reign of Louis XIV.[289] The flowers in Donneau de Visé's tribute also carried floral symbolism to new heights in glorifying Louis XIV's person, his reign, and his kingdom. His choice of flowers to carry his proposal to the king was a wise one. But as we have seen, it was not an original one: even the king's official panegyrists had exploited the iconographical potential presented by the king's flower gardens. Centuries-old floral symbolism was energized and expanded through the mania for florists' flowers. The popularity of flowers in the seventeenth century made the use of floral symbolism and iconography particularly resonant with courtiers who both would have comprehended floral symbolism and have themselves cultivated expensive flowers or built elaborate gardens.[290] The great value placed on flowers in early modern France enabled the king to appropriate and exploit flowers and their symbolism to glorify his reign. For the blossoms flourishing in the king's gardens cast Louis XIV as the greatest floriculturist, able to obtain flowers from all over the world and to provide a suitably luxurious setting for their successful cultivation. As Donneau de Visé and the many other royal panegyrists made clear, the king's parterres were a living demonstration that his reign was a golden age, an eternal springtime equal to, or perhaps even surpassing, that of antiquity.

Flowers and floral symbolism also complemented the various other guises in which Louis XIV and his *académistes* cast his rule. Charles Le Brun painted them upon the ground before Louis XIV's early hero and model, Alexander the Great. And Louis XIV as Apollo, or the Sun King, used his powerful warmth to bring flowers to bloom in a perpetual spring. When the king was celebrated as Louis le Grand later in his rule, the sheer number of exquisite and fashionable flowers crowning the king's glories, required no further mythological construct to communicate the greatness of the king. Indeed, as the floral expenditures at Trianon and Marly and Donneau de Visé's *Histoire de Louis le Grand* make clear, flowers were increasingly incorporated into celebrating the king in the later years of his reign when, as many have argued, mythology and allegory ceased to embody the power to persuade.[291] Flowers contained none of the difficulties entailed in comparing the aging king to a youthful Greek hero, a pagan sun god, or a divine magician in an increasingly Cartesian and mechanistic culture, although they conveniently and beautifully complemented all three.

Having attained, in addition to aesthetic fashionability, botanical desirability, and outright mercantile and geographical power, a degree of symbolic complexity and iconographical malleability, flowers had become an economical choice (figuratively speaking) for writing the "histoire du roi"[292] for an increasingly complex and sophisticated audience. That audience, for whom taste and reason were paramount, would have admired and recognized in the royal flower gardens not the work of a magician king, but rather the curiosity, taste, and sheer horticultural will of their glorious ruler. For flowers flourished with equal brilliance in the world of the Ancients *and* the Moderns. That is, they spoke eloquently of the glory of the king both in the ancient realm of mythology and history, and in the modern parterre of the curious florist. As the 1689 ballet *Palais de Flore* performed at the Trianon proclaimed, "the Palace of Flora and Eternal Springtime which until now have [existed] only in the imagination of the Poets, are [now] veritably found here,"[293] in the gardens of Louis XIV.

Epilogue

After the death of Louis XIV, the royal garden at Toulon fell into disuse. No records of bulb shipments dated after 1715 have been discovered.[1] By 1776 the garden had been forgotten by the monarchy and royal gardeners so that when on 2 February 1776 a Monsieur Aublet wrote to the comte d'Angeviller with the aspiration of acquiring the garden, he felt it necessary to explain its history to the count: "King Louis XIV acquired during his reign . . . some small terrain that he reunited and enclosed by very high walls that still exist in a very good state. He formed there a garden for furnishing him with spring flowers, because at the time one could not [produce] enough heat, to supply the temperature of the climate. Oranges were also raised in this garden to furnish the supply for the orangery of Versailles, and rare plants were cultivated there for the garden of the king. During the minority of the happy memory of King Louis XV the garden was forgotten."[2] In the eighteenth century, he continued, the intendant of Toulon had used the garden for himself, but eventually the plot was rented "to a peasant who planted cabbages there."[3]

Aublet then outlined his own plans for the garden, beginning with a profession of his love and dedication to the study of botany: "[Because of] the love that I have for botany . . . , this passion that I possess to a high degree, of desiring to be useful all of my life, I propose to reunite the garden of the king, to the royal Jardin des plantes in Paris and to the orangery of Versailles to form there nurseries for different oranges, of genres and of species, and of rare and useful and curious plants that cannot flower and be raised in Paris. . . . I would reassemble with facility all this."[4] Aublet believed that he would be successful in his venture because he had directed gardens before. In addition, he promised to "find the moments to scan the Alps, the mountains of the province and make a collection of all [their] agreeable products." Aublet finally concluded by arguing that the restoration of the garden would actually cost the king very little. Aublet himself planned to absorb most of the costs, while sharing his specimens and learning with the king's gardeners and botanists at the Jardin des plantes.

An investigation into the status of the garden by the king's secretaries determined that the garden had in fact been rented in 1764 for a period of twenty years to "Monsieur Joseph Lieutard Seigneur de Chateauredon Lieutenant . . . honnoraire de la seneschaussée de Toulon." Shortly after taking possession, however, he died and the garden was rented to the widow of Monsieur du Tillet, as Aublet had reported, for a period of nine years that was set to expire in the following January. The "Memoire concernant le jardin du roy situe au terroir d'hyeres" summed up the result of the investigation, while explaining the recent history of the garden. In the end, the "Memoire" granted the lease to Aublet on condition that he pay 4,000 livres in rent, replace all of the dead trees, keep it full of orange and other fruit trees, and comply with several other minor conditions.[5] It is unclear whether or not Aublet succeeded with his plans, but he did begin a botanically inclined correspondence with gardeners at the Jardin des plantes in Paris.

The ignominious decline of the royal garden in Toulon after the death of Louis XIV demonstrates that the botanical and floricultural needs of the French monarchy had changed, as had the kings' ability to encourage and harness the production of luxury goods. Like the eighteenth-century curious florists who became more interested in fashioning themselves as amateur "scientists," the eighteenth-century scientist-king Louis XV, who puttered in his private Versailles apartments concocting perfumes, played at botany by assembling at Choisy every sort of hyacinth (the most popular flower in the eighteenth century) that he could obtain. In 1747 and 1748, the gardeners charged with the care and cultivation of the royal gardens at the château of Choisy set about acquiring bulbs to fulfill the king's desire to create a grand floral display at the château. The gardeners began by compiling a list of "names and residences of the curious florists of Paris."[6] Apparently, however, the Parisian sources were not capable of fulfilling the floral demands of Choisy, and it was necessary to broaden the search. They turned to northern France for some, ordering hundreds of anemones and ranunculi from Normandy.[7] In 1751, for example, 5,300 anemones, ranunculi, jonquils, and narcissi were bought in Caen for 2,799 livres (shipping included).[8] But French growers could not supply all of the species needed. In March 1747, Jacques Anges Gabriel, the royal architect redesigning the château and its gardens, requested permission from Monsieur Le Normant de Tournehem, the "Directeur et Ordonnateur general des Bâtimens du Roy," for the flower gardener to bring from Holland 100 to 120 livres worth of *marcottes*, or cuttings, for carnations in order that the species could be reproduced "in perpetuity."[9] And it was in Holland that the royal gardeners located the species that the king most wanted for Choisy: hyacinths. Hyacinths were, after all, the most fashionable flowers in the eighteenth century, prompting some to compare their popularity to that of tulips in the seventeenth century. The king's gardeners therefore solicited the help of Jean Agges Scholten in Amsterdam, who launched a successful search on the king's behalf. In August 1748, Scholten wrote to Tournehem to inquire how to pay for and ship a package containing two small boxes of hyacinth bulbs he had purchased for Choisy. In his letter he explained the care he took in carrying out "the honor of your orders."[10] "When I made the purchase of the bulbs," he explained, "I was informed by our curious and amateurs in flowers in order that I know who, of all of our florists in Haarlem, were the best suited and the most honest gentlemen." He concluded that Dirck and Pieter Voorhelm were "the most renowned, and the only possessors of certain hyacinths," such as the rare "La gloire des fleurs supreme, Grandeur Triomphante Thiara, [and] Roy des Nêgres."[11]

The choice of the Voorhelms was a good one, for the relationship between the royal flower gardeners and the Haarlem growers would last for decades. Every year, Louis XV's gardeners would place an order for hyacinth bulbs from the Voorhelms' catalogue, such as the 1751 edition of their *Catalogus der Schoonste Tulpaan, Hyacinten, Ranuncules, Anemones, en dandere Bol-Bloemen.*[12] From the Dutch placard, the French gardeners transcribed and translated into French the list of hyacinths available for purchase along with their prices. From the list, they selected several hundred bulbs, always including a selection of blue, pink, and white double-blossomed varieties.

The hyacinth bulbs were intended for Louis XV's latest building project, a series of renovations and additions to the Château de Choisy. Situated on the banks of the Seine a short distance from Paris, the small palace was built in 1680 by Jacques II Gabriel for Mademoiselle de Montpensier and was accompanied by gardens designed by André Le Nôtre. The château eventually passed into the hands of the princesse de Conti, the legitimated daughter of Louis XIV.[13] At the death of the princess, Louis XV purchased the château for 100,000 écus in 1739. During the 1740s, the king concentrated on renovating the interior of the palace. In the 1750s he employed Jacques Anges Gabriel to build additional structures on the property, including stables and a "petit château," a smaller, single-story auxiliary palace that included lodging for the king as well as for Madame de Pompadour.[14]

Louis XV's building projects at Choisy in many ways mirrored the changes he had already made to the palace at Versailles. During the regency of Philippe d'Orléans, the court had abandoned Versailles for Paris. But Louis XV returned to Versailles upon attaining his majority and almost immediately began renovating the grand political palace of his great-grandfather to reflect his own personal interests and tastes. Eager to maintain a private life beyond the public, ceremonial existence of the king of France at court, he constructed a series of smaller rooms above his official apartments that included a library and laboratories.[15] Louis XV was a well-educated and intellectually curious man. His library, catalogued in 1730, contained more than 2,500 printed works and forty manuscripts, with numerous volumes on history, geography, the sciences, and religion.[16] The king also collected historical artifacts, maps, and scientific instruments. He was interested in astronomy, meteorology, medicine, and botany. Not only did he continue to patronize the Jardin des plantes in Paris, but he also created a botanical garden at Trianon in which the specimens were organized according to the new principles of Linnaeus.[17]

The palace of Choisy similarly reflected the king's "enlightened" interests: the king added a library and a private garden that included an orangery, a menagerie, ponds stocked with red fish from China, and sumptuous flower gardens. To shelter and encourage the plants intended for his garden, the king constructed a greenhouse at Choisy. The flower parterres were filled with ranunculi and anemones, among other species. But two of the beds, *plates-bandes*, or long, simple, rectangular beds, were covered with iron ribs that could support cloth coverings to shield their contents from rain and cold. Under the iron ribs were planted tulips and, most importantly, the king's hyacinths.

Within the long, thin *plates-bandes*, the bulbs were organized into rows of four, five, or six of the same color. Then the rows alternated between the three dominant hyacinth colors: blue, white, and pink. According to a 1754 planting plan for the "most beautiful or premiere bed of double hyacinths," rows of four blue hyacinths were flanked by a row of five white bulbs on one side, and a row of five pink bulbs on the other, thereby creating a pattern of "white, blue, pink, blue, white, blue, pink, blue," and so forth, for sixty-five rows.[18] The nearly 293 bulbs required to complete the plan were all named varieties such as the "Commandeur de Flora" and "La Cour de France" that constituted the first white row. The plan likely functioned not only as instruction as to how the bulbs should be planted, but also as a guide to the identification of each variety, for it was necessary to monitor which varieties succeeded and which did not. Selected from the Voorhelms' catalogue, the varieties named on the planting plan were not selected from among the cheaper bulbs available. Rather, they were expensive varieties, some costing as much as 30 livres (when 2 sous—20 sous per livre— could feed a family for a day). The gardeners estimated the total cost for the hyacinth bed at "around 6,000 [French] livres." Such expenditure was annual— the plan for the same bed in 1755 called for varieties totaling 6,388 livres.[19]

No direct indictment of Louis XV's hyacinths was levied, but contemporaries did remark upon the royal expenditures for the projects at Choisy. Rene Louis de Voyer, the marquis d'Argenson, wrote in his journal on 26 February 1752, "It is decided and declared that, despite the present misery, they are going to build a stairway at the château de Choisy and build it double, as is the one at Muette. . . . There is going to be an outcry."[20] Only days later, on 2 March 1752, the marquis returned to the subject:

> They began yesterday to demolish the façade of Choisy on the [side] of the court . . . where the stairway will go. The king undertook a voyage to Choisy in order [to see] before him the beginning of the destruction: thus they embarked on this business that will cost millions. What is to be said of this approach? Nothing good, it is mutiny, it is to defy the public who suffers through great shortages, it is an affectation of final impenitence against the necessity of conduct of economy. However we commit all these things with a good heart, with a sensitive heart, with some wisdom, but the bravado and the affection dominate us. . . .
>
> It is calculated that, since 1726 when the cardinal de Fleury began his ministry, to the present, the buildings [department] showed expenditures of 350 million, all to make nothing but nests for rats, to build and to destroy. It is the château of Choisy that is the largest theater of such variations; there is not a year when they do not destroy in order to rebuild that which they change the following year.[21]

In one entry, d'Argenson tried to deflect the blame for the building projects away from the king: "They always complain, in public, about buildings whose taste and expense are augmented each day. Choisy is going to be rebuilt, the old and the new [parts] of which are falling down at the same time. . . . This is attributed to Madame de Pompadour, but that is wrong: it is not at all from personal taste, it is in order to please and amuse the king that she throws him into these enterprises the execution of which is entrusted to her uncle."[22] Although Madame de Pompadour, too, took pleasure in gardening and botany—and like her predecessors, the mistresses of Louis XIV, was depicted in a portrait as the goddess Flora—attributing decisions and power to the royal mistress was hardly a good defense for Louis XV who was regularly pilloried for allowing his favorite too much influence in political matters.

Edmond Jean François Barbier, another memoirist, tried to put a more positive spin on the building projects. He wrote in his journal in October 1750:

> At Choisy, there is considerable work being done in order to make changes and augment what is there. The expenditures for building are very considerable nevertheless without making any respectable monument; but, to consider it well [fairly], these expenses do not do great harm to the state; the [construction work] gives life and work to a great number of workers who, on the other hand, spread their gains in all the neighboring villages in order to live. They sell stone and wood; it is a circulation of silver to a great number of people in the kingdom that imperceptibly returns into the coffers of the king by the taxes and duties on everything that they consume. Besides, the king has many princesses not all of whom are married . . . , and to whom, at a certain age, he will have to give houses in the countryside.[23]

Barbier was, therefore, able to see in the rebuilding of Choisy a means by which the king's spending both distributed his wealth, stimulated the ecomony, and replenished the royal treasury.

The same could not be said of Louis XV's hyacinth bulbs that were imported at great expense from Haarlem. Louis XV's great-grandfather, Louis XIV, and his minister Colbert had established the mercantilist system for the cultivation of bulbs in Toulon in order to supply the royal garden with bulbs yet limiting the outflow of currency and unnecessary contact with the Dutch. The gardeners of Toulon, as we have seen, purchased seeds and small bulbs, including hyacinths, for low prices from Mediterranean sources. The bulbs were then raised to maturity and shipped to Versailles and the Trianon. But this mercantilist system, as Aublet's account illustrates, was allowed to fall apart during the regency and was never revived. The hyacinth parterres of Louis XV reveal the king to be a man of fashion and of rigorous botanical and horticultural curiosity. But, situated oddly between the royal scientific botanical garden (the Jardin des plantes) and the pleasure garden, the mail-order beds of hyacinths suggest the indulgence of the whims of an amateur scientist-king, with little to say about his reign, his power, or his glory. The garden neither rivaled the floral displays of Louis XIV's Trianon nor matched the scientific integrity of the Jardin des plantes, though it pretended to do both.

The changing use of planted flowers by the French monarchy reflected the changing use of floral symbolism and floral motifs in the eighteenth century. The emergence of the rococo meant continued visual celebration of the natural world, but individual flowers and floral species were less likely to be distinguishable in profuse displays of Rousseauian idyllic wildernesses. Floral motifs dominated mass-produced decorative items, including newly popular wallpaper and printed fabrics.[24] Although flowers were clearly a favorite decorative element, they had lost their uniqueness, the specialness, exoticism, and rarity. La Chesnée Monstereul's fear that tulips would become common had come true. Flowers were still collected, but the heyday of the curious florist had passed.

Many Enlightenment florists became less concerned with the cultural distinction displayed by assembling a collection and breeding new flowers, than about the scientific knowledge to be gained from them. Robert-Xavier Mallet's 1775 *Beauté de la Nature, ou fleurimanie raisonnée* defended floriculture on professional terms: "If he takes a taste for human or veterinary medicine, whether for surgery or pharmacy, the knowledge of botany is indispensable for him."[25] Meanwhile, English florists complained that English flower shows were dominated by the working class because they were more accustomed to devoting the requisite sort of diligent labor and attention needed to bring prize-winning flowers to bloom.[26] When in 1771 Jean-Jacques Rousseau wrote his *Letters on the Elements of Botany: Addressed to a Lady*, for the instruction of a young girl in the principles of amateur botany, the place of flowers in French culture had come full circle.[27] Botany was recommended as an appropriate amateur scientific pursuit for young women. Botany textbooks were produced specifically for women, as were even greater numbers of books for flower painting. By the 1830s, the sentimental "language of flowers" was invented for women who incorporated it into expressions of love and friendship. Government patronage of botany and public gardens continued. Indeed, the Jardin des plantes was flourishing. But in 1805 Empress Josephine, not her husband, sponsored the creation of the gardens at Malmaison where *her* collection of 250 different roses was planted and famously recorded in paint by Redouté.[28] For men, the cultural cachet of floriculture had declined in favor of the hard sciences, and the world of flowers was ceded once again to women.

Extract of the Inventory . . . by Sieur Cottereau of Flowering Plants and Bulbs that He Offers to Furnish for the Gardens of the Royal Households

Extrait de l'estat presenté a Monseigneur par le Sieur Cottereau des plantes et oignons de fleurs qu'il offre fournir Pour les Jardins des maisons Royalles, que J'ay Remarquée aveq [*sic*] depuis et Olivier Jardiniers de Sa Majesté, et les Sieurs Magnoles de Montpellier, Brement, Laminoye, Cruchet, et Huby Jardiniers habiles et curieux, tant pour les qualitez desd. Plantes que pour les prix, au Roulle le 26ᵉ xᵇʳᵉ 1684.

Premierement
Oignons et plantes de fleurs propres
Pour planter dans le Jardin de Trianons.

Demandes d'Olivier

100	Énemosnes blanches doubles de lait de la grande éspece grosse chaconne comme le poulée au Raison de 30 s piece monte a	150#
100	Renoncules blanche double de la grande éspece quy doivent avoir chaconne 7 a 8 Janves a 30 s piece fait	150#
100	Autres Renoncules Blanches doubles foüettées de Rouges et viollet de pareilles grosseurs a 30 s piece monte a	150#
100	Autres Renoncules de la tàrmodoquinà variée de Rouge d'Italie de pareilles grosseur, nest pas connüe j'ay 40 s piece monte a	200#
100	Autres Renoncules Bleüe Jaunes odorantes et d'Italye de pareilles grosseur cette plantes nest pas connüe jay, a 40 s piece monte a	200#
1000	Autres Renoncules du bagadet, dont la fleur est plus grande que les autres Renoncules des oignons de pareilles grosseur que cy dessus a 10# le cent monte a	100#
1000	Autres Renoncules géant de Rome de pareilles grosseur panache a 10# le cent monte a	100#

1000	Autres Renoncules Bagadet panache Bosuert de pareilles grosseurs a 8# le cent	80#
1000	Autres Renoncules jaulnes caltapa lustry—doubles de la grande éspeces de pareille grosseur a 10# le cent monte a	100#
4500	TOTAL	1230#

Autres oignons de fleurs qu led. Sieur Cotereau offre de fournir et de choisir tres beaux, des qualities et prix quy seront cy après dites, et que Monseigneur peut s'il luy plaist ordonner quy soyent choisir et Envoyer d'Hollande, de Flandre et de Provence s'il ne desire Lad. Quelle Cottereau les fournissent.
Sçavoir
Led. Sr Cotereau offer des pastout blans—Olivier en demende pour Trianon, la quantite de . . .

400	Couteront 60# le cent de 5 a 6 pouces des tous, Il y en a en Flandre et Hollande cy	240#
400	Pastout bleüe de pareille grosseur a 50# le cent Il y a en Flandre et Hollande cy	200#
5000	Jacintes blanches precosse de 4 a 5 pouce de detous a 63 le cent, Il y en a en Provence cy	300#
5000	Jacintes Romaines de pareilles grosseur a 8# le cent, Il y en a Provence, cy	400#
100	Autres Jacintes Blanches doubles de pareilles grosseur a 60# le cent cy	60#
20000	Oignons de tubereuses de 5 a 6 pouces de tous a 3# le cent Monsiegneur ma fait ecrire de sa part a Mr de Vauvray d'en Envoyer—10,000 de Gennes et 10,000 de Provence, Le prix dud. Sr Cotereau est de	600#
4000	Jonquilles simples grandes éspeces printanierres d'Italye de 2 a 3 pouces de tous a 20# le Million. Il y en a, en genes, et en Provence cy	80#
10000	Narcisses Constantinoples doubles de la grande éspece de 5 a 6 pouces de tous a 3# le cent, Il y en a, a Gennes et en Provence cy	300#
44900	TOTAL	2180#

Continuation de fourniture de plantes que led. Sr Cotereau offer de faire que
Monseigneur peut sil luy plaist . . . laisser fournir aud. Cottereau

200	Narcisses du Japon couleur de chair de 3 pouces de tous a 50# le cent cy	100#
200	Autres narcisses du Japon couleur de feu de pareilles grosseur a 50# le cent cy	100#
500	Autres narcisses dit bagadet fort doubles, un peu jaunes dedans de pareilles grosseur, a 10# le cent cy	50#
1500	Autres narcisses galices Rouges Jaunes odorant simples a 30 s le cent cy10 s.	22#
1500	Autres narcisses spherique tradex simple de 2 a 3 pouces de tous a 2# le cent cy	30#
1000	Iris de la grande espece de deux a 3 pouces de tous a 2# le cent	20#
4000	Autres Iris de perse de pareille grosseur a 2# le cent cy	80#
1000	Fretilaires peringuins précose dit bourdelois tardif de 2 a trois pouces de tous a 3# le cent cy	30#
1000	Autres fretilaires pour pres de pareil grosseur a 3# le cent cy	30#
1000	Autres fretilaires blancs de pareille grosseurs a 3# le cent cy	30#
1000	Autres fretilaires panaches noir de pareil grosseur a 3# le cent cy	30#
500	Émerocales Jaune de 4 a 5 pouces de tous a 10# le cent cy	50#
500	Émerocales Rouges de pareil grosseur a 10# le cent cy	50#
500	Émerocales Violette de pareil eschantillon a 10# le cent cy	50#
500	Émerocales Blanches de pareil grosseur a 10# le cent cy	50#
500	Émerocales de couleur de ponceau de pareil grosseur a 10# le cent cy	50#
1000	Martagons pomponion de pareil grosseur a 10# le cent cy	100#
100	Lis asfodelle odorante Blanequer quy est une plante a Raçines a 40# le cent cy	40#
100	Lis asfodelle couleur de Citron a 40# le cent cy	40#
100	Autres lis asfodelles Jaunes a 40# le cent cy	40#
12	Couronnes Imperialles Jaunes grande espece de six a sept pouces de tous, a 3# piece cy	36#
1000	Colchiques a fleur doubles des 3 a 4 pouces de tous a 5# le cent cy	50#

1000	Autres colchiquese gris le lin de pareil grosseur a 5# le cent cy	50#
1000	Autres colchiques couleur de pourpre de mesme grosseur a 5# le cent cy	50#
1000	Autres colchiques Jaunes de pareil grosseur a 5# le cent cy	50#
1000	Autres colchiques bleu de pareil grosseur a 5# le cent cy	50#
50	Ciclamen a fleur jaune de 8 a 10 pouces de tous a 3# piece cy	150#
12	Autres cyclamen bleu de bonne odeur de pareil grosseur a 20# piece cy	240#
100	Dent de chien a fleur blanche et gris de lin c'est une plante a Racine a 10# le cent	10#
500	Éleborre Rouge pris a 3# le cent cy	15#
12	Arbres nomme grand sambacq proper a plantes une allée quy porte des fleur de blanches odorante comme un oranger de 3 a 4 pouces de tous par la tige sur 3 pieds de hauteur, Il sera levé en motte de terre a 20# piece cet arbre nest pas connu cy	240#
12	Arbre tulips d'un pouce ½ de tous et d'un pied de hauteur, Il y en a un petit au Jardin des Simples, a 20# piece cy	240#
12	Àcasis d'egipte a fleur blanche de 2 a 3 pouce de tous a 20# piece cy . . . Il en faut envoyer de la graine a Trianon	240#
10	Colutéade a fleur Jaune odorante d'un pouce de tous et de 2 piedes de hauteur a 3# La piece cy	30#
30	Baumes des alpes ou Rodendros, quy est un abrisseau quy garde sa feuille a fleur Rouge a 3# la piece cy	90#
12	Astragalues d'Afrique a fleur Jaune, odorante[,] c'est une plante a Racine, Il y en . . . au Jardin des Simples, a 3# La piece cy	36#
12	Autres astragalues de Sivie a fleur de purpre de pareil grosseur a 3# piece cy	36#
12	Caracola quy est unne [sic] plante a Racine a fleur, blanche et violette odorante a 3# piece cy . . . Il en faut envoyer de la graine a Trianon, Il y en . . . Jardin des Simples	36#
12	Immortelles Rouges vivasse hautes de 2 pied portant beaucoup de branches a 3# la piece cy	36#
12	Talaspiq vivasse toujours verd quy fleurir Jaune a 3# la piece cy	36#
12	Pieds d'epatique double blanche de 12 a 15 cüilletons de grosseur a 10# le pied cy	120#

24	Autres pied de d'Epatiques doubles Rouges de pareille grosseur a 3# le pied cy	72#
6	Marcottes d'oeüillet de couleur de citron doubles pour a 10# piece	60#
6	Autres marcottes d'oüillet de double couleur, de Citron panache de sa belle a 10# piece cy	60#
22558	TOTAL	3025#10s.

Orangers citroniers et autres arbustes Rares que Olivier ne desire point avoir a Trianon et que dupuis Receva pour l'orangerie de Versailles s'il plaist a Monseigneur. . . .

2	Orangers quy ont la feuille d'entelée large de quatre doits quy porte de fruit grosse comme la teste de 3 a 4 pouces de tous sur 3 piedes de hault, led. Sr Cotereau ne peut pas. Dire le prix a Cause de leurs Rareté, scavoir sy Monseigneur en desire.	
2	Autres orangers, don't le fruit a divers goust de pareil grosseurs et hauteur, ne peut par aussy en dire les prix	
2	Autres orangers portant leurs fruits plus gros que les portugals, tres beau de pareil grossuer et hauteur, ne peut pas aussy, en dire le prix	
2	Autres orangers portant les oranges fort grosses dont [sic] le Jüs est aigre et doux de pareil grosseurs et hauteurs, ne peut pas aussi dire le prix	
2	Citroniers lime douces portant le fruit, Extraordinairement gros et plat de pareilles grosseurs et hauteur, ne peut pas aussy dire le prix	
2	Autres Citroniers nommes Cédres, don't le des Citrons perent trios ou quatres livres le suç, et doux de pareil grosseur et hauteur, ne peut pas aussy dire le prix.	
4	Palmiers Éstoillé de 3 pieds de tiges de hauteur et des 8 a 10 pouces de tous en caisse ou en mote a 20# piece cy	80#
4	Autres palmiers masles de pareilles hauteurs et grosseurs levez en mottes ou en caisses a 12# piece cy	48#
4	Autres palmiers semelles de pareilles, hauteurs et grosseurs a 10# piece cy	40#
	TOTAL	168#

Plants Included in Jean Donneau de Visé's
Histoire de Louis le Grand

1. L'Arbre qui produit la mirre.
2. L'Arbre qui produit l'encens.
3. La Rameau d'or.
4. L'Anemone.
5. L'Oranger.
6. La Gentiane.
7. Le Genevrier.
8. Le Tournesol.
9. La Chene.
10. La Tubereuse.
11. Le Romarin.
12. La Lisimachie.
13. Le Grand Cedre.
14. Le Pavot.
15. L'Olivier.
16. L'Iris ou Flambe.
17. L'Amandier.
18. L'Arbre qui produit la baume.
19. Le Trefle Odorant.
20. Le Lis.
21. L'Palmier.
22. La Rose.
23. La Plantane.
24. Le Cinnamome.
25. Le Chevre-feuil.
26. Les Feuilles d'Acanthe.
27. L'Oeillet.
28. La Violette.
29. L'Ambrosie.
30. L'Heliotrope Grand.
31. L'Laurier.
32. La Grenadier.
33. Le Jasmin.
34. La Pensée.
35. Le Grand Narcisse.

NOTES

Introduction

1. Jean Donneau de Visé, *Histoire de Louis le Grand, contenüe dans les rapports qui se trouvent entre ses actions, & les qualités, & vertus des fleurs, & des plantes*, 1688, Bibliothèque Nationale de France, Manuscrits, fonds français 6995.

2. Donneau de Visé, *Histoire de Louis le Grand*, 34. "Dès que l'on commence à publier les grand projets que vous faites souvent pour le repos de la Terre, et pour l'avantage, et la gloire de la France, on est surpris . . . au premier bruit qui se repand de ces projets, qui ne font que d'éclore. Mais quand on vient à les examiner dans la suite, et qu'ils commencement à produire les effets, pour lesquels ils ont été concus, c'est alors qu'ils paroissent plus extraordinaires, et qu'on en découvre avec plaisir la grandeur, et la beauté, et comme les biens qu'ils font naitre, sont de longue durée, on comparer à mes fleurs, qui naissent dans une saison et durent dans l'autre." All translations, unless otherwise noted, are by the author.

3. Donneau de Visé, *Histoire de Louis le Grand*, 46. "Le dénombrement des qualités, et des vertus, par les quelles je contribüe à la sante des hommes, seroit trop long à faire en leur faveur, et ceux qui ont entrepris de faire votre Panégyrique, sont souvent demeurés aux seuls titres de vos actions principales, et leur ouvrages n'ont pas laissé d'étre de la grosseur qu'ils avoient résolu de les faire, en s'étendant sur chacune."

4. Isaac de Benserade. *Ballet des Saisons. Dansé à Fontainebleau par sa Majesté le 23 juillet 1661* (Paris: Robert Ballard, 1661), 18. "La jeune vigeur du Printemps// A dissipé le mauvais temps,// Tous ces vents mutins & fantasques// Qui parmy des broüillards épais// Causoient de se grandes bourasques// On esté bannis pour jamais,// Et dans l'air il a mis un profonde Paix.// Cette Saison qui plaist si fort// R'envoye aux froids climats du Nort// L'Hyver qui vous livroit la guerre// Et produit pour nostre bonheur// Au plus noble endroit de la Terre// La grande & l'immortelle fleur// Qui par toute l'Europe épandra son odeur." The king would, of course, fail to preserve the "profonde Paix" in Europe, but Benserade unknowingly anticipated the fame and notoriety of the king's future flower gardens.

5. Renatus Rapinus [René Rapin], *Of Gardens. Four Books*, trans. John Evelyn (London: T.R. and N.T., 1673), 234–237.

6. The phrase "culture of flowers" is a deliberate reference to the title of Jack Goody's book, which attempts to recover the broader uses and meanings of flowers across history and around the world. See Jack Goody, *The Culture of Flowers* (Cambridge: Cambridge University Press, 1993).

7. Olivier de Serres, *Le Théâtre d'agriculture et mesnage des champs. D'Olivier de Serres, Seigneur du Pradel. Troisième Edition, reveuë et augmentée par l'auteur*, 3rd ed. (Paris: Abr. Saugrain, 1605), 500–501. "Le Bouquetier est composé de toutes sortes de plantes, herbes, fleurs, arbustes par compartiments és parterres, & eflevé en voisures & cabinets, selon les inventions & fantasies des seigneurs, plus pour plaisir que pour profit."

8. Etienne Binet, *Essay des merveilles de nature, et des plus nobles artifices, pièce très-necessaire à tous ceux qui font profession d'eloquence* (Rouen: Romain de Beauvais, 1621), frontispiece.

9. De Serres, *Le Théâtre d'agriculture*, 571.

10. Abbé de Vallemont [Pierre Le Lorrain], *Curiositez de la nature et de l'art sur la vegetation: ou l'agriculture, et le Jardinage dans leur perfection* (Paris: Claude Cellier, 1705), 92.

11. Keith Thomas, *Man and the Natural World: Changing Attitudes in England, 1500–1800* (London: Allen Lane, 1983) most notably explored man's changing attitudes toward nature, its flora, and fauna in early modern England. Also important is D. G. Charlton, *New Images of the Natural in France: A Study in European Cultural History, 1750–1800* (Cambridge: Cambridge University Press, 1984), which considers the effects of Enlightenment thinking on the understanding of the natural world, and Simon Schama's monumental *Landscape and Memory* (New York: Alfred A. Knopf, 1995), in which early modern Europe figures largely. Of these works, only Thomas's *Man and the Natural World* devotes attention directly to flowers.

12. See Antoine Schnapper, *Le Géant, la licorne, et la tulipe. Histoire et histoire naturelle* and *Curieux du Grand Siècle. Oeuvres d'art*, vols 1 and 2 of *Collections et collectionneurs dans la France du XVIIe siècle* (Paris: Flammarion, 1988, 1994); and Krzysztof Pomian, *Collectors and Curiosities: Paris and Venice, 1500–1800*, trans. Elizabeth Wiles-Portier (Cambridge, Mass.: Polity Press, 1990). Also important are Peter N. Miller, *Peiresc's Europe: Learning and Virtue in the Seventeenth Century* (New Haven, Conn.: Yale University Press, 2000); Paula Findlen, *Possessing Nature: Museums, Collecting, and Scientific Culture in Early Modern Italy* (Berkeley: University of California Press, 1994); and Lisa Jardine, *Worldly Goods: A New History of the Renaissance* (London: Macmillan, 1996).

13. Carolyn Merchant, *The Death of Nature: Women, Ecology, and the Scientific Revolution* (San Francisco: HarperSanFrancisco, 1990) influenced many important subsequent studies on women and science. Londa Schiebinger, *The Mind Has No Sex? Women and the Origins of Modern Science* (Cambridge, Mass.: Harvard University Press, 1989) considers the importance of women and their craft tradition to early science; Patricia Phillips, *The Scientific Lady: A Social History of Women's Scientific Interests 1520–1918* (New York: St. Martin's Press, 1990) looks specifically at the contributions of notable women in the sciences. Most recently, Ann B. Shteir, *Cultivating Women, Cultivating Science: Flora's Daughters and Botany in England 1760–1860* (Baltimore, Md.: Johns Hopkins University Press, 1996) traces women's traditional work with herbal, vegetable, and flower gardening to the prominent role played by a few exceptional women in the formative years of the science of botany.

14. See Jean-Marie Apostolidès, *Le Roi-machine: Spectacle et politique au temps de Louis* XIV (Paris: Les Editions de Minuit, 1981); Jean-Pierre Néraudau, *L'Olympe du Roi-Soleil: Mythologie et idéologie royale au Grand Siècle* (Paris: Société d'Edition "Les Belles Lettres," 1986); Peter Burke, *The Fabrication of Louis XIV* (New Haven, Conn.: Yale University Press, 1992); Chandra Mukerji, *Territorial Ambitions and the Gardens of Versailles* (Cambridge: Cambridge University Press, 1997); and Abby E. Zanger, *Scenes from the Marriage of Louis XIV: Nuptial Fictions and the Making of Absolutist Power* (Stanford, Calif.: Stanford University Press, 1997).

15. Wilfrid Blunt's *The Art of Botanical Illustration* offers a conventional but invaluable review of print, painting, and botany, while Gill Saunders' *Picturing Plants* attempts to interpret the development of botanical representations in the context of the changing cultural demands of the study of plant life. Lucia Tongiorgi Tomasi's *An Oak*

Spring Flora, an invaluable reference, offers lengthy treatment of many of the painted and printed masterpieces of floral representation. Germaine Greer's *The Obstacle Race*, Whitney Chadwick's *Women, Art, and Society*, and Roszika Parker and Griselda Pollock's *Old Mistresses* have all recognized the gendered notions of botanical illustration and flower and still life painting. See Wilfrid Blunt, *The Art of Botanical Illustration: An Illustrated History* (New York: Dover, 1994); Gill Saunders, *Picturing Plants: An Analytical History of Botanical Illustration* (Berkeley: University of California Press in association with the Victoria and Albert Museum, London, 1995); Lucia Tongiorgi Tomasi, *An Oak Spring Flora: Flower Illustration from the Fifteenth Century to the Present Time: A Selection of the Rare Books, Manuscripts and Works of Art in the Collection of Rachel Lambert Mellon* (Upperville, Va.: Oak Spring Garden Library; New Haven, Conn.: Yale University Press, 1997); Germaine Greer, *The Obstacle Race: The Fortunes of Women Painters and Their Work* (New York: Farrar, Straus, Giroux, 1979); Whitney Chadwick, *Women, Art, and Society* (London: Thames and Hudson, 1990); and Roszika Parker and Griselda Pollock, *Old Mistresses: Women, Art, and Ideology* (London: Routledge & Kegan Paul, 1981).

16. Simon Schama's "Perishable Commodities," Norman Bryson's *Looking at the Overlooked*, and Paul Taylor's *Dutch Flower Painting 1600–1720* all offer interpretations of flower paintings as cultural artifacts and fine art, though primarily in the Dutch tradition. Taylor attempts an intriguing analysis of the flower painting in relationship to the tulip mania and fashion for flowers in Dutch culture. For French flower painting, Michel Faré's *Le Grande Siècle de la nature morte en France* and Michel Faré and Fabrice Faré's *La Vie silencieuse en France* are the most thorough. The flower in the decorative arts was also the subject of a collection of articles published under the title *Flower into Art*. See Simon Schama, "Perishable Commodities: Dutch Still-Life Painting and the 'Empire of Things,'" in *Consumption and the World of Goods*, ed. John Brewer and Roy Porter (London: Routledge, 1993), 478–488; Norman Bryson, *Looking at the Overlooked: Four Essays on Still Life Painting* (Cambridge, Mass.: Harvard University Press, 1990); Paul Taylor, *Dutch Flower Painting 1600–1720* (New Haven, Conn.: Yale University Press, 1995); Michel Faré, *Le Grand Siècle de la nature morte en France: Le XVIIe siècle* (Fribourg: Office du livre; Paris: Société française du livre, 1974); Michel Faré and Fabrice Faré, *La Vie silencieuse en France: La nature morte au XVIIIe siècle* (Fribourg: Office du livre, 1976); and Vibeke Woldbye, ed., *Flowers into Art: Floral Motifs in European Painting and Decorative Arts* (The Hague: SDU Publishers, 1991).

17. See Georgina Masson, "Italian Flower Collectors' Gardens in Seventeenth-Century Italy," in *The Italian Garden: Dumbarton Oaks Colloquium on the History of Landscape Architecture*, ed. David R. Coffin (Washington, D.C.: Dumbarton Oaks, 1972), 61–80; Elisabeth Blair MacDougall, *Fountains, Statues, and Flowers: Studies in Italian Gardens of the Sixteenth and Seventeenth Centuries* (Washington, D.C.: Dumbarton Oaks, 1994); Mark Laird, *The Formal Garden: Traditions of Art and Nature* (London: Thames and Hudson, 1992); Mark Laird, "Ornamental Planting and Horticulture in English Pleasure Grounds, 1700–1830," in *Garden History: Issues, Approaches, Methods*, ed. John Dixon Hunt (Washington, D.C.: Dumbarton Oaks, 1989); Mark Laird, "'Our Equally Favorite Hobby Horse': The Flower Gardens of Lady Elizabeth Lee at Hartwell and the 2nd Earl Harcourt at Nuneham Courtenay," *Garden History: The Journal of the Garden History Society* 18.2 (Autumn 1990): 103–154; Mark Laird and John H. Harvey, "'A Cloth of Tissue of Divers Cloth': The English Flower Border, 1660–1735," *Garden History: The*

Journal of the Garden History Society 21.2 (Winter 1993); Mark Laird, *The Flowering of the Landscape Garden: English Pleasure Grounds, 1720–1800* (Philadephia: University of Pennsylvania Press, 1999); and Brent Elliott, *Flora: An Illustrated History of the Garden Flower* (Ontario: Firefly Books, 2001).

18. Jennifer Bennett's *Lilies of the Hearth: The Historical Relationship Between Women and Plants* is a survey of the gendered notions of flowers in the western tradition. Christine Velut's *La Rose et l'orchidée: les usages sociaux et symboliques des fleurs à Paris au XVIIIe siècle* describes how flowers were used in Enlightenment France. And Beverly Seaton's *The Language of Flowers: A History* is a study of the nineteenth-century sentimental "language of flowers." See Jennifer Bennett, *Lilies of the Hearth: The Historical Relationship Between Women and Plants* (Camden East, Ont.: Camden House Publishing, 1991); Christine Velut, *La Rose et l'orchidée: les usages sociaux et symboliques des fleurs à Paris au XVIIIe siècle* (Paris: Découvrir, 1993); Beverly Seaton, *The Language of Flowers: A History* (Charlottesville: University Press of Virginia, 1995).

19. Jack Goody, *The Culture of Flowers* (Cambridge: Cambridge University Press, 1993), 427.

20. See Goody's *The Culture of Flowers*, chapter 6, "Icons and Iconoclasm in the Renaissance."

21. Anne Goldgar, *Tulip Mania* (New York: Alfred A. Knopf, 2004). Already in print is Goldgar's article, "Nature as Art: The Case of the Tulip," in *Merchants and Marvels: Commerce, Science, and Art in Early Modern Europe*, ed. Pamela H. Smith and Paula Findlen (New York: Routledge, 2002), 324–346.

22. Bourdieu's work has contributed greatly to my understanding of the means by which consumption creates identity in early modern Europe. See Pierre Bourdieu, *Distinction: A Social Critique of the Judgement of Taste*, trans. Richard Nice (Cambridge, Mass.: Harvard University Press, 1984); and Pierre Bourdieu, *The Field of Cultural Production: Essays on Art and Literature*, ed. Randal Johnson (New York: Columbia University Press, 1993).

Chapter 1. Disorderly Flowers

1. For an analysis of the history of the publications, see Alice Stroup, *A Company of Scientists: Botany, Patronage, and Community at the Seventeenth-Century Parisian Royal Academy of Sciences* (Berkeley: University of California Press, 1990), chapters 6 and 8.

2. Bibliothèque du Muséum d'Histoire Naturelle, ms. 450, quoted in Stroup, *A Company of Scientists*, 82, note 43. The work "ne la represente pas masle par la racine mais plustost femelle et avec une affectation ridicule. Il la faut corriger."

3. For similar representations of the mandragore, see B[asilius] Besler, *Mandragora foemina*, (1613) Bibliothèque Nationale de France (hereafter B.N.), Cabinet des Estampes, Jd 79 fol., and Johann Theodor de Bry, *Mandragora femina*, in *Florilegium novum* (1612), reproduced in Tomasi, *An Oak Spring Flora*, 51.

4. Jennifer Bennett explains: "The plant was so 'human,' it was said to shriek when pulled from the ground, a sound that would kill any harvester who heard it. Elaborate rituals once surrounded the harvest of mandrake, including tying the plant to a dog so that the dog, rather than a person, would be killed by the sound of the plant. In another tradition, three circles were drawn around mandrake with the tip of a sword, and the

would-be harvester then danced around the plant, reciting words of love." Bennett, *Lilies of the Hearth,* 65.

5. Henri Boguet (d. 1619) is quoted as reporting the use of "mandragora or some other narcotic drought" for such purposes by Bennett, *Lilies of the Hearth,* 65.

6. Ancient Romans, in particular, had a highly developed flower trade in order to fill the great demand for flowers used in a variety of Roman cultural institutions. Flower growers used heat to force the blossoming of roses and other flowers, thereby extending the growing season. For more on classical floriculture, see Goody, *The Culture of Flowers,* chapter 2, "In the Beginning: Gardens and Paradise, Garlands and Sacrifice."

7. See Goody, *The Culture of Flowers,* 28–72 and Jean-Marie Pelt, *Fleurs, fêtes et saisons* (Paris: Fayard, 1988).

8. See Ian Maclean, *The Renaissance Notion of Woman: A Study in the Fortunes of Scholasticism and Medical Science in European Intellectual Life* (Cambridge: Cambridge University Press, 1980).

9. See P. Meyvaert, "The Medieval Monastic Garden," in *Medieval Gardens,* ed. Elisabeth Blair MacDougall (Washington, D.C.: Dumbarton Oaks, 1986); and Goody, *The Culture of Flowers,* 124–126.

10. Botanic gardens were established in the 1540s at Padua and Pisa and at Bologna in 1567. See Harold J. Cook, "Physicians and Natural History," in *Cultures of Natural History,* ed. N. Jardine, J. A. Secord, and E. C. Spary (Cambridge: Cambridge University Press, 1996), 96.

11. Kenneth Woodbridge, *Princely Gardens: The Origins and Development of the French Formal Style* (New York: Rizzoli, 1986), 100.

12. Ibid., 104.

13. See Stroup, *A Company of Scientists,* 89–102.

14. John Prest, *The Garden of Eden: The Botanic Garden and the Re-Creation of Paradise* (New Haven, Conn.: Yale University Press, 1981), 6.

15. Ibid., 54–55.

16. See Goody, *The Culture of Flowers,* 166–205, for the best discussion of flowers in Puritan England.

17. Cesare Ripa, *Iconologia: Or, Moral Emblems* (London: P. Tempest, 1709; repr. New York: Garland, 1976), 10.

18. Ibid., 33.

19. Ibid., 79.

20. Jean Laignet, *Il faut mourir,* seventeenth century B.N., Cabinet des Estampes, Tf 7.

21. *Vanitas* paintings were most common in the Dutch tradition, but could be found in French still lifes, most notably in the work of Jacques Linard. For discussions of still life painting and the *vanitas* tradition, see Bryson, *Looking at the Overlooked;* Faré, *Le Grande Siè de la naure morte en France;* Schama, "Perishable Commodities"; Taylor, *Dutch Flower Painting.*

22. *See Taylor,* Dutch Flower Painting, chapter 4, "Painters in a Market."

23. Poussin actually completed two compositions featuring Flora. In 1630 he completed the *Triumph of Flora,* a painting that illustrated the goddess of flowers drawn in a chariot pulled by putti and accompanied by flower-bearing attendants. The painting

found its way into the royal collection by the end of the seventeenth century and is now in the Louvre. Jean-Aimar Piganiol de La Force, *Nouvelle description des chasteaux of parcs de Versailles of de Marly* (Paris: Florentin & Pierre Dulaine, 1701), 149.

24. Anthony Blunt, *Art and Architecture in France, 1500–1700* (London: Penguin Books, 1982), 279.

25. Troy Thomas, "'Un fior vano e fragile': The Symbolism of Poussin's *Realm of Flora*," *Art Bulletin* 68.2 (June 1986): 235.

26. Despite the relatively unusual moralizing tone that Poussin's interpretation of Ovid suggests, there was, according to H. Bardon, a "querelle d'Ovide" in the seventeenth century between those who took pleasure in his work and those who found it paganistic and amoral. See H. Bardon, "Sur l'influence d'Ovide en France au 17ème siècle," in *Atti del convegno internazionale Ovidiano, Sulmona, maggio 1958* (Rome: Istituto di Studi Romani Editore, 1959), 76.

27. Charles de La Chesnée Monstereul, *Le Floriste François traitant de l'origine des-tulipes, de l'lordre qu on doit observer pour les cultiver & planter* (Caen: Eleazer Mangeant, 1654), 193–194: "La plus belle & vertueuse Femme du monde (aussi bien que les Tulipes) sera delaissée pour une laidure, qui clochera de fatigue d'avoir porté sur son dos sa bosse pleine de pistoles. . . . Quoy disent ces gens du temps, à quoy bon ces beautez passageres; quelle utilité rapporte la beauté des Femmes & des Fleurs; ne voit-on pas que leur lustre se passe en un instant, & que la possession en est tres courte."

28. Franciscus de Grenaille, *Les Plaisirs des dames dediez à la Reyne de la Grande Bre-taigne* (Paris: Gervais Clovsier, 1641), 4: "si vous sentez leur odeur, vostre ame en restera si ravie qu'elle n'aura plus de force pour regarder les couleurs."

29. Constance Classen, David Howes, and Anthony Synnott, *Aroma: The Cultural History of Smell* (London: Routledge, 1994), 48–49.

30. Ibid., 13–30.

31. Ibid., 52.

32. The Venerable Benedicta of Notre-Dame-du-Laus's fragrant body was reported in P. Guérin's *Vies des saints*, cited in Classen et al., *Aroma*, 53.

33. Antoine Furetière, *Dictionnaire universel des arts et des sciences* (La Haye: n.p., 1690), s.v. "odeur." The word *odeur* could be used in reference to "choses morales, & signifie, Bonne ou mauvaise reputation."

34. Pierre Richelet, *Dictionnaire François contenant les mots et les choses plusieurs nou-velles remarques sur la langue Françoise . . .* (Geneva: Jean Herman Widerhold; repr. Geneva: Slatkine Reprints, 1970), s.v. "odeur."

35. Furetière, *Dictionnaire*, s.v. "parfum." Furetière wrote, "PARFUM, se dit figuré-ment des choses qui flatten agreablement l'esprit. Le *parfum* des loüanges. La priere monte au ciel comme un agreeable *parfum*."

36. Jacques Bénigne Bossuet, bishop of Meaux, *Traité de la concupiscence* (1693–1694; repr. Paris, 1879), 8. Quoted in Annick Le Guérer, *Scent: The Mysterious and Essential Powers of Smell*, trans. Richard Miller (London: Chatto & Windus, 1993), 163.

37. By the later seventeenth century, flowers were joined by perfume or incense burners in allegorical representations of the sense of smell. See, for example, two late seventeenth-century Parisian prints from the B.N., Cabinet des Estampes, Oa 56, clichés c.1565 and c. 1552. Abraham du Pradel's *Le Livre commode contenant les adresses de la ville de Paris et le trésor des almanachs pour l'année bissextile 1692* (repr. Geneva: Minkoff

Reprint, 1973), 97–98, directed Parisian shoppers to *parfumeurs* hawking their wares in the streets, Provençal merchants selling orange and flower water, and to the Orangerie on the rue de l'Arbre sec at the sign bearing the royal device where one could purchase the finest "eau de Fleurs d'Oranges." The interest in perfumes expanded to include amateur manufacture of perfumes. Simon Barbe published *Le Parfumeur François, qui enseigne toutes les manieres de tirer les odeurs des fleurs; & à faire toutes sortes de compositions de parfums* . . . (Lyon: Thomas Amaulry, 1693) and *Le Parfumeur François, ou l'art de parfumer avec les fleurs & composer toutes sortes de Parfums tant pour l'odeur que pour le goût* (Paris: Simon Augustin Brunet, 1699). Dedicated to Monseigneur, the Grand Dauphin, the work was an instructional manual "pour le divertissement des Personnes de qualité, l'utilité de celles qui recüeillent des fleurs, & necessaire aux Gantiers, Perruquiers, & Marchands de Liqueurs."

38. *L'Odorat*, 1689, B.N., Cabinet des Estampes, Oa 56 pet. fol. "J'aime bien a sentir les Fleurs,// C'est un regal pour les coquettes.// Mais elles donnent des vapeurs,// Ainsi j'aime mieux les fleurettes."

39. Furetière, *Dictionnaire*, s.v. "fleurette." The entry reads, "FLEURETTE. s.f. qui ne se dit qu'au figuré de certains petits ornemens du langage, & des termes doucereux dont on se sert ordinairement pour cajeoller les femmes. C'est un diseur de *fleurettes*. Il conte *fleurettes* à cette Dame, c'est à dire, Il luy fait l'amour."

40. The original reads, "Ses regards toutes fois ont beaucoup de malices,// Et sont des autres sens les subtils enchanteurs." Abraham Bosse, *L'Odorat*, seventeenth century, Metropolitan Museum of Art, New York, Dick Fund, 1930, 30.54.27.

41. Grenaille, *Les Plaisirs des dames*, "Epistre," n.p. Grenaille's book was dedicated to Henrietta Maria, queen of England, in hopes that it would help the queen protect her honor while in France "pendant que les hommes sont occupés à faire le guerre."

42. Ibid., 3. Grenaille wrote that the suitor hoped that "l'odeur des fleurs purifiant le cerveau de sa maistresse, y produise l'image de son Amant."

43. Ibid., 27. "Le Bouquet & le sein qui le porte sont deux sujets de corruption mis l'un prez de l'autre."

44. Ibid., 12. Grenaille explained: "Que comme ce ne sont pas les couronnes qui embellissent les testes, mais plustost les testes qui embellissent les Couronnes, on doit croire pareillement qui c'est le sein d'une Dame qui embellit un Bouquet, & non pas les Bouquet qui embellit le sein d'une Dame. Que s'il y a des gorges qu'on doive couvrir, il y en a d'autres que la beauté doit laisser découvretes, & qu'il est bien difficile de rendre invisibles les deux montaignes d'amour."

45. Furetière, *Dictionnaire*, s.v. "bouquet." "On dit proverbialement d'une maison, qu'elle a le *bouquet* sur l'oreille; pour dire, qu'elle est à vendre: & d'une fille; pour dire, qu'elle est à marier. On dit aussi, Donner le *bouquet* à quelcun, quand on l'engage à donner un bal ou un repas à une compagnie: &, Rendre le *bouquet*, quand il s'acquitte de son devoir. On dit aussi, qu'une femme fait porter le *bouquet* à son marie, quand elle lui est infidelle."

46. [Pierre-Joseph Buc'Hoz, after Barbier], *Toilette de Flore, ou essai sur les plantes & les fleurs qui peuvent servir d'ornement aux dames* (Paris: Vilade, 1771), preface, n.p. Buc'Hoz wrote, "les fleurs sont aujourd'hui une [sic] de leurs principaux ornements."

47. For example, Buc'Hoz explained that the aster could be raised in pots "pour orner les Toilettes des Dames dans cette saison [Fall]," while the narcissus could "former des

bouquets & pour orner les Toilettes." Buc'Hoz wrote that flowers were useful "pour orner les Toilettes des Dames." Buc'Hoz, *Toilette de Flore*, 8, 43.

48. Ripa, *Iconologia*, 72.

49. Thomas Bartholin, *Bartholinus Anatomy; Made From the Precepts of His Father, and From the Observations of All Modern Anatomists, Together with His Own* (London: Published for Nicholas Culpeper and Abdiah Cole by John Streater, 1668), 68.

50. The description of women's bodies through agricultural terms was neither unique to early modern France, nor has it disappeared today.

51. For more on the influences of cultural assumptions, stereotypes, and misogyny on the understanding of the female body, see Londa Schiebinger, *The Mind Has No Sex? Women in the Origins of Modern Science* (Cambridge, Mass.: Harvard University Press, 1989), chapters 7 and 8; and Londa Schiebinger, *Nature's Body: Gender in the Making of Modern Science* (Boston: Beacon Press, 1993).

52. Furetière, *Dictionnaire*, s.v. "fleur." Wrote Furetière, "On appelle aussi *fleurs*, les purgations ordinaires des femmes, leurs mois, leurs menstruës."

53. Ibid., s.v. "fleur." "On dit aussi, que la virginité est une *fleur* qu'on ne cueille qu'une fois."

54. Jean Le Pautre, seventeenth century B.N., Cabinet des Estampes, Ed 42e, fol., tome 5, cliché E007144. The woman responds to his overtures saying, "Que si vous aviez pris un baiser sur ma bouche// Vous me pourriez causer la perte de mes fleurs."

55. Nicolas Venette, *Tableau de l'Amour dans l'etat du mariage* (Cologne: Claude Joly, 1710), 65. Venette wrote, "c'est une belle fleur conservée chetement dans un jardin muré de toutes parts."

56. See Bennett, *Lilies of the Hearth*, 73–75, and Goody, *The Culture of Flowers*, 155–156: "The image of a virgin as a flower in an enclosed garden was present in ancient Israel as well as in Rome. In the art and literature of medieval Europe the Virgin Mary was sometimes visualised as the enclosed garden, sometimes as a rose in that garden; she was a rose (often white) without thorns. . . . The Virgin was associated with living flowers in quite another way. Just as gardens were 'christianised' by being brought into the monastery, flowers were baptised with 'Christian names.' The marigold is one of many flowers likened to the Virgin Mary after the increasing popularity of her cult in the eleventh century."

57. In Catholic communities, motherhood was not more highly esteemed than living a life of chastity in a convent. Yet the example set by the Virgin Mary, born without the stain of original sin herself, and her miraculous impregnation with Jesus Christ, was unattainable for even the most chaste women. For most, then, motherhood within marriage was the best one could do. See, for example, Maclean, *The Renaissance Notion of Woman;* Hufton, *The Prospect before Her;* Elisja Schulte van Kessel, "Virgins and Mothers between Heaven and Earth," in *A History of Women in the West*, vol. 3, *Renaissance and Enlightenment Paradoxes*, ed. Natalie Zemon Davis and Arlette Farge (Cambridge, Mass.: Belknap Press of Harvard University Press, 1993), 132–166.

58. The name Floralia was also given to a poetry contest held in the city of Toulouse. Dating to the fourteenth century, the contest was held in the first days of May. In its earliest years, the poems were composed in *langue d'oc*. In the early sixteenth century, French became the required language. In 1694 Louis XIV awarded the society letters patent by which he promised royal support for the society which became the

Académie des jeux floraux. Winners were presented with floral medals of precious metals, including the golden Violet, the silver Eglantine, or the silver Marigold. For more on the Floralia of Toulouse, see John Charles Dawson, *Toulouse in the Renaissance: The Floral Games; University and Student Life; Etienne Dolet (1532–1534)* (New York: Columbia University Press, 1921); and François Gélis, *Histoire critique des jeux floraux depuis les origines jusqu'à leur transformation en académie (1323–1694)* (Geneva: Slatkine, 1981).

59. Ovid, *Fasti*, trans. Sir James George Frazer, 2nd ed. G. P. Goold, vol. 5 (Cambridge, Mass.: Harvard University Press, 1989), v. 331–354.

60. *Fasti*, v. 193–214.

61. Ibid.

62. The stories of Flora's transformed lovers make up much of Ovid's *Metamorphoses* and Flora's story in the *Fasti*. Among those metamorphosed into flowers are Hyacinthus from whose blood sprouted the purple iris or hyacinth after Hyacinthus was slain by Apollo (*Fasti*, v. 223–225; *Metamorphoses*, x. 162–219); Narcissus, who died enamored of his own image, became the flower bearing the same name (*Fasti*, v. 225–226; *Metamorphoses*, iii. 402–510); Crocus and Smilax, who became the crocus and smilax (or yew), respectively, as a result of their doomed love affair (*Fasti*, v. 227; *Metamorphoses*, iv. 283); Attis, whose blood brought forth violets (*Fasti*, v. 227; *Metamorphoses*, iv. 223); Adonis, whose blood was transformed into the red anemone (*Fasti*, v. 227; *Metamorphoses*, x. 710–739); Ajax, who killed himself after losing to Ulysses in a speaking contest for the arms of Achilles; and Clytie, who became a heliotrope or sunflower and followed the movements through the sky of her beloved Apollo (*Metamorphoses*, iv, v. 185–290). Flora also takes credit for the creation of Mars, son of Juno, which she facilitated by touching the abdomen of Juno with a flower, perhaps the lily (*Fasti*, v. 229–262).

63. According to Held, "In the foreward of his *De Claris Mulieribus* [Boccaccio] alludes to the questionable morals of Flora by saying that alongside such chaste characters as Penelope, Lucretia, and Sulpitia the reader will find women with the 'grandissimo, ma sceleratissimo ingegno' of Medea, Flora, and Sempronia. When he came to the chapter on Flora, he inscribed it with brutal directness: 'De Flora Meretrice, Dea Florum et Zephiri Conjuge.'" Held continues, "Flora the harlot is mentioned also in the fourth book of Boccaccio's *Genealogy of the Gods*, in the chapter on Zephyrus." *Genealogie Deorum Gentilium Libri* (Scrittori d'Italia, n. 200), vol. 1 (Bari: n.p., 1951), 218. See Julius S. Held, "Flora, Goddess and Courtesan," in *De Artibus Opuscula XL: Essays in Honor of Erwin Panofsky*, ed. Millard Meiss, 2 vols. (New York: New York University Press, 1961), vol. 1, 208–209.

64. Giovanni Boccaccio, *Concerning Famous Women*, trans. Guido Guarino (New Brunswick, N.J.: Rutgers University Press, 1963), 139.

65. Ibid., 140.

66. Ibid., 140–141.

67. Jean-Pierre Néraudau, "La Présence d'Ovide aux XVIe et XVIIe siècles ou la survie du prince de poésie," in *La Littérature et ses avatars: Discrédits, déformations et réhabilitations dans l'histoire de la littérature*, ed. Yvonne Bellenger (Paris: Klincksieck, 1991), 18–23.

68. According to Néraudau ("La Présence d'Ovide," 16), among the greatest translations of Ovid in the seventeenth century were those of Nicolas Renouard in 1606, Thomas Corneille in 1669, and Isaac de Benserade in 1676.

69. Bardon, "Sur l'influence d'Ovide," 76.

70. Lilian Zirpolo, "Botticelli's *Primavera*: A Lesson for the Bride," in *The Expanding Discourse: Feminism and Art History*, ed. Norma Broude and Mary D. Garrard (New York: Icon Editions of Harper Collins, 1992), 100–109.

71. See Zirpolo, "Botticelli's *Primavera*," for a brief survey of the various interpretations of the painting.

72. Mirella Levi D'Ancona, *Botticelli's "Primavera": A Botanical Interpretation Including Astrology, Alchemy and the Medici* (Florence: Leo S. Olschki Editore, 1983), 25–67.

73. Ibid., 44–46.

74. Held, "Flora, Goddess and Courtesan," 212.

75. Maître de Flore, *Triumph of Flora*, c. 1560, private collection, Italy. Anonymous, *Allegory of Love*, c. 1560–1570, Louvre. Both paintings are reproduced in Roy Strong, *The Cult of Elizabeth: Elizabeth Portraiture and Pageantry* (London: Thames and Hudson, 1977), figures 34 and 35.

76. Ripa, *Iconologia*, 27.

77. Abraham Bosse, *Four Seasons*, seventeenth century, Metropolitan Museum of Art, New York, D. 1055, Whittelsey Fund, 1957. "Dedans le Printemps de vôtre age,// Suivez cet amour qui vous suit.// Menagez bien ces fleurs quil vous don[n]e pour gage// Ou bien ne les perdez que pour avoir du fruit."

78. Rituals associated with spring are explored in Pelt, *Fleurs, fêtes et saisons*, pt. 2, "Le Renouveau."

79. Venette, *Tableau de l'amour*, 147–148. Venette wrote: "C'est cette aimable saison où toute la Nature par son verd & par ses fleurs ne respire que production. Alors le sang boüillonne dans les veines de l'un & de l'autre sexe. . . . Nous pouvons donc dire que le Printems est la saison où les hommes & les femmes sont plus amoureux."

80. Natalie Zemon Davis writes: "The young May queens in their flowers and white ribbons begged for money for dowries or for the Virgin's altar, promising a mere kiss in return. Some May customs that were still current in early modern Europe, however, point back to a rowdier role for women. In rural Franche-Comté during May, wives could take revenge on their husbands for beating them by ducking the men or making them ride an ass; wives could dance, jump, and banquet freely without permission from their husbands; and women's courts issued mock decrees. . . . Generally, May—Flora's month in Roman times—was thought to be a period in which women were powerful, their desires at their most immoderate. As the saying went, a May bride would keep her husband in yoke all year round. And in fact marriages were not frequent in May." Davis, *Society and Culture in Early Modern France* (Stanford, Calif.: Stanford University Press, 1975), 141.

81. Jean Le Blond, *Le Printemps*, B.N., Cabinet des Estampes, Oa 46. The caption reads: "Au retour du Printemps reprennent leur verdure// Les arbres, que l'Hyver avoit rendu chenus;// Les rayons du Soleil bannissent la froidure,// Et le bel Adonis fait l'amour à Venus."

82. H. Bonnart, *Le Printemps,* c. 1722, B.N., Cabinet des Estampes, Oa 57. The caption reads, "Flore, accompagnée de deux Zéphirs qui badinent avec elle: Les Poetes ont feint que c'estoient ces vents agréables qui ramenoient le Printemps, et que de leurs amours avec Flore, naissoient les fleurs qui embelissent cette Saison."

83. Ménagier de Paris, *A Medieval Home Companion: Housekeeping in the Fourteenth Century*, trans. and ed. Tania Bayard (New York: HarperPerennials, 1991), 76–86.

84. The *Maison Rustique*, heavily derived from Varro, Pliny, and Columella, was orignialy composed in Latin by Charles Estienne, and was first published in 1554 under the title *Praedium rusticum, in quo cuiusuis soli vol culti vel inculti plantarum vocabula ac descriptiones, earumque conserendarum atque excolendarum instrumenta suo ordinae describuntur in adolescentulorum, bonarum literarumstudiosorum gratiam* (Lutetiae: Apud Carolum Stephanum, 1554). It was translated into French by his son-in-law Jean Liebault in 1564 under the title *L'Agriculture et maison rustique*. The work was quickly regarded as a classic and appeared in numerous editions. It was translated into English as early as 1600 by Richard Surflet and published as Charles Stevens and John Liebault, *Maison Rustique, or, The Countrie Farme* (London: E. Bollifant, 1600). For more on its significance, see Woodbridge, *Princely Gardens*.

85. Estienne and Liebault, *Maison Rustique, or The Countrie Farme*, 51.

86. Ibid., 51–53.

87. Ibid., 51–53, 300.

88. See Alicia Amherst, *A History of Gardening in England* (London: Bernard Quaritch, 1895), 101; Bennett, *Lilies of the Hearth*, 33; George Gibault, *L'Ancienne corporation des maitres jardiniers de la ville de Paris*, (Paris: L. Maretheaux, n.d.); and George Gibault, *La Condition et les salaires des anciens jardiniers*, (Paris: Librairie agricole de la Maison Rustique, 1898).

89. Quoted in George Gibault, "Les *Jonchées* à Notre-Dame et à la maison aux piliers" (Paris: Librairie Ancienne H. Champion, 1912), 3–8. Colette la Moinesse was employed "pour joncher d'herbe verte, depuis le mois de mai jusqu'à la fin de septembre plusieurs salles de l'ancien Hôtel de Ville."

90. For a lengthier discussion of the waning and waxing of the fashion for floral crowns from antiquity to the early modern period, see Goody, *The Culture of Flowers*, chapters 2, 3, 5–7.

91. George Gibault, *Les Couronnes de fleurs et les chapeaux de roses dans l'antiquité et au moyen age* (Orléans: Paul Pigelet, n.d.), 3.

92. Étienne Boileau, *Le Livre des métiers XIIIe siècle* (Geneva: Slatkine Reprints, 1980), LXXVI. Boileau wrote: "les femmes allainet chercher des fleurs dans les jardins de la banlieue, les tressaient en couronnes et les vendaient par la ville."

93. Archives Nationale de France (hereafter A.N.), Série Minutier Central (hereafter MC), XXVI, R. 62.

94. A.N., MC, XXVI, R. 67.

95. A.N., MC, XXXVI, R. 108.

96. A.N., MC, XXXVI, R. 184. Flocourt was identified as "bouquetière de la Reine . . . pour le service du roi, de la reine et du duc d'Anjou."

97. For Linard's paintings, see Faré, *Le Grand Siècle de la nature morte en France*.

98. *Nicolas de Larmessin*, Les Costumes grotesques et les métiers de Nicolas de Larmessin, XVIIe siècle (c. 1695); repr., ed. Paul Ahnne (Paris: Editions Henri Veyrier, 1974).

99. See Denis Diderot, *Recueil des planches, sur les sciences, les arts liberaux, et les arts méchaniques, avec leur explication*, vol. 3 (Paris: Briasson, David, Le Breton, 1765), s.v. "fleuriste artificial"; and Charlotte Paludan, "A Beguiling Similarity: A Contribution to the History of Artificial Flowers," in *Flowers into Art*, Woldbye, 116–126.

100. A.N., MC, XXXV, R. 186.

101. A.N., MC, xxxv, R. 197.

102. A.N., MC, xxxv, R. 209.

103. A.N., MC, xxxv, R. 188.

104. A.N., MC, xxxv, R. 193.

105. This practice was common in many trades for, as Olwen Hufton writes, "No one contested the right of wives and daughters to work in a shop or at a stall leased in the name of the husband and father." Hufton, *The Prospect before Her,* 95. See also Olwen Hufton, "Women, Work and Family," in *A History of Women in the West,* vol. 3, *Renaissance and Enlightenment Paradoxes,* ed. Davis and Farge, 22–26; and Wendy Gibson, *Women in Seventeenth-Century France* (Basingstoke: Macmillan, 1989), 107–112.

106. See Diderot, *Recueil des planches,* s.v. "fleuriste artificial"; and Paludan, "A Beguiling Similarity."

107. A.N., MC, xxxv, R. 185; and xxxv, R. 212.

108. Full membership as a master in the *jardinier* guild was limited to men, although widows of gardeners could continue in the trade following the death of their husbands. They were not, however, permitted to take apprentices. Jacques Savary des Bruslons, *Dictionnaire universel de commerce,* 2 vols. (Paris: Jacques Estienne, 1723–1739), vol. 2, 382–383.

109. A.N., MC, xxxv, R. 185; and LXXIII, 284. Alix and Langot were identified as "jardinier[s] au faubourg St. Jacques."

110. A.N., MC, xxxv, R. 217.

111. A.N., MC, xxxv, R. 206.

112. A.N., MC, xxxv, R. 185. Dufour was identified as "aussi maîtresse bouquetière chapelière de fleurs."

113. The *bouquetières* preserved the *bouquetière-chapelière* name. Although they sold fresh flowers, they also sold artificial flowers and were therefore counted among the *marchands merciers* and *plumassiers.* See Savary des Bruslons, *Dictionnaire,* vol. 1, 442.

114. The *bouquetières* were one of three exclusively female Parisian guilds, the linen-drapers and *couturières* being the others. See Gibson, *Women in Seventeenth-Century France,* 107.

115. Goody, *The Culture of Flowers,* 216.

116. *Statuts et ordonnances des maistresses bouquetières-chapeliers en fleurs de cette ville & faux-bourgs de Paris* (Paris: V.H. Lambin, 1698), articles 2, 6. According to the statutes, "Nulle fille ou femme ne poura parvenir à la Maistrise qu'elle n'ait fait son temps d'apprentissage chez l'une des Maistresses Bouquetiere pendant quatre années."

117. As vendors in Les Halles, *bouquetières* were identified with the *Dames de la Halle* and *poissard* literature associated with them. See René S. Marion, "The *Dames de la Halle:* Women and Community in Late Eighteenth-Century Paris," *Proceedings of the Annual Meeting of the Western Society for French History* 17 (1990): 140–145.

118. *Statuts et ordonnances,* articles 8–11. According to the statutes, only flower sellers could sell "bouquets, chapeaux, couronnes, guirlandes de fleurs."

119. Ibid., articles 8, 10.

120. Savary des Bruslons, *Dictionnare,* vol. 1, 442, s.v. "bouquetière." Bruslons's entry on flower sellers reads, "On appelle ainsi à Paris, ces femmes établies dans les halles & marchez de la Ville, ou aux portes des principales Eglises, qui agencent, font & vendent des bouquets de fleurs naturelles pour la parure des Dames. . . . On ne met

pas néantmoins de ce nombre les Bouquetières ambulantes, qui vont par les ruës présenter aux passans quelques fleurs, pour exciter leur charité, & en obtenir quelque
aumône; celles-ci couvrant leur mendicité sous cette espece de petit trafic; & les
autres faisant un commerce reglé de leurs fleurs, & de leurs bouquets, où elles trouvent un gain considerable."

121. Ibid., vol. 1, 442.

122. *Statuts et ordonnances,* article 18.

123. Nehemiah Adams wrote in *The Boston Common, or Rural Walks in Cities*
(Boston: George W. Light, 1838), "The 'flower-girl' is as common personage in a French
city as the pette dealer in apples and beer is among us."

124. The public voice of the flower sellers in the market place has been studied by
René Marion in "The *Dames de la Halle.*"

125. The two works are discussed in Goody, 221–224. Recall, too, that in George
Bernard Shaw's 1913 play *Pygmalion,* the character Eliza Doolittle was a flower seller in
the local marketplace.

126. The identification of the woman flower seller as a sexual being was not new.
In ancient Rome, writes Jack Goody (*The Culture of Flowers,* 59, 62), "flower girls, as
later in history, were often objects of delight, partly because they were selected for their
looks, partly because of the attraction of their wares, and partly because of the nature
of their commerce, which brought them into direct relations with their clients." He continues, "Both the wearing and the selling of flowers were associated not only with sex,
but with the sale of sex."

127. Grenaille, *Les Plaisirs des dames,* 28. "Ainsi donc si les fleurs entrent dans un
bouquet, ce n'est pas un effect de leur inclination, mais du caprice de la Bouquetiere, qui
entretient les folies d'un homme, pource qu'elles sont utiles à l'entrentie de sa vie."

128. Sara F. Matthews Grieco, *Ange ou diablesse: La représentation de la femme au XVIe
siècle* (Paris: Flammarion, 1991). For a summary of the images she studies, see tables 19
and 20 on pages 392 and 393 of her study.

129. Still prominent Aristotelian oppositions placed women clearly in the realm
of nature while men were associated with culture. For a more subtle analysis of the philosophical, theological, and juridical understanding of woman in this period, see Maclean,
The Renaissance Nation of Woman.

130. Merchant, *The Death of Nature,* 144.

131. See Frances Yates, *Astraea: The Imperial Theme in the Sixteenth Century* (London: ARK Paperbacks, 1985), 29–87.

132. Robert Krueger in *The Poems of Sir John Davies,* ed. Robert Krueger, (Oxford:
Clarendon Press, 1975), 354.

133. Yates, *Astraea,* 66–68.

134. Davies, *The Poems of Sir John Davies,* 76.

135. Portrait attributed to Marcus Gheeraerts I, c. 1585, Duke of Portland, Welbeck
Abbey. It is reproduced in Roy C. Strong, *Portraits of Queen Elizabeth I* (Oxford:
Clarendon Press, 1963), plate XI.

136. Jacobus de Fornazi, seventeenth century B.N., Cabinet des Estampes, Collection Hennin, tome 12 (2ème partie), cliché G151549. "Maintenant que tu es Reine en
la Royauté// Du plus grand Roy des Rois cett'heureuse Alliance// Promet rendre les fruits
bien heureuse à la France// Des fleurs qu'elle a conioincts aux flairs de ta beauté."

137. Anonymous engraving, *Je couvre de mon ombre toute la terre*, seventeenth century, B.N., Cabinet des Estampes, Qb 1. Cl.

138. Firens, *La Representation du Mariage accordé entre les Tres-puissans Roys de France et d'Angleterre pour Charles Prince de Walles [sic] Duc de Cornu, avec Madame Henriette Marie, soeur du Tres—chretien Roy de France et de Naverre [sic] Lous XIII, l'an 1624 au mois de Novembre*, 1624, B.N., Cabinet des Estampes, N 2, folio, vol. 814, cliché D 164516. "Rose pourprine [sic] a Venus consacrée//Ores conioincte a la fleur argentée// De ce beau lis, pourtraict de chasteté.// Que voules vous, que de cest hymenée// Nous esperions q'une race bien née// Q'un fils parfaict en valeur et bonté."

139. Ben Jonson, "Chloridia," in *The Complete Masques*, ed. Stephen Orgel (New Haven, Conn.: Yale University Press, 1969), 47.

140. Erica Veevers, *Images of Love and Religion: Queen Henrietta Maria and Court Entertainments* (Cambridge: Cambridge University Press, 1989), 127.

141. Goody, *The Culture of Flowers*, 177.

142. Zanger writes: "At this early stage of his 'reign' [1657–1658], the king was still under the tutelage of Mazarin, and his portrayal reflects his connection both to the minister and to the players of the larger political arena. Indeed, portraits of the king associated with military triumph relied heavily on the depiction of other bodies: his ministers and generals, his family, French soldiers, and the allegories of vanquished disorder. As a marriage treaty was negotiated . . . , Louis XIV's power was promoted by displaying his marital (and hence mortal *qua* sexual) body. In this shift, Louis XIV's political body was further framed and complemented by supporting characters and props." On the marriage itself, Zanger writes: "Representations of the queen were crucial to nuptial fictions' displays of the king's prowess. In the story of the marriage treaty, the queen was both a subordinate symbol in the kinship exchange and a dynamic force or potential player in her own right. Nuptial images are thus both malleable signs and less predictable agents of signification. This dialectic is also a property of the vehicles used to project the fictions of marriage. The central purveyor of the nuptial fiction, the occasional pamphlet, was both a manipulatable (privileged) prop for displaying the king and an entity that could manipulate for profit." Abby E. Zanger, *Scenes from the Marriage of Louis XIV: Nuptial Fictions and the Making of Absolutist Power* (Stanford, Calif.: Stanford University Press, 1997), 13–14, 98.

143. The painting is now in the Salon de l'Oeil-de-boeuf in Versailles. For an explication of the painting, see Néraudau, *L'Olympe du Roi-Soleil*, 95–103.

144. The painting is in the Musée de Congnac Jay in Paris.

145. Elisabeth Charlotte, duchesse d'Orléans, *A Woman's Life in the Court of the Sun King: Letters of Liselotte von der Pfalz, 1652–1722*, trans. and intro. Elborg Forster (Baltimore, Md.: Johns Hopkins University Press, 1984), 55–56.

146. Ibid., 78.

Chapter 2. Refashioning the Culture of Flowers in Early Modern France

1. Charles de La Chesnée Monstereul, *Le Floriste françois, traittant de l'origine des tulipes de l'ordre qu'on doit observer pour les cultiver & planter* (Caen: Eleazar Mangeant, 1654), 34.

2. Phyllis E. Crump, *Nature in the Age of Louis XIV* (London: George Routledge & Sons, 1928), 25. The importation of French bulbs for British royal gardens continued

after the restoration of the British monarchy. In 1661, for example, Gabriel Mollet, of the famous Mollet family of French gardeners who, with his brother André, worked for the British royal family, imported from his nephew Charles in Paris a substantial number of anemones, ranunculi, and narcissi. For a discussion of the Mollet's work for the royal family, as well as a list of the flowers imported from Paris, see Laurence Pattacini, "André Mollet, Royal Gardener in St James's Park, London," in *Garden History: The Journal of the Garden History Society* 26.1 (Summer 1998): 3–18.

3. Carolus Clusius, or Charles de l'Ecluse, was a sixteenth-century Flemish botanist who studied and collected plant species native to Europe, but also cultivated and collected rare species imported from the East. He counted among his patrons members of the Fugger family and Emperor Maximilian II. In the late sixteenth century, he established a botanical garden in Leiden where his tulips captured the attentions of persons from all over Europe interested in plants. His publications, *Rariorum aliquot Stirpium per Hispanias observatarum Historia* and *Rariorum Plantarum Historia*, mark a watershed in the emergence of the discipline of botany. For a brief description of his work, see Wilfrid Blunt, *The Art of Botanical Illustration: An Illustrated History* (New York: Dover, 1994), 63–64.

4. F.B.'s work was unusual in the amount of space (over forty pages) devoted to a defense of flowers and flower collecting within his flower gardening manual. It was not uncommon for flower gardening manuals to include such discussions, but most were limited to a few sentences or paragraphs. F.B. Sieur de l'Ecluse, *La Flore sainte et l'apologie de Flore et des floristes contre les critiques: Avec un traité de la culture des principales fleurs* (Saumur: Isaac & Henry Desbordes, 1675).

5. The story of the rose's elevation to queen of the realm of flowers was recounted repeatedly. Scudéry named the rose "Royne des Fleurs" in verses recounting the Ovidian myths of metamorphoses that served as a dedication to Sieur de la Chesnée Monstereul's *Le Floriste françois, traittant de l'origine des tulipes, de l'ordre qu'on doit observer pour les cultiver & planter* (Caen: Eleazar Mangeant, 1654), n.p. The story was recounted in verse at greater length in Louis Liger's *Le Jardinier Fleuriste et historiographe, ou la culture universelle des fleurs, arbres, arbustes, & arbrisseaux, servans à l'embelissement des Jardins*, 2 vols. (Paris: Chez Damien Beugnie, 1704),vol. 2, 369–374.

6. F.B., *La Flore sainte*, 64–65. The entire passage reads: "Et d'autant que les anciens Auteurs, qui ne connoissoient pas quantité de Fleurs, d'une beauté excellente, que nous avons en ces derniers Siècles, avoient donné à la Rose (à cause de sa vive couleur, de sa douce odeur, & de son abondance) le titre de Reine des Fleurs, faisant une Monarchie semblable à celle des Amazones, qui ne vouloient point de Roy. Maintenant que le régne de ces Inocentes est finy, il est à propos de faire un Roy, & d'en donner le titre à l'Oeillet, pour regnir en Monarque, & tenir préférablement les reînes de cette Monarchie: Et à cette fin, composer une Cour illustre, quoy-que toùûjours tributaire de l'Empire de Flore, ou plûtôt du ressort, ou sous l'invocation de Saint Flore, (sans préjudicier à la sainte allusion qui se pourroit faire de la Fleur à la Sainteté.)"

7. See Levi D'Ancona, *Botticelli's "Primavera," 20*; and Mirella Levi D'Ancona, The Garden of the Renaissance: Botanical Symbolism in Italian Painting (Florence: Leo S. Olschki, 1977) for exhaustive studies of the very specific symbolism of individual floral species as used in Renaissance painting. Levi D'Ancona relies upon an extensive group of classical texts and Renaissance interpretations of them in this study of their symbolism.

These precise symbolic meanings of flowers perhaps constituted a veritable "language of flowers" that was incorporated into Renaissance iconography. Jack Goody (*The Culture of Flowers*, 179–181) suggests that this floral code could have served as the basis for Ophelia's seemingly incoherent list of flowers she distributes to the king and queen once she has gone mad in *Hamlet*. Certain species of flowers did connote specific sentiments in Renaissance Europe. This study, however, is primarily concerned with broader, more general meanings attached to the cultivation and collection of flowers.

8. F.B., *La Flore sainte*, 64.

9. The Salic Law has recently been reinterpreted by Sarah Hanley, "Identity Politics and Rulership in France: Female Political Place and the Fraudulent Salic Law in Christine de Pizan and Jean de Montreuil," in *Changing Identities in Early Modern France*, ed. Michael Wolfe with a foreword by Natalie Zemon Davis (Durham, N.C.: Duke University Press, 1997).

10. F.B., *La Flore sainte*, preface, n.p. "Ce qu'ils font comme Critiques & censeurs à l'égard de tout es les autres choses, ils le font encore à l'égard de la fleur, & de la passion que quantité d'honnêtes gens ont pour elle, qui est sans doute la plus pure & la plus innocente de toutes les passions."

11. Ibid.

12. Ibid., 7–8. "Joignez à l'utilité qu'on reçoit des Fleurs, l'ancienne coûtume de faire & de porter des couronnes, des guirlandes & des bouquets, principalement pour les filles, à qui elles servent d'ornement. Strabon dit, que cette coûtume vint premierement de Vibonne, en Calabre, où Proserpine se retira pour l'abondance des Fleurs qui y étoient: Et Ovide donne à Europe cette occupation de faire des festons & des guirlandes, dans les prairies de la Phénicie, lors qu'elle fut ravie par Jupiter. Pline au I. Livre de son histoire dit, que les premiers qui diversifiérent les couronnes de fleurs, furent les Sicyoniens, à l'imitation de cette fameuse bouquetiére Glycéra, qui fut aimée d'un excellent Peintre de Sicyone, nommé Plausias, qui tâchoit d'imiter en ses tableaux les bouquets qu'elle façonnoit, avec tant d'art, & qui la représenta dans un tableau . . . si bien ornée de chapeaux de fleurs, qu'on ne pouvoit rien voir de plus admirable."

13. Ibid., 10–11. "L'Eglise de Jésus Christ a suivi l'usage de l'antiquité, puisque d'un consintement unanimie, & par une coûtume que le Ciel a luy-même authorisée, l'on se sert des Fleurs pour décorer les Temples, les Autels, & les Ornemens sacrez; qu'on en parséme les Eglises & les ruës, dans les Processions solennelles; qu'on en embellit les torches & les flambeaux, & qu'on en couronne les images des Saints, comme n'y ayant rien dans toute la Nature de plus pure, de plus simple, de plus innocent, dont on puisse faire à Dieu d'agréables offrandes."

14. Ibid., 12. "Quel aveuglement est le vôtre, de ne pas l'état que le Ciel fait de la Fleur, puisque Dieu a bien vouleu changer du pain en fleur, par un miracle surprenant, en faveur d'un innocent Fille, & inspirer une troupe de Religieuses à changes le nom d'une des leurs Soeurs, en celuy de Flore, pour la substituër à une Divinité Payenne, & donner par ce moyen une Patrone Sainte aux Floristes, laquelle ils peuvent honorer sans crime, & cultiver ainsi la Fleur tout saintement?"

15. The Saint Flora that F.B. cited was only one of a number of saints of that name. An Italian hagiographer by the name of Bozio cited the same Flora as F.B., a thirteenth-century nun in the order of Saint Jean de Jerusalem, while a nineteenth-century "encyclopédie théologique" included at least nine Saint Floras, one of which was that of F.B.

See Bozio, *Les Vies des saincts, et des sainctes de l'ordre de sainct Jean de Jérusalem*, trans. J. Baudoin (Paris: Jean du Hamel, 1631), 132–139; and J. P. Migne, ed., *Encyclopédie Théologique*, vol. 40 (Paris: Chez l'Editeur, 1850), s.v. "Flor."

16. F.B., *La Flore sainte*, "Eloge de Sainte Flore," n.p. Flora's sanctity had been revealed by God through the miraculous transformation of bread she was secretly supplying to starving villagers into "tres-belles & riches Fleurs de Lys & des Roses."

17. Alfred Franklin, *Dictionnarie historique des arts, métiers et professions excercé dans Paris depuis le treizième siècle* (Paris: Librairie universitaire française et étrangère, 1906), 98, 406.

18. Estienne and Liebault, *Maison Rustique*, 300.

19. Nicolas de Bonnefons, *Le Jardinier François, qui enseigne à cultiver les arbres, & herbes potageres; avec la maniere de conserver les fruicts, & faire toutes de confitures, conserves, & massepans. Dédié aux dames*, 5th ed. (Amsterdam: Jean Bleau, 1654), 100.

20. N. Valnay, *Connoissance et culture parfaite des tulippes rares, des anemones extra-ordinaires, des oeillets fins, et des belles oreilles d'ours panachées* (Paris: Laurent d'Houry, 1688), "Avertissement," n.p. "Quel goût y a-t'il en comparaison dans d'autres curiositez plus à la mode, dans les Tableaux, les Medailles & les Porcelaines. Regardez-les tant qu'il vous plaira, vous verrez toujours la même chose. La varieté & ce jeu annuel des Fleurs sont bien plus satisfaisans. Toutes les beautez de l'Art de la Peinture sont dans le dessein, l'execution & le coloris. Je défie l'Academie de Peinture entiere d'imaginer en Fleur aussi à propos que le naturel, d'executer dans la derniere perfection ce qu'il nous montre, & d'approcher jamais du coloris des Fleurs. Un tableau est toujours un, un oignon se multiplie. On donne à son amy une rare Fleur, & on l'a à soy; ce sont plusieurs originaux aussi se communiquement, l'art ne va point là. Une Medaille toute usée, dont ce défaut fait en partie le merite, quel-qu'ancienne qu'elle soit, est toujours moderne à l'égard des Fleurs; elles sont de la creation du monde. S'il plaisoit aux Sçavans de raisonne sur elles, comme sur une Medaille qui ne prouve jamais rien de tout ce que leur sçavoir leur fait debiter, leur Dissertations plairoient également. Il en est de meme à proportion des Porcelains, & des autres raretez qui sont en vogue, & quand on voudra que la raison se mesle des goûts, les belles Fleurs teindront le premier rang parmy les plaisirs de la veüe."

21. As with so many cultural and intellectual developments in the Renaissance and early modern periods, the Italians led the way in the study of natural history. Paula Findlen writes, "The collecting of antiquities and the passion for natural objects appeared in Italy before any other part of Western Europe; in both instances, a strong historicizing impulse on the part of Italian Renaissance humanists precipitated these activites." Findlen, *Possessing Nature: Museums, Collecting, and Scientific Culture in Early Modern Italy* (Berkeley: University of California Press, 1994), 1.

22. Some scholars trace the interest in natural history specimens to an even earlier era. Lorrain Daston and Katherine Park see natural history specimens as part of the culture of wonder and marvels that dates to the twelfth century when, according to them, an increase in the number of ancient texts written on the natural world sparked new interest while the emergence of cities, the increased sophistication of bureaucracies and court culture, and the establishment of schools and universities allowed for the creation of an audience curious about the wonders of the natural world. See Daston and Park, *Wonders and the Order of Nature (1150–1750)* (New York: Zone Books, 1998).

23. The role of consumption and commodities shaping Renaissance culture is

explored in Lisa Jardine, *Worldly Goods: A New History of the Renaissance* (London: Macmillan, 1997).

24. In fact, historians have attributed to these collectors a role in the transformation of the means of study to include a greater emphasis on observation and experience. Findlen (*Possessing Nature*, 1) writes: "These two activities—collecting and the interrogation of nature—met in the studies of naturalistics such as Ulisse Aldrovandi (1522–1605) and Athanasius Kircher (1602–1680), resulting in new attitudes toward nature, as a collectible entity, and generating new technologies of investigation that subsequently transformed natural history." Similarly, Peter Miller writes: "Antiquaries were characterized by an almost obsessive devotion to reconstructing the material culture and imaginative forms of the ancient world. . . . Their most decisive contribution to the way the past was studied was in emphasizing the value of non-literary sources and developing rules for using them. Three sorts of intellectual practice were typical: collection, observation, and comparison." Peter N. Miller, *Peiresc's Europe: Learning and Virtue in the Seventeenth Century* (New Haven, Conn.: Yale University Press, 2000), 8.

25. Findlen, *Possessing Nature*, 105.

26. See, for example, the Salon Bleu of Madame de Rambouillet.

27. Miller (*Peiresc's Europe*, 50–51) writes: "The commitment to sociability as a practice of moral excellence that complemented the life of learning could hardly be extended much beyond the world of neo-Stoics and monkish scholars and was dropped. What remained was what we might term the 'momentum' of the practice but not its meaning: constancy without self-mastery, conversation without improvement, and friendship without philosophy. This, too, is part of the history of civil society." He continues: "This revolution of style against substance broke out in Paris in the 1620s and was marked by the opening of a *salon* in which Latin and learning were equally discouraged and which was dominated by worldly values of the sort that Corneille represented in his early comedies. . . . Why this happened in the 1620s is a significant unresolved question."

28. See Erica Harth, *Cartesian Women: Versions and Subversions of Rational Discourse in the Old Regime* (Ithaca, N.Y.: Cornell University Press, 1992) for women's scholarly contributions to salon culture.

29. Miller (*Peiresc's Europe*, 46) writes that there was a "shift in the center of gravity of civil life in seventeenth-century France and England from aristocratic, Latinate, erudite, and male 'academics,' to the mixed-gender and explicitly non-erudite *salons*.

30. Findlen (*Possessing Nature*, 144) writes that in Italy, "As Aldrovandi's catalogue of visitors suggests, more strongly than any other document emerging from the collecting culture of the period, the emerging scientific culture largely excluded women from its official representations. On the one hand, the strength of courtly models and the importance of courtiers as naturalists, collectors, and visitors allowed a limited place for women, not as participants in this discourse but as an audience whose presence facilitated the civil conversation of men. On the other hand, the organization of his catalogue of visitors allowed no place in which to record such encounters [with women], nor would they have added to his standing in the republic of letters. . . . The invisibility of women and servants underscores the social function of Aldrovandi's catalogue, which did not indiscriminantly record all visitors. Each entry was a calculated attempt to enhance the reputation of the museum and its creator, by collecting people of worth within its pages."

31. Jean-Louis Flandrin, "Distinction through Taste," in *A History of Private Life*, ed. Philippe Ariès and Georges Duby, vol. 3, *Passions of the Renaissance*, ed. Roger Chartier, trans. Arthur Goldhammer (Cambridge, Mass.: Belknap Press of Harvard University Press, 1989), 307.

32. La Chesnée Monstereul, *Le Floriste françois*, preface, n.p.

33. The term *fleuriste* was a new one in the seventeenth century. It is not included in the *Dictionnaire de l'ancienne langue française et de tous ses dialectes du IXe au XVe siècle*, or in the *Dictionnaire de la langue française du siezième siècle*. According to the *Dictionnaire étymologique et historique de la langue française*, "fleuriste" dates to the seventeenth century. It is in common usage during the seventeenth century, as illustrated through countless flower gardening manuals, and it was included in Antoine Furetière's *Dictionnaire universel*. See Frédéric Godefroy, *Dictionnaire de l'ancienne langue française et de tous ses dialectes du IXe au XVe siècle* (Paris: F. Vieweg, 1885); Edmond Huguet, *Dictionnaire de la langue française du siezième siècle* (Paris: Librairie M. Didier, 1973); Emmanuèle Baumgartner and Philippe Ménard, *Dictionnaire étymologique et historique de la langue française* (Paris: La Pochothèque, 1996), s.v. "fleuriste;" Antoine Furetière, *Dictionnaire universel des arts et des sciences* (La Haye: 1690), s.v. "fleuriste."

34. For more on Morin and his brother René, see Marjorie F. Warner, "The Morins," *National Horticultural Magazine* (1954): 168–176.

35. Pierre Morin, *Catalogues de quelques plantes à fleurs qui sont de présent au jardin de Pierre Morin le jeune, dit Troisième; fleuriste, scitué au faux-bourg Saint Germain, proche la Charité* (Paris: François le Cointe, 1651).

36. The term *jardinier fleuriste* was identified as a subdivision of the master gardener guild in eighteenth-century Paris. See Franklin, *Dictionnaire historique*, 406.

37. For a discussion of the emergence of the phrase, see David Tarver and Brent Elliott, "Des Fleuristes aux sociétés horticoles. Histoire des expositions florales," in *L'Empire de Flore: Histoire et représentations des fleurs en Europe du XVIe au XIXe siècle*, ed. Sabine van Sprang with the collaboration of Gerda De Brabandere (Brussels: Renaissance du Livre, 1996), 115–117.

38. Valnay, *Connoissance et culture parfaite des tulippes rares*, 4, 55.

39. Ibid., avertissement [n.p.].

40. J. L[aurent], *Abregé pour les arbres nains et autres* (Paris: Charles de Sercy, 1683). He wrote for those "Curieux en ces sortes de choses."

41. Ballon and Garnier, "d'après Barbier," *Nouvelle instruction facile pour la culture des figuiers. Où l'on apprend la maniere de les élever, multiplier & conserver, tant en caisses, qu'autrement. Avec un traité de la culture des fleurs* (Paris: Charles de Sercy, 1692), 113. Ballon and Garnier's 1692 flower gardening treatise addressed the great "nombre des personnes qui en sont curieuses" about flowers.

42. Robert-Xavier Mallet, *Beauté de la Nature, ou fleurimanie raisonnée* (Paris: Didot, le jeune, 1775), n.p. Mallet wrote his book "pour l'avantage des Curieux Fleuristes."

43. Furetière, *Dictionnaire*, s.v. "fleuriste." The entry reads: "FLEURISTE. C'est une personne qui est curieuse en fleurs rares, ou celle qui en fait trafic. Ce *fleuriste* a un beau carreau de tulipes."

44. Thomas Corneille, *Le Dictionnaire des arts et des sciences* (1694; repr. Geneva: Slatkine Reprints, 1968), s.v. "fleuriste."

45. For a brief overview of the publication of the dictionaries, see Alain Rey, "Linguistic Absolutism," in *A New History of French Literature*, ed. Denis Hollier (Cambridge, Mass.: Harvard University Press, 1994), 373–379.

46. Furetière, *Dictionnaire*, s.v. "curieux." The French reads: "CURIEUX, se dit aussi de celuy qui a ramassé les choses les plus rares, les plus belles et les plus extraordinaires qu'il a pu trouver tant dans les arts que dans la nature. C'est un *curieux* de Livres, de médailles, d'estampes, de tableaux, de fleurs, de coquilles, d'antiquités, de choses naturelles."

47. *Dictionnaire de l'Académie française* (Paris: 1694), s.v. "curieux." The entry reads: "CURIEUX, EUSE. adj. Qui a beaucoup d'envie et de soin d'apprendre, de voir, de posséder des choses nouvelles, rares, excellentes etc. *Fort curieux. extrêmement curieux. curieux de sçavoir, il est curieux. il est curieux de fleurs, de tulipes, curieux de nouvelles. curieux de peintures, de tableaux, de médailles. curieux de livres, de bustes. elle est curieuse en habits, curieuse en linge.*" For a discussion of the entry, see Krzysztof Pomian, *Collectors and Curiosities: Paris and Venice, 1500–1800*, trans. Elizabeth Wiles-Portier (Cambridge, Mass.: Polity Press, 1990), 55. Note that the Académie limited women's curiosity to clothing and linens. Despite the strong symbolic connections between women and flowers, little evidence has emerged that seventeenth-century French women were engaged in flower collecting.

48. Pomian, *Collectors*, 45–64.

49. Ibid., 53–60.

50. The tulip mania is discussed in greater detail in Wilfrid Blunt, *Tulipomania* (London: Penguin Books, 1950); Ernst Heinrich Krelage, *Drie Eeuwen Bloembollenexport de geschiedenis van den bloembollenhandel en der hollandsche bloembollen tot 1938* (The Hague: Rijksuitgeverij, 1946); N. W. (Nicolaas Wilhelmus) Posthumus, "The Tulip Mania in Holland in the Years 1636 and 1637," *Journal of Economic and Business History* 1:3 (May 1929): 434–466; and Simon Schama, *The Embarrassment of Riches: An Interpretation of Dutch Culture in the Golden Age* (N.p.: Fontana Press, 1988), 351–365. The seventeenth-century pamphlet literature of the Dutch tulip mania is reprinted in E. H. Krelage, *De pamfletten van den tulpenwindhandel, 1636–1637* (The Hauge: M. Nijhoff, 1942). Popular prints also ridiculed the tulip speculators. The most famous of such images is Crispin de Passe the Younger's *Floraes Mallewagen* of 1637, which is reproduced in Schama, *Embarrassment of Riches*, 365.

51. La Bruyère includes the expense of flowers in his attack on *fleuristes* (discussed below), and John Evelyn mentions in his description of Gaston, duc d'Orléans's flower gardens that the duke's flowers had cost him a small fortune. Evelyn wrote, "Towards the grotto and stables [of the duke's garden at the Luxembourg palace], within a wall, is a garden of choyce flowers, in which the Duke spends many thousand pistoles." John Evelyn, *The Diary of John Evelyn Esq. From 1641 to 1705–6, with Memoir*, ed. William Bray (London: W. W. Gibbings, 1890), 58.

52. Pomian, *Collectors*, 56–59. According to Pomian, the Académie viewed curiosity with less esteem than Furetière who, incidentally, had been thrown out of the Académie française for writing his own dictionary while the Académie continued to work (though more slowly) on theirs. See also Rey, "Linguistic Absolutism."

53. René Descartes, *Discours de la méthode pour bien conduire sa raison et chercher la vérité dans les sciences = Discourse on the Method of Conducting One's Reason Well and*

of Seeking the Truth in the Sciences. A Bilingual Edition and Interpretation of René Descartes' Philosophy of Method, ed. and trans. George Heffernan (Notre Dame, Ind.: University of Notre Dame Press, 1994), 98–99. Pomian writes: "the principles supposedly governing from within knowledge itself were used to justify the need to keep curiosity within well-defined limits. To this end, Descartes condemned blind curiosity in favour of research carried out in accordance with the rules of method. He even went as far as to say that seeking truth without due regard being paid to these rules was worse than not seeking it at all." Pomian, *Collectors*, 62.

54. Ibid., 61.

55. "Le Bouquet est une production des hommes aussi bien que du Ciel & de la terre. L'agréement de nos Dames vient des soucis de plusieurs grands Iardiniers. Il y a des esprits dont la curiosité est amoureuse qui ont quelquefois moins de soin de leur maison que d'un parterre, & qui s'oublient de l'entretien de leur vie pour entretenir des fleurs. On dit qu'une rose nasquit de la blessure du pied de la Deesse de l'Amour, mais c'est la main de ceux dont ie parle qui fait naistre toutes les autres beautez terrestres. Si l'air semble nous menacer de quelque tempeste, ils craignent plus pour leur iardin que pour leur personne, & ils ne desirent pas de beaux iours pour vivre longtemps, mais pour voir vivre leurs oeillets. Le matin il les salvent avec l'Aurore, ils d'edaigneroient de voir le Soleil aux prix d'eux s'il ne leur devoit donner un nouvel éclat, & la nuit qui est la mere du repos est le sujet de leur inquietude, pource qu'ils craignent que sa froideur n'étouffe ces rares beautez que la chaleur vivifie. Au reste quand le Ciel ne leur envoye pas sa rosée, ils forment une pluie sur la terre qu'ils distillent avecque des arroisoirs. Ils taschent de surpasser la nature par artifice, & neatmoins leur artifice agit tousiours par les forces de la nature. Ils ne se contentent par mesme d'eslever leurs Creatures dans des Iardins, ils les portent encor dans leurs cabinets, & les font vivre sans violence en les tirant hors de leur élement. Ils font communément ce que Semiramis fit appeller miracle, c'est à die des parterres suspendus en l'air." Grenaille, *Les Plaisirs des Dames*, 5–6.

56. Schnapper, *Le Géant, la licorne, la tulipe*, 43.

57. Jean de La Bruyère, *Les Caractères de Theophraste traduite du Grec: avec les caractères ou les moeurs de ce siècle*, 6th ed. (Paris: Estienne Michallet, 1691), 483–484. "Le fleuriste a un jardin dans un Fauxbourg, il y court au lever du soleil, & il en revient à son coucher; vous le voyez planté, & qui a pris racine au milieu de ses tulippes & devant la *solitaire* [a tulip]; il ouvre de grands yeux, il frotte ses mains, il se baisse, il la voit de plus prés, il ne l'a jamais vûë si belle, il la le coeur épanoüi de joye; il la quitte pour *l'orientale*, delà il va à la *veuve*, il passe au *drap d'or*, de celle-cy à *l'agathe*, d'où il revient enfin à la *solitaire*, où il se fixe, où il se lasse, où il s'assit, où il oublie de dîner; aussi est-elle nuancé, bordée, huilée, à pieces emportées, elle a un beau vase ou un beau calice, il la contemple, il l'admire; Dieu & la nature sont en tout cela ce qu'il n'admire point, il ne va pas plus loin que l'oignon de sa tulippe qu'il ne livreroit pas pour mil écus, & qu'il donnera pour rien quand les tulippes seront negligées, & que les oeillets auront prévalu. Cet homme raisonnable, qui a une ame, qui a un culte & une religion, revient chez soy fatigué, affamé, mais fort content de sa journée; il a vû des tulippes."

58. Valnay, *Connoissance et culture parfaite des tulippes rares*, 55. "Je sçay que Monsieur le Prince & Monsieur le Marquis de Seignelay en ont plusieurs [anemones], mais je ne sçay s'ils en sont curieux."

59. La Chesnée Monstereul, *Le Floriste françois*, 199–200. In the chapter "De la Difference qu'il y a entre les veritables Floristes & les curieux ignorans," La Chesnée
Monstereul distinguishes "vrais Floristes, d'avec un certain tas de gens qu'un peu de
curiosité porte à aimer les fleurs."

60. Ibid., 200. The imposter, wrote La Chesnée Monstereul, was like a "vain
amoureux qui croyent meriter les affections des Dames, sans avoir la peine de les
acquerir, & posseder le tresor de leur beauté sans qu'il leur couste auxune chose."

61. Ibid., 200–201. "Ce sont Floristes lesquels moins descrets que les Abeilles qui
visitent les fleurs sans les endommager, vont comme des pourrceaux foüillans & pico-
rans nos parterres pour en enlever les richesses par leur authorité ou demandes importunes; & après qu'ils ont ravy ces beautez contre le gré de ceux qui les conservent, veulent
passer entre les vrais Floristes. . . . Ce sont gens qui sacrifient à des Dieux inconnus, &
qui dans le Temple de Flora adorent des Divinitez qui leur sont estrangeres. Ce sont
Curieux ignorans qui possedent des tresors sans en connoistre la valeur; & enfin ce sont
personnes qui demeurans dans l'admiration de tant de diverses couleurs qui se rencontrent aux Tulipes, s'arrestent à la contemplation de leurs beautez, & croyent estre bien
sçavans quand ils begueient de toutes ces choses."

62. Ibid., 201–202. The ignorant curious recognized neither "cause ny la dignité du
sujet dont ils se rendent adorateurs." Having served metaphorically as a "Chimique, qui
separe le pur de l'impur, pour connoistre la dignité de l'un, par le mépris de l'autre. . . ,"
La Chesnée Monstereul explained, "je veux rebuter ces gens là, sans admettre dans le
Catalogue de vrais Floristes."

63. Samuel Gilbert, *The Florists Vade-mecum* (London: Thomas Simmons, 1682),
"Epistle to the Reader," n.p.

64. Despite the connections between women and flowers explored in Chapter 1,
this is the only instance I have found connecting flower collection and cultivation to an
accusation of effeminacy. It is possible that Gilbert's statement reflects the participation of English women in the collection of flowers, the most famous of whom were Mary
Capel, duchess of Beaufort, and Mary Delany. English gardeners also wrote a number
of gardening manuals for women (see Chapter 3). See Gloria Cottesloe, *The Duchess of
Beaufort's Flowers* (Exeter, Eng.: Webb & Bower, 1983); and Ruth Hayden, *Mrs. Delany:
Her Life and Her Flower Collages* (London: British Museum Press, 1992). English gardening manuals for women include Charles Evelyn, *The Lady's Recreation: Or, the Third
and Last Part of the Art of Gardening Improv'd* (London: J. Roberts, 1717).

65. Henry Van Oosten, *The Dutch Gardener: Or, The Compleat Florist* (London: D.
Midwinter and T. Leigh, 1703), preface, n.p.

66. *La Culture des fleurs* (Bourge en Bresse: Joseph Ravoux, 1692), preface, n.p. "De
toutes les occupations où l'Esprit se délasse le plus innocement, celle de Fleuristes fait
sans doute aujourduy d'empressement d'un grand nombre des plus honnêtes gens de
toute sort d'Etat. Il seroit inutile de faire remarquer icy, qu'il est peu de plaisir de ceux
même que les plus moderez, & les plus sevéres se permettent sans scrupule, ou l'Ame
partage moins ses sentiments avec le Corps, qui celuy dont l'éclat, l'odeur, & la varieté réuliere des parterres récompensent les peines, & l'assiduité de ceux qui se mélent
de les Cultiver."

67. Ibid, conclusion, n.p. He suggested that "on regarderoit le Ciel comme le
Pere des Fleurs, la Terre comme leur Mere, & l'Air & l'Eau comme leur nourriture. Quoy

qu'il en soit nous ne voyons pas que nos Soyes, & nos Laines, nos Toiles, ny nes Etoffes, ny même les Coloris les plus vifs, & les plus éclatants de ceux que l'Europe emprunte des autres parties du Monde, ayent encore trompé la veüe jusqu'a luy faire confondre les enventions de l'Art avec les productions, dont la nature pare les Compartiments de nos Parterres."

68. Ibid. "Savez-vous bien (Mon cher Lecteur) que vostre parterre, est une figure de vostre Ame, & qu'un jour il vous servira de condamnation dans les Jugements de Dieu, si vous avez negligé de cultiver la Plante de son Jardin qu'il vous-même, & si vous avez preferé la culture de toutes les Fleurs dont je viens de vous entretenir. . . . Le Monde est le Jardin, où plutôt la Pepiniere de ce grand Dieu, c'est de là qu'il tire tous les jours des Fleurs pour les mettre sur les Autels de sa gloire, & pour en faire les ornements de son Paradis."

69. Renati Rapini, *Hortorum libri IV cum Disputatione de Cultura Hortensi* (Paris: Typographia Regia, 1665).

70. Elfreida Dubois, "René Rapin: L'homme et l'oeuvre" (Ph.D. diss., Faculté des Lettres et Sciences Humaines de Paris, 1970; Lille: Université de Lille, Service de Reproduction des Thèses, 1972), 202–213.

71. Renatus Rapinus [René Rapin], *Of Gardens. Four Books*, trans. John Evelyn (London: T. R. and N. T., 1672), preface, n.p.

72. Ibid.

73. Ada Segre has suggested that F.B.'s moralizing is rooted in the controversial Jansenist movement in seventeenth-century France. See Ada Segre, "Le Retour de Flore: Naissance et évolution des jardins de fleurs de 1550 à 1650," in *L'Empire de Flore: Histoire et représentations des fleurs en Europe du XVIe au XIXe siècle*, ed. Sabine van Sprang with the collaboration of Gerda De Brabandere (Brussels: Renaissance du Livre, 1996), 179.

74. Many Protestant sects, especially the English Puritans, were deeply suspicious of flowers because they were so heavily incorporated into Catholic rituals. See Jack Goody, *The Culture of Flowers* (Cambridge: Cambridge University Press, 1993), 166–205.

75. Pierre Bourdieu, *Distinction: A Social Critique of the Judgement of Taste*, trans. Richard Nice (Cambridge, Mass.: Harvard University Press, 1984), 11.

76. Schnapper wrote: "S'agissant de fleuristes, une telle ignorance serait moins grave, puisqu'ils semblent peu soucieux de hiérarchie sociale. Cette curiosité traverse en tous les cas les milieux sociaux les plus variés, depuis le Roi-Soleil jusqu'au modest apothicaire." Schnapper, *Le Géant, la licorne, et la tulipe*, 213.

77. Jean-Baptiste Dru, *Catalogue des plantes* (Lyon: Guillaume Barbier, 1653), 13. "Mais comme deux moyens servent à l'acquisition des Fleurs, l'argent & l'exchange, je pratiqueray fidelement celuy-cy, & seray encore plus aise qu'on se serve de l'autre: & pour ne point denier à autray la mesme satisfaction que j'en desire recevoir, j'accommoderay en toutes les deux facons, ceux qui souhaitteront (aussi bien que je le desire moy-mesme) de contenter cette loüable curiosité. Ces choses sont aymées si generalement de tout le monde, que non seulement les enfans dans un âge exempt de passions, tesmoignent d'en avoir une tres-puissante pour elles: . . . entre les plus sensez, ceux qui les considerent les mons, venans à jetter de hazard les yeux dessus, en soint surpris, & y trouvent des sujets dignes de leur agréement & de leur admiration. Je ne sçaurois exprimer le nombre des personnes d'esprit, que charmée des agreables divertissements

que fournissent les plants, se sont données à leur culture, pour se distraire de leurs plus grandes affaires & de leurs estudes plus serieuses: & mesme il s'en est trouvé quelques-unes qui en ont fait leur principale occupation, leur plus chere estude & leur divertissement tout ensemble."

78. Liger, *Le Jardinier Fleuriste et historiographe*, vol. 1, 36–37. Liger wrote: "Un Jardinier Fleuriste qui doit être naturellement curieux, doit satisfaire honnêtement la curiosité de ceux qui lui demandent à voir les fleurs se son jardin. Persuadé qu'il doit être, que ces sortes de gens se donneront bien de garde d'en cüeillir aucune: & pour prevenir ceux qui moins honnêtes, portent indescretement la main sur une fleur, pour la ravir à l'insçu du Maître, il fera graver ces deux vers sur la porte de son jardin."

79. For more on Jean Robin, see Marjorie F. Warner, "Jean and Vespasien Robin, 'Royal Botanists,' and North American Plants, 1601–1635," *National Horticultural Magazine* 35.4 (October 1956): 214–220.

80. John Evelyn, *The Diary of John Evelyn*, 59.

81. Dru, *Catalogue des plantes*.

82. Jacques Contant and Paul Contant, *Les Oeuvres de Jacques et Paul Contant pere et fils maistres apoticaires de la ville de Poictiers* (Poitiers: Julian Thoreau et veuve d'Antoine Mesniers, Imprimeurs ordinaires du Roy, & de l'Université, 1640).

83. Schnapper, *Le Géant, la licorne, et la tulipe*, 223–224. Charles Clusius (Charles de l'Ecluse) was the early Flemish botanist credited with spreading tulips throughout Europe.

84. Ibid., 231.

85. Guy de La Brosse, *Description du jardin royal des plantes Médicinales, establ) par le Roy Louis le Juste, à Paris, contenant le catalogue des plantes qui y sont de présent cultivées, ensemble le plan du jardin* (Paris: n.p., 1636), 21. "Les deux premieres [parterres] & plus prochaines du logis sont plantée de toutes sortes d'arbrisseaux tousious verds, & de plantes vivaces, tant à fleurs plaisantes qu'autres, & les deux autres de plusieurs sortes d'arbrisseaux se despoüillant de feuilles l'hyver."

86. Schnapper, *Le Géant, la licorne, et la tulipe*, 247.

87. Ibid., 213. Schnapper has mined the letters of Peiresc for his reconstruction of the world of collecting in the seventeenth century. See pages 237–247 for a discussion on seventeenth-century collecting specifically devoted to Peiresc and his friends.

88. Ibid., 214.

89. Ibid., 214.

90. L[ouis] B[oulanger], *Jardinage des Oeillets* (Paris: Louis Boulanger, 1647), dedication, n.p. Boulanger dedicated his work to Geoffrey Lullier, "Chevalier Seigneur d'Orgeval & de Mal-maison, Conseiller du Roy en ses Conseils d'Estat & Privé, & Maistre des Requestes Ordinaires de son Hostel." Boulanger wrote: "Comme tres-fidel & ancien magistrate de nos Roys, toutes vos laborieuses occupations n'ayants pour but que d'immortaliser les fleurs de lis de la France, & vos innocens divertissements s'occupants à cultiver les oeillets du paradis terrestre de vostre agreable sejour de Paris."

91. Valnay, *Connoissance et culture parfaite des tulippes rares*, 7–8, 55, 88. The Monsieur de Valnay was himself the "Controlleur de la Maison du Roy," and his flower gardening manual identified among the Parisian curious Monsieur Desgranges, "Controlleur general de la Tresorie de la Maison de sa Majesté," Monsieur Caboud, "Avocat au Conseil," Messieurs Descoteaux and Breart, "Officiers du Roy," Monsieur le Verrier,

"Gressier de Consuls," and Monsieur Charpentier, "Lieutenant General de Compeigne."

92. Martin Lister reported that in the duc D'Aumont's private garden were "parterres well filled with flowers; yet there was only one sort in each, such as tulips, &c." Lister, *An Account of Paris, at the Close of the Seventeeth [sic] Century* (London: Black, Young, & Young, 1823), 158–159.

93. Schnapper, *Le Géant, la licorne, et la tulipe*, 46.

94. La Chesnée Monstereul, *Le Floriste françois*, 249.

95. Kenneth Woodbridge, *Princely Gardens: The Origins and Development of the French Formal Style* (New York: Rizzoli, 1986), 155.

96. Fouquet obtained anemones from his brother in Italy. Schnapper quotes a 1656 letter from his brother to Nicholas in which he writes, "Vous serez peut-être mieux pourvu en anémones qu'homme de France." Schnapper, *Le Géant, la licorne, et la tulipe*, 47.

97. Schnapper, *Le Géant, la licorne, et la tulipe*, 213; and Orest Ranum, *The Fronde: A French Revolution, 1648–1652* (New York: W. W. Norton, 1993), 271. Reports of the cultivation of flowers while in exile or prison may have been a fashionable trope. For, as Elizabeth Goldsmith has demonstrated, exile was presented by Madame de Sévigné in heroic terms in which the exiled person passed his or her time in an idyllic pastoral setting. See Elizabeth Goldsmith, *Exclusive Conversations: The Art of Interacting in Seventeenth-Century France* (Philadelphia: University of Pennsylvania Press, 1988), "Talking in the Garden," 123–132.

98. Ibid., 194.

99. See Chapter 5.

100. The Sun King's relationship with flowers is discussed extensively in Chapter 5.

101. Valnay (*Connoissance et culture parfaite des tulippes rares*, n.p.) wrote, "La connoissance de ces Fleurs est fondée sur des beautez si essentielles & si sensibles, que je plains leur merite, quand je considere que plusieurs personnes de qualité de ce païs-cy & qui paroissent avoire du goût, n'en sont point touchez."

102. Ibid., "Avertissement," n.p. "Avant le regne de Louis XIV y connoissoit-t'on la beauté des Jardins? Il semble que les Arts & leur suitte se soient reservez de tout temps pour fleurir dans celuy-cy, & que parce que nostre Monarque merite d'autres courrones que tous les Heros, il nous soit né de plus belles Fleurs qu'on n'en ait jamais veu, pour servir de modeles aux habiles Artisans de ses trophées."

103. *La Culture des fleurs*, preface, n.p. The author wrote: "C'en est plus dire qu'il n'en faloit, pour soûtenir l'estime, que le soin des Fleurs s'est exquise dans le comerce du Monde; depuis que le plus grand des Roys & des Heros, qui peut en Souverain disposer des modes, aussi bien que de tout ce qui est de sont gout, et a fait l'objet de ses empressements pendant les loisirs que l'interest public luy accorde pour se délasser."

104. I first explored this topic in a paper presented at Dumbarton Oaks and subsequently published. See Elizabeth Hyde, "Flowers of Distinction: Taste, Class, and Floriculture in Seventeenth-Century France," in *Bourgeois and Aristocratic Cultural Encounters in Garden Art, 1550–1850*, ed. Michel Conan (Washington, D.C.: Dumbarton Oaks, 2002), 77–100.

105. Pierre Goubert, *The Ancien Régime: French Society, 1600–1750*, trans. Steven Cox (New York: Harper Torchbooks, 1974), 180.

106. Bourdieu (*Distinction*, 69) argues that the conflict between the *doctes* and the *mondain* is not surprising: "It is no accident that the opposition between the 'scholastic' (or 'pedantic') and the *mondain*, the effortlessly elegant, is at the heart of debates over taste and culture in every age: behind two ways of producing or appreciating cultural works, it very clearly designates two contrasting modes of acquisition, and, in the modern period at least, two different relationships to the educational system."

107. "Le plaisir qu'il y a d'en efleuer quelque beau & rare, outre le profit qu'il apporte à son Maistre, est de le veoir visité de plusieurs Iardiniers, esperans en tirer quelque douceur, & courtisé de quantité de personnes de condition & de merite, qui viennent en examiner toutes les parties, remarquer le feuillage, dintinguer les couleurs, & trouver, ou chacher les defauts, selong l'esprit genereux, ou envieux qui l'anime. Et ce avec le petite poinçon d'argent qui en developpe les merveilles, pour ne pas alterer sa beauté par l'attouchement d'une main eschaufée. Ie souhaitte souvent cette bonne fortune à tous ceux qui le cultivent, à la charge qu'ils le feront tirer au naturel par quelque adroit pinceau, & qu'ils nous en conserveront la race, sinon en effet du moins en peinture." Boulanger, *Jardinage des oeillets*, 24–25.

108. La Chesnée Monstereul, *Le Floriste françois*, 180–181. "Si les Tulipes estoient renduës communes," he lamented, "ce seroit encor oster le plus loüable commerce qui se pratique entre les Hommes, & les priver de la plus douce societé qu'il y aye entre les gens d'honneur." He continued: "Combien leur rareté donne-t'elle deconnoissance aux Esprits curieux? combien d'agreable visites? combien de douces conversations? & combien de solides entretiens? Certainement c'est la plus douce vie du monde, & un tres agreable entretien que de mediter entre les fleurs, & considerer les merveilleux effets de la Nature, & la puissance de son Autheur."

109. La Chesnée Monstereul, *Le Floriste françois*, 181–182. "Les Holandois en consequence de leur religion pratiquent un autre ordre, ils font assemblée tous les ans à certain jour qu'ils remarquent lors que les Tulipes sont en leur perfection; & aprés avoire esté visiter les Jardins des Floristes, à la sortie d'un festin quils font entr'eux, ils elisent un de la compagnie, qui est Juge des differents qui naissent l'année à cause de leurs fleurs."

110. See Ruth Duthie, "English Florists' Societies and Feasts in the Seventeenth and First Half of the Eighteenth Centuries," *Garden History: The Journal of the Garden History Society* 10.1 (Spring 1982): 17–35; E. Charles Nelson, "The Dublin Florists' Club in the Mid Eighteenth Century," *Garden History: The Journal of the Garden History Society* 10.2 (Fall 1982): 142–148; and D. Tarver and Brent Elliott, "Des Fleuristes aux sociétés horticoles. Histoire des expositions florales," in *L'Empire de Flore* (as above, note 73), 115–137.

111. The commercial flower trade is discussed in this chapter, women flower sellers in Chapter 1.

112. Antoine Schnapper writes, too, that "Leur commune passion crée chez les fleuristes une sociabilité, pour employer un terme à la mode." Schnapper, *Le Géant, la licorne, et la tulipe*, 218.

113. See Daniel Gordon, *Citizens without Sovereignty: Equality and Sociability in French Thought, 1670–1789* (Princeton, N.J.: Princeton University Press, 1994), 53, 33–42.

114. See Dena Goodman, *The Republic of Letters: A Cultural History of the French Enlightenment* (Ithaca, N.Y.: Cornell University Press, 1994).

115. See Anne Goldgar, *Impolite Learning: Conduct and Community in the Republic of Letters, 1680–1750* (New Haven, Conn.: Yale University Press, 1995).

116. Miller, *Peiresc's Europe*, 11.

117. Ibid., 50.

118. Gordon, *Citizens Without Sovereignty*, 9–42.

119. *Nouveau traité de la civilité qui se pratique en France parmi les honnêtes-gens. Nouvelle Edition revuë, corrigée, & de beaucoup augmentée par l'Auteur* (Paris: Chez Louis Josse and Charles Robustez, 1728), 159.

120. The *Hortorum libri IV* was not translated into French until 1773 as Rapin, *Les Jardins*, trans. Gazon-Dourxigué (Paris: Cailleau, 1773).

121. Renatus Rapinus, *Of Gardens*, 70. For more on Rapinus, see Dubois, "René Rapin."

122. Gaston was a notable participant in Parisian salon culture, where his flowers indeed may have become the topic of conversation.

Chapter 3. Cultivating the Flower

1. Dru, *Catalogue des Plantes*, 13. "Ie ne sçaurois exprimer le nombre des personnes d'esprit, qui charmées des agreables divertissemens que fournissent les plantes, se sont données à leur culture, pour se distraire de leurs plus grandes affaires & de leurs estudes plus serieuses: & mesme il s'en est trouvé quelques-unes qui en ont fait leur principale occupation, leur plus chere estude & leur divertissement tout ensemble. Les Fleuristes (ie nomme ainsi les personnes qui ioignent la connoissance des Fleurs à la connoissance des Fleurs à la intelligence de leur culture) demeurent tous d'accord que la Tulipe s'esleve absolument sur les autres fleurs par un empire legitime."

2. *Dictionnaire de l'Académie française* (1694), s.v. "connoissance." The entry reads: "Connoissance. S.f.v. Idée, imagination qu'on a de quelque chose, de quelque personne. *La connoissance du bien & du mal. la connoissance qu'on a d'un homme. je na'y aucune connoissance de cette affaire. cela est de ma connoissance, de la connoissance de tout le monde. cela est venu à ma connoissance. je n'en ay aucune connoissance. bienheureux qui a la connoissance de Dieu. il a la connoissance des pierreries, des tableaux. la connoissance des affaires. il a acquis, il possede toutes les belles connoissances.*"

3. *Dictionnaire de l'Académie française* (1694), s.v. "intelligence." The entry reads: "Intelligence. S.f. Faculté intellective, capacité d'entendre, de comprendre. *Cet homme a l'intelligence dure, vive, prompte, tardive &c. il a de l'intelligence, peu d'intelligence.*"

4. Antoine Schnapper observes that D'Argenville did not discuss floriculture in the first edition of his gardening manual, apparently considering it to be less important to the practice of gardening. Readers, however, felt otherwise, and D'Argenville revised the second edition, published in 1713, to include a section devoted to the cultivation of flowers. See Schnapper, *Le Géant, la licorne, et la tulipe*, 45.

5. Antoine-Joseph Dezallier d'Argenville, *La Théorie et la pratique du jardinage, où l'on traite à fond des beaux jardins appellés communément les jardins de plaisance et de propreté*, 3rd ed. (La Haye: Jean Martin Husson, 1739), 263–264. "La curiosité en fait de fleurs, roule principalement sur les Tulippes, les Anémones, les Renoncules, les Oreilles d'Ours & les Oeillets. Les Curieux ne font guère de cas de nos autres fleurs, qui, quoique moins variées dans leurs espèces, ne leur cèdent en rien pour la vivacité des couleurs, la belle forme, l'odeur, la durée & l'agrément qu'elles fournissent aux jardins: ce sont ces Tulippes, ces Anémones &c., qui leur demandent tant de soin & tant de pein, pour avoir le plaisir de les voir durer douze ou quinze jours au plus. Qu'on s'imagine un homme

mistérieux, toujours inquiet, toujours craintif, qui se relève la nuit dans les gelées pour couvrir ses fleurs, qui laboure, arrose & sarcle ses plates-bandes continuellement, qui en passe les terres au crible fin, & les prépare différement pour chaque espèce, qui fait un mémoire écrit par ordre de ses plates-bandes, avec les noms & portrait de chaque fleur, qui aussitôt que les fleurs sont passées, lève leurs oignons, & les serre dans des boîtes & tiroirs chacun dans sa case, & en enveloppe d'autres dans du papier, & qui par dessus tout cela garde ses fleurs comme un trésor, & n'en laisse approcher qu'avec des yeux jaloux, on aura une idée véritable d'un grand Fleuriste; c'est par là que ces Curieux parviennent à un si grande entêtement de leurs fleurs, qu'ils ont estimé un oignon de Tulippes jusqu'à cent pistoles & plus, & même pour rendre leurs beaux oignons unique, ils ont souvent la malice d'en écraser les caïeux."

6. Liger, *Le Jardinier Fleuriste*, 36–37.

7. Charles Loyseau, *A Treatise on Orders* (*Traité des ordres et simples dignitez*, 1610), in John W. Boyer and Julius Kirshner, gen. eds., *University of Chicago Readings in Western Civilization. Vol. 7. The Old Regime and the French Revolution*, ed. Keith Michael Baker (Chicago: University of Chicago Press, 1987), 26.

8. Goubert, *The Ancien Régime*, 166.

9. Although Jonathan Dewald has argued that "In high French society landed property failed to acquire the symbolic functions that it had long had in England because the realm of property could not be seen as beyond the reach of political constraint, as a source of independent identity." But he continues, "This did not mean that French nobles turned away from land altogether, or that they lost interest in their country houses. We have seen the enthusiasm for building that touched old and new families alike in the seventeenth century. The Condés, we saw, spent a fortune beautifying their palace at Chantilly, and numerous other families behaved in similar ways." Jonathan Dewald, *Aristocratic Experience and the Origins of Modern Culture: France, 1570–1715* (Berkeley: University of California Press, 1993), 163.

10. Furetière, *Dictionnaire*, s.v. "honneste." The *honnêtic homme*, the "homme de bien," the "galant homme, qui a pris l'air du monde, qui sait vivre."

11. Ibid., s.v. "honnestet." The *honnête homme* was governed by "les regles de la bien-scance, des bonnes moeurs."

12. Ibid. The successful *honnête homme* perfected "une maniere d'agir juste, sincere, courtoise, obligeante, civile."

13. John Evelyn, *The Diary*, 58. See Woodbridge *Princely Gardens*, 138, for his assertion that André Le Nôtre was then in the employ of Gaston and may have instituted the work schedule.

14. Bourdieu (*Distinction*, 56); "Tastes (i.e., manifested preferences) are the practical affirmation of an inevitable difference. . . . and tastes are perhaps first and foremost distates, disgust provoked by horror or visceral intolerance ('sick-making') of the tastes of others."

15. Dezallier d'Argenville, *La Théorie*, 263–264.

16. See Chapter 2 for La Bruyère's censure of the activities of the *curieux fleuriste* in a harsh critique of fashion.

17. See Jean-Louis Flandrin, "Distinction Through Taste," in *Passions of the Renaissance*, ed. Roger Chartier, vol. 3, *A History of Private Life*, ed. Philippe Ariès and Georges Duby, trans. Arthur Goldhammer (Cambridge, Mass.: Belknap Press of Harvard Uni-

versity, 1989), 307. Fashion is intimately related to the display of taste through consumption. Fernand Braudel writes: "I have always thought that fashion resulted to a large extent from the desire of the privileged to distinguish themselves, whatever the cost, from the masses who followed them; to set up a barrier. . . . Fashion is also a search for a new language to discredit the old, a way in which each generation can repudiate its immediate predecessor and distinguish itself from it." Fernand Braudel, *Civilization and Capitalism, Fifteenth to Eighteenth Centuries*, vol. 1, *The Structures of Everyday Life: The Limits of the Possible*, trans. Siân Reynolds (New York: Harper & Row, 1981), 324.

Taste and consumption were inseparably linked in the increasingly acquisitive seventeenth century. Writes Flandrin, "Good taste, partly a matter of what one was and partly of what one had, is the first of all these criteria to involve the individual as consumer." Flandrin, "Distinction," 307.

18. José Antonio Maravall discusses the importance of novelty to the baroque in *Culture of the Baroque*. According to Maravall, "The baroque proclaimed, cultivated and exalted novelty. . . . Because in the baroque the pedagogy and all modes of directing human behavior endeavored to reach the individuals' extrarational levels and from there to move them and integrate them into the supporting groups of the prevailing social system, one of the most important means was attracting attention through the suspense of novelty whenever no risk was involved. The new pleased, the never-before-seen attracted, the invention making its debut fascinated; but this would only be permitted in apparent challenges that would not affect the underlying foundation of beliefs holding up the absolute monarchy's social framework. On the contrary, in making use of these novelties as a vehicle, the persuasive propaganda in favor of the established order was more easily introduced." José Antonio Maravall, *Culture of the Baroque: Analysis of a Historical Structure*, trans. Terry Cochran, foreword by Wlad Godzich and Nickolas Spadacinni (Minneapolis: University of Minnesota Press, 1986), 227.

19. Ibid., 225.

20. See Wilfrid Blunt, *Tulipomania*; Penelope Hobhouse, *Gardening Through the Ages: An Illustrated History of Plants and Their Influence on Garden Styles from Ancient Egypt to the Present Day* (New York: Simon & Schuster, 1992), 96, 98, 118–119; David Stuart and James Sutherland, *Plants from the Past: Old Flowers for New Gardens* (London: Penguin Books, 1987), 226–228; Paul Taylor, *Dutch Flower Painting, 1600–1720* (New Haven, Conn.: Yale University Press, 1995), 2.

21. Quoted in Wilfrid Blunt, *Tulipomania*, 7–8.

22. Taylor, *Dutch Flower Painting*, 2.

23. Ibid.; Hobhouse, *Gardening*, 96.

24. Hobhouse, *Gardening*, 96.

25. La Chesnée Monstereul, *Le Floriste françois*, 18–20.

26. See Pierre Vallet, *Le Jardin du Roy Tres Chrestien Henry IV Roy de France et de Navare dédié à la Royne* (Paris: n.p., 1608), plates 1–9, plate 89.

27. The tulipmania is discussed in greater detail in Wilfrid Blunt, *Tulipomania*; Krelage, *Drie Eeuwen Bloembollenexport*; Posthumus "Tulip Mania in Holland"; Schama, *Embarrassment of Riches*, 351–365; and Anne Goldgar, "Nature as Art: The Case of the Tulip," in *Merchants and Marvels: Commerce, Science, and Art in Early Modern Europe*, ed. Pamela H. Smith and Paula Findlen (New York: Routledge, 2002), 324–346.

28. Valnay, *Connoissance et culture parfaite des tulippes rares*, n.p. Valnay wrote, "Je

me suis attaché particulierement à la Tulippe rare, à l'Anemone extraordinaire, à l'Oeillet fin & à l'Oreille d'ours panachée, & j'en cheris si fort la connoisance & la Culture, que j'ay entrepris d'en parler."

29. Pierre Morin, *Catalogues de quelques plantes a fleurs*, 4–16, 17, 20–23, 47–48.

30. Ballon and Garnier, *Nouvelle instruction*.

31. P[ierre] Morin, *Remarques necessaires pour la culture des fleurs. Diligemment observées par P. Morin, avec un catalogue des plantes rares qui se trouvent à present dans son Jardin* (Paris: Charles de Sercy, 1658), 79–80. Morin noted: "La couleur l'odeur sont les deux principales qualitez qui font aimer les Fleurs: mais sçavoir la quelle des deux est preferable, c'est un question. Il y a des personnes qui n'aiment gueres les Fleurs, si elles ne sentent bon, & ceux-cy preferent tousiours l'Oeillet à la Tulippe. D'autres, au contraire, n'en font point d'estat, si elles ne sont reustsuës des plus riches couleurs, c'est à dire des plus vives, & avec cela bien diversifiées. Ceux-cy estimeront plustost la Tulippe, que la Rose ou l'Oeillet."

32. F.B., *La Flore sainte*, 103–4. According F.B., these "principalles fleurs" alone "peut suffire pour orner un Jardin, contenter la passion d'un Curieux, & composer une belle Monarchie, relevant de l'Empire de Flore." Other flowers, he explained, were like the stars compared to the sun, "les simples sujets auprés des Princes, & les soldats auprés des Généraux d'Armées."

33. Morin, *Catalogues de quelques plantes a fleurs*, preface, n.p. Morin explained: "Entre les plus belles Fleurs, il n'y en a point qui se diversituen [sic] en tant de couleurs & manieres que les Tulippes: ce qui les a fait nommer à bon droit Reines des Fleurs."

34. P. Cos, *Verzameling van een meenigte tuipaanen, naar het leven geteekend met hunne naamen, en swaarte der bollen, zoo als die publicq verkogt zijn, te Haarlem in den jaare A. 1637, door P. Cos, bloemist te Haarlem* (Haarlem, 1637), plates 2, 24.

35. Ibid., plates 24, 54.

36. Ibid., plate 33.

37. In 1641 a ship's carpenter in Amsterdam could earn a wage from 20 to 40 stuivers per day, with 20 stuivers equaling one guilder. According to these calculations, then, a "Viceroy" tulip could therefore cost between 1,500 and 4,200 days of the ship carpenter's labor. Wage and currency information from A. Th. van Deursen, *Het kopergeld van de gouden eeuw*, vol. 1, *Het dagelijks brood*, quoted and translated in Taylor, *Dutch Flower Painting*, 3.

38. La Chesnée Monstereul, *Le Floriste françois*, 181: "Les Tulipes ont toûjours esté en tres grande consideration, & particulierement chez les Flamans & Holandois . . . qui en l'année 1637 les penserent faire entrer en commerce, comme les Diamans & les Perles: mais les Estats par un maxime politique le diffendirent; en sorte que le vent & revente publique en estant interdite, on en est venu aux eschanges & ventes particulieres."

39. Ibid., 206. "Il est sans doute que la Tulipe peut legitimement s'eslever au dessus des autres fleurs, & prendre le mesme rang entr'elles, que le soleil fait entre les Astres; puis qu'avec les Curieux elle passe pour l'Imperatrice des fleurs."

40. Valnay, *Connoissance et culture parfaite des tulippes rares*, 38–39. "Voilà de six sortes de tulippes qu'on peut marquer avec trois couleurs de laines. On a son memoir sur lequel on écrit. Les tulippes liées de laine blanche, sont les couleurs printanieres, celles liées de laine noire sont les panachées printanieres, celles liées de laine rouge sont les hazards parfaits, celles liées de laine blanche & laine noire sont les hazards pour seconde

planche, celles liées de laine blanche & laine rouge sont les couleurs triées, & laine noire sont les tulippes pour graines."

41. Nicholas Van Kampen, and Son, *The Dutch Florist: or, True Method of Managing All Sorts of Flowers with Bulbous Roots*, 2nd ed. (London: R. Baldwin, 1764), 48–51.

42. Mallet, *Beauté de la Nature*, 153–155. Although Mallet explained: "Le goût est très inconstant dans cette fleur: quant à moi, je ne tiens n'aime que les bizarres dans toutes les couleurs." He continued, "La beauté de la Tulipe consiste essentiellement dans la forme de son gobelet & dans la beauté de sa plante. Il faut que son verd ne soit ni trop long, ni trop court, ni trop large, & qu'il se couche un peu sur terre. Sa tige doit ête modérément haute dans les bizarres, moins que celle des baguettes rigeaux qu'on aimoit autrefois: il semble qu'on les reprend. . . . Les couleurs & les panaches des Tulips doivent être tranchées nettes, à grosses plaques, étant aussi brillantes en dehors qu'en dedans. Les six pétales qui forme sa corole, doivent être épaisses, régulièrement arrangées, saisant bien le gobelet."

43. Van Kampen, *The Dutch Florist*, 50.

44. La Chesnée-Monstereul, *Le Floriste françois*, 19. La Chesnée-Monstereul maintained that tulips had "une odeur assez agreable." He explained: "Si la Tulipe avoit conservé en ces païs froids l'odeur suave qu'elle a son Isle, son utilité & sa beauté feroient dire avec verité que cette fleur possederoit en elle toutes les perfections des autres."

45. Etienne Binet, *Essay des merveilles de nature, et des plus nobles artifices* (Rouen, 1621; repr. ed. Marc Fumaroli, Evreux: Association du theâtre de la ville d'Evreux, 1987), 316. Binet suggested: "Nature a bien fait ne leur donnant nulle odeur, car si avec tant de beauté, elle y eut infuses les douceurs des fleurs odoriferantes, les hommes qui n'en sont fols qu'à demy, en eussent esté tout à fait, et amoureux esperduëment."

46. Boulanger, *Jardinage des oeillets*, "Au Lecteur," n.p. "Jusqu'à present les Fleurs ont tousiours disputé// Qui porteroit le sceptre en leur petit empire,// Le combat est finy, l'oeillet l'a merité,// Et ce petit Livret n'est que pour vous le dire."

47. Ibid., 7–8. "D'autres l'appellent giroflée, d'autant qu'elle respend une suave odeur de clou-de-girofle, & que plusieurs eslevent avec si grand soin & curiosité qu'il semble aujourd'huy qu'estant presque le dernier venu, il soit le premier en estime, d'autant qu'il ne se desrobe point à nos yeux l'espace de neuf ou dix mois, comme fait la tulippe (si fort neantmoins en estime) pour montrer puis apres huit ou dix jours son escarlatte rayonnante, & son esmail de diverses couleurs, puis qu'en tout temps il estalle une belle verdure, donne des fleurs au plus fort de l'hyver, & n'ensanglante point nos mains en le ceuillant comme fait la rose par ses espines."

48. Brent Elliott, *Flora: An Illustrated History of the Garden Flower* (Buffalo, N.Y.: Firefly, 2001), 57. Stuart and Sutherland, *Plants from the Past*, 117.

49. See also John Grimshaw, *The Gardener's Atlas: The Origins, Discovery, and Cultivation of the World's Most Popular Garden Plants* (Buffalo, N.Y.: Firefly Books, 2002), 46–53 for more on the *dianthus* class.

50. Boulanger, *Jardinage des oeillets*, 26. Boulanger wrote: "L'interest & la curiosité ont inventé plusieurs moyens de panacher & camarer de diverses couleurs les Fleurs de os [sic] Jardins."

51. Mallet, *Beauté de la Nature*, ix–xi. "Comme l'Oeillet est la fleur du plus grand mérite & la plus difficile à cultiver, il sera l'objet principal & le plus détaillé de mon premier Traité."

52. Boulanger, *Jardinage des oeillets*, 102.

53. Valnay, *Connoissance et culture parfaite des tulippes rares*, 88–89. Valnay wrote: "Monsieur Morin y Monsieur Charpentier, Lieutenant General de Compeigne ont écrite de l'Oeillet, je n'en écris pas aprés eux, parce qu'ils n'en ont pas dit assez; au contraire j'en parle seulement pour montre que la culture de cette fleur n'est point une chose si penible que ces Auteurs l'on faite. Il semble à voir la grosseur de leurs Traitez, Y leurs longues dissertations sur la moindre regle qui souvent est inutile, qu'il faille une étude d'application gesnante pour le gouvernement de l'Oeillet. Rien moins que cela, l'experience nous met au dessus de tous leurs travaux, & l'on gouverne à present avec plus de facilité deux ou trois cens pots d'Oeillets, qu'on n'en gouvernoit, selon eux, une trentaine."

54. *Nouvelle instruction pour la culture des fleurs* (Paris: Claude Barbin, 1695), 58. The author explained: "Le Pot contribue beaucoup à la beauté de l'oëillet & à sa conservation. *Prémierement* à sa beauté, car plusieurs se servent de pots ou trop grands ou trop petits & s'aperçoivent visiblement de ce defaut. Si le pot est trop grand l'Oëillet prend aussi trop de nourriture, & pousse de fortes racines, mais un petit bouton qui ne fait pas une grosse fleur. Si le pot est trop petit, l'Oëillet manques de nourriture & restraint si fort ses racines, que le montant ne profite pas.

Le pot le plus convenable doit être d'une mediocre grandeur, plus étroit pas le bas que par le haut, contenant environ autant de terre qu'il en peut contenir en la forme d'un chapeau."

55. Mallet, *Beauté de la Nature*, 32. "Je conseille aux Etrangers la forme des pots que je vais indiquer comme étant la plus convenable. Savoir: la hauteur, dix pouces; la largeur supérieure, six pouces; l'inférieure, trois pouces; sur les deux côtés supérieurs il s'y trouve deux ans pour faciliter à les prendre. . . ."

56. See, for example, Jan Breughel's *Garden of Flora*, reproduced in *Il Giardino di Flora: Natura e simbolo nell'immagine dei fiori* (Geneva: Sagep Editrice, 1986), 14.

57. Valnay, *Connoissance et culture parfaite des tulippes rares*, 108. Valnay wrote: "La premiere fleur estant toûjours la plus large, elles est l'unique esperance du Curieux, il neglige le reste."

58. *Nouvelle instruction pour la culture des fleurs*, 81.

59. Thomas Hale [John Hill], *Eden: or, a Compleat Body of Gardening* (London: T. Osborne, T. Trye, S. Crowder, H. Woodgate, 1757), 534.

60. Mallet, *Beauté de la Nature*, 19–20. Mallet wrote: "Personne ne peut disconvenir qu'il est sans contredit la plus belle & la plus brillante de toutes les fleurs, sans vouloir cependant faire aucun mépris des autres belles fleurs. Outre que l'Oeillet est très-varié dans ses couleurs, il est la plante la plus agréable à la vûe, tant par sa forme que par sa verdure & la majesté de sa tige. . . . Son odeur douce, aromatique & gracieuse surpasse tous les parfums du monde. On doit admirer ses couleurs, ses nuances, la régularité de ses traces, & sa forme admirable. Il est enfin la fleur des fleurs, qui peut être offerte de préférence aux plus grandes Princesses de la terre."

61. Ibid., n.p. Mallet wrote: "Il vend ses Oeillets dont la plûpart gagnés par lui des graines qu'il sème dupuis long-temps, en trois classes différentes, savoir:// Ceux de la première espèce, six francs la marcotte.// De la second, trois livres.// De la troisième, trent sols.// Il se réserve en outre des espèces d'une beauté rare dont il ne marque pas les prix."

62. Stuart and Sutherland, *Plants from the Past*, 74–78 for a discussion of the species included under the label "anemone."

63. John Rea, *Flora: Seu De Florum Cultura. Or, a Complete Florilege Furnished With all Requisites Belonging to a Florist*, 2nd. ed. (London: George Marriot, 1676), 117.

64. Valnay, *Connoissance et culture parfaite des tulippes rares*, 54. Valnay added, "La facilité qu'il y à connoistre les beautez de l'anemone, & même à élever, nous a donné beaucoup plus de Curieux de cette Fleur, que de la Tulippe. Quelques-uns ne veulent pas que ce grand nombre de Curieux d'Anemones viennent de la cause que je dis, Y pretendent que la preferance qu'ils donnent à cette fleur, luy attire plus de partisans. J'aime & connois à fond ces deux fleurs; mais l'une a beaucoup plus de goût & delicatesse que l'autre."

65. See Elliott, *Flora*, 107 and Stuart and Sutherland, *Plants from the Past* 74–77.

66. Valnay, *Connoissance et culture parfaite des tulippes rares*, 51. Valnay explained, "Les Anemones nous sont venuës des Indes; Monsieur Bachelier grand Curieux de Fleurs les en apporta il y a environ quarante ans . . . Nos illustres Curieux visitoient assidûment le Jardin de Monsieur Bachelier, parce qu'ils sçavoient plusieurs raretez."

67. Jean Donneau de Visé, *Histoire de Louis le Grand*, 23. "Il y a pres de cinquante ans que le premiere Anemone fut aportée des Indes en France, par M[onsieur] Bachelier, grand curieux de fleurs. On admira sa fleurison, la vivacité, & l'email de ses fleurs. La beauté de l'Anemone qui a de la graine en abondance, augmenta pendant huit ou dix années, & durant tout ce têms la M[onsieur] Bachelier n'en ayant voulu, ny vendre, ny donner, on trouva moyen de luy en surprendre, & les belles Anemones cultivées devinrent au point de perfection, ou elles sont, & furent encore plus admirées, & recherchées."

68. Schnapper, *Le Géant, la licorne, et la tulipe*, 41.

69. See Woodbridge, *Princely Gardens*, 300–305, for a comparative look at ornamental plants mentioned in major gardening texts.

70. Valnay, *Connoissance et culture parfaite des tulippes rares*, 51–2. Valnay wrote that those "Curieux" who visited the garden of Monsieur Bachelier "furent émerveillez de voire la fleurison des Anemones. La merite de la nouveauté & la vivacité de l'émail de ces fleurs ravirent."

71. Quoted in Schnapper, *Le Géant, la licorne, et la tulipe*, 40. He wrote, "de toutes les plantes, il me semble que la variété des Anémones passe toutes les autres; il est vrai qu'avoir de tout dans un jardin fait bel effet."

72. Argued by Antoine Schnapper to be an addition by Jean de la Quintinie to his *Instructions pour les jardins fruit et potager* (Paris, 1690) in Schnapper, *La Géant, la licorne, et la tulipe*, 334.

73. *Nouvelle instruction pour la culture des fleurs*, 25. The anemone, explained the author, "doit être grosse, & pommée; & il faut que la peluched fasse le dome comme le pavot."

74. Quoted in Schnapper, *Le Géant, la licorne, et la tulipe*, 47. The author added: "Il y a des Anémones qui varient, qui sont panachées une année par grandes pièces emportées sur les grandes feüilles, les béquillons bordés, une autre année tout sera larmoyé, & une autre année les grandes feüilles seront tiquetées, & les béquillons purs. Ces Anémones sont préférables à d'autres, car par leurs mêmes oignons vous aurez des différences, comme si c'étoit d'autres plantes."

75. Ballon and Garnier, *Nouvelle instruction*, 229–230. Ballon and Garnier wrote: "Pour commencer par les Anemones, leur beauté dépende en premier lieu de la disposition de leur fanne: plus elle est frisée, plus elle est jolie; sa tousse basse & bien garnie

fait sur tout plaisir à voir. Une Anemone pour être belle, doit être grosse & pommée, & grande à proportion de sa grosseur. Elle doit porter sa fleur sans baisser. Le briliant de son coloris est une qualité qu'elle n'aime pas moins que les autres Fleurs; non pas qu'il n'en faille avoire que de couleur de feu, incarnat, blanches & autres couleur éclatantes; il y en a de brunes merveilleuses."

76. Pierre Morin, *Catalogues de quelques plantes a fleurs*, 40–41. This discussion is very similar to that in Dru, *Catalogue des plantes*, 37–38. Morin explained: "Il se void une grande varieté d'Anemones: les unes portant larges fueilles en leur verdure, qu'on nomme anemones lierrées, les autres menuës qu'on dit à fueille de Persil, aucunes à fleurs simples, autres doubles, & de tant de couleur que c'est merveilles. Les doubles à fueilles de Persil sont encore divisées en deux especes: Car il y a plusieurs (& sont les plus vulgaires) qui portent d'ordinaires en leurs fleurs cinq ou six grandes & larges fueilles, qui environnent une infinité d'autres fueilles étroites qu'on nomme Pluche, ou Panne: & aucunes d'icelles portent encore beaucoup de menus filaments courts, qui se tiennent attachez par le pied dans la fleur entre lesdites grandes fueilles & Pluche, l'environnant de toutes parts: ce qu'on peut nommer Fraise, ou cordon. Les autres Anemones doubles à fueille de Persil ne portent pas de larges fueilles en leur fleurs, ne Pluche, ne Fraise aussi: Mais leur fleur est composée d'une multitude de fueilles de moyen largeur, à la maniere de celles des Anemones lierrées; & l'on nomme celles-cy Hermafroites [sic], à cause qu'elles participent de la nature desdites Anemones pluchées en leurs fueillages, & des lierrées en leurs fleurs."

77. James Justice, *The British Gardener's Director, Chiefly Adapted to the Climate of the Northern Counties: Directing the Necessary Works in the Kitchen, Fruit and Pleasure Gardens, and in the Nursery, Green-House, and Stove* (Edinburgh: A. Kincaid, J. Bell, and R. Fleming, 1764), 325.

78. William Hanbury, *A Complete Body of Planting and Gardening*, vol. 1 (London: Edward and Charles Dilly, 1770–1771), 308.

79. Most of the florists' varieties of anemones, particularly the doubles, have been lost. Stuart and Sutherland, *Plants from the Past*, 77.

80. Van Kampen, *The Dutch Florist*, 1.

81. Mallet, *Beauté de la Nature*, 124. "Comme la Jacinthe double est la fleur qui dispute par sa beauté la préférence aux Oeillets, quoiqu' injustement, il n'est que trop juste de la placer dans le second rang des fleurs du premier order: c'est pourquoi j'en donnerai sa culture qui est toute simple, en suivant celle des Oeillets."

82. George Voorhelm, *Traité sur la jacinte. Contenant la maniere de la cultiver suivant l'expérience qui en a été faite* (Haarlem: I. & J. Enschedé, 1752); *Traité sur la connoissance et la culture des jacintes, par l'auteur du "Traité des Renoncules" imprimé à Paris chez Lottin* (Avignon: Louis Chambeau, 1765); and Saint Simon, *Des Jacintes, de leur anatomie, reproduction et culture* (Amsterdam: n.p., 1768). Reproduced in Krelage, *Drie Eeuwen Bloembollenexport*, 613.

83. Elliott, *Flora*, 88, 119–120; and Stuart and Sutherland, *Plants from the Past*, 156.

84. Mallet, *Beauté de la Nature*, 127. "La Jacinthe double se tire donc de Haerlem en Holland; on la vend à présent également à Paris & dans plusieurs Villes de la Flandre & du Brabant."

85. Archives Nationales (hereafter A.N.), Maison du roi O^{1}2102^{11}.

86. Mallet, *Beauté de la Nature*, 124. "Nous avons obligation de cette plante aux

Hollandois; c'est à force de la semer, qu'ils sont parvenus à nous fournir les belles variétés que nous admirons."

87. Ibid. He added, however, that "il semble que chaque Pays ne soit favorable qu'à certaines plantes: nous avons l'avantage sur eux dans les Oeillets."

88. Hanbury, *A Complete Body of Planting*, 293.

89. Ibid., 299–300.

90. Krelage, *Drie Eeuwen Bloembollenexport*, 587.

91. Hanbury, *A Complete Body of Planting*, 299.

92. Ibid.

93. John Parkinson, *Paradisi in Sole: Paradisus Terrestris* (London: Humphrey Lownes and Robert Young, 1629); repr. as *A Garden of Pleasant Flowers* (New York: Dover, 1976), 8–10.

94. Stuart and Sutherland, *Plants from the Past*, 203.

95. Hanbury, *A Complete Body of Planting*, 293.

96. Justice, *The British Gardener's Director*, 303.

97. A Florist, *A Treatise on the Culture and Management of the Bear's Ear, or Auricula Ursi. With Directions for Raising It from Seed* (Bath: L. Bull, J. Wallis, 1782), preface, n.p.

98. Ibid., 39.

99. Valnay, *Connoissance et culture parfaite des tulippes rares*, 122. Valnay wrote, "L'Oreille d'Ours est Française."

100. Ibid., 123. He wrote: "nous ne sommes pas les premiers qui en avons connu les beautez. Il faut rendre justice à qui elle est deuë, les Flamans s'y sont plus attachez que nous; ce sont eux qui ont élevé à l'Isle en Flandres les premiers panachées; mais aprés leurs avoir acheté, nous avons beaucoup semé, & nous sommes à present aussi riches qu'eux en cette fleur."

101. Mallet, *Beauté de la Nature*, 144–45. "Les Liégois sont nos maîtres dans ce genre de fleurs, tant pour le goût que pour les espèces; quoique cette fleur soit naturellement Françoise, les Flamands en font plus de cas que nous, qui préférons les Oeillets & les Jacinthes doubles."

102. A Florist, *A Treatise on the Culture and Management of the Bear's Ear*, 39–40.

103. Stuart and Sutherland, *Plants from the Past*, 204–205.

104. Hanbury, *A Complete Body of Planting*, 293.

105. Mallet, *Beauté de la Nature*, 144–145. Mallet wrote that the flowers were of a "belle couleur & agréable à la vûe."

106. Thomas Mawe *Every Man His Own Gardener. Being a New, and Much More Complete Gardener's Kalendar [sic] Than Any One Hitherto Published*, 6th ed. (London: William Griffin, 1773), 165.

107. Ibid., 165–166.

108. Guénin, *Traité de la culture parfaite des oreilles d'ours ou auricules* (Paris, 1738); reproduced in Duthie, "English Florists' Societies and Feasts," 24.

109. A Florist, *A Treatise on the Culture and Management of the Bear's Ear*, 29.

110. Ibid., 29.

111. Ibid., 35.

112. Dezallier D'Argenville, *La Théorie et la pratique du jardinage*, 263–264.

113. Valnay, *Connoissance et culture parfaite des tulippes rares*, 52–53. Valnay wrote, "mais l'ardeur des autres Curieux fut Trop vehemente pour un terme si long. . . . L'invention

dont un de nos Curieux Consiller au Parlement se servit, pour avoir de la graine d'Anemones, malgré les durs refus de Monsieur Bachelier est trop spirituelle pour estre tuë. Cette graine ressemble estrémemente à de la bourre, elle en porte même le nom, & quand elle est tout à fait mûre, elle s'attache facilement aux étoffes de laine; ce Conseiller alla voire les fleurs de Monsieur Bachelier lorsque la graine des Anemones estoit tout à fait mute, il y alla en robbe de drap de Palais, y commanda à son Laquais de la laisser traîner. Quand ces Messieurs furent vers les Anemones, . . . la conversation sur une plante qui attachoit la veuë ailleurs & d'un tour de robbe, on effleura quelques têtes d'Anemones qui laiserent de leurs graines à l'étoff. Le Laquais instruit reprit aussi-tost la queuë de la robbe, la graine se cacha dans les relis, & Monsieur Bachelier qui ne se doutoit de ren ne s'apperçut de quoy que ce soit."

114. For more on the Dutch tulip market, see Goldgar, "Nature as Art: The Case of the Tulip;" Schama, *Embarrassment of Riches*, 358–62; and Wilfrid Blunt, *Tulipomania*, 14–15.

115. Justice, *The British Gardener's Director*, 434.

116. Ibid., 434–435.

117. A.N., Minutier Central (hereafter MC), CV 329.

118. Jacques Savary des Bruslons, *Dictionnaire universel de commerce*, vol. 2 (Paris: Jacques Estienne, 1723), 382.

119. Georges Gibault, *L'Ancienne corporation des maitres jardiniers de la ville de Paris* (Paris: L. Maretheux, n.d.), 10.

120. Franklin, 406.

121. Savary des Bruslons, *Dictionnaire universel*, vol. 2, 382–383.

122. See Alicia Amherst, *A History of Gardening in England* (London: Bernard Quaritch, 1895), 101; Bennett, *Lilies of the Hearth*, 33; Georges Gibault, *L'Ancienne corporation des maitres jardiniers de la ville de Paris*; and Georges Gibault, *La Condition et les salaires des anciens jardiniers* (Paris: Librairie agricole de la Maison Rustique, 1898).

123. Savary des Bruslons, *Dictionnaire universel*, vol. 2, 381–382.

124. Abraham du Pradel (pseudonym of Nicolas de Blegny), *Le Livre commode contenant les adresses de la ville de Paris et le trésor des almanachs pour l'année bissextile 1692*; repr. (Geneva: Minkoff Reprint, 1973), 79. Pradel directed his readers to the faubourg Saint Antoine for gardeners "qui sont commerce de fleurs, Arbres, & Arbustes pour l'ornement des Jardins."

125. Ibid., 79. He also recommended consulting the Sieur Billette, "Jardinier du Roy" (whose wife was "Bouquetière de Sa Majesté") for "tres-belles fleurs . . . & de tres-beaux arbustes."

126. Ibid., 79–80.

127. Liger, *Le Jardinier Fleuriste*, 378–379. Liger advertised the services of a Madame le Fevre, "marchande de graines," who, in addition to selling vegetable and herb seeds, offered "toutes sortes de graines de plus belles fleurs, des Anemones de toutes espéces, & des plus rares, des Tulipes des plus estimées, & des plus fines Renoncules."

128. Abraham du Pradel, *Le Livre commode*, 79–80.

129. Giovanni Battista Ferrari, *De Florum Cultura* (Rome: Stephanus Paulinus, 1633). For more on Ferrari, see Tomasi, *An Oak Spring Flora*, 116–121.

130. George London and Henry Wise, eds. and trans., *The Retir'd Gard'ner*, vol. 2 (London: Jacob Tonson, 1706), 295–297.

131. John Ellis, *Directions for Bringing Over Seeds and Plants, from the East-Indies and Other Distant Countries, in a State of Vegetation* (London: L. Davis, 1770), 11, 1.

132. The market was unable, for example, to supply Louis XIV with the flowers necessary to furnish his extensive gardens. See Chapter 4 for a discussion of the network of nurseries established by the king to fill his own floral needs.

133. Wilfrid Blunt, *The Art of Botanical Illustration*, 91.

134. Quoted in Krelage, *Drie Eeuwen Bloembollenexport*, 270. Sweerts wrote: "Messieurs s'il y a quelcun qui desire d'achepter de ces Livres, Plantes ou fleurs: narrée en ces dicts Livres, ils se trouveront à la foire de Francfort devant le Roemer: ou maison de la ville, dedans la boutique de l'Autheur Emanuel Sweerts, Mais apres, la foire a Amsterdame . . . Emanuel Sweerts demeurant sur le Bloemgracht."

135. Woodbridge, *Princely Gardens*, 104.

136. Dru, *Catalogue des plantes*, 12–13.

137. See Warner, "The Morins."

138. Valnay, *Connoissance et culture parfaite des tulippes rares*, 7–8, 55, 89, 125.

139. Claude Mollet, *Théâtre des jardinages* (Paris, 1670); quoted in Antoine Schnapper, *Le Géant, la licorne, et la tulipe*, 219. Mollet wrote: "J'ay veu que quelques Jardiniers curieux se fréquentoient les uns les autres amiablement, & faisoient recherche de ce qu'ils pourvoient avoir en leurs Jardins, pour voir s'ils avoient quelques espèces de fleurs ou de fruits que l'un ou l'autre n'eust point, afin de s'en entre accommoder."

140. A Florist, *A Treatise on the Culture and Management of the Bear's Ear*, 39–40.

141. For discussion of Van Kampen's price list, see Taylor, *Dutch Flower Painting* 2–10; and Krelage, *Drie Eeuwen Bloembollenexport*, 273.

142. A.N., Maison du Roi O^{1}2102^{11}, cotte 3.

143. A.N., Maison du Roi O^{1}2102^{11}.

144. *Annonces, affiches et avis divers, ou Journal Général de France*, 29 November 1781 (no. 333), 2749. Regnault would "garnit de Fleurs les tables des appartemens & les renouvelle." I thank Rebecca Spang for bringing this reference to my attention.

145. Hubert François Bourguignon d'Anville Gravelot, *Gentlemen Discussing Tulips*, preparatory drawing for Fréard du Castel, *L'Ecole du Jardinier Fleuriste*, 1764. Dumbarton Oaks Research Library and Collection, Washington, D.C.

146. The two impulses in flower collecting do not differ from collecting in general. See Schnapper, *Le Géant, la licorne, et la tulipe*, 41.

147. Pierre Morin, *Catalogues de quelques plantes a fleurs*.

148. Pierre Morin, *Remarques necessaires pour la culture des fleurs*. Morin's work included extensive lists of different "fleurs odiferentes," "fleurs des meilleurs odeurs," "herbes odoriferentes," "plantes bulbeuses," "plantes tubereuses plus curieuses," "plantes genouïlleuses," and then finally "quelques plantes a fleurs."

149. Stuart and Sutherland, *Plants from the Past*, 227.

150. Boulanger, *Jardinage des Oeillets*, 26. Boulanger explained: "L'interest & la curiosité ont inventé plusieurs moyens de panacher & camarer de diverses couleurs les Fleurs de vos Jardins, comme de faire des roses verdes, jaunes, & bleües, & mesme en bien peu de temps donner deux ou trois coloris à un oeillet, outre son teint naturel."

151. Ibid., 74–77, 204.

152. Johann Gregor Mendel did not demonstrate the principles of heredity through selective breeding of sweet peas until the nineteenth century.

153. For a discussion of the theological underpinnings of early modern European attitudes towards nature, see Keith Thomas, *Man and the Natural World: Changing Attitudes in England, 1500–1800* (London: Allen Lane, 1983), 17–36.

154. He adds, in reference to painting: "If the cultivation of painting aroused the interest of baroque individuals up to such a point, it was not because using paintbrushes made it possible for one to acquire a capacity to imitate nature; rather, in manipulating them the artist obtained the ability to re-form and remake that which was given in nature." Maravall, *Culture of the Baroque*, 231, 260.

155. Hugh Plat, *The Garden of Eden. Or, An Accurate Description of all Flowers and Fruits Now Growing in England, With Particular Rules How to Advance Their Nature and Growth, as Well as in Seeds and Herbs, as the Secret Ordering of Trees and Plants* (London: William Leake, 1653), 85–86.

156. See chapters on "Colori aggiunti, e mutati ne'fiori," "colori aggiunti, e mutati ne'fiori," and "Odori corretti, e aggiunti a fiori," in book 4 of Giovanni Battista Ferrari, *Flora ouero Cultura di Fiori*, trans. from Latin by Lodovico Aureli Perugino (Rome: Pier' Ant. Facciotti, 1638).

157. Boulanger, *Jardinage des Oeillets*, 26. "Par exemple," wrote Boulanger, "ayent pulverisé de la terre grasse, cuitte au soleil, & l'arousant puis apres l'espace de quinze ou vingt jours d'une eau rouge, jaune, ou autre teinture, lors que l'on y aura semé la graine de cette Fleur d'une couleur contraire à cet arrousoir artificiel."

158. Ibid., 26–27. Carnation seeds were mixed with chicory roots in hopes of producing a blue carnation "autant beau, qu'il estoit rare."

159. Stephen Blake, *The Compleat Gardeners Practice, Directing the Exact Way of Gardening. In Three Parts, the Garden of Pleasure, Physical Garden, Kitchen Garden* (London: Thomas Pierrepoint, 1664), 69–71.

160. Ibid., 21.

161. Ibid., 23.

162. Ibid., 72.

163. Henry van Oosten, *The Dutch Gardener*, 185–186.

164. Boulanger, *Jardinage des Oeillets* 27. Boulanger wrote of the attempts to "ravy les yeaux des ignorants ne sçachans pas la cause de ces diverses peintures," concluded that such violations of the bulbs "quelque temps cause souvent la mort à la tige qui luy a donné la vie, punissant ainsi la curiosité d'une main trop hardie."

165. Ibid., 29. "Ce qui fait, mon cher Lecteur, qui je vous invite d'en recognoistre l'Autheur, pour aduoüer ingenuement avec moy, à moins d'estre un aveugle volontaire, qui Dieu a tellement composé toutes les creatures que l'on ne peut en examiner la moindre, sans y rencontrer aussi-toit quelque trait sur-naturel de son amour & sa puissance, bien plus adroitement que cet Ancien, y ayant gravé par tout son image, que l'eternité ne pourra jamais effacer."

166. Rea, *Flora*, 9.

167. Justice, *The British Gardener's Director*, 439–441.

168. Ibid.

169. Dionys Dodart, *Memoires pour servir a l'histoire des plantes* (Paris: Imprimerie Royale, 1676), 435. Dodart wrote: "La necessité où l'on est de trouver des termes propres, sur tout dans les Descriptions, nous a fait penser à prendre la liberté d'introduire

quelques nouvelles manieres de parler, ou de rétablir quelques vieux mots lors que nous manquerons des mots propres."

170. Ibid., 18–19. Boulanger discussed the "divers noms que les Curieux luy ont donné." He continued: "Quand j'aurois la memoir aussi heureuse que Themistocle qui salüoit tous ses citoyens chacun par son propre nom. Que comme Cyrus & le Scipion j'appelerois tous les soldats d'une grande armée par leurs surnoms de guerre. Et qu'avec Cyneas Ambassadeurs de Pyrrhus, je parlerois à tout le Senat, & le peuple Romain apostrofant les Senateurs, & tous ses assistans les uns apres les autres par leurs noms."

171. Boulanger, *Jardinage des Oeillets*, 19–20. Boulanger remarked: "Luy seul ordonne des armées entieres de Capitaines & de Soldats. Sans battre le tambour il leue des Regimens de Suisses. Luy seul est Gouverneur de plusieurs villes, de Roüen, de Tours, de Bordeaux. Il compose des Republiques & des Royaumes, de Parisiens, de Picards, & de Portugais. Sans changer de Religion, il est aujourd'huy Capucin, & demain Huguenot, ou Anti-huguenot."

172. La Chesnée Monstereul, *Le Floriste françois*, 33.

173. This unidentified "Demoiselle" is the only example of a female flower collector in France that I have come across.

174. La Chesnée Monstereul, *Le Floriste françois*, 33–35.

175. Ibid., 35. Boulanger reported that "Monseigneur le Cardinal Richelieu, qui aprés ses grandes occupations alloit délasser son esprit entre les fleurs, & le bel émail des Jardins, ne dédaigna pas de donner le nom au Jean Scime, au Gaignepain, & à la Chanceliere."

176. Ibid., 237, 245, 249. La Chesnée Monstereul listed the "Monstereulle, . . . panachée d'un violet cramoisy vif, sur beaucoup de blanc," "Virginie, . . . panachée d'incarnadin sur de blanc, avec des pieces détachées qui semblent de gouttes de sang," and one named after the Cardinal himself, "Richelieu," which was richly striped with "violet lavé sur du blanc."

177. Ibid., 31–32. "De toutes les espèces & sortes de Tulipes, il y en a qui se parangonnent, & sont celle qui deviennent plus belles en se perfectionnant: alors les Curieux, auxquels elles arrivent, leur peuvent donner un nom; & conservant toûjours celuy de leur espece, adjouster celuy de Parangon. Par exemple, on peut dire une telle parangonnée, ou parangon un tel, pourueu [sic] que le nom qu'ils donneront soit adjouster à celuy de l'espece (ce qui demeurera toûjours pour regle generalle) & que le nom soit conuenable à la forme, couleur, & perfection de la Tulipe . . . ainsi que Monsieur Robin donna le nom d'Agate Robin à une Tulipe Agate qui se perfectionna, & à laquelle (s'estant plus embellie) on a donné depuis le nom d'Agate Royalle. L'Agate Morin a esté nommée par Monsieur Morin l'aisné, aprés s'estre parangonnée. Est ainsi chacun doit nommer les Tulipes par jugement, & non par fantaisie."

178. Ibid., 35–36. "Quelqu'un me dira peut-estre qu'il a remarqué qu'on a donné divers noms aux Tulipes, quoy qu'elles soient assorties de mesmes couleurs; & que parant la difference seroit seulement au nom, & non pas aux couleurs."

179. Valnay, *Connoissance et culture parfaite des tulippes rares*, 39–40. Explained Valnay: "Il faut donner des noms à vos plus belles tulippes, vous pouvez attendre si vous voulez que vos hazards ayent panaché nettement deux années de suite, afin de ne les point nommer inutilement; mais il faut décrire vos principaux hazards parfaits pour voir l'année ensuite leur constance, leur progrés ou leur diminution. Auquel cas au lieu de leur

laines, il faudra y lier au pied de petits morceaux de carter, sur chacun desquels il y aura un chiffre relatif à vostre memoir, sur lequel vous serez leurs portraits.

Ainsi par exemple, il faudra écrire numero 1. couleur bijare, nuancée de tané brun & clair, panachée de tres-beau jaune d'or par grandes pieces emportées, moyen vase ou grand vase, belle forme, haute tige ou moyenne, fond verd cerclé ou autrement, estamine de bleu enfoncée, pivoits jaunes claires, brunis par en haut, hazard de 1688, & de mesme pour autres numeros."

180. John Cowell, *The Curious and Profitable Gardener* (London: Weaver Bickerton, Richard Montagu, 1730), 46–48.

181. Van Kampen, *The Dutch Florist*, 40–41.

182. Ibid., 41.

Chapter 4. Cultivating the Man

1. The *hôtel* is at 58, rue Charlot. The panels comprising La Hyre's series are now dispersed among museums and private collections. See *Revue de l'art: Plafonds Parisiens du xviie siècle* 122, no. 4 (1998): 78.

2. The painting is now in the National Gallery, London. Laurent de La Hyre, *Allegorical Figure of Grammar*, 1650, NG6329, bequeathed by Francis Falconer Madan. The inscription reads "Vox litterata et articvlata debito modo pronvnciata."

3. Maryanne Cline Horowitz traces the history of the relationship between the metaphor of seeds and plants as learning through the Renaissance and early modern period. She believes that "the vegetative language of seeds of virtue and knowledge among humanists and artists contributes to the formation of a concept of a renaissance of arts and letters. Visual imagery, as well as written texts, make explicit the vegetative symbolism inherent in humanist models of how the human mind develops." See Maryanne Cline Horowitz, *Seeds of Virtue and Knowledge* (Princeton, N.J.: Princeton University Press, 1998), 96.

Similarly, Rebecca W. Bushnell sees a connection between the humanist educational goals and methods and horticultural metaphors: "I take the metaphor of nurture or cultivation at its face value, examining how educational and gardening theory and practice intersected in the gardening tropes that were used to describe a child's development and training." Bushnell investigates the role of the teacher as gardener, writing, "the frequent comparison of a teacher and a gardener underlines the uncertain authority of teachers and thus the fragility of their power to shape the student's self." In addition, she explores the notion of "the early sixteenth-century image of the text as a garden from which the reader harvests material for 'fruit.'" See Rebecca W. Bushnell, *A Culture of Teaching: Early Modern Humanism in Theory and Practice* (Ithaca, N.Y.: Cornell University Press, 1996), 75, 81–82, 119.

4. Jacques Revel writes: "Between the ethic of the salon and that of the court, between the belief in a birthright and the assumption of quality, lay a difficult middle ground. Absolutist society contained groups outside the court that aspired to emulate various models of perfection: lower-ranking nobles, provincials, and various elites who had linked their fate to that of the monarchy. Numerous treatises were published on such subjects as 'the happiness of the court and true felicity of man' (Dampmartin, 1592), 'the art of raising the nobility to virtue, knowledge, and other exercises appropriate to its condition' (Grenaille, 1642), and the 'courtly spirit' (Bary, 1662). . . . But aspiring courtiers

differed from the 'happy few' of the hôtel de Rambouillet, however, and had little in common with those already designated by royal election. Unlike the former, they had to believe that grace was not a birthright but something that could be learned. And unlike the latter, they had to invent qualities that would compensate for the deficiencies of their birth; while respecting the importance of social appearances, they somehow had to revive the notion of individual merit." Jacques Revel, "The Uses of Civility," in *A History of Private Life*, vol. 3, *Passions of the Renaissance*, ed. Roger Chartier, 195–196.

5. Roger Chartier, "From Texts to Manners, A Concept and Its Books: *Civilité* Between Aristocratic Distinction and Popular Appropriation," in *The Cultural Uses of Print in Early Modern France*, trans. Lydia G. Cochrane (Princeton, N.J.: Princeton University Press, 1987), 74, 82.

6. Ibid., 86–87. Chartier continues: "A double danger threatens this unstable equation: Either the individual fails to act as his rank and the circumstances demand . . . or he fails to have sentiments that conform with his visible behavior. Then *civilité* becomes pretense; it changes from a legitimate representation to a hypocritical mask."

7. Furetière, *Dictionnaire*, s.v. "cultiver." "On dit fig. *Cultiver les Arts & les* Sciences, pour dire, Les faire fleurir. . . . "On dit fig. *Cultiver l'esprit. Cultiver la memoire. Cultiver le jugement*, pour dire, Les exercer, apporter du soin à les perfectionner. On dit aussi, *Cultiver la connoissance, l'amitié, la bienveillance, l'affection de quelqu'un. Cultiver ses amis.*"

8. *Dictionnaire de l'Académie française* (1694), s.v. "cultiver." "Il faut *cultiver* l'esprit des jeunes gens, leur memoire, en leur donnant de bonnes instructions. . . . On dit en ce sens, *Cultiver* l'amitié, la connoissance."

9. Flandrin writes: "The Middle Ages had prized courtliness above all other qualities. In later years such criteria as civility, urbanity, and politeness came into vogue. Talking well was prized in the Renaissance and remained so thereafter. The seventeenth century invented good taste. . . . Good taste, partly a matter of what one was and partly of what one had, is the first of all these criteria to involve the individual as consumer. No doubt this had something to do with the fact that the great lords lost the major part of their old political and military powers in the seventeenth century; thus their primary role became that of great consumers. And the various classes that composed the social elite in the seventeenth and eighteenth centuries found it easiest to communicate with one another by means of consumption and luxury." Jean-Louis Flandrin, in *Passions of the Renaissance*, ed. Roger Chartier (as above, note 4), 307.

10. Ridiculing social climbing was a central theme to Molière's *Georges Dandin* (1668) and *Le Bourgeois Gentilhomme* (1670).

11. La Chesnée Monstereul, *Le Floriste françois*, 200–201.

12. *Nouveau traité pour la culture des fleurs, qui enseigne la maniere des les cultiver, multiplier, & les conserver selon leurs especes; avec leurs proprietez merveilleuses, & leurs vertus medecinales, divisé en trois livres* (Paris: Charles de Sercy, 1682), 11. The author wrote, "car cet agreable Theatre de la Déesse des Fleurs, a beaucoup de grace quand la beauté de ses Fleurs est accompagnée d'une exacte politesse." Authorship of the text is disputed. Antoine Schapper has argued against the attribution of the work to Pierre Morin, suggesting that it was drawn from an Italian work by A. Mandirola published in Ferrara in 1652. See Schnapper, *Le Géant, la licorne, et la tulipe*, 340.

13. Quoted in Georges Gibault, *Les Anciennes lois relatives au jardinage* (Paris: Imprimerie de la cour d'Appel, L. Maretheux, 1912), 5. The edict read: "Pour ce que

plusieurs propriétaires et locatifs jettent des eaux par leurs fenestres, esquelles y a jardins, pots d'oeillets, romarins, marjolaines et autres choses, dont pourroit advenir inconvénient, et aussi qu'on ne peut bonnement voir d'où les dites eaux sont jetées: nous défondons à toutes personnes de quelque état, qualité ou conditions qu'elles soient, de mettre aux fenestres aucuns pots ne jardinet, sur peine de cent sols parisis d'amende."

14. Louis Mercier, *Tableau de Paris, nouvelle édition*, vol. 6 (Amsterdam, 1783), 137.

15. Ibid., 136. Mercier wrote: "L'Amour de la campagne & de l'agriculture, commun à tous les hommes, se manifeste encore dans l'immense tas de pierres qu'habite le Parisien. Il éleve en l'aire un petit jardin de trois pieds de long; il place sur ses fenêtres un pot de fleurs; c'est un petit tribut qu'il envoie de loin à la nature. . . . Il cultive dans une caisse l'oeillet & la rose. Six pouces de verdure le consolent de la perte des tapis émaillés, & remplacent l'aspect des bois épais & fleuris."

16. Ibid., 137. Explained Mercier, the pots were taken inside, then "il la replace quand il est passé." Window boxes were of particular consolation, continued Mercier, to women who chose not to venture into the streets and public gardens of the city: "La femme qui ne quitte pas la chambre, épie cette heure fortunée, & sourit de joie quand le calice d'une fleur isolée vient à s'ouvrir à l'astre du jour. Elle appelle sa voisine pour contempler avec elle ce phénomene."

17. Hugh Plat, *The Garden of Eden, Or, An Accurate Description of All Flowers and Fruits Now Growing in England, With Particular Rules How to Advance Their Nature and Growth, as Well as In Seeds and Herbs, as the Secret of Ordering of Trees and Plants* (London: William Leake, 1653), 44.

18. Ibid., 50–52.

19. Thomas Fairchild, *The City Gardener. Containing the Most Experienced Method of Cultivating and Ordering such Ever-Greens, Fruit-Trees, Flowering Shrubs, Flowers, Exotick Plants, & c. as Will Be Ornamental, and Thrive Best in the London Garden* (London: T. Woodward and J. Peele, 1722), 64. The duchess of Beaufort was known for her fine flowers.

20. Ibid., 64–65.

21. Nicholas Van Kampen and Son, *The Dutch Florist; Or, True Method of Managing All Sorts of Flowers with Bulbous Roots*, 2nd. ed. (London: R. Baldwin, 1764), 90.

22. Ibid., 91–92.

23. Ibid., 90–91.

24. Justice, *The British Gardener's Director*, 292.

25. Ibid., 293.

26. Robert Furber, *The Flower Garden Display'd in above 400 Curious Representations of the Most Beautifull Flowers; Regularly Dispos'd in the Respective Months of their Blossom* (London: R. Montagu, J. Brindley, C. Corbett, 1734), 126–128.

27. Ibid., 133–134.

28. Van Kampen, *The Dutch Florist*, 90.

29. Ibid., 94.

30. Garden historian Mark Laird has explored the creation of such theatrical displays in "Theatres of Flowers: The Art and Science of Eighteenth-Century Floral Display," *Text of the Clusius Lectures* (Leiden: Clusiusstichting, 1997), 5–19. See also his *The Flowering of the Landscape Garden: English Pleasure Gardens, 1720–1800* (Philadelphia: University of Pennsylvania Press, 1999).

31. Robert-Xavier Mallet, *Beauté de la Nature, ou fleurimanie raisonnée* (Paris: Didot, le jeune, 1775), 152–153. Mallet explained: "c'est la première fleur qui entre au théâtre de celles du premier ordre: ensuite c'est la Renoncule en pyramide, & puis l'Oeillet qui l'accomplit." He continued: "De façon qu'un Fleuriste qui donne dans ces trois genres de fleurs, avec connoissance & précision, peut, presque sans interruption, avoir l'agrément de pouvoire garnir ses théâtre depuis le mois d'Avril jusqu'à la fin d'Août."

32. Valnay, *Connoissance et culture parfaite des tulippes, rares*, 44. Valnay "trouvé par là le moyen de faire voir ensemble, & commodement un amas de panachées mêlées suivant leurs couleurs differentes & arrangées les unes prés autres, de maniere ... d'un seul coup d'oeil vous divertissez la veuë de tout ce qu'un tres-grand jardin peut produire de raretez."

33. Ibid., 44–46. Valnay wrote, "Au milieu d'une salle sur une tres-grande table, il fait un theater de cinq ou six gradins larges de quatre à cinq pouces & élevés les unes des autres de même hauteur, il les couvre d'un tapis vert, & il cüeille ses panachées parfaites qu'il met chacune dans une petite fiole avec de l'eau aprés les avoir entierement épanoüies. Il arrange ensuite toutes ces fioles sur ces gradins. Il cüeilles pour cela ses Tulippes quand elles ont esté quelques temps en fleur, s'il les coupoit trop tost elles ne tiendroient pas épanoüies dans l'eau, elles se resserreroient incessamment. ... Ces theatres ... font un effet extraordinairement agreable."

34. Dezallier D'Argenville, *La Theorie et la pratique du jardinage*, 51–52. "Un autre façon que les curieux, & sur tout les fleuristes de profession, mettent en oeuvre, pour voir plus commodement & pour assemblage de planches ou de degrez qui vont toujours en s'élevant les uns derriére les autres, ensorte que l'oeil & la main se puissent porter partout sans aucun obstacle. On le reserve particulierement pour les oreilles d'ours & pour les oeillets; & comme ces fleurs ont plus besoin que les autres d'être garenties à propos de la pluie, & du grand Soleil, le theater est toujours accompagné d'un petit toit de planches ou de toile cirée. ... Il y a encore des curieux, qui ont une autre espece de theater qu'ils appellent la pyramide des fleurs: après que les plus belles ont paré quelque tems leur parterre, ils les coupent & les exposent dans des phioles sur les degrés d'une pyramide qu'ils font construire exprés au milieu de leur sale, & là avec le secours de l'eau & de l'ombre ils en prolongent de beaucoup la durée."

35. Woodbridge, *Princely Gardens*, chapters 3 and 4.

36. Ibid., 84–87.

37. Charles Stevens [Estienne] and John [Jean] Liébault, *Maison Rustique, or The Countrie Farme*, trans. Richard Surflet (London: E. Bollifant, 1600), 300.

38. Ibid., 301.

39. Ibid.

40. Ibid., 323, 328–347.

41. Ibid., 201.

42. Claude Mollet, *Théâtre des jardinages* (Paris: Charles de Sercy, 1678), 174. This work exists in manuscript at Dumbarton Oaks, RBR 0-2-5, 1643. "Les fleurs basses, comme Violettes de toutes sortes de Marguerites, ou Pasquerettes, Armeries, Camamilles doubles, Anemones, Jacinthes, Primveres, Pensées, & toutes sortes de petites fleurs basses, sont fort propres pour planter dedans toutes sortes de compartimens tant en broderie qu'autres, pourveu que le Jardinier observe la cimmetrie."

43. André Mollet, *Le Jardin de plaisir* (Stockholm: Henry Kayser, 1651), n.p. "Il is

expedient de le separer en deux parties, sçavoir; l'une pour les fleurs arbustes, comme Rosier Genest d'Espagne, caprifolia, oeillets d'Inde, Pivoines, & autres grands fleurs, lesquelles ofusqueroient les basses estant meslees ensemble; & l'autre partie pour les fleurs basses, & plus rares, comme oeillets, Girofleës doubles, couronnes imperialles, Martagons, Tulippes, Anemones, ranunculs, auriculs, Iris, & autres, lesquelles deux parties se peuvent encor diviser, pour mieux mettre chasque escpece a part."

44. Ibid., n.p. "Le dessin 8 est aussi un parterre en broderie de 40 toises au carré; sa fontaine octagonal, de 7 toises de diamètre; les plates-bandes de 6 pieds avec les quartes de cercle au milieu, au centre desquels sont marqués les huit piédestaux pour y poser des figures. Et, au milieu desdites plates-bandes, on peut planter, par especes, des petits arbrisseaux toujours verts et bien tondus, entre lesquels on peut planter toutes sortes de fleurs basses, comme tulipes, anémones, renoncules et autres."

45. Daniel Rabel, *Theatrum Florae* (Paris: Apud Petrum Firens, 1627), frontispiece. The work was first published in 1622, then again in 1627 and 1633. The banner reads, "The Lord's Delights. Naught else was worth hoping for." For more on Rabel, see Tomasi, *An Oak Spring Flora*, 69–73.

46. Johann Walther, *Florilège de Nassau-Idstein*, 1663, B.N., Cabinet des Estampes, Rès. Ja 25, fol. 2.

47. Jean Franeau, *Jardin d'hyver ou cabinet des fleurs* (Douay: Pierre Borremans, 1616), plate 7. Wilfrid Blunt argues that Franeau's illustrations were taken directly from Crispin de Passe's popular works. See Wilfrid Blunt, *The Art of Botanical Illustration*, 91–104.

48. Louis Liger, *Le Jardinier Fleuriste et historiographe* (Paris: Damien Beugnie, 1704); trans. George London and Henry Wise as *The Retir'd Gardn'ner*, 2 vols. (London: Jacob Tonson, 1706), 264–265.

49. Ibid., 266–267.

50. S.A., *Jardinier portatif, ou la culture des quatre classes de jardins, et de l'éducation des fleurs* (Rouen: Antoine Ferrand, 1784), 112–113. "Il y a des curieux qui, après avoir tracé des pieces de parterres ou plates-bandes destinées pour les fleurs, en font un calcul pour savoir ce que les compartiments peuvent en contenir, étant plantées à quatre doigts l'une de l'autre, & qui, non contents de cela, platent également & à distances égales les fleurs qui sont printanieres, comme d'autre qui viennent en été ou plus tard, afin que, se succédant les unes aux autres, leurs jardins paroiessent toujours garnis de fleurs. D'autres pour planter réguliérement, tirent auparavant sur une carte le dessein & le plan de leurs jardins, & à mesure qu'ils plantent les oignons & les racines dans les planches ou plates-bandes de leurs parterres, ils les marquent de la même maniere dans celles qui sont figurées sur la carte, afin de mieux connoître la qualité des fleurs qu'ils ont mises en chaque planche ou plate-bande."

51. *Nouveau traité pour la culture des fleurs* (1682), 7. He suggested that "les Tulippes & les Anemones [peuvent] estre placées autour des Planches proche les bordures, & les autres Fleurs au milieu, meslées avec d'autres especes: Et ainsi dans chaque Planche la diversité des Fleurs sera gaye & tres plaisant à la veuë."

52. Ibid., 10–11.

53. John Rea, *Flora, seu De Flora Cultura*, 2nd. ed. (London: George Marriot, 1676), 9.

54. Ballon and Garnier, *Nouvelle instruction facile pour la culture des figuiers* (Paris:

Charles de Sercy, 1692), 152. Ballon and Garnier wrote: "arranger & assortir les Oignons par le mêlange des differentes couleurs, [pour] l'effet en étant trés-agreable quand les Fleurs sont venuës."

55. J[ean] L[aurent], *Abregé pour les arbres nains et autres* (Paris: Charles de Sercy, 1683), 117–118. J.L. suggested: "Ensuite, proche desdites bordures & à distance au moins de quatre bons doigts & plus d'icelles y planter des bouquet d'oreilles d'ours, éloignez l'un de l'autre de demy pied & plus, entre lesquels ils planteront des Iris de Perse, des Jonquilles doubles & simples, des Crocus, des Perse-neiges, des Bizantines, des Jacintes blanches, bleuës, des musquez à faire des parfums, & des Marguerites de diverses couleurs, & ce par égale portion: dans le reste & les milieux d'aucunes desdites planches, il y faut planter des Tulippes, comme il est dit cy-devant, en d'autres toutes Oreilles d'Ours, en d'autres touts Epatiques doubles, en d'autres tous Ciclamennes, . . . Fretilairs . . . , en d'autres toutes Amarantes, en d'autres toutes Anemones, en d'autres tous Ranoncul."

56. Ibid., 120. "Le bon ordre pour faire de beaux Jardins à Fleurs, est d'y éviter la confusion, comme aussi d'y garder une grande symmétrie, c'est à dire à accommoder & ranger si bien les Fleurs, qu'il y en ait toûjours des opposées & en pareille quantité, & nombre de planches qui répondent l'une à l'autre."

57. See, for example, *Nouveau traité pour la culture des fleurs* (1674), 4.

58. André Mollet, *Le Jardin de plaisir*, 33: "plantes-bandes de 6 pieds, avec des carreaux de pierre d'espace en propres à y poser de pots, ou vases pleins de fleurs."

59. Prudence Leith-Ross, in "A Seventeenth-Century Paris Garden," *Garden History: The Journal of the Garden History Society* 21.2 (Winter 1993): 150–157, argues convincingly that Symonds' sketch in the British Library is of Morin's garden.

60. Pierre Morin, *Catalogues de quelques plantes à fleurs* (Paris: François le Cointe, 1651).

61. Pierre Morin, *Remarques necessaires pour la culture des fleurs* (Paris: Charles de Sercy, 1658).

62. Ibid., 141–144.

63. John Evelyn, *Diary*, 59.

64. Reproduced in Leith-Ross, "A Seventeenth-Century Paris Garden," 152–153.

65. B.N., Cabinet des Estampes, *Maniére de planter les fleurs*, Va 78g, cliché B 11189; reproduced and discussed in Mark Laird, *The Formal Garden: Traditions of Art and Nature* (London: Thames and Hudson, 1992), 43–44, and Mark Laird, "Ornamental Planting and Horticulture in English Pleasure Grounds, 1700–1830," in *Garden History: Issues, Approaches, Methods*, ed. John Dixon Hunt (Washington, D.C.: Dumbarton Oaks, 1992), 243–279.

66. A.N., Maison du Roi O^{1}2102^1.

67. I have not yet been able to determine what the "bosuelle" refers to or was. However, the verb "bossuer" can mean to deform. It is possible, then, that "bosuelle," as it is often used in conjunction with "tulipe," refers to a "broken," or variegated tulip.

68. Olivier likely refers to Olivier Fleurant, *jardinier* at Trianon, or his son, André Olivier Fleurant, who also appears in the royal account books as a royal gardener. See Jules Guiffrey, *Comptes des bâtiments du roi sous le règne de Louis XIV*, vols. 3–5 (Paris: Imprimerie Nationale, 1891–1901).

69. Archives Nationales (hereafter A.N.), Maison du Roi O^{1}2101^1. The garden was to be colorful "en tout sesons [*sic*]."

70. *Nouveau traité pour la culture des fleurs* (1674), 11.

71. Wilfred Blunt, *The Art of Botanical Illustration*, 106–107.

72. *Les Fleurs dans le jardin au XVIIe siècle*, 15–25 June 1974 (Versailles: Ecole Nationale Supérieure d'Horticulture, 1974). The paintings are now in the Muséum d'Histoire Naturelle in Paris.

73. Wilfred Blunt, *The Art of Botanical Illustration*, 107.

74. Tomasi, *An Oak Spring Flora*, 70 and Schnapper, *Le Géant, la licorne, et la tulipe*, 58; Wilfrid Blunt, *The Art of Botanical Illustration*, 107–108. Some images in the album are reproduced in Gérard Aymonin, *Daniel Rabel: Cent fleurs et insectes*, introduction by Antoine Schnapper (Arcueil, France: Anthese, 1991).

75. Saunders, *Picturing Plants*, 41. See also Nicholas Barker, *The Hortus Eystettensis: The Bishop's Garden and Besler's Magnificent Book* (London: British Library Publications, 1994). Selected paintings by Besler have been published as *The Besler Florilegium: Plants of the Four Seasons* (New York: H. N. Abrams, 1989).

76. The two copies are now in the Bibliothèque Nationale de France (with sixty-five paintings) and the Victoria and Albert Museum (133 flower paintings) in London. Gil Saunders contends that a third copy existed in the collection of the Darmstadt Landesbibliothek, but was destroyed in World War II. See Saunders, *Picturing Plants*, 41, note 1. For more on the Walther paintings, see also Wilfrid Blunt, *The Art of Botanical Illustration*, 123–125; and *Les Fleurs dans le jardin au XVIIe siècle*.

77. Wilfrid Blunt, *The Art of Botanical Illustration*, 109.

78. Tallement des Réaux, quoted in Denis Lopez, *La Plume et l'épée: Montausier 1610–1690* Biblio 17 (Paris,: Papers on French Seventeenth-Century Literature, 1987), 125. The *Guirlande* has since been celebrated as "une des plus illustres galanteries qui ayent jamais esté faittes."

79. Lopez, *La Plume et l'épée*, 124.

80. Lopez argues in his study of the work that the poems were gathered into manuscript form in 1633–1634, but not copied and bound into their final form until 1641. He contends, too, that Montausier might have seen a similar illustrated collection of poems in Italy.

81. Prior to the collation of the poems with Robert's paintings, the verses were gathered in the late 1630s into a single document and copied. Three versions of the manuscript in this earlier form exist, two in the Bibliothèque Nationale and one in the Bibliothèque de l'Arsénal. See Lopez, *La Plume et l'épée*, 121, note 12.

82. Jarry (1620–1674) also worked for La Fontaine and was appointed "écrivain et noteur de la musique du roi." See Lopez, *La Plume et l'épée*, 123, note 17.

83. Charles de Montausier et al., *Guirlande de Julie* (1641), manuscript, Bibliothèque Nationale de France. Portions of the manuscript have been reproduced in Irène Frain's incomplete *La Guirlande de Julie présentée par Irène Frain, suivie d'un Dictionnaire du Langage des Fleurs aux fins de chiffrer et déchiffrer vos tendres messages floraux* (Paris: Robert Laffont, Bibliothèque Nationale, 1991).

84. Although the work remained privately owned until 1991, several editions of the poems were published in the eighteenth and nineteenth centuries. The Bibliothèque Nationale de France acquired the book in 1991 for 4 million francs, officially appending the work to the French patrimony for the first time since its creation. See Denis Lopez,

"Scudéry et la *Guirlande de Julie*," in *Les Trois Scudéry: Actes du Colloque du Havre, 1–5 octobre 1991*, ed. Alain Niderst (Paris: Klincksieck, 1993), 69.

85. Gaston frequented Rambouillet's salon and therefore could have seen Robert's work for Montausier there.

86. Louis K. Horowitz, "Pastoral Fiction," in *A New History of French Literature*, ed. Denis Hollier (Cambridge, Mass.: Harvard University Press, 1994), 258–259.

87. Anthony Blunt, "The Précieux and French Art," in *Fritz Saxl, 1890–1948: A Volume of Memorial Essays from His Friends in England*, ed. Donald James Gordon (London: Thomas Nelson and Sons, 1957), 328. Indeed, Blunt credits Rambouillet and her circle with establishing the fashion for the use of fresh flowers and their inclusion in portraits. I believe, however, that this ignores trends in still life painting and portraiture already in practice before Rambouillet's flower-filled *chambre bleue* became famous. The room was also notorious, as suggested by its name, for its blue color as reported by Tallement des Réaux. For more on the *chambre bleue* and fashionable colors of the seventeenth century, see Alain Mérot, *Retraites mondaines: Aspects de la décoration intérieure à Paris au XVIIe siècle* (Paris: Le Promeneur, 1990), 60.

88. For more on the relationship between the garden and preciosity, see Anne Desprechins, "Les jardins de *Clélie*," in *Les Trois Scudéry*, ed. Alain Niderst, 433–441; and Elizabeth Goldsmith, *Exclusive Conversations: The Art of Interacting in Seventeenth-Century France* (Philadelphia: University of Pennsylvania Press, 1988), "Talking in the Garden," 123–132.

89. Quoted in Mérot, *Retraites mondaines*, 75. "Tout est magnifique chez elle, et même particulier; . . . ses cabinets sont pleins de mille raretés, qui font voir le jugement de celle qui les a choisies; l'air est toujours parfumé dans son palais: diverses corbeilles magnifiques pleines de fleurs font un printemps continuel dans sa chambre."

90. Quoted in Mérot, *Retraites mondaines*, 76. Montpensier wrote of an "antre . . . entouré de grands vases de cristal, pleins des plus belles fleurs du printemps, qui durent toujours dans les jardins qui sont auprès de son temple."

91. Michel Faré and Fabrice Faré, *Peintres de fleurs en France du XVIIe au XIXe siècles* (Paris: Musée du Petit Palais, Palais des Beaux-Arts de la ville de Paris, 1979), 4–5; and Madeleine Pinault, *Le Peintre et l'histoire naturelle*, trans. Philip Sturgess (Paris: Flammarion, 1990).

92. Linard was a Parisian flower painter active in the first half of the seventeenth century. For more on Linard, see Michel Faré, *Le Grand Siècle de la nature morte en France: Le XVIIe siècle* (Fribourg: Office du livre; Paris: Société française du livre, 1974).

93. Evelyne Saint-Paul, *L'Hôtel de Sully* (Paris: Caisse Nationale des Monuments Historiques et des Sites; Rennes: Editions Ouest-France, 1993), 15.

94. Reproduced in *Le Marais: Mythe et realité. Exposition: Hôtel de Sully 30 avril–30 août 1987* (Paris: Caisse Nationale des Monuments Historiques et des Sites, 1987).

95. Reproduced in Woodbridge, *Princely Gardens*, 106.

96. One might posit here that the taste for painted floral decorations was an extension of the elaborate floral borders woven into tapestries. Painted flowers frequently surround history paintings and portraits as they surrounded the central figures on tapestries. And of course the *mille fleurs* tapestries are testimony to the taste for floral background designs. In addition, tapestries often featured pastoral subjects such as the

chase, falconry, or days spent in the countryside. For more on the representations of the outdoors in tapestry, see Ronald Rees, *Interior Landscapes: Gardens and the Domestic Environment* (Baltimore, Md.: Johns Hopkins University Press, 1993), 28–36.

97. See photographs of the floral decor of Cormatin in "Chateaux et jardins, numéro spécial des *Connaissance des arts,*" *Connaissance des arts* (Paris: 1990): 56–63; and "L'Eclat de Cormatin," in *Maison et jardin* (February 1994): 56–63.

98. Lucretia de Planta, "Le Comte de Bussy et sa cour d'illustres," in *Les Heures Bourguignonnes du Comte de Bussy-Rabutin* (Autun: Musée Rolin, 1993), 54–60.

99. Bussy-Rabutin did not, however, include these women as a form of flattery. Underneath each portrait Bussy painted their names and short descriptions of the women that were hardly flattering. To describe Catherine-Henriette d'Angennes de la Loupe, comtesse d'Olonne, who was featured in his *Histoire amoureuse des Gaules,* Bussy wrote, "Catherine d'Angennes comtesse d'Olonne la plus belle fame de son tems, mais moins fameuse pour sa beauté, que pour l[']usage qu'elle en fit." Quoted in De Planta, "Le comte de Bussy et sa cour d'illustres," in *Les Heures Bourguignonnes,* 55.

100. For example, rich floral garlands were incorporated into the decoration of the Hall of Mirrors.

101. The fresco was destroyed in the eighteenth century. Jane Davidson Reid, *The Oxford Guide to Classical Mythology in the Arts, 1300–1990* (Oxford: Oxford University Press, 1993), 434.

102. Pierre Dan reports, "De cette Antichambre ou Cabinet l'on passe à la Chambre du Roy, où est sur la cheminée un fort beau Tableau, representant la Deesse Flora; & est du feu sieur de Bois," in his *Le Tresor des merveilles de la maison royale de Fontainebleau* (Paris: Sebastien Cramoisy, 1642), 142–144. The painting, after a period of absence, has been returned to Fontainebleau and hangs there today. The work was apparently very popular, as several copies of it were rendered in the seventeenth century, one of which is now in the Fogg Art Museum, Harvard University. For more on Ambroise Dubois, see Sylvie Béguin, "L'art de peinture et de sculpture d'Ambroise Dubois à Fontainebleau," *Revue du Louvre et des Musées de France* 3 (1979): 229–233; and Sylvie Béguin, "Deux peintures d'Ambroise Dubois," *La Revue du Louvre* (1965).

103. Despite the relatively unusual moralizing tone that Poussin's interpretation of Ovid suggests, there was, according to Henry Bardon, a "querelle d'Ovide" in the seventeenth century between those who took pleasure in his work and those who found it paganistic and amoral. See H. Bardon, "Sur l'influence d'Ovide en France au 17ème siècle," *Atti del convegno internazionale Ovidiano, Sulmona, maggio 1958* (Rome: Istituto di Studi Romani Editore, 1959), 76.

104. Antoine Schnapper, *Curieux du Grand Siècle. Oeuvres d'art,* vol. 2, *Collections et collectionneurs dans la France du XVIIe siècle* (Paris: Flammarion, 1994), 210.

105. A drawing by Le Sueur in the Musée de Besançon has been identified by Alain Mérot as a plan for the ceiling. Denis Lavalle, "Plafonds et grands décors peints dans les hôtels du Marais au XVIIe siècle," in *Le Marais: mythe et realité,* 182.

106. Lavalle, "Plafonds et grands décors," 193.

107. Ibid.

108. Michel Le Möel, *L'Architecture privée à Paris au grand siècle* (Paris: Commission des travaux historiques de la ville de Paris, 1990), 198–199. Colbert lived at this address (5 rue du Mail).

109. Ibid., 202, 208.

110. Mérot, *Retraites mondaines*, 55.

111. Alain Mérot explains the convenience of mythology in such expressions: writing "Les sujets mythologiques sont commodes: ils permettent la flatterie sans insistance comme l'amplification brillante; ils donnent au décorateur une grande liberté, par leur abondance et leur facilité d'adaptation aux convenances de l'architecture et du programme. . . . La mythologie redevient alors un langage image." See Alain Mérot, "La Place des sujets mythologiques et leur signification dans le décor peint, à Paris, dans la première moitié du XVIIe siècle," in *La Mythologie au XVIIe siècle. Centre Méridional de Rencontres sur le XVIIe siècle. 11e Colloque, janvier 1981*, ed. Claude Faisant (Marseille: A. Robert, 1982), 224.

112. The work of Alain Mérot is helpful here. He writes: "La prolifération des images et le mélange, au sein d'un même espace, de catégories apparemment hétérogènes peuvent d'abord s'expliquer par la notion de microcosme: comme les cabinets de collectionneurs où sont réunies toutes les 'curiosités' possibles . . . , les décors du Grand Siècle se veulent un monde en miniature et peuvent en refléter les aspects principaux. D'où cette organisation caractéristique en séries et en strates autour d'un thème donné et le rôle joué par les éléments naturels—fleurs, oiseaux, paysages . . .—en contrepoint à l'histoire ou à la mythologie. Bien plus, les différents domaines communiquent entre eux au sein d'un vaste système de correspondances symboliques. . . . Les gens du monde—c'est-à-dire une aristocratie raffinée et tous ceux qui tentent, plus ou moins adroitement, de l'imiter—privilégient un mode de connaissance non livresque, aisé, synthétique, où les diverses qualités ou attributs des êtres et des choses sont mis en rapport. Ainsi une déesse, une femme, une fleur, une pierre précieuse, une couleur, un astre peuvent servir à de subtiles alliances." Mérot, *Retraites mondaines*, 183–184.

113. The most comprehensive studies of French still life paintings are Michel Faré, *Le Grand Siècle de la nature morte en France*, and Michel Faré and Fabrice Faré, *La Vie silencieuse en France: La nature morte au XVIIIe siècle* (Fribourg: Office du livre, 1976).

114. Michel Faré, *Le Grand Siècle de la nature morte*, 86.

115. Quoted in Taylor, *Dutch Flower Painting*, 78. Taylor quotes and discusses Félibien in the context of the theory of still life painting in the Netherlands.

116. See Chapter 1.

117. Simon Schama, "Perishable Commodities: Dutch Still-life Painting and the 'Empire of Things,'" in *Consumption and the World of Goods*, ed. John Brewer and Roy Porter (London: Routledge, 1993), 486.

118. Schama, "Perishable Commodities," 486.

119. Taylor, *Dutch Flower Paintings*, 195.

120. Norman Bryson, *Looking at the Overlooked: Four Essays on Still Life Painting* (Cambridge, Mass.: Harvard University Press, 1990), 108.

121. I therefore would not apply Bryson's conclusion that "the Dutch painters of still life . . . make no use of painting as a vehicle for bringing to the world the uniqueness of a personal vision" to early modern France. Bryson, *Looking at the Overlooked*, 135.

122. Reproduced in Goody, *The Culture of Flowers*, 172.

123. Reproduced in Frain, *La Guirlande de Julie*, 68.

124. Reproduced in Woodbridge, *Princely Gardens*, 96.

125. Anthony Blunt, "The Précieux and French Art," 335.

126. Both portraits are reproduced in Frain, *La Guirlande de Julie*, 15 and 51.

127. Richard Brilliant explains in *Portraiture* that "Allegorical portraiture, by its very nature, tends to make observation abstract, to displace perception from its objects, and to engender emblematic images which transmute the substance of a person into ideas, words, and conceits, gathered around a named person." See Brilliant, *Portraiture* (Cambridge, Mass.: Harvard University Press, 1991), 104.

128. Orest Ranum has suggested that the exchange of flowers between mother and child in eighteenth-century portraits is represented "to note the fragility of childhood and the all-too-frequent deaths of these supposedly fragile creatures." Ranum, "Intimacy in French Eighteenth-Century Family Portraits," *Word and Image: A Journal of Verbal/Visual Enquiry* 6.4 (October–December 1990): 364.

129. See Chapter 1 for a discussion of women and flowers.

130. Robert Brilliant argues in his theoretical study of the genre of portraiture (which he identifies as "a particular phenomenon of representation in Western art that is especially sensitive to changes in the perceived nature of the individual in Western society") that the genre "requires a high degree of cooperation and collusion among the participants in a social encounter. Cooperation is found in the exchange of the meaningful, but not necessarily true, indications of status and role that establish the social identity manifested by one person and so understood by another. Collusion is the end result of the tacit agreement that whatever a person represents himself or herself to be, or to be like, will be taken at face value, at least at the beginning of the exchange." Brilliant, *Portraiture*, 8, 89.

131. For the implications of and interpretation of Henrietta Maria as Flora, see Stephen Orgel, ed., *Ben Jonson: The Complete Masques* (New Haven, Conn.: Yale University Press, 1969), and Erica Veevers, *Images of Love and Religion: Queen Henrietta Maria and Court Entertainments* (Cambridge: Cambridge University Press, 1989).

132. Reproduced in Néraudau, *L'Olympe du Roi-Soleil*, plate A.

133. See Daniel S. Russell, *The Emblem and Device in France* (Lexington, Ky.: French Forum, 1985).

134. Pierre Le Moyne, *De l'Art des devises. Par le P. Le Moyne de a Compagnie de Jesus. Avec divers receuils de devises du mesme autheur* (Paris: Sebastien Cramoisy & Sebastien Mabre Cramoisy, 1666), preface, n.p. Flowers were suitable, according to Le Moyne, "dans les Festes de la Cour, dans les entrées du Roys & des Reynes, & dans les autre occasions, où avec le peinture & la broderie, avec les marbres & les dorures."

135. Ibid., 380. Le Moyne writes: "C'est le titre que je donne à ce second Recueil de Devises faites sur diverses Fleurs. Et quoy qu'il y en ait quelques unes qui ne sont que simples Inscriptions: elles n'en vallent pas moins, ny n'ont moins cousté à faire: & c'est le droit de la plus forte partie, de tirer l'intitulation à elle. On n'en a point fait graver les Figures; parce que l'imagination se les peut assez faciliment representer, sans le secours de la graveure."

136. Ibid. Le Moyne explained that "en chaque Devise la Fleur parle; toutes ses paroles ont double sens; & ne luy appartiennent pas plus qu'à la Personne pour qui elle parle."

137. Ibid., 386. According to Le Moyne: "Il ne se voit point de tissure plus délicate que celle de l'Anemone: le chaud & le froid l'offencent également. . . . C'est la propre figure d'une Ame tranquile & moderée: aussi incapable d'excez que de deffaut: qui

n'agit ny chaudement, ny avec froideur: qui se tient tousiours éloignée des extremitez: & qui ne donne jamais de prise à aucune passion."

138. Ibid., 387. "J'ay le corps delicat, comme j'ay le coeur tendre;// A mon temperament mon esprit est égal;// Le plus petit excez me tient lieu d'un grand mal;// Et mon instinct me porte à m'en deffendre.// Quoy que je tienne du Soleil,// J'évite avec un soin pareil,// Soit l'extréme chaleur, soit l'extréme froidure;// Et le tissu d'air temperé,// Dont me composa la Nature,// Ne souffre rien qui ne soit moderé."

139. Mérot, *Retraites mondaines*, 103.

140. Brigitte Maurice-Chabard, "Le Salon des Devises," in *Les Heures Bourguignonnes* (as above, note 99), 80.

141. Interestingly, Bussy was not the only "exile" with whom flowers were associated. It was reported in verses by Georges de Scudéry that the Grand Condé cultivated carnations in Vincennes during the Fronde. Scudéry's poem was entitled "Sur des pots de fleurs que le Prince de Condé cultivait à Vincennes." See Faré and Faré, *Peintres de fleurs en France du XVIIe au XIXe siècles*, 2; Orest Ranum, *The Fronde: A French Revolution, 1648–1652* (New York: W. W. Norton, 1993), 271. The most famous prisoner of the seventeenth century, Nicolas Fouquet, reportedly also grew flowers in his captivity, as if flowers sympathetically commented upon his character.

142. Bryson, *Looking at the Overlooked*, 60.

143. Abraham Bosse, *Le Iardin e la Noblesse Françoise dans lequel ce peut ceuillir leur manierre de Vettements* (Paris: Melchior Tavernier, 1629), title page.

144. Guillaume Budé, *Le livre de l'institution du prince*, in Claude Bontems, Léon-Pierre Raybaud, and Jean-Pierre Brancourt, *Le Prince dans la France des XVIe et XVIIe siècles* (Paris: Presses Universitaires de France, 1965), 91. Budé addressed François I: "comme si j'estoye en ung grant pré au mois de may et je cueilloye les fleurs plus insignes par odeur ou couleur ou émminentes sur les autres pour en faire ung chapellet et le présenter à vostre majesté ou lieu d'ung grant présent que ung homme riche pourroit donner qui auroit de quoy le faire, ce que je n'ay pas."

For discussions of Budé's text, see Orest Ranum, *Artisans of Glory: Writers and Historical Thought in Seventeenth-Century France* (Chapel Hill: University of North Carolina Press, 1980), chapter 1, "Men of Letters: Sixteenth-Century Models of Conduct," 26–57; and Timothy Hampton, "Guillaume Budé Addresses to Francis I the Manuscript of *Le Livre de l'institution du prince*: Humanist Models for Thought and Action," in *A New History of French Literature*, ed. Hollier, 91. I thank Professor Orest Ranum for referring me to Budé's use of the floral metaphor.

145. Furetière, *Dictionnaire*, s.v. "fleur." "On appelle *fleurs* de Rhetorique, les figures, les ornements du discours. Il s'est servi de toutes les fleurs de sa Rhetorique pour me persuader son opinion. les *fleurs* de bien dire." Furetière added: "Ce mot a servi aussi de titre à plusieurs livres. Les *Fleurs* des Saincts. les *Fleurs* Poëtiques, &c."

146. Maryanne Cline Horowitz explores the role of these florilegia in the humanist pedagogy: "Humanist educators encouraged florilegia based on fresh readings of classical authorities and encouraged thinking of ethics in the context of historical examples. The process of storing uplifting quotations molds both the mind and the character, and characters so molded articulate memorized sayings and worthy examples for emulation at the moment of important ethical decisions. More important than the published versions, which simplify the secondhand acquisition of classical culture, is the training of

students to make their own copybooks from their readings of the classics." Horowitz, *Seeds of Virtue*, 105–106.

147. See Dawson, *Toulouse in the Renaissance*; and François Gélis, *Histoire critique des jeux floraux*.

148. *Le Parterre de la rhetorique Françoise, emaillé de toutes les plus belles fleurs d'eloquence qui se montrent dans les oeuvres des orateurs tant anciens que modernes, ensemble le verger de poësie, ouvrage tres-utile à ceux qui veulent exceller en l'un et l'autre art* (Lyon: C. de La Rivière, 1659).

149. Pierre Le Moyne, *Les Peintres Morales* (Paris, 1640).

150. Puget de La Serre, *Le Bouquet des plus belles fleurs de l'eloquence cueilly dans les jardins des sieurs Du Perron, Coiffeteau, Du Vair, Bertaud, D'Urfé, Malerbe, Daudiguier, La Brosse, Du Rousset, La Serre* (Paris: P. Billaine, 1624), frontispiece. Reproduced in Marc Fumaroli, *L'Age de l'éloquence: Rhétorique et 'res literaria' de la Renaissance au seuil de l'époque classique* (Paris: Albin Michel, 1994), plate 23.

151. Etienne Binet, *Essay des merveilles de nature, et des plus nobles artifices, piece très-necessaire à tous ceux qui font profession d'eloquence* (Rouen: Romain de Beauvais, 1621), frontispiece. Reproduced in Fumaroli, *L'âge de l'éloquence*, plate 12.

152. Binet, *Essay*, 296. "La Nature esmaillant les campagnes, les Peres fleurdelisant leurs escrits, contre-tirant toutes ses mignardises, ont fait un si noble paralelle de beauté, que de vray ce sont des miracles, et tous deux sont plus beaux l'un que l'autre. Mais quelle vergongne de voir qu'on ne sçait pas parler de ces belles beautez; et quelle fantasie de sçavoir leurs noms en Grec et en Latin, et en François ne sçavoir ny les noms, ny les parties des Fleurs, ny parler de choses si delicates, et si ordinaires! Quand les plus huppez ont dit la Rose, le Lis, et l'Oeillet, le Bouton, et la fueille, ce petit bouton renferme toute leur science, car ils sont au bout de leur sçavoir, et rebattent les aureilles les greslant de redites importunes et ignorantes. Je vous veux deslier la langue, afin que vous puissiez, dire deux mots bien à propos."

153. Francesco Colonna, *Hypnerotomachie ou discours du Songe de Poliphile*, trans. and ed. Robert de Lenoncourt and Jean Martin (Paris: I. Keruer, 1546); Pietro Crescenzi, *Le Bon Mesnagier* (1540); Charles Estienne and Jean Liébault, *L'Agriculture et la maison rustique* (1570), trans. Richard Surflet as *Maison Rustique, or The Countrie Farme* (London: E. Bollifant, 1600); and Olivier de Serres, *Le Théâtre d'agriculture et mesnage des champs* (Paris: Abr. Saugrain, 1605).

154. Jacques Boyceau, *Traité du jardinage selon les raisons de la nature et de l'art* (Paris: Michel Vanlochom, 1638); Claude Mollet, *Théâtre des jardinages*; and André Mollet, *Le Jardin de plaisir*.

155. Boyceau, *Traité*, 82. Boyceau imagined "qui aura les fontaines enrichies, les canaux & ruisseaux enjolivez, les grottes & lieux sousterrains, les vollieres, les galleries ornées de peinture & sculpture, l'orangerie, les allée & promenoirs mieux agencez, couvert ou découverts, les pelouses & preaux pour les jeux de ballon, & exercises de la personne, . . . bien disposez és environs des parterres."

156. Liger, *La Jardinier Fleuriste*, 36–37.

157. Nicolas de Bonnefons, *Le Jardinier François*, 5th ed. (Amsterdam: Jean Blaeu, 1654), 6. "C'est pourquoy (MESDAMES) j'espere que vous me sçavrez gré de vois avoire dressé cette instruction, je l'ay fait imprimer en petit Volume, afin que vous le puissiez

porter sans incommodité, pour confronter le travail de vos Jardiniers avec ce petit Livre, & juger de leur capacité ou negligence."

158. Interestingly, several gardening texts were printed especially for women in England, including Charles Evelyn, *The Lady's Recreation: or, the Third and Last Part of the Art of Gardening Improv'd* (London: J. Roberts, 1717), the introduction of which stated: "As the curious Part of Gardening in general, has been always an Amusement chosen by the greatest of Men, for the unbending of their Thoughts, and to retire from the World; so the Management of the Flower-Garden in particular, is oftentimes the Diversion of the Ladies, where the Gardens are not very extensive, and the Inspection thereof doth not take up too much of their Time." Yet when John Evelyn translated and published Bonnefons's work in 1672 as *The French Gardiner*, he deleted the author's dedication to women. For more on English women's gardening texts, see June Taboroff, "'Wife, unto thy garden': The First Gardening Books for Women," *Garden History: The Journal of the Garden History Society* 11.1 (Spring 1983): 1–5.

159. Pierre Morin, *Remarques necessaires pour la culture des fleurs* (Bourge en Bresse: Joseph Ravoux, 1692); and N. Valnay, *Connoissance et culture parfaite des tulippes rares* (Paris: Laurent d'Houry, 1688).

160. L[ouis] B[oulanger], *Jardinage de oeillets* (Paris: Louis Boulanger, 1647); De La Chesnée Monstereul, *Le Floriste françois*; Guénin, *Traité de la culture parfaite des oreilles d'ours ou auricules* (Paris: n.p., 1738); George Voorhelm, *Traité sur la jacinte. Contenant la maniere de la cultiver suivant l'expérience qui en a été faite* (Harlem: I. & J. Enschedé, 1752); and Maximilian Henri, Marquis de Saint Simon, *Des Jacintes, de leur anatomie, reproduction et culture* (Amsterdam: n.p., 1768).

161. Wilfrid Blunt, *The Art of Botanical Illustration*, 31–44.

162. For more on herbals, see Agnes Arber, *Herbals: Their Origin and Evolution* (Cambridge: Cambridge University Press, 1938).

163. Wilfrid Blunt recounts the early uses of line engraving and etching in botanical works in *The Art of Botanical Illustration*, chapter 8, "The Early Etchers and Metal-Engravers."

164. The term *florilegium*, translated literally as "flower books," was long used to describe collections of verse. The application of the term to books containing flower illustrations was therefore a less figurative although newer use of the term.

165. For an analysis of the format of the florilegium, see Gill Saunders, *Picturing Plants: An Analytical History of Botanical Illustration* (Berkeley: University of California Press in association with the Victoria and Albert Museum, London, 1995), 41.

166. Pierre Vallet, *Le Jardin du Roy Tres Chrestien Henry IV Roy de France et de Navare dédié à La Royne* (Paris, n.p., 1608), 19. The work's flowers "ne redoutent les froides haleines de l'hyver, ni les secousses des vents, ni mesme que l'aspérité des rayons du soleil des desseche & flestrisse."

167. Ibid., 1. One engraving in the copy in the collection of the Dumbarton Oaks Research Library and Collection has been painted in the prescribed colors; several others have been traced. The copy in Houghton Library, Harvard University, has not been utilized in such a manner. The work provided patterns for "ceux qui voudront peindré ou enluminer, ou broder & faire tapisserie" in floral designs.

168. Blunt, *The Art of Botanical Illustration*, 98–99.

169. Wilfrid Blunt has traced the use of Crispin de Passe's engravings to Franeau's *Jardin de l'Hyver*, Parkinson's *Paradisus*, Anselm de Boodt's *Florum, Herbarum, ac Fructuum Selectiorum Icones*, and Matthew Merian's 1641 reedition of Johann Theodor De Bry's *Florilegium Novum* (the original edition of which copied plates from Vallet's work). See Blunt, *The Art of Botanical Illustration*, 91–104.

170. François Langlois, *Livres de fleurs, ou sont representés touttes sortes de tulippes, narcisses, iris, et plusieurs autres fleurs avec diversités d'oiseaux, mouches, et papillons, le tout fait apres le naturel* (Paris: Jean le Clerc, 1620).

171. For more on Rabel, see Tomasi, *An Oak Spring Flora*, 69–73, Wilfred Blunt, *The Art of Botanical Illustration*, 107–108, and Schapper, *Le Géant la licorne, et la tulipe*, 57–58.

172. Franeau, *Jardin d'hyver*, 3–4. Franeau explained in the dedication of the work his purpose in writing it: "Mais comme les Jardins & parterres domestiques, parmy la rigueur d'un rud & froid Hyver, parmy ses glaces, gresles & nieges, sont rendus plus steriles, & que lors la Nature nous retire ses jeus fleuris, . . . j'ay à desein representé du crayon de ma plume aucuns Fleurons plus signalez, pour en faire participer ceste triste saison." "C'est pourquoy," he added, "que sur la porte ou frontispiece de ces foibles traits & pourtraits, je luy ay mis ceste inscription de Jardin d'hyver, ou cabinet des fleurs."

173. The connection between *cabinets* and gardens is explored in John Dixon Hunt, "Curiosities to Adorn Cabinets and Gardens," in *The Origins of Museums: The Cabinet of Curiosities in Sixteenth- and Seventeenth-Century Europe*, ed. Oliver Impey and Arthur MacGregor (Oxford: Clarendon Press, 1985), 193–203.

174. Gill Saunders has similarly argued that "Florilegia were in a sense catalogues of collections, for a garden (certainly in the seventeenth century) was a collection of ephemeral exhibits, beautiful, often rare and exotic, imported or otherwise acquired at great cost. Some florilegia were records of specific gardens." See Saunders, *Picturing Plants*, 41.

175. Thomasina Beck has demonstrated that surviving early modern works of embroidery containing floral patterns and garden scenes can be traced directly to specific illustrations from early florilegia and gardening manuals. Floral themes were used so extensively in England that the phrase "to flower" came to mean "to embroider." According to Rozsika Parker, "By 1740 the terms 'to embroider' and 'to flower' were interchangeable. In Samuel Richardson's *Pamela* the narrator wrote to her parents that 'Mrs. Jervis shewed my master the waistcoat I am flowering for him.'" See Thomasina Beck, *The Embroiderer's Gardens* (New York: Viking Press, 1979); and Thomasina Beck, *The Embroiderer's Flowers* (N.p.: David & Charles, 1992); and Rozsika Parker, *The Subversive Stitch: Embroidery and the Making of the Feminine* (New York: Routledge, 1989).

176. Vallet, *Le Jardin du Roy Tres Chrestien Henry IV Roy de France et de Navare dédié à La Royne*, dedication, n.p. He wrote: "Le nom de Printemps perpetuel luy seroit autant couenable, pource que les fleurs dont il est embelli ne redoutent les froides haleines de l'hyver, ni les secousses des vents, ni mesme que l'asperité des rayons du soleil des desseche & flestrisse, leur ostant l'honneur que Flore leur avoit faict porter à leur naissance, ces fleurs ne peuvent & doivent estre que vostres, ayans esté imitées de celles qui croissent dedans les superbes & delicieux iardins, que sa Majesté fait cultiver par Jehan Robin son herboriste, qui m'a fait part de ce que nature y produisoit de plus beau selo les temps, le soing duquel ne poet tant faire que l'inconstance des saisons n'en esteigne par fois la durée, & les plaisir que vous en pourriés."

177. Ibid., 18. "Advertissement a Ceux qui voudront peindré ou anluminer, ou broder & faire tapisserie sur ce present livre."

178. The copy is to be found in the Dumbarton Oaks Research Library and Collection, Washington, D.C.

179. Saunders, *Picturing Plants*, 55.

180. Ibid., 55, 61.

181. Nicolas Cochin, *Livre nouveau de fleurs tres util pour l'art d'orfevrier et autres* (Paris: Baltazar Moncornet, 1645).

182. François Le Febvre, *Livres de fleurs & de feullies pour servir a l'art d'orfevrerie invente par François le Febvre maistre orfevre à Paris* (Paris: Baltazar Moncornet, 1635); and Jean Vauquier, *Livre de fleurs propre pour orfevres et graveurs* (Blois, 1680; repr. London: Bernard Quaritch, 1888).

183. Maria Sibylla Merian, *Neues Blumen Buch allen Kunstverständigen Liebhabern su Lust, Nutz und Dienst* (Nürnburg: Joh. Andrea Graffen, 1680; repr. Leipzig: Insel Verlag, 1966). To understand the place of this work in the context of Merian's research, see Natalie Zemon Davis, *Women on the Margins: Three Seventeenth-Century Lives* (Cambridge, Mass.: Harvard University Press, 1995), 145–146.

184. Catherine Perrot, *Les Leçons royales ou la maniere de peindre en mignature les fleurs & les oyseaux, par l'explication des livres de fleurs & d'oyseaux de feu Nicolas Robert fleuriste* (Paris: Pierre de Bats, 1687); and *Traité de la mignature* (Paris: Arnoult Seneuze, 1693).

185. Perrot does not name a specific volume of Robert's work. She might, however, have had in mind his *Receuil des Plantes* or his *Variae ac Multiformes Florum Species*, a pattern book.

186. Perrot, *Les Leçons royales*, "Avis," n.p. She explained: "Quoique Monsieur Robert, dont je suis l'Eleve, ne soit pas le seul Fleuriste qui ait excelé, neanmoins j'ai toûjours preferé ses Ouvrages à ceux des autres Fleuristes, parce qu'il a le mieux representé le Naturel des Fleurs & des Oyseaux."

187. Ibid., "Epistre," n.p. Perrot named the dauphine as one of "toutes les personnes de qualité, qui ont de l'inclination pour la Peintre en Mignature," although she added that "Les personnes vulgaires ne seront pas moins obligées d'avoire agreables ces Leçons."

188. Claude Boutet, *Ecole de la mignature, dans laquelle on peut aisément apprendre à peindre sans maître. Avec le secret de faire les plus belles couleurs: l'or bruni & l'or en coquille. Nouvelle édition, augmentée* (Lyon: François du Chesne, 1679), 87, 3.

189. Ibid., 87. He explained that flowers were particularly agreeable to paint "non-seulement par l'éclat de leurs différentes couleurs, mais aussi par le peu de tems & de peine qu'on employe à les faire." He added that "la plus grande partie des personnes de qualité qui se divertissent à peindre, s'en tiennent aux Fleurs."

190. For more see Alain Corbin, *The Foul and the Fragrant: Odor and the French Social Imagination*, trans. Miriam L. Kochan, Ray Porter, and Christopher Prendergast (Cambridge, Mass.: Harvard University Press, 1986).

191. Simon Barbe, *Le Parfumeur François, qui enseigne toutes les manieres de tirer les odeurs des fleurs; & à faire toutes sortes de compositions de parfums* (Lyon: Thomas Amaulry, 1693), "Au Lecteur," n.p. Barbe's work was intended "pour le divertissement de la Noblesse." His work was therefore intended for those "personnes de condition & celles

qui ont un honnête loisir rempliront leur temps & se desennuyeront en campagne, lors qu'ils employeront l'abondance des fleurs à faire des parfums à juste prix."

192. F.L.D.T.R., *Secrets pour teindre la fleur d'immortelle en diverses couleurs, avec la maniere de la cultiver* (Paris: Charles de Sercy, 1690), 16–17, 29–31, 34–37.

193. An advertisement for the series is included in Morin, *Remarques necessaires pour la culture des fleurs*, n.p.

194. Boulanger, *Jardinage des oeillets*, 148–149. "Enfin pour terminer ces pieuses pensées, la plus belle fleur, & l'oeillet le plus pompeux qui jamais la nature ait produit, n'a pas esté immortel, mais apres quinze jours, ou un mois d'esclat, apres les estonnemens de tous les curieux, apres tout la vanité de ceux qui l'on eslevé, apres dis-je tant de soins & de caresses. Cette fleurs est flestrie, & cet oeillet est fané; si bien qui ce n'est plus qu'un peu de paille & de fumier. Estrange Catastrofe de toutes les beautez de l'univers, & de l'homme mesme qui en est la principale piece, lequel durant sa vie ayant obey comme un sujet, ou commandé en souverain; ne laisse enfin apres sa mort à la posterite, qui le triste ressouvenir de ses ans trop tost escoulés; & quelques pitoyables tombeaux, pour eterniser la memoire de ses plus glorieuses conquestes. Tombeaux eslevez sur des pretieuses Colomnes de Porphyre & de Marbre, enrichis des plus rares pieces de l'antiquité, & venerables pour la multitude de leurs figures & statuës presque vivantes & animées; mais enfin (nonobstant leur superbes Epitalames) qui ne proteront iamais un Epitaphe plus veritable que celuy-cy. / Homo tanquam flos agri sic efflorescit, / Et omnis gloria eius tanquam flos faeni. FIN."

195. Ibid., "Approbation," n.p. The approbation read: "Ce livre intitulé, *Le Jardinage des oeillets*, fait & composé par L.B. pour sa curiosité, & pour l'exacte observation de la nature, & de la culture de l'oeillet, meslangé de quelques considerations morales, merité d'estre imprimé."

196. La Chesnée Monstereul, *Le Floriste françois*, "Approbation," n.p. They found "rien trouvé contraire à la foy de l'Eglise Catholique, Apostolique & Romaine, ny aux bonnes moeurs."

197. Ibid., 203. "Ce divin Autheur de toutes choses ayant au troisième jour creé les Plantes," Chesnée Monstereul explained: "entre lesquelles la Tulip sans doute paroissoit comme la premiere en dignité, & le plus bel ornement du paradis terrestre; faisant (selon le texte de Moyse) une sorte de reflexion sur ses divins Ouvrages, considerant leur beauté, & la perfection en laquelle il les avoit creés, les jugea bons."

198. *La Culture des fleurs* (Bourge en Bresse: Joseph Ravoux, 1692), 205. "Je prie ceux qui liront ce Traité de faire reflection sur les merveilles de la Nature dans la seule production des Fleurs, & de considerer que sans le Peché, elles ne nous auroient jamais rien couté: Toute la Terre seroit un Jardin de delices, on ne connoitroit point de Ronces, ny d'Epines, ny de Chardons."

199. Ibid., 205. The author implored his fellow florists to "cherchons la donc ensemble, mon cher Lecteur, cultivons la, avec celle de nos coeurs, & en faisons un Bouquet, qui est la seule union, à la quelle nous devons buter, avec la grace de Jesus-Christ, auquel nous devons tous nos desirs, toutes nos pensées, toutes nos affections, Et semper, & upique gratias agere."

200. La Chesnée Monstereul, *Le Floriste françois*, preface, n.p.

201. René Rapin, *Of Gardens*, trans. John Evelyn, 5.

202. Ibid., 18–19.

203. Liger, *Le Jardinier Fleuriste*, trans. George London and Henry Wise as *The Retir'd Gard'ner*, 323.

204. Michel Foucault, *The Order of Things: An Archaeology of the Human Sciences* (New York: Vintage Books, 1973), 125–131.

205. See Blunt, *The Art of Botanical Illustration*, 92–93.

206. This idea is explored more fully in Chapter 2, where I argue that floriculture conferred cultural distinction on a wide variety of people in early modern France, from curious gardeners, to apothecaries, to doctors, and further up the social scale to nobles and even the king. The diminishing differences between the two cultural ideals upheld by *doctes* and *mondains* is discussed by Pierre Bourdieu, *Distinction*, 73.

Chapter 5. Cultivating the King

1. N. Valnay, *Connoissance et culture parfaite des tulippes rares, des anemones extraordinaires, des oeillets fins, et des belles oreilles d'ours panachées* (Paris: Laurent d'Houry, 1688), 123–124. Valnay wrote: "Les panachées sont si nouvelles que lorsque Monsieur le Chevalier de Saint Mory cet illustre & grand Curieux en enyoya [*sic*] des fleurs au Roy en 1685. Sa Majesté qui les admira fut surpris qu'il y eut de si jolies Fleurs en ce païs qui luy fussent inconnunës."

2. Ibid., "Avertissement," n.p. "Avant le regne de Louis XIV y connoissoit-t'on la beauté des Jardins? Il semble que les Arts & leur suitte se soient reserverz de tout temps pour fleurir dans celuy-cy, & que parce que nostre Monarque merite d'autres courrones que tous les Heros, il nous soit né de plus belles Fleurs qu'on n'en ait jamais veu, our servir de modeles aux habiles Artisans de ses trophées."

3. See Peter Burke, *The Fabrication of Louis XIV* (New Haven, Conn.: Yale University Press, 1992); Jean-Marie Apostolidès, *Le Roi-machine: Spectacle et politique au temps de Louis XIV* (Paris: Les Editions de Minuit, 1981); Louis Marin, *Portrait of the King*, trans. Martha M. Houle, foreword by Tom Conley (Minneapolis: University of Minnesota Press, 1988).

4. Scholars have long speculated on the degree to which Louis XIV himself made decisions for architectural, artistic, and iconographical projects. Recent scholarship has demonstrated that at times the king showed substantial interest in building programs, though often decisions were left to his ministers and the academies. See, for example, Robert W. Berger, *A Royal Passion: Louis XIV as Patron of Architecture* (Cambridge: Cambridge University Press, 1994).

5. Anthony Blunt, *Art and Architecture in France, 1500–1700* (London: Penguin Books, 1982), 347. For a more thorough treatment of the series of paintings, see Donald Posner, "Charles Le Brun's *Triumphs of Alexander*," *Art Bulletin* 41 (September 1959): 237–248. The canvases were so large that no permanent location to display them could be found until they were placed in the Galerie d'Apollon in the Louvre in the eighteenth century. *Le Louvre: The Palace and Its Paintings: An Interactive Visit to the World's Grandest Museum* (Paris: Réunion des Musées Nationaux, 1995), CD-ROM.

6. Julius Held and Donald Posner, *Seventeenth and Eighteenth Century Art: Baroque Painting, Sculpture, Architecture* (Englewood Cliffs, N.J.: Prentice-Hall; New York: Harry N. Abrams, n.d.), 163.

7. Burke, *The Fabrication of Louis XIV*, 28, 68–69, 131.

8. Georges Gibault, *Les Fleurs nationales et les fleurs politiques* (Paris: Librairie et imprimerie Horticoles, 1904), 23.

9. Alice M. Coats, *Garden Shrubs and Their Histories* (New York: Simon and Schuster, 1992), 173.

10. Colette Beaune, *The Birth of an Ideology: Myths and Symbols of Nation in Late-Medieval France*, ed. Fredric L. Cheyette, trans. Susan Ross Huston (Berkeley: University of California Press, 1991), 202, 215. According to one version of the fourteenth-century tale, God sent to Clovis a shield bearing three lilies on a blue background that Clovis carried into battle against the Goths at the battle of Tobiac. Another version told by the monks of Joyenval claimed that a hermit attempting to avoid military service was given the shield who took it to Clovis where his Christian wife Clotilda persuaded him to accept it and, after the military victory, to convert to Christianity.

11. Furetière, *Dictionnaire*, s.v. "lis." Furetière wrote: "Les Critiques qui en ont écrit [on the *fleur de lys*] sont Chiflet, le Pere Tristau de Saint Amand, le Pere Ferrand, de la Roque, de Ste. Marthe, Du Tillet en son Recueil sur l'Oriflambe, Du Cange sur l'Histoire de Joinville, le Pere Menestrier, & le Pere Rousselet Jesuïte, qui a ramassé ce que tous les autres Auteurs on dit sur les fleurs de *lis*."

12. Ibid., s.v. "lis." Furetière continued: "Lis, se dit figurément, & poëtiquement du Royaume de France, qu'on appelle *l'Empire des lis*, à cause de ses Armes, comme on dit aussi *l'Aigle*, pour l'Empire, *la Rose*, pour l'Angleterre, & c." The entry continues: "Elle a pris naissance des *lis*; Voit. pour dire, elle descend des Rois de France. Jamais Prince des *lis* ne fut si triomphant; Main. pour dire, jamais Roi de France, &c. Cette valeur extrême par qui refleurissent nos *lis*, ne sera plus rien; Voit. pour dire, par qui les affaires de France prosperent. Ces sortes d'expressions sont plus de la poësies que de la prose; du moins il faut s'en servir rarement."

13. Johanne Jacobo Chiflet, *Lilium Francicum, Veritate Historica, Botanica, et Heraldica Illustratum* (Antwerp: Balthasaris Moreti, 1658). Chiflet was not the only one to question the origins of the *fleur-de-lys*. Jean Tristan, sieur de Saint-Amant et du Puy d'Amour, also cited by Furetière, suggested the emblem was originally a symbol of hope, stemming from its medical uses, and that its tri-partite structure called to mind the Trinity. See Schnapper, *Le Géant, la licorne, et la tulipe*, 209.

14. For discussion of the importance of Italian style to the development of French garden history, see Woodbridge, *Princely Gardens*.

15. Ibid., 104.

16. Reid, *The Oxford Guide to Classical Mythology in the Arts, 1300–1990* (1993), 434.

17. Woodbridge, *Princely Gardens*, 104.

18. Vallet, *Le Jardin du Roy Tres Chrestien Henry IV* (Paris: n.p., 1608).

19. Ibid., 19. Vallet wrote to Marie: "vous estes la fleur de toutes les Roynes, qui ont devancé ce siecle, que vous rendez heureux, vous estes ceste divine fleur de Florence, qui unie avec les lys de France par arrest du Ciel, à produict des fleurons de vie, des fleurons de salut, . . . des fleurons de paix."

20. For more on this painting, see Sylvie Béguin, "Deux peintures d'Ambroise Dubois," *La Revue du Louvre* (1965): 183–190.

21. Anonymous engraving, *Je couvre de mon ombre toute la terre*, B.N., Cabinet des Estampes, Qb 1.

22. A copy of the engraving, *Equestrian Portrait of Henri IV, 1600,* by Jacques de Fornazeris, is in the collection of the Boston Museum of Fine Arts, accession number 1984.143, Stephen Bullard Memorial Fund.

23. Pierre Dan, *Les Tresor des Merveilles de la maison royale de Fontainebleau* (Paris: Sebastien Cramoisy, 1642), 144. Dan reported seeing "sur la cheminée un fort beau Tableau, representant la Deesse Flora."

24. The painting was apparently quite popular. In addition to the original by Dubois, now displayed again at Fontainebleau, at least two other copies were made, one of which was presented by the late Sydney Freedberg, professor of art history at Harvard University, to the Fogg Art Museum, Harvard University, Cambridge, Mass.

25. Woodbridge, *Princely Gardens,* 104.

26. See Marjorie F. Warner, "Jean and Vespasien Robin, 'Royal Botanists,' and North American Plants, 1601–1635," *National Horticultural Magazine* 35.4 (October 1956): 214–220. Jean published two catalogues of his collection including *Catalogus stirpium tam indigenarum quam exoticarum quae Lutetiae coluntur a J. robino botanico regio* (Paris: P. A. Prato, 1601) and *Enchiridion Isagogicum ad facilem notitiam stirpium, tam indigenarum, quam exoticarum, quoe coluntur in horto D.D. Joannis et Vespasiani Robin, botanicorum regiorum* (Paris: Apud P. de Bresche, 1623).

27. Marjorie F. Warner argues that the second volume by Vallet was published in 1624. Warner, "Jean and Vespasien Robin," 217–218.

28. The garden is now the *Jardin des plantes* (renamed during the French Revolution), and its collections are part of the adjoining Muséum national d'histoire naturelle. For more on the role of the Robins in the early years of the garden, see Warner, "Jean and Vespasien Robin."

29. Guy de La Brosse, *Description du Jardin Royal des Plantes Médicinales, estably par le Roy Louis le Juste, à Paris, contenant le catalogue des plantes qui y sont de présent cultivées, ensemble le plan du jardin* (Paris: n.p., 1636), 21–22. According to La Brosse: "Les plantes sont tellement disposées en leurs quarreaux & les parterres de tel cimmetrie, qu'elles y sont ordonnées en leurs especes selon leurs genres, de sorte que quiconque connoist une espece peut assurément dire que le genre comme est là dedans."

30. "Reception faite a la reine au Louvre où leurs maistez prennent le frais sur un des balcons," 1616. B.N., Cabinet des Estampes. The heading reads, "L'Excellence des celestes et royalles fleur de lys et comment elles furent tranmises du ciel. Pour estre mises dans lescu de France."

31. The original French reads: "O qu'à nostre Repos ses Travaux sont utiles!// Par eux de toutes parts on voit ensevelis// Ces Insectes puans, et ces vilains Reptiles// Qui tachent de ternir la beauté de nos LIS.// POUR conserver ces Fleurs Royales et Divines,// (Tresor cher aux François et Gage precieux)// Il ne se lasse point d'arracher les espines,// Que sement dans nos Cham[p]s les mains de Factieux."

32. Richelieu was, as discussed in Chapter 2, a collector of flowers. At his château of Rueil, a large parterre accessible from the main rooms of the palace included a "jardin de fleurs" in which was a collection of fashionable flowers and especially tulips. See Woodbridge, *Princely Gardens,* 154–155; and Alfred Cramail, *Le Château de Ruel et ses jardins sous le Cardinal de Richelieu et sous la duchesse d'Aiguillon* (Fontainebleau: E. Bourges, 1888), 6–9.

33. Bourbon kings continued to add paintings of flowers, birds, and other natural history phenomena until the Revolution, after which the French government con-

tinued to add *vélins* and patronize painters of natural history until 1905. The *vélins* are now in the collection of the Muséum d'histoire naturelle. Among the painters employed by the Bourbon monarchs on the *vélins* project were Daniel Rabel, Nicolas Robert, Jean Joubert, Claude Aubriet, Madeleine Basseporte, and Gerard van Spaëndonck. For more on the collection of the *vélins*, see Wilfrid Blunt, *The Art of Botanical Illustration;* and Madeleine Pinault, *Le Peintre et l'histoire naturelle,* trans. Philip Sturgess (Paris: Flammarion, 1990).

34. "Memoire general de toutes les feuilles de miniatures d'oyseaux et de plantes que j'ay fait faire pour Monseigneur," in *Pièces de comptabilité relatives aux miniatures de plantes et d'oiseaux qui Colbert exécuter à Le Roy à Bailly et à Villement,* B.N., Manuscrits, fonds français 5662.

35. Madeleine de Scudéry, *La Promenade de Versailles* (Paris: C. Barbin, 1669; reprint, Geneva: Slatkine Reprints, 1979), 88. Scudéry writes, "Ce magnifique jardin, aussi bien que les autres, a ses vases de fleurs sur ses terrasses."

36. Wrote Saint-Simon on the occasion of Le Nôtre's death, "Il disait des parterres qu'ils n'étaient bons que pour les nourrices qui ne pouvant quitter leurs enfants, s'y promenaient des yeux et les admiraient du deuxième étage." Duc de Saint-Simon, *Mémoires (1691–1701), Additions au Journal de Dangeau,* vol. 1, ed. Yves Coirault (Paris: Gallimard, 1983), 739.

37. In describing the visit to the Trianon, the part of the garden best known for its flowers, Louis XIV suggested: "On arrival [via the canal], climb the slopes, pausing at the top to point out the three water jets, the canal and the end of it near the Menagery. Proceed straight to the fountain in the middle of the lower parterre to show the house. After this, go inside, entering by the peristyle from which there is a view of the avenue, and from the garden you see the courtyard; next visit the rest of the house as far as the room at the top of the gallery. Return to the same room at the end of the gallery to enter the springs. And then pass through the gallery to go to Trianon-sous-bois. Proceed as far as the terrace above the cascade. And then leave by the room at the end of the gallery on the side of the wood. Walk along the terrace as far as the corner. From where the canal can be seen; after the room at the end of the wing, turn to look at the château, the woods and the canal. Go out and pass along the main building on the side of the offices as far as the central avenue. On reaching the middle of the house, point out the dark wood, the great jet and the pool visible through the shade. Go straight down on to the grass lawn and stop at the end of the shady avenue to look at the surrounding jets. Pass by the fountain in the small grove to reach the lower cascade. Walk up the avenue to the top. And then cross the lower parterre by the avenue leading to the horseshoe. Go down it to board the boats which take you to Apollo [in the main park]." Louis XIV, *The Way to Present the Gardens of Versailles,* intro. Simone Hoog, trans. John F. Stewart (Paris: Editions de la Réunion des Musées nationaux, 1992), 60–65.

38. The most important sources for recovering the history of flowers in the gardens of Louis XIV are the *Comptes des bâtiments du roi sous le règne de Louis XIV,* compiled in the nineteenth century by Jules Guiffrey, and documents preserved in the Archives Nationale de France (hereafter A.N.), Série O, Maison du Roi sous l'Ancien Régime (hereafter Maison du Roi). See Jules Guiffrey, *Comptes des bâtiments du roi sous le règne de Louis XIV,* 5 vols. (Paris: Imprimerie Nationale, 1881–1901).

39. For survey histories of Versailles, see Guy Walton, *Louis XIV's Versailles*

(Chicago: University of Chicago Press, 1986), and Ian Dunlop, *Royal Palaces of France* (London: Hamish Hamilton, 1985).

40. Jean-Marie Apostolidès has suggested that the decoration of Versailles was deliberately intended to draw upon the example of the *fêtes*: "Pour maintenir la noblesse en état permanent de 'courtisanerie,' Louis XIV fera transformer le parc de Versailles à partier des décors éphémères de grand divertissements de 1664, 1668 et 1674. Ce n'est pas l'architecture du château qui inspire les décorations de la fête, mais au contraire l'esprit des fêtes qui sera inscrit dans le palais et les jardins, de façon à faire de Versailles un sanctuaire de sémiophores aussi imposant qu'une cathédrale médiévale." Apostolidès, *Le roi-machine*, 112.

41. See Chapter 4 for more on the use of flowers in interior decoration.

42. Jean-Aimar Piganiol de La Force, *Nouvelle description des chasteaux et parcs de Versailles et de Marly* (Paris: Florentin & Pierre Dulaune, 1701), 13–14, 18.

43. Ibid., 149. Piganiol de La Force reported, "Sur la cheminée, il y a le Triomphe de Flore, par le Poussin."

44. His collecting in these items was guided by Louis-Marie de Rochebaron, the duc D'Aumont, who himself collected flowers. See Schnapper, *Le Géant, la licorne, et la tulipe*, 270.

45. The "Mem[oire] g[e]n[er]al de toutes les fueilles de miniatures d'oyseaux et de plantes que j'ay fait faire pour Monseigneur" lists the paintings of flowers and birds executed by the dauphin's order in the 1670s. B.N., Manuscrits français 5226.

46. Guiffrey, *Comptes des bâtiments*, vol. 1, 769, 1438.

47. Abraham du Pradel (pseudonym of Nicolas de Blegny), *Le Livre commode contenant les adresses de la ville de Paris et le trésor des almanachs pour l'année bissextile 1692* (Paris: Chez le veuve de Denis Ninon, 1692; repr., Geneva: Minkoff, 1973), 79.

48. *Bouquetières* had been in royal service at least as early as the early seventeenth century. In 1619 a Françoise Meusnier was apprenticed to Marguerite François, "ouvrière de la Reine en fleurs," A.N., Série Minutier Central (hereafter MC), xxxvi, R. 108, while in 1650 a business agreement was made between Marie Flocourt, "bouquetière de la reine," and Perrette Duquesne "pour le service du roi, de la reine et du duc d'Anjou," A.N., MC, xxxvi, R. 184.

49. Guiffrey, *Comptes des bâtiments*, vol. 3, 461. Lambert was paid for porcelain *cuvettes* "qu'il a livrées dans les cheminées de l'appartement de la Reyne pour y mettre des fleurs."

50. Walton, *Louis XIV's Versailles*, 24.

51. Jules Guiffrey, *Inventaire générale du mobilier de la couronne sous Louis XIV (1663–1715)*, vol. 2 (Paris: Au siège de la Société, 1886), 116. The entry recorded "cent soixante unze autres bouquets de diverses sortes de fleurs de la Chine, faits d'un seul enroulement de cordons de soye." For more on artificial flowers, see Charlotte Paludan, "A Beguiling Similarity: A Contribution to the History of Artificial Flowers," in *Flowers into Art: Floral Motifs in European Painting and Decorative Arts*, ed. Vibeke Woldbye (The Hague: SDU Publishers, 1991), 116–126. Also of great importance for the history of artificial flower making is the article on the craft in Denis Diderot's *Encyclopédie*, in which the manufacture of artificial flowers is extensively illustrated. See *Recueil des planches, sur les sciences, les arts libéraux, et les arts méchaniques, avec leur explication*, vol. 3 (Paris: Briasson, David, Le Breton, 1765), s.v. "fleuriste artificiel."

52. It is possible that the plumes of artificial flowers adorned the finials of bed

canopies, as illustrated in Peter Thornton, *Seventeenth-Century Interior Decoration in England, France and Holland* (New Haven, Conn.: Yale University Press, 1978), 103.

53. "Plan général des jardins, bosquets, et pieces d'eau du petit Parc de Versailles, avec la situation des statues, et des vases de marbre, et de metal," design by Girard, *fontanier du roy*, engraving by Raymond (Paris: Demortain, 1714). B.N., Cabinet des Estampes, Va 422 (Ft. 4), H 186435. Although this plan was made late in the reign of Louis XIV, the segments of the garden under consideration here were largely unchanged from Le Nôtre's early expansion of the gardens. Indeed, this structure remained intact through the Bourbon reign. See, for example, the "Plan de Versailles dedié a Monseigneur le Comte de Noailles" of 1767 on which the "parterres de fleurs à l'Angloise" is similarly named the "Parterre des fleurs" (B.N., Cabinet des Estampes, Va 422 [Fr 4] Yvelines, H 186438).

54. Etienne Allegrain, "View of the North Parterre," in Louis XIV, *The Way to Present the Gardens of Versailles*, 66–67.

55. Pierre-André Lablaude, *The Gardens of Versailles*, preface by Jean-Pierre Babelon (London: Zwemmer, 1995), 65.

56. Guiffrey, *Comptes des bâtiments*, vol. 2, 1030.

57. A.N., Maison du Roi O^{1}2102^1 cotte 4.

58. Guiffrey, *Comptes des bâtiments*, vol. 3, 447.

59. Ibid., vol. 3, 590.

60. Ibid., vol. 3, 739.

61. Ibid., vol. 3, 591.

62. Apostolidès writes: "Ce n'est pas l'architecture du château qui inspire les décorations de la fête, mais au contraire l'esprit des fêtes qui sera inscrit dans le palais et les jardins, de façon à faire de Versailles un sanctuaire de sémiophores aussi pmposant qu'une câthedral médievale." See Apostolidès, *Le Roi-machine*, 112.

63. Clagny was a small château built by Louis XIV near Versailles for Madame de Montespan. Flower expenditures for Clagny did not continue through the 1680s as Montespan gradually lost favor. Indeed, when she left court in 1691, her son the duc du Maine took over the palace. Its gardens were described by Madame de Sévigné after a visit: "the garden is ready. You know Le Nôtre—he has left a little, dark wood which makes a perfect effect; there's a forest of orange trees in large tubs—then, to hide the tubs, on both sides of them there are palissades covered with tuberoses, roses, jasmine and carnations; a beautiful, surprising, enchanting idea—everybody loves this spot." Quoted in Nancy Mitford, *The Sun King* (London: Penguin Books, 1994), 50.

64. A.N., Série Maison du Roi O^{1}2102^1 cotte 4.

65. These calculations are based on Guiffrey, *Comptes des bâtiments*, vols. 1–5. Each entry consists of a payment recorded for a specific flower or "diverse flowers." In the case where a payment lists several species of flowers by name, each species counts as one entry.

66. These figures, too, were culled from Guiffrey's *Comptes des bâtiments*. 163,529 livres spent on flowers represents only .2 percent of the 82,245,744 livres necessary to build, decorate, furnish, and maintain Versailles, the Trianon, Marly, Clagny, the *pepinière du Roule*, Jardin royales des plantes médicinales, and the Jardin du roi at Toulon. However, the figure of 163,529 livres represents only the *purchase* of flowers; the total expenses of 82,245,744 livres includes the wages of gardeners, costs of reworking the land, furnishing gardens with fountains, statues, trellises, vases, urns, trees, and a myriad of other expenses required in completing and maintaining the magnificent gardens. At the same

time, as a point of reference, it is estimated that André Le Nôtre received 9,640 *livres* annually for his services to the king, a sum comparable to that spent annually on flowers. For more on Le Nôtre see Thierry Mariage, *L'Univers de Le Nôstre* (Brussels: Pierre Mardaga, 1990), 116–117.

67. Alfred Marie, *Naissance de Versailles: Le chateau, les jardins*, vol. 2 (Paris: Editions Vincent, Fréal & Cie., 1968), 198, plate 95.

68. Quoted ibid., vol. 2, 203.

69. Pierre de Nolhac, *Versailles and the Trianons* (New York: Dodd, Mead, 1906), 341–342.

70. Lablaude, *The Gardens of Versailles*, 103.

71. Louis Marin argues, too, that the Trianon palace must be interpreted as a permanent manifestation of the royal fête. The fête, Marin asserts, showcases the king's role as magician. The Trianon mirrored the fête in demonstrating the king's magical powers: first, the palace and its gardens were constructed so rapidly that it astonished courtiers; and, second, the continual presence of flowers in the Trianon gardens, whatever the season, pointed to the king's power over "Time" itself. Marin, *Portrait of the King*, 193–195.

72. André Félibien, *La Description du château de Versailles* (Paris: Antoine Vilette, 1694), 84–85. Wrote Félibien: "Ce palais fut regardé d'abord, de tout le monde, comme un enchantement; car n'ayant été commencé qu'à la fin de l'Hyver il se trouva fait au Printemps, comme s'il fût sorty de terre avec les fleurs des Jardins qui l'accompagnent."

73. See slightly varying representations in B.N., Cabinet des Estampes, H 186630, Va 424 Ft. 4; and Perelle's representation of the garden reproduced in Lablaude, *The Gardens of Versailles*, 105.

74. Quoted ibid., 104.

75. Guiffrey, *Comptes des bâtiments*, vol. 1, 705.

76. Abraham Bosse, *L'Odorat*.

77. See Michel de Montaigne, "On Smells," *Essays*, trans. with intro. by John Michael Cohen (London: Penguin Books, 1958), 133; and Jacques Ferrand, *A Treatise on Lovesickness*, 1623; repr. trans. and ed. Donald A. Beecher and Massimo Ciavolella (Syracuse, N.Y.: Syracuse University Press, 1990), 244.

78. Jean Baptiste Colbert, *Lettres et instructions de Colbert*, vol. 5, quoted in Alfred Marie, *Naissance de Versailles*, vol. 2, 225. Colbert wrote: "Visiter souvent Trianon, voir que Le Bouteux ayt des fleurs pour le Roy pendant tout l'hyver, qu'il y ayt le nombre de garçons auquel il est obligé et le presser d'achever tous les ouvrages de l'hyver. Il faut me rendre compte toutes les semaines des fleurs qu'il aura. Visiter souvent Trianon et prendre garde que toutes les réparations soyent bien faites."

79. The separation of Trianon expenses from those of Versailles probably came about upon the building of an elaborate nursery on the grounds of Trianon specifically for the purpose of supplying its gardens.

80. Guiffrey, *Comptes des bâtiments*, vol. 1, 669, 804, 876.

81. Ibid., vol. 1, 422, 540, 541.

82. Woodbridge, *Princely Gardens*, 225–232.

83. According to the *Comptes des bâtiments*, "grands fumiers pour couvrir les fleurs cet hiver" and "quatre cent paillassons . . . pour recouvrir les fleurs," and "100 cloches de verre . . . à eslever et à conserver des fleurs à Trianon" were purchased in 1692 and 1690. Guiffrey, *Comptes des bâtiments*, vol. 3, 672, 456.

84. Simone Hoog in Louis XIV, *The Way to Present the Gardens of Versailles*, 99.

85. Woodbridge, *Princely Gardens*, 229–231.

86. Piganiol de La Force, *Nouvelle description*, 359–361. Piganiol de La Force reported: "les dehors de ce palais enchanté, répondent à la propreté & à la magnificence du dedans, & qu'aprés les jardins de Versailles & de Marly, rien au monde n'aproche de l'arangement & de la beauté de ceux de Trianon. Dans la saison des fleurs tout est parfumé, & on ny respire que violettes, qu'oranges, & que jasemins."

87. Guiffrey, *Comptes des bâtiments*, vols. 2, 3.

88. I have not been able to identify what a "tulipe bosuelle" was. It is possible, however, that since the verb *bossuer* could mean "to deform," used in conjunction with "tulipe" it referred to "broken," or variegated tulips.

89. Guiffrey, *Comptes des bâtiments*, vol. 2, 1019, 1025–1027.

90. Ibid., vol. 2, 1216, 1217, and vol. 3, 134, 135.

91. B.N., Cabinet des Estampes, Va 78 f t.2, cliché B11189. A discussion and original watercolor reconstruction of the Trianon border can be found in Laird, *The Formal Garden*, 43–44; and Laird, "Ornamental Planting and Horticulture in English Pleasure Grounds," 243–77.

92. André Le Nôtre, "Description du Grand Trianon en 1694, par André Le Nostre," in Ragnar Josephson, "Le Grand Trianon sous Louis XIV d'après des documents inédits," *Revue de l'histoire de Versailles et de Seine-et-Oise* (1927): 20. Le Nôtre explained that the small parterre was a "jardin particulier quy est toutjours plein de fleurs que l'on change touts les saisons dans des pots et jamais on ne void de feuille morte ny arbrisseaux quy ne soit en fleurs; il faut que lon [sic] change plus d'eux (1) millions de pots porté prix et raporté continuellement."

93. Georges Louis Le Rouge, *Les Curiositez de Paris, de Versailles, de Marly, de Vincennes, de S. Cloud, et des environs* (Paris: Saugrain, 1716), 349. Le Rouge advised his readers to "Regardez de cet appartement le petit parterre royal avec un bassin au milieu: ce beau lieu, qui est rempli de fleurs des plus rares & des plus belles dans toutes les saisons, persuade qui l'hyver n'en sçauroit approcher."

94. Guiffrey, *Comptes des bâtiments*, vol. 3, 134, 311, 739.

95. Indeed, his successor and grandson, Louis XV, assembled at Choisy a huge collection of rare hyacinths. For more on the gardens at Choisy, see the Epilogue.

96. *Mercure Galant* (1673), quoted in Marie, *Naissance de Versailles*, vol. 2, 203. The *Mercure Galant* reported: "Presque tous les grands seigneurs qui avaient des maisons de campagne en avaient fait bâtir dans leur parc et les particuliers au bout de leur jardin; les bourgeois avaient fait habiller des masures en Trianon, ou du moins quelque cabinet ou quelque guérite."

97. Martin Lister, *An Account of Paris, at the Close of the Seventeeth [sic] Century* (London: Black, Young, & Young, 1823), 180.

98. Woodbridge, *Princely Gardens*, 234.

99. Liselotte von der Pfalz, duchesse d'Orléans to Sophie, electress of Hanover, 24 April 1712. In Elisabeth Charlotte, duchesse d'Orleans, *A Woman's Life in the Court of the Sun King: Letters of Liselotte von der Pfalz, 1652–1722*, trans. Elborg Forster (Baltimore: Johns Hopkins University Press, 1984), 191.

100. Lister, *An Account of Paris*, 180–181.

101. A.N., Maison du roi O^{1}2101^1 cotte 4, 2.

102. Guiffrey, *Comptes des bâtiments*. Calculations are my own, but are based on Guiffrey's indices.

103. Ibid., vol. 3, 450.

104. Ibid., vol. 4, 770.

105. Ibid., vol. 4, 656. Loitron was charged with "l'entretien, plant et culture des fleurs rares et autres du nouveau jardin de Marly."

106. Ibid., vol. 4, 997, 1105, 1215; vol. 5, 75.

107. Emile Magne, *Le Château de Marly, d'après des documents inédits* (Paris: Calmann-Lévy, 1934), 157–160.

108. Woodbridge, *Princely Gardens*, 234.

109. For more on the idea of the king as collector, see Antoine Schnapper, "The King of France as Collector in the Seventeenth Century," in *Art and History: Images and Their Meaning*, ed. Robert I. Rotberg and Theodore K. Rabb (Cambridge: Cambridge University Press, 1988), 185–202.

110. For more on the relationship between the *cabinet* and the garden, see Hunt, "Curiosities to Adorn Cabinets and Gardens," in *The Origins of Museums*, ed. Impey and MacGregor, 193–203. For more on the *cabinet* in the château, see Mérot, *Retraites mondaines*.

111. Magne, *Le Château de Marly*, 166; and Dunlop, *Royal Palaces of France*, 160–161.

112. Guiffrey, *Comptes des bâtiments*, vol. 5, 719, 812.

113. Néraudau, *L'Olympe du Roi-Soleil*, 248.

114. Lister, *An Account of Paris*, 180.

115. Guiffrey, *Comptes des bâtiments*, vol. 1, 470. The Trumel in question was most likely Antoine Trumel who had served as the flower gardener at Vaux-le-Vicomte and in 1670 was given the responsibility for organizing the *pépinière du Roule*. For more on the Trumels, see Woodbridge, *Princely Gardens*, 225–228.

116. Guiffrey, *Comptes des bâtiments*, vol. 1, 477–478.

117. Ibid., vol. 1, 473.

118. Ibid., vol. 1, 540, 835.

119. Ibid., vol. 1, 669.

120. Ibid., vol. 2, 1019.

121. Ibid., vol. 2, 1030, 1213.

122. Ibid., vol. 3, 134.

123. Ibid., vol. 1, 683. Subleau was reimbursed for money spent "pour achat de livres, fleurs et autres curiositez de Levant pour le service de S.M."

124. Ibid., vol. 1, 735.

125. A.N., Maison du Roi O¹2102¹ cotte 4. The document was titled "facture d'une boëte de plantes et graines pour le jardin du Roy."

126. Guiffrey, *Comptes des bâtiments*, vol. 3, 311. Truitté was paid for "plantes de fleurs qu'il va chercher sur les montagnes de Dauphiné et Piedmont pour le jardin de Trianon."

127. Aubert Aubert du Petit Thouars, *Notice historique sur la pépinière du roi au Roule* (Paris: Gueffier, 1825), 1.

128. Lister, *An Account of Paris*, 187–189.

129. A.N., Maison du Roi O¹2102¹ cotte 7. For the Trianon, Cottereau promised he could produce 100 double white anemones, 100 double white ranunculi, 100 double white ranunculi flecked with pink and violet, 100 blue and yellow aromatic ranunculi,

1,000 ranunculi "du bagadet dont la fleur est plus grande que les autres," and 1,000 ranunculi "géant de Rome de pareilles grosseur panaché."

130. A.N., Maison du Roi O[1]2102[1] cotte 7, 2–3.

131. A.N., Maison du Roi O[1]2102[1] cotte 7.

132. A.N., Maison du Roi O[1]2103 and O[1]2104.

133. B.N., *Cabinet des Estampes*, Va 424 f t. 4, cliché H 186658–61.

134. The *serres* incorporated into the structure of the Trianon nursery would have been heated rooms with as many windows as possible for light. The "greenhouse" as we know it today, contructed almost entirely of glass, did not come into existence until much later. For additional reading on the history of greenhouses, see John Hix, *The Glass House* (London: Phaidon, 1974); and May Woods and Arete Swartz Warren, *Glass Houses: A History of Greenhouses, Orangeries, and Conservatories* (London: Aurum Press, 1988).

135. A.N., Maison du Roi O[1]2124[1] cotte 3.

136. A.N., Maison du Roi O[1]2124[1], cotte 1. The Toulon garden was purchased to "élever oignons de fleurs qu'il faut fournir tous les ans pour les jardins des Maisons Royalles."

137. A.N., Maison du Roi O[1]2124[1] cotte 3.

138. A.N., Maison du Roi O[1]2124[1] cotte 1 and O[1]1905[3] no. 3.

139. A.N., Maison du Roi O[1]2102[1] cotte 4.

140. A.N., Maison du Roi O[1]2124[1].

141. A.N., Maison du Roi O[1]2124[1].

142. A.N., Maison du Roi O[1]2102[1] cotte 4.

143. A.N., Maison du Roi O[1]2102[1] cotte 4.

144. A.N., Maison du Roi O[1]2102[1] cotte 4.

145. A.N., Maison du Roi O[1]2102[1] cotte 4.

146. A.N., Maison du Roi O[1]2102[1] cotte 4.

147. A.N., Maison du Roi O[1]2102[1] cotte 4.

148. A.N., Maison du Roi O[1]2102[1] cotte 4.

149. A.N., Maison du Roi O[1]2102[1] cotte 4.

150. A.N., Maison du Roi O[1]2124[1] cotte 2.

151. Jean-Baptiste Colbert died in 1683 after he had orchestrated the purchase of the Toulon garden.

152. A.N., Maison du Roi O[1]2124[1] cotte 2. Colbert wrote: "Je suis obligé M. de vous informer que des oignons de Narcisse de Constantinople, de totus albus, d'hyacintes romaines et de jonquilles montant le tous à 21 miliers qui ont esté ennoyer de Toulon le 10 juillet dernier, il y en a la plus grande partie qui ne porterant point parceque ce ne sont que des cayeux qui ne pouront fleurir. . . . Je vous supplie d'obliger le jardinier du jardin de Toulon à ne donner que des oignons portans, parcequ'autre qu'ils ne servent à rien, la voiture côute au Roy et il tant mieux en avoir moins et qui'ls soient bons."

153. A.N., Maison du Roi O[1]2124[1] cotte 2. He reminded De Vauvré: "Par l'etablissement de ce jardin suivant le memoire que vous envoyastes [*sic*] à M. de Louvois le 15 septembre 1683. L'on fournissoit tous les ans 65,000 oignons l'on n'en a fourni cette année que 24,000 y compris 3,000 tubereuses, et la dépense du jardin est égale."

154. A.N., Maison du Roi O[1]2102[1] cotte 4.

155. A.N., Maison du Roi O[1]2124[1].

156. See Du Pradel, *Le Livre commode*, 97–98.

157. See Guiffrey, *Comptes des bâtiments*, vol. 2, 894.

158. Chandra Mukerji, "Reading and Writing with Nature: A Materialist Approach to French Formal Gardens," in *Consumption and the World of Goods*, ed. John Brewer and Roy Porter (London: Routledge, 1993), 456–457.

159. Ovid, *Metamorphoses*, trans. Mary Innes (London: Penguin Classics, 1955), 99–101.

160. Jean Donneau de Visé, *Les Amours du soleil, tragedie en machines, representée sur le Theatre du Marais* (Paris: Claude Barbin, 1671), prologue, n.p. "Ce Dieu leur fait connoistre qu'elles ne peuvent estre abandonnées, que leur gloire croistra toûjours, & que les Dieux doivent donner à la France un grand Roy qui doit faire des choses étonnantes pour elles, qui fera refleurir les Sciences & les beaux Arts, & qui recompensera le merite de tous ceux qui en auront. Il les invite de donner tous leurs soins à travailler pour sa gloire, de le placer par avance au Temple de Memoire, & de le mettre au dessus de tous les demy-Dieux."

161. Ibid., n.p. The muses responded by promising their continued service, "qu'elles le peindront si bien dans leurs Ouvrages, que le Portrait ne s'en perdra jamais."

162. Ibid., Act 5. In the course of *Les Amours du soleil*, the complicity of the muses, Art, and Nature were demonstrated, for the fifth act took place in the gardens of the king of Persia where "pour l'embellissement des quelles l'Art & la Nature sembloient avoire épuisé leurs merveilles." The garden, according to the descriptions provided by Donneau de Visé, included "vases remplis des fleurs en confusion" and an arcade, the herms of which carried on their heads "corbeilles d'or pleines d'un nombre infiny de fleurs diferentes, dont la vivacité réjouit la veuë."

163. F.B., *La Flora sainte*, 55. F.B., Sieur de L'Ecluse asserted that the "invincible Louis . . . rend honneur à Fleurs . . . dans ses Jardins de Versailles, & de ses autres Palais."

164. Valnay, *Connoissance et culture parfaite des tulippes rares*, "Avertissement," n.p.; and *La Culture des fleurs*, preface, n.p.

165. *Mercure Galant*, December 1686, 115–117. The ambassador saw a flower-filled "galante Maison" that was "destiné pour y conserver toutes sortes de fleurs tant l'Hiver que l'Esté, l'Air y seconde si bien la Nature, qu'il en est remply en toutes Saisons." The ambassador was even taken to the Cabinet des Parfums: "Le Cabinet des Parfums leur plût extrémement, car ils aiment fort les odeurs, & ils admirerent la maniere de parfumer avec des fleurs."

166. Académie des inscriptions & belles-lettres, *Médailles sur les principaux événements du règne entier de Louis le Grand: avec des explications historiques* (Paris: Imprimerie royale, 1702).

167. Frances A. Yates, *The French Academies of the Sixteenth Century* (London: Routledge, 1988), 301.

168. The phrase "histoire du roi" was used by the *académistes* themselves to describe their primary goal of controlling the image of Louis XIV both during his reign and for posterity. Peter Burke discusses the idea of the "histoire du roi" in his *Fabrication of Louis XIV*, 7.

169. Dionys Dodart, *Mémoires pour servir à l'histoire des plantes* (Paris: Imprimerie royale, 1676). According to Wilfrid Blunt, the text and plates were not published together until the eighteenth century. He adds that the work was never sold publicly and is therefore very rare. Blunt, *The Art of Botanical Illustration*, 111–112.

170. Nicole Castan, "The Public and the Private," in *Passions of the Renaissance*, ed. Roger Chartier, trans. Arthur Goldhammer, 419–422.

171. Schnapper discusses the king's *Cabinet des Curiosités* arranged in the kings apartments in Versailles in "The King of France as Collector in the Seventeenth Century," 196–198. For a broader discussion of the cultural meaning of the *cabinet* in French residences, see Mérot, *Retraites mondaines*, 167–176. Discussions of the relationship between architectural configuration of rooms and their social function in the seventeenth-century apartment can be found in H. M. Baillie, "Etiquette and the Planning of Royal Apartments in Baroque Palaces," *Archaeologia* 101 (1967): 169–199, and Norbert Elias's chapter on "The Structure of Dwellings as an Indicator of Social Structure" in his *The Court Society*, trans. Edmund Jephcott (New York: Pantheon Books, 1983).

172. Hunt, "Curiosities to Adorn Cabinets and Gardens," 193–203.

173. Anonymous, *A Lady, possibly Madame de Montespan, in a richly decorated interior*, c. 1670, Victoria and Albert Museum, London.

174. Pamela Cowen argues that the blue and white décor, together with the documented bed, makes it possible to identify this as the Trianon de Porcelaine. See Pamela Cowen, "The Trianon de Porcelaine at Versailles (newly discovered painting provides clues about the furnishings of the extinct building), *[The Magazine] Antiques* 143 (January 1993): 136–143. The Trianon de Porcelaine was torn down in 1686 and replaced by the Trianon de Marbre (the Grand Trianon).

175. See Chapter 1.

176. Frances A. Yates, *Astraea: The Imperial Theme in the Sixteenth Century* (London: ARK Paperbacks, 1985), 67–69.

177. Ibid., 123.

178. Ibid., 208–214. Yates argues that representations of Henri as the "Gallic Hercules" also drew upon the qualities of Astraea. She also suggests that Honoré d'Urfée's *L'Astrée* referred generally to order enjoyed by France in the reign of Henri IV.

179. Ovid, *Metamorphoses*, 32.

180. Virgil's fourth eclogue which predicted the birth of a child who would usher in a new golden age, and described a flower-filled utopia. Virgil wrote, "But for thee, child, the Earth untilled, as her first pretty gifts,// Shall put forth straying ivy and foxglove everywhere,// and arum lilies mingled with smiling acanthus flowers.// . . . Of themselves// From the ground whereon thou liest shall spring flowers for thy delight." Publius Virgilius Maro, *The Eclogues and the Georgics*, trans. R. C. Trevelyan (Cambridge: Cambridge University Press, 1944), 14, lines 18–23.

181. Michel de Marolles, *L'Siècle d'or*, seventeenth century, B.N., Cabinet des Estampes, Oa 46. The caption at the print explained, "DURANT le Siecle d'or, Siecle chery du Ciel,// Flore eternellement se couronnoit de roses."

182. N[icolas] Bonnart, *L'Aage d'or*, late seventeenth century, B.N., Cabinet des Estampes, Oa 58 pet. fol., c 1958. The caption reads: "Nous est representé soubs l'Embleme d'une belle, et jeune fille simplement vetüe, carressant un mouton a qui elle met une guirlande de fleurs, et joüant avec un enfant pour marquer l'innocence des moeurs de ce siècle, la ruche d'abeilles represente la douceur, et l'union; l'olivier est le simbole de la paix qui regnoit alors."

183. According to Jean-Pierre Néraudau: "En 1638, pour célébrer le naissance de

Louis XIV, c'est à la quatrième églogue de Virgile que Campanella emprunte ses accents prophétiques, faute de trouver chez Ovide le mème envers un enfant providential, et pourtant les thèmes mythologiques qui illustreront le pouvoir de Louis XIV viennent presque exclusivement des *Métamorphoses.*" Jean-Pierre Néraudau, "La présance d'Ovide aux XVIe et XVIIe siècles ou la survie du prince de poésie", in *La Littérature et ses avatars: Discrédits, déformations et réhabilitations dans l'histoire de la littérature,* ed. Yvonne Bellenger (Paris: Kincksieck, 1991), 13–39, 15.

184. Others have reached similar conclusions, though with less attention paid to the importance of flowers to the evocation of eternal spring and the king's iconographical scheme. Antoine Schnapper's interpretation of the paintings commissioned for the Trianon in the late seventeenth century led him to conclude that it was a palace dedicated to love, a country house of delights for the king. Drawing on Julius Held's work on the goddess Flora, Schnapper interprets the "loves" of the gods and the preoccupation with Flora and springtime at Trianon as a celebration of love and pleasure. For Jean-Pierre Néraudau, the Trianon was the king's expression of his reign as one of "eternal springtime," in which mythology and flowers promised perpetual abundance and fertility in the kingdom of the Sun King. Louis Marin gives greater consideration to the king's power in the creation of the Trianon and the king's mastery of the seasons, suggesting that the Trianon was a place where the king could work and display his most powerful magic. That magic, explains Marin like Néraudau, was used in the creation of perpetual springtime. See Held, "Flora, Goddess and Courtesan," in *De Artibus Opscula XL,* ed. Millard Meiss, vol. 1, 209; Antoine Schnapper, *Tableaux pour le Trianon de Marbre, 1688–1714* (Paris: Mouton, 1967), 45; Néraudau, *L'Olympe du Roi-Soleil,* 249–253; and Marin, *Portrait of the King,* 193–195.

185. *Les Plaisirs de l'île enchantée* (Paris: Robert Ballard, 1664), repr. in Molière, *Oeuvres complètes,* ed. Georges Couton, vol. 1 (Paris: Gallimard, 1971), 751.

186. Ibid. The garden was decorated by a "nombre infini de ses fleurs."

187. Ibid., 757. The golden age was typically associated with flowers. The golden age, or "*l'siècle d'or,*" wore gilded armor, which "était encore paré des diverses fleurs qui faisaient un des principaux ornements de cet heureux âge."

188. Ibid., 762.

189. Ibid., 762. The allegory of Spring was also accompanied by twelve attendants who "couvert de fleurs, portaient, comme des jardiniers, des corbeilles peintes de vert et d'argent, garnies d'un grand nombre de porcelaines, si remplies de confitures et d'autres choses délicieuses de la saison."

190. Ibid., 763. Spring said: "Entre toutes les fleurs nouvellement écloses// Dont mes jardins sont embellis,// Méprisant les jasmines, les oeillets et les roses,// Pour payer mon tribut j'ai fait choix de ces lis,// Que de vos premiers ans vous avez tant chéris.// Louis les fait briller du couchant à l'aurore;// Tout l'univers charmé les respecte et les craint;// Mais leur règne est plus doux et plus puissant encore,// Quand ils brillent sur votre teint."

191. Ovid, *Metamorphoses,* 32; and Virgil, *Eclogue IV,* line 6.

192. Woodbridge, *Princely Gardens,* 227.

193. Guiffrey, *Comptes des bâtiments,* vol. 1, 305. Michel Le Bouteux was paid for "les festons, bouquets et ornemens de fleurs qu'il a fourni pour la décoration des salles du festin du bal et de la collation."

194. André Félibien, *Relation de la fête de Versailles du dix-huit juillet mille six cent soixante-huit,* 1668, 1674; repr. Martin Meade, ed. (N.p.: Editions Dédale, Maisonneuve et Larose, 1994), 36–37.

195. Ibid., 44.

196. Ibid., 66. "Sur la grande corniche qui régnait autour de ce salon étaient rangés soixante-quatorze vases de porcelaine, remplis de diverses fleurs," while "de cette corniche et du tour que formait l'ouverture du dôme pendaient plusieurs festons de toutes de fleurs."

197. Ibid., 72.

198. Ibid., 76, 78.

199. Guiffrey, *Comptes des bâtiments,* vol. 1, 305.

200. Ibid., Félibien, *Relation de la fête,* 111–112, 113. Guests were treated to the sight of porcelain pots filled with "une infinité de diverses fleurs que par des festons, aussi des fleurs, disposés d'une manière qui les faisaient beaucoup paraître parmi les arbres aux quels ils étaient attachés," and "festons des fleurs."

201. Ibid., 114. The theater included "la fontaine de marbre qui est au milieu de cette cour était environnée de girandoles et de vases pleins de fleurs et dans le bassin même, six grand vases de porcelain remplis de fleurs."

202. Ibid., 114–115. Félibien remarked: "Ainsi l'architecture de ces bâtiments éclairés de tant de lumières et la disposition ingénieuse de tant de lustres et de girandoles entremêlés parmi l'agréable variéte des arbres et des fleurs faisaient un riche ornement à ce théâtre."

203. Ibid., 117–119. According to Félibien, "l'on trouve toujours les printemps," and, "tout ce qu'on y voit a des beautés particulières et l'air qu'on y respire est parfumé des fleurs les plus odiférantes."

204. Ibid., 120–121. The party continued in the *salle du Conseil* where "l'île était bordée de soixante-treize guéridons de fleurs portant des girandoles de cristal."

205. Ibid., 130, 132, 130.

206. Ibid., 135.

207. Ibid., 140, 142, 143–153.

208. In seventeenth-century France, the idealized, fantastical pastoral idea of nature was immensely popular within elite circles, who by celebrating the pastoral hearkened back to their origins as *noblesse d'épée,* the ancient landed, agricultural, and militarily based nobility. For only one discussion of this, see Roger Chartier, *Forms and Meanings: Texts, Performances, and Audiences from Codex to Computer* (Philadelphia: University of Pennsylvania Press, 1995), 60. For a look at the trend among the nobility in constructing châteaux and elaborate gardens on their recently acquired large estates in the region around Paris, see Mariage L'Univers de Le Nôstre, 23–38.

209. Two studies of the royal celebrations at the court of Louis XIV consider the grand fêtes in the context of the quite full annual calendar of royal and civic entertainments: Sabine du Crest, *Des Fêtes à Versailles: Les divertissements de Louis XIV* (Paris: Aux Editions Klincksieck, Amateurs des Livres, 1990); and Marie-Christine Moine, *Les Fêtes à la cour du Roi Soleil, 1653–1715* (Paris: Editions Fernand Lanore, 1984).

210. Jean-Marie Apostolidès writes, for example, "Ces fêtes présentent, dans un court laps de temps, une réunion de tous les «plaisirs» accessibles au XVIIe siècle." Apostolidès, *Le Roi-machine,* 94.

211. Roger Chartier argues that the elaborate staging of the *fêtes* allowed the court to demonstrate its social superiority over the rest of society by comparing the staging of Molière's *George Dandin* lavishly for the 1668 Versailles spectacle and more starkly later in Paris. See Chartier, "From Court Festivity to City Spectators," in *Forms and Meanings*, chapter 3.

212. The symbolic and economic importance of royal consumption is explored by Chandra Mukerji: "It turns out that the history of French formal gardens is a particularly rich place for seeing the complex culture of court and commerce that appeared in seventeenth-century France. Gardens are forms of material culture inscribing affluence and power." The material culture and commerce of the gardens were evident, maintains Mukerji, in the purchase and manipulation of land and in the collection of plants and statuary to decorate the gardens. See Mukerji, "Reading and Writing with Nature," 440, 450.

213. Apostolidès writes: "La fête tranche sur le rythme de la vie ordinaire de la cour par l'abondance des produits qu'on y consomme en quelques jours. . . . Pendant la fête sont concentrés en un même lieu tous les produits que la technique et le commerce permettent d'obtenir à l'époque: vêtements de luxe, objects d'art d'Italie ou de France, fleurs de Hollande, épices d'Amerique ou d'Orient, porcelains de Chine, bois et métaux précieux d'Afrique ou d'Amérique du Sud. Cependent, quelle que soit leur origine, ces objects n'apparaissent pas comme des merchandises; ils ne sont ni pensées ni utilisé comme des produits de l'économie." Apostolidès, *Le Roi-machine*, 105. I take issue, however, with his identification of the flowers used as of Dutch origin. As is made clear earlier in this chapter, Louis XIV and Colbert went to great lengths to produce their own flowers. And French *fleuristes*, as discussed in Chapter 2, took great pride in the French superiority in cultivating certain species.

214. See Chapter 1 for a discussion of flowers as symbols of the brevity of life.

215. Roger Chartier has described the fêtes as "entertainment calculated to overwhelm the senses." Chartier, *Forms and Meanings*, 45.

216. *Les Plaisirs de l'île enchantée* (Paris: Robert Ballard, 1664); repr. in Molière, *Oeuvres complètes*, 751. They explained that Versailles was "un château qu'on peut nommer un palais enchanté, tant les ajustements de l'art ont bien secondé les soins que la nature a pris pour le rendre parfait."

217. Ibid., 751. Nature was improved through the imposition of "sa symétrie, la richesse de ses meubles, la beauté de ses promenades et le nombre infini de ses fleurs, comme de ses orangers, rendent les environs de ce lieu dignes de sa rareté singulière."

218. Chartier, *Forms and Meanings*, 59.

219. Isaac de Benserade, *Ballet des Saisons: Dansé à Fontainebleau par sa Majesté le 23 juillet, 1661* (Paris: Robert Ballard, 1661), 4.

220. Benserade's text reads: "L'une (M. de Sully, Flore) represente Flore,// Et la même par dessus,// Represente Madame encore;// Et cela c'est dire plus,// Que Junon, Pallas & Venus,// Qui firent devant un Homme// Tant de bruit pour une Pomme." Isaac de Benserade, *Balet Royal de Flore, Dansé par Sa Majesté en 1669* (n.p., n.d.), 41. Madame, Henrietta of England, had captured the affections of the king and was represented as Flora in Nocret's mythological portrayal of the royal family. According to Charles I. Silin, Henrietta of England was to have performed the role of Flora in the ballet herself, but when she became pregnant, she was replaced by Marie-Antoinette Servien, duchesse

de Sully. Charles I. Silin, *Benserade and His Ballets de Cour* (Baltimore: Johns Hopkins University Press; London: Humphrey Milford, Oxford University Press; Paris: Société d'Edition "Les Belles Lettres," 1940), 387–388.

221. Benserade, *Balet Royal de Flore*, 399. Jupiter and Destiny sang: "Jeunes Lys, qui semblez ne faire que d'éclore,// Vous avez deux brillans emplois;// Vous couronenz l'amour sur le beau teint de Flore:// Et sur le front de plus puissant des Rois,// Qui traîne aprés lui la Victoire,// Vous couronnez la Gloire."

222. *Psyché, tragedi-comédie et ballet dansé devant Sa Majesté au mois de janvier 1671*, in Molière, *Oeuvres complètes*, vol. 2; or *Recueil des opera, des ballets, et des plus belles pièces en musique, qui ont été représentées devant sa Majesté Tres-Chrétienne*, vol. 1 (Amsterdam: Abraham Wolfgang, 1690), 28. Flora said to Venus: "Ce n'est plus le tems de la Guerre;// Le plus puissant des Rois// Interrompt ses Exploits// Pour donner la Paix à la Terre.// Descendez, Mére des Amours,// Venez nous donner de beaux jours."

223. Philippe Quinault, *Atys. Edition critique*, ed. Stéphane Bassinet (Geneva: Librairie Droz, 1992), 56–57. Flora and Time sang: "Les plaisirs à ses yeux ont beau se présenter,// Si-tôst qu'il voit Bellone, il quitte tout pour elle;// Rien ne peut l'arrester// Quand la Gloire l'apelle."

224. Michel Richard Delalande, *Le Palais de Flore dansé à Trianon devant Sa Majesté le 5 janvier 1689*, in *Receuil des sujets et paroles d'une partie des ballets, dansez devant sa Majesté* (Paris: Christophe Ballard, 1709), 7. "Le Palais de Flore & le Printemps eternel qui jusques à present n'avoient esté que dans l'imagination des Poëtes, se trouvent veritablement icy. Le Theatre de Trianon ne sçauroit avoir de plus superbe decoration que Trianon mesme. L'éclat des Marbres, & les beautez de l'Architecture attachent d'abord la veuë sur cette grande façade appellée le Peristile; & le plaisir redouble lorsque par les ouvertures de ses Arcades, entre plusieurs rangs de riches Colonnes, on découvre ces Fontaines, ces Jardins, & ces Parterres toujours remplis de toutes sortes de fleurs. On ne se souvient plus qu'on est au milieu de l'Hiver, ou bien l'on croit avoir esté transporté tout d'un coup en d'autres Climats, quand on voit ces delicieux objects qui marquent si agreablement la demeure de Flore."

225. All had come to the Trianon palace "se reposer dans ce beaux lieux."

226. I maintain that a portrait of the young Mademoiselle de Blois (1677–1749) in costume attributed to Pierre Mignard is indeed a depiction of the king's daughter in her role as Flora. In the portrait, Mademoiselle de Blois stands in the gardens of Versailles, accompanied by her pearl-earringed spaniel and a brightly colored exotic bird, and is herself crowned with flowers. In her skirt, she gathers jasmines or tuberoses and orange blossoms. The legitimized daughter of Louis XIV by his mistress became the duchesse d'Orléans when she married Philippe II, the duc d'Orléans and regent, in 1692.

227. Delalande, *Le Palais de Flore dansé à Trianon devant Sa Majesté le 5 janvier 1689*, 14. "A l'aspect de Flore// Hastez-vous d'éclore.// Venez en ses belles mains,// Moissons odorantes,// Richesses riantes,// Roses, Jasmines,// Anemones, Amarantes.// Aimables fleurs venez orner// Le front victorieux qu'elle veut couronner."

228. Ibid., 14. "Tout fleurit sur nos rivages// Nos jardins sont toûjours verds.// Jamais de trise Hivers// Nous ne sentons les outrages.// Nostre Printemps dure toûjours.// Nous n'avons que de beaux jours."

229. *Zephire et Flore. Opéra*, in *Recueil des opera, des ballets, et des plus belles pièces en*

musique, vol. 2, 368. The prologue took place in a theater that "représente le nouveau Palais de Trianon, avec ses Jardins."

230. Ibid., Prologue, 370. A zephyr labeled the gardens the "lieux les plus beaux de son charmant Empire."

231. Ibid., 372. The theater was transformed into an exotic country in Assyria on the banks of the Euphrates where "L'éclat & l'Abondance des fleurs dont elles sont semées, les peut faire prendre aisément pour l'endroit le plus agréable de l'Empire de Flore."

232. Ibid.," 394–395. "Laisse en paix ces tendres Amans,// Jupiter par mes soins veut finir leur tourmens.// Voi s'élever sur la ruine// De ton séjour afreux,// Un Palais brillant & pompeux// Qu'à leur bonheur le Ciel destine."

233. Ibid., 394. In the middle of the seventh scene, the theater again changed, this time into a "Palais magnifique tout orné de fleurs," which was decorated with gold vases filled with "ces fleurs illustres dans lesquelles plusieurs Héros de la Fable ont été metamorphosez, comme Adonis, Narcisse, & sur tout Clytie qui vient d'changée en Souci."

234. For a thorough discussion of the paintings at Trianon, see Antoine Schnapper, *Tableaux pour le Trianon de Marbre, 1688–1714.*

235. For more on the style of seventeenth-century French still life, see Michel Faré, *Le Grand Siècle de la nature morte en France; Norman Bryson,* Looking at the Overlooked; and Paul Taylor, *Dutch Flower Painting.*

236. Ovid, *Metamorphoses,* 101.

237. The sunflower was most famously and conspicuously used in Anthony Van Dyck's (1599–1641) self-portrait of 1633 in which he expressed his position as painter to the Charles I, king of England, by depicting himself holding his gold chain of honor together with a large sunflower.

238. Schnapper, *Tableaux pour le Trianon de Marbre,* 79.

239. Ibid., 80–81.

240. The mythological source for the depicted meeting of Juno and Flora is uncertain.

241. Jacques Bailly, *Devises pour les tapisseries du roi,* manuscript (1668); repr. ed. Marianne Grivel and Marc Fumaroli (Paris: Herscher, 1988).

242. Ibid., 19. "Un Girasol, avec ce mot COELESTES SEQVITVR MOTVS, pour dire que sa Majesté se conduit par les mouvement du Soleil qu'il regard toujours."

243. Ibid., 19. "Malgré l'Element qui m'enserre,// Et la loy du destin qui m'attache à la Terre,// Dans le plus haut des cieux sont mes tendres amours,// Du divin autheur de ma vie// J'ay toûjours la trace suivie,// Et la suivray toûjours."

244. Ibid., 20. "Sa majesté qui se plaist dans les choses grandes et elevées va droit à la gloire, ainsi que le Sapin qui se plaist sur les montagnes les plus hautes, & qui s'éleve droit en haut sans jamais se gauchée."

245. Ibid., 25. The swallow signified spring because, "cet oyseau . . . ramener le Printemps avec luy."

246. Ibid., 25. "On peut dire de mesme que le Roy a ramené le beau temps & la Paix apres use longue & ennuyeuse guerre."

247. Ibid., 26. The device of the border of spring flowers was included "pour signifier que . . . la terre aime les Fleurs comme ses premiers productions & celles qui font son plus bel ornement."

248. Ibid., 26. "Sa Majesté n'est pas moins l'Amour & l'ornement de toute la terre."

249. Ibid., 28. "Il se trouve dans la Rose de la beauté & de la fierté tout à la fois, & elle est comme une image de la Paix & de la guerre jointes ensemble, la mesme chose se peut dire des Course de bagues & Carrousels qui sont des jeux, mais des jeux militaires ou il faut beaucoup de force & d'adresse dans les armes, avec beaucoup de bonne mine & de bonne grace, qui sont des choses qui se rencontrent souverainement en sa Majesté."

250. Ibid., 28. "A mon air attrayant, doux, charmant, agreable,// De plaisir on se sent toucher,// Mes traits en mesme temps rendent redoutable,// Sans amour & sans crainte on ne peut m'aprocher;// Aussy parmy l'horreur des armes// On ne vit jamais tant de charmes."

251. Ibid., 31. The white lily was the "symbole de la candeur & de la sincerité esté choisy pour representer le procedé noble, sincere & genereux de sa Majesté dans toutes ses Actions."

252. Ibid. "Rejetton glorieux d'une tige sublime,// Je monte vers le Ciel d'un effort magnanime,// Et brille d'un éclat qui n'a rien d'emprunte;// Rien de ce que je suis aux mortels ne se cashe,// Mon front toujours ouvert aussy bien que sans tache// Sert de parfait symbole à la sincerite."

253. Ibid., 40. The snowdrop "s'epanoüit au milieu de la neige & malgré les rigueurs de l'hyver." The manuscript continued: "Ce qui peut se dire de la gloire de sa Majeste que tous les obstacles ne peuvent empescher d'eclatter, & que fleurit au milieu de difficultez."

254. Ibid. "Ce n'est qu'aux saisons favorables// Que l'on voit mes semblables// Par leur brillant éclat les regards attirer;// Pour moy qui ne voit point d'aprés fort adversaire,// C'est dans le temps le plus contraire// Que je fleuris le plus & me sais admirer."

255. Ibid., plate 43, 105. The machinery "surpasse les forces naturelles."

256. Ibid. "Quel merveilleux objet, quel auguste miracle,// Par son rapide cours surmontant tout obstacle,// Ravit les yeux & les esprits?// D'un art victorieux sa force est animée,// Et de ses mouvemens la Nature charmée// L'admire & luy cede le prix."

257. The qualities of the king celebrated by the flowers were not dissimilar to the qualites of other, more conventional histories of the king. According to Malina Stefanovska, French kings were regularly represented as Christian kings who both loved and feared God, and as militarily successful. "Later in the century," writes Stefanovska, "other values came to the fore: princes were extolled for their civility and their love of arts, traits which brought them closer to the contemporary *honnête homme*." See Malina Stefanovskak, "A Monumental Triptych: Saint-Simon's *Parallèle des trois premiers rois Bourbons*," *French Historical Studies* 19.4 (Fall 1996): 933; and Michael Tyvaert, "L'Image du roi: Légitime et moralité royales dans les histoires de France au XVIIe siècle," *Revue d'histoire moderne et contemporaine* 21 (October–December 1974): 521–547.

258. Jean Donneau de Visé, *Histoire de Louis le Grand, contenüe dans les rapports qui se trouvent entres ses actions, & les qualités, & vertus des fleurs, & des plants*, B.N., Manuscrits, fond français 6995.

259. In January 1687 Paris and the rest of France celebrated Louis XIV's recovery from surgery to remove a fistula.

260. Donneau de Visé, *Histoire de Louis le Grand*, 1.

261. Ibid., 9–10. "Quoique les saisons nous séparent nous avons aujourd'huy forcé l'ordre de la nature pour paraître devant un Prince qui a toujours surmonté les obsta-

cles qu'elle a formés, quand pour reculer l'execution de ses grands desseins, elle a opposé les glaces de plus rudes Hivers, . . . & refusé de donner tout ce qui étoit nécessaire pour l'embélissement du superbe, & délicieus Palais, qui fait aujourdhui l'admiration de toute la Terre."

262. See, for example, Jean Franeau's *Jardin d'hyver ou cabinet des fleurs contenant en XXVI elegie les plus rares et signalez fleurons de plus fleurissans parterres* (Douay: Pierre Borremans, 1616) as another example of the book as a means of enjoying flowers year round.

263. Donneau de Visé, *Histoire de Louis le Grand*, 11–12. "Nous pouvons . . . assembler aujourdhui, non pour élire un Roi, mais pour travailler à l'histoire d'un Monarque, qui doit être loüé par tout ce que la Terre produit, puisque tout la Terre luy est redevable. Quioque nous soyons de différens pays, nous sommes toutes françoises d'inclination, ou plutôt nous vous sommes toutes devoüées, étant toutes d'accord pour vous loüer."

264. Ibid., 12. "Dieu leur donne sa bénédiction, le Ciel, & la Terre comme le Pére, & la Mére des Plantes; la Terre leur donne le corps, & le Ciel l'ame."

265. Ibid., 13. "Dieu avoit fait l'homme comme une plante de raison & de sagesse."

266. Ibid., 16–20.

267. Ibid., 23. "Il y a pres de cinquante ans que la premiere Anemone fut aportée des Indes en France, par M[onsieur] Bachelier, grand curieux de fleurs. On admira sa fleurison, la vivacité, & l'email de ses fleurs. La beauté de l'Anemone qui a de la graine en abondance, augmenta pendant huit ou dix années, & durant tout ce têms la M. Bachelier n'en ayant voulu, ny vendre, ny donner, on trouva moyen de luy en surprendre, & les belles Anemones cultivées devinrent au point de perfection, ou elles sont, & furent encore plus admirées, & recherchées. Elles suportent le froid, & valent mieux quand elles y sont un peu endurcies. On compte plus de vingt sorts d'Anemones, qui ont des noms de Royaumes, de Provinces, de Villes, & de particuliers. . . . Elles ont des qualites, & des vertus médicinales."

268. Ibid., 22. The plant boasted, "Le Ciel vous a donne à la France dans le temps qu'on m'a aportées des Indes."

269. Ibid., 22. "Vous ne sortiez qu'à peine du berceau, que le grand nombre de vos vertus naissants fut predire votre grandeur; Vous nétiez enfant que par votre age, et des ce tems la, on remarqua une douce et charmante vivacité, qui animoit votre esprit. Votre Jeunesse parut moderée vous montrates toujours prest à quiter les plaisirs pour les affaires, et vos inclinations qui étoient toutes d'un homme sage, et meur; vous attirent l'estime de tout le monde; de sorte que si on eut eu a former des souhaits pour vous on n'auroit pu désirir autre chose, que de voir la fin repondre à de si heureux commencemens. Ma beauté s'est perfectionée en France pendant huit ou dix annees; Vous continuâtes à vous former vous meme et à travailles pour desirir ce qui nous vous voyons aujourdhuy."

270. Ibid., 22. "Quoy que ceux qui avoient l'honneur de vous approcher connoissent la solidité de votre esprit, ils n'en savoient pas toute la profondeur. Le ministre qui vous aydoit alors à suporter les poids des affairs de votre Etat, voulut convaincre quelques personnes d'un esprit distingué de la pénétrations du votre. Il les fit cacher, et vous ayant entretenu d'affaires qui demandoient tous les misonnemens d'un Politique consomme, les furent surpris qui demandoient tous les misonnements d'un Politique consomme, ils furent surpris de la force, avec laquelle ils vous entendirent raisonner. La mort de ce Ministre vous decouvrit tout entier, et vous parutes tout d'un coup le plus sage et le plus grand

des Rois. Vous ne comtez votre regne que depuis ce tems la de meme que je ne comte celuy de ma beauté que depuis qu'on a pris plaisir a me cultiver en France."

271. Ibid. "Je foisonne en graines," said the anemone, as "Le nombre infiny de vos actions de piété en inspire la pratique, presque a tous ceux qui les regardent avec attention. Ces examples en excitent d'autres à les imiter, ainsy vous étes cause que nombre des verteuse se multiplie."

272. Ibid. "On me donne les noms des Royaumes et des Provinces, où je regne avec éclat, ainsy que de ceux qui m'ont mise en réputation," while adding to the king, "On vous donne ceux de conquerant de pacifique, de Pieux, avec une infinité d'autres, suivant les actions qui vous les font meriter."

273. Ibid. "Tous les souverains sont batir dans leurs Palais des lieux pour me loger; et comme vous les surpassez tous en magnificence, on peut dire que celuy que vous m'avez fait élever n'apoint de parieul."

274. Ibid., 24. "Mon feüillage est toujours vert et vous étés toujours vous meme, c'est à dire, toujours ferme, dans ce que la justice, la prudence, et votre grande ame vous font entreprendre."

275. Ibid. "Toutes mes parties ont des qualités utiles au corps de l'homme touts vos vertus qui sont les qualité de votre ame, sont incessament du bien à tous les hommes."

276. Ibid. The orange continued, "j'aime le soleil, parceque je tiens de sa chaleur, tout ce qui me fait estimer, c'est dire assez que je ne saurois vivre sans vous puisque vous representez ce grand Astre, et que vous avez tant de raports avec luy, qu'on ne le nomme plus sans penser à vous."

277. Ibid., 30. "Celuy qui m'est resté me convient parfaitement puisque je me tourne tous les matins vers l'astre que vous representez. Je le suis pendant le jour, et le soir je me tourne vers l'occident, pour attendre son retour. Des qu'il s'éclipse je perds tout mon éclat, mes feüilles et mes fleurs deviennent pasles, et ma racine meme, se ressent de ces eclipse. Vos peuples en font de meme à votre égard. Ils perdent tout leur joye, et deviennent languissans, lorsqu'ils vous voyent ménacé de la moindre maladie, qui seroit une Eclipse pour eux, puisqu'il le vous déroberoit quelque tems à leur veuë. Tous leurs mouvemens, toutes leurs craintes, et tous leurs regards, sans cesse attachés sur vous, comme les miens le sont sur cet Astre, marquent un attachement inviolable pour vous, une grand fidélité, et un fort amour."

278. Ibid., 54. "La droiture de votre ame, s'attire tous les jours mille louanges."

279. Ibid. "Je multiplie beaucoup; jamais souverain n'agrandi ses Etats autant que vous avez fait: vos conquétes ont plus donné de villes à la France que tous les Rois vos prédecesseurs ensemble n'en ont pris pendant leurs regnes."

280. Ibid., 58. "Nous sommes d'un grand ornement aux Jardins; vous en étes un grand à l'Univers."

281. Ibid. "Mon sirop purge sans violence, vous purgez votre Etat de toutes sortes de vices, sans verser de sang. . . . La nature m'a donné des Epines pour me deffendre, vous avez non seulement de nombreuses troupes, pour deffendre vos Etats; mais encore pour faire toutes sortes de conquétes, quand il vous plaira de vous couronner de nouveaux laurieurs."

282. Ibid., 34. "Dès que l'on commence à publier les grand projets que vous faites souvent pour le repos de la Terre, et pour l'avantage, et la gloire de la France, on est surpris . . . au premier bruit qui se repand de ces projets, qui ne font que d'éclore. Mais quand

on vient à les examiner dans la suite, et qu'ils commencement à produire les effets, pour lesquels ils ont été concus, c'est alors qu'ils paroissent plus extraordinaires, et qu'on en découvre avec plaisir la grandeur, et la beauté, et comme les biens qu'ils font naitre, sont de longue durée, on peut avec justice les comparer à mes fleurs, qui naissent dans une saison et durent dans l'autre."

283. Ibid., 46. "Le dénombrement des qualités, et des vertus, par les quelles je contribüe à la sante des hommes, seroit trop long à faire en leur faveur, et ceux qui ont entrepris de faire votre Panégyrique, sont souvent demeurés aux seuls titres de vos actions principales, et leur ouvrages n'ont pas laissé d'étre de la grosseur qu'ils avoient résolu de les faire, en s'étendant sur chacune."

284. Ibid., 68. "Les peintres ne peuvent représenter toutes mes couleurs, à cause de leur grand nombre, et de leur varieté. Ces meme peintres ny tout ce que votre régne a de plus fameuse historiens ne sauroient receuillir toutes vos actions, quelque éclat qui les fasse remarquer, et il leur en échapera toujour beaucoup malgré tous les soins qu'ils prennent, pour n'en point laisser perdre. Si j'ay beaucoup de noms différens, ceux qui veulent faire votre Eloge, manquent de termes pour vous loüer, et ne sauroient trouver d'Epithetes pour toutes les choses extraordinaires dont doivent être remplis tous les panegyriques qu'on fait de vous."

285. Ibid., 85. "On ne me doit plus regarder comme leur Reine puisqu'elles ne reconnoissent plus que vous pour leur Souverain."

286. Ibid., 11–12. "Quoique nous soyons de diférens pays, nous sommes toutes françoises d'inclination, ou plutôt nous vous sommes toutes devoüées, étant toutes d'accord pour vous loüer."

287. Ibid., 86. "Celles que les pays étrangers nous ont fournies, brillent aujourd'huy en France, avec plus d'eclat qu'elles n'ont jamais fait dans les lieux d'ou elle tirent leur origine."

288. Louis XIV had invaded the Netherlands in 1672.

289. Donneau de Visé's fortunes were also helped by the death of Colbert and ascendancy of Louvois as the *surintendant des bâtiments*. See Burke, *The Fabrication of Louis XIV*, 92.

290. Antoine Schnapper argues that collecting was not an effective means of persuasion: "The idea—in my view, largely erroneous—that a picture collection is an important means of propaganda comes from the confusion of two distinct, albeit related, notions: collecting and patronage. Commissioning a new work, and thus having control over its iconography, is not the same thing as acquiring an existing work." He continues: "As far as art collections are concerned, they are really, at best, no more than secondary means of royal propaganda." The reputation of the king was best served, according to Schnapper, when a unified scheme glorifying specific accomplishments of the king himself was implemented, as in the Galerie des Glaces in Versailles. See Schnapper, "The King of France as Collector," 200–201. I would, however, ascribe a much more important role to the king as collector. I maintain that by engaging in collecting, as demonstrated through this study of the king as a collector and cultivator of flowers, the king was performing for his courtiers in a means or language immediately relevant to their interests, to their culture.

291. Burke argues that the shift away from mythological representations of the king came around 1680. Apostolidès argues that it came earlier, in 1674. See Burke, *The Fab-*

rication of Louix XIV, 131; Apostolidès, *Le Roi-machine,* 135–147. For a summary of Apostolidès' interpretation of the iconography of Louis XIV, see his "From Roi Soleil to Louis le Grand," in *A New History of French Literature,* ed. Denis Hollier, 314–320.

292. Here I use the term "economically" in two senses. Though the king's flowers were indeed expensive and required tremendous upkeep, they were inexpensive in comparison to the grander building and artistic schemes. Flowers were an "economical" choice to honor the king too because they embodied such a wide variety of qualities and symbolisms.

293. "Du Palais de Flore dansé à Trianon devant sa Majesté le 5 janvier 1689," in *Recueil des sujets et paroles d'une partie des ballets.*

Epilogue

1. It is possible that the garden's productivity was interrupted by the War of the Spanish Succession (1702–1714). In 1707 Eugene of Savoy and a large Anglo-Dutch naval force attempted to attack the French naval base in Toulon. Louis XIV had directed Marshal Tessé to fortify the city, however, and the siege was unsuccessful. Nonetheless, it would not be difficult to imagine that the Toulon gardens were not a high priority during the lengthy, resource-draining war. For a description of the siege, see John B. Wolf, *Louis XIV* (New York: W. W. Norton, 1968), 548–550.

2. Archives Nationale (hereafter A.N.), Maison du Roi O^{1}2110 cotte 3. Monsieur Aublet to Comte d'Angeviller, 2 February 1776. "Le Roy Louis XIV acquit pendant son regne à hiére en provence quelques petits terrains quil reunit et fit entourer de murs assez eléves qui exitent encore en assez bon état. Il en forma un jardin pour lui fournir de primveres, parceque dans le temps l'on ne protiquoit [sic] point de serres, pour supplier à la temperature du climat. On elevoit aussi à ce jardin des oranges pour fournir à l'entretien de l'orangerie de Versailles, et on y cultivoit des plantes rares pour le jardin du Roy. Pendant la minorité d'heureuse memoire du Roy Louis XV ce jardin fut oublié."

3. A.N., Maison du Roi O^{1}2110 cotte 3. Monsieur Aublet to Comte d'Angenviller, 2 February 1776. "M[onsieur] l'intendant de Toulon fit usage des fleurs et des fruits de ce jardin. Feu M[onsieur] . . . lieutenant de la seneschaussée de ce païs, profiter des chargements, qui survienent dans l'administration; il se fit adjuger moyenant la somme de 600# [livres] le jardin. M[adame] du Tillet sa veuve tres riche, et encore veuve d'un lieutenant . . . [rented] ce jardin à un païsan du lieu qui y plante des choux."

4. A.N., Maison du Roi O^{1}2110 cotte 3. Monsieur Aublet to Comte d'Angeviller, 2 February 1776. "L'amour que j'ai pour la botanique . . . , cette passion poussée [sic] au plus haut d'degré, . . . desiront être utile toutes ma vie, me fait proposes de reunir le jardin du Roy, un jardin royal des plantes de Paris et a l'orangerie de Versailles, pour y former de pepinieres de differentes orangers, des genres et des especes, de plantes rares utiles et curieuses, qui ne peuvent fleurir et être elévées à Paris. Ou elles y languissent, qu'on y perd et qu'on ne peut souvent le reprocure. Je rassemblerois avec facilité tout ce qui avoit dans l'archipel du levant et terre ferme. Je connois le temps necessaire pour les envoyer à Paris. La culture m'en est connüe, ce ne sera pas le premier jardin que je d'irigerois, je serai dans ma . . . ce qui prolongera mesjours, vivant avec de belles plantes, cela me permettra de me rendre toujours utile. Je trouverai de moments pour parcourir les alpes, les montagnes de la province et de faire une collection de tout agréable produit dans les trois regnes."

5. A.N., Maison du Roi O^{1}2110 cotte 3.

6. "Nommes et demeures des Curieux fleuristes de Paris," A.N., Maison du roi O^{1}1352. The list includes "Messieurs Bontems [,] rue et Barriere de Montreuil,[,] Rossignol, meme rue[,] Fournier, meme rue," and "Du Chemin pour les renoncules." In the faubourg St. Honoré, the gardeners identified "Frère Louis aux Jacobins[,] Benier, et Dupuis, sur le Boulevard au bout de la rue des Capucines[,] Le Comte, pres la Magdeleine[,] La Chapelle, meme rue[,] Noél [,] place Cambray[,] Le Jardinier de Ste. Genevieve[,]" and "M. Le Marquis de Gouvernay."

7. "Fleurs apropos de atirer de Normandie sur le memoire envoyée par M. Louvet pour Garnir quatres planches du jardin fleuriste de Choisy," M. Billaudet, 9 avril 1750." A.N., Maison du roi O^{1}1352^5.

8. "Memoire d'oignons de fleurs fournis pour le Jardin fleuriste de Château de Choisi par order de Monsieur le Normant de Tournehem, Directeur et Ordonnateur general des Bâtimens par le nommé La Croix au mois d'Aout 1751." A.N., Maison du roi O^{1}1352^{37}.

9. Gabriel to Monsieur Le Normant de Tournehem, 17 March 1747. A.N., Maison du roi O^{1}1352.

10. He took the opportunity of his letter to explain the care he took in carrying out "l'honneur de Vos orders j'ay enfin execute votre commission pour les jacintes." Jean Agges Scholten to M. Le Normant de Tournehem, 19 August 1748. A.N., Maison du roi, O^{1}1352^2.

11. Ibid. "Quant que de faire l'achapt des ses oignons," he explained, "je metois informé de nos curieux & amateurs de fleurs, pur savoir, qui de tous nos fleuristes de Haarlem estoient, les mieux assortis & les plus honnetes gens." He discovered that Dirck and Pierre Voorhelm were "les plus rénommez, et uniques possesseurs de certaines jacintes."

12. *Catalogus der Schoonste Tulpaan, Hyacinten, Ranuncules, Anemones, en andere Bol-Bloemen, Te bekomen by Dirk en Pieter Voorhelm, Bleomisten tot Haarlem,* 1751. A.N., Maison du Roi. O^{1}1352.

13. [Georges Louis Le Rouge], *Curiosités de Paris, de Versailles, Marly, Vincennes, Saint Cloud, et des Environs. Nouvelle Édition, Augmentée de la Description de tous les nouveaux Monumens, Edifices, & autres Curiosités, avec les changemens qui ont été faites depuis environ vingt ans,* vol. 2 (Paris: Chez Les Librairies Associés, 1771), 323.

14. For a summary of Louis XV's work on Choisy, see Michel Antoine, *Louis XV* (Paris: Fayard, 1989), 550–551. For a more thorough study of Choisy, see Mme. B. Chamchine, "Le Château de Choisy," thèse de doctorat à la Faculte des Lettres de l'Université de Paris (Paris: Jouve, 1910).

15. See Jean-Claude Le Guillou, "La création des Cabinets et des Petits Appartements de Louis XV au château de Versailles, 1722–1738," *Gazette des Beaux-Arts* 105 (April 1985): 137–146.

16. Antoine, *Louis XV*, 413.

17. Ibid., 422–425.

18. "Plan Pour la plus belle ou premiere Planche des Jacinthes doubles," 11 July 1754. A.N., Maison du roi O^{1}1352^{74}.

19. "Etat des fleurs qu'il faut tirer de hollande et qui soyent arrives a Choisy dans tout le courant du mois de septembre prochain pour le nouveau Fleuriste du Roy," 4 August 1755. A.N., Maison du roi O^{1}1352^{77}.

20. Rene Louis de Voyer, marquis d'Argenson, *Journal et mémoires du Marquis d'Argenson*, ed. E. J. B. Rathery, vol. 7 (Paris: Chez Mme Veuve Jules Renouard, Librairie de la Société de l'Histoire de France, 1865), 123. "Il est decide et declare que, malgré la misère présente, l'on va abattre l'escalier du château de Choisy et y bâtir un double, comme on a fait à la Muette, puis l'on dit q ue le vieux emporte le neuf, puis ayant fait la doublure, l'on fait aussi l'étoffe à neuf. Ceci va beauoup faire crier."

21. Ibid., 127–128. "On a commencé hier à abattre la façade de Choisy sur la cour, avec les petites ailes où était l'escalier. Le Roi a entrepris ce voyage de Choisy pour faire commence devant lui cette destruction: ainsi l'on est embarqué dans cette affaire qui coûtera plusieurs millions. Que dire de cette demarche? Rien de bon, c'est mutinerie, c'est braver le public qui souffre de la grande pénurie, c'est une affectation d'impénitence finale contre la nécessité de conduite de d'économie. Cependant nous commettons toutes ces choses avec un bon Coeur, avec un Coeur sensible, avec quelque sagesse, mais la bravade et l'affectation nous dominent; on place l'honneur à ne se render à aucunes remonstrances et à n'avoir pour amis que les gens qui affectent l'esprit au leur de ceux qui en ont la réalité. On a calculé que, depuis 1726 où le cardinal de Fleury a commence son ministère jusqu'à present, les bâtiments ont monté en dépense à trios cent cinquante millions, le tout pour ne faire que des nids à rats, à faire et à défaire. C'est le château de Choisy qui est le plus grand theater de ces variations; il n'y a point d'année où l'on ne détruise pour rebâtir ce que l'on change encore l'année suivante."

22. Ibid., vol. 6 (1864), 5–6. "On se plaint toujours, dans le public, des bâtiments dont le gout et la dépense augmentent chauqe jour. On va rebâtir Choisy, dont le vieux et le nouveau tombent à la fois. A Compiègne, on va bâtir un château dans toutes les formes. On attribue ceci à Mme de Pompadour, mais on a tort: ce n'est point par gout personnel, c'est pour plaire et pour amuser le roi qu'elle le jette dans ces enterprises don't l'exécution est confiée à son oncle."

23. Edmond Jean François Barbier, *Journal historique et anecdotique du règne de Louis XV*, ed. A. de la Villegille, vol. 3 (Paris: Chez Jules Renouard, 1851), 176. "A Choisy, on travaille aussi considérablement pour changer ce qu'on y fait et pour augmenter. Les dépenses des bâtiments sont très-considérables sans que l'on fasse néanmoins aucun monument respectable; mais, à le bien considerer, ces dépenses ne font pas grand prejudice à l'État; cela fait vivre et travailler un grand nombre d'ouvriers qui, d'un autre côté, répandent leur gain dans tous les villages voisins pour vivre. Cela fait vendre des pierres et des bois; c'est une circulation d'argent à un grand nombre de gens dans le royaume qui revient insensiblement dans les coffres du roi par les taxes et les impôts sur tout ce qui se consomme. D'ailleurs, le roi a beaucoup de princesses qui ne sont pas toutes mariées, à beaucoup près, et à qui, à un certain âge, il faudra des maisons de campagne."

24. See Christine Velut, *La Rose et l'orchidée: Les usages sociaux et symboliques des fleurs à Paris au XVIIIe siècle* (Paris: Découvrir, 1993).

25. Robert-Xavier Mallet, *Beauté de la Nature*, 269. He wrote: "Si . . . il prend du goût pour la Médecine humaine ou vétérinaire, soit pour la Chiurgurie ou la Pharmacie, la connoissance de la Botanique lui est indispensable."

26. Keith Thomas, *Man and the Natural World: Changing Attitudes in England, 1500–1800* (London: Allen Lane, 1983), 229.

27. Jean-Jacques Rousseau, *Letters on the Elements of Botany: Addressed to a Lady* (London: B. White and Son, 1785).

28. Georges Teyssot, "The Eclectic Garden and the Imitation of Nature," in *The Architecture of Western Gardens: A Design History from the Renaissance to the Present*, ed. Monique Mosser and Georges Teyssot (Cambridge, Mass.: MIT Press, 1991), 366–367.

SELECTED BIBLIOGRAPHY

PRIMARY SOURCES

Manuscripts

Paris, Archives Nationale de France
Série AJ¹⁵. Muséum d'histoire naturelle.
Série O¹. Maison du Roi sous l'Ancien Régime.
Série MC. Minutier central des notaires de Paris.

Paris, Bibliothèque Nationale de France
Manuscripts
De Visé, Jean Donneau. *Histoire de Louis le Grand, contenüe dans les rapports qui se trou-*
  vent entre ses actions, & les qualités, & vertus des fleurs, et des plantes. 1688. Fonds
  français 6995.
Montausier, Charles de, et al. *La Guirlande de Julie.* 1641. Fonds français N.A.F. 19142.
Pièces de comptabilité relatives aux miniatures de plantes et d'oiseaux qui Colbert exécuter à
  Le Roy à Bailly et à Villement. 1668–1674. Fonds français 5662.
Cabinet des Estampes
Walther, Johann. *Florilège de Nassau-Idstein.* 1663. Rès. Ja 25, fol. 2.

Wageningen Agricultural University Library, Special Collections Department
Cos. P. *Verzameling van een meenigte tulipaanen, naar het leven geteekend met hunne naa-*
  men, en swaarte der bollen, zoo als die publicq verkogt zijn, to Haarlem in den jaare A.
  1637, door P. Cos, bleomist te Haarlem. 1637.

Washington, D.C., Dumbarton Oaks Research Library and Collection
Abregée des principes de botanique contenant la methode des Tournefort, le sisteme de Linneaus,
  et les familles d'Adanson. 1768.
Garzoni, Giovanna. *Piante Varia.* c. 1650.
Gravelot, Hubert François Bourguignon D'Anville. *Gentlemen Discussing Tulips.* 1764.
Mollet, Claude. *Théâtre des plans et jardinages.* 1643.
Streatfeild, Harriet. *Silvia's Flower Garden in Which is Contained the Most Easy and*
  Expeditious Manner of Raising a Collection of Flower's and Flowering Shrubs in nat-
  ural Soils (Without the Assistance of Hotbeds) Proper to Adorn a Small Garden and a
  Little Wilderness. Together With a Kalendar Showing the Monthly Works Directed to
  be Performed in This Treatise, Also, What Months Flower's are in Bloom. 1735.

Printed Works

Académie des inscriptions & belles-lettres. *Médailles sur les principaux événements du règne*
  entier de Louis le Grand: avec des explications historiques. Paris: Imprimerie royale, 1702.

Adams, Nehemiah. *The Boston Common, or Rural Walks in Cities.* Boston: George W. Light, 1838.

Annonces, affiches et avis divers, ou Journal Général de France. 1781.

Ardène, Lucia. *Traité de la culture des renoncules, des oeillets, des auricules, et des tulipes.* Paris: Savoye, 1744.

Aristote Jardinier. *Instruction pour le jardin potager. Avec l'Art de cultiver les fleurs et pour cultiver et gresser les arbres fruitiers.* Paris: Charles de Sercy, 1678.

Aubert du Petit Thouars, Aubert. *Notice historique sur la pépinière du roi au Roule; Faisant suite à un Discours sur l'enseignement de la botanique, prononcé dans cet etablissement, le 24 mai 1824.* Paris: Gueffier, 1825.

Bailly, Jacques. *Devises pour les tapisseries du roi.* 1668. Reprint, edited by Marianne Grivel and Marc Fumarolo. Paris: Herscher, 1988.

———. *Diverses fleurs mises en bouquets dessinées et gravées par J. Bailly, Peinture du Roy.* Paris: Bailly, n.d.

Ballon and Garnier, "d'après Barbier." *Nouvelle instruction facile pour la culture des figuiers. Où l'on apprend la maniere de les élever, multiplier & conserver, tant en caisses, qu'autrement. Avec un traité de la culture des fleurs.* Paris: Charles de Sercy, 1692.

Barbe, Simon. *Le Parfumeur François, ou l'art de parfumer avec les fleurs & composer toutes sortes de Parfums tant pour l'odeur que pour le goût.* Paris: Simon Augustin Brunet, 1699.

———. *Le Parfumeur François, qui enseigne toutes les manieres de tirer les odeurs des fleurs; & à faire toutes sortes de compositions de parfums. Avec le secret de purger le tabac en poudre; & le parfumeur de toutes sortes d'odeurs. Pour le divertissement de la noblesse, l'utilité des personnes religieuses & necessaire aux baigneurs & perruquiers.* Lyon: Thomas Amaulry, 1693.

Barbier, Edmond Jean François. *Journal historique et anecdotique du règne de Louis XV.* Edited by A. de la Villegille. Paris: Chez Jules Renouard, 1851.

Bartholin, Thomas. *Bartholinus Anatomy; Made From the Precepts of His Father, and From the Observations of All Modern Anatomists, Together with His Own.* London: Published for Nicholas Culpeper and Abdiah Cole by John Streater, 1668.

Benserade, Isaac de. *Balet Royal de Flore. Dansé par Sa Majesté en 1669.* N.p., n.d.

———. *Ballet des Saisons. Dansé à Fontainebleau par sa Majesté le 23 juillet, 1661.* Paris: Robert Ballard, 1661.

———. *Ballet du Temps. Dansé par le Roy le dernier jour de novembre 1654.* In *Recueil des sujets et paroles d'une partie des ballets, dansez devant sa Majesté.* Paris: Christophe Ballard, 1709.

Berain, Jean. *Ornemens inventez par J. Berain.* Paris: Chez Monsieur Thuret, 1700.

Besler, Basil. *The Besler Florilegium: Plants of the Four Seasons.* New York: H. N. Abrams, 1989.

Binet, Etienne. *Essay des merveilles de nature, et des plus nobles artifices, pièce très-nécessaires à tous ceux qui font profession d'eloquence.* Rouen: Romain de Beauvais, 1621.

———. *Essay des merveilles de nature, et des plus nobles artifices, pièce très-nécessaire à tous ceux qui font profession d'eloquence.* Reprint, edited by Marc Fumaroli. Evreux: Association du théâtre de la ville d'Evreux, 1987.

Blake, Stephen. *The Compleat Gardeners Practice, Directing the Exact Way of Gardening. In Three Parts. The Garden of Pleasure, Physical Garden, Kitchen Garden.* London: Thomas Pierrepont, 1664.

Boileau, Étienne. *Le Livre des métiers, XIIIe siècle*. Geneva: Slatkine Reprints, 1980.

Bonnefons, Nicolas de. *The French Gardiner: Instructing How to Cultivate All Sorts of Fruit-Trees, and Herbs for the Garden: Together with Directions to Dry, and Conserve them in their Natural: An Accomplished Piece, Written Originally in French, and Now Transplanted into English, by John Evelyn Esq, Fellow of the Royal Society*. Translated by John Evelyn. London: Benj. Tooke, 1672.

———. *Le Jardinier François, qui enseigne à cultiver les arbres et herbes potagers; avec la maniere de conserver les fruicts, & faire toutes sortes de confitures, conserves & massepans. Dédié aux dames*. 5th ed. Amsterdam: Jean Blaeu, 1654.

Bosse, Abraham. *Le Iardin de la Noblesse Françoise dans lequel ce peut ceuillir leur maniere de Vettemens*. Paris: Melchior Tavernier, 1629.

B[oulanger], L[ouis]. *Jardinage des oeillets*. Paris: Louis Boulanger, 1647.

Boutet, Claude. *Ecole de la mignature, dans laquelle on peut aisément apprendre à peindre sans maître. Avec le secret de faire les plus belles couleurs: l'or bruni & l'or en coquille. Nouvelle édition, augmentée*. Lyon: François du Chesne, 1679.

Boyceau, Jacques. *Traité du jardinage selon les raisons de la nature et de l'art. Devisé en trois livres ensemble divers desseins de parterres, pelouzes, bosquets, et autres ornements servans à l'embellisement des jardins*. Paris: Michel Vanlochom, 1638.

Bozio [Bosio]. *Les Vies des saincts, et des sainctes de l'ordre de sainct Jean de Jerusalem*. Translated by J. Baudoin. Paris: Jean du Hamel, 1631.

Bradley, Richard. *A Philosophical Account of the Works of Nature. Endeavouring to Set Forth the Several Gradations Remarkable in the Mineral, Vegetable, and Animal Parts of the Creation. Tending to the Composition of a Scale of Life. To Which is Added, an Account of the State of Gardening, as it is Now in Great Britain, and other Parts of Europe: Together with Several New Experiments Relating to the Improvement of Barren Ground, and the Propagating of Timber-Trees, Fruit-Trees, & c. With Many Curious Cutts*. London: W. Mears, 1721.

Brice, Germain. *Description nouvelle de ce qu'il y a de plus remarquable dans la ville de Paris*. Paris: N. Le Gras, 1684.

Brookshaw, George. *Groups of Flowers, Drawn and Accurately Coloured After Nature, with Full Directions for the Young Artist. Designed as a Companion to the Treatise on Flower Painting*. 2nd ed. Thomas McLean, 1819.

———. *A New Treatise on Flower Painting, or Every Lady Her Own Drawing Master: Containing Familiar and Easy Instructions for Acquiring a Perfect Knowledge of Drawing Flowers With Accuracy and Taste. Also Complete Directions for Producing the Various Tints*. London: Longman, Hurst, Rees, Orme, and Brown, J. Booth, J. Lepard, 1816.

Buc'Hoz, Pierre-Joseph. *Bouquets de Flore ou recueil de bouquets et d'autres objets d'histoire naturelle*. Paris: Buc'Hoz, n.d.

———. *Collection coloriée des plus belles variétés de tulipes qu'on cultive dans les jardins des fleuristes. Ou entrènnes de Flore aux amateurs*. Paris: Buc'Hoz, 1781.

———. *Dissertations sur les sorbiers et les viournes, auxquelles on a joint un supplément aux réflextions sur le robinier*. Paris: la Dame Buc'hoz, 1804.

———. *Le Jardin d'Eden, le paradis terrestre renouvellé dans le Jardin de la Reine à Trianon. Ou collection des plantes les plus rares, que se trouvent dans les deux hémisphéres. Pour servir à l'intelligence de l'histoire générale et oeconomique des 3 règnes. Et faisant le supplément de la collection précieuse et coloriée des fleurs qui se cultivent tant dans les jardins de la Chine que dans ceux de l'Europe. Et des dons merveilleux et diversement coloriés de la nature dans le règne végétal.* 2 vols. Paris: Buc'Hoz, 1783.

————. *Toilette de Flore, ou essai sur les plantes & les fleurs qui peuvent servir d'ornement aux dames; contenant les différentes manières de préparer les essences, pommades, rouges, poudres, fards & eaux de senteurs; auquel on a ajouté différents recettes, pour enlever toutes sortes de tachés sur le ligne & sur les étoffes, &c. & c.* Paris: Vilade, 1771.

Camerio, Joachim. *Symbolorum et emblematum ex re herbaria desumtorum centuria una collecta.* Frankfort: Johannes Ammony, 1661.

Catelan, [Laurent]. *Rares et curieux discours de la plante appelle mandragore, de ses espèces, vertus et usages.* Paris: 1638.

Chiflet, Johanne Jacobo. *Lilium Francicum, Veritate Historica, Botanica, et Heraldica Illustratum.* Antwerp: Balthasaris Moreti, 1658.

Cochin, Nicolas. *Livre nouveau de fleurs tres-util pour l'art d'orfevrier et autres.* Paris: Baltazar Moncornet, 1645.

Colonna, Francesco. *Hypnerotomachie ou discours du Songe de Poliphile, deduisant comme amour combat a l'occasion de Polia. Soubsz la fiction de quoy l'aucteur monstrant que toutes choses terrestres ne sont que vanité, traicte de plusieurs matieres profitables, & dignes de memoire.* Translated and edited by Robert de Lenoncourt and Jean Martin. Paris: I. Keruer, 1546.

Contant, Jacques, and Paul Contant. *Les Oeuvres de Jacques et Paul Contant pere et fils maistres apoticaires de la ville de Poictiers.* Poitiers: Julian Thoreau et veuve d'Antoine Mesniers, Imprimeurs ordinaires du Roy, & de l'Université, 1640.

Contant, Paul. *Le Jardin et cabinet poétique de Paul Contant, apothicaire de Poitiers.* Poitiers: 1609.

Cook, Moses. *The Manner of Raising, Ordering, and Improving Forrest-Trees: Also, How to Plant, Make and Keep Woods, Walks, Avenues, Lawns, Hedges, & c.* London: Peter Parker, 1676.

Cooke, Samuel. *The Complete English Gardener: Or, Gardening Made Perfectly Easy.* London: J. Cooke, 1780.

Corneille, Thomas. *Le Dictionnaire des arts et des sciences.* 1694. Reprint, Geneva: Slatkine Reprints, 1968.

Cotin, Charles. *Les Nopces Royales.* Paris: Pierre le Petit, 1640.

The Country-man's Recreation, or the Art of Planting, Graffing, and Gardening, in Three Books. London: William Shears, 1654.

Courtin, Antoine de. *Nouveau traité de la civilité qui se pratique en France parmi les honnête-gens. Nouvelle Edition revuë, corrigée, & de beaucoup augmentée par l'Auteur.* Paris: Chez Louis Josse and Charles Roubustez, 1728.

Cowell, John. *The Curious and Profitable Gardener by John Cowell, of Hoxton.* London: Weaver Bickerton, Richard Montagu, 1730.

Crescenzi, Pietro. *Le Bon Mesnagier.* 1540.

La Culture des fleurs, ou il est traitté generalement de la maniere de semer, planter, transplanter et conserver toutes sortes de fleurs et arbres ou arbrisseaux à fleurs, connus en France. Et de douze maximes generales desquelles il est necessaire d'être instruit ou pratiquer utilement cette sorte d'agriculture. Bourge en Bresse: Joseph Ravoux, 1692.

Dalibard, Thomas François. *Florae Parisiensis Prodromus, ou Catalogue des Plantes qui naissent dans le environs de Paris, rapportées sous les denominations modernes et anciennes, et arrangées suivant la méthode sexeulle de M. Linneaus. Avec l'explication en françois de tous les termes de la nouvelle nomenclature.* Paris: Durand, 1749.

Dan, Pierre. *Les Tresor des Merveilles de la maison royale de Fontainebleau.* Paris: Sebastien Cramoisy, 1642.

D'Argenson, Rene Louis de Voyer, marquis. *Journal et mémoires du Marquis d'Argenson.* Edited by E. J. B. Rathery. Paris: Chez Mme. Veuve Jules Renouard, Librairie de la Société de l'Histoire de France, 1865.

Delafleur, N. B. *Nicolas Guillelms a Florae Lotharingus.* Rome, 1630.

Delalande, Michel Richard. *Le Palais de Flore dansé à Trianon devant Sa Majesté le 5 janvier 1689.* In *Receuil des sujets et paroles d'une partie des ballets, dansez devant Sa Majesté.* Paris: Christophe Ballard, 1709.

De Lille, Jacques. *The Garden; or, the Art of Laying Out Grounds.* Translated by James Powell. London: T. Cadell, 1789.

Descartes, René. *Discours de la méthode pour bien conduire sa raison et chercher la verité dans les sciences = Discourse on the Method of Conducting One's Reason Well and of Seeking the Truth in the Sciences. A Bilingual Edition and Interpretation of René Descartes' Philosophy of Method.* Edited and translated by George Heffernan. Notre Dame, Ind.: University of Notre Dame Press, 1994.

Descemet, Jean. *Catalogue des plantes du jardin de Mrs. les apoticaires de Paris, suivant leur genres et les caracteres des fleurs, conformément à la Méthode de Monsieur Tournefort, dans ses instituts.* N.p.: n.p., 1759.

De Visé, Jean Donneau. *Les Amours du soleil, tragedie en machines, representée sur le Theatre du Marais.* Paris: Claude Barbin, 1671.

Dezallier D'Argenville, Antoine-Joseph. *La Théorie et la pratique du jardinage, où l'on traite à fond des beaux jardins apellés communément les jardins de plaisance et de propreté.* 3rd ed. La Haye: Jean Martin Husson, 1739.

Dicksons & Co. *Nurserymen, Seedsmen, and Florists. A Catalogue of Hot-House, Green-House, and Hardy Plants; Flowering and Evergreen Shrubs, Fruit and Forest Trees, and Herbaceous Plants, Alphabetically Arranged According to the Linnaean System.* Edinburgh, 1792.

Diderot, Denis. *Encyclopédie, ou dictionnaire raisonné des sciences, des arts et des métiers.* Paris: Briasson, David, Le Breton, Durand, 1751.

———. *Recueil des planches, sur les sciences, les arts libéraux, et les arts méchaniques, avec leur explication.* Vol. 3. Paris: Briasson, David, Le Breton, 1765.

Dodart, Dionys. *Mémoires pour servir à l'histoire des plantes.* Paris: Imprimerie royale, 1676.

Dru, Jean-Baptiste. *Catalogue des plantes, tant des Tulipes que des autres fleurs qui se trouvent au jardin du Sieur Jean-Baptiste Dru, Herboriste du Roy, demeurant proche la Déserte à Lyon. Troisiesme édition, augmentée de quantité de plantes, & des noms d'une partie des couleurs qui manquoient en la précédente impression.* Lyon: Guillaume Barbier, 1653.

Du Boullay, Michel. *Zephire et Flore. Opéra.* In *Recueil des opera, des ballets, et des plus belles pièces en musique, qui ont été représentées devant sa Majesté Tres-Chrétienne. Derniere edition. Corrigée & augmentée de plusieurs pièces qui n'avoient pas été imprimées jusques à présent.* 2 vols. Amsterdam: Abraham Wolfgang, 1690.

Du Castel, Fréard. *L'Ecole du Jardinier Fleuriste.* Paris: Panckoucke, 1764.

Du Pradel, Abraham [Nicolas de Blegny]. *Le Livre commode contenant les adresses de la ville de Paris et le trésor des almanachs pour l'année bissextile 1692.* Paris: Chez le veuve de Denis Ninon, 1692. Reprint, Geneva: Minkoff Reprint, 1973.

Duret, Claude. *Histoire admirable des plantes et herbes esmeruillables et miraculeuses en nature: mesmes d'aucunes qui sont vrays zoophytes, ou plant-animales, plantes & animaux tout ensemble, pour avoir vie vegetative, sensitive & animale.* Paris: Nicolas Buon, 1605.

[Du Vivien]. *Le Jardin de Hollande planté & garni de fleurs, de fruits, et d'orangeries; où l'on enseigne, comment on peut élever & cultiver toutes sortes de fleurs les plus curieuses; telles que sont les tulipes, les oeuillets [sic], les hiacinthes, les narcisses, les oreilles d'ours, & c.* Amsterdam: Les Freres Wetstein, 1721.

Ellis, John. *Directions for Bringing Over Seeds and Plants from the East Indies and Other Distant Countries, in a State of Vegetation: Together with a Catalogue of Such Foreign Plants as are Worthy of Being Encouraged in our American Colonies, for the Purpose of Medicine, Agriculture, and Commerce. To Which is Added, the Figure and Botanical Description of a New Sensitive Plant, Called Dionoea Muscipula: or, Venus's Fly-Trap.* London: L. Davis, 1770.

[Estienne], Charles, and Jean Liébault. *Maison Rustique, or The Countrie Farme.* Translated by Richard Surflet. London: E. Bollifant, 1600.

Evelyn, Charles [John Lawrence]. *The Lady's Recreation: Or, the Third and Last Part of the Art of Gardening Improv'd.* London: J. Roberts, 1717.

Evelyn, John. *The Diary of John Evelyn, Esq. From 1641 to 1705–6, with Memoir.* Edited by William Bray. London: W. W. Gibbings, 1890.

F.B. Sieur de l'Ecluse. *La Flore sainte et l'apologie de Flore et des floristes contre les critiques: Avec un traité de la culture des principales fleurs.* Saumur: Isaac and Henri Desbordes, 1675.

F.L.D.T.R. *Secrets pour teindre la fleur d'immortelle en diverses couleurs, avec la maniere de la cultiver. Pour faire des pastes de differentes odeurs fort agreables. Et pour contrefaire du marbre au naturel propre pour toute sorte d'ouvrages figurez.* Paris: Charles de Sercy, 1690.

Fairchild, Thomas. *The City Gardener. Containing the Most Experienced Method of Cultivating and Ordering such Ever-Greens, Fruit-Trees, Flowering Shrubs, Flowers, Exotick Plants, &c. as Will Be Ornamental, and Thrive Best in the London Garden.* London: T. Woodward and J. Peele, 1722.

Félibien, André. *La Description du château de Versailles.* Paris: Antoine Vilette, 1694.

———. *Relation de la fête de Versailles du dix-huit juillet mille six cent soixante-huit. Les Divertissements de Versailles donné par le roi à toute sa cour au retour de la conquête de la Franche-Comté en l'année mille six cent soixante-quatorze.* 1668, 1674. Reprint, edited by Martin Meade. N.p.: Editions Dédale, Maisonneuve et Larose, 1994.

Ferrand, Jacques. *A Treatise on Lovesickness.* 1623; Reprint, translated and edited by Donald A. Beecher and Massimo Ciavolella. Syracuse, N.Y.: Syracuse University Press, 1990.

Ferrari, P. Giovanni Battista. *Flora ouero Cultura di Fiori.* Translated by Ludovico Aureli Perugino. Rome: Pier' Ant. Facciotti, 1638.

———. *Flora, seu De Florum Cultura.* Rome: Stephanus Paulinus, 1633.

Ferris, C. F. *The Parterre: or Whole Art of Forming Flower Gardens.* London: Edward Bull, 1837.

Florist, A. *A Treatise on the Culture and Management of the Bear's Ear, or Auricula Ursi. With directions for Raising it from Seed.* Bath: L. Bull, J. Wallis 1782.

Franeau, Jean. *Jardin d'hyver ou cabinet des fleurs contenant en XXVI elegie les plus rares et signalez fleurons de plus fleurissans parterres: illustre d'exellentes figures representantes au naturel les plus belles fleurs des jardins domestiques*. Douay: Pierre Borremans, 1616.

Furber, Robert. *A Short Introduction to Gardening; or, A Guide to Gentlemen and Ladies in Furnishing their Gardens. Being Several Useful Catalogues of Fruits and Flowers*. London: H. Woodfall, 1733.

———. *Twelve Months of Flowers*. London: n.p., 1730.

———. *The Flower Garden Display'd in above 400 Curious Representations of the Most Beautifull Flowers; Regularly Dispos'd in the Respective Months of their Blossom*. London: R. Montagu, J. Brindly, C. Corbett, 1734.

Furetière, Antoine. *Dictionnaire universel des arts et des sciences*. La Haye: n.p., 1690.

Garden Amusements, for Improving the Minds of Little Children. New York: Samuel Wood, 1814.

Gardiner, John, and David Hepburn. *The American Gardener Containing Ample Directions for Working a Kitchen Garden Every Month in the Year; and Copious Instructions for the Cultivation of Flower Gardens, Vineyards, Nurseries, Hop-yards, Green Houses, and Hot Houses*. Washington, D.C.: Samuel Smith, 1804.

Garton, James. *The Practical Gardener, and Gentleman's Directory, for Every Month in the Year*. Dublin: H. Saunders, D. Chamberlaine, J. Potts, W. Sleater, and J. Williams, 1770.

Gilbert, Samuel. *The Florist's Vade-mecum. Being a Choice Compendium of Whatever Worthy Notice Hath Been Extant for the Propagation, Raising, Planting, Encreasing and Preserving the Rarest Flowers and Plants that Our Climate and Skill (in Mixing, Making and Meliorating Apted Soils to Each Species) Will Persuade to Live With Us*. London: Thomas Simmons, 1682.

Gilman, Caroline. *The Lady's Annual Register and Housewife's Memorandum, 1838*. Boston: T.H. Carter, 1837.

Grace, Thomas François. *Jardinier portatif, ou la culture des quatre classes de jardins, et de l'éducation des fleurs. Nouvelle edition, revue, corrigée, augmentée, & exactement expliquée par un amateur, de plusieurs articles nouveaux*. Rouen: Antoine Ferrand, 1784.

Grenaille, Franciscus de, Sieur de Chatounieres. *Les Plaisirs des dames dediez à la Reyne de la Grande Bretaigne*. Paris: Gervais Clovsier, 1641.

Groen, Jan van der. *Le Jardinier hollandois où sont décrites toutes sortes de belles maisons de plaisance et de campagne; et comment on les peut planter semer, et embellir de plusieurs herbes, fleurs, et arbres rares*. Amsterdam: Marc Doornick, 1669.

Guénin. *Nouveau traité de la culture parfaite des oreilles d'ours ou auricules*. Paris: n.p., 1738.

Guiffrey, Jules. *Comptes des bâtiments du roi sous le règne de Louis XIV*. 5 vols. Paris: Imprimerie Nationale, 1881–1901.

———. *Inventaire générale du mobilier de la couronne sous Louis XIV (1663–1715)*. Paris: Au siège de la Société, 1886.

La Guirlande ou les fleurs enchantées, acte de ballet, représenté pour la première fois par l'Académie Royale de Musique, à la Suite des Indes Galantes, le mardy 21 septembre 1751. Paris: V. Delormel & Fils, 1751.

Hale, Thomas [John Hill]. *Eden: or, a Compleat Body of Gardening*. London: T. Osborne, T. Tyre, S. Crowder, H. Woodgate, 1757.

Hanbury, William. *A Complete Body of Planting and Gardening.* 2 vols. London: William
    Hanbury, 1770–1771.

Harris, Walter. *A Description of the King's Royal Palace and Gardens at Loo. Together with
    a Short Account of Holland. In Which There are Some Observations Relating to their
    Diseases.* London: R. Roberts, 1699.

Hill, Thomas. *The Gardener's Labyrinth.* London: John Wolfe, 1586.

Hughes, William. *The Flower Garden.* London: William Crook, 1672.

———. *The Flower Garden and Compleat Vineyard.* 3rd. ed. London: William Crook,
    1683.

Inventaire des merveilles du monde rencontrées dans le palais du Cardinal Mazarin. Paris:
    Rolin de la Haye, 1649.

Jacque, M. *Vases Nouveaux Composées par M. Jacque, Peinture et Dessinateur en la Man-
    ufacture Royale Gobelins.* Paris: Daumont, n.d.

Jaubert, Pierre. *Dictionnaire raisonné universel des arts et metiers, contenant l'histoire, la descrip-
    tion, la police des fabriques et manufactures de France & des pays etrangers: ouvrage utile
    a tous les citoyens.* 4 vols. Paris: Didot, 1773.

Jombert, Charles Antoine. *Les Delices de Versailles et des maisons royales, ou recueil de veue
    perspectives des plus beaux endroits des châteaux, parcs, jardins, fontaines et bosquets de
    Versailles, Marly, Meudon, Saint-Cloud, Fontainebleau, Chantilly, Sceaux, Maisons,
    & c. En deux cent planches, dessinées & gravées pour la plupart par les Perelle, pere &
    fils. Le Tout enrichi de courtes descriptions.* Paris: Chez l'auteur, 1766.

Jonson, Ben. *Ben Jonson: The Complete Masques.* Edited by Stephen Orgel. New Haven,
    Conn.: Yale University Press, 1969.

[Jouy, Etienne]. *The Paris Spectator; or, l'hermite de la Chaussée-D'Antin. Containing
    Observations upon Parisian Manners and Customs at the Commencement of the Nine-
    teenth Century.* Translated by William Jerdan. 3 vols. London: Longman, Hurst,
    Rees, Orme, and Brown, 1815.

Justice, James. *The British Gardener's Director, Chiefly Adapted to the Climate of the North-
    ern Counties, Directing the Necessary Works in the Kitchen, Fruit, and Pleasure Gar-
    dens, and in the Nursery Green-House, and Stove.* Edinburgh: A. Kincaid, J. Bell, R.
    Fleming, 1764.

Kampen, Nicholas Van, and Son. *The Dutch Florist; Or, True Method of Managing All
    Sorts of Flowers with Bulbous Roots.* 2nd ed. London: R. Baldwin, 1764.

La Brosse, Guy de. *Advis pour le jardin royal des plantes médicinales.* Paris: N.p., 1631.

———. *Description du Jardin royal des plantes médicinales, estably par le Roy Louis le
    Juste, à Paris, contenant le catalogue des plantes qui y sont de présent cultivées, ensem-
    ble le plan du jardin.* Paris: n.p., 1636.

———. *Catalogue des plantes cultivées à présent au jardin royal des plantes médicinales.* Paris,
    1641.

La Bruyère, Jean de. *Les Caractères de Theophraste traduits du Grec: avec les caractères ou les
    moeurs de ce siècle.* 6th ed. Paris: Estienne Michallet, 1691.

La Chesnée Monstereul, Charles de. *Le Floriste françois, traitant de l'origine des tulipes,
    de l'ordre qu'on doit observer pour les cultiver & planter.* Caen: Eleazar Mangeant,
    1654.

La Fayette, Madame de. *The Secret History of Henrietta, Princess of England First Wife* of Philippe, Duc d'Orleans Together With Memoirs of the Court of France for the Years 1688–1689. Translated by J. M. Shelmerdine. New York: Howard Fertig, 1993.

Langlois, François. *Livres de fleurs, ou sont representés toutes sortes de tulippes, narcisses, iris, et plusieurs autres fleurs avec diversités d'oiseaux, mouches, et papillons, le tout fait après le naturel.* Paris: Jean le Clerc, 1620.

La Quintinie, Jean de. *The Compleat Gard'ner; or, Directions for Cultivating and Right Ordering of Fruit-Gardens and Kitchen-Gardens; With Divers Reflections on Several Parts of Husbandry. In Six Books . . . To Which Is Added His Treatise of Orange-Trees, With the Raising of Melons, Omitted in the French Editions.* London: Matthew Gillyflower, 1693.

Larmessin, Nicolas de. *Les Costumes grotesques et les métiers de Nicolas de Larmessin, XVIIe siècle.* c. 1695. Reprint, edited by Paul Ahnne. Paris: Editions Henri Veyrier, 1974.

La Serre, Puget de. *Le Bouquet des plus belles fleurs de l'eloquence cueilly dans les jardins des sieurs Du Perron, Coiffeteau, Du Vair, Bertaud, D'Urfé, Malerbe, Daudiguier, La Brosse, Du Rousset, La Serre.* Paris: P. Billaine, 1624.

L[aurent], J[ean]. *Abrégé pour les arbres nains et autres.* Paris: Charles de Sercy, 1683.

Lawson, William. *The Country House-Wive's Garden.* London: E. Brewster and George Sandridge, 1653.

———. *A New Orchard and Garden. Or the Best Way for Planting, Grafting, and to Make Any Ground Good, for a Rich Orchard: Particularly in the North Parts of England.* London: Roger Jackson, 1618.

Le Febvre, François. *Livres de fleurs & de feuilles pour servir a l'art d'orfevrerie invente par François le Febvre maistre orfevre à Paris.* Paris: Baltazar Moncornet, 1635.

Le Moyne, Pierre. *De l'Art des devises. Par le P. Le Moyne de la Compagnie de Jesus. Avec divers recueils de devises du mesme autheur.* Paris: Sebastien Cramoisy & Sebastien Mabre Cramoisy, 1666.

———. *Les Peintres Morales, ou les passions sont representees par tableaux, par characteres, & par questions nouvelles & curieuses.* Paris: Sebastien Cramoisy, 1640.

Le Rouge, Georges Louis. *Les Curiositez de Paris, de Versailles, de Marly, de Vincennes, de S. Cloud, et des environs, Avec les Adresses pour trouver facilement ou ce qu'ils renferment d'agreable & d'utile. Ouvrage enrichi d'un grand nombre de Figures.* Paris: Saugrain, 1716.

———. *Curiosités de Paris, de Versailles, Marly, Vincennes, Saint Cloud, et des Environs. Nouvelle Édition, Augmentée de la Descroption de tous les nouveaux Monumens, Edifices, & autres Curiosités, avec les changemens qui ont été faites depuis environ vingt ans.* Paris: Chez Les Librairies Associés, 1771.

Liger, Louis. *Le Jardinier Fleuriste et historiographe, ou la culture universelle des fleurs arbres arbustes, et arbrisseaux, servans à l'embellisement des Jardins.* 2 vols. Paris: Chez Damien Beugnie, 1704.

Lister, Martin. *An Account of Paris, at the Close of the Seventeeth [sic] Century: Relating to the Buildings of that City, its Libraries, Gardens, Natural and Artificial Curiosities, the Manners and Customs of the People, Their Arts, Manufactures, &c.* London: Black, Young & Young, 1823.

London, George, and Henry Wise, ed. and trans. *The Retir'd Gard'ner.* 2 vols. London: Jacob Tonson, 1706.

Loris, Daniel. *Le Thresor des parterres de l'univers, contenant les figures et poutraict des plus beaux compartimens cabanes et labyrinthes des jardinages, tant à Allemandé qu'à la françoise. Avec le maniere de les construire compasser et former dextrements.* Geneva: Estienne Gamonet, 1629.

Louis XIV. *The Way to Present the Gardens of Versailles.* Introduction by Simone Hoog. Translated by John F. Stewart. Paris: Editions de la Réunion des Musées nationaux, 1992.

Loyseau, Charles. *A Treatise on Orders.* In *University of Chicago Readings in Western Civilization. Vol. 7. The Old Regime and the French Revolution.* Edited by Keith Michael Baker, 13–31. Chicago: University of Chicago Press, 1987.

Maddock, James. *The Florist's Directory, A Treatise on the Culture of Flowers: To Which Is Added, A Supplementary Dissertation on Soils, Manures, & c.* London: J. Harding, 1822.

Mallet, Sieur Robert-Xavier. *Beauté de la Nature, ou fleurimanie raisonnée, concernant l'art de cultiver les oeillets ainsi que les fleurs de premier et second ordre, servant d'ornemens pour les parterres; avec une dissertation sur les arbrisseaux choisis: fondé sur une longue expérience.* Paris: Didot, le jeune, 1775.

Markham, Gervase. *The English Hous-Wife, Containing the Inward and Outward Vertues Which Ought to be in a Compleat Woman.* London: E. Brewster, George Sawbridge, 1656.

Marquié, Père. *Catalogue des fleurs.* Toulouse: Marquié, 1800.

Mawe, Thomas. *Every Man His Own Gardener.* 6th ed. London: William Griffin, 1773.

Meader, James. *The Planter's Guide: or, Pleasure Gardener's Companion. Giving Plain Directions With Observations, for the Proper Disposition and Management of the Various Trees and Shrubs for a Pleasure Garden Plantation.* London: G. Robinson, 1779.

Meager, Leonard. *The English Gardener: Or, A Sure Guide to Young Planters and Gardeners in Three Parts,* London: P. Parker, 1670.

Ménagier de Paris. *A Medieval Home Companion: Housekeeping in the Fourteenth Century.* Translated and edited by Tania Bayard. New York: HarperPerennials, 1991.

Menestrier, Claude François. *Le Printemps Victorieux. De l'hyver et de l'autonne, sur le different qui estoit entre ces trois saisons, pour recevoir l'Hymen de leurs, Altesses Royalles. Comedie Heroique. Jouée devant leur AA. RR. au College de la Compagnie de Jesus.* Chamery: F.F. Du-Four, 1663.

Mercier, Louis. *Tableau de Paris, nouvelle édition.* 12 vols. Amsterdam: n.p., 1783.

Mercure Galant. 1672–1715.

Merian, Maria Sibylla. *Neues Blumen Buch allen Kunstverständigen Liebhabern su Lust, Nutz und Dienst.* Nürnburg: Joh. Andrea Graffen, 1680. Reprinted, Leipzig: Insel Verlag, 1966.

Miller, Philip. *The Gardener's Dictionary.* 2nd ed. London: Printed for the Author, 1733.

Molière. *Oeuvres complètes.* Edited by Georges Couton. 2 vols. Paris: Gallimard, 1971.

Mollet, André. *Le Jardin de plaisir, contenant plusieurs desseins de jardinage tant parterres en broderie, compartimens de gazon, que bosquets, & autres. Avec un abbregé de l'agriculture, touchant ce qui peut estre le plus utile & necessaire a la construction & accompagnement dudict jardin de plaisir.* Stockholm: Henry Kayser, 1651.

Mollet, Claude. *Théâtre des jardinages, contenant une methode facile pour faire des pepinieres, planter, elever, enter, gresser, & cultiver toutes sortes d'arbres fruitiers avec les fleurs qu'il faut mettre dans les parterres qui servent à l'embellissement des jardins.* Paris: Charles de Sercy, 1678.

Monicart, Jean-Baptiste de. *Versailles immortalisé par les merveilles parlantes des bâtimens, jardins, bosquets, parcs, statues, groupes, termes, et vases de marbre, de pierre, et de métaux, pieces d'eaux, tableaux et peintures que sont dans les châteaux de Versailles, de Trianon, de la Menagerie, et de Marly.* Paris: Etienne Ganeau et Jacques Quillau, 1720.

Montaigne, Michel de. *Essays.* Translated by J. M. Cohen. London: Penguin Books, 1958.

Morin, Pierre. *Catalogues de quelques plantes à fleurs qui sont de présent au jardin de Pierre Morin le jeune, dit Troisième; fleuriste, scitué au faux-bourg Saint Germain, proche la Charité.* Paris: François le Cointe, 1651.

———. *Remarques necessaires pour la culture des fleurs. Diligemment observées par P. Morin, avec un catalogue de plantes rares qui se trouvent à present dans son jardin.* Paris: Charles de Sercy, 1658.

———. *Remarques necessaires pour la culture des fleurs.* Bourge en Bresse: Joseph Ravoux, 1692.

Mortain, Gilles de. *Les Plans, profils, et elevations, des ville, et château de Versailles, avec les bosquets, et fontaines, tels quils sont a present; levez sur les lieux, dessinez et gravez en 1714 et 1715.* Paris: Chez Demortain, 1716.

Nouveau traité de la civilité qui se pratique en France parmi les honnêtes-gens. Nouvelle Edition revuë, corrigée, & de beaucoup augmentée par l'Auteur. Paris: Chez Louis Josse and Charles Robustez, 1728.

Nouveau traité de la culture des oreilles d'ours ou auricules. Paris and Brussels: chez Gilles Stryckwant, 1738.

Nouveau traité pour la culture des fleurs. Paris: Charles de Sercy, 1674.

Nouveau traité pour la culture des fleurs, qui enseigne la maniere de les cultiver, multiplier, & les conserver selon leurs especes; avec leurs proprietez merveilleuses, & les vertus medecinales, divisé en trois livres. Paris: Charles de Sercy, 1682.

Nouvelle instruction pour la culture des fleurs. Paris: Claude Barbin, 1695.

Oosten, Henry Van. *The Dutch Gardener: Or, The Compleat Florist.* London: D. Midwinter and T. Leigh, 1703.

The Orchard, and the Garden: Containing Certaine Necessarie, Secret, and Ordinarie Knowledges in Grafting and Gardening. London: Adam Islip, 1596.

Orléans, Elisabeth Charlotte, duchesse d'. *A Woman's Life in the Court of the Sun King: Letters of Liselotte von der Pfalz, 1652–1722.* Translated by Elborg Forster. Baltimore: Johns Hopkins University Press, 1984.

Ovid. *Fasti.* Vol. 5. *Ovid in Six Volumes.* Translated by James George Frazer. 2nd ed. Edited by G. P. Goold. Cambridge, Mass.: Harvard University Press, 1989.

———. *Metamorphoses.* Translated by Mary Innes. London: Penguin Classics, 1955.

"Du Palais de Flore dansé à Trianon devant sa Majesté le 5 janvier 1689." In *Recueil des sujets et paroles d'une partie des ballets, dansez devant sa Majesté.* Paris: Chrisophe Ballard, 1709.

Le Parfumeur Royal, ou traité des parfums. Des plus beaux secrets qui entrent dans leur composition, & de la distillation des eaux de senteur & autres liqueurs précieuses. Paris: Saugrain, 1741.

Parkinson, John. *Paradisi in Sole: Paradisus Terrestris.* London: Humphrey Lownes and Robert Young, 1629. Reprinted as *A Garden of Pleasant Flowers.* New York: Dover, 1976.

Le Parterre de la rhetorique Françoise, emaillé de toutes les plus belles fleurs d'eloquence qui se montrent dans les oeuvres des orateurs tant anciens que modernes, ensemble le verger de poësie, ouvrage tres-utile à ceux qui veulent exceller en l'un et l'autre art. Lyon: C. de La Rivière, 1659.

Perrot, Catherine. *Les Leçons royales ou la maniere de peindre en mignature les fleurs & les oyseaux, par l'explication des livres de fleurs et d'oyseaux de feu Nicolas Robert fleuriste.* Paris: Pierre de Bats, 1687.

————. *Traité de la mignature.* Paris: Arnoult Seneuze, 1693.

Piganol de La Force, Jean-Aimar. *Nouvelle description des chasteaux et parcs de Versailles et de Marly.* Paris: Florentin & Pierre Dulaine, 1701.

Pillement, Jean. *A New & Useful Collection of the Most Beautiful Flowers, on 20 Copper Plates, Drawn after Nature.* London: Robert Sayer, 1762.

Plat, Hugh. *The Garden of Eden, Or, An Accurate Description of All Flowers and Fruits Now Growing in England, With Particular Rules How to Advance Their Nature and Growth, as Well as in Seeds and Herbs, as the Secret Ordering of Trees and Plants.* London: William Leake, 1653.

Prévost, Jean-Louis. *Collection des fleurs et des fruits, peints d'après nature, par Jean-Louis Prevost, et tirés de son porte-feuille. Avec un discours d'introduction sur l'usage de cette collection dans les arts et les manufactures, suivi d'un précis historique sur l'art de la broderie, et d'une vue générale sur toutes les manières de peindre depuis l'antiquité jusqu'à nous par P. M. Gault-de-Saint-Germain;* avec une explication des planches par Ant.-Nic. Duchesne. Paris: Vilquin, 1805.

Pye, Mrs. Jael Henrietta Mendez. *A Short Account of the Principal Seats and Gardens, In and About Twickenham.* London, 1760.

Quinault, Philippe. *Atys. Edition critique.* Introduction and notes by Stéphane Bassinet. Geneva: Librairie Droz, 1992.

Rabel, Daniel. *Theatrum Florae In quo ex toto orbe selecti Mirabiles Venustiores ac praecipui Flores Tanquam Ab ipsus Deae sinu proferuntur.* Paris: Pierre Mariette, 1627.

Rapin, René. *Les Jardins.* Translated by Gazon-Dourxigué. Paris: Cailleau, 1773.

Rapinus, Renatus [René Rapin]. *Of Gardens. Four Books.* Translated by John Evelyn. London: T. R. and N. T., 1673.

Rapini, Renati [René Rapin]. *Hortorum libri VI cum Disputatione de Cultura Hortensi.* Paris: Typographia Regia, 1665.

Rea, John. *Flora; seu De Florum Cultura. Or, a Complete Florilege Furnished With All Requisites Belonging to a Florist. The Second Impression Corrected, With Many Additions and Several New Plates.* 2nd ed. London: George Marriot, 1676.

Recueil des opera, des ballets, et des plus belles pièces en musique, qui ont été représentées devant sa Majesté Tres-Chrétienne. Derniere edition. Corrigée & augmentée de plusieurs piéces qui n'avoient pas été imprimées jusques à présent. 2 vols. Amsterdam: Abraham Wolfgang, 1690.

Recueil des sujets et paroles d'une partie des ballets, dansez devant sa Majesté. Paris: Christophe Ballard, 1709.

Richelet, Pierre. *Dictionnaire Francois, contenant les mots et les choses, plusieurs nouvelles remarques sur la langue françoise.* Geneva: Chez Jean Herman Widerhold, 1680. Reprint, Geneva: Slatkine Reprints, 1970.

Ripa, Cesare. *Baroque and Rococo Pictorial Imagery. The 1758–60 Hertel Edition of Ripa's "Iconologia."* New York: Dover, 1971.

———. *Iconologia: or, Moral Emblems.* London: P. Tempest, 1709. Reprinted, New York: Garland, 1976.

Robertson, William. *Designs in Architecture, for Garden Chairs, Small Gates for Villas, Park Entrances, Aviarys, Temples, Boat Houses, Mausoleums, and Bridges; With Their Plans, Elevations, and Sections, Accompanied With Scenery &c.* London: R. Ackermann's Repository of Arts, 1800.

Rousseau, Jean-Jacques. *Letters on the Elements of Botany: Addressed to a Lady.* London: B. White and Son, 1785.

S.A. *Jardinier portatif, ou la culture des quatre classes de jardins, et de l'éducation des fleurs. Nouvelle edition, revue, corrigée, augmentée, & exactment expliqué par un Amateur, de plusieurs articles nouveaux.* Rouen: Antoine Ferrand, 1784.

Saint-Aubin, Charles Germain de. *Art of the Embroiderer.* Translated by Nikki Scheuer. Los Angeles: Los Angeles County Museum of Art, 1983.

Saint-Marc, Trial, and Laval. *La Fête de Flore. Pastorale en un acte; représentée devant Sa Majesté, à Fontainebleau, le Jeudi 15 Novembre 1770.* Paris: P. Robert, Christophe Ballard, n.d.

Saint-Simon, Maximilien Henri, marquis de. *Des Jacintes, de leur anatomie, reproduction et culture.* Amsterdam: n.p., 1768.

Saint-Simon, duc de. *Mémoires (1691–1701), Additions au Journal de Dangeau.* Edited by Yves Coirault. 7 vols. Paris: Gallimard, 1983.

Sales, François de. *Les caracteres ou les peintures de la vie et de la douceur du bien-heureux François de Sales Evéque & Prince de Geneve. Livre premier. Sa Vie exterieure par le Sr. Nicolas de Hauteville.* Lyon: Claude Prost, 1661.

Savary des Bruslons, Jacques. *Dictionnaire universel de commerce.* 2 vols. and Supplement. Paris: Jacques Estienne, 1723–1730.

Scudéry, Madeleine de. *La Promenade de Versailles.* Paris: C. Barbin, 1669. Reprint, Geneva: Slatkine Reprints, 1979.

Sercy, Charles de, ed. *Théâtre du Jardinage.* 7 vols. Paris: Charles de Sercy, 1683.

Serres, Olivier de. *Le Théâtre d'agriculture et mesnage des champs. D'Olivier de Serres, Seigneur du Pradel. Troisième Edition, reveuë et augmentée par l'auteur. Ici est représenté tout ce qui est requis et nécessaire pour bien dresser, gouverner, enrichir et embellir, la maison rustique.* 3rd ed. Paris: Abr. Saugrain, 1605.

Silvestre, Israel. *Recueil général du chasteau de Versailles.* 1664–1689.

Statuts et ordonnances des maitresses bouquetières-chapeliers en fleurs de cette ville & fauxbourgs de Paris. Paris: V.H. Lambin, 1698.

Tessier, Louis. *Livre de principes de fleurs, dédié aux dames.* Paris: Chez la Veuve Chereau, 1770.

Tradescant, John. *Musaeum Tradescantianum: Or, A Collection of Rarities.* London: Nathanael Brooke, 1661.

Traité de la maniere de semer dans toutes les saisons de l'année toutes sortes de graines & plantes, tant potageres que fleurs & oignons de fleurs, graines d'arbres & autres. Avec un idée ou description d'une maison de campagne. Paris: Charles de Sercy, 1689.

Traité sur la connoissance et la culture des jacintes, par l'auteur du "Traité des Renoncules" *imprimé à Paris chez Lottin.* Avignon: Louis Chambeau, 1765.

Trusler, John. *The Garden-Companion For Gentlemen and Ladies; Or, A Calendar, What Should Be Done Every Month, in the Green-House, Flower, Fruit, and Kitchen-Garden.* 4th ed. London: R. Baldwin, 1782.

Vaillant, Sebastien. *Botanicon Parisiense ou denombrement par order alphabetique des plantes, qui se trouvent aux environs de Paris compris dans la carte de la prevoté & de l'election de la dite ville par le Sieur Danet Gendre année 1722. Avec plusieurs descriptions des plantes, leurs synonymes, le tems de fleurir & de grainer et une critique des auteurs de botanique.* Leyden, Amsterdam: Jean & Herman Verbeek and Balthazar Lakeman, 1727.

Vallemont, Abbé de [Pierre Le Lorrain]. *Curiositez de la nature et de l'art sur la vegetation: ou l'agriculture, et le jardinage dans leur perfection.* Paris: Claude Cellier, 1705.

Vallet, Pierre. *Le Jardin du Roy Tres Chrestien Henry IV Roy de France et de Navare dédié à La Royne.* Paris: N.p., 1608.

Valnay, N. *Connoissance et culture parfaite des tulippes rares, des anemones extraordinaires, des oeillets fins, et des belles oreilles d'ours panachées.* Paris: Laurent d'Houry, 1688.

Vauquier, Jean. *Livre de fleurs propre pour orfevries et graveurs.* Blois, 1680. Reprinted, London: Bernard Quaritch, 1888.

Venette, Nicolas. *Tableau de l'amour dans l'état du mariage.* Cologne: Claude Joly, 1710.

Virgilius Maro, Publius. *The Eclogues and the Georgics.* Translated by R. C. Trevelyan. Cambridge: Cambridge University Press, 1944.

Voorhelm, George. *Traité sur la jacinte. Contenant la maniere de la cultiver suivant l'expérience qui en a été faite.* Haarlem: I. & J. Enschedé, 1752.

Whately, Thomas. *Observations on Modern Gardening, Illustrated by Description.* Dublin: John Exshaw, 1770.

Secondary Sources

Agnew, Jean-Christophe. "Coming up for Air: Consumer Culture in Historical Perspective." In *Consumption and the World of Goods.* Edited by John Brewer and Roy Porter, 19–39. London: Routledge, 1993.

Amherst, Alicia. *A History of Gardening in England.* London: Bernard Quaritch, 1895.

Anderson, Alexander Walter. *The Coming of the Flowers.* New York: Farrar, Straus and Young, [1951].

Antoine, Michel. *Louis XV.* Paris: Fayard, 1989.

Apostolidès, Jean-Marie. *Le Roi-machine: Spectacle et politique au temps de Louis XIV.* Paris: Les Editions de Minuit, 1981.

Appleby, Joyce. "Consumption in Early Modern Social Thought." In *Consumption and the World of Goods.* Edited by John Brewer and Roy Porter, 162–173. London: Routledge, 1993.

Arber, Agnes. *Herbals: Their Origin and Evolution.* Cambridge: Cambridge University Press, 1938.

Arminjou, Catherine, and Nicole Blondel. *Principes d'analyse scientifique: Objets civils domestiques.* Paris: Imprimerie national, 1984.

Aymonin, Gérard. *Daniel Rabel: Cent fleurs et insectes*. Introduction by Antoine Schnapper. Arcueil, France: Anthese, 1991.

Baer, Winfried. "Botanical Décors on Porcelain." In *Flowers into Art: Floral Motifs in European Painting and Decorative Arts*. Edited by Vibeke Woldbye, 82–92. The Hague: SDU Publishers, 1991.

Baillie, H. M. "Etiquette and the Planning of Royal Apartments in Baroque Palaces." *Archaeologia* 101 (1967): 169–199.

Bardon, Françoise. *Le Portrait mythologique à la cour de France sous Henri IV et Louis XIII: Mythologique et politique*. Paris: A. & J. Picard, 1974.

Bardon, Henry. "Sur l'influence d'Ovide en France au 17ème siècle." In *Atti del convegno internazionale Ovidiano, Sulmona, maggio 1958*, 69–83. Rome: Istituto di Studi Romani Editore, 1959.

Barker, Nicholas. *The Hortus Eystettensis: The Bishop's Garden and Besler's Magnificent Book*. London: British Library Publications, 1994.

Baumgartner, Emmanuèle, and Philippe Ménard. *Dictionnaire étymologique et historique de la langue française*. Paris: La Pochothèque, n.d.

Bayley, Peter. "Resisting the Baroque." *Seventeenth-Century French Studies* 16 (1994): 1–14.

Bazin, Germain. *Les Fleurs vues par les peintres*. Lausanne: Edita, La Bibliothèque des arts, 1984.

Beaune, Colette. *The Birth of an Ideology: Myths and Symbols of Nation in Late-Medieval France*. Edited by Frederic L. Cheyette. Translated by Susan Ross Huston. Berkeley: University of California Press, 1991.

Beck, Thomasina. *The Embroiderer's Flowers*. N.p.: David & Charles, 1992.

———. *The Embroiderer's Gardens*. New York: Viking Press, 1979.

Béguin, Sylvie. "L'art de peinture et de sculpture d'Ambroise Dubois à Fontainebleau." *Revue du Louvre et des Musées de France* 3 (1979): 229–233.

———. "Deux peintures d'Ambroise Dubois." *La Revue du Louvre* (1965).

Bell, Susan Groag. "Women Create Gardens in Male Landscapes: A Revisionist Approach to Eighteenth-Century English Garden History." *Feminist Studies* 16.3 (Fall 1990): 471–491.

Bending, Stephen. "William Mason's 'An Essay on the Arrangement of Flowers in Pleasure-Grounds.'" *Journal of Garden History* 9.4 (1989): 217–220.

Beneš, Mirka and Dianne Harris, editors. *Villas and Gardens in Early Modern Italy and France*. Cambridge: Cambridge University Press, 2001.

Bennett, Jennifer. *Lilies of the Hearth: The Historical Relationship Between Women and Plants*. Camden East, Ont.: Camden House Publishing, 1991.

Berger, Robert. *A Royal Passion: Louis XIV as Patron of Architecture*. Cambridge: Cambridge University Press, 1994.

Berrall, Julia S. *A History of Flower Arrangement*. London: Studio Publications, 1953.

Blair, Ann. *The Theater of Nature: Jean Bodin and Renaissance Science*. Princeton, N.J.: Princeton University Press, 1997.

Bloom. New York: Metropolitan Museum of Art, 1995.

Bluche, François, ed. *Dictionnaire du Grand Siècle*. Paris: Fayard, 1990.

Blunt, Anthony. *Art and Architecture in France, 1500–1700*. London: Penguin Books, 1982.

———. "The Précieux and French Art." In *Fritz Saxl, 1890–1948: A Volume of Memor-

ial Essays from His Friends in England. Edited by Donald James Gordon, 326–339. London: Thomas Nelson and Sons, 1957.

Blunt, Wilfrid. *The Art of Botanical Illustration: An Illustrated History*. New York: Dover, 1994.

———. *Tulipomania*. London: Penguin Books, 1950.

Bonnassieux, Pierre. *Le Chateau de Clagny et Madame de Montespan*. Paris: Alphonse Picard, 1881.

Bontems, Claude, Léon-Pierre Raybaud, and Jean-Pierre Brancourt. *Le Prince dans la France des XVIe et XVIIe siècles*. Paris: Presses Universitaires de France, 1965.

Bourdieu, Pierre. *Distinction: A Social Critique of the Judgement of Taste*. Translated by Richard Nice. Cambridge, Mass.: Harvard University Press, 1984.

———. *The Field of Cultural Production: Essays on Art and Literature*. Edited with an introduction by Randal Johnson. New York: Columbia University Press, 1993.

Boureau, Alain. "Books of Emblems on the Public Stage: *Côté jardin* and *côté cour*." In *The Culture of Print: Power and the Uses of Print in Early Modern Europe*. Edited by Roger Chartier. Translated by Lydia G. Cochrane, 261–289. Princeton, N.J.: Princeton University Press, 1989.

Braudel, Fernand. *Civilization and Capitalism, Fifteenth to Eighteenth Centuries*. Vol. 1. *The Structures of Everyday Life: The Limits of the Possible*. Translated by Siân Reynolds. New York: Harper & Row, 1981.

Breen, T. H. "The Meaning of Things: Interpreting the Consumer Economy in the Eighteenth Century." In *Consumption and the World of Goods*. Edited by John Brewer and Roy Porter, 249–260. London: Routledge, 1993.

Brilliant, Robert. *Portraiture*. Cambridge, Mass.: Harvard University Press, 1991.

Browne, Janet. "Botany for Gentlemen: Erasmus Darwin and *The Loves of the Plants*." *Isis* 80 (1989): 593–621.

Bryson, Norman. *Looking at the Overlooked: Four Essays on Still Life Painting*. Cambridge, Mass.: Harvard University Press, 1990.

———. *Word and Image: French Painting of the Ancien Régime*. Cambridge: Cambridge University Press, 1981.

Burgers, Jacqueline. *Wenceslaus Hollar: Seventeenth-Century Prints from the Museum Boymans-van Beuningen, Rotterdam*. Alexandria, Va.: Art Services International, 1994.

Burke, Peter. *The Fabrication of Louis XIV*. New Haven, Conn.: Yale University Press, 1992.

———. "*Res et verba*: Conspicuous Consumption in the Early Modern Period." In *Consumption and the World of Goods*. Edited by John Brewer and Roy Porter, 148–161. London: Routledge, 1993.

Bushnell, Rebecca W. *A Culture of Teaching: Early Modern Humanism in Theory and Practice*. Ithaca, N.Y.: Cornell University Press, 1996.

———. *Green Desire: Imagining Early Modern English Gardens*. Ithaca, N.Y.: Cornell University Press, 2003.

Chadwick, Whitney. *Women, Art, and Society*. London: Thames and Hudson, 1990.

Chamchine, B. "Le Château de Choisy." Thèse de doctorat à la Faculty des Lettres de l'Université de Paris. Paris: Jouve, 1910.

Charlton, Donald Geoffrey. *New Images of the Natural in France: A Study in European Cultural History, 1750–1800*. Cambridge: Cambridge University Press, 1984.

Chartier, Roger. *Forms and Meanings: Texts, Performances, and Audiences from Codex to Computer*. Philadelphia: University of Pennsylvania Press, 1995.

———. "From Texts to Manners, A Concept and Its Books: *Civilité* between Aristocratic Distinction and Popular Appropriation." In *The Cultural Uses of Print in Early Modern France*. Translated by Lydia G. Cochrane. Princeton, N.J.: Princeton University Press, 1987, 71–109.

———, ed. *Passions of the Renaissance*. Vol. 3. *A History of Private Life*. Edited by Philippe Ariès and Georges Duby. Translated by Arthur Goldhammer. Cambridge, Mass.: Belknap Press of Harvard University Press, 1989.

Christensen, Charlotte. "The Flowers' Metamorphoses." In *Flowers into Art: Floral Motifs in European Painting and Decorative Arts*. Edited by Vibeke Woldbye, 107–115. The Hague: SDU Publishers, 1991.

Christout, Marie-Françoise. *Le Ballet de Cour au XVIIe siècle. The Ballet de Cour in the 17th Century*. Geneva: Editions Minkoff, 1987.

———. *Le Ballet de Cour de Louis XIV 1643–1672*. Paris: Editions A. and J. Picard, 1967.

Classen, Constance, David Howes, and Anthony Synnott. *Aroma: The Cultural History of Smell*. London: Routledge, 1994.

Coats, Alice M. *Garden Shrubs and Their Histories*. New York: Simon and Schuster, 1992.

———. *The Treasury of Flowers*. New York: McGraw-Hill, 1975.

Coats, Peter. *Flowers in History*. New York: Viking Press, 1970.

Colvin, Christina, and Charles Nelson. "'Building Castles of Flowers': Maria Edgeworth as Gardener." *Garden History: The Journal of the Garden History Society* 16.1 (Spring 1988): 58–70.

Conan, Michel, editor. *Bourgeois and Aristocratic Encounters in the Garden*. Washington, D.C.: Dumbarton Oaks Research Library and Collection, 2002.

———. "The Conundrum of Le Nôtre's *Labyrinthe*." In *Garden History: Issues, Approaches, Methods*. Edited by John Dixon Hunt, 119–151. Washington, D.C.: Dumbarton Oaks Research Library and Collection, 1989.

Connaissance des arts. 1990.

Corbin, Alain. *The Foul and the Fragrant: Odor and the French Social Imagination*. Translated by Miriam L. Kochan, Roy Porter, and Christopher Prendergast. Cambridge, Mass.: Harvard University Press, 1986.

Cottesloe, Gloria. *The Duchess of Beaufort's Flowers*. Exeter, Engl.: Webb & Bower, 1983.

Cowen, Pamela. "The Trianon de Porcelaine at Versailles (newly discovered painting provides clues about the furnishings of the extinct building)." *The Magazine Antiques* 143 (January 1993): 136–143.

Cramail, Alfred. *Le Château de Ruel et ses jardins sous le Cardinal de Richelieu et sous la duchesse d'Aiguillon*. Fontainebleau: E. Bourges, 1888.

Crump, Phyllis E. *Nature in the Age of Louis XIV*. London: George Routledge & Sons, 1928.

Cunnington, C. Willett, and Philis Cunnington. *Handbook of English Costume in the Eighteenth Century*. Philadelphia: Dufour Editions, 1957.

Currie, C. K. "The Archaeology of the Flowerpot in England and Wales, *circa* 1650–1950."

Garden History: The Journal of the Garden History Society 21.2 (Winter 1993): 227–246.

Davis, Natalie Zemon. *Society and Culture in Early Modern France*. Stanford, Calif.: Stanford University Press, 1975.

———. *Women on the Margins: Three Seventeenth-Century Lives*. Cambridge, Mass.: Harvard University Press, 1995.

Davis, Natalie Zemon, and Arlette Farge, eds. *Renaissance and Enlightenment Paradoxes*. Vol. 3. *A History of Women in the West*. Edited by Georges Duby and Michelle Perrot. Cambridge, Mass.: Belknap Press of Harvard University Press, 1993.

Dawson, John Charles. *Toulouse in the Renaissance: The Floral Games; University and Student Life; Etienne Dolet (1532–1534)*. New York: Columbia University Press, 1921.

DeJean, Joan. *Tender Geographies: Women and the Origins of the Novel in France*. New York: Columbia University Press, 1991.

Delumeau, Jean. *Une Histoire du paradis*. Paris: Fayard, 1992.

Desprechins, Anne. "Les jardins de *Clélie*." In *Les Trois Scudéry. Actes du colloque du Havre*. Edited by Alain Niderst, 433–441. Paris: Klincksieck, 1993.

Dewald, Jonathan. *Aristocratic Experience and the Origins of Modern Culture: France, 1570–1715*. Berkeley: University of California Press, 1993.

Dubois, Elfrieda. "Mythe et allégorie dans la représentation de la nature: L'art du jardin et son évocation dans la poésie." In *La Mythologie au XVIIe siècle. 11e Colloque, Janvier 1981. Centre méridional de rencontres sur le XVIIe siècle*. Edited by Claude Faisant, 209–218. Marseille: A. Robert, 1982.

———. "René Rapin: L'homme et l'oeuvre." Ph.D. dissertation, Faculté des Lettres et Sciences Humaines de Paris, 1970. Lille: Université de Lille, Service de Reproduction des Thèses, 1972.

Du Crest, Sabine. *Des Fêtes à Versailles: Les divertissements de Louis XIV*. Paris: Aux Amateurs des livres, Diffusion, Klincksieck 1990.

Dunlop, Ian. *Royal Palaces of France*. London: Hamish Hamilton, 1985.

Duthie, Ruth. "English Florists' Societies and Feasts in the Seventeenth and First Half of the Eighteenth Centuries." *Garden History: The Journal of the Garden History Society* 10.1 (Spring 1982): 17–35.

———. "Florists' Societies and Feasts after 1750." *Garden History: The Journal of the Garden History Society* 12.1 (Spring 1984): 8–38.

Elias, Norbert. *The Court Society*. Translated by Edmund Jephcott. New York: Pantheon Books, 1983.

Elliott, Brent. *Flora: An Illustrated History of the Garden Flower*. Buffalo, N.Y.: Firefly Books, 2002.

Elsner, John, and Roger Cardinal, eds. *The Cultures of Collecting*. Cambridge, Mass.: Harvard University Press, 1994.

Faré, Michel. *Le Grand Siècle de la nature morte en France: Le XVIIe siècle*. Fribourg: Office du livre; Paris: Société française du livre, 1974.

Faré, Michel, and Fabrice Faré. *Peintres de fleurs en France du XVIIe au XIXe siècles*. Paris: Musée du Petit Palais, Palais des Beaux-Arts de la ville de Paris, 1979.

———. *La Vie silencieuse en France: La nature morte au XVIIIe siècle*. Fribourg: Office du livre, 1976.

Findlen, Paula. *Possessing Nature: Museums, Collecting, and Scientific Culture in Early Modern Italy*. Berkeley: University of California Press, 1994.

Flandrin, Jean-Louis. "Distinction through Taste." In *Passions of the Renaissance*. Edited by Roger Chartier, 265–307. Vol. 3. *A History of Private Life*. Edited by Philippe Ariès and Georges Duby. Translated by Arthur Goldhammer. Cambridge, Mass.: Belknap Press of Harvard University Press, 1989.

Les Fleurs dans le jardin au XVIIe siècle. Exhibition at Versailles, 15–25 June 1974. Versailles: Ecole Nationale Supérieure d'Horticulture, 1974.

Foucault, Michel. *The Order of Things: An Archaeology of the Human Sciences*. New York: Vintage Books, 1973.

Frain, Irène. *La Guirlande de Julie présentée par Irène Frain, suivie d'un Dictionnaire du Langage des Fleurs aux fins de chiffrer et déchiffrer vos tendres messages floraux*. Paris: Robert Laffont, Bibliothèque Nationale, 1991.

Franklin, Alfred. *Dictionnaire historique des arts, métiers et professions exercés dans Paris depuis le treizième siècle*. Paris: Librairie universitaire française et étrangère, 1906.

Freedberg, David, and Jan de Vries, eds. *Art in History, History in Art: Studies in Seventeenth-Century Dutch Culture*. Santa Monica, Calif.: Getty Center Publication Programs, 1991.

Friedman, Ann. "What John Locke Saw at Versailles." *Journal of Garden History* 9.4 (1989): 177–198.

Fumaroli, Marc. *L'Age de l'eloquence: Rhétorique et 'res literaria' de la Renaissance au seuil de l'époque classique*. Paris: Albin Michel, 1994.

———. *L'Ecole du Silence: Le sentiment des images au XVIIe siècle*. Paris: Flammarion, 1994.

Galinou, Mireille, ed. *London's Pride: The Glorious History of the Capital's Gardens*. Introduction by Roy Strong. London: Anaya Publishers, 1990.

Ganay, Ernest. *André Le Nostre 1613–1700*. Paris: Editions Vincent, Fréale & Cie, 1962.

———. *Bibliographie de l'art des jardins*. Paris: Bibliothèque des Arts Décoratifs, 1989.

Gélis, François. *Histoire critique des jeux floraux depuis les origines jusqu'à leur transformation en académie (1323–1694)*. Geneva: Slatkine, 1981.

Gélis, Jacques. *History of Childbirth: Fertility, Pregnancy and Birth in Early Modern Europe*. Translated by Rosemary Morris. Boston: Northeastern University Press, 1991.

Il Giardino di Flora: Natura e simbolo nell'immagine dei fiori. Geneva: Sagep Editrice, 1986.

Gibault, Georges. *L'Ancienne corporation des maitres jardiniers de la ville de Paris*. Paris: L. Maretheux, n.d.

———. *Les Anciennes lois relatives au jardinage*. Paris: Imprimerie de la cour d'Appel, L. Maretheux, 1912.

———. *Les Anciens jardins de Fontainebleau: Etude historique et archéologique*. Paris: Librairie Horticole, 1913.

———. *Les Anciens jardins du IVe arrondissement*. Paris: Imprimerie Deplanche, 1906.

———. *La Condition et les salaires des anciens jardiniers*. Paris: Librairie agricole de la Maison Rustique, 1898.

———. *Les Couronnes de fleurs et les chapeaux de roses dans l'antiquité et au moyen age*. Orléans: Paul Pigelet, n.d.

———. *Etude sur la bibliographie et la littérature horticoles anciennes*. Paris: L. Maretheux, 1905.

———. *Les Fleurs, les fruits et les légumes dans l'ancien Paris*. Orléans: P. Pigelet, n.d.

———. *Les Fleurs nationales et les fleurs politiques*. Paris: Librairie et imprimerie Horticoles, 1904.

———. *Les* Jonchées à Notre-Dame et à la maison aux piliers. Paris: Librairie Ancienne H. Champion, 1912.

———. *Les Origines de la culture forcée*. Paris: Société Nationale d'Horticulture de France, 1898.

———. *Les Rues de Paris, qui rappellent par leur nom des souvenirs horticoles*. Orléans: P. Pigelet, [1900].

Gibson, Wendy. *Women in Seventeenth-Century France*. Basingstoke: Macmillan, 1989.

Godefroy, Frédéric. *Dictionnaire de l'ancienne langue française et de tous ses dialectes du IXe au XVe siècle*. Paris: F. Vieweg, 1885.

Goldgar, Anne. *Impolite Learning: Conduct and Community in the Republic of Letters, 1680–1750*. New Haven, Conn.: Yale University Press, 1995.

———. *Tulip Mania*. New York: Alfred A. Knopf, 2004.

Goldsmith, Elizabeth. *Exclusive Conversations: The Art of Interacting in Seventeenth-Century France*. Philadelphia: University of Pennsylvania Press, 1988.

Goodchild, Peter. "John Rea's Gardens of Delight: Introduction and the Construction of the Flower Garden." *Garden History: The Journal of the Garden History Society* 9.2 (Fall 1981): 99–109.

Goodman, Dena. *The Republic of Letters: A Cultural History of the French Enlightenment*. Ithaca, N.Y.: Cornell University Press, 1994.

Goody, Jack. *The Culture of Flowers*. Cambridge: Cambridge University Press, 1993.

Gordon, Daniel. *Citizens without Sovereignty: Equality and Sociability in French Thought, 1670–1789*. Princeton, N.J.: Princeton University Press, 1994.

Greer, Germaine. *The Obstacle Race: The Fortunes of Women Painters and Their Work*. New York: Farrar, Straus, and Giroux, 1979.

Grieco, Sara F. Matthews *Ange ou diablesse: La représentation de la femme au XVIe siècle*. Paris: Flammarion, 1991.

Grimshaw, John, Bobby Ward, consultant. *The Gardener's Atlas: The Origins, Discovery, and Cultivation of the World's Most Popular Garden Plants*. Buffalo, N.Y.: Firefly Books, 2002.

Hahn, Roger. "Louis XIV and Science Policy." In *Sun King: The Ascendance of French Culture during the Reign of Louis XIV*. Edited by David Lee Rubin, 195–207. Washington, D.C.: Folger Books, 1992.

Hall, Elizabeth. "The Plant Collections of an Eighteenth-Century Virtuoso." *Garden History: The Journal of the Garden History Society* 14.1 (Spring 1986): 6–31.

Hanley, Sarah. "Identity Politics and Rulership in France: Female Political Place and the Fraudulent Salic Law in Christine de Pizan and Jean de Montreuil." In *Changing Identities in Early Modern France*. Edited by Michael Wolfe with a foreword by Natalie Zemon Davis. Durham, N.C.: Duke University Press, 1997.

Hardie, Dee. "The Feminine Rose Mystique." *House Beautiful* (September 1992): 154.

Harth, Erica. *Cartesian Women: Versions and Subversions of Rational Discourse in the Old Regime*. Ithaca, N.Y.: Cornell University Press, 1992.

Harvey, John H. "Gillyflower and Carnation." *Garden History: The Journal of the Garden History Society* 6.1 (1978): 46–57.

Hayden, Ruth. *Mrs. Delany: Her Life and Her Flower Collages.* London: British Museum Press, 1992.

Hazard, Paul. *The European Mind: The Critical Years, 1680–1715.* Translated by J. Lewis May. New York: Fordham University Press, 1990.

Held, Julius S. "Flora, Goddess and Courtesan." In *De Artibus Opuscula XL: Essays in Honor of Erwin Panofsky.* Edited by Millard Meiss. 2 vols. New York: New York University Press, 1961.

Held, Julius, and Donald Posner. *17th and 18th Century Art: Baroque Painting, Sculpture, Architecture.* Englewood Cliffs, N.J.: Prentice-Hall; New York: Harry N. Abrams, n.d.

Henrey, Blanche. *British Botanical and Horticultural Literature Before 1800. Comprising a History and Bibliography of Botanical and Horticultural Books Printed in England, Scotland, and Ireland from the Earliest Times Until 1800.* London: Oxford University Press, 1975.

Les Heures Bourguignonnes du Comte de Bussy-Rabutin. Autun: Musée Rolin, 1993.

Hix, John. *The Glass House.* London: Phaidon, 1974.

Hobhouse, Penelope. *Gardening Through the Ages: An Illustrated History of Plants and Their Influence on Garden Styles from Ancient Egypt to the Present Day.* New York: Simon & Schuster, 1992.

Hoeniger, F. David. "How Plants and Animals Were Studied in the Mid-Sixteenth Century." In *Science and the Arts in the Renaissance.* Edited by John W. Shirley and F. David Hoeniger, 130–148. Washington, D.C.: Folger Shakespeare Library, 1985.

Hollier, Denis, ed. *A New History of French Literature.* Cambridge, Mass.: Harvard University Press, 1994.

Horowitz, Maryanne Cline. *Seeds of Virtue and Knowledge.* Princeton, N.J.: Princeton University Press, 1998.

Hufton, Olwen. *The Prospect Before Her: A History of Women in Western Europe 1500–1800.* New York: Alfred A. Knopf, 1995.

Huguet, Edmond. *Dictionnaire de la langue française du seizième siècle.* Paris: Librairie M. Didier, 1973.

Hunt, John Dixon. "Curiosities to Adorn Cabinets and Gardens." In *The Origins of Museums: The Cabinet of Curiosities in Sixteenth- and Seventeenth-Century Europe.* Edited by Oliver Impey and Arthur MacGregor, 193–203. Oxford: Clarendon Press, 1985.

———. "Some Different 'Manieres de montrer les jardins'—A Review Essay." *Seventeenth-Century French Studies* 10 (1988): 122–135.

Hunt, John Dixon and Michel Conan, eds. *Tradition and Innovation in the French Garden.* Philadelphia: University of Pennsylvania Press, 2002.

Hunt, John Dixon, and Joachim Wolschke-Bulmahn, eds. *The Vernacular Garden.* Washington, D.C.: Dumbarton Oaks Research Library and Collection, 1993.

Hyde, Elizabeth. "The Cultivation of a King, or the Flower Gardens of Louis XIV." In *Tradition and Innovation in the French Garden.* Edited by John Dixon Hunt and Michel Conan, 1–21. Philadelphia: University of Pennsylvania Press, 2002.

———. "Flowers of Distinction: Taste, Class, and Floriculture in Seventeenth-

Century France." In *Bourgeois and Aristocratic Encounters in the Garden.* Edited by Michel Conan, 77–100. Washington, D.C.: Dumbarton Oaks Research Library and Collection, 2002.

———. "Gender, Flowers, and the Baroque Nature of Kingship." In *Villas and Gardens in Early Modern Italy and France.* Edited by Mirka Beneš and Dianne Harris, 225–248. Cambridge: Cambridge University Press, 2001.

Jardine, Lisa. *Worldly Goods: A New History of the Renaissance.* London: Macmillan, 1996.

Jardins d'Opéra. Paris: Bibliothèque Nationale de France, 1996.

Josephson, Ragnar. "Le Grand Trianon sous Louis XIV d'après des documents inédits." *Revue de l'histoire de Versailles et de Seine-et-Oise* (1927): 5–24.

———. "Rélation de la visite de Nicodème Tessin à Marly, Versailles, Clagny, Rueil et Saint-Cloud." *Revue de l'Histoire de Versailles et de Seine-et-Oise* (1926): 150–167, 274–300.

Kearns, Edward John. *Ideas in Seventeenth-Century France: The Most Important Thinkers and the Climate of Ideas in Which They Worked.* Manchester: Manchester University Press, 1979.

Keohane, Nannerl. *Philosophy and the State in France.* Princeton, N.J.: Princeton University Press, 1980.

Koerner, Lisbet. "Linnaeus' Floral Transplants." *Representations* 47 (Summer 1994): 144–169.

Krelage, Ernst Heinrich. *Drie Eeuwen Bloembollenexport de geschiedenis van den bloembollenhandel en der hollandsche bloembollen tot 1938.* The Hague: Rijksuitgeverij, 1946.

———. *De pamfletten van den tulpenwindhandel, 1636–1637.* The Hague: M. Nijhoff, 1942.

Lablaude, Pierre-André. *The Gardens of Versailles.* Preface by Jean-Pierre Babelon. London: Zwemmer, 1995.

Laird, Mark. *The Flowering of the Landscape Garden: English Pleasure Grounds, 1720–1800.* Philadelphia: University of Pennsylvania Press, 1999.

———. *The Formal Garden: Traditions of Art and Nature.* London: Thames and Hudson, 1992.

———. "Ornamental Planting and Horticulture in English Pleasure Grounds, 1700–1830." In *Garden History: Issues, Approaches, Methods.* Edited by John Dixon Hunt, 243–279. Washington, D.C.: Dumbarton Oaks Research Library and Collection, 1992.

———. "'Our Equally Favorite Hobby Horse': The Flower Gardens of Lady Elizabeth Lee at Hartwell and the 2nd Earl Harcourt at Nuneham Courtenay." *Garden History: The Journal of the Garden History Society* 18.2 (Autumn 1990): 103–154.

———. "Theatres of Flowers: The Art and Science of Eighteenth-Century Floral Display." In *Text of the Clusius Lectures.* Clusiusstichting, 1997, 5–19.

Laird, Mark, and John H. Harvey. "'A Cloth of Tissue of Divers Colours': The English Flower Border, 1660–1735." *Garden History: The Journal of the Garden History Society* 21.2 (Winter 1993): 158–205.

Lavalle, Denis. "Plafonds et grands décors peints dans les hôtels du Marais au XVIIe siècle." In *Le Marais: Mythe et réalité*, 179–196. Paris: Caisse Nationale des Monuments Historiques et des Sites, 1987.

Lecuir, Jean. "Minerve-Pallas dans la médaille royale d'Henri IV et de Marie de Medicis." In *La Mythologie au XVIIe siècle. 11e Colloque, Janvier 1981. Centre méridional de rencontres sur le XVIIe siècle.* Edited by Claude Faisant, 225–233. Marseille: A. Robert, 1982.

Le Dantec, Denise, and Jean-Pierre Le Dantec. *Reading the French Garden: Story and History.* Translated by Jessica Levine. Cambridge, Mass.: MIT Press, 1990.

Le Guérer, Annick. *Scent: The Mysterious and Essential Powers of Smell.* Translated by Richard Miller. London: Chatto & Windus, 1993.

Le Guillou, Jean-Claude. "La création des Cabinets et des Petits Appartements de Louis XV au château de Versailles, 1722–1738." *Gazette des Beaux-Arts* 105 (April 1985): 137–146.

Leith-Ross, Prudence. "A Seventeenth-Century Paris Garden." *Garden History: The Journal of the Garden History Society* 21.2 (Winter 1993): 150–157.

Le Moël, Michel. *L'Architecture privée à Paris au Grand Siècle.* Paris: Commission des travaux historiques de la ville de Paris, 1990.

Lesueur, Pierre. *Les Jardins du château de Blois et leur dépendances.* Blois: C. Migault, 1906.

Levi D'Ancona, Mirella. *Boticelli's "Primavera": A Botanical Interpretation Including Astrology, Alchemy and the Medici.* Florence: Leo S. Olschki Editore, 1983.

———. *The Garden of the Renaissance: Botanical Symbolism in Italian Painting.* Florence: Leo S. Olschki, 1977.

Leyzour, Philippe le. "Myth and Enlightenment: On Mythology in the Eighteenth Century." In *The Loves of the Gods: Mythological Painting from Watteau to David.* Edited by Colin B. Baily with the assistance of Carrie A. Hamilton, 20–31. Fort Worth, Tex.: Rizzoli, 1992.

Longstaffe-Gowan, R. Todd. "Private Urban Gardening in England, 1700–1830." In *The Vernacular Garden.* Edited by John Dixon Hunt and Joachim Wolschke-Bulmahn, 47–75. Washington, D.C.: Dumbarton Oaks Research Library and Collection, 1993.

———. "Proposal for a Georgian Town Garden in Gower Street: The Francis Douce Garden." *Garden History: The Journal of the Garden History Society* 15.2 (Fall 1987): 136–144.

Lopez, Denis. *La Plume et l'épée: Montausier, 1610–1690.* Biblio 17. Paris: Papers on French Seventeenth-Century Literature, 1987.

———. "Scudéry et la *Guirlande de Julie.*" In *Les Trois Scudéry. Actes du Colloque du Havre, 1–5 octobre 1991.* Edited by Alain Niderst. Paris: Klincksieck, 1993.

Le Louvre: The Palace and Its Paintings: An Interactive Visit to the World's Grandest Museum. CD-ROM. Paris: Réunion des Musées Nationaux, 1995.

MacDougall, Elisabeth Blair. *Fountains, Statues, and Flowers: Studies in Italian Gardens of the Sixteenth and Seventeenth Centuries.* Washington, D.C.: Dumbarton Oaks Research Library and Collection, 1994.

———. "A Paradise of Plants: Exotica, Rarities, and Botanical Fantasies." In *The Age of The Marvelous.* Edited by Joy Kenseth, 145–157. Hanover, N.H.: Hood Museum of Art, Dartmouth College, 1991.

McGowan, Margaret M. *Ideal Forms in the Age of Ronsard.* Berkeley: University of California Press, 1985.

Maclean, Ian. *The Renaissance Notion of Woman: A Study in the Fortunes of Scholasticism and Medical Science in European Intellectual Life.* Cambridge: Cambridge University Press, 1980.

Magne, Bernard. "Le Procès de la mythologie dans la querelle des Anciens et des Modernes." In *La Mythologie au XVIIe siècle. 11e Colloque, Janvier 1981. Centre méridional de rencontres sur le XVIIe siècle.* Edited by Claude Faisant, 49–56. Marseille: A. Robert, 1982.

Magne, Emile. *Le Château de Marly d'après des documents inédits.* Paris: Calmann-Lévy, 1934.

Maison et jardin. February 1994.

Le Marais: Mythe et realité. Exposition: Hôtel de Sully 30 avril–30 aout 1987. Paris: Caisse Nationale des Monuments Historiques et des Sites, 1987.

Maravall, José Antonio. *Culture of the Baroque: Analysis of a Historical Structure.* Translated by Terry Cochran. Foreward by Wlad Godzich and Nickolas Spadacinni. Minneapolis: University of Minnesota Press, 1986.

Mariage, Thierry. *L'Univers de Le Nôstre.* Brussels: Pierre Mardaga, 1990.

Marie, Alfred. *Naissance de Versailles: Le château, les jardins.* 2 vols. Paris: Editions Vincent, Fréal & Cie., 1968.

———. *Versailles au temps du Louis XIV. Troisième partie: Mansart et Robert de Cotte.* Paris: Imprimerie Nationale, 1976.

Marin, Louis. *Portrait of the King.* Translated by Martha M. Houle. Foreward by Tom Conley. Minneapolis: University of Minnesota Press, 1988.

Marion, René S. "The *Dames de la Halle*: Women and Community in Late Eighteenth-Century Paris." *Proceedings of the Annual Meeting of the Western Society for French History* 17 (1990): 140–145.

Masson, Georgina. "Italian Flower Collectors' Gardens in Seventeenth-Century Italy." In *The Italian Garden: Dumbarton Oaks Colloquium on the History of Landscape Architecture.* Edited by David R. Coffin, 61–80. Washington, D.C.: Dumbarton Oaks Research Library and Collection, 1972.

Maza, Sarah. "The Rose-Girl of Salency: Representations of Virtue in Prerevolutionary France." *Eighteenth-Century Studies* 22.3 (Spring 1989): 395–412.

Merchant, Carolyn. *The Death of Nature: Women, Ecology, and the Scientific Revolution.* San Francisco: HarperSanFrancisco, 1990.

Mérot, Alain. "La Place des sujets mythologiques et leur signification dans le décor peint, à Paris, dans la première moitié du XVIIe siècle." In *La Mythologie au XVIIe siècle. 11e Colloque, janvier 1981. Centre méridional de rencontres sur le XVIIe siècle.* Edited by Claude Faisant, 219–224. Marseille: A. Robert, 1982.

———. *Retraites mondaines: Aspects de la décoration intérieure à Paris au XVIIe siècle.* Paris: Le Promeneur, 1990.

Meyenburg, Bettina von. "'Saying It With Flowers': The Flower as an Artistic Motif from the Late Middle Ages until the Baroque." In *Flowers into Art: Floral Motifs in European Painting and Decorative Arts.* Edited by Vibeke Woldbye, 37–56. The Hague: SDU Publishers, 1991.

Meyer, Gerald Dennis. *The Scientific Lady in England 1650–1760: An Account of Her Rise, With Emphasis on the Major Roles of the Telescope and Microscope.* Berkeley: University of California Press, 1955.

Migne, J.-P. *Encyclopédie Théologique, ou série de dictionnaires sur toutes les parties de la science religieuse, offrant en français la plus claire, la plus facile, la plus commode, la plus variée et la plus complète des théologies.* 50 vols. Paris: Chez l'Editeur, 1850.

Millen, Ronald Forsyth, and Robert Erich Wolf. *Heroic Deeds and Mystic Figures: A New*

Reading of Rubens' "Life of Maria de' Medici." Princeton, N.J.: Princeton University Press, 1989.

Miller, Peter N. *Peiresc's Europe: Learning and Virtue in the Seventeenth Century.* New Haven, Conn.: Yale University Press, 2000.

Mitford, Nancy. *The Sun King.* London: Penguin Books, 1994.

Moine, Marie-Christine. *Les Fêtes à la cour du Roi Soleil, 1653–1715.* Paris: Editions Fernand Lanore, 1984.

Mongan, Agnes. "A Fête of Flowers: Women Artists' Contribution to Botanical Illustration." *Apollo* 119 (April 1984): 264–267.

Mosser, Monique, and Georges Teyssot, eds. *The Architecture of Western Gardens: A Design History from the Renaissance to the Present.* Cambridge, Mass.: MIT Press, 1991.

Mukerji, Chandra. *From Graven Images: Patterns of Modern Materialism.* New York: Columbia University Press, 1983.

———. "Reading and Writing with Nature: A Materialist Approach to French Formal Gardens." In *Consumption and the World of Goods.* Edited by John Brewer and Roy Porter, 439–461. London: Routledge, 1993.

———. *Territorial Ambitions and the Gardens of Versailles.* Cambridge: Cambridge University Press, 1997.

Nelson, E. Charles. "The Dublin Florists' Club in the Mid Eighteenth Century." *Garden History: The Journal of the Garden History Society* 10.2 (Fall 1982): 142–148.

Néraudau, Jean-Pierre. *L'Olympe du Roi-Soleil: Mythologie et idéologie royal au Grand Siècle.* Paris: Société d'Edition "Les Belles Lettres," 1986.

———. "La Présence d'Ovide aux XVIe et XVIIe siècles ou la survie du prince de poésie." In *La Littérature et ses avatars: Discrédits, déformations et réhabilitations dans l'histoire de la littérature.* Edited by Yvonne Bellenger, 13–39. Paris: Klincksieck, 1991.

Nolhac, Pierre de. *Versailles and the Trianons.* New York: Dodd, Mead, & Co., 1906.

Paludan, Charlotte. "A Beguiling Similarity: A Contribution to the History of Artificial Flowers." In *Flowers into Art: Floral Motifs in European Painting and Decorative Arts.* Edited by Vibeke Woldbye, 116–126. The Hague: SDU Publishers, 1991.

Pardailhé-Galabrun, Annik. *The Birth of Intimacy: Privacy and Domestic Life in Early Modern Paris.* Translated by Jocelyn Phelps. Philadelphia: University of Pennsylvania Press, 1991.

Parker, Rozsika. *The Subversive Stitch: Embroidery and the Making of the Feminine.* New York: Routledge, 1989.

Parker, Rozsika, and Griselda Pollock. *Old Mistresses: Women, Art, and Ideology.* London: Routledge & Kegan Paul, 1981.

Pattacini, Laurence. "André Mollet, Royal Gardener in St. James's Park, London." *Garden History: The Journal of the Garden History Society* 26.1 (Summer 1998): 3–18.

Pavière, Sydney H. *A Dictionary of Flower, Fruit, and Still Life Painters.* 4 vols. Leighon-Sea: F. Lewis, 1962.

Peintres de fleurs en France du XVIIe au XIXe siècles, 12 mai–2 septembre 1979. Paris: Musée du Petit Palais, Palais des Beaux-arts de la Ville de Paris, 1979.

Pelt, Jean-Marie. *Fleurs, fêtes et saisons.* Paris: Fayard, 1988.

Percy, Joan. "Maria Elizabetha Jacson and Her *Florist's Manual.*" *Garden History: The Journal of the Garden History Society* 20.1 (Spring 1992): 45–56.

Phillips, Patricia. *The Scientific Lady: A Social History of Women's Scientific Interests 1520–1918*. New York: St. Martin's Press, 1990.

Pillivuyt, Ghislaine, with the collaboration of Pauline Mercier and Doris Jakubec. *Flacons de la séduction: L'art du parfum au XVIIIe*. Lausanne: Bibliothèque des Arts, 1985.

Pinault, Madeleine. *Le Peintre et l'histoire naturelle*. Translated by Philip Sturgess. Paris: Flammarion, 1990.

Pomian, Krzysztof. *Collectors and Curiosities: Paris and Venice, 1500–1800*. Translated by Elizabeth Wiles-Portier. Cambridge, Mass.: Polity Press, 1990.

Posner, Donald. "Charles Le Brun's *Triumphs of Alexander*." *Art Bulletin* 41 (September 1959): 237–248.

Posthumus, N. W. "The Tulip Mania in Holland in the Years 1636 and 1637." *Journal of Economic and Business History* 1.3 (May 1929): 434–466.

Prest, John. *The Garden of Eden: The Botanic Garden and the Re-Creation of Paradise*. New Haven, Conn.: Yale University Press, 1981.

Rabb, Theodore. *The Struggle for Stability in Early Modern Europe*. New York: Oxford University Press, 1975.

Ranum, Orest. *Artisans of Glory: Writers and Historical Thought in Seventeenth-Century France*. Chapel Hill: University of North Carolina Press, 1980.

———. *The Fronde: A French Revolution, 1648–1652*. New York: W. W. Norton, 1993.

———. "Intimacy in French Eighteenth-Century Family Portraits." *Word and Image: A Journal of Verbal/Visual Enquiry* 6.4 (October–December 1990): 351–367.

———. *Paris in the Age of Absolutism*. Bloomington: Indiana University Press, 1979.

Rees, Ronald. *Interior Landscapes: Gardens and the Domestic Environment*. Baltimore, Md.: Johns Hopkins University Press, 1993.

Reid, Jane Davidson. *The Oxford Guide to Classical Mythology in the Arts, 1300–1990*. Oxford: Oxford University Press, 1993.

Revel, Jacques. "The Uses of Civility." In *Passions of the Renaissance*. Edited by Roger Chartier, 167–205. Vol. 3. *A History of Private Life*. Edited by Philippe Ariès and Georges Duby. Translated by Arthur Goldhammer. Cambridge, Mass.: Belknap Press of Harvard University Press, 1989.

Revue de l'art: Plafonds Parisiens du XVIIe sièle. 122.4 (1998).

Rey, Alain. "Linguistic Absolutism." In *A New History of French Literature*. Edited by Denis Hollier, 373–379. Cambridge, Mass.: Harvard University Press, 1994.

Ribeiro, Aileen. *Dress in Eighteenth-Century Europe, 1715–1789*. London: B. T. Batsford, 1984.

Ritterbush, Philip C. "The Organism as Symbol: An Innovation in Art." In *Science and the Arts in the Renaissance*. Edited by John W. Shirley and F. David Hoeniger, 149–167. Washington, D.C.: Folger Shakespeare Library, 1985.

Rochelle, Mercedes. *Mythological and Classical World Art Index*. Jefferson, N.C.: McFarland & Company, 1991.

Rothstein, Natalie. *Silk Designs of the Eighteenth Century in the Collection of the Victoria and Albert Museum, London, with a Complete Catalogue*. London: Thames and Hudson, 1990.

Rubin, David Lee, ed. *Sun King: The Ascendance of French Culture During the Reign of Louis XIV*. Washington, D.C.: Folger Shakespeare Library; London: Associated University Presses, 1992.

Russell, Daniel S. *The Emblem and Device in France.* Lexington, Ky.: French Forum, 1985.

Saint-Paul, Evelyne. *L'Hôtel de Sully.* Paris: Caisse Nationale des Monuments Historiques et des Sites; Rennes: Editions Ouest-France, 1993.

Saisselin, Rémy. *The Enlightenment against the Baroque: Economics and Aesthetics in the Eighteenth Century.* Berkeley: University of California Press, 1992.

Saunders, Gill. *Picturing Plants: An Analytical History of Botanical Illustration.* Berkeley: University of California Press in association with the Victoria and Albert Museum, London, 1995.

Schama, Simon. *The Embarrassment of Riches: An Interpretation of Dutch Culture in the Golden Age.* N.p.: Fontana Press, 1988.

———. *Landscape and Memory.* New York: Alfred A. Knopf, 1995.

———. "Perishable Commodities: Dutch Still-Life Painting and the 'Empire of Things.'" In *Consumption and the World of Goods.* Edited by John Brewer and Roy Porter, 478–488. London: Routledge, 1993.

Schiebinger, Londa. *The Mind Has No Sex? Women in the Origins of Modern Science.* Cambridge, Mass.: Harvard University Press, 1989.

———. *Nature's Body: Gender in the Making of Modern Science.* Boston: Beacon Press, 1993.

———. "The Private Life of Plants: Sexual Politics in Earl Linnaeus and Erasmus Darwin." In *Science and Sensibility: Gender and Scientific Enquiry 1780–1945.* Edited by Marina Benjamin, 121–143. Cambridge, Mass.: Basil Blackwell, 1991.

Schnapper, Antoine. *Curieux du Grand Siècle. Oeuvres d'art.* Vol. 2. *Collections et collectionneurs dans la France du XVIIe siècle.* Paris: Flammarion, 1994.

———. *Le Géant, la licorne, et la tulipe. Histoire et histoire naturelle.* Vol. 1. *Collections et collectionneurs dans la France du XVIIe siècle.* Paris: Flammarion, 1988.

———. "The King of France as Collector in the Seventeenth Century." In *Art and History: Images and Their Meaning.* Edited by Robert I. Rotberg and Theodore K. Rabb, 185–202. Cambridge: Cambridge University Press, 1988.

———. *Tableaux pour le Trianon de Marbre, 1688–1714.* Paris: Mouton, 1967.

Scott, Katie. "D'un Siècle à l'autre: History, Mythology, and Decoration in Early Eighteenth-Century Paris." In *The Loves of the Gods: Mythological Painting from Watteau to David.* Edited by Colin Bailey, 32–59. Kimball Art Museum, Fort Worth, Tex.: Rizzoli, 1992.

Seaton, Beverly. *The Language of Flowers: A History.* Charlottesville: University of Virginia Press, 1995.

Segal, Sam. *Flowers and Nature: Netherlandish Flower Painting of Four Centuries.* The Hague: SDU Publishers, 1990.

Shteir, Ann B. "Botany in the Breakfast Room: Women and Early Nineteenth-Century British Plant Study." In *Uneasy Careers and Intimate Lives: Women in Science, 1789–1979.* Edited by Phina G. Abir-Am and Dorinda Outram, 31–43. New Brunswick, N.J.: Rutgers University Press, 1987.

———. *Cultivating Women, Cultivating Science: Flora's Daughters and Botany in England 1760–1860.* Baltimore: Johns Hopkins University Press, 1996.

Silin, Charles I. *Benserade and His Ballets de Cour.* Baltimore, Md.: Johns Hopkins University Press; London: Humphrey Milford, Oxford University Press; Paris: Société d'Edition "Les Belles Lettres," 1940.

Smith, Pamela H. and Paula Findlen, eds. *Merchants and Marvels: Commerce, Science, and Art in Early Modern Europe*. New York: Routledge, 2002.

Sprang, Sabine van, comp., with Gerda De Brabandere and Elisabeth Lauwers-Derveaux. *L'empire de flore: histoire et représentation des fleurs en Europe du XVIe au XIXe siècle*. Brussels: Renaissance du Livre, 1996.

Stefanovska, Malina. "A Monumental Triptych: Saint-Simon's *Parallèle des trois premiers rois Bourbons*." *French Historical Studies* 19.4 (Fall 1996): 933.

Stroup, Alice. *A Company of Scientists: Botany, Patronage, and Community at the Seventeenth-Century Parisian Royal Academy of Sciences*. Berkeley: University of California Press, 1990.

Stuart, David. *The Plants That Shaped Our Gardens*. Cambridge, Mass.: Harvard University Press, 2002.

Stuart, David, and James Sutherland. *Plants from the Past: Old Flowers for New Gardens*. London: Penguin Books, 1987.

Symbolique et botanique: Le sens caché des fleurs dans la peintre au XVIIe siècle: [Exposition] Caen, 9 juillet–26 octobre 1987, Musée des beaux arts de Caen. Caen: Le Musée, 1987.

Taboroff, June. "'Wife, unto thy garden': The First Gardening Books for Women." *Garden History: The Journal of the Garden History Society* 11.1 (Spring 1983): 1–5.

Taylor, Paul. *Dutch Flower Painting, 1600–1720*. New Haven, Conn.: Yale University Press, 1995.

Thomas, Keith. *Man and the Natural World: Changing Attitudes in England, 1500–1800*. London: Allen Lane, 1983.

Thomas, Troy. "'Un fior vano e fragile': The Symbolism of Poussin's *Realm of Flora*." *Art Bulletin* 68.2 (June 1986): 225–236.

Thornton, Peter. *Seventeenth-Century Interior Decoration in England, France and Holland*. New Haven, Conn.: Yale University Press, 1978.

Tocanne, Bernard. *L'Idée de nature en France dans la seconde moitié du XVIIe siècle: Contribution à l'histoire de la pensée classique*. [Paris]: Klincksieck, 1978.

Tomasi, Lucia Tongiorgi. *An Oak Spring Flora: Flower Illustration from the Fifteenth Century to the Present Time: A Selection of the Rare Books, Manuscripts and Works of Art in the Collection of Rachel Lambert Mellon*. Upperville, Va.: Oak Spring Garden Library; New Haven, Conn.: Yale University Press, 1997.

Trout, Andrew. *City on the Seine: Paris in the Time of Richelieu and Louis XIV*. New York: St. Martin's Press, 1996.

Tyvaert, Michael. "L'Image du roi: Légitime et moralité royales dans les histoires de France au XVIIe siècle." *Revue d'histoire moderne et contemporaine* 21 (October–December 1974): 521–547.

Veevers, Erica. *Images of Love and Religion: Queen Henrietta Maria and Court Entertainments*. Cambridge: Cambridge University Press, 1989.

Velut, Christine. *La Rose et l'orchidée: Les usages sociaux et symboliques des fleurs à Paris au XVIIIe siècle*. Paris: Découvrir, 1993.

Wagner, Peter. "Flower Gardens, Flower Fashions and Illustrated Botanical Works: Observations on Fashion from a Botanist's Point of View." In *Flowers into Art: Floral Motifs in European Painting and Decorative Arts*. Edited by Vibeke Woldbye, 9–23. The Hague: SDU Publishers, 1991.

———. "*Icones Florae Danicae*: The 'Plant Illustrators' of Flora Danica and the 'School of Illumination for Women.'" In *Flowers into Art: Floral Motifs in European Painting and Decorative Arts*. Edited by Vibeke Woldbye, 93–100. The Hague: SDU Publishers, 1991.

Walton, Guy. *Louis XIV's Versailles*. Chicago: University of Chicago Press, 1986.

Warner, Marjorie F. "The Morins." *National Horticultural Magazine* (1954): 168–176.

———. "Jean and Vespasien Robin, 'Royal Botanists,' and North American Plants, 1601–1635." *National Horticultural Magazine* 35.4 (October 1956): 214–220.

Weil, Mark S. "Love, Monsters, Movement, and Machines: The Marvelous in Theaters, Festivals, and Gardens." In *The Age of the Marvelous*. Edited by Joy Kenseth, 159–178. Hanover, N.H.: Hood Museum of Art, Dartmouth College, 1991.

Westergaard, Hanne. "The Immortal Motif." In *Flowers into Art: Floral Motifs in European Painting and Decorative Arts*. Edited by Vibeke Woldbye, 25–36. The Hague: SDU Publishers, 1991.

Woldbye, Vibeke, ed. *Flowers into Art: Floral Motifs in European Painting and Decorative Arts*. The Hague: SDU Publishers, 1991.

Wolf, John B. *Louis XIV*. New York: W. W. Norton, 1968.

Woodbridge, Kenneth. *Princely Gardens: The Origins and Development of the French Formal Style*. New York: Rizzoli, 1986.

Woods, May, and Arete Swartz Warren. *Glass Houses: A History of Greenhouses, Orangeries, and Conservatories*. London: Aurum Press, 1988.

Yates, Frances. *Astraea: The Imperial Theme in the Sixteenth Century*. London: ARK Paperbacks, 1985.

———. *The French Academies of the Sixteenth Century*. London: Routledge, 1988.

Zanger, Abby E. *Scenes from the Marriage of Louis XIV: Nuptial Fictions and the Making of Absolutist Power*. Stanford, Calif.: Stanford University Press, 1997.

Zirpolo, Lilian. "Botticelli's *Primavera*: A Lesson for the Bride." In *The Expanding Discourse: Feminism and Art History*. Edited by Norma Broude and Mary D. Garrard, 100–109. New York: Icon Editions of Harper Collins, 1992.

INDEX

Page references to figures and plate numbers are in boldface italics.

ACKNOWLEDGMENTS

This project could not have been completed without the support of numerous institutions, colleagues, and friends. I began my research with a Summer Fellowship at Dumbarton Oaks Research Library and Collection in Washington, D.C. A Krupp Foundation Fellowship in European Studies from the Minda da Gunzberg Center for European Studies at Harvard University provided me with funding to spend an academic year conducting research in Paris. While in Paris, I was grateful to be a scholar at the Graduate Research Institute at Reid Hall. A summer travel grant from the Department of History at Harvard University was also helpful. The transformation of my initial research into this book was completed with the assistance of very generous fellowships from the National Endowment for the Humanities and the American Philosophical Society.

Portions of this work have appeared in earlier publications. Parts of Chapter 1 were published as "Gender, Flowers, and the Baroque Nature of Kingship" in *Villas and Gardens in Early Modern Italy and France*, edited by Mirka Beneš and Dianne Harris and published by Cambridge University Press. An earlier version of Chapter 2, "Flowers of Distinction: Taste, Class, and Floriculture in Seventeenth-Century France," was included in *Bourgeois and Aristocratic Encounters in the Garden*, edited by Michel Conan and published by Dumbarton Oaks Research Library and Collection. And portions of Chapter 5 appeared in *Tradition and Innovation in the French Garden*, edited by John Dixon Hunt and Michel Conan and published by the University of Pennsylvania Press. I thank these presses for permission to draw on my articles for this book.

The intellectual journey that has become this book began many years ago at West Virginia University where Dennis H. O'Brien and Elizabeth Hudson sparked my interest in early modern Europe. At Harvard University, Simon Schama helped shape my understanding of cultural history and encouraged me to think as broadly about flowers as possible. From Olwen Hufton I learned to think more critically about the sources available to the historian for understanding the early modern period. Patrice Higonnet graciously read drafts of my dissertation and has continued to be a helpful advocate. Ann Blair's optimism, close reading of my work, and wise insights have been crucial in making revisions. Finally, this work would not have been completed without the measureless advice and support of Abby Zanger. In addition to pressing me to find the courage to labor on, she has been a patient teacher in emboldening me to think more analytically about the material I have uncovered. Together these generous scholars have contributed greatly to the crafting of what I hope is a richly textured exploration of early modern French culture.

Numerous colleagues and friends have helped move this project forward by inviting me to contribute papers and deliver talks, commenting on conference papers, sharing manuscripts of their own, and keeping ever alert for references to flowers. Great thanks therefore go to Mirka Beneš, Rebecca Bushnell, Anne Goldgar, Anthony Grafton, Mark Laird, Susan Taylor Leduc, Susan Lively, George Longenecker, Linda Lott, Lisa Perella, Orest Ranum, Rebecca Spang, Alice Stroup, Lucia Tongiorgi Tomasi, Leslie Tuttle, and Joachim Wolschke-Bulmahn. I am particularly grateful to Joseph O'Donnell, who first alerted me to the existence of the Donneau de Visé manuscript. And I am greatly indebted to John Dixon Hunt, editor of the Penn Studies in Landscape Architecture series, for his interest in my work, and to Jo Joslyn, Ted Mann, Noreen O'Connor, and everyone at the University of Pennsylvania Press for their patience and assistance in bringing the work to print.

In bringing this work to fruition, I have also incurred a great number of personal debts to those who have been a source of sustaining friendship, encouragement, and understanding. I therefore extend heartfelt personal thanks to Caroline Castiglione, Julia Landweber, Susan Lively, Debra Martin, Abby Zanger, Joan and Daniel Boyle, Mary Dawn Milne, my grandmothers E. Clarissa Hyde and Vivian McConnell, and my sister Emily H. Skiles and her family. For peace of mind, I also thank Kangaroo Kids. Chelsea, and especially Meredith and now Lauren, have served as a constant source of entertainment, amazement, and diversion. My husband, Craig Boyle, has been patient, devoted, and willing to support me and the project in whatever manner he can. For all of these things I will be forever grateful and devoted in return. Finally, I think it is not too far-fetched to argue that the seeds of this project on flowers were planted many years ago in my parents' greenhouses. For this, and for their loving and unwavering support, I thank them.